D1223364

Justice Joseph Story, by Gilbert Stuart (1819).
Courtesy Harvard Law School.

Supreme Court Justice

Joseph Story

Statesman of the Old Republic

R. Kent Newmyer

The University of North Carolina Press

Chapel Hill and London

Both the initial research and the publication of this work
were made possible in part through grants from the National
Endowment for the Humanities, a federal agency whose
mission is to award grants to support education, scholarship,
media programming, libraries, and museums, in order to bring
the results of cultural activities to a broad, general public.

© 1985 The University of North Carolina Press

Manufactured in the United States of America

Library of Congress Cataloging in Publication Data

Newmyer, R. Kent

  Supreme Court Justice Joseph Story.

  (Studies in legal history)
  Bibliography: p.
  Includes index.
  1. Story, Joseph, 1779–1845. 2. Judges—United States
—Biography. I. Title. II. Series.
KF8745.S83N48 1985   347.73′2634 [B]   84-11886
ISBN 0-8078-1626-4   347.3073534 [B]

For My Family,

Jody, Dan, Tim, and Jenny

Contents

Acknowledgments

Some years ago, as I sat pondering the Crowninshield papers at the Peabody Museum in Salem, Massachusetts, an old man sat down across the table from me. He desperately needed a shave and, in truth, looked totally down, out, and bedraggled. He fixed me with a disconcerting stare for some time before asking if I were the person working on Joseph Story. I confessed my presumption, whereupon he fired several remarkably informed questions at me that led me to conclude he was an unfrocked history professor—or perhaps a crashed biographer of Judge Story. Having queried me and found me wanting, not to say speechless, he rose abruptly. "Young man," he said with a grim intensity as he turned to leave, "studying Joseph Story could ruin your career!"

How true the old fellow's prophecy concerning my "career" has rung is not for me to say. But I can say that if I have avoided ruin in writing this biography of Justice Story, it is in no small part because so many kind people helped me along the way. It is a pleasure to thank them—with deep apologies to anyone I have missed and without imputing to any of them any of the shortcomings of my book.

I recall with special warmth the generous encouragement given me from the outset by my teacher, Professor Emeritus Kenneth Rossman of Doane College, Crete, Nebraska. My colleagues at the University of Connecticut have also been most generous in their support and intellectual camaradarie. Particular thanks are due to A. William Hoglund for his wise counsel and to Richard D. Brown, Richard O. Curry, and Hugh Macgill (of the University of Connecticut School of Law) for their critical reading of select chapters of the manuscript. Harry Stout offered me useful criticisms on the entire work and listened with immense patience to what I fear was an incessant babble about my work in progress. My student and friend Harlow Sheidley gave me a very trenchant critical appraisal of the whole manuscript in which she shared with me her deep knowledge of New England conservatism in the early nineteenth century. I am indebted, too, for the critical insights on select chapters given me by Aviam Soifer, Boston University School of Law. Erwin Surrency, Temple University Law School, kindly shared with me his knowledge of early American equity. Fred Konefsky of the Faculty of Law and Jurisprudence of New York University at Buffalo made helpful suggestions on the entire manuscript, as did Donald Roper of the State University of New York at New Paltz.

Allan Ward, of the History Department at the University of Connecticut, generously translated Story's Latin correspondence for me. Thanks also go to Jan Bittner, who typed the final draft of the entire book, and to Daniel LePage, who helped me check footnotes and bibliography. To Jennifer Newmyer, for her always cheerful clerical assistance, goes her father's love and gratitude.

Because Story's papers and other essential sources were voluminous and widely scattered, my indebtedness to librarians is immense. The staff of the University of Connecticut Library has been most helpful in acquiring materials, tracing down remote leads, and, in general, standing ready to answer all queries. Most especially, I thank Mohini Mundkur, Robert Vrecenak, and Barbara Allen, of the library of the University of Connecticut School of Law. I am much obliged, too, to the librarians in the legal reference section of the Connecticut State Library.

I remember with gratitude the generous efforts of the staff of the Massachusetts Historical Society—and especially of Miss Winifred V. Collins and the late Warren G. Wheeler, who hauled out vast quantities of materials with never-ending patience. The dedicated staff of the Manuscript Division of the Library of Congress, the National Archives, and the Federal Records Center, Waltham, Massachusetts, made working at those places an exhilarating experience. Most helpful, also, were the librarians at the Boston Athenaeum, the Massachusetts State Archives, the Dartmouth College Library, Houghton and Widener libraries of Harvard University, the Harvard University Archives, and the Library of Harvard Law School. My thanks go also to the staffs of the American Antiquarian Society, the Essex Institute (Salem), the Peabody Museum (Salem), and the Marblehead Historical Society, as well as the Pierpont Morgan Library of New York City, the Free Library of Philadelphia, the Library of the College of William and Mary, the Historical Society of Pennsylvania, the Maryland Historical Society, the Library of Allegheny College (Allegheny, Pennsylvania), and the Sterling Library of Yale University. I appreciate the willingness of the New York Historical Society, the William Clements Library of the University of Michigan, and the Library of the University of Texas to make the Story material in their collections available to me on microfilm.

As is customary, I have stated my indebtedness to scholars in the footnotes, but I want to express a special sense of gratitude to fellow biographers of Story who in one way or another have inspired and aided me: to Henry Steele Commager, Gerald T. Dunne, and especially to James McClellan, whose careful scholarship helped bridge the gaps in my own knowledge. I have also been the beneficiary of a revolution in legal historiography without which my efforts at self-education would surely have failed. Among those whose work has been particularly helpful are Maxwell Bloomfield, Robert Cover, E. Merrick Dodd, Paul Finkelman, Tony

Freyer, Gerard Gawalt, Morton Horwitz, Willard Hurst, Leonard Levy, William Nelson, Oscar and Mary Handlin, Harry Scheiber, and William Wiecek.

Several other friends and supporters deserve mention. Among them is Julia Shepard, who spent several long months putting several thousand Supreme Court cases on computer cards. John Jenswold kindly assisted me in ordering the information about the students who studied under Story at Harvard Law School.

I remember kindly, as well, those who guided me in my early work on Story: Aubrey C. Land, who suggested the topic to me; the late James Sellers, of the University of Nebraska, who directed my dissertation; and Peter Coleman, whose trenchant criticism of early drafts was an eye-opener. Maurice Baxter, Maxwell Bloomfield, and Morton Horwitz came to my aid, later, with timely support. Finally, I want to express my gratitude to G. Edward White, editor of Studies in Legal History, for his generous efforts in bringing the manuscript to press, and to Lewis Bateman, Gwen Duffey, and others of the University of North Carolina Press for seeing it through production. To Janis Bolster for her superb copyediting go my profound thanks and admiration. I also much appreciate Jean Hankins's fine job of indexing.

I gratefully acknowledge the financial support extended me by the University of Connecticut Research Foundation and thank the American Council of Learned Societies for a Grant-in-Aid and especially the National Endowment for the Humanities for a Research Fellowship and for an additional grant in support of publication. Thanks go to the *American Journal of Legal History* and the *DePaul Law Review* for permitting me to publish portions of articles that appeared in their pages. I appreciate, too, the permission granted me to use reproductions of Story portraits owned by Harvard Law School, the Library of Congress, and the Massachusetts Historical Society.

My deepest gratitude is reserved for my wife, Jody Chalupa Newmyer. For several summers and during sabbatical leaves we traveled to the libraries and manuscript depositories of the eastern United States. Thanks to her typing skill, I was able to plunge, exorbitantly, I'm afraid, into the sources. Throughout the long period of writing and rewriting, she stood by as copyeditor, proofreader, and literary critic-of-the-last-resort. I like to think it was a labor of love. How else can I explain her cheerful willingness to spend a boiling Philadelphia summer at the "sumptuous" Hotel Morris, where a suite of rooms went for all of twenty-six dollars a week?

Introduction

It would be nice if every struggling scholar could experience a great moment of revelation in which his or her life's work would be made manifest—like Edward Gibbon's epiphany in Rome as he sat musing amid the ruins of the Capitol or Perry Miller's vision that came while unloading oil barrels in the Congo. The less gifted of us, I suspect, are doomed to discover the meaning of our life's work while doing it, to gain whatever inspiration we can from a gradual process of self-education that comes with research and writing. Such at any rate has been the nature of my years with Joseph Story, and I confess to a strange sense of gratitude to the old judge for being such a demanding teacher and such good company.

Most assuredly, I had no notion of the problems and the pleasures that lay in wait for me when in the late 1950s I set out to study Justice Story's political and constitutional thought. I came to the chore with a vast ignorance of what I needed to know and with a bias as well. My heroes were Jefferson, Jackson, Wendell Phillips, and Lincoln, though even then I found John Marshall hard to resist. The historians I most admired were Charles Beard, Carl Becker, and Vernon Parrington. Like Parrington, as much as I could be like him, I was quite prepared, as an unreconstructed Nebraska populist, to see Joseph Story and his friends with a cold and critical eye.

I have not lost affection for my old heroes (though Jefferson and Jackson have worn less well than Phillips and Lincoln) and the more I learn about Daniel Webster, the more I cherish my democratic prejudices. But twenty years in the trenches, so to speak, have left me with a deep admiration for Story—his seemingly superhuman accomplishments, his generosity, his idealism, his love of country, and his fundamental decency. What I discovered as I struggled to understand him, moreover, was the wisdom of the old-fashioned rules of historiography: the need for historians to get out of their own skin, to avoid anachronism, to judge by past, not present, standards. Studying Story transported me to an age quite distinct from that of Beard and Becker and even of Lincoln and Phillips (who was Story's student at Harvard Law School, class of 1833). The judge belonged to that generation touched by the idealism of the American Revolution. He grew up with the Republic, intermingled his ambition with its fate. Story brought to bear his own special genius, to be sure, but his singular talent would not have blossomed so brilliantly or produced so copiously except for the rich soil of republican culture.

The challenge as I came to perceive it, then, was to present Story's manifold accomplishments as a politician, lawyer, judge, legal educator, and publicist in the context of republicanism, which during Story's lifetime was itself undergoing radical transformation. This I have aimed to do in a single volume (though a second was tempting) and in language that is understandable (despite the technical nature of the subject). The balance struck between law and history I hope will make the work of some interest to students of law as well as historians and perhaps even to general readers with an interest in early national history.

The confining limits of a single volume as well as my general approach have led me to be selective in emphasis. A word about these matters here might be useful. I have dealt only with those aspects of Story's personal life—family background, childhood, education—which shaped his public life. In treating his public life, which for Story largely subsumed his private life, I have consistently looked for symbiotic connections between his law and the real world. Story's law practice, for example, is seen not just as a part of early nineteenth-century legal culture in Massachusetts but as Story's self-conscious reaction to the rise of political parties. Even the judge's pioneering efforts in legal education at Harvard Law School, as well as his outpouring of legal treatises, had important political connotations. Both must be understood, I argue, as part of the counterrevolution of Massachusetts conservatives in the 1820s.

Story's jurisprudence also had an intellectual, scientific, or "juristic" dimension, to use Charles Sumner's word. "Legal science" was another contemporary phrase, and because it will appear at various places in my analysis some clarification is in order. Legal science was a cultural given in the early nineteenth century, which is to say that it was rarely defined with precision. Sometimes it was used descriptively, at other times normatively; often it was mere rhetoric. Most often it meant simply systematic law— the mirror opposite, that is to say, of the haphazard, pluralistic, localized nature of early national jurisprudence. In this respect, legal science stood for legal reform: the clarification and rational ordering and effective dissemination of legal principles. Sir William Blackstone's *Commentaries* was the model, and therefore eighteenth-century rationalism melded with the conviction that legal order was God-given. This moral, ordered legal universe was also—for Story, at least, and I think his age as well—infused with practical purpose. Legal science was applied science, and here it became, as I see it, a subfield of what contemporaries called the science of government.

It followed, for Story, that judging was to govern, to bring legal principles to bear on the great political and economic problems of the age. My treatment of Story's numerous opinions, both at Washington and on circuit in New England, aims to highlight the practical cast of his legal science. Though I have not shunned legal categories, formal doctrinal analysis per se gets only limited attention. I have dealt with the institutional aspects of the Supreme Court only as they influenced or were influenced by Story. Throughout I have tried to avoid the case-by-case format, although Story's most important opinions in both private and public law receive extended treatment. Here as elsewhere, my concern is less with law itself than with the interaction of Story's law and his perception of history. Accordingly, I have when possible organized chapters around such themes as sectionalism, slavery, nationalism, economic growth—problems with which Story as a judicial statesman grappled. Special attention is given to Story's experience on the New England circuit, because it was there at the trial level that law and history most obviously intersected.

In treating the historical context of Story's law, republicanism has been a constant point of reference, so that a definition of this illusive term is also required. When I began the book, studies of republicanism in the early national period were almost nonexistent, and even in 1973, when I wrote on the *Charles River Bridge* case as a "crisis in republicanism," there were as yet few major studies; most notable were Douglass Adair's marvelously heuristic essays and Gordon Wood's seminal work, *The Creation of the American Republic, 1776–1787* (1969). Since then (but not always in time for me to make use of them) a spate of fine studies on the subject have appeared by such scholars as Joyce Appleby, Lance Banning, Nathan Hatch, Michael Kammen, Drew McCoy, and Robert Shalhope, to mention only some. None of these works presumes to explore fully the relation of law to republican culture. Nor do I presume to do so.

Republicanism figures in my account because it figured in Story's life. By "republicanism" I mean not a narrow creed or doctrine but a set of collectively held and often vaguely defined general assumptions about American government and society: what it was as well as what it ought to be. The starting point of speculation was the American Revolution itself. Indeed, in the simplest sense republicanism denotes the government that resulted from American independence, a government that repudiated kingly authority and settled sovereignty on the people themselves. The doctrine of popular sovereignty, however, raised as many problems as it settled. The people were sovereign, but were they virtuous and wise enough to govern? Some Americans tended toward a democratic answer; others favored an aristocratic solution. What arrangement of power within the federal system most comported with republican principles, and which branch of government was most favored? The Constitution was not so much the end of this debate as the beginning. And behind the debate lay increasingly contrary notions of republican society itself, one rooted in agrarianism with its great champions in the South and the other rooted in Northern commerce. As sectionalism worked to fracture republican unity, so did the debate over political parties, which threatened or promised (depending on which side one took) to substitute common sense and compromise for ideological purity as the modus operandi of American government.

All this is to say that republicanism, at least as it figures here, is not a monolithic ideology so much as a cultural matrix generated by the American Revolution within which Americans debated questions of government, law, economics, and all else. The debate oscillated between polarities: between individualism and community, between agrarian and commercial values, between states' rights and nationalism, between the South and the North. Republicanism was a cultural dialogue or, more precisely perhaps, the shared ground bounded by the polarities of disagreement on which the debate raged. Americans had to agree in order to debate. What they agreed on, and it was the bedrock of republican ideology, was that a successful revolution and a bountiful providence had marked out the American republic for a special destiny. Those touched by this revolutionary vision were compelled to think and act boldly, comprehensively, idealistically, and passionately—to see the nation in providential terms and themselves as instruments of civic regeneration. Matters large and small, as with the old Puritans, were plotted on the curve of history and took on a cosmic morality.

It is to republicanism in this broad sense that I refer; it energized Story and infused his great work. Indeed, it would appear from Story's career that republicanism was particularly congenial to law and lawyers: It dethroned a king and raised a constitution in his place. By asserting equality over social class as the calculus of government, republicanism put a premium on contract law as the primary means of social cohesion. A society under law tended to translate into a social order in which lawyers ruled. Story saw this connection, I argue, but legal power for him was a means, not an end. His great objective was to secure the American Revolution, to protect his vision of republican society from the corrosive impact of the nineteenth century. This purpose gave unity to his life and to his legal system, and accordingly it is an important objective of this book to explore this interconnectedness: of his republican education with his later career; of his work as judge, teacher, and scholar; of his opinions themselves; and of his jurisprudence with his vision of republican society.

Story's vision was put forth in nationalist terms, but his nationalism, though deeply felt, was shaped by his New England experience. This sectional nationalism, moreover, rested squarely on the fault line of historical change, for New England was the cutting edge of a social transformation that challenged and finally engulfed much that Story cherished. Ironically, the age that invited him to build his system of republican law also doomed the enterprise to impermanence. Story was great because he captured the unique lawmaking, system-building potential of the early republic. His fame was fleeting because the republican age in America was remarkably evanescent. Much that Story created lasted beyond his lifetime; some stands even today as a tribute to his genius. But his grand vision of the old republic resting on the foundations of a moral, scientific law is a relic on Clio's junkpile. Thus Story's life's work seen in its entirety might, if I have done the job I set out to do, be a useful bench mark from which to measure the transformation of the old republic.

Kent Newmyer
Storrs, Connecticut
Summer 1983

Supreme Court Justice
Joseph Story

Chapter 1

A Republican Education

Each new being is received into a style of life prepared by tradition and held together by tradition, and at the same time disintegrating because of the very nature of tradition. We say that tradition "molds" the individual, "channels" his drives. But the social process does not mold a new being merely to house-break him; it molds generations in order to be remolded, to be reinvigorated, by them.
　　　Erik Erikson, *Young Man Luther*

Now, Joe, I've sat up and tended you many a night when you were a child, and don't you dare not to be a great man.
　　　Mehitable Pedrick Story to
　　　Joseph Story

"I am not sorry at the beating of our classmate," confessed Arthur Maynard Walter, Harvard 1798, to his friend William Smith Shaw. "The fellow has deserved a flogging this long while, & I hope he will now be satisfied." The unfortunate target of Hersey Derby's right hook and Walter's vindictive pen was Joseph Story. Walter went on to say, over the protests of his more moderate friends, that in addition to very modest talents and morals that would not bear discussion, this fellow Story had a dangerously "wicked mind." Such a "great scoundrel" most assuredly was not among those few "worthies" whose friendship and esteem were worth having.[1]

Such hatred and ostracism, on the surface, are difficult to understand and harder to justify. There were, of course, personal explanations: Walter's peevishness and Story's brashness; the tendency of Harvard undergraduates toward cliquishness; and, as Story put it, the "little strifes, jealousies and rivalries of college life."[2] Walter was especially miffed that Story, who graduated with second honors, got laurels that he, Walter, in his own opinion better deserved. Class standing was not the real problem, however, and neither was social class: Both Story and Walter were young gentlemen of standing and privilege, as their graduation from Harvard itself indicated. The nub of the matter was values, ideology. By 1803, when Walter excommunicated Story from respectable society, he and Shaw—self-styled "the most orthodox young men in Boston"[3]—had become subalterns in the "Headquarters of good principles," as Josiah Dwight dubbed the Federalist establishment that ruled Massachusetts.[4] Story had become a zealous convert to the rising party of Thomas Jefferson. The divisive issue was not republicanism, to which new orthodoxy both Federalists and Republicans pledged their loyalties, but how its guiding principles should be applied, how preserved. Because parties agreed so passionately on the basic values, they disagreed as vehemently on their application.[5] What made Story "wicked" and immoral was simply that he had "very mistaken ideas of the revolution," that he was one of the deluded mob who "ascribes too much to that villain, the debauchee of J[efferson] who by every art & intrigue under the insidious cloak of patriotism was endeavoring to destroy what Jay & others by patience, perseverence and magnanimity were exerting themselves to build."[6]

Petty differences among Harvard students, it would seem, had come to turn on a fundamental schism in republican culture itself. Not only had Story put a false gloss on republican culture, then, but to Walter's greater distress, he had internalized his perception of history and had begun to act on his interpretation. Significantly—as it provided the ideological underpinning of his remarkable legal career—he had by the time of his graduation from Harvard in 1798 taken on himself the burden of securing the truth of the American Revolution. And not just conserving it; what was true of Erikson's Luther was no less true for Story: He aimed to and would in fact pass on to subsequent generations much more than he received from the preceding one.[7] But first let us consider the inheritance.

1. Time, Place, and Family: Crucible of Republicanism

The American Revolution, more than any other event in American history, transformed those whom it touched, both the generation that made it and the one that inherited the burden of preserving it. Never in American history, before or since, were the fundamental principles of society and government so thoroughly debated, so brilliantly articulated. Because institutions were being shaped and precedents formed, those principles had a relevance unusual to ideological constructions. The republican culture crystallized by the Revolution was not monolithic; it was full of tension and contradictions, as the culturally laden dispute between Walter and Story suggests and the nineteenth century proves.[8] But the integrating impact of the American war was extraordinary. Not all Americans agreed on the definitive meaning of their revolution, but few doubted that such a clear and certain meaning existed—and that deviation from it was heresy. For the moment at least, history had been tidied up: Republicanism was hypostatized by the dramatic birth of a new nation, sanctified by the blood of martyrs.

That Joe Story was a republican, then, was not in the least remarkable. Along with Shaw and Walter, Jefferson and Hamilton, he could, unless he were nothing at all, hardly have been anything else. What else needs explaining was the special gloss he put on republican ideology, the intensity of his commitment to it, the fruitful identification of his life with the fate of the new nation. The answers lie not only in the unique educative force of a revolutionary age but in the refracting prisms through which he saw it, the various and mutually fortifying instruments by which the Revolution educated its children. Activating Story's genius were time, place, and family: It mattered that he was born on 10 September 1779 (three years after independence and two before the defeat of the British at Yorktown), in Marblehead, in Essex County, Massachusetts (where the Revolution was a way of life); that he graduated from Harvard in 1798 (when that institution was on fire with republican zeal); that he was the first son of Mehitable Pedrick and Elisha Story (indomitable patriots both).

Little is known about the early Pedricks except that they were plain folk who settled on Marblehead Neck sometime in the seventeenth century. By the mid-eighteenth they had risen from obscurity, thanks to Story's maternal grandfather, John Pedrick, who was one of Marblehead's "opulent" mercantile gentlemen with a stately house on lower Washington Street at the corner of Pickett, near the Old North Church (First Church of Christ). Family tradition attributed his mobility to "enterprize and decision of character," to ambition and self-reliance. ("He had no fear of anything that the Almighty ever put on this earth," Story's mother once said of her father.)[9] These traits of personality and social enterprise he left to his daughter, who, if behavior constitutes genetic evidence, passed them on to her eldest son. As for the Pedrick fortune, that most of it was lost during the Revolution undoubtedly goes far to explain the old man's Tory inclinations.

The Storys on the other hand were relative newcomers to Marblehead, having resided in Boston since the early 1700s and before that most likely in Ipswich (though the connecting evidence is circumstantial).[10] What is known is that William Story of Ipswich married Sarah Foster sometime before 1681 and that he was a carpenter by trade. From obscure beginnings came a steady ascent. William, Jr., one of the five children of William and Sarah, followed his father's trade, manifesting some entrepreneurial talents to boot—enough at any rate, to acquire a modest estate of twelve acres, a house, an orchard, and a mill, which he sold in March 1689/90 in order to pursue the main chance. With his wife, Susannah Fuller Story, William, Jr., moved first to Concord and after that Roxbury and then to Brookline.[11] Elisha Story of Boston was in all probability the son of William Story, Jr., and Susannah Fuller Story of Brookline. On his death Elisha Story willed his Boston real estate along with some shares in New Hampshire lands bought on speculation to his son William and daughter Lydia in equal shares when they came of age.[12]

This William (Elisha's son and Joseph's grandfather) propelled the family upward into Boston's colonial gentry—and brought it down by his importunate and untimely place-seeking politics. Speculation in Boston real estate along with office holding in the British colonial bureaucracy appear to have been the main levers of advancement that lifted the Story family from their artisan anonymity.[13] Beginning with a modest inheritance (for which, in good entrepreneurial spirit, he contested with his sister in the Suffolk County Court of Common Pleas),[14] he bought and sold regularly and with enough success to acquire a pew in Old South Church and change his title from "Gentleman" (as it was listed in the land records of March 1743) to "Esquire" (as listed in August 1762).[15] His presence alongside Samuel Adams at the Boston Caucus of 1763 marked him as not only a man of some authority but one of Whiggish sentiments (which is the way his grandson remembered him). He was also deputy registrar of the much-hated Vice-Admiralty Court in Boston.

Whiggish politics and a place in the British colonial establishment were not of course mutually exclusive in the 1760s, but the balancing act became increasingly precarious, as Story discovered on 26 August 1765 when the Stamp Act mob, after sacking the homes of Lieutenant-Governor Thomas Hutchinson and Customs Comptroller Benjamin Hallowell, destroyed his office and burned his papers. Why is not clear, since Story was only a bit-player in the drama of empire unfolding in Boston. As deputy registrar, Story may simply have been a convenient target for anti-British sentiment. Possibly the attack was a carefully calculated effort to destroy records of debt and other incriminating evidence against Massachusetts merchants. But the indisputable fact was that William Story, who stood with Sam Adams in 1763, stood with Thomas Hutchinson in 1765.[16]

The patriot mob delivered the first blow to William Story's ambitions; the British delivered the second in 1768 (or 1769) when they dismissed him from his position at the Vice-Admiralty Court—the result, it would appear, of the fall from grace of John Temple, the surveyor general of customs in Boston and Story's patron. Out of a job, hounded by litigants aiming to recover prize money lost during his tenure as deputy registrar,[17] Story retreated to his wife's place in Ipswich, from which he continued to campaign for office. The most he could get from Hutchinson and the establishment, who now distrusted his Whiggism as much as the radicals distrusted his Loyalism, was letters of introduction to Treasury officials in London, where Story betook himself in early 1772 in a last desperate quest for royal appointment. That step failing, Story seems to have turned to blackmail. While in London, he had seen or heard of the famous letters discovered by Benjamin Franklin in which Hutchinson writing to Thomas Whately recommended a tougher policy against the colonies. Story may in fact have carried the letters back to Franklin's radical friends in Boston, who finally used them to topple Hutchinson from power and to convince doubters of the evil duplicity of British authorities.[18]

Threatening to disclose the contents of those letters (if indeed he did so) could hardly have aided Story's quest for a place, because the contents were soon common knowledge. Having Hutchinson as an enemy did, however, turn into a timely asset that may explain how Story got a position as naval commissioner during the Revolution. However that may have been, his dreams of greatness were surely in tatters. After the war he retreated to Marblehead, where his sons resided and where he died quietly in 1799. The swirling forces of revolution, passing him by just as they had John Pedrick, created a generation gap in the Story family to match the fissure of empire. The result was that family history for Joseph Story would begin with his father and mother, both of whom in their own ways fought valiantly for national independence. Their son would grow up not only chronologically but psychologically with the new nation.

Beginnings are of course never entirely new in history or biography. But a decisive break seems to have occurred for the Storys when William Story's son Elisha left Boston for Marblehead in 1770 with his first wife, Ruth Ruddock Story. He left in part because Boston had too many physicians, although he had already impressed people with his ability and clearly came to Marblehead with the strongest recommendations. Possibly he came to escape the shadow of his father's social and political eclipse, which looked darker as the Patriot cause brightened. Marblehead, however, had its own attractions in 1770. Great culture it lacked, but with nearly five thousand people it ranked second only to Boston in Massachusetts and New England and sixth among the cities of British North America.[19] In fishing it was first. In the boom times before the Revolution 150 schooners employing seven to eight hundred sailors sailed semiannually for Georges Banks. Working folk left at home were employed in one or another aspect of the fishing and shipping industry. Complementing fishing was an ocean-borne commerce, especially with the British West Indies, and a vigorous coastal trade as well, augmented in off-seasons by fishing vessels. Revenue in paid-in specie from Marblehead fishing and shipping made it a special financial asset in a specie-short economy and in addition laid the foundation for a remarkable local aristocracy. Not all of the merchant-shippers achieved the opulence of Robert "King" Hooper or Jeremiah Lee, but good wine, English finery, and stately homes on Washington Street clearly testified to Marblehead's importance. The sixty or so families of "quality" set well above the working people of the village supplied quite enough polite company and good living for the modest republican tastes and limited free time of Elisha Story.

As a matter of course, Dr. Story became part of the Marblehead aristocracy, with a comfortable three-story house on Washington Street. He was, after all, the only physician in the village; his brother Isaac was minister of the Second Congregational Church and a public figure of visibility; his fathers-in-law (both Ruddock and Pedrick) were gentlemen of substance.

Political office had little attraction for Story, but he was deeply involved in village life. Ministering to the physical welfare of the entire village took most of his time, but he would become a leading champion of educational reform (perhaps because of his son's unhappy experience with the local educational establishment). Only two years after arriving he spoke out boldly in favor of smallpox inoculation against powerful local opposition. For this he got caught up on the losing side in Marblehead's famous "Small Pox War," which resulted in the popular repudiation of the champions of inoculation and the burning of the hospital they had built for the community on Cat Island.[20] Story continued to serve the people who abused him, however. As a member of the Tuesday Evening Club, he also rubbed minds with the likes of Elbridge Gerry, Jeremiah Lee, and John Glover—prominent men, Whigs all, and Patriots-to-be.[21]

Dr. Story's ambivalent position as a patrician serving the masses (and sometimes, as in the Small Pox War, the mob) bears a remarkable parallel to the role of his son as republican judge in a democratic country. Judge Story's first lessons in conservative leadership may well have been learned at home. Elisha Story was assuredly a model public, republican servant. Class for him was not an occasion for indulgence and easy living but an opportunity and an obligation to serve. Serve he did, but the lessons which that service taught his son were republican, not conservative. Elisha Story was an American Patriot. He and his wife and Marblehead itself conspired to teach Joseph Story the republican lessons of the Revolution.

Even before his arrival, Marblehead was caught up in the struggles of empire, pulled into the vortex by its dependence on the sea and its connections with Boston.[22] Merchants and shippers were forced to take a stand. Some, like John Pedrick, who prospered under the economic arrangements of the old empire, were reluctant to join the radical clamor against Britain's new colonial policy. Others, like the Gerrys and the Lees, who might profit from change or at least were less locked into the old system, argued for a more forceful stand. Accordingly, Marblehead oscillated. The Stamp Act elicited strong anti-British sentiment, but the bold town-meeting resolutions called forth by that act were largely forgotten in the wake of its repeal. Marblehead's reaction to the Townsend duties, despite the pressure from Boston radicals, was restrained, but anti-British feeling surged forth again during the Tea Act crisis and the closing of Boston's port so that finally Marblehead came out firmly for independence, even though at this late stage some local merchants and shippers demurred.

Once committed, Marblehead stood forth gallantly—and paid a heavy price. Its thriving Atlantic trade was all but destroyed by the war, and so was much of its fishing industry. Joseph Story's "earliest recollections," in fact, were of a place "greatly impoverished," gripped in "an apparently irretrievable decline."[23] After the war venturesome merchants like Gerry would seek opportunity elsewhere; during it Marblehead's unemployed fishermen flocked to the ranks of Washington's army, inspired, no doubt, by the memory of the British blockade of Marblehead harbor, by the stationing of Redcoats in the village in January 1775, and by the landing of a British regiment on Homan's Beach the following month.[24] Marblehead marched a whole regiment to war, and when it was over "15 per cent of the population consisted of widows and fatherless children."[25]

Young Story was nourished on accounts of Marblehead bravery, of military heroes and great statesmen. One such hero was Robert Wormsted, who even before hostilities made a one-man stand against British occupation by disarming six British regulars with a walking cane.[26] More famous were John Glover and his "amphibious regiment" of Marblehead fishermen, who saved the Revolution by ferrying Washington's army across the East River after the battle of Long Island in August 1776 and who several months later ferried them back across the Delaware to rout the Hessians at the battle of Trenton.[27] As a statesman there was Elbridge Gerry, who as signer of the Declaration of Independence, delegate to the Philadelphia convention, governor of the state, and vice-president gave Marblehead a voice in the councils of state and nation. For the young men of the village, proximity to greatness made it seem accessible. To say that Joseph Story was born in Marblehead in 1779, then, is to make him a special child of the Revolution.

Revolutionary Marblehead supplied the raw materials for a republican education, but it did not teach the lesson to everyone. For example, when Edward Bowen was born (like Joseph Story) in Marblehead in 1779, his father wrote in his journal that he wanted his son, "if he should live," to "remember that his father had no hand in the destruction of his country, which was once the best for a poor man in the known world, but now the worst."[28] Elisha Story had a hand in that "destruction," but he looked on it as the creation of a new country and wanted *his* son to share in its blessings. Accordingly, Elisha Story and his wife drew out for their eldest son the republican lessons that Marblehead offered, made family the instrument by which they became traits of his personality.

When Elisha Story arrived in Marblehead in 1770, he and Ruth Ruddock Story had one child, a son named John, and over the next eight years they added seven more children. The last died at birth in 1778 with his mother. The next year Dr. Story married Mehitable Pedrick, who fortunately for the young widower had just been jilted by a Mr. Fosdick, a "prominent" citizen of Portland. She was, according to family tradition, quite inconsolable—for all of a few days. Then in an act of will that proved prophetic, she simply "made up her mind to forget her former love and to marry the first promising man who came along,"[29] who was Dr. Story.

Very beautiful and equally vivacious and energetic, Mehitable Story was a force to reckon with. She would outlive her famous son by two years and may have been one of the few people who could outtalk him. Though she was only nineteen when she married Elisha, she readily assumed the burden of taking care of her husband (for which act he heartily praised her in his will) and his children, although family rumor had it that "there was not much love lost between the stepchildren and their new mother."[30] Her first son was Joseph; after him she had ten other children, six girls and four boys, the last of whom was born in 1799, one year after Joseph had graduated from Harvard. While having babies with great regularity, she also managed her household during a period of relative privation. There were no servants, a luxury to which she was used (and which after the Revolution she would again have), and she attended personally to the sewing, mending, and cooking with great efficiency and no complaints—and with a contagious enthusiasm for the revolutionary cause. Intelligent, talkative, and, if her grandson is to be trusted, a bit imperious,[31] she brought to life for her son the tradition of patriotism and sacrifice that Marblehead offered the nation.

Assuredly, the hero of the young wife's revolutionary tales (though we do not have documents to prove it) was Elisha Story. His patriotic record was made for telling. Born in 1743, he was eighteen when James Otis let fly the barbs of his patriotic oratory against the Writs of Assistance; he was twenty-two when his father's office was attacked by the Boston mob, old enough to read the lesson of history as he watched his father grovel unsuccessfully for a place in a British colonial establishment that was itself in a state of advanced decay.

When exactly Elisha Story concluded that independence was the wave of America's future we do not know. But in 1773, at the age of thirty, only one year after his father went to England in a last-ditch effort to salvage a position with the British establishment in Boston, Elisha daubed on Indian war paint and helped toss ninety thousand pounds' worth of English tea into Boston Harbor. He became a full-fledged member of the Sons of Liberty in Boston and was elected by them, along with others, to steal the British cannon positioned on Boston Common. His single-handed disarming of the Redcoat picket and the success of the mission of stealth for liberty were among the favorite war tales in the Story household. Elisha also defied British authority by supporting the American seaman who had killed a British officer when the officer tried to impress him. He fought at Concord and Lexington; at Bunker Hill he was in the trenches with his friend and colleague, Dr. Joseph Warren, fighting first before ministering to the wounded. He was a surgeon in Colonel Little's Essex Regiment and served with Washington at Long Island, White Plains, and Trenton.[32]

An early resignation in 1777, in protest over the inefficiency and mismanagement of the medical department, did not diminish his patriotic stature, and his return to Marblehead brought the Revolution into the Story household. Elisha Story had been present at the creation, and through him so was his young son. When he praised liberty, celebrated the virtues and greatness of Washington, and glorified the new nation, which things he did with enthusiasm, Joseph listened. For Joseph, Elisha Story was truly a founding father.

2. Self-Mastery and Self-Improvement: The Crucible of Ambition

History, place, family: Conjoined and mutually enhancing, they wove into the very texture of Story's being those most essential qualities of republican ideology—patriotism, a belief in virtue, and the tradition of public service. It was assumed that the republican citizen who served his country (no less than the seventeenth-century Puritan who covenanted to serve God and his community) would bring to that duty a disciplined mind and a purified heart. It made sense, then, that those forces which taught community service also coalesced to build character and inculcate private virtue and self-mastery. The method of conversion, as Emerson would rediscover, was introspective self-purification. In republican New England no less than in Puritan New England, then, individualism was inseparable from community responsibility. The public and the private man, in the final shakedown of cultural values, were inseparable. Public service, as in the classical *res publica*, ennobled private ambition.[33]

The old Calvinist doctrines of privation and inner struggle were assuredly alive in Joseph Story's Marblehead, in his uncle's church, no less, where he went dutifully every Sunday to be scourged with New Light brimstone. Even the cultural austerity and solitude of Marblehead, which turned Story into himself, invited introspection. But mostly the message of service and the technique of self-discipline were taught by his family.[34] What we know of the daily give-and-take in the Story household, the complex interaction among its members, who themselves were constantly changing and who moved against a shifting backdrop of events, is scanty, mostly secondhand and after the fact. But available evidence—wills, an epitaph, short autobiography, scattered letters, and family tradition preserved by a history-minded grandson—all point to a family imbued with republican values and determined to pass them on as usable instruments of personal achievement and social action.

Story's family was a uniquely persuasive educational institution for several reasons, not the least of which was Marblehead itself, both its deficiencies (which enhanced family influence) and its strengths (which the family drew on and refracted). By common agreement Marblehead was quaint and picturesque. All granite it was, too, with scarcely a place to bury the dead and no place to sink a plow. The boulders on Sewell's Point jutted out defiantly into the Atlantic, giving the village its name and defining the tone of life, which for most of its people was hard and barren. Marblehead, whatever it was, rested mainly on the backs of plain folks: the fishermen who risked their lives on Georges Banks and Fundy Bay and their wives and children who cleaned, dried, and packed the cod they brought back, if indeed they made it back. They were a "peculiar race," to use Story's words, "generous, brave, humane, honest, straightforward, . . . sagacious in their own affairs, but not wise beyond them; confiding and unsuspecting; hospitable by nature, though stinted in means; with a love of home scarcely paralleled; . . . frugal and laborious; content with their ordinary means."[35] A less generous assessment was made by the Reverend William Bentley of Marblehead's First Church, who found them dangerously superstitious, with "little knowledge of moral life"—"as profane, intemperate, & ungoverned as any people on the Continent."[36]

That Marblehead, in its post-revolutionary decline, was uncouth did not mean that it had no capacity to educate. The patriotic traditions were still alive and doubly so, no doubt, on great moments, as when Washington visited there in 1789. Joseph could still hear accounts of patriotic valor on the village streets and in the local barbershop where as a boy he was allowed to speechify. The plain fishermen had lessons to teach, too, and Story listened—even perhaps when they chafed at deferential rule, which all agreed they had a tendency to do. ("I was their companion, and often in their society," Story later remembered about the seamen of Marblehead.)[37] There were other enticements in Marblehead, too, at least to youngsters with imagination like Story and a family tradition of tale-telling. The village in fact had a fully developed panoply of "ghosts, hobgoblins, will-o'-wisps, apparitions, and premonitions" and an enduring belief in "the Pixies of Devonshire, the Boggle of Scotland, and Northern Jack o' Lanthorn," not to mention a real live devil in old Uncle Diamond.[38] And of course there was plenty of solitude to ponder these and other providences.

But solitude had its drawbacks, too. Only twenty miles from Boston, Marblehead, once the communication network of the Revolution was dismantled, might as well have been two hundred. It had no newspaper, and the post, Story remembered, came only "*once* or *twice* a week" and that "tardily."[39] The ships brought goods, dreams maybe, but no ideas. "Few books were to be found, and few scholars were nurtured on its rocky shores."[40] There were only two formal institutions in the village that bore on Story's early education. One was Marblehead Academy, which, as we shall note shortly, helped Story prepare for Harvard. The other was the Second Congregational Society of Uncle Isaac, which the family dutifully attended and where Story's religious impulses took on some institutional structure.

But in religion, as in most else, it was Story's family that made the strongest impression, and it was one at considerable odds with the truth dispensed from the pulpit of the Second Congregational Church. Minister Isaac Story, it appeared, was not touched by the warming humanitarian currents of liberal Christianity of the sort championed by Marblehead's William Bentley. He was, as Joseph remembered with obvious distaste, "inclined in his preaching to dwell on the terrors of the law, upon man's depravity, and eternal torments. . . ." What young Story took home from this Calvinist bombardment was a God "of terror, and not of love, . . . a being whom I was to propitiate, rather than a parent of whom I was to ask blessings."[41] Story seemed to be saying that he expected God to resemble his own kind and gentle father—and indeed, in the religion taught at home, exactly this anthropomorphic transfiguration took place.

The Story household was deeply and meaningfully religious. There were family prayers both morning and evening, and "on Sunday, after the public afternoon service was over, all the family, including the servants, were assembled in one room, and he [Dr. Story] then read a printed sermon of some English divine, and concluded the day with reading a portion of the New Testament, and with a prayer."[42] The God prayed to, however, was not the Reverend Isaac's New Light God of wrath and power. Elisha Story was frankly Arminian and did not mind contradicting his brother— and leaving the implications of such an open rupture of authority for Joseph to ponder. It was, however, not so much what Elisha Story said about religious beliefs that counted as how he applied them in his own life. Elisha was loving and gentle, hopeful about humanity and tolerant even of Catholics (a stance that verged on heresy in eighteenth-century New England). The liberal qualities of Joseph's God so closely resembled those of Elisha that it is hard to doubt the connection of the two. Joseph never gave up entirely, however, the Augustinian image of a great struggle between good and evil that he was all too ready to secularize and impose on his own age. There remained also a strong vestigial dose of Calvinist gloom in his makeup, alongside a deep respect for the idealism of the early Puritans (which he shared with most other intellectuals of New England). But his religion, long before he formalized it at Harvard, was liberal, Unitarian, and deeply felt.

If religion was a family affair, so was republicanism itself (and thus it is not surprising that family became the basic unit in Story's mature conception of republican society).[43] Again it was Story's father, a "very decided republican," who set the tone, but it was family in a larger cultural sense that conveyed the special meaning of republicanism. Family for the Storys was not bloodline, status, pedigree. Nowhere in Story's autobiography or in his correspondence and public writings is there any concern whether the family line in America began with the carpenter William of Ipswich or the carpenter Elisha of Boston or whether the Storys were descended from aristocrats driven out of England during the Restoration of James II (a theory suggested by some genealogical accounts). As noted already, even grandfathers William Story and John Pedrick, both of whom clung too long to the Lion's tail, seem to have been rather distant figures. The republican function of Story's family was not to perpetuate itself but to launch its members successfully into society, to inculcate the virtues of self-discipline, self-reliance, and ambition. Story was taught (to paraphrase David Reisman) not to succeed his father, as much as he loved and admired him, but simply to succeed. Such was the cultural import of Elisha Story's advice to Joseph, as the latter recounted in 1833 while passing the same republican advice on to his son:

> I was about your age (fourteen) when my father first began to give me his confidence, and to treat me as one entitled to it. He freely conversed with me on all his hopes and his situation in life and taught me to feel the importance of firmness, sound morals, and ambition of excellence. He told me, that I should be obliged to depend on my own exertions for my success in life; that he should leave little or no property, and that I must study to fit myself for my profession in life. I never forgot his advice and kindness; it was present to me at all times, and gave a new turn to my thoughts. From that time I began to think that I ought to cease to be a *mere boy*, and to struggle for distinction as a man.[44]

The point—and it was confirmed by Elisha Story's will distributing his modest estate in equal shares among many children[45]—was that the family was not a shield and buckler against society but a springboard into it. But the family was not to worry: Society was fluid and mobile; the continent was rich; and Joseph, the eldest in the second family, was a young man of great promise. His father had helped create the new empire for freedom. Should not his son share in its bounty, and maybe even help direct its destiny? The pursuit of these possibilities would carry the son like the father into the party of Jefferson, and carry him as well into a head-on collision with aristocratic Arthur Walter, who, like the party he belonged to, misperceived the main direction of American history.

In its individualistic bent, Story's family was nineteenth century in orientation;[46] in size and structure it resembled the family of the seventeenth century. Elisha Story had eighteen children in all; seven by his first wife and eleven by his second; nine boys and nine girls in all and on Joseph's side five boys and six girls. Structurally the Story family corresponded to the quasi-extended-nuclear model, which is to say, that the parents and their offspring lived under one roof, with aunts, uncles, cousins, and grandparents nearby enough to count but not close enough to destroy the nuclear line of authority. Both grandfathers were living in Marblehead, but they do not, perhaps because of their tainted patriotism, seem to have figured greatly in Joseph's life. Of the various aunts and uncles, the Reverend Isaac Story left the only documented impression: partly a negative one because of his doom-and-gloom Calvinism and partly a positive one in his ambition for his kin and his championship of civic humanism modeled after George Washington.

Story grew up in the bustling household on Washington Street, where the authority of the parents was undiminished, except possibly by the sheer size and complexity of the family. Owing to his two marriages and the youth of his second wife, Elisha's children differed widely in age and in fact resembled two families—which tendency Mehitable may have exacerbated by favoring her own.[47] Because of the wide age differential among the Story children, it is likely that no more than seven or eight lived at home at any one time. Joseph occupied a unique position among his brothers and sisters and one that most likely affected his socialization. As the first son of a second marriage he was the baby to his older half brothers and sisters, and at the same time a possible object of resentment (though there is no mention of any). On the other hand, he was the eldest son of Mehitable and Elisha and the protector of his younger siblings, a responsibility that encouraged him to identify with his father and develop an early sense of fatherhood. Kinship connections also supplied Story with his closest friends. Until he left Salem for Cambridge in 1829, his sisters and their husbands—Mehitable, who married William Fettyplace; Eliza, who married Capt. Joseph White; and Harriet, whose husband was Stephen White —were his best friends and closest confidants.

If in size the Story family looked to the past, the lines of authority and the relationship between Elisha and Mehitable looked to the future.[48] Elisha Story, one infers from extant documents, was the dominant influence on his son, but it was not because he was the kind of family patriarch sanctioned by Puritan notions of social hierarchy. The sort of equality that characterized the relationship of father and mother defies easy classification. Mehitable Story was not a liberated woman by modern standards. As a young woman she was immediately saddled with the responsibilities of raising a large family, which she quickly augmented with the eleven children of her own. The doctor's profession kept him busy, too, so that his wife was "servant, seamstress, housekeeper, schoolmistress and lady" all at once.[49] What was important—and Elisha Story's will makes the point explicit—was that she got credit for what she did,[50] and authority to educate and shape her family as well. Mehitable was the ruling spirit in the family, and hence the Story household was full of warmth, vivacity, talk. Those, and they were many, who testified to the incredible energy of Mr. Justice Story, to his restless curiosity and his unquenchable capacity for talking, could not doubt that he was Mehitable Pedrick Story's son.

Story was also very much his father's son in physical appearance as in much else. Joseph remembered his father as "not so tall as I am and rather of a stronger and fuller build. He must have been an uncommonly handsome man in his youth (and indeed so I have always heard); for when I first recollect him with distinctness, though then quite bald, his face was still of great masculine beauty and attractiveness. His eyes were blue and of singular vivacity and sweetness, his eyebrows regularly arched, and a fine nose, and an expressive mouth, gave a perfect harmony to his features"[51]—a perfect description, too, of Joseph Story at the same age, as a look at early portraits verifies (see the Chester Harding portrait accompanying Chapter 3).

Elisha Story, it would seem, taught by gentler means than his wife, so that his "bland" manner balanced off Mehitable's more energetic, determined style. He was, according to his son's account, "not a man of genius" but (as became a practicing physician who moved daily among the real people) a "man of plain, practical sense" with "quick insight into the deeds of men" and a "great and natural tact and sagacity with little pretense to learning."[52]

This decent, gentle, and wise man's standing with his family was based on character, not on patriarchal authority. He was "kind and indulgent to his children, partaking of all their pleasures, and busy in protecting their innocent amusements. . . ."[53] There was so much gentleness about him that to them he seemed more a companion than a parent. Unlike Cotton Mather, who preached the truth to his children at every turn, Dr. Story quietly acted it out for them to see. What his son Joseph saw he tells us in a poem written in 1805 on his father's death:

> Firm, yet humane, benevolent, yet just,
> Here rest, dear Shade, and mingle dust with dust;
> Warm was thy heart with generous feelings fir'd,
> For truth and virtue every deed inspir'd:
> Prompt to the calls of woe, thy anxious eyes
> Dwelt on the widow's cares, the orphan's cries,
> Thy smile o'er sickness threw the charm of health;
> Kind as a parent, faithful to the end,
> In all that wins, as husband, patriot, friend.
> While o'er thy grave I bend with grief sincere,
> And drop with pious awe the filial tear,
> Not, as the hopeless, mourn I o'er thy doom,
> Nor linger pause in melancholy gloom.
> In that blest world, where pain, and sorrow cease.
> Thy soul has rest, in everlasting peace;
> Thy bright career suspends the rising sigh,
> And bids me live like thee, like thee, to die.[54]

The Story household, with its diffusion of authority, its tolerance, the egalitarian relationship of husband and wife, taught a republican lesson on authority.[55] In contrast to the style common in many of the Federalist families of the time, there was little institutionalized deference to parents, no "honored Papa" or "honored Mamma."[56] "Childhood" was permitted (in anticipation of the nineteenth century), and the old Puritan habit of crushing young wills was gone.[57] There was "no domestic tyranny" and "no curious prying into abuses, no magnifying of pecadilloes into crimes." Dr. Story "avoided seeing any freak unless it bore a stamp of immorality"[58]—a category that, as it turned out, did not include midnight sorties by Joseph and his brothers into the family larder: It must be the family dog, Dr. Story obligingly told a visiting neighbor on one such occasion, pretending not to notice his children's feet sticking out from under the kitchen table.

Because there was no oppressive authoritarianism in the Story family, it must not be inferred that there were no restraints or givens. On the contrary: Between the lines one reads Mehitable Story's character, again anticipating her son's exactly, as a natural didact, an intrepid, somewhat self-righteous moralizer. Elisha Story, too, for all his gentleness stood firm on the virtues, the ethics, and the moral life stressed by liberal Christianity. The elder Story was prejudiced against prejudice, firm in a "constant hatred of religious persecution," in his "inextinguishable love of freedom of opinion and inquiry in matters of religion."[59] The givens were that God was benevolent and man rational and the nation sacred. On these values indifference was not tolerated, opposing views were not represented.

It is doubtful whether Story's parents found time in their busy lives to read Rousseau's *Emile* with its naturalistic theory of education, its emphasis on the traits of simplicity, self-reliance, and independence.[60] That Story celebrated it so exuberantly suggests that his family practiced much of what Rousseau preached (minus his antifeminism, to be sure).[61] In any case, there was no youthful rebellion against parental authority, no generation gap, in Story's childhood. Emphasis in the Story household, as in *Emile* and the theories of Maria and Richard L. Edgeworth (other authorities for education in the new republic),[62] was on family environment, learning by emulation. It was mainly through this method, at any rate, that Story learned to know who he was, where he stood, and what he wanted. Because his family lived what it taught, there was no chasm of hypocrisy to discourage learning or to separate generations. Values were not forced but assimilated. There were clear limits and firm boundaries on the one hand, and freedom to grow, maneuver, and test on the other.

The freedom Story had in which to find himself, no less important than the limits, was a function of life in Marblehead. It was also a luxury afforded by the privileged position of Dr. Story. Farm youngsters in the hinterland, unless they were unusually well off, went to work with the family at the age of eight or nine, and the sons and daughters of Marblehead's fishing families were recruited early on to cut, salt, and dry the cod. Unlike his poor contemporaries (but exactly like his future friend and Harvard classmate William Ellery Channing, who cherished his "solitude" too),[63] Story had space and freedom. His father's capacious house meant that he had some privacy at home. There was no hay to harvest or fish to dry, so like Channing in Newport Story could wander, think, plan, and dream— all of which Marblehead invited him to do. He remembered many years later what it meant to do so:

> My delight was to roam over the narrow and rude territory of my native town; to traverse its secluded beaches and its shallow inlets; to gaze upon the sleepless ocean; to lay myself down on the sunny rocks and listen to the deep tones of the rising and falling tide; to look abroad, when the foaming waves were driven with terrific force and uproar against the barren cliffs or the rocky promontories, which everywhere opposed their immovable fronts to resist them; to seek, in the midst of the tremendous majesty of an eastern storm, some elevated spot where, in security, I could mark the mountain billow break upon the distant shore, or dash its broken waters over the lofty rocks which here and there stood along the coast naked and weather-beaten. But still more was I pleased, in a calm summer day, to lay myself down alone on one of the beautiful heights which overlook the harbor of Salem, and to listen to the broken sounds of the hammers in the distant ship-yards, or to the soft ripple of the murmuring wave; or to gaze on the swelling sail, or the flying bird, or the scarcely moving smoke, in a reverie of delicious indolence.[64]

Indolence and solitude: these were not qualities ordinarily celebrated in the republican catechism. But in an age of growing individualism, solitude in league with nature was an acceptable means to the end of selfhood. Story put the idea to work, even wrote about it, long before Emerson turned it into a philosophy. Solitude was power, said Story in his ambitious poem "The Power of Solitude."[65] It was the catalyst that permitted him to sort out and integrate ideas of virtue, ambition, history; truths learned at home, in church, at Marblehead Academy. In his "solitary rambles" he carried Young's *Night Thoughts*[66] ("darkness visible")[67] along with Uncle Isaac's images of hell's fire, a mixture that, together with a roaring nor'easter off Fort Sewell, could conjure up some frightening images. Solitude, then, tempted Story to become an avowed romantic, but he was a rationalist as well. (Before he wrote the poem to solitude he wrote one to reason, which in a not unreasonable romantic gesture he later burned.)

The view of life Story put together on his solitary wanderings was in fact a series of polarities, oscillations between the Calvinist world view of his uncle and the hopeful one of his father, between optimism and pessimism, between heart and mind. In the freedom of his youth he mastered contesting ideas and passions and in the process gathered energy for public life. But private and public life were hardly separable, or if they must be deemed polarities then there was, in Story's case at least, a well-traveled path between them. With a revealing ease the solitary beachcomber, rock-climber, shipwatcher, became the golden-haired boy-orator of the Marble-head barbershop who impressed the likes of old Mr. Hawkes with his precocity.[68] Later the poet who (in the tradition of the Reverend Edward Taylor of Westfield) would poetize privately to assuage the grief felt on the death of his children would double as one of the writing-est, talking-est public men in America. Words made in solitary study opened the door to public greatness in the print culture of the young republic, as Story, the most prolific legal publicist in the nineteenth century, would prove.[69]

There is evidence that his "greatness" was a matter of strategy. Ambition, perhaps even more than talk, was an abundant quantity in the Story family. Elisha Story aimed to be the best doctor around, and the evidence is that he was, especially in obstetrics. Aspiration jumps out from Isaac Story's printed sermons, his high-flown patriotic orations, and from his admonition to his minister brother Daniel to save the new West from sin.[70] Mutual encouragement in fact was a family staple. When Joseph's half brother William succeeded in business, his full brother Isaac congratulated him on the fact that "letters are no longer directed to the simple Mr. Story, but to Mr. William Story, Merchant, Boston."[71] (That was little more than a half century after old William Story of Boston made it from "Mr." to "Esquire.") Place-seeking in the largest sense may in fact have been one aspect of family that transcended the revolutionary break. And Joseph Story was a special target of this family aspiration: "his father's pride and joy, his mother's own delight," as an old ballad put it. Story's Christian name said as much: "Joseph" in New England was a name, following Gen. 37:3−8, often reserved for the first sons of second marriages, where it stood for special blessing and signified a hope for distinction.[72]

Significantly, the only quotation directly attributable to Story's mother is on exactly this theme: "Now, Joe," she is reputed to have said, "I've sat up and tended you many a night when you were a child, and don't you dare not to be a great man." His father also had special hopes for Joseph, treated him from a young age with a special "confidence" and, as Story proudly remembered, filled him with "an ambition for excellence" and urged him to struggle for "distinction as a man."[73] Dr. Story assigned Joseph a special position of guardianship of his mother in his will, too, not because she needed help but as a "special confidence in his affections, skill and abilities."[74] The burden was not just to succeed but to be great. Even Marblehead, whose decline instilled in Story the deep desire to escape to something better, joined the refrain.

The place to escape to greatness, experience showed, was Harvard College—or rather (since 1780), to signify *its* aspirations, Harvard University. Master Joseph Story was almost ready for the new world of books and learning and the likes of Arthur Maynard Walter and his esteemed "circle of worthies."

3. Harvard University: Self-Mastery Proved, Aspiration Vindicated

The village of Marblehead, however else it educated Story, did little to prepare him for that new world of letters. Solitude had its limits as well. ("I saw few persons, & heard still fewer," he complained retrospectively.) [75] Book learning, such as there was, fell to Marblehead's newly established academy. Story's presence there signified his father's ability to pay (though the fees generally were not steep), his ambition for his son, and his hopes that a college education would lead him into one of the learned professions.

What else it meant is not so clear. On the one hand, the academy was a considerable step up from the primitive and sporadic public education that New England provided its working poor. On the other, it was a notch below established academies like those in Andover, Exeter, or Worcester (where John Adams taught as a young man) and well beneath the Boston Public Latin, where Story's father went. Not much is known of the school, but if it followed the pattern of eighteenth-century academies it lumped students of a wide age range together, so that they learned from one another as well as from the instructors, who were often poorly equipped and almost always poorly paid. [76]

At the head of Marblehead Academy was the Reverend Mr. William Harris, later president of Columbia University, who taught elocution when he was not laying on the ferrule. Young Michael Walsh, the usher, handled all the rest; luckily, he was an able and deeply concerned teacher, and a special friend to young Story. Walsh taught the rudiments of arithmetic and taught them well if one judges from his *Mercantile Arithmetic*,[77] which was one of the most popular texts of the early nineteenth century. He handled Greek and Latin grammar, too, well enough for Story to attribute to him his own foundation in classical learning.[78] Judging from the few extant letters between them, Walsh whetted Story's appetite for learning and his determination to excel. The overworked young tutor also taught English grammar and literature, but Story seems to have learned these mainly on his own or with his mother's help, working from Dr. Viscemius Knox's *Elegant Extracts*, which included excerpts from such authors as Addison, Burke, Chesterfield, Franklin, and Montesquieu (among "Prosaic writers") and Goldsmith, Gray, Crabbe (all of whom Story praised), Milton, Pope, Shakespeare, Smollet, and Swift (among the "Votaries of the Muses").[79] As for elocution, which in response to the civic-minded age was already a staple at Harvard, Joseph probably learned as much from his mother and from his regular appearances at the local barbershop as he did from the autocratic Reverend Mr. Harris. Talking at any rate was not something he had to learn.

Besides Walsh's friendship and Dr. Knox's book, Story remembered little he liked about the academy except athletics (which he entered into enthusiastically) and the company of female students (who, along with his mother, taught him some early lessons about the equality of women "in their studies and acquirements.")[80] What struck him most vividly about the school was Harris's brutality. In the fall of 1794, when he was fifteen and in his last year at the academy, Story "chastized" one of his fellow students at the school for "some boyish affair." Unfortunately, the lad boarded with Harris, who lay in wait for revenge and soon found the occasion in some "slight peccadillo" of Story's. He was brought before the whole school and beaten on the hands with a ruler, all the harder and longer because, out of pride, he refused to cry out. Story forgave Harris many years later—"heartily forgave him"—but he never forgot the ritual of humiliation. Nor did Elisha Story, who, having abjured education by humiliation at home, was not about to tolerate it in school. He immediately withdrew his son from the academy and made plans for his early admission to Harvard at the ensuing winter term.[81]

So it was that Story traveled to Cambridge with his uncle Isaac in the late fall of 1794 to see where he stood regarding admission. He arrived with the "flush of hope" on his cheeks, only to have it wiped off by the formidable Reverend Joseph Willard, president of Harvard, who informed the village scholar how much he did not know. Story was "glum, disconsolate, mortified" to hear that not only would he have to stand the regular entrance examination, but he would also be tested on all the studies covered by the freshman class during the fall term.[82] Besides English grammar, rhetoric, and logic, there were Sallust, the *Odes* of Horace, Livy, three books of Xenophon's *Anabasis*, and two books of Homer's *Iliad*. All this in six weeks?

Joseph returned to Marblehead in a deep depression, but in even less time than it took his mother to recover from her lost love, he resolved to meet the test. Like Achilles off to the siege of Troy, he girded himself for battle. By cramming most of the night every night (as his younger brother Isaac testified) and clipping off five recitations each morning (memorized the night before) to the town schoolmaster, he covered the entire ground, leaving three weeks for general review. Self-discipline paid off. Story conquered Harvard's entrance exam like "the hero who conquers in battle, the orator who triumphs in the senate."[83] The first skirmish confirmed his confidence and intensified his appetite for glory—an appetite that, one senses, was already a bit excessive for the measured tastes of Arthur Walter.

Looking back at college education before the turn of the century and judging it by mid-nineteenth-century standards, Edward Everett was amazed at the simplicity of it, though he also noted that a college degree still "constituted a person at once a member of an intellectual aristocracy."[84] Even Story had to agree that Harvard education in the 1790s was more "confined and limited than at present," in 1843.[85] He did not concede that it was therefore deficient. True, Harvard was a backwater compared to the great universities of England and Europe; even against Princeton it could not hold its own. There were only five professors counting President Willard; the great burden of instruction, as well as supervision, counseling, and moral uplift, was thus left to a handful of tutors, most of whom were recent graduates and all of whom were overworked, underpaid, and, with one exception, transient. The library was small and so was the student body. All but a handful of the student body—173 strong when Story graduated in 1798—came from a radius of fifty miles. No New Yorkers at all attended the college from 1737 to 1790;[86] during Story's day they were still exotic birds. The great influx of Southern students was still half a century away.

Nor was provinciality much relieved by the surroundings: Cambridge was still a country village remembered by Harvard students primarily, it appears, for its pretty girls, who were decidedly off limits to them. Boston offered little help, partly because it was inaccessible to most students (even though the West Boston Bridge was built in 1792) and partly because it had not outgrown its own intellectual and cultural limitations. Not surprisingly, venturesome and bold spirits like Joseph Dennie (later of *Portfolio* fame) preferred "rustification among the country girls" to Harvard's meager fare. Others celebrated college days and college friends more than Harvard's book learning. Even William Ellery Channing, who was grateful for what he got at Harvard but whose spirit and ambition had already begun to soar, had to confess finally that Cambridge was intellectually confining.[87]

In contrast, Joseph Story of Marblehead thought it was "Elysium" and relished it with an uncritical passion. "I awoke, as it were, from a dream," he remembered vividly years later. "Everything was new to me. I seemed to breathe a higher atmosphere, and to look abroad with a wider vision and more comprehensive power. Instead of the narrow group of a village, I was suddenly brought into a large circle of young men engaged in literary pursuits, and warmed and cheered by the hopes of future eminence."[88] If a good education is convincing students that education is good, that learning is worthwhile, then Harvard for Joseph Story was a great university.

Clearly the "seminary," as a few of the old-timers still called it, fitted

Story's needs. More to the point, it complemented and augmented the republican education he had begun in Marblehead. Harvard supplied an intellectual excitement, a ferment of ideas, not because its curriculum embodied the final word on truth and culture (though it presumed to do so) but because it did not and could not. Harvard University, like New England—indeed, like American society—was in the throes of republican transformation; old and new coexisted on uneasy terms. "Old forms were outgrown," William Ellery Channing observed "and new ones had not taken their place."[89] A creative tension was felt everywhere: tentatively in the faculty, more strongly among the tutors, and most of all between the students and the faculty and administration. Among the students themselves there was also a growing ideological conflict. This conflict was exacerbated by the disparity between Harvard's official curriculum and the world of underground books and ideas, pursued more avidly, no doubt, because they were discouraged by the administration. The struggles between Calvinism and liberal religion, between secularism and religiosity, were not new at Harvard in the 1790s, of course. But the unfinished business of the American Revolution gave the debate new relevance, which was intensified further for Harvard students of the 1790s by the debate over the French Revolution. Willy-nilly Harvard found itself, not unlike young Story himself, grappling toward an education fit for the republican age.[90]

The transformation was uneven, but old forms were on the wane. For example, the practice of classifying students at Harvard according to the social position of their families was dropped during the early stages of the Revolution in favor of a more republican listing by alphabet. Dropped also was the aristocratic dress code that sanctioned frilled cuffs and class markings. Social distinctions among Harvard students did not disappear completely, however, and may help explain both the general clannishness of Harvard students and that of the special group to which Story belonged. He remembered, at any rate, and with great distaste, that he entered at the "fag end" of his class. But more to the point, he recalled with relish the republican side of Harvard in the 1790s: the open, competitive drive for excellence that permitted bright, industrious young men to gain distinction without regard to social pedigree.

Harvard or at least Harvard students responded to the republican age, which cried out for young men of ability to lead the nation. Intellectual combat was everything and more that organized athletics would become. The enforced isolation of Cambridge and the small and homogeneous nature of the student body added further incentive to what Story called the "powerful impulse to . . . ambition" and the "generous spirit of emulation" that came in its wake. The natural arena for Harvard's intellectual gladiators was the classroom, then, where the now much-denigrated system of formal class recitation prevailed. "This general assemblage of the whole class in the same room at the same time had, in my judgment," wrote Story, "the most beneficial influence. In the first place, it enabled the whole class clearly and accurately to ascertain the relative scholarship and attainments of each scholar; and thus one great source of jealousy, the suspicion of partiality on the part of the college faculty, was either extinguished or greatly mitigated, and I do not hesitate to say that the relative rank then assigned to the various members of the class by their own classmates was generally correct, impartial, and satisfactory."[91]

For young Story, well trained in barbershop declamation but eager for a larger and more discriminating audience, public recitation was a godsend. There were some painful moments to be sure, as when his self-taught Latin pronunciation called forth derisive laughter from classmates. When Story laughed they laughed less, and when the instructor reminded them that he knew his lessons better than they did, the laughter stopped altogether. Knowledge, even for a lowly freshman, was a kind of power, and it helped Story overleap what was left of the social pecking order of the not-so-good old colonial days.

His growing reputation as a scholar, along with his natural garrulousness and high spirits, also helped him break the social ice formed by his late arrival. Story seems never to have penetrated the exclusivist circle of Arthur Walter, William Smith Shaw, and William Ellery Channing, though he and Channing held one another in high mutual esteem. Most likely he did not belong to the Porcellian Club, either, which unlike the other, "working clubs" was organized around social status and dedicated to fun. But Story had his own circle of congenial friends and admirers. Joseph Tuckerman, whom Boston would later celebrate as the originator of the "ministry at large," was one of his dearest friends, along with C. P. Sumner, the father of Charles Sumner, future senator from Massachusetts and one of Story's favorite students at Harvard Law School. Other college chums who turned into longtime friends were Humphrey Devereaux, Leonard Woods, Richard Sullivan, William Williams, Jonathan French, and Samuel P. Fay.

College socializing was a crucial part of Story's education, but he never abandoned his penchant for solitude. Strolling under the college elms and wandering by the Charles were favorite pastimes. Poetizing, too, increasingly attracted his attention, and he even tried his hand at painting (attempts that his artist son later found promising). But mostly he studied, which duty he approached in a state of mind that mixed the Puritan with the Roman. Like Channing and unlike other college students of the age, he drank no alcohol, a habit he maintained until he met John Marshall, whose irresistible logic convinced him that a glass of Madeira somehow fell within the jurisdiction of the Supreme Court. As for the other forms of dissipation, "I passed through the dangerous period," he boasted, "without a stain or reproach."[92] He rhapsodized ardently about the local "goddesses," to be sure, but for him, unlike the rakish Dennie, female breasts heaved only with "divine sentiments" and "delicacy of thought."[93] And late nights were for books. Coming home to Massachusetts Hall from a convivial night among friends, Tuckerman often found his indomitable roommate still bent over the books. If some of his classmates went to the yard pump to sober up after a night in Boston (whose charms some, like Leverett Saltonstall and James Dunning, found irresistible) they might well have run into him splashing his face with water to salvage another hour of study. What they no doubt failed to understand was that for Joe Story (as for Mr. Justice Story) work and play were indistinguishable.

A good deal of the intellectual world that Story set out to master with such determination went back to colonial times and beyond, but the changes, most of which were accretional, were important too. Greek and Latin were the foundations of Harvard's curriculum in the 1790s as they had been in the seventeenth century, and were studied all four years. Story remembered especially struggling through Xenophon's *Anabasis* and two books of the *Iliad* for Greek, and for Latin, Sallust and a few books of Livy. For the sheer joy of it he read the *Odes* of Horace[94] (which were banned earlier in the century because of their corrupting secularism). Hebrew was offered to freshmen, but they could, and did, with the permission of their parents avoid it, so that it became more and more a special course for ministers-to-be—who were becoming a decided minority of the student body. There was in Story's day one French course available, but as a true measure of Federal New England's affinity to France, it was taught only once a week by a nonresident instructor.[95] Whether Story took the course is not clear, but he did read French. To his regret he read neither German nor Hebrew.

With reason honed, sensibilities refined, and republican virtue fortified by the classics, Story and his friends were allowed to delve deeper into the traditional liberal arts. From arithmetic the first year he graduated to algebra (taught from Nicholas Saunderson's textbook). Euclidean geometry was standard fare beginning with the junior year, put there, one of Story's classmates believed, "to measure our strength." (One of Story's carefully constructed proofs still rests in the Harvard University Archives.) Beyond Euclid were conic sections, spheric geometry, and trigonometry. Somewhat related to mathematics but more practical in approach was the senior course in astronomy. History and history's lessons, it was assumed, would be learned in part from the classics. More directly there was, as part of the official fare, Abbé Millot's *Elements d'histoires*, immortalized by one victim as "the most utterly worthless and contemptible work of that kind or any other extant"—which may explain why interested students turned increasingly to the works of Edward Gibbon, Francis Ferguson, and Charles Rollin (the latter of whose *Ancient History* was a standard source of American ideas about ambition).[96]

Seniors, whether bound for the ministry or not, got a substantial taste of theology via Philip Doddridge's ubiquitous *Lectures* (which by Story's time had replaced the work of the more tedious Wollebius).[97] Locke's *Essay concerning Human Understanding* was still a staple, and most students seem to have encountered William Paley, whose work on natural philosophy argued for the permeation through all society of unifying Christian moral values, a holistic notion that became stock-in-trade in Story's legal system and that would find itself increasingly at odds with nineteenth-century facts of economic life. Running parallel to all this and required of freshmen and sophomores was logic (Aristotelian as well as Ramist), taught from Isaac Watts's *Logic*. Declamation and elocution, practiced daily in recitations and informally in Harvard's speaking clubs, were refined by Blair's *Lectures on Rhetoric and Belles Lettres*, whose emphasis on heart as well as mind attested to the presence of Scottish Enlightenment ideas and forecast the coming of Unitarianism.[98] The idea here and elsewhere at Harvard that reason and emotion, heart and mind, need not part company was entirely congenial to Story's inclination (just as it had been to John Marshall's earlier).[99]

Although Harvard's curriculum had quietly responded to the forces of liberalism and secularism during the century, much else remained traditional[100]—not least the faculty. President Willard had done much to put the school on a sound footing in the hectic period after the Revolution. He was a distinguished classicist—a "sound scholar," Story called him—as well as a competent mathematician and astronomer. He was also a Calvinist in theology who was "stiff and unbending" in the face of the radical ideas of the 1790s. "Cold and foreboding in his demeanor," Story recalled, he still addressed Harvard undergraduates as "children." When he appeared in the Yard, bewigged and bedecked in smallclothes, he expected hats to come off—and they did.[101]

Eliphalet Pearson (known to some of his students as "Elephant") came to Harvard from Phillips Academy in 1785 as Hancock Professor of Hebrew and other oriental languages; when enrollment in those courses waned he taught principles of English grammar and composition. Story thought him an "excellent critic," but he was also, as his campaign for the presidency of Harvard in 1805 and his opposition to Henry Ware for the position of Hollis Professor of Divinity indicated, an opponent of creeping liberalism at Harvard. The Hollis Professor during Story's years was the Reverend David Tappan, who was less formidable and more moderate in his Calvinism but who also resisted further concessions to liberal religion. Professor Samuel Webber, who taught mathematics, was more receptive to liberalism than Willard and Tappan, maybe because he was less in a position to do anything about it. He was also less overbearing than "Elephant" Pearson, but he was uninspiring and, in Story's words, "unconquerably distant" (in the eighteenth-century style). Whatever excitement was generated by teaching, then, came mainly from young tutors like John Popkin and Levi Hedge, whom Story remembered with gratitude.[102] But even they were expected to distance themselves from the students so as not to interrupt their "espionage" duties.

Story never rebelled against the rule of the "*regime* of the old school," as he called it,[103] either the courses or the men who taught them. Innocence perhaps, a family-bred faith in authority maybe, or simply his starvation for learning and deeply engrained work habits kept him enthusiastic for what might appear—was in fact already under attack as being—thin gruel. Story and others no doubt tolerated Harvard's formal requirements more easily because they were only one part of education at Harvard. Outside formal courses, sometimes as an outgrowth of them and at other times in opposition to them, was a world of ideas generated and sustained by the students themselves, who in many ways were more receptive to the new and often radical ideas of the eighteenth century than their teachers. What they taught themselves, in their private friendships (as for example that of Story and Woods),[104] in the Speaking Club, the Phi Beta Kappa Society, or Adelphi ("working clubs" in which students criticized one another's literary productions), cannot be known for sure. The transforming ideas of the Scottish Enlightenment never swept Willard's Harvard as they did Witherspoon's Princeton, but "Scottish texts" were introduced in 1792 by Professor Tappan,[105] and there is evidence that Hume and Ferguson were being read. Gibbon's *Decline and Fall* was a favorite with some, too, despite an official interdict. Its grand ironic style and passionate sense of time and change, of human error and folly, were a refreshing relief from Millot's insipid teleology. Shakespeare (who was, as Channing noted, extremely popular among the undergraduates) joined Gibbon in affirming the complexity of human nature and moral truth. Gibbon and Shakespeare, along with Scottish common sense, could only have blurred Calvin's version of human nature and human history.

A healthy and un-Calvinist debate was also taking place over the meaning of human nature as Locke's psychology undercut medieval categories of mind, only to be challenged by Berkeley, Hume, and Richard Price. The latter's works circulated freely in the Harvard underground; Story's friend William Williams confessed that they saved him from Locke.[106] The English romantics got a hearing, too, in the works of Goldsmith and Southey. Story liked both of them, though not to the exclusion of Pope (who was also a favorite of his future friend and colleague John Marshall). Even further away from the world of Joseph Willard and his friends were the writings of German romantics like Goethe, which were making their way among Harvard students at this time and which Story appears to have read in translation. Most disruptive of the old ways were the political radicalism of Tom Paine (whose *Rights of Man* appeared only three years before Story entered Harvard) and the radical social theories of Rousseau, William Godwin, and Mary Wollstonecraft. Not many tasted this forbidden fruit, but a few such ideas went a long way—far enough at least for the conservative-minded to call forth Bisset, Bolingbroke, and Burke as antidotes. ("So much dignity in the man, so much proud authority," gushed Walter about the latter.)[107]

How exactly and to what result Story engaged in the cultural dialogue it is impossible to say with precision. Clearly he did not neglect Harvard's standard offerings: He graduated second in his class behind Channing (with each arguing that the other deserved first place).[108] That he went beyond the requirements is verified by Walter's caustic retrospective evaluation. Story, he said, was a "young man who has really read much, but who has digested nothing; who takes for granted what he finds in books, but never appeals to the experience of his mind, as the correct standard of truth."[109] In his wide-ranging pursuit of knowledge, Story undoubtedly sampled the Jacobinical literature of the 1790s, as Walter later claimed. There is, however, serious question that he believed as much of it as Walter alleged. It is true that Story read the Bible less than was expected, and he expressed great admiration for Rousseau shortly after graduating in 1798 (though significantly it was *Emile* and not the *Social Contract* that he named). But certainly his moral sensibilities would have been just as offended as Walter's with that "errant jade" Mrs. Wollstonecraft, as the young conservatives called her. William Smith Shaw's distress at the notion of a community of property, too, was a sentiment that Story most certainly shared. There is no evidence for, and considerable against, the notion that he accepted Tom Paine as a hero, particularly in light of the difficulty he had with Thomas Jefferson even while he was working to elect him. Washington and Adams were his heroes, not Jefferson, Paine, or Robespierre.

What we see, if we extrapolate from Walter's constant carping and note Woods's friendly suggestion that Story put more stock in the Bible, was a young man who plunged headlong into the swift current of new ideas, and this is how he saw himself. That he believed what he read, that he oscillated between romanticism and rationalism (as he would later between Federalism and Jeffersonian Republicanism), merely meant that he had not resolved the tensions present in the intellectual culture of the age. If there was still play in the joints of Story's intellectual system, he did settle two things at Harvard. First, he made a decisive and permanent move away from the Calvinism of Isaac Story and Harvard's "ancient regime"— from their stingy view of human nature and increasingly unrepublican notions of material progress.[110] More congenial to his own buoyant nature was his father's religious liberalism, which he found reinforced by his subversive reading at Harvard and probably even more by his iconoclastic friends, who in no way appeared to be passive sinners in the hands of an angry God. Story's conversion to Unitarianism did not obliterate all traces of his early Calvinism, to be sure, though such traces are found more in his secular intellectual system than in his religion. Story's view of history as a great struggle between good and evil, for example, retained more than a little Calvinist teleology. A concern for morality and ethics had, in Story's Unitarianism, replaced the theological emphasis of early Calvinism. What remained was a belief in the permeating quality of that morality (as we shall see in his approach to the common law) and a willingness to judge his enemies accordingly (as we shall see in his unforgiving hatred of Thomas Jefferson).

Story's religion, which stands in stark contrast to his later political philosophy, was warm, generous, and Arminian.[111] God for Story as for Massachusetts Unitarianism remained a personal God, not a cosmic force, a New Testament God of benevolence, forgiveness, and love. Story never spoke much of miracles, unlike his future colleague at Harvard, Andrews Norton, but he believed in salvation and life after death—the greatest miracle of all. Never in his deepest gloom did he doubt that he would be saved or that he would see those he loved in Heaven. Whether he was prepared to see Andrew Jackson there he never said, but the democratic nature of his religious belief led him to that possibility. Certainly the generous view of man revealed in Story's Unitarianism was congenial to the new age of rationality and consistent with the republican conviction that people with God's help might control their own destinies. Temporarily, at least, Story was moving toward a view of American history that would carry him away from Walter, Shaw, and company and into the party of Thomas Jefferson.

Story's second conversion at Harvard, not unconnected to the first, was to scholarship, to the life of the mind. His commitment to rationalism, it must be emphasized, did not crowd out the romantic in him or eliminate the poet. Heart and mind were as yet in a friendly state of tension, just as science and religion, emotion and reason, had been for Jonathan Edwards a half century before. The combination was a function of Story's complex personality as well as his course of studies; it made perfect sense that his scholarship at Harvard should have been recognized by his being designated the class poet, and that the poem he wrote for graduation in 1798 should have been called "Reason." Story's belief in the illimitable progress of human reason[112] may have been at odds with the cyclic theory of history preached by David Tappan at commencement, but it did not contradict his newfound religion or his romantic idealism. One cannot observe the central role of scholarship, of science, in Story's life—in shaping his career choice of law over politics, in determining his work as judge and jurist—without sensing the formative impact of the Harvard years and the relevance of the old learning. It was not accidental that Justice Story, when faced with what he firmly believed to be the crisis of the survival of the Republic in the 1820s, should have turned to education and to Harvard University as instruments of salvation.

4. A Civic Humanist at Harvard: A Young Man of the Republic

"He who has been able, by the force of his talents and the examples of his virtues, to identify his own character with the solid interests and happiness of his country; he who has lived long enough to stamp the impression of his own mind upon the age, and has left on record lessons of wisdom for the study and improvement of all posterity; he, I say, has attained all that a truly great man should aspire to."[113] So declared Story in his eulogy of Chief Justice John Marshall in October 1835. In bringing talent, virtue, character, and wisdom to public service Marshall embodied the essence of republican statesmanship. But Story, it is clear from the context of his words, was not writing just about the chief justice. Among others who fit the definition of greatness were Newton, Locke, Epaminondas, Scipio, Justinian, and Washington. And Joseph Story? Not quite, perhaps—or rather, not yet. But if Story was not writing *about* himself, he was writing *for* himself. Here in his tribute to his dearest friend was his formula for fame and immortality. Here too, only slightly disguised, was a statement of his own ambition. Story assumed that biography and history might merge, that individual ambition might serve national greatness. It was a lesson taught by the American Revolution as refracted by Marblehead, by Elisha Story, and by Harvard University; it was the most republican part of his republican education.

The age in which Story grew up was obsessed with the question of ambition, greatness, fame—all rooted in the history and logic of a successful revolution. No other generation in American history had the distinctive honor of being present at the birth of the nation. No other generation, or so it must have seemed to contemporaries, had so defied historical odds to impose its will on history. How could a disunited collection of colonies with barely more than three million people, with a raggle-taggle army led by a mere tobacco planter and a handful of ships for a navy, defeat the greatest military and naval power in the world? Against all odds they had done just that. Participation in that singular and almost inexplicable effort gave heroism a new standard and bestowed a legacy of emulation on the succeeding generation. Young Story and others whose lives were coterminous with that of the young nation and who grew up with it were invited to serve its cause, mix their lives with its. The challenge was to secure the Revolution against a hostile world, to extend its principles through national institutions and national law, to spread a republican culture over a vast and waiting continent. What John Adams wrote three years before Story was born still made sense: What an age for "lawgivers," exulted Adams. "When, before the present epoch, had three millions of people full power and a fair opportunity to form and establish the wisest and happiest government that human wisdom can contrive?" [114] The founders had done their work; a new generation of statesmen must do its. And because there was so much to be done, the possibility of shaping history was real. A man achieved success, as Story saw it, by identifying his own character and talents "with the solid interests and happiness of his country." [115] Ambition directed to selfish ends might ruin the republic; ambition directed to public good might save it. As Portius in Addison's much-read *Cato* put it to Story and his friends at Harvard: "Thy life's not thy own, when *Rome* demands it." [116]

The classics taught Story and his compatriots much about the glories of public service, the temptations of power, the dangers of ambition gone wrong. So did Shakespeare, Francis Bacon, and the still-fresh arguments of the eighteenth-century English polemicists that had nourished America's revolutionary inclinations. But the American republic, as thoughtful students and would-be statesmen understood, was not Greece or Rome or eighteenth-century England either. To accommodate this fact, America, or at least New England, developed its own homegrown catechism of political ethics, one forged by the Revolution from an amalgam of social and political experience, Calvinist theology, and pulpit language into a new secular religion, a civic humanism. [117] In this unique code of republican behavior, God joined Americans in their struggle for liberty and justice. But He demanded in return (shades of the covenant) that they purify themselves. Religious morality became a civic necessity on which national survival depended. It followed that one served God by serving one's country, that public service took on the sanctity and the passion of a godly quest. In a way that Cotton Mather (the author of *Magnalia Christi Americana*) would have understood, the fate of the new republic was projected onto the great tradition of Western history in which good and evil were engaged in a life-and-death struggle.

The transforming impact of civic humanism came home to Story from every quarter and in overlapping and reconfirming regularity. Marblehead in its own crude way taught him the lessons of heroism and public service. What the village told him of sacrifice was confirmed in the vivid accounts of his mother and the example of a Patriot father who was a party to the creation of his country. Even his uncle Isaac, who preached patriotism and praised George Washington as a gift of God, confirmed the notion that one served God by serving one's country.[118]

Harvard University amplified the theme. Education no less than religion responded to the imperative of the Revolution, and tiny Harvard, without any deliberate plan or educational theory, became a vehicle of republican transformation. The republicanization of Harvard began long before Story got there; for example, the corporation of the college voted on 9 July 1771 to invite John Hancock "to dine in the Hall, whenever there is a public entertainment there"—this immediately following Hancock's rejection by Governor Hutchinson as a member of the Supreme Council of the province.[119] War came home to Harvard when Washington mustered his tiny army on Cambridge Common in the summer of 1776, when military action forced the college into temporary quarters at Concord. Harvard showed its patriotic colors in small ways by abandoning public commencement and quartering troops in college dormitories, and in large ones by sending its young men to fight. Even incidental practices such as abandoning frilled cuffs for blue homespun and dropping the practice of ranking students by social class signified the revolutionary spirit of Harvard College.

That spirit was still present when Story arrived in 1794, and not surprisingly. After all, the Peace of Paris was only eleven years old. Story roomed in Massachusetts Hall, which only a few years before had housed American soldiers. And most of all there was a new revolution to keep memories of the old one alive. The French Revolution forced Americans to debate the meaning of their own revolution; the world war that came in its wake created an environment distinctly hostile to republican institutions. Americans divided on the great issues of the day and so did Harvard students. Locke, Paine, Hutcheson, Hume, Price, Gibbon, and all else took on a new meaning. Even the old curriculum assumed an urgent relevance. History turned into prophecy; political philosophy into a practical guide for would-be statesmen; liberal learning became the foundation of the science of government, not because the administration willed it but because the young men of Harvard imbibed the heady spirit of the age.

It was, as Story put it, the "intra-moenial influence of college life."[120] Students read history for themselves, drew their own conclusions about controlling it—however much Tappan might warn them about the inevitability of cyclic decline. When Story remembered his friend Channing as being "ambitious of distinction," he was talking about himself and most of the rest of his classmates, with their "incentive to exertion" and "lofty ambition of excellence."[121] Scholarship assumed a centrality in Story's life, not just for its own sake but because it counted in the real world.

Excellence had its own rewards, no doubt, and the praise of fellow students given honestly and openly was surely gratifying. But the point was not lost on Harvard students that John Adams, class of 1755, was now president of the United States. Adams's example drove home what the age already took for granted: that statesmen were also intellectuals, that governance was a science informed by the study of the classics, history, logic, philosophy, and religion. It was not just the dress code that went out the window but the notion of aristocratic leisure itself. When plain citizens were expected to take a rational stand on public issues, when lawyers were often legislators and judges, and when ministers were a political force to reckon with, the life of public responsibility could not easily be shirked.

This message came home with special force to Harvard students in 1798 on the occasion of the quasi-naval war with France. Harvard rallied to support President Adams in his struggle to uphold American honor and neutral rights against the encroachments of France, and the first and second scholars of the graduating class of 1798 led the way. William Ellery Channing, the bolder of the two, insisted (against the stern advice of the administration) on making his valedictory a political statement supporting the foreign policy of John Adams. Only after threatening not to appear at all in the ceremony was he permitted to speak, and he spoke, according to one contemporary, with stern and knowing glances at the disgruntled faculty in attendance.[122]

Story had no occasion to be quite so courageous, but he supported Channing wholeheartedly and joined other Harvard students in signing a petition supporting Adams against France and his domestic critics. As the class poet, moreover, he went on record with his patriotism. When his class gathered for the last time in the college chapel on 21 June 1798, they sang these words by Story to the tune of "Rise Columbia":

> While discord's bloody flag unfurl'd,
>   O'er *Europe*, war his torrent pours,
> Rolls vollied thunder round the world,
>   From *Boreat* climes to *India's* shores,
>   *Rise, united,* Harvard's *band,*
>   *Rise, the bulwark of our land.*

> Shall *Galia's* clan our coast invade,
>   With hellish outrage scourge the main,
> Insult our nation's neutral trade,
>   And we not dare our rights maintain?
>   *Rise, & c*

>   .   .   .   .

> Beneath the *shade* by *wisdom* taught
>   The *arts* unfold their virgin charms;

> And, fir'd by genius, nervous Thought
> In Triumph grasp his *classic* arms.
> *Rise*, & c
>
> To guard this *pantheon* of the globe,
> While peace displays her rainbow vest,
> While, leagued with justice, swells the *robe*,
> And great in valor, nods the *crest*.
> *Rise*, & c
>
> Let freedom's voice round earth proclaim,
> *Cabal* shall ne'er *divide* our realm,
> While *time* can trumpet GEORGE's fame,
> Or ADAMS guide our *Union's* helm.
> *Rise*, & c
>
> Should fierce *invasion's* powers combine;
> To guard *Columbia*, great and free,
> E'en *Bunker*, rent by bursting mine,
> Would *float* an *Andes* o'er the sea.
> *Then, united*, Harvard's *band*,
> *Rise, the bulwark of your land.*[123]

Story's bad poetry is a telling document whose audacious assumption is that "Harvard's band" counted in the scales of national history. Not every student at Harvard aspired to such relevance, to be sure, and not all those who aspired achieved it. But there was, judging by the care with which they followed each other's careers, a collective pressure to succeed.[124] Walter's friend Nathaniel Lord, perhaps the most ambitious authority on class ambitions, noted only one sluggard in the lot. And he counted with pride just among his acquaintances in the class of 1798 twenty who pursued professional careers (five in law, five in divinity, three in medicine, and seven in teaching).[125]

The commitment of many, moreover, was to greatness, not merely success. In addition to Story (who shortly after graduation admitted that "ambition is truly the food of my existence, and for that alone life is desirable"),[126] there was Channing, who confessed a deep "love of country" and who was already aiming to influence its spiritual life—as in fact he did. Joseph Stevens Buckminster, two years behind Story and Channing, had a similar goal and (as biblical scholar and preacher at the Brattle Street Church) was already on his way to fame when he died in 1812. Buckminster's Phi Beta Kappa address at Harvard in 1809, "The Danger and Duties of Men of Letters," captured the noble principles that guided his life, no doubt the ones he imparted to young Daniel Webster, whom he taught briefly at Phillips-Exeter. Where Buckminster and Channing concentrated on the moral side of republican culture, Washington Allston, class of 1800, attended to the aesthetics. Allston died in 1843 with his great canvas *Belshazzar's Feast* (a dire prophecy about the republic) still unfinished, but his painting added significantly to the standing of American art. Arthur Walter's great plans for republican letters were cut short by an early death but not before his contribution to the founding of the Boston Athenaeum. His friend Shaw was also a moving force in that notable enterprise, as well as being among the founders and supporters of the Boston *Monthly Anthology*, a literary periodical devoted to the elevation and purification of republican letters. Even Joseph Dennie overcame his early resistance to learning and went on to touch the course of national letters as the talented editor of the *Port Folio*. Story's closest friend, Joseph Tuckerman, another late bloomer, pioneered in the field of Christian public service as Boston's famous "minister at large." And these were only some.

As for Story: Harvard and its students did not have to teach him about ambition, but the aspiration he brought from home was intensified and directed by college life and, judging by letters from his friend and tutor Michael Walsh, given a decided civic cast. Writing in 1794 (in Latin, as befitted the themes of public virtue and service to country), Walsh urged "dear Joseph" to "reach your goal as I argue. Pay attention to your studies as it is desirable that you always be a leader for the rest in the literary game."[127]

Three years later, in the midst of the passionate debate over the French Revolution and the growing foreign policy crisis, the goal of leadership turned from literature to statecraft and the salvation of the republic. "You estimate," wrote Walsh to Story on Independence Day, 1797, with an eye on past glories and the great Washington, "what attitude we boys have towards those who met the dangers of that time, by a divine nod as it were, rose up on behalf of the dignity of our country. 'O fortunate ones to whom he was a general in war and President in peace'—that man, I mean, who however often tempted, never sullied his reputation but now in the evening of his life increases his virtue with praise. May a long time remain for a life led usefully and, departing from this light, may he rise up again with increased splendor. Alas, when will we find an equal?"[128] Never, it was clear. But as the ship of state sailed into troubled seas, a new generation of leaders would be called on to take the helm. The hope, Walsh continued in another Latin letter the following day, was "that boys apply themselves to their studies so that when those men reach their heavenly abode, the fatherland, looking upon its young men, will rejoice."[129]

Rome called: six months later in his soaring eulogy on Washington, Story publicly owned the covenant of republicanism. All the symbolic trappings of civic humanism New England style were there, along with copious references to classical Greece and Rome, as befitted a new A.B.

from Harvard. With an exuberance that outdid his uncle Isaac's, the young orator canonized Washington on the spot. He was made to embody not only the "hereditary heroism" of ancient Greece and Rome, the "celerity of CAESAR," and the "prudence of FABIUS" but the morality of a Christian saint as well: Story referred to "our departed Savior" and the "sainted shade." "Like the resurrection angel, Washington rolled back the stone from the sepulcher of Reason," intoned Story in perfect synchronization with the new religion of republicanism, "dissolved the cerements of slavery, and led forth America to sovereignty and independence." The challenge to the new generation was to "enkindle in the hearts of our youth the spirit of freedom, the firmness of conduct, the activity of intellect, and the integrity of patriotism, that spoke, that blazoned, that convinced, in the character of Washington."[130]

In a penetrating insight about the operation of fame in early national history, Douglass Adair noted that in choosing their heroes, men revealed their own estimation of themselves, took their stand in history.[131] In choosing Washington, in the unselfconscious didacticism of his celebratory rhetoric, Story confessed his own lofty ambition to shape history, to assume the mantle of leadership left by the dead founder. Arthur Walter, among others, might think that Story aimed too high for his "modest" talents, but they did agree on one thing: With Tappan, whose lecture on cyclic history and the fate of republics both heard on graduation day, they agreed that the legacy of the Revolution was in danger and that a new generation must step into the breach. Cyclic history for republicans, like original sin for the Puritans, led not to passivity but to action. In praising Washington, Story stood witness to his belief that men of virtue and wisdom could shape history, that the duty of great leaders, as Hamilton said, was to march ahead of events. Like Erikson's Luther, Story was determined not just to accept the heritage he received from the fathers, from his father, but to "reinvigorate it." He, Joseph Story, eldest son of Mehitable and Elisha Story of Marblehead, A.B. Harvard 1798, soon-to-be student of law with the Honorable Samuel Sewall, was ready to march.

Chapter 2

Law over Politics

I cannot disguise that I had lost relish for political controversy, and found an entire obedience to party projects required such constant sacrifices of opinion and feeling, that my solicitude was greatly increased to withdraw from the field, that I might devote myself with singleness of heart to the study of law, which was at all times the object of my admiration and almost exclusive devotion.
Joseph Story to William Story,
23 January 1831

Sitting in the "gladsome light of Jurisprudence," the political world seemed to be lighted by squibs and fire-rockets.
William W. Story on his father

The period from the 1760s to the end of the War of 1812 in Massachusetts, as in the rest of the nation, was, despite its scope and complexity, of a single piece. Change and confusion followed inevitably in the wake of independence and the new freedom it brought. Massachusetts as much as any state felt the exhilarating impact of this freedom and the anxious chaos that came with it. Eleven of the fifty years between the Stamp Act and the Treaty of Ghent were spent in war and at least another ten in talking about it. While fretting for the survival of the nation, Massachusetts was working out its own version of republican government under the new constitution of 1780, a process that found the state oscillating violently between high-flown nationalism and states' rights tainted with threats of secession. Connected with Massachusetts's shifting politics were transforming economic changes: first the radical expansion of seaborne commerce that came with the end of British mercantilism, and then a revolution in manufacturing stimulated by the pressure of Jefferson's embargo. Economic change begat social division, too, and with the French Revolution, new interest groups and finally new political parties assumed ideological positions that identified self-interest with civilization.

In this period of turbulence, when uncertainty and potential went hand in hand, it is not surprising that Joseph Story and his ambitious classmates at Harvard were deeply concerned with the matter of governance and leadership. How, by whom, and according to what process should individuals formulate and administer the rules that would govern them individually and collectively? With his mind's eye on Saint Washington, the Founding Fathers, and his own father—on the great work to be done and the fame to be won—Story chose the legal profession.

Law suited his temperament and talents, but with him the profession took on a larger moral and ideological coloration. Like hundreds of his contemporaries, Story chose to pursue law and politics simultaneously; unlike most of them he came to see the two as not only practically incompatible but, in the republican scheme of things, fundamentally contradictory. Ten years of practicing both and an unexpected appointment to the Supreme Court led him to choose law over politics and "withdraw from the field."[1] But he carried with him two indelible impressions: One was that political parties, and to some extent the legislative branch where they operated most conspicuously, were inefficient, if not immoral and unrepublican, and quite unable to guide the American people safely through the troubled age. The other impression, fashioned in contrast to the first, was that law pursued as a science, administered by lawyers and judges, was a corrective to party government and possibly even an alternative to it—one uniquely compatible with republican principles.

In choosing law, then, Story chose not just a way of making a living but a way of governing, a way of life. Why he drew such cosmic conclusions is a question worth exploring because it reveals his holistic frame of mind and that of the age. The union of idealism and rationalism was translated into a romantic view of legal science that proved to be the starting point of his theory of judging and that remained a basic premise of his system of jurisprudence.

1. Apprentice at Law

Story took from Harvard, with its sustaining circle of friends, an accumulation of ideas and values prepared by a previous generation and passed on to him through family and folk wisdom and structured by formal education. Experience and book learning, intertwined with his own genius and personality, merged inextricably with his own sense of identity. His belief that man was noble was a projection of his own high assessment of himself; his conviction that history was controllable stemmed from a faith in his own ability to master it—part and parcel of a healthy, not to say bumptious, sense of self. Story came forth, then, to use Erik Erikson's apt phrase, "as a bearer of fresh energy."[2] It was also true that the capacity of his ideas to organize and explain experience had not really been tested, as his constant critic Arthur Walter noted. Nor had his talent been validated and accepted by the community he proposed to serve and shape.

The testing came with formative intensity from 1798 to 1805, the seven years after graduation, when in Story's own words the "feverish restlessness and unbridled passions of youth" gave way to manhood.[3] During these years he chose a wife, Mary Lynde Oliver, and lost her to death on

22 June 1805. His father's death only two months later thrust him deeper in gloom and further away from youthful dreams of happiness. He also chose a profession and studied it; chose a political party and served it; and confronted the swirling, shifting, and hostile society of Essex County: guardedly at first in the law offices of Samuel Sewall in Marblehead and Samuel Putnam in Salem; vigorously and passionately as a young lawyer-politician on the make. In one year, when he was twenty-six, he lost his wife and father, was elected to the state house of representatives, and saw the publication of his first scholarly work on the law, a volume of select pleadings.[4] Success did not erase his grief or restore his idyllic vision of happiness, but it helped him survive and rekindled his determination to make the law do great things.

Even at this early stage (despite the tears shed over Lord Coke and complaints about dusty folios) law was the staple of his existence, an "almost exclusive devotion." When exactly he committed himself to it is not clear, but certainly it was no later than his senior year at Harvard, for he went directly from graduation in June 1798 to apprenticeship in Sewall's office in Marblehead. Story never philosophized about his choice of profession, but his reasons can be readily surmised. Elisha Story made it clear very early that there would be little or no inheritance and that his son would have to prepare himself for a profession. Trade was out of the question, then, and so was literature, though Story loved the subject and at Michael Walsh's urging fashioned himself a "leader" at Harvard. Medicine was a possibility, of course, as was the ministry. He may well have been discouraged from the former by his father's career as a village doctor, if not by his advice, as well as by his own hankering after political fame, which the law would better serve. For the ministry he had as models his uncle Isaac and Harvard friends like Channing, Tuckerman, and Buckminster.

It cannot be denied that Story had a preachy and moralizing disposition, but the law could be a moral discipline, too, even a Christian one, as Story would soon argue. It was even more talky than preachy, a characteristic that suited his garrulous disposition; its potential as a science was even greater. More important, especially to a young man who aspired to fame, honor, and public service, the law and the legal profession in Massachusetts held out, as one recent scholar has put it, the "promise of power."[5] At least five of the Harvard Class of 1798 got the message, according to Nathaniel Lord's incomplete survey.[6] What these young men perceived, what the previous generation of lawyer-politicians had already discovered (and what the clergy increasingly feared) was that, in a society caught up in economic revolution, given to individual competition and materialism, lawyers would be the brokers of power.

Story chose law, regardless of the growing antilawyer sentiment in Massachusetts and despite grim advice that there were already too many lawyers. As for the commonplace warning that learning it by apprenticeship was haphazard, dreary, and lonely, it was all too true. Canaan may indeed lie "before your view," as Lord's poetic admonition to law students put it,

> But deserts must be travers'd through
> Before you rest secure.[7]

For Story the deserts were the "dry and technical principles, the dark and mysterious elements of the feudal system, the subtle refinements and intricacies of the middle ages of the common law, and the repulsive and almost unintelligible forms of processes and pleadings, for the most part wrapped up in black-letter, or in dusty folios."[8]

His guide over these trackless wastes was Samuel Sewall, a prominent, practical-minded, Federalist lawyer who was (unfortunately for Story's education) serving his party in Congress. Sewall was also a champion of social order who believed firmly in the right and duty of the elite to rule, sentiments distinctly at odds with the ideas of Elisha Story's son, who at that time was singing the beauties of Rousseau, Southey, Junius, and the German romantics.[9] Then there was Marblehead again. Without his Harvard friends, with college days behind him, with literary studies "ravished" from him, it was a "hard lot." What remained was the law to master and his ambition ("truly the food of my existence"): "It is the part of cowardice to shrink, and of imbecility to hesitate. I have determined, and will execute."[10]

Apprenticeship training in law, though always parochial, varied according to the talents and self-reliance of the student and the practice and library of the teacher—and his willingness and ability to teach. Story was relatively fortunate, although Sewall was no Edmund Trowbridge, the great lawyer-teacher of Essex County, and no Theophilus Parsons either. One problem, as Story complained, was that Sewall's duties in Congress kept him in Philadelphia about half the year. On top of that, he was a practical rather than a "philosophical" lawyer who, unlike a William Wirt or a David Hoffman, had no carefully devised comprehensive plan of study. He did have a wide-ranging commercial practice, however, and an impressive grasp of the requirements for success, the latter of which he passed on to his young ward in February 1799. There were, Sewall wrote assuredly, two ways to approach the law: One was "to begin with practice, such as writing in an attorney's office, & thereby a considerable stock of knowledge may be, as it were, mechanically obtained." The other, made possible by "the publication of Blackstone's Comms.," was "to examine the theory & General doctrines and the origins of the Municipal Law [i.e., national law], and descending from generals to particulars, to discover afterwards the partial applications & limits of the system. . . ."[11]

Sewall thought the second course "the easiest & Pleasantest" and finally "the most thoro' and certain course," and he set his young apprentice to work. First there were the "theory and general doctrines," for which Story turned to the English legal classics. For him as for Marshall, Webster, William Plumer, Roger Taney, James Kent, John Q. Adams, James Wilson, and Theophilus Parsons, not to mention Abraham Lincoln and the thousands of nineteenth-century lawyers who followed them, Blackstone's *Commentaries* was the primer.[12] Story devoured "this most elegant of all commentaries" with no difficulty. Not so with *Coke upon Littleton*, the next work on Sewall's "must" list, but the two works were to be studied in tandem. Blackstone by Sewall's reckoning would show Story "what is the law of England, whether originating in immemorial usage or in known statutes,"[13] and thus provide the starting point for reasoning about American law. In addition, it would give Story, as it gave others, the tools of legal language, a compendium of guiding principles, an introduction to English legal history, and a vision of law as a science—that is to say, as a system of interrelated principles and rules.[14]

Blackstone was about the law. *Coke upon Littleton*, in addition to providing the foundation of real property law, was the very essence of it. Mastering Coke separated the mere student from the scientific lawyer.[15] Fresh from the elegant Blackstone (not to mention "the lightest fiction, the enticing novel, the still more enticing romance"), Story took the solitary plunge into Coke using Hargrave's and Butler's notes. After many "bitter tears" of frustration he emerged victorious. "I felt that I breathed a purer air," he recalled, "and that I had acquired a new power." After Coke even Fearne's treatise, *Contingent Remainders and Executory Devises*, seemed simple, and Story dutifully made "a manuscript of all its principles."[16] It is likely that he also studied Espinasse on Nisi Prius (much praised among Massachusetts lawyers for its clarity and practicality). James Sullivan's *History of Land Titles in Massachusetts* (1801) also appeared in time to be of use to Story. Among other law-office standards were Comyns's *Digest* (which laid out basic legal principles with supporting authorities) and Bacon's *Abridgment* (the closest thing to the modern legal encyclopedia). The great natural law commentators Grotius, Puffendorf, and Vattel figured prominently in Story's education, but they appear to have come somewhat later.

Treatise learning in any case, as Sewall made clear, was not the end but the beginning, a preparation for the reports themselves.[17] And case law for the most part meant more English law, because, as Story remembered, there were only five or six volumes of American reports available and none for Massachusetts until 1805. First, advised Sewall from Philadelphia, there were the reports of Plowden and Saunders, the latter of which Story read "repeatedly" with an eye to special pleading, which became his "favorite pursuit."[18] "Coke's reports, if you can borrow a modern edition of them, are well worth our attention, even to go through them as a course of reading," advised Sewall, but they were to be read with an eye to what had been overruled. Foster's Crown cases, notable for their technical mastery and unusual clarity of principle, deserved "a very strict attention" and should, Sewall advised, be studied alongside appropriate sections of Hawkins's *Pleas of the Crown*. With Foster as a "model of judicial legislation" (as one scholar put it), Story could make critical sense of the reports of Salkeld, Vinton, Raymond, Strange, Wilson, Burrows, and the like— "all to be read," declared Sewall, "and if you please in the order they are mentioned."[19]

To cover this ground he read fourteen hours a day for months on end and to the point of nervous exhaustion. Fortunately, his capacity for solitude and Harvard-formed study habits were still intact. Sheer ambition, as he said more than once, kept him going, too, but he also treated himself now and then to literature and poetry, all the more precious because of their contrast with the "dusty folios" of black letter. Poetry and friendship not only spelled him from the drudgery of law but kept alive his romantic temperament and youthful search for perfection. "My throbbing heart can never be at rest," he confessed to his friend Fay, after two and a half years of law study. "The visions of the future have not yet been discolored by the disappointments of the past, and I am alternately the veriest knight-errant in romance, and the most despondent monk in Christendom."[20]

In the monkish part of his life, he was faced with bringing some order out of the diverse strands of his reading: the rational Blackstone, the arcane Coke, the diffuse and fragmentary reports—all foreign law, particularly as it applied to the period after independence. English law could of course be cited with considerable authority in reference to the colonial law of Massachusetts, and English authorities still counted for much after independence, too. But they were no longer binding, and so the subject of American law and American practice was left to be worked out.

What American lawyers needed to know was what worked for their clients and even more specifically what the judges before whom they argued accepted as law. With few printed reports (and thus few written opinions), with fewer treatises on American law and no digest at all, this was a staggering problem. The working lawyer's key to survival, if not success, was his form or commonplace book (such as those given by Theophilus Parsons to his students), wherein practicing lawyers mobilized English precedent under the main heads of law with a running count of leading American cases as an indication of what worked in court.

As a practicing lawyer Story would start his own. Sewall unfortunately had none to loan. He did agree, however, apparently at Story's request, "to review" with him "the elementary treatises which you have read, and assist you in arranging your learning."[21] There is no evidence that Sewall really made good his promise, and it was not until Story studied with Samuel

Putnam in Salem, during the last few months of his apprenticeship, that he really got a chance to "talk" law. "He read much yet we talked more," remembered Putnam many years later, "and I believe in my heart, that even *then* he did the greater part of it." [22]

Reading and talking were crucial, but practical experience was the heart of the apprenticeship method. How well it worked, of course, depended on the nature of the mentor's practice and the scope of responsibility allowed. Some apprentices did little more than tend the office, chase down debtors, and copy writs, and Story performed his share of this drudgery. It was in fact a part of his education. Subtle changes in the prerevolutionary system of common-law pleading were under way, but litigation in Massachusetts courts was still initiated by such ancient writs as trespass, trover, debt, covenant, assumpsit, and replevin, each with its unique language and special function. [23] Copying and serving writs was mastering the tools of the trade.

Fortunately for Story, he was able to do more. Both Sewall and Putnam had burgeoning practices, and both needed help—especially Sewall, who was gone a good bit of the time. The result was that Story got quickly into the business of lawyering. After less than a year at the books, he was charged with commencing "some actions at the office" and generally handling business for his absent teacher. On at least one occasion, and probably many more, he traveled to Ipswich to enter actions at the April term of the Court of Common Pleas. "In cases where defences are made," Sewall instructed his young assistant, "particularly my case ag. Green, . . . agree to a demurrer if you can get it and if not you must admit a continuance." "Engage business," he added, and if there were any problems "manage with the aid of Mr. [William] Prescott or Mr. Putnam." And of course collect the fees: "3 or 4 dollars in advance" for entering an action "where the success of the action or the ability of the party is questionable." [24]

Story prepared cases, too, thus returning unavoidably to the great questions of American jurisprudence. Pressed with doing real law, he saw the logic of Sewall's course of study: From Blackstone, other treatise writers, and the reports, one mastered, as Sewall put it, "the law of England as a system of political and moral and economic rules." Then one had to discover what part of English law was actually, that is, legally, in force. Here Sewall had some conventional wisdom (which would later make its way into Story's own theory of the transplantation of the common law). Assume, he advised, "that all the Rules of the English law, that is of the common law system as modified by the Statute law, and in use & force at the departure of our fathers from their native country, and which have been found applicable to the forme of society and govt., and the state of property adopted by them in this acquired territory, became the laws of the land. . . . Look then for changes effected by the Engl. Parlt. in which the colonies were expressly named. . . ." Also account for changes "admitted by the courts of law here, as modifications of the common law in certain instances, altho enacted at a much later period than the emigration of our ancestors."[25]

The study of English law was practical as well as intellectual, then, but the problem still remained of determining "to what extent and in what particulars" the rules of English law had been adopted in Massachusetts—this without reports, digest, and treatises. The "question," declared Sewall, is "to be fully answered only by experience." Study the statutes of Massachusetts, and for "those variations which are to be argued from neglect or disuse of particular rules" observe "the Practise of the Courts" and listen "to the conversations or arguments of professed lawyers."[26] Attending the courts was what Story was already required to do. Listening, given his propensity to talk, may have been more of a problem, but doubtless Sewall, Putnam, and "professed" lawyers like William Prescott could hold their own. Story's own passion for learning did the rest.

Story finished out his apprenticeship in the Salem law office of Samuel Putnam, where he went in January 1801 upon Sewall's appointment to the state supreme court. Putnam's office was in his home, and Story was welcomed into the family circle in what was the beginning of a lifelong personal and professional friendship. He continued his reading and talking and, as Putnam recalled, was "frequently interrupted by the examination of the Books touching the cases which were offered for my consideration."[27] By July 1801, when he was formally admitted to the Essex bar, he had done everything involved in the practice of law except argue cases at the bar.

If a good education is one that equips its recipient to do what has to be done, then Story's law-office education was an excellent one. He learned the theory and was at home in the practical application of it. He was ready to do business. But he learned more, too. Three years of apprenticeship had left him with a deep love of the law and a lasting admiration of legal science.

In defining the latter Story laid hold of the whole system of judicial lawmaking that would guide his career. Scientific law assumed the mastery of rules and principles, but it was not legal taxidermy (the preservation of fixed rules) or a legal version of natural history (the hierarchical organization of legal rules). Law in America was a process of creation, a process, as Sewall reminded him, of "descending from generals to particulars." And it was in this transforming process that one "must be most scientific."[28] Principles and rules learned from the great legal system of England, from the Continent, from ancient Rome, were to be mastered so they could be modified to meet the needs of the American people. Coke, Blackstone, Grotius, and other publicists played a part, but so did such practical-minded merchant-shippers as the Crowninshields of Salem, who knew what they wanted the law to do. So also did lawyers and judges, who understood the special manner in which principle and practice must interact. The vision of making American law into a great system was there, thanks to Blackstone, but before that glorious consummation lay the creative work of transformation.

2. Lawyer as Politician: "A Bonaparte in Modesty and Ambition"

Story opened his law office in Salem in the summer of 1801, in the Deliverance Parkman house at the corner of North and Main streets. At the same time, after cautiously avoiding politics for three years, he committed himself actively to the Jeffersonian Republicans, or the Antifederalists, as they were still called in Essex County. A look at the number of lawyers in the legislature or the lawyer-dominated structure of Federalist power that controlled seaboard Massachusetts made it clear that a joint career in law and politics was possible and profitable.[29]

Being a lawyer in politics was one thing, however; being a Republican lawyer something else. Massachusetts at the turn of the century was solidly Federalist, and Essex County, boasting stalwarts like Timothy Pickering and Theophilus Parsons, more unbendingly so than the rest. As for the legal profession itself, Story could "scarcely remember more than four or five lawyers in the whole state, who *dared* avow themselves republican." In Essex County all the lawyers and judges were Federalists until Story made his audacious debut.[30] In addition to controlling the profession and monopolizing legal office, Massachusetts Federalists also dictated the dominant legal ideology, which is to say that they appropriated law to bolster the standing social, economic, and political order.[31] Driven to condemn what they could not share, Story's chosen party, or at least the radical wing of it, stirred up popular hatred against lawyers and judges by depicting them as parasites and aristocrats.

But why should an aspiring lawyer like Story join a party notorious for its distrust of lawyers, particularly as that party was not only outside power in New England but beyond the pale of respectability as well? The answer lies, no doubt, in his father's strong preference for the party of Jefferson.[32] But the Republicans were also congenial to his own romantic and idealistic view of man. In fact, a Unitarian who liked Rousseau, Southey, and the German romantics and who had a fierce sense of social justice could hardly have been anything but a Republican, seeing that the Federalists branded such liberal views as un-Christian, un-American, Frenchified heresies. More even than professional exclusivism (which Story quickly broke down by the sheer force of his talent), it was the Federalists' intolerance, their monopolizing control of society and constrictive view of American history, that made him a Republican.

Nowhere was Federalist exclusivism more virulent or more forcefully assaulted than in Salem at the turn of the century, where the ruling Federalist elite, the Ornes and Derbys with their in-laws and professional allies, were challenged by the Crowninshield family and theirs.[33] George Crowninshield and his sons began as moderate Federalists who supported John Adams. But when the pro-English commercial policies of the Hamilton-Pickering wing of the party threatened their economic interests, they shifted to the party of Jefferson. Economics quickly turned into politics and politics into ideology as the Crowninshields spearheaded Republican party organization in Salem and Essex County. Willy-nilly, Salem had become a battleground between those who held political-economic power and those who wanted access to it. In the conflict the community itself was politicized so that churches, newspapers, and even dancing groups and social clubs were identified by political affiliation.[34]

In this environment Story learned the basic lesson of his political career: that there was no neutral ground. Not to join, not to obey, was to oppose. That lesson came home to Story while he was an apprentice in Putnam's office, still "studiously avoiding politics." Dr. Story unknowingly set the stage for his son's political debut when he criticized an article in the Federalist *Salem Gazette* that had attacked local Republican social clubs as "schools where decency and modesty were laid aside, and Deism and Wolstonecraftian principles were the order of the day."[35]

What followed as young Story was caught up in an ascending spiral of action, reaction, and deepening response is a perfect illustration of Silvan Tompkins's theory of the dynamics of commitment.[36] First he leaped to the defense of his father and the Salem Republicans, and for that act of loyalty found himself branded publicly as a "deist, a defender of suicide, an eccentric phenomenon, a violent Jacobin."[37] Convinced of the purity of his political principles and "the virginity of his life,"[38] he demanded a retraction. "I must have reparation for the insult & Satisfaction of my honor," he wrote angrily to his friend Fay from Salem, and to make his point asked him to get a "good brace" of pistols even though he was "unused *wholly* to arms and would only apply to them as dernier resort."[39] Fortunately for the future of American law, the matter was settled without trial by arms, but Story, as Jacob Crowninshield put it later, was "marked out for destruction."[40]

As it turned out, Story thrived on combat or at least managed to survive it. But there were casualties along the way, among the first of which was the love of Lydia Pierce, whose family had no use for reputed Jacobins. The ardent young lover did not give up easily, however. Having "been of late taught, that objections would probably arise on your part, originating in religious & political differences of opinion," Story wrote the girl's guardian, "I have therefore requested this appeal to yourself. . . ." His "appeal" was a fervid outpouring of sentiment and frustration testifying to his honorable intentions, his love of Christianity (which he admitted having once doubted), and his patriotism. As for his politics: Not only had he given "public approbation to Washington and Adams" but he had supported "Pinkney and Pickering." "While not on the extreme, of what are denominated federal principles," he declared himself to be "a *federalist* in the noblest sense."[41] Politics and love made him grovel, but to no avail. As another plaintive letter to Lydia herself indicated, the old man and possibly the girl herself remained unmoved.[42]

Story was moved, however—off neutral ground into the political fray as a zealous partisan of the nascent Republican party. The Federalist *Salem Gazette* recorded his presence at the Fourth of July Republican celebration in 1801, where presumably he joined the Reverend William Bentley and the Crowninshields in their toast to Thomas Jefferson: "The Sage without dishonor, and the Patriot without reproach."[43] Thereafter he was in the thick of battle in Essex County as the Republicans fought their way to power. We see him as secretary of the Republican Town Committee endorsing Republican candidates for the purity of their cause. On a more earthy level he urged that "every republican . . . personally go to every ward in Lynnfield" and appeal directly to the voters, many of whom were "deluded . . . to their most important interests."[44] On 29 October 1802 he was the key speaker at the first popular caucus held by the Salem Republicans, and thereafter "Orator Jo" (as the Crowninshields affectionately called him) led the charge in the battle of political rhetoric—adding further to his reputation as a raving Jacobin.[45]

Indeed, the ridicule of the *Gazette* became so virulent and personal that Story, with Richard and Benjamin Crowninshield, stormed into editor Thomas C. Cushing's residence one Saturday evening in November 1802 and demanded public retraction. Instead of getting satisfaction, he was pilloried in a subsequent issue of the paper as a ruffian and a bully and exposed as a writer of anonymous political tracts for the rival Republican paper, the *Salem Register*, edited by William Bentley and supported by the Crowninshields.[46] Story's articles in fact heated up the newspaper war, especially the one accusing Benjamin Pickman (at that time Story's Federalist rival for the post of naval officer at Salem) of having advocated life terms for congressmen and the president.[47] This charge, with Story's public attack on the Federalist town overseers for accusing one of his friends of fraud, led directly to his being physically assaulted by Hersey Derby, the son of "King" Derby, whose frequent scuffles marked him as the Federalist avenger. Story was knocked down twice and kicked before he escaped to a friend's house. He had, in the words of his old classmate William Smith Shaw, become a "notorious character."[48]

Beaten, bruised, and "notorious" though he was, Story stayed on the political firing line, writing, speaking, organizing, and hustling votes as the Salem Antifederalists turned Jeffersonian Republicans and finally by 1805 fought their way to dominance in Essex County. Never during this period of partisan activity did he theorize about political parties or defend them on principle; quite likely he agreed with Jacob Crowninshield that the Federalists were a "faction" that would disappear with the victory of the wise and the good.[49] Like the Crowninshields, too, he found the focus of his politics shifting only gradually from local to national issues, from expediency to ideology. Story seems never to have been enthusiastic about Jefferson himself, though he moved a long way from his grudging concession to Capt. Ichabod Nichols in 1801 that the president was not really a criminal or an "enemy to his country." He did of course send Jefferson copies of his poem *The Power of Solitude* and his *Selection of Pleadings*, along with some flowery compliments. And while he never appeared to talk of "our beloved Jefferson," as his friend G. W. Prescott did, he did defend Jefferson's administration as "virtuous."[50]

Story had, with the help of the lunatic thinking of Timothy Pickering and company and the personal attacks on himself, come at least temporarily to identify the Republican party with republican principles.[51] In his passionate oration of 4 July 1804, he was willing to defend national Republican policy, most noticeably the controversial acquisition of Louisiana.[52] Story's stand here went to the heart of his politics. The Federalist party opposed the acquisition of Louisiana not for constitutional reasons, though they thought Jefferson's constitutional reasoning was illogical, but because they feared that new western states would strengthen democracy, further slavery and Southern influence, and diminish the role of Massachusetts in the Union. It was a position that radiated decadence: As Story's friend Channing put it, the Federalists "wanted a just confidence in our national institutions. They wanted that faith, which hopes against hope, and which freedom should inspire. By not confiding in the community, they lost its confidence."[53]

The Federalists wanted to stop history with themselves on top; Story wanted it to move on so he could get to the top. It was a question of ambition—for himself and, inseparably, for his country. He may have joined the party because of his father, but he stayed there as long as he did because the Republican party in Salem and in Washington was the party of the future: of hope, of mobility and opportunity, of nationalism.[54]

The benefits of this Republicanism for Story were tangible and immediate. His alliance with the Crowninshield family brought him friends, comfort, and protection from Federalist efforts to destroy him, a destruction that, declared Jacob Crowninshield, "shall not be."[55] Politics, for all of his later complaints against them, also satisfied Story's urge for public performance, for it must be inferred that a man who talked for three hours at the drop of a hat enjoyed doing so. Service to party also sent patronage his way. As early as September 1802 Jefferson was being pressured for "a Commission for Joseph Story, as a Commr of Bankruptcy" in Massachusetts, and the next year Story was offered a position as naval officer in Salem.[56] The first job evaporated with the repeal of the Bankrupt Act of 1801. Story turned down the second, as he explained to Gabriel Duvall (his future colleague on the Supreme Court), partly because it would not bring in much money but mainly for "professional considerations."[57]

Story had aspirations other than law, to be sure, almost as many as his friend Artemas Sawyer, who had "ambition to be everything but a villain."[58] Literature was still much on his mind, as the audacious publication of his poem *The Power of Solitude* indicated; his oratorical ambition was already well known, if not universally appreciated; and his desire to figure in public councils was still much alive, though not to the exclusion of his passionate desire for domestic bliss. Still, what moved him most, what kept him going when all else failed, was his desire to excel in law, a profession "employing the noblest faculties of the human mind and systematizing its boldest operations."[59] Being a naval officer in Salem, however gratifying it was as a mark of party support, simply did not mesh with professional goals.

Being a Republican in Federalist Massachusetts and an ally of the Crowninshields did mesh, however, despite apparent contradictions. But there were some costs involved. Temporary estrangement from his old teacher Samuel Putnam was one, as the Crowninshields, with good reason, considered him an enemy. Story's friendship with Sewall seems to have been melted, too, by political heat, though Sewall later admitted to Theophilus Parsons that he had never doubted Story would rise to the top despite Federalist opposition. Story felt that opposition, however: "the extreme degree" of Federalist "virulence," as he put it, "the manifest attempts to close against me the doors of professional eminence."[60] As late as June 1805 he talked of leaving "the petty prejudices and sullen coolness of New England" for the more congenial professional atmosphere of Baltimore, where his old chum Nathaniel Williams lived.[61]

But this was mostly talk. By 1805, when Story grumbled about leaving, he had in fact established himself as one of the up-and-coming attorneys of Essex County—no small feat, considering that the Essex bar was one of the ablest and best organized in the state. Story began humbly, however. At the July term of the Court of Common Pleas in Ipswich, the term in which he was admitted, he entered only one case, and at the October term only four more. The Justice of the Peace Records of Thomas

Bancroft of Salem suggest, too, that he took whatever business came along, even a case like *Hower* v. *Prince*, argued on 2 November 1801, which netted his client all of ten cents' damages.[62]

Business picked up rapidly, however, especially in the Court of Common Pleas, which was the center of legal practice in Essex County. It was a county-wide institution that held sessions at Salem (beginning in June), Newburyport (beginning in September), and Ipswich (beginning in July, March, and December). It was also the primary trial court of civil jurisdiction, although it did hear appeals from the justices of the peace and also entertained jurisdiction over minor criminal offenses. Only a small portion of cases entered in this court ever went to trial because of a curious system of pleading that permitted the case to be taken on appeal to the superior court before judgment.[63] Still, the court was essential to the commercial operations of Essex. Docketing a debt case, even if that case were continued from one term to the next and even if it never came to trial, was a means by which creditors put debtors on notice, established a lien for future damages, and put pressure on them to settle out of court. Essex County lawyers played a vital role, therefore, in the economic life of the community.

Debt litigation in the Court of Common Pleas was also bread on the table for lawyers. Not only did they receive a fee for entering and arguing a case in court (a minimum of $5.00 for a solo lawyer during Story's early years at the bar), but they also received a fee for continuing it on the docket ($0.33 per case for each day the court was in session).[64] A steady source of income required lawyers to enter as many cases as possible on the docket and keep them there as long as possible, a system that meant attending the various sessions of the court throughout the county. Story did this. By the end of the September term at Newburyport in 1806, he had docketed at least 460 cases, including continuances.[65] Not surprisingly, his Fee Book, fragmentary though it is, records a steadily increasing income (confirmed in later autobiography) for these early years.[66]

And business begat business. The simplest debt action, even cases before the justice of the peace, established a relationship between lawyer and client that could lead to new cases or spill over into in-office counseling about estates, wills, and the whole raft of social and economic problems that a busy property-owning community confronted.[67] As a leading practitioner in the Court of Common Pleas, Story was, then, a defender, adviser, and litigator for hundreds of Essex County citizens—a mediator and facilitator for the rich, the "middling," and even the poor.

But the rich counted for more than the poor in American law and lawyering. And politics counted, too, at least in Essex County and certainly in Story's case. His connection with the Crowninshields gave him access to both wealth and power that was greatly significant in his professional ascendancy. He would no doubt have succeeded without the Crowninshields. His booming business in the Court of Common Pleas indicated as much, and so did his growing practice outside Essex County and his impressive victories over established greats like Jeremiah Mason and William Prescott.[68] His reputation as a scientific lawyer and thus his business were also enhanced by the publication in 1805 of his *Selection of Pleadings in Civil Actions*. Talent counted, it is clear, but connections paved the way, and being in-house counsel for the Crowninshields was a very rich plum. By 1800 that enterprising family had become the chief rival of Federalist shippers in Salem. Commercial competition soon spilled over into real estate, banking, and insurance, not to mention politics,[69] all generating legal business. Occasionally they called on other lawyers, but Story was their man in Salem. Even the scanty records that remain find him pressing Crowninshield debtors (often for substantial sums) and advising the brothers on securing liens against bankrupt political friends.[70] When Richard and Benjamin stormed the house of editor Cushing of the *Gazette*, Story was at their side, did most of the talking, and no doubt advised on what could and could not be done at law.

Legal business often came through political channels, too, as when Republican lawyer James Sullivan advised Republican minister William Bentley to turn to "our mutual and valuable friend Mr. Story" in case a civil action for damages needed to be brought in Essex County. It made political and legal sense that Story should defend Nathaniel West (son-in-law of "King" Derby) in his notorious divorce case, which in addition to exposing the philandering and greed of West signaled the breakup of the Derby family and the rise of the Crowninshields. Story also handled important economic matters, as in cases like *Appleton* v. *Crowninshield* (1807), in which he represented family interests in court.[71] When the Crowninshields retaliated against Federalist exclusivism by chartering their own bank and marine insurance company, they called on Story to advise them and draw up the papers of incorporation.

By helping the Crowninshields Story helped himself, then, so that by 1805, when they consolidated their political and economic dominance in Salem, he had established himself as one of Essex County's leading lawyers, as well as a justice of the peace, a banker, and a member of the local school committee.[72] He achieved these things not merely by keeping his desk neat, attending court punctually, and having his friends ask the judge for continuances (advice that William Wirt only half-humorously proffered as the key to professional success).[73] What Story learned in Essex County, what he got from his Crowninshield connection besides fees and a professional toehold, was an insight into the working relationship between lawyers and entrepreneurs, between law and capitalism. This was the "experience" that, Sewall taught him, would be the key to adjusting English law to American needs. When as judge, teacher, and legal publicist Story made national law serve American capitalism, he drew on this lesson from his early lawyering.

3. A "Pseudo-Republican": A Dubious Politician

Joseph Story loved the law and courted that jealous mistress with a passion. But he loved literature, too, and still longed for literary fame. He sought public acclaim but yearned intensely for the respite of domestic bliss. He cherished solitude, as his poem tells us, but needed the company of friends. He was a moralist to the point of prudery, even to the point of rebuking his women friends for playful cheating at cards, yet he admitted to having doubted Christianity. He was hypersensitive to political criticism, and yet he fought in the political arena and gained a reputation among proper people in Salem as a "political heretic." He expected the best from mankind, but thought men, if not "madmen," then "knaves or dupes." Truly he was a "knight-errant in romance," and at the same time the "most despondent monk in Christendom." [74]

Even when he turned conservative, Story was never a monolithic personality; in this early period, in fact, he was a bundle of contradictions. Yet there was—as he defied the world, mingled with "the crowd" he feared, and confronted himself—a sorting out of priorities. One thing to go was his aspiration for literary greatness, shot down rudely by his old Harvard critics who now controlled the *Monthly Anthology and Boston Review*. That periodical aimed to create a distinguished national literature, and the author of *The Power of Solitude*, who had taken immense pains to get his work before the public, was not invited to participate. [75] Story got the message and, like Blackstone and Mansfield before him, took a "lawyer's farewell to the muse." Poetizing remained a lifelong outlet for his emotions, but henceforth he wrote for himself only or for his friends. *The Power of Solitude*, with Story's approval, fell into well-deserved obscurity, except for the single copy that for some mysterious reason remained chained to a table at Harvard Law School. [76]

Story also took a realistic measure of his romantic view of life. He did not give it up entirely, but the perfectionist view of mankind was tempered by experience: by moving among the "mob," which was already becoming a favorite word; by witnessing the "petty tyranny" of Federalist gentlemen from whom more might have been expected; by practicing law, which presented the world in constant litigation.

Most sobering of all, as it came in the midst of his brightest dreams of happiness, was the sudden death on 22 June 1805 of his wife, Mary Lynde Oliver, after only seven months of marriage. Little is known of

Mary except that she was the daughter of the Reverend Thomas F. Oliver and Sarah Oliver, who was the daughter of William Pynchon, who was a prominent prerevolutionary lawyer. In Story's autobiography, written nearly three decades after her death, Mary appeared briefly and distantly as "an elegant and accomplished woman, full of fine sense, and interesting in her person and manners. . . ."[77] In 1805 he was crushed by the sense of loss. "Joy has forever departed and left me the miserable victim of despondency," he confessed to his close friend Samuel Fay three months after Mary's death. "In losing my wife I have lost the companion of my studies, the participator of my ambition, the consoler of my sorrows, and the defender of my frailties." Even religion could not console him as it would do later. "My tears and my groans are ineffectual," he cried out. "She has left me forever, and the grave has closed between us."[78]

Slowly and painfully, with the help of friends and the therapy of incessant labor, Story reawakened to life. In 1808 he married Sarah Waldo Wetmore, whose father, William Wetmore, was a judge in the Court of Common Pleas in Boston and a man of some prominence in the city's conservative establishment. Sarah had been a close friend of Story's and Mary's and, as he explained to his brother-in-law Joseph White, Jr., "esteem has ripened into affection."[79] Natural buoyancy returned and with it a renewed optimism, but for all that, Story was not the same. He had crossed a "great divide" in his psychic life. The tragedy of Mary's death, followed in two months by his beloved father's, hurried him to manhood.[80] Survival confirmed his own identity; loneliness left him with nothing to do but work. Having lost control over the private portion of his life, he seemed obsessed with his career in law and politics. Some if not all the idealism that he had lavished on his dreams of personal happiness now infused his public philosophy.

Yet even here, perhaps especially here, there were tensions and contradictions to be resolved. Story began his legal and political careers with the notion that they were complementary, and so in many ways had they proved to be. But there was a growing disjunction between the profession of law as Story conceived of it and the role of a Republican politician as the imperatives of political parties and professional politicians defined it. Story felt the tension increasingly in the years after 1805, as Republican legislator and especially as congressman from Essex South during the embargo crisis. He never ceased practicing the art of politics during these years, and he reaped a handsome reward for his efforts, including an appointment to the Supreme Court of the United States. But his misgivings about party government also made him a special kind of politician and, more important, invited him to contrast the art of politics with the science of law: The latter fitted readily into the prevailing notion of science of government; the former did not.

In retrospect it is tempting to see the conflict between the lawyer and the politician in Story as inevitable. Perhaps, as Benjamin Waterhouse suggested, the man who follows the "laborious and dull study" of law simply "looses [*sic*] the tact of a politician."[81] Maybe Story's personality was simply not suited for political life. Certainly his aggressive morality, his hypersensitivity, and his monolithic vision of truth were at odds with the earthy, often vulgar, always accommodating character of party politics. There was also the problematic nature of his commitment. It is perfectly understandable that Story should have become a Republican because he hated Essex County Federalism, but negative reference is a tenuous basis for lasting party allegiance. Even more tenuous would it be if hatred of Federalism itself were youthful rebellion, part of a process by which he defined himself by striking out against Federalist exclusivism. Youthful rebellion ends with youth; being a Republican to spite Federalism boded ill for continued allegiance to party.

So, even more, did being a Republican for the sake of ambition. The Republican party helped Story be successful, but his very success permitted him to act independently of party and made him impatient with party demands. As more than one of his Republican colleagues noted, the more successful he became, the less Republican he was. His final and ironic act of accepting the rewards of party (that is, his appointment to the Supreme Court) in order to repudiate party appears simply to be the working out of a long-standing calculus of personal advancement along lines congenial with personality and personal preference. And undeniably it was partly that.

But it was more, too. Repudiating politics was an intellectual decision as well as a practical and personal one. Story took the measure of party government during a period when political parties were in the process of development, when their position in the scheme of republican government was very much unsettled. The Founding Fathers opposed parties, but parties existed, nevertheless, and after the election of 1800 with a measure of legitimacy.[82] Still, the matter was in doubt: The notion that party was synonymous with faction was very much alive. Party was considered by many (including many active party organizers) to be self-interested, unnecessary, unpatriotic, unconstitutional, a passing aberration that would disappear with time (or, more accurately, when one's own party gobbled up its opponent).[83]

Transitional politics denied Story a ready rationalization of his partisan behavior. Without an established tradition of party government to discourage first questions and philosophical reckoning, without an ideology of party to fall back on, Story ended up measuring his political actions and those of his fellow politicians against the idealistic notions of scientific, republican government fashioned during the Revolution.

Still, he continued to play a leading role in local party organization as political confidant and legal adviser of the Crowninshields and as a member of the Salem Town Committee (of which he was chairman in 1806). As a measure of his reputation with both the party organization and the Crowninshields, he was nominated unanimously to replace Jacob Crowninshield in Congress in 1808. In the state house of representatives, where legal training and oratorical ability were at a premium among Republicans, Story rose rapidly to a position of party leadership.[84] As a regular member of the committee appointed to answer the governor's message, he was in a position to articulate party legislative policy. His position on the key committees of the house, especially the Judiciary Committee, allowed him to translate policy into law. As Republicans cashed in political power for a share in corporate and banking privileges, Story was there with legal expertise, though sometimes he disagreed with party strategy (as in 1811 when the Republicans memorialized against the recharter of the First Bank of the United States).[85] When sensitive and statesmanlike discretion was required, as it was in the settlement of the disputed election of 1806 and the impeachment of Moses Copeland in 1807, the party called on Story because of his legal knowledge and his reputation for fairness.[86] He was also on hand for less pleasant duty. When the reputation of the Republican party was on the line in the embargo crisis, for example, it was Story who went forth to the hustings to grapple with Federalist ideologues.

He was elected speaker of the house in 1811 because of his statesmanship and because he was a party warhorse. His farewell address to the house on 17 January 1812 ignored the latter entirely. With a court appointment in his pocket, he could warn his former colleagues against "power and ambition," advise them to "check intemperate debate" and to perfect "established rules, which invite liberal discussion"—reforms that, when the pending crises of war came, would permit "the flame kindled in the Revolution" to "burn with inextinguishable splendor."[87]

Coming in the midst of rumors (which were untrue) that Story had engineered the notorious redistricting of the legislature to favor his party, his words appeared to some as the worst sort of hypocrisy. They were not that, but they were the sentiments of a disillusioned party man who had come to believe that the kind of party behavior he had seen in the state legislature and in Congress was uncongenial to republican government.

Story's misgivings, as his farewell speech vaguely suggests, arose from the nature of legislative government itself: its unwieldy size (the state house of representatives in 1806 had 481 members), its ramshackle organization, and its vulnerability to short-run constituent self-interest. His main complaint, however, was not with the legislative branch per se but with the way the political parties controlled legislative business. What party needed from its members, especially those in legislative office, was loyalty and discipline. Story believed that independence of action was the foundation on which the republican science of government rested. The problem was how to be a practical Republican politician and a rational, impartial statesman at the same time. It was not a problem that he solved, as complaints from his own party and compliments from the Federalists suggest.

Take, for example, his double role in the disputed gubernatorial election of 1806.[88] The Federalist candidate, Caleb Strong, seems clearly to have won the election over Republican James Sullivan, and he ultimately took office, but the election was so close that it appeared to turn on disputed returns from several towns. Story was a member of the joint committee composed of five Republicans and two Federalists appointed to settle the question. To the great satisfaction of the Federalists (and to his own credit), he refused to vote the party line and, when the issue came to the floor of the house, made a "candid and animated" defense of his nonpartisan conduct. His speech and his final vote for Strong were noted with approval by the *Columbian Centinel* and the *New England Palladium*, both Federalist papers.[89]

Even more lavish was the praise given Story by the *Boston Gazette* in March 1807, this time for his efforts in defeating Republican attempts to circumvent the governor's revisionary powers over legislation. Against this "*daring* and *foul* play," reported the Federalist editor, Story appealed to the "virtue left in the majority," to the hope "that there was a line of conduct, beyond which they would scruple to proceed."[90] The account was addressed to the voters with the implication that Federalists ought to support Story. Republican leaders were distressed and agreed no doubt with the Reverend William Bentley of Salem, who already had Story pegged as a Republican whose reputation was "doubtful."[91]

Bentley had in mind, among other transgressions, Story's flagrant deviation from Republican party orthodoxy on judicial reform, an issue that pitted law against politics in the most obvious way. Massachusetts Republicans were not uniformly anti-bench and bar, nor could they afford to be, given their aspirations for the commercial and political power that the law could help them get.[92] But the Republican party, following the ideological habits of the age and the lead of the national party, was saddled with an antilawyer bias kept alive by outspoken critics like John Leland and Benjamin Austin, who condemned lawyers and Federalists without distinguishing between the two.

But Story was a lawyer and, what was worse, a lawyer who agreed with leading Federalists that legal reform was crucial. The Republican party was willy-nilly pitted against it, at least until Story's appearance in the legislature in 1805. Because he was committed to judicial reform, because he was the dominant figure on (and for several years chairman of) the house Judiciary Committee, and because he was a leader of the Republican majority in the legislature, Story held the key to success. Theodore

Sedgwick—associate justice of the state supreme court, dedicated Federalist, and longtime leader of the movement for judicial reform—made the point to Story himself: "On you, doubtless," he said, "more than any other man success depends."[93]

Sedgwick and Story were in fact collaborators with Samuel Sewall on a comprehensive bill altering the circuits and reforming jurisdiction and the appellate process that came out of Story's committee in 1806[94] and that in various forms came before the legislature over the next few years. The reform movement failed, but Story's willingness to strengthen the power of the judges (at the expense of the jury and indirectly of the legislature) was a measure of his willingness to defy party principles and discipline. So was the bill to establish a separate equity court in Massachusetts, which Story drafted and introduced in 1808.[95] Chancery jurisdiction was seen, despite Story's arguments to the contrary, as giving almost unlimited discretionary jurisdiction to the judges and was thus antithetical to the democratic inclinations of Massachusetts Republicanism.

More successful and therefore more politically controversial was Story's effort to put the salaries of the judges on a "permanent and honorable" basis, as the constitution of 1780 seemed to require. Neither the $1,233.33 which the chief justice received nor the $1,166.66 salary of the associate justices was "honorable" in 1805; and the annual legislative supplement of a few hundred dollars not only failed to make them so but subjected the judges to legislative whim in what appeared to be a flat contravention of the constitutional mandate. After consulting with Federalist leaders Samuel Sewall and Theophilus Parsons, and after learning that the latter would not serve as chief justice of the supreme court unless adequate compensation were given him, Story introduced in the house a bill for increased salaries.[96] He also took the lead in the "animated and vehement" debate that followed. Indeed, as he remembered it, "the bill must have been lost but for my efforts."[97] Three years later, when Chief Justice Parsons threatened to resign on the issue of compensation, it was Story again who saved the day, and again after consultation with Parsons, the "desperate party leader" of Massachusetts Federalism, as John Q. Adams called him,[98] and the driving force behind the consolidation of judicial authority in Massachusetts.

Federalists, not surprisingly, liked such "independence." The Federalist *Columbian Centinel* for 17 June 1809 praised his statesmanship. When he went to Washington as lobbyist for the New England Yazoo claimants in the spring of 1807, he got a warm letter of endorsement from Federalist leader H. G. Otis, who praised his "salutary spirit of independence" from the Republican party and noted that "a little attention from the right sort of people will be very useful to him & to us."[99] George Cabot, one of the most respected of New England Federalists, joined the praise and suggested that Story was a young man "well worth the civil attention of the most respectable Federalists."[100]

For Republican purists like William Bentley, Story's independence from party was tantamount to defection to the enemy:

> While young Adams is working into political favor [Bentley wrote in his diary on 24 February 1808] young Story of the Law in this town is working out. He began with a great fury. But as soon as he reached as far as the public fervour could carry him, as far as the H. of Rep. he was not content to lead his brethren but fell out imme- diately into the hands of the opposition & dared to come forward with a project of salaries for the Judges which the opposition could not in the days of their glory obtain. He gained it by surprise & from the confidence of his friends. They were alarmed. He could not open his eyes. He dared still to venture & next time came with three bills of Judicature. The last of which was the bill for the establishment of a Court of Equity. They were rejected as far as they had his patron- age, & as he confessed he had lost all influence in the house, to con- sole him, he was sent to manage the mad Yazoo business in the face of the most violent prejudices & the vote not to give him a hearing was 77 to 27.[101]

When the Federalists refused to oppose Story's election to Congress in the fall of 1808, Bentley thought the worst. "I would sooner trust the vilest opposer than a secret enemy & hypocrite," he wrote after the Repub- lican caucus in May that chose Story, "or a man that would sell one at any price." The Federalists wanted no candidate for the simple reason that "JS will answer as well for them as any man they can chuse."[102]

Bentley's criticism was a good index of party development, but it was also unfair. He failed to see that judicial reform was much needed and that it would have benefited both parties and the people as well. That Story might have acted from principle and conviction was not considered, nor was the fact that he acted at considerable risk, as it was the Republicans and not the Federalists who had power and gifts to bestow. On one point, however, Bentley was right: Story was not behaving as party leaders were expected to behave.

After Story's two months in Congress, Thomas Jefferson had to agree. The embargo, passed by the Tenth Congress in December 1807, was the issue. The immediate occasion for that policy was the outrageous attack in June 1807 by the British frigate *Leopard* on the American public ship *Chesapeake*, which resulted in the impressment and death of American sailors. Behind British arrogance was the fact that Great Britain and France under Napoleon were locked in a struggle for national survival, not to mention control of Europe and world empire. Both powers were hostile to republican government, and American neutral rights had no status in the mind of either except as such rights were congenial to national self-interest, as determined by the fortunes of war.

Against the naval power of England and the military might of France, the United States could muster no navy to speak of and less of an army. The country divided profoundly over what to do and whom to like. Jefferson's embargo came partly from his idealistic commitment to the theory of peaceful economic coercion, a tradition that went back to the protests against English commercial policy before the Revolution. The embargo was partly sheer realism, too, a recognition of American weakness and unpreparedness, a temporary measure designed to protect American ocean shipping from seizure and give the country time to build a navy for the war that seemed unavoidable short of surrendering neutral rights and national honor.[103]

Its success in any case depended on the determination and ability of the administration to enforce the law (which would ultimately pit Story against the president) and the willingness of the people to obey it. The embargo called forth party behavior in its most virulent form. New England Republicans freely borrowed ideology from the national party while they pursued local interests; now they were expected to follow the national party (with its Southern contingent and Southern president) on an issue that demanded heavy sacrifice from their own constituents. Congressman Story from Republican, commercial Essex County was on the firing line, conspicuously so in light of his already "doubtful" loyalty to his party. He bit the bullet but only after further traumatic reckoning about the role of party in republican government—a reckoning shaped by a feckless Congress and an indecisive president.

Story arrived late for the second session of the Tenth Congress and left early, but he stayed long enough to win the undying enmity of Thomas Jefferson. The president's assessment of Story's Republicanism, given to Henry Dearborn, was harsher even than Bentley's:

> The Federalists, during their short-lived ascendancy, have nevertheless, by forcing us from the embargo, inflicted a wound on our interests which can never be cured, and on our affections which will require time to cicatrize. I ascribe all this to one pseudo-republican, Story. He came on (in place of Crowninshield, I believe) and staid only a few days; long enough, however, to get complete hold of Bacon, who giving in to his representations, became panic-struck, and communicated his panic to his colleagues, and they to a majority of the sound members of Congress. They believed in the alternative of repeal or civil war, and produced the fatal measure of repeal. This

is the immediate parent of all our present evils, and has reduced us to a low standing in the eyes of the world.[104]

That one man might be thought to have done so much was a tribute to his power, however backhanded the compliment. But the truth of the matter was considerably more complicated and more revealing of Story's ambiguous relationship with party. He had been an avid defender of neutral rights, national honor, and Jeffersonian foreign policy since the British admiralty court's decision on the *Essex* in 1805. By applying the "rule of 1756" (which held that trade not open in peace could not be open in war) and the doctrine of the "continuous voyage" (which interdicted the neutral carrying trade between France and the French West Indies), that decision struck a deadly blow at American neutral shipping. Story was outraged at British arrogance and extended wholehearted support to Jefferson's administration, which he was certain would devise "measures firm and just, resolute yet cool," that would "control infringements on our national independence."[105]

To aid in the formulation of policy, Story drafted a forceful legal argument refuting the *Essex* decision that was forwarded through the Salem Town Committee and Benjamin Crowninshield to Congress and President Jefferson.[106] His arguments were too lawyerlike for the Reverend William Bentley and not enough so for Samuel Putnam, who thought it was presumptuous of Republicans to have opinions on international law and smiled at his former pupil's grave "talk," his "Jurists" and "Publications." Story had little chance, either, of reaching rigid Federalists like Timothy Pickering or Fisher Ames, who had concluded that Great Britain "had a better right to exist, than neutrals have to trade."[107] Perhaps Story was a bit full of himself, as Putnam intimated, but he also brought scholarship to the service of American policy, along with some hardheaded economic facts learned in the Salem countinghouse of the Crowninshields. The British would not tow international law in the wake of their sea power; the United States would not recognize "the authority of any one nation to legislate for the rest."[108] Ideas might count; scholarship might be practical; lawyers might be statesmen.

Story's reasoning in the *Essex* controversy brought him to defend the embargo as among the "firm and resolute" measures of a "virtuous" administration. When the Federalists in the Massachusetts legislature attacked the embargo in their Wheaton Resolutions introduced in the house of representatives in June 1808, he defended the administration with a "display of luminous argument and classical diction," one democratic paper noted, unsurpassed in "the annals of parliamentary debates." Story signed and probably drafted his party's response to the resolutions, upholding the embargo not only for its practical aspects but on constitutional and ideological grounds as well.[109] He hit the hustings, too, at Salem in a three-hour "everlasting" speech (as Samuel Putnam complained) and "in almost every town in the District." Everywhere he was "eulogising Mr. Jefferson and his administration" and, as his old teacher noted with dismay, "abusing Federalists" with a "zeal" that could not be comprehended "without witnessing it on the spot."[110]

Story continued to "abuse" Federalists and defend the embargo once he got to Washington, too, contrary to Jefferson's blanket charge of disloyalty. Only four days after his arrival in Washington, in fact, he was convinced from a perusal of confidential dispatches "that the embargo did produce great effect in England, and that it would have occasioned abandonment of the orders" but for the "deeply criminal" efforts of Federalists to deceive the people, obstruct negotiations, and in general put "our country at the footstool of a foreign power."[111] On 28 December, Story publicly supported the embargo again as "a wise measure," and on 17 January 1809 he vouched for the integrity of Jefferson in urging its passage.[112] Against doubters back home he defended the motives of Southern Republicans, too, refuting charges that they were hostile to the interests of Northern commerce.[113] Story also supported administration efforts in January 1809 to close loopholes in the enforcement of the embargo and even helped draft supplementary legislation on the subject—this though he knew with certainty that his own section would oppose such draconian measures.[114]

It is true, as Jefferson claimed, that Story did come to favor repeal, though that sentiment did not distinguish him from many Republicans in Congress, including some from the South. He was moved, too, as Jefferson claimed, by sentiment from his constituents in Essex, whose opinions he assiduously attended to, though it is hard to see why and in what way such deference to constituents should offend a democratic President.[115] If Story warned others that there was a question how long his own section would support the embargo with its new amendments, he was saying only what was true and what John Quincy Adams and others were also saying. As for his central role in the repeal, he was gone before the great debate took place, leaving Ezekiel Bacon to take the full heat of presidential lobbying. What really stuck in Jefferson's craw was the final decision to repeal on 4 March (which Bacon defended). Story was willing, against his own inclination, to settle for 1 June.[116]

If Story did not single-handedly secure the repeal of the embargo, wherein and to what extent, one must ask, was he a "pseudo-republican"? Certainly he was not on the embargo issue a pseudo-Republican because he was a crypto-Federalist. Nor was it that he failed to defend the embargo publicly, or his party or his president: He championed all of them effectively and consistently before and after he got to Washington. Story consulted public opinion, played the role of the people's representative, and compromised like a good politician.

He was in fact a Republican politician, and that was the nub of the problem, at least from his own point of view. He did not like what he was doing for his party and resented the fact that it wanted more—not only his vote but his soul, if one listens to the judgmental Bentley. When he asked to go to Washington with a free hand on the embargo,[117] it was clear that he did not want to be bound by either party dictates or public opinion (though he was willing to listen to both). There can be no doubt that he resented and resisted the pressure put on him and Bacon during the last hectic days of the struggle over repeal, pressure that both he and Bacon referred to as relentless.[118] He despaired that the whim and stubbornness of a president who refused to lead should have reduced foreign policy to a question of personal vanity, which the debate over the repeal date finally became.

In short, Story was willing to support the embargo and his party but on his terms and not theirs. And his terms, as it turned out finally, were emphatically not theirs or at least not President Jefferson's. In the letter in which he bestowed "complete" confidence in the administration, back in 1805, he registered his opposition to "an *absolute non-intercourse*" because "it would cripple our Commerce without giving us material advantage."[119] When the embargo came, Story supported it, not because he changed his mind but because he considered it to be a temporary holding action (as Jefferson himself seems also to have believed). As such, the embargo would pressure Great Britain and France to repeal their acts against neutral trade; it would allow time for diplomatic negotiations to that end and would, at the same time, protect American shipping from seizure on the high seas. Finally, it would permit the nation to prepare for war if diplomatic negotiations failed. Story's position on the embargo, like those of many of his countrymen, varied in response to the negotiations, which in turn followed the course of military events on the Continent.

But on one fundamental point he was resolutely consistent, and it was this point that separated him finally from administration leaders and his own party in Washington: Story was willing if not eager to go to war to maintain commercial rights and national honor. He "deprecated" war, to be sure, as he confessed to Jacob Crowninshield on 4 January 1806, "but if peace is to be bought by surrender of our rights or our commerce, I should not hesitate to fly from its embraces."[120] He made the same point in his memorial of 1806. Indeed, in addressing the regimental officers at Salem shortly before he went to Washington, he advocated public instruction in military science and urged the militia to ready itself for action. "It is a sound axiom to which the statesman of every description pays homage," he declared at one point in his speech, "that the rights & liberties of a nation depend upon its ability to enforce them. Internal weakness invites the aggressions of foreign foes, and sometimes gives them all the benefits of conquest even at the moment of negotiation."[121]

Story was also a consistent and outspoken advocate of increased naval power, in his memorial of 1806 and as a member of the Massachusetts house. His demand for a naval establishment, which he reiterated forcefully during his few weeks in Congress, was probably as important in alienating Jefferson as was the embargo issue and assuredly damaged his standing with the economy-minded Southern wing of the party.[122]

Story's militant nationalism was the clue to his final disillusionment with party government, Federalist and Republican alike. After laboring mightily for months, after debate, cajolement, maneuver, compromise, heaving, and tugging, the party system, his party, his president, brought forth a mouse of a foreign policy. Story listlessly accepted the repeal of the embargo and the limp policy of nonintercourse that replaced it, but it was a far cry from the manly response he considered the only viable alternative to the embargo.

That a party should ask so much of his independence and produce so little settled his mind: "I am no advocate for a party," he exclaimed to Fay during the midst of the debate over repeal and after analyzing the various factions at work, "and what I see of party spirit satisfied me, that we have pressed our differences beyond what the good of our common country will allow." He would not, he added, "continue in public councils for a salary of $10,000 per annum."[123] With telling symbolism and no compunction whatsoever, he cut short his visit to the seat of national power in time to attend the February term of the Massachusetts supreme court.[124]

This rejection of party was not mere bombast or a temporary disaffection, although Story went back to the Massachusetts legislature and continued in the state party organization. There, almost in proportion as his influence in party councils rose, he found the demands of allegiance irksome, inconvenient, and, worse, intellectually intolerable. The embargo experience had made more apparent what he had increasingly grown to suspect: that political maneuvers in the legislative arena could not produce a policy commensurate with the needs of the community, be it state or nation.

Story's sentiments were shared by many as part of a vital antiparty tradition that went back to the Constitution and forward to Washington's Farewell Address.[125] Furthermore, his theory on the pathology of party government was an anvil on which he hammered out his notions of judicial government. In that metaphor the iron was the legal culture of Massachusetts as Story experienced it, and the hammer was his driving ambition to form and shape. The final product, lacking little but the finishing touches, was a notion that lawyers, judges, the courts, and the common law were a corrective to, even an alternative to, the bumbling work of politicians and legislatures. Over the art of politics and the artful dodging of the demagogue, Story chose the science of the law.

4. Scientific Law: Lawyers as Creative Statesmen

Story was appointed to the Supreme Court of the United States on 15 November 1811, two months after his thirty-second birthday. Because he was the youngest man ever to be appointed, because he came with no judicial experience and only ten years of law practice, it might be assumed that his views on judging were largely unformed and highly malleable and thus, so the assumption runs, vulnerable to the irresistible and controlling influence of Chief Justice John Marshall. Neither the primary assumption nor its corollary is true: A decade of practice might not be much, but it was enough to give substance and direction to Story's thinking about the law (which would be both nationalistic and scientific) and about judging (which would follow logically from the process of judicial lawmaking he saw operative in Massachusetts).

The Essex County Court of Common Pleas remained his professional base of operations in the period after 1805, although he argued cases before the state supreme court and before the federal courts in the area, John Davis's district court and the federal circuit court, and on one occasion before the U.S. Supreme Court. How he balanced practice in these various courts with the other aspects of his profession can be seen by taking 1809 as a typical year. In the various terms of the Court of Common Pleas for that year, Story had 169 actions on the docket, of which 93 were continuances.[126] Most of the cases that actually came on for trial were cases of debt involving a cross-section of the community: mariners, cordwainers, ship carpenters, housewrights, painters, blacksmiths, yeomen, physicians, husbandmen, cabinetmakers, leather dressers, boatbuilders, brickmakers, hatters, sailmakers, watchmakers, and common laborers. Merchants and traders were the most common litigants. The amount of debt, which generally followed the social status of the litigants, ranged from a few dollars to several hundred and in one case $1,474; damages at issue varied from $0.01 (paid by Bill Gray for taking a chaise for a joyride) to $10,000 (which Story kept his client from paying in a trespass case involving a lost schooner).

Among the handful of cases not involving debt in 1809 was one action in which Story successfully pressed a claim for a house and land for his mother as executrix of Elisha Story's estate. Only one of his many litigants before the Court of Common Pleas in 1809 was a corporation, the Union Marine and Fire Insurance Company, the issue being a simple default on a note. The most interesting case in 1809 was Story's defense of Joseph Smith, accused of defaming Timothy Pickering by lumping him in with Aaron Burr and Benedict Arnold. His victory must have been gratifying, because both Pickering and Putnam, who pressed the case, had been busy maligning Story's stand on the embargo. The case was the only one Story argued that year that was appealed to the Supreme Judicial Court, though there is no evidence that it ever came to trial.

Story's extensive practice in the Court of Common Pleas was supplemented by probate business and a wide-ranging chamber practice that included such clients as the Crowninshield family and other leading businessmen. He also developed a substantial and rewarding appellate practice before the Supreme Judicial Court. In 1809, for example, while he argued 118 cases in Common Pleas, he had eight before the supreme court, all at the November term of the court in Essex. Four were debt cases (one action of covenant, three of assumpsit). There was one action of replevin (concerning a stray cow), and in one of three criminal trials Story got quack "Dr." Sam Thompson acquitted even though his home remedies (which included coffee, "well-my-quistle," and "ramcats") ended the life of poor Ezra Lovett, Jr.[127]

Others of the thirty-five cases that Story argued before the Supreme Judicial Court from March 1806 to November 1812[128] were more important and wide-ranging. There were questions of state citizenship (in which Story discoursed learnedly on treaty law and an extensive range of English, French, and Continental legal principles), maritime insurance, bottomry bonds, real actions, and a number of traditional debt cases. As *amicus curiae* in one criminal action, he argued unsuccessfully against the grand jury's swearing of John Tucker, drawing his argument from the records of the Burr treason trial in Richmond that he troubled to get and study.[129] Four of Story's cases at the supreme court level involved corporations; all were debt cases, although one dealt with corporate agency, an area of law in which as justice he would pioneer.[130]

He also practiced regularly before the U.S. district court (held at Salem and Boston) and the U.S. circuit court (held at Boston only). The more lucrative of the two for him was John Davis's district court, generally referred to simply as the "admiralty" court, because it dealt almost exclusively with maritime matters. Mariner's wages, import and custom violations, actions on bottomry bonds and merchant bonds, salvage, and prize were standard fare for Story, although in 1805 he had one case each of bankruptcy, common debt, and counterfeiting. After 1807, violations of the embargo and nonintercourse laws became the staple.[131] Counsel were not consistently listed in the district court docket and minute books, but it is clear that Story had a lively business there, though it never rivaled those of Samuel Dexter and William Prescott. He had only one case each in 1805, 1806, and 1807; six cases docketed in 1809 (both in Salem and in Boston) listed him as counsel. By 1809 the number had grown to twenty, and by 1810 it was thirty.[132] Most of these cases concerned violations of federal import, customs, or embargo laws, so he most often appeared for the defendant, often with Prescott, who became his closest friend in the Essex County bar.

In the circuit court, to which Story was admitted in June 1806, he competed with such established lawyers as Dexter, Rufus G. Amory, John

Lowell, George Blake, James Sullivan, Charles Jackson, Harrison G. Otis, and Theophilus Parsons. Story argued only a half dozen cases, among them *Fletcher* v. *Peck*, but they added to his income (which was a handsome $7,000 per year by 1811) and no doubt brought him some "court house applause." [133]

Lobbying for the New England Yazoo land speculators was a feather in his cap as well as a supplement to his professional income. His duties took him to Washington, where he pressured key congressmen to rescue his clients. There he met Jefferson for the first time and introduced himself to the justices of the Supreme Court and other leading figures in the capital. His Yazoo connections also included J. Q. Adams, George Blake, and Perez Morton, all of whom were lawyers for the New England Mississippi Land Company and all of them, not coincidentally, candidates for the position on the Supreme Court that Story finally got.[134] Story also argued the Yazoo side in *Fletcher* v. *Peck* (1810) before the Supreme Court, a step that introduced him to Robert Goodloe Harper, a leading Maryland Federalist. Arguing this great case before the Supreme Court may have helped him get his appointment to it. Certainly it marked him as one of the leading lawyers of New England. It was also a measure of his deep involvement with the New England business community, which, to the Reverend William Bentley's disgust, had come to include Republicans as well as Federalists.

Story's professional success came largely from his relationship with this community, because he supplied what it needed. New England businessmen needed a reformed legal system. Cases continued interminably (as debt cases were in the Court of Common Pleas) were not objectionable when debtors were neighbors and suits were considered a means of bringing pressure for payment short of actual litigation to judgment. Numerous appeals, wide-ranging jury power over both law and fact, and unreported decisions—all of which were characteristic of the unreformed Massachusetts judicial system in the first decade of the nineteenth century—were tolerable when business was dominated by family firms, local in scope, and governed by the general moral standards of the community (which a jury verdict could bring to bear on each case). But new efficiency-minded entrepreneurs like the Crowninshields and the Lowells did business in new ways and on a new scale, and law was pressured to follow suit.[135] Old areas of law like marine insurance were transformed as American commerce expanded and corporations entered the field. New areas like agency took shape as the network of business relations expanded beyond region and family and grew in complexity. Corporation law exploded as corporations increasingly entered the field of productive enterprise.

Judicial reform, in short, meant new technically sufficient law effectively administered. With large sums of money at risk in national and international markets, community standards of economic morality casually and haphazardly enforced would no longer do. Law had to come into action *before* litigation as well as during it. Businessmen who sought to deploy capital efficiently needed a body of rational rules that they knew in advance and that they knew would be enforced. The lawyers and judges who succeeded were those who could deliver that kind of law. Legal science and legal scholarship, it followed, were good for business, and scientific lawyers were likely to be successful ones.

Story got this message and acted on it, although scientific practice was not the only reason for his success. Simple punctuality, dependability, careful management, and even good manners also paid off. His open, congenial personality was a positive factor, too, though it should be said that congeniality did not prevent him, as one shocked witness attested, from some aggressive lawyering.[136] Story also formed good relationships with other lawyers, a requirement for a successful practice in Essex County. Statewide circuit riding, with the bar following the Supreme Judicial Court on its perambulations, no longer existed, but routine attendance at all sessions of the Court of Common Pleas drew together the lawyers in Essex County and, in matters of business, often demanded their cooperation. A good many cases in that court, in fact, and in the Supreme Judicial Court as well, were argued in tandem to ease the burden of entering actions and attending court.

Story served as joint counsel with a large number of Essex County lawyers during his career—with his friends, with famous lawyers and those of modest talent, with Federalists as well as Republicans. With his colleagues he was, even at this early stage, helpful and always ready with scholarly advice. He was well known, too, for his cooperation with adversaries. The habit of the Essex bar at this time, as Samuel Putnam recalled, was "to disclose freely to the adverse counsel, the points which were to be controverted, or admitted—whereby much expense to clients was saved. What out of Court was agreed to be admitted was always admitted on trial; and so much trouble and expenses of witnesses were prevented. No traps were set." In all of this Story "played his part" with earnestness and "good breeding."[137] In fact, he quickly became a leader, serving as examiner for the admission of new members in 1806 and as county attorney in 1807 (a choice that, though the position was appointive, was also a measure of his general stature and popularity). Friendships made at the bar bridged ideological and generational gaps and lasted throughout Story's life. Some, like those with William Prescott and Nathan Dane, would blossom into active and productive collaboration.

Professionalism shaped Story's practice, as did his work habits and personality. Still, the key to his success, as well as to his later style of judging, was his commitment to scientific law. He was finally, as Charles Sumner put it, a lawyer who went beyond "the applause of the court-house, the approbation of clients, 'fat contentions, and flowing fees.'"[138] Even as a practitioner, Story saw law from the broad perspective of a jurist. He practiced law at the trial and appellate level, before state and federal courts, as prosecutor and defender. As a general practitioner he was forced to master land law, commercial law, prize and admiralty law, civil law, and criminal law. He was at home in equity and began to lay the foundations for his later mastery of conflict of laws. By viewing law as a whole, he saw the need for and the possibility of making it rational and systematic. Even while he was a student he pledged himself to reform. As legislative leader he led the way: in restructuring the court system; in putting judicial salaries on a permanent and honorable basis; in securing the talents of Theophilus Parsons, who more than any other person during this formative period was responsible for the rational ordering of Massachusetts decisional law. His effort to establish a separate equity court with a distinct body of equity law was a valiant effort to modernize Massachusetts jurisprudence, even though it failed to pass.

Story's legal publications also marked him as a scientific reformer, one who, as the *Monthly Anthology* put it in a review of one of his works, aimed at relieving the "necessities of the profession."[139] Beginning with his joint anonymous *American Precedents of Declarations* (1802) and more effectively in his *Selection of Pleadings in Civil Actions* (1805)[140] and his editions of Chitty on Bills and Notes (1809), Abbott on Shipping (1810), and Lawes on Assumpsit (1811), Story aimed to put up-to-date, relevant law within the convenient reach of practitioners who were increasingly overwhelmed with the lawbooks they could not buy and the cases they could not organize. His method, following essentially the advice given him by Samuel Sewall, was to select leading English decisions and show, by extensive annotation and reference to relevant American decisions, how they applied to the United States. In an age when American case law was in its infancy (and still largely unreported) it made sense to mobilize principles wherever they could be found, in ancient black letter or modern English decisions and treatises. And how better to carry the day in Chief Justice Parsons's court than to cite the judge's own Yankee exegesis on that law, as Story did almost exclusively in *American Precedents*.[141]

What Story advised other lawyers to do in his books he did himself. Indeed, the reason he could publish so much so early was that his scholarship grew out of the necessities of his practice. Take, for example, his work on pleading. Story loved the intricacies of the subject itself—reason enough to write a book. But special pleading was also very much in use in Massachusetts.[142] Story, like Parsons, saw it for what it was: a means for bringing legal issues into exact focus so that judges might, without hindrance of juries, clarify legal principle. Principle for Story the scholar and Story the practicing lawyer was the name of the game. In making principles available for others in his published scholarship, he was also making them available for himself.[143]

Principled argument was also the hallmark of his advocacy. In his very first case before the Supreme Judicial Court (at the November 1806 session in Salem) we find him ranging over several centuries of English and Continental law to show that Asa Kilham was an alien who could not vote in a town election.[144] In *Appleton* v. *Crowninshield* the young scholar took on both Samuel Dexter and William Prescott, two of the most respected lawyers in the commonwealth. Story's masterful display of learning convinced the court. Equity was with the plaintiff, declared Judge Isaac Parker, but Story's sources were better. On appeal he was even more profuse in citing authorities and, to the distress of reporter Dudley A. Tyng, in reading and expounding them at inordinate length. He lost the case, but his erudition managed to shake the confidence of Judge Parker on some key points of law. Story also won the praise of the court for the "zeal" of his argument and "the labor bestowed" on it.[145]

Story's scholarship showed, too, in the U.S. circuit court in Boston, as is indicated by the praise of William Minot: "We had at the Circuit Court last week," he wrote Leverett Saltonstall, "a very favorable specimen of your Essex bar; Story was particularly brilliant, I think he has more of the copia Dicendi than any man I ever saw, a very torrent [of] words flowed fast as his utterance & the best chosen words too. His fault is to make too many points & to dwell too long on those points. Good faults you will say in a lawyer."[146]

"Good faults" indeed they were, and they surely contributed to Story's impressive victory over Jeremiah Mason in the Superior Court of Rockingham County in New Hampshire and in *Rust* v. *Low* (argued first at the November 1808 term of the Supreme Judicial Court in Essex County and again at the November 1809 term).[147] In the latter Story was defending against an action brought by the plaintiff to recover his cattle, which had strayed into the defendant's field and were being held hostage to damages. On the crucial question whether a New England farmer was required to fence his fields against cattle of strangers, Story traveled back to Hale and Fitzhugh. Armed with ancient learning he surprised William Prescott (who thought he was home safe) and astonished Chief Justice Parsons (who was tickled at Story's arrogance) by showing that Lord Hale (on whom Prescott had relied) had misconstrued Fitzhugh. When the chief justice rendered judgment in the case at the Suffolk session of the court, he adopted these doctrinal revisions but without the slightest reference to Story's contribution; it gave Story a hearty laugh (at least later) and caused reporter Tyng to marvel at the quaint vanity of Parsons. Story had literally *found* some law.

In *Rust* v. *Low* the problem was simply to discover the correct English rule of law and apply it; in other cases an American modification of the inherited principle was the order of the day; in yet others, like *Fowler* v. *Bott*,[148] Story had to admit that the absence of relevant English cases and controlling American decisions left the question open. In all cases the principles fit because they were useful. They were useful because they were available. In all cases, too—even those where there was no clearly applicable principle—legal science was at the heart of the lawyering process. Constructing principle from the cases, even if the final result had to be tested instrumentally, was the essence of legal reasoning.

In reasoning thus, Story never stopped to ponder whether he was "finding" law or "making" it. The two were in fact not mutually exclusive at this stage in the development of American common law. He could hardly have been blind, however, to the fact that the lawyers and judges of Massachusetts were creating a new body of law for a new age and a new people. Whether the old law was Gothic, Norman, Roman, Saxon, or the "work of Westminster Hall, from time immemorial," it was "now sweetened to suit Yankee tastes, as a mixture altogether incomparable."[149] What remained of the old law was not so much the substance as the method by which it was recovered and reconverted. This "taught tradition of the common law" Story brought with him to the Supreme Court of the United States.

Justice William Cushing's death in September 1810, gruesomely anticipated for months, set off a flurry of office seeking that, according to one account, turned Washington City into a veritable Polish Diet. Story was a contender for the position.[150] He was a New Englander with an admirable command of maritime and commercial law, both of which the circuit-riding obligation of Supreme Court duties required. In only ten years he had risen to the top of the state bar and was the most promising and prolific legal scholar in New England (though James Sullivan's *Land Titles* was probably more significant than any of Story's early works). The main obstacle was politics, which, except for chance and the good sense of President Madison, would have done him in.

Story later recalled that his appointment came "quite unexpectedly" and without his solicitation.[151] In fact, he wanted the job badly and had an active champion in Ezekiel Bacon, who kept him informed and urged him not to "assist in kicking over your own dish" by supporting any of the various candidates put forth.[152] The threat to Story's "dish" was not Story, however, but Thomas Jefferson. The ex-president, who had influence with Madison, wanted an "unequivocating republican." On that score he distrusted both Bacon and Story but especially Story, who was "too young" and worse was both a "pseudo-republican" and a "tory."[153]

Madison was less fearful of the judiciary than Jefferson, more nationalistic and personally less involved. Still, there were political considerations.

Accordingly, the first offer went to Levi Lincoln of Massachusetts, an able lawyer and solid Republican; then, passing over Gideon Granger, the offer went to Alexander Wolcott, for reasons of party service, one must conclude, rather than judicial potential; and finally it went to J. Q. Adams (whose defection from Federalism was much appreciated). Lincoln turned down the office on account of failing eyesight; Wolcott's nomination was wisely rejected by the Senate; and J. Q. Adams said no because he wanted to be president.

Story finally got the nod because he was a Republican, even if a "doubtful" one, because he was admirably qualified, and very possibly because President Madison saw a congeniality between his own and Story's nationalism. He accepted the offer without the slightest trace of wounded pride at being fourth in line. He could leave politics and be free, as he put it, quoting Cowper, "from the loop-holes to gaze upon the world."[154]

Public reaction to Story's nomination varied pretty much according to perceptions of his politics. Bentley thought his "promotion is a reasonable relief when his political reputation has deserted him."[155] Orthodox Federalist Josiah Quincy was enraged that a "country pettifogger" should be appointed to the Supreme Court.[156] The conservative editor of the *Columbian Centinel* was less alarmed, and remarkably prescient about the fragility of Story's commitment to democracy. "Your Speaker, STORY" he wrote "is nominated a Supreme Court Judge—If I know anything of him, I hope he will be appointed, and will accept. Two as excellent Judges as adorn our bench, when nominated were held to be as democratic as Mr. S."[157]

Story accepted the position because of the "high honor attached to it, the permanence of the tenure, the respectability, if I may so say, of the salary," and because he had used up his political capital. But most of all, he took it because it allowed him "to pursue, what of all things I admire, juridical studies." What he brought with him to the new job were some well-developed notions of judicial government, which contrasted sharply at every point with political lawmaking as he perceived it. Legislators, unlike common-law judges, had no obligation to be consistent and no method of achieving consistency if they desired it. Statute law, if one judged from the embargo, turned not on principle but on power. Political power, moreover, was calculated simply in terms of votes, and votes were influenced by party pressure and often by misinformed and volatile public opinion. While politicians in Massachusetts and Washington were haggling, jobbing, and gerrymandering for power, and while the interests of the people went begging, the common law of Massachusetts was being reformed to the contours of American needs.

So at any rate Story perceived it. Law and politics for him were different ways of doing things: One was based on principle and science and the other on compromise and short-term self-interest. Instead of the confusion and chaos of the legislative chamber, there was the rational order and friendly competition of the courtroom; instead of backbiting, vote-seeking politicos, there were the William Prescotts and Samuel Dexters of the Essex bar; in contrast to demagogues like Thomas Jefferson stood quiet statesmen like Theophilus Parsons and John Marshall. Judging was a way of governing. Even before becoming a judge, Story, following the logic of Madison in *Federalist* 51, had begun to take a proprietary interest in being one.

Justice Joseph Story, by Chester Harding (probably 1828).
Courtesy Massachusetts Historical Society.

Chapter 3

Mr. Justice Story:
Scholar at War

The men who were the first opposers of British tyranny are mostly gone. They dared to think—they dared to speak—they dared to unite, not fearing the wrath of kings. *These men were the chariots of our American* Israel, *and as the horsemen thereof.* The Elijahs *have passed the spheres, and they call on our* Elishas *to take up their mantles.*
Columbian Centinel,
2 November 1811

Let us extend the national authority over the whole extent given by the Constitution. Let us have great military and naval schools; an adequate regular army; the broad foundations laid of a permanent navy; a national bank; a national system of bankruptcy; a great navigation act; a general survey of our ports, and appointment of port-wardens and pilots; Judicial Courts which shall embrace the whole constitutional powers; national notaries; public and national justices of the peace, for the commercial and national concerns of the United States. By such enlarged and liberal institutions, the Government of the United States will be endeared to the people, and the factions of the great states will be rendered harmless.
Story to Nathaniel Williams,
22 February 1815

The Joseph Story who looks out of Harding's 1828 portrait is a study in paradox: piercing, almost mischievous blue eyes and balding head (after his father), a strong expressive mouth (which threatens to break into a hearty laugh or, more likely, an animated soliloquy), a symmetrical oval face radiant with vitality. Generous, warm-hearted, and gregarious, a passerby would rightly surmise. In the faint curl of the lips, echoed by arched brows and the stern line of the jaw, that passerby might also see a latent puritanism in which firmness and resolve merged with self-satisfaction touched with smugness.

Minus the learned self-control of twenty-some years, this might be the youth whom Arthur Walter found so full of himself, or the young politico whose soaring ambition later offended the captious Reverend William Bentley, or the zealous young attorney hungry for distinction. Take away a little confidence and a few years, add a bit of hair, and you have the new appointee to the U.S. Supreme Court who in January 1812 bade a Washington-like farewell to his former colleagues in the Massachusetts house of representatives. He warned his friends of the "approaching storms" of war, with "perils which may truly be said to try men's souls." He prayed that the fame and achievements of the revolutionary saints were still alive, that "the memory of their deeds shall animate their children boldly to dare, and gloriously to contend for their injured country."[1] For Story it was the Revolution again: A new Elisha was on his way to the capital.

Story's farewell address was better autobiography than prophecy. The War of 1812—prosecuted by a weak administration weakened further by bitter New England opposition, full of humiliation (as the British drove the government from its capital), devoid of military glory except for isolated naval victories and a battle won after the war was over, concluded by a treaty that settled nothing—was not a return to patriotic purity. If the war had a message it was that the Revolution had already receded, that provincialism was alive and well in the nineteenth century, that the spirit of republicanism was a fragile, perishable thing.

But Story was right on one matter: The crisis called forth men of action and permitted—indeed, invited—them to shape events. If the government's slackness and New England's disloyalty discouraged Story's romantic hopes, they also fortified his personal determination to serve his country—to save it. It was not much of a war, but it was the only one he knew and it added a kind of reckless daring to his efforts. What the war showed Story was a country that needed unifying, energizing national institutions. Victory, even if it were qualified, made them possible. If Congress and the presidency proved feeble, then the Supreme Court would lead the way, once it consolidated its own powers.

1. Settling In: "A Calm but Ambitious Self-Possession"

Story left for the "wilderness of Washington" (as he once called it)[2] in late January 1812, allowing himself a couple of weeks to navigate the five hundred miles of winter roads. He had made the trip four times before, twice on Yazoo business, once as a congressman, and once in 1810 as a lawyer in *Fletcher* v. *Peck*. These visits predisposed him against leaving Salem, the warmth and security of family and friends. As for the city of Washington, it may have had its Capitoline Hill and its River Tiber, but it most assuredly was not Rome. It had in fact changed little since Story was last there, which is to say that Goosecreek (as the natives called the Tiber) still turned the city into a swamp in the spring, separating the branches of government more convincingly than ever the Constitution did. Summer still brought heat and fever that drove away all except those too poor to leave. As yet there were few residential structures, and the capitol itself was closer to being burned by the British (in 1814) than it was to completion.

Story could not have brought Sarah and the family even if he had wanted to, and he did not. Less than a year previously their daughter Caroline, aged three, had suddenly died, leaving both parents depressed and bereaved—"choked in still despair," as he mourned in verse.[3] Taking Sarah was out of the question; leaving doubly painful. But the wound had begun to heal. Young Joseph was healthy; Sarah was expecting again; and the prospect of high office was therapeutic. Story oscillated wildly between humility (as in his farewell to the Massachusetts house) and confidence, between apprehension about the burdens of the justiceship and exhilaration at the prospects of fame that it held out.

Once the Court convened, Story had little time to worry or need to, as he quickly settled in. Matriculation was quite painless, thanks in no small part to the kindness of his new colleagues and to their simple and informal style of living and working. With the exception of Gabriel Duvall (with whom he had already corresponded) he was at least briefly acquainted with the justices, having "supped and dined" with them in 1808 and argued before them in 1810. He had been favorably impressed particularly with Brockholst Livingston and Bushrod Washington ("boyish in appearance" but "profound as a lawyer"). Both would be close to him personally and intellectually. But it was the chief justice who impressed him the most and who undoubtedly did the most to ease the anxiety of his first few days. "I love his laugh," he wrote to Fay after meeting Marshall in 1808; "it is too hearty for an intriguer, and his good temper and unwearied patience are equally agreeable on the bench and in the study"[4]—and in their common boardinghouse, too, where justices, bachelors and family men alike, boarded and slept during the Court's brief session, when they were not being wined and dined by Washington's social elite.

It was hectic and cramped but for a few weeks each year quite pleasant, especially for the new justice. After only a short time he reported home that "the judges here live with perfect harmony, and as agreeably as absence from friends and families could make our residence. Our intercourse is perfectly familiar and unconstrained, and our social hours when undisturbed with the labor of law, are passed in frank conversation, which at once enlivens and instructs."[5] Thanks to his earlier visits, Story was also familiar with most of the leading lawyers at the Supreme Court bar, including Luther Martin, William Tilghman, Jared Ingersoll, Alexander J. Dallas, Peter S. DuPonceau, Charles Lee, and William Rawle. Robert G. Harper (fellow counsel in *Fletcher*) and Samuel Dexter from Massachusetts he knew well.[6] Those he did not know he soon met in the courtroom on the basement floor of the north wing, where closeness and intimacy were unavoidable.

Story was as much at home with his new judicial duties as he was with his new colleagues. "You ask me how the ermine rests upon my shoulder," he wrote his old friend Nat Williams after the Court had been sitting only a few days; "I answer with more ease than I expected. I am more at home than I looked to be in so novel an employment." His first case, he went on to say, was the *Holland Land Company* case, "which lasted five days," and was "extremely intricate and laborious." Though it was on the equity side of the Court, where he had little experience, he was, through "steady attention," able to grasp the issue. He was gratified and relieved that his "first strong views" were also those of brother Washington and the Court.[7]

His maiden opinion came on 24 February in *U.S.* v. *Crosby*, a land case that came up from his own circuit and that, prophesying his later reputation, dealt with conflict of laws. The question, whether the *lex loci contractus* or the *lex loci rei sitae* governed in the disposal of real estate, was resolved in a tidy and confident three paragraphs in favor of the law of the place.[8] Not a spectacular debut, perhaps, but it was, as he recounted to Samuel Fay, enough to relieve his anxiety: "I begin to feel the weight of depression with which I came here insensibly wearing away, and a calm but ambitious self-possession gradually succeeding in its place. Some difficulties which I anticipated have vanished at the touch, and some which I have to meet have been vanquished without extraordinary labor. I am, therefore, comparatively happy, and begin to feel encouragement, that by diligence, care, and patience, I may not dishonor the elevated station assigned to me."[9]

His only other opinion that term, out of some forty for the whole Court, came in *Marsteller* v. *McClean*, where he handled a question of pleading with great dispatch and a little touch of that "self-possession" which his great opinions would all manifest.[10]

With survival assured and anxiety relieved, Story could take measure of his new colleagues and the institution on which he would serve for thirty-three years. The prospect on both counts was mixed. The Court that gathered for the 1812 term was not calculated to impress, at least on the basis of its record. In the eleven years of Marshall's tenure as chief justice, there had been only a handful of significant lawmaking decisions and none on the great question of congressional power. With the exception of Marshall, who spoke for the Court in its few great moments, none of the justices could claim more than solid judicial competence, and some decidedly less. Things had got so bad with sickness and unfilled vacancies, in fact, that the Court adjourned for the entire 1811 term for want of a quorum. A pessimist about judicial power like John Jay earlier might have concluded, not unreasonably, that the Court's basement "apartment" in the north wing was an accurate measure of its institutional future, one designed both architecturally and politically by Thomas Jefferson.

A more upbeat interpretation was possible, however, particularly if one looked at the faltering presidency of Madison during the war years or the chaos of Congress without the ordering structure of party—all of which Story did. To this one had to add the modest scale of all political institutions in the early republic. The Court was not yet great, but greatness was within reach. Rapid turnover among the justices, which had debilitated judicial energy, ceased with the appointments of Duvall and Story, and the Court headed into the most stable decade in its history. Questions generated by the war gave the Court a chance to act. In acting it could draw freely on judicial authority staked out in *Marbury* v. *Madison* and left standing by Justice Samuel Chase's acquittal on impeachment charges in 1805 and by Marshall's victorious encounter with executive authority in the Burr treason trial in 1807. When Jefferson left the presidency, moreover, he took with him his hatred of Marshall and his distrust of the Court. Backed by a nationalist president, the Court's show of force in *U.S.* v. *Peters* (1809) and *Fletcher* v. *Peck* (1810) took on prophetic significance. The Court's powers were not yet so firmly settled that they could not be undone by ineptitude, but the Court seemed blessed with a rich future.

The future looked the brighter because of the men on the Court and the way they lived and worked together. Boardinghouse living, which divided congressmen into distinct blocs and regional units, actually worked to overcome the sectional and ideological divisions among the justices, fusing their work and leisure and strengthening their sense of institutional identity.[11] The Court heard arguments, Story recalled of the 1812 term, from eleven to four o'clock.[12] Cases were mooted as they came up, in part no doubt because written briefs were not uniformly submitted and deliberations benefited from immediacy. Story remembered the interchanges in conference as freewheeling, a "pleasant and animated interchange of legal acumen." Judicial conferences took place "at our lodgings and often come to a very quick, and I trust, a very accurate opinion, in a few hours."[13] The dynamics of the conference were determined, it can be inferred, by Marshall's effort to avoid separate opinions and dissents. Much if not all of the Court's collective reasoning, then, was carried on orally without formal exchange of memorandums or draft opinions, as on the modern Court. This practice, in addition to impoverishing history, put a premium on memory, quick scholarly recall, and talk—qualities that Story had in abundance.

Personality, character, charisma, and experience took on special meaning in such face-to-face encounters, and here Marshall had the edge. The brethren were a varied lot, made so by the politics of appointment and the logic of circuit duties (which ensured sectional representation and a range of legal specialties). John Marshall and Bushrod Washington were Federalists appointed by John Adams, the former with a Federalist mandate to rescue the country from the party of Jefferson, which swept the other branches in the election of 1800. Marshall and Washington were considered "one judge" by the Jeffersonians. They were bound together by ties of place, a shared experience at William and Mary, where they both listened to George Wythe's law lectures, and a common conservative ideology. There was also a shared reverence for President Washington: Bushrod was the president's favorite nephew as well as his executor and heir; Marshall, his biographer, was attached by an almost filial affection that went back to the Revolution.

Story could have had no better recommendation to these two Virginia nationalists than his own love of union, his own reverence for Washington—unless it was Jefferson's hatred of him, which surely was no secret to his Federalist colleagues. Story's "doubtful" reputation among the Republicans, on the other hand, may have put some distance, at least initially, between him and William Johnson and Thomas Todd, who were put on the Court by Jefferson with the hope that they would undo the stranglehold Marshall was reputed to have on his colleagues. Todd, as it turned out, was neither equipped nor inclined to challenge the chief justice and became instead, as Story later noted, a steadfast supporter of "the constitutional doctrines which Mr. Chief Justice Marshall promulgated, in the name of the Court."[14] Johnson was more up to the job.[15] Not only was he independent, honest, and intellectually pugnacious, but he was more democratic than Marshall (or Story) and had more doubts about judicial omniscience and more faith in legislative government. Insofar as there was an ideological dimension to the Court's conference proceedings it was due to the presence of the crusty South Carolinian. Fortunately for the working unity of the Court, he shared with its majority a reverence for the Constitution and (even more than Marshall himself) a firm nationalist determination to expand the powers of Congress.

Brockholst Livingston, the third of Jefferson's appointees, was a Federalist turned Republican, who with Burr and Clinton organized the new party in New York after 1800. With Livingston, however, as with the other Republican appointees (excepting Johnson), shared values of national union and national capitalism were more important determinants of judicial behavior than fragile and evanescent party affiliation. Gabriel Duvall, who came on the Court with Story, was the fifth Republican, but his politics really did not matter: He less than any other justice was inclined to challenge the law or ideology of the nationalist majority.

Background, education, and professional experience varied considerably as a result of geographical differences. But even here there was unity in diversity.[16] Five of the Court were Southerners: The chief justice and Washington were Virginians, as was Todd, although he grew up in Kentucky; Johnson came from South Carolina and Duvall from Maryland. Only Livingston and Story were left to represent the North. Story was the sole New Englander, and as we shall see this status gave a peculiar dimension to his nationalism. Washington, Duvall, and Todd belonged to the planter class by birth. Todd, however, did not share in the family estate, and Marshall was closer to the business community of Richmond than to the great planters of the Tidewater. William Johnson's father was a blacksmith, but through marriage, ability, and ambition he rose into the slaveholding elite. Livingston came by his aristocracy naturally, as scion of the Manor branch of the New York clan (which connected him both with John Jay, whom he hated and who preceded him on the Court, and with Smith Thompson, who succeeded him). Aside from Story only Johnson and Washington had graduated from college, although all had classical educations.

Measured against the general populace, the Marshall Court stood for modest privilege. Judged by its operating procedures and social profile and compared to English or Continental standards of class and power, it was decidedly provincial—or, as the Americans liked to say, republican. In truth, the Court in 1812 was less than awesome. Marshall was the only proven jurist, and his achievements had come at the price of a dominance that was not healthy. Beyond the chief justice lay a confusion of specialties and a disparity of talents that threatened to weaken the Court as an institution. The Southern justices were at home in the law of real property, particularly as it related to slavery, but all, even Marshall, were weak in admiralty and maritime law and much less knowledgeable of general commercial law than Story or Livingston. Prize, the law of neutral rights, international law—all of which would figure prominently in the war years— were with the exception of Story terra incognita for the justices. Todd's forte lay almost exclusively, if one judges from his Kentucky experience and his written opinions on the Court, in the peculiar and intricate area of Virginia-Kentucky land litigation, and Duvall never really laid claim to any area of expertise during his twenty-three years on the Court.

Still, there was in the assembled justices a roughhewn practical vitality, as well as a kind of intellectual unity supplied by a common training and shared professional experience. All received their legal education by apprenticeship, though, as noted, Marshall and Washington both attended the law lectures of George Wythe at William and Mary. Great variation in quality and substance resulted, of course, because apprenticeship education built in provincialism. But in the "taught tradition of the common law" the justices had a common legal language, and in the problem of adapting inherited law to American needs, a common functional frame of legal reference.

The members of the Marshall Court also shared wide-ranging general experience in government. Five of the seven had served either in state legislatures or in Congress or both, not counting Todd, who was secretary to the Kentucky legislature without being an elected member. Two (Story and Johnson) were speakers of the lower house of their respective state legislatures. All the justices except Washington, Marshall, and Story had prior judicial experience at the state supreme court level. None except Story laid any real claim to formal legal scholarship, though Bushrod Washington was so inclined. Marshall and Johnson were biographers, Marshall of Washington and Johnson of General Nathanael Greene. All knew firsthand the role that law played, or might play, in the lives of the American people.

There was strength in diversity, too, despite some weak links in personnel. Together the justices covered the whole spectrum of law (except for equity, perhaps), and thanks to Marshall's genius for leadership, "together" was the way the Court worked, at least until the institutional crisis of the mid-1820s. Marshall was clearly the catalytic force on the Court at the time of Story's ascension and afterward as well. His credentials as a revolutionary hero and celebrated diplomat, as well as his seniority, judicial experience, and qualities of mind, gave him authority without his having to demand it.

He was a great lawyer without being a legal scholar or a lawyer's lawyer. His training—six months with George Wythe and a brief stint as judge advocate in the revolutionary army—was shoddy even by apprenticeship standards, closer to that of Andrew Jackson than that of Story. But he learned by doing, and (contrary to the myth fostered by Marshall's modesty and indifference to reputation) he was a master, if not of the common law in all its arcane intricacies, then of the common-law mode.[17] Behind his success was a rapid, impeccably logical mind (as even Thomas Jefferson had to concede), an unsurpassed capacity for extracting issues from facts and fashioning legal doctrine to fit them. His sensitivity to the nuances and rhythms of written language, his capacity for compelling argument, was Lincolnesque—which is to say that it was tough, logical, clear, eloquent, and graceful all at once and always appropriate to the chore at hand.

It was important, then, that Marshall wrote 147 of the Court's 171 opinions up to 1811, including all of the important ones, but that is not the whole point. The Court, as Marshall himself made clear, reasoned together, worked collectively, even when Marshall assembled the final product.[18] He did not usurp the duties of his associates but, by virtue of his patience, grace, and gentle humor, brought forth what they had to give. And this was the key to Story's easy matriculation as well as his contribution to the Marshall Court. The chief justice saw him for the legal genius that he was and harnessed his energy to the collective work of the Court, even if it meant, as it did, surrendering some of his own preeminence.

Here then, with John Marshall presiding, were the men with whom Story would live and work, without change until Livingston's death in 1823. Despite his differences, or rather because of them, he was ideally equipped to fit in. The Judiciary Act of 1789, which defined the circuit duties of Supreme Court justices, contemplated that each justice would bring a knowledge of local-sectional law to the Court.[19] Coming from the New England circuit, Story contributed a background in maritime and commercial law, and in these matters he very quickly became the Court's expert in residence. And because maritime law would dominate the Court's work during the war years and commercial law thereafter (as New England would be the cutting edge of American economic change in the early nineteenth century), Story was assured a quick and lasting position of prominence in the Court's deliberations. His knowledge of comparative law (and thus conflict of laws) was much in demand, too, as would be his growing command of equity.

Story's scholarship could be somewhat overpowering and had the potential of alienating some of his colleagues. Sometimes it did, but Marshall was a master at soothing ruffled egos. More harmonizing still was the justices' pervasive commitment to the tradition of public service rooted in the American Revolution. Despite disparities in age, talent, and experience, all of them belonged to the revolutionary generation: Washington, Marshall, Duvall, Todd, and Livingston had served either in their state militias or in the Continental line or both; Marshall, Washington, and Duvall had seen combat. All five had served in some capacity on the state level during the 1780s, too, when state particularism and social and economic disorganization and national debility threatened to destroy the Revolution. Story (who was four years old in 1783) and Johnson (who was twelve) were too young to join directly in the revolutionary effort, but both participated vicariously through their fathers: William Johnson, Sr., was a member of the Liberty Tree Society in Charleston and Elisha Story was an "Indian" at the Boston Tea Party; both served with distinction in the army. That their sons should celebrate the virtues of the revolutionary saints simultaneously in 1812, Story in Boston and Johnson in Charleston, was fitting and logical. Differences in personality, legal doctrine, and conceptions of judicial duties were not homogenized simply by remembrance of the Revolution, of course. But it mattered considerably that these disagreements took place in the context of revolutionary patriotism. This shared sentiment would lose its force as distance from the Revolution increased, but while it lasted it created an environment that permitted the wisdom and charm of John Marshall to work their harmonizing magic.

With Marshall's help, Story settled quickly and easily into the life and work of the Court. His presence also altered the dynamics of the institution. He did not challenge Marshall's position as leader. Nor did such impressive performances as his opinion in *Martin* v. *Hunter's Lessee* (1816) diminish the chief justice's position as the authoritative expounder of the Constitution. But other things did shift: the division of labor on the Court; the distribution of power among the justices; and, one must presume, the flow of ideas in conference that gave final form to the opinions themselves and to the decisions of the Court. Story was heard immediately, forcefully, and not always in unison with his brethren, including the chief justice. Story did join Marshall and the majority on many of the great issues arising from the war. But he also dissented seven times in the six years from 1812 through 1817. His opinions for the majority signaled the presence of a new force on the Court, and his dissents not only challenged the ideological posture of the majority but proved the independence of the new justice from the chief justice whom he revered and from the Federalists of New England who opposed the war and expected their man in Washington to do the same.

2. An Independent Judge on Circuit

The impact of the War of 1812 on American law has never been assessed, but the relationship between the two was as important as it was complex.[20] The war was a watershed between the revolutionary age, when the very durability of the nation was the overriding issue, and the new nationalist period that ushered in rapid economic change and continental expansion. The war that unleashed the pent-up economic energies of America also generated both the nationalist decisions of the Marshall Court and, albeit temporarily, the nationalist sentiment sufficient to sustain them. The war was a bonanza for Story because the new precedent-making questions in prize law, neutral rights, wartime executive powers, and international law fell exactly into his area of expertise.

But riding the first circuit during the war, being New England's representative on the Court, had drawbacks as well as advantages and presented Story a challenge that went beyond legal learning and doctrinal advancement to the integrity of the judicial system itself. Story and his section— including many of the men he most admired, whose esteem he cherished, whose company he enjoyed, and with whom he would later associate in the cause of conservatism—differed passionately over "Mr. Madison's War," as John Lowell branded it.[21] Massachusetts Federalists looked on the war as an assault on New England interests and culture, the culmination of a Southern president's anticommercial, pro-French policy. Antiwar activities became a badge of sectional and party honor: Federalist governor Strong, who defeated Gerry on the war issue in 1812, proclaimed a day of fasting and humiliation to protest it and thereafter did everything in his power to resist the war effort and embarrass the Republican administration. Strong, with the advice of Story's friends on the state supreme court, in fact refused to place the state militia under national control (an effort Story would answer fifteen years later with a ringing assertion of national power in *Martin* v. *Mott*).[22] The Massachusetts house, six months after Story urged it to rekindle its revolutionary zeal, joined in an "address to the People of the State," urging them to "meet and consult together" to demonstrate their "disapprobation of this war."[23]

Story was embarrassed by and disgusted with the flagrant obstructionism of his state. His position on war had been unequivocal from the first British insult to American honor; he had been a leading advocate of military and naval preparedness; and when war came he embraced it as a revolutionary patriot. The man who condemned Clinton simply because he stood for peace in the election of 1812[24] was apoplectic about Federalist obstructionism, which he considered nothing less than an effort to "inflame animosities between the Northern and Southern people" that would lead to a "severance of the Union." The proposal of the Massachusetts house for a state convention he thought was "unquestionably designed to pave the way." "I abhor their conduct!" he exclaimed to Nat Williams, "Gracious God! That the people who led the van in the Revolution, should be the first to sell their liberties to a few designing, ambitious men, who hate even the name of patriotism!"[25]

Disaffected leaders and a doubting populace were not problems Story could ignore. As justice of the Supreme Court on circuit in New England, he was the most immediate representative—indeed, the personification— of national authority. The laws he was charged to uphold and administer were hated by the people he knew, respected, and loved and who counted on him for relief. The question was not just whether he could maintain the authority of those laws, difficult as that was, but whether, given his own feelings, he could do so with fairness and objectivity and respect for procedural regularity.

He saw the "mean and miserable" effort to undermine the authority of the Court and the country and made up his mind:

> I have determined to do my duty, and if popular odium follows, I shall at least have the consolation that I have satisfied my own judgment. I can perceive a path, which, without a great sacrifice of what the world would deem equity, might make me a very popular Judge of the Court at this moment; but I have great fears as to the character of a popular Judge in these times. I prefer to meet present prejudices, rather than hereafter to suffer the deepest regrets for judgments which I could not sustain upon principles of law or upon conscientious error of reasoning.[26]

New England's blatant disregard of the law and Story's firm determination to uphold it might well have led him to fiat judging, the categorical and unadorned assertion of power (and he was in fact accused of just this). He sought wisely instead to gain respect for the law by making it not only firm but fair—and by exploring its moral and educative potential, which was particularly rich at the trial level.

Story's opinions, as we shall see, rarely missed an opportunity to instruct and lecture, but they were of necessity addressed to a narrow audience. Not so with charges to the grand juries impaneled in each district of the circuit to inquire into and bring presentments in all crimes against the United States. The justice on circuit could, if he chose, give only a perfunctory statement of the law to the jury, leaving the main job of legal explication to the government's attorney (a practice later to become common). Story chose instead—after the manner of eighteenth-century judges and in the style of Chief Justice Parsons, from whom he probably learned the technique[27]—to give a general charge that mixed a plainspoken exposition of the laws to be upheld with a bracing lecture on sound policy and public morality. That mode suited his talent for oratory, his inclination for moral didacticism, his fear of excessive jury power. It also permitted him to exploit fully the educative potential of his authority as a Supreme Court justice on circuit.

During the war years the law-and-order charge was a major weapon against Federalist demagoguery and "the present prejudices" of New England. And treason against the United States, not surprisingly, was a frequent theme of these legal sermons. The problem was to balance force with rule of law. Story was guided by his reading of the treason trials of Bollman and Swartwout and Burr. Doubtless he knew of Jefferson's excessive efforts to procure convictions. He was present when William Giles of Virginia lashed out at Marshall for his narrow definition of treason. Giles's attempt to circumvent the Court's power by insisting on the right of the legislature to define the crime, Story thought, "laid the axe at the root of judicial power"—a position that anticipated his stand in *Martin* v. *Hunter's Lessee*.[28] Accordingly, Story warned New England jurors against the "persecuting zeal of prerogative and the fury of popular action" that would inflame "trivial crimes into the enormity of treason."[29]

But there was a war on, and Story's legal definition of treason took on a tone quite distinct from that of the *Bollman* and *Burr* opinions, though he borrowed from both. The American law of treason was not the harsh political law of the English. Agreed: But it must be adequate to prevent the destruction of the Union and the subversion of the legal order—and here Story spoke directly to Massachusetts Federalists and particularly to the resolution of the Massachusetts legislature that counseled open resistance. Treason, following Marshall in *Burr*, required the actual levying of war;

conspiring to subvert the government by force, though it was a crime, was not treason. But if conspiracy came into the open it was treason. If it did, the "quantum of force" to be employed was not the issue. Here Story subtly shifted from Marshall in *Burr* to Marshall in *Bollman*, whose somewhat harsher doctrines he preferred.[30] To assemble with force "destined or arranged and armed in a warlike manner" was an overt act; "enlisting and marching" were overt acts; "attacking the public forces upon a march or in quarters with a *designed* opposition to the authority of the Government" was levying war; so was joining with such rebels or furnishing them with arms or provisions. Treason might in fact exist "without the presence or actual employment of arms or other military weapons"; under certain circumstances mere numbers are enough. Nor did treason require that "the direct purpose or design of the conspirators should be the overthrow of the Govt. itself. All combinations to effect by force or violence any object of a general & national concern—as to dismember the Union,—to compel a change of the administration—to coerce the repeal of an obnoxious law— or the adoption of a favorite law—or to resist or oppose the execution of any general act or statute of the U. S.—all such combinations amount in law to a conspiracy to levy war—and if carried into effect by actual insurrection or by assembling in force for *actual* rebellion are overt acts of levying war."[31]

And lest New England should miss the point he added, "It is wholly immaterial, whether the grievance be real or imaginary—or the Law be unjust, burthensome or oppressive or the contrary. . . ." The point was simply that no individuals "should take upon themselves the redress of grievances by *force* or control the public will by military terror or violence."[32] Thirty years later he would say basically the same thing to Thomas Dorr and his followers and make it the basis of the American doctrine of martial law.

Taken in its largest sense, Story's charge, which he delivered to the grand juries in each of the districts of his circuit, was a primer on the role of law and the duties of citizens in a republic at war. There was, he warned (echoing the Reverend David Tappan's jeremiad of 1798 and anticipating his own during the 1820s), a tendency in human affairs toward "utter instability." Law, devised by man in his rational moments, was the buffer against social disintegration and a bulwark against man's inconstant virtue. Without it "good men would be everywhere expelled from office and bad men under colour of some captivating delusions would seize the reigns of power." Without law, vice would corrupt the sources of domestic virtue, then "seize upon popular feelings through every root and branch of the political system." Next to fall would be the sanction of religion and the rights of private property. "Anarchy would succeed, & on its ruins tyranny would erect its throne, and as with a sponge, wipe away the very name and remembrance of liberty." And if law supported virtue, then good men with virtue had to support the law. Such was the "glorious privilege" of citizenship on which the republic itself was founded.[33]

If Story's contemplation of social disorder seems excessively Manichean, it must be remembered that he had lived for a decade amid persistent rumors of disunion and stood witness since 1807 to open violation and outspoken contempt of national commercial regulations—this by the men and the party who in the next breath praised the rule of law.

On circuit he confronted New England's ingrained habit of law defiance head on. Illicit trade was a case in point, in regard first to the embargo and nonintercourse laws and then, with an imperceptible shift of gears, to the wartime interdict on trade with the enemy. From 1809 to 1826 the Court tried nearly fifty such cases, and on the 1812 circuit, embargo cases, backlogged because of Cushing's death, were the most numerous category Story faced.[34] They were among the most difficult, too, because he not only knew many of the merchants and shippers involved and their lawyers but was personally torn between his dislike of the embargo and his hatred of those who broke the law. Convicting under the embargo and nonintercourse laws after they had been repealed only made the task of enforcement more onerous, the temptation to be lenient greater. In any case, the responsibility was his: Under the admiralty side of his jurisdiction, the cases were ordinarily tried without jury.[35]

In *The Orono*, which came before him in May 1812 at the circuit court in Boston, the dilemma was even more difficult because it involved an exercise of authority by the president who had just appointed him. At issue was the legal effect of President Madison's proclamation of 9 August 1809, which revived the embargo system against Great Britain. By the eleventh section of the act of 1 March 1809, commonly called the Non-Importation Act, the president was authorized to suspend the embargo with any nation that repealed its commercial restrictions on the United States. Acting under the authority of this act and on the assumed validity of the Erskine Treaty, Madison resumed commercial relations with Great Britain. When George Canning repudiated the Erskine Treaty as a breach of authority on Erskine's part, Madison, by presidential proclamation on 9 August 1809, revived the embargo against Great Britain.

The problem was that the act of 1 March 1809 contained no authorization for a revival, unless such executive authority could be inferred from the power to suspend the embargo. Story had "the most entire respect for the executive," sympathized with his "multiplicity of cares," but he said no to such an exercise of power. "I take it to be an incontestable principle," he declared, "that the President has no common law prerogative to interdict commercial intercourse with any nation; or to revive any act, whose operation had expired." Such authority "must be derived from some positive law; and when that is once found to exist, the court have nothing to do with the manner and circumstances under which it is exercised."[36] The Federalist editor who, upon Story's election to Congress back in 1808, prophesied that "he will never submit to become a 'back stairs' minion of Executive influence" must have been pleased with his prescience.[37]

Story's independence and attachment to principle are all the more impressive because he could be accused of having succumbed to popular pressure. Such an inference, however, is not justified. Far from opposing wartime executive power, Story was a champion of it, as a look at his other wartime opinions makes clear. Also, he demonstrated not the slightest hesitancy to decree convictions under the embargo and nonintercourse laws when the facts were clear concerning the complicity of the accused.[38] He was not reluctant, either, to grant a liberal interpretation of authority for the enforcement of the commercial laws when the intent of the legislature was certain. Thus, in *The Bolina* and again in *U.S.* v. *Sears*, he refused to obstruct the operation of the embargo by encumbering enforcing officers with technical restraints.[39]

To be sure, the Court would not tolerate an invasion "of the rights of citizens under color of office."[40] Nor when the legislature spoke ambiguously, *spargere ambiguas voces*, would the Court "hunt through dark and doubtful passages, to catch a glimmering meaning, whereby to load the citizens with penalties and forfeitures." In doubtful cases, that is to say, "the words are to be expounded in favor of the citizen, and against the legislature."[41]

But Story was as realistic about power as he was about legislative incompetence, and he was a bit elitist as well: Power was a necessary attribute of governing; discretion must be allowed those who rule. His axiom of construction laid down in *U.S.* v. *Sears* on this subject adumbrated a theory of constitutional power that would be Story's hallmark and the Marshall Court's too—once it caught up with him. "In the nature of things . . . ," he said of customs officials, "they must have some implied powers." And because the legislature cannot enumerate all their powers, "it may be safely assumed, that they may exercise all powers necessary and proper to effectuate the manifest intentions of the law connected with the duties of their office."[42] This broad exercise of power, it is clear from trading-with-the-enemy cases, Story was willing—indeed, anxious—to extend to the judiciary itself.

Neither the embargo nor the nonintercourse system succeeded in severing the commercial relationship between New England and Great Britain, and the declaration of war in 1812 was hardly more effective. Trading with Great Britain was not only a way of economic survival for New England merchants and shippers but a way of protesting what they thought was an unnecessary and unjust war. And they pursued illicit trade with a variety of well-practiced techniques that went back to the defiance of British commercial regulations in the 1760s and 1770s and up through the embargo years.

Story knew these techniques of defiance as well as anyone. He knew that the attempt to enforce the unpopular commercial law in the face of such hostility would plunge him into "political discussions" of an explosive nature. He knew also that sectional self-interest would have to give way to the war effort, and he put his section on warning. "War puts every individual of the respective governments themselves," he said in *The Rapid and Cargo*, "in a state of hostility with each other." Enemies are enemies in every respect, including trade, which by definition cannot "subsist in a state of utter hostility."[43]

The Rapid involved a blatant effort to bring British goods into Boston by stealth, although Story's friend William Prescott argued, with a straight face, presumably, that the merchandise in question had been "rescued" from the possession of the enemy. In *The Julia* the guise—that the vessel was sailing legally under a license issued by the British vice-admiral at Halifax—was only slightly more sophisticated (as licensing was permitted only in a limited number of emergency circumstances). Repeating the principle asserted in *The Rapid*—that "in war all intercourse between the subjects and citizens of the belligerent countries is illegal, unless sanctioned by the authority of the government, or in the exercise of the rights of humanity"—Story went on to excoriate New England's "cupidity," which led it to think that an American citizen might by means of a foreign license "carve out for himself a neutrality on the ocean, when his country is at war. . . ."[44]

Much more challenging than cases of sailing under foreign license were those involving falsified ships' papers, simulated shipwreck, and collusive capture, all of which devices were regularly employed by New Englanders to circumvent the law. Ambiguous evidence, complicated factual environment, and the wide discretion allowed the judge by admiralty and maritime law were calculated to put Story on the firing line.

The Bothnea. Janstoff, a case of collusive capture, makes the point and shows Story's ability as a trial judge as well.[45] The facts were deceptively simple. On about 24 November 1813 two ships sailing under a Swedish flag with Swedish papers (which were admitted by both parties to have been simulated) left British Halifax for New London, Connecticut, under a British license and with British-manufactured goods on board. Both vessels were captured by a small American privateer, the *Washington*, on the alleged ground that they were engaged in transporting British goods into the United States in violation of the interdict on trade with Great Britain that came with the War of 1812.[46] Upon arrival the vessels were seized by the collector for alleged collusive capture and fraudulent violation of the nonimportation act. The captors instigated action in the District Court of Massachusetts against both vessels as fairly taken prize of war, but in the first instance confined themselves "to the endeavor to obtain an order for further proof."[47] The motion was overruled and the vessels and cargoes condemned to the government. The case was appealed to Story's circuit court, where the motion for further proof was renewed.

The difficulty was that these seemingly simple facts could yield two contradictory interpretations, or as Justice Johnson put it later after hearing the arguments on appeal before the full court, "scarcely a feature of it may not be indifferently pronounced the lineament of guilt or innocence."[48] One interpretation, based on a literal reading of the facts, saw the case as a simple one of illegal trade and justifiable capture and condemnation in favor of the captors. On the other hand, common knowledge of the inventive ways employed by New Englanders to avoid the interdict on British trade and the unusual success of such efforts suggested that the voyage was undertaken with the plan that it be interrupted by capture. By the anticipated decree of condemnation, British goods would be brought into the United States under the protective color of patriotism and with the unavoidable compliance of the federal courts.

A number of unusual circumstances surrounding the case gave the government real reason for suspecting the validity of the capture and for looking beyond the ships' papers to sustain its suspicions. First, given the alleged purpose of smuggling, the ships were most inadequately prepared for contingencies. The ships' papers were given such poor clothing of neutrality that a simple perusal penetrated the guise and established the illegality of the voyage. The ships were entirely unarmed and could not repel even small privateers despite the fact that the captains had been explicitly warned about them. Moreover, each ship had on board an American citizen, who as a loyal American upon arrival in New London would assuredly have divulged the entire operation to authorities. Further suspicions were excited because neither American was willing to account in any detail for his being in Halifax and making the voyage and because, by process of elimination, a case could be made for their being the mysterious agents to whom secret dispatches found among the papers had been addressed.

There were, secondly, questionable circumstances surrounding the capture itself: It was made "in the very mouth of British territory"; there was no evidence of resistance or attempt to escape (the *Bothnea* did not even alter course, though it saw the capture of the *Janstoff*); and there was no attempt to destroy the ships' papers despite their incriminatory contents. Finally, all the captured crewmen were put ashore, leaving only the single American on each vessel as a witness, despite the fact that there was a bounty on such prisoners and that the prize act and presidential instructions required that at least the master and principal officers of the captured vessels be brought in.[49]

Warranted as government suspicions might have been, however, they rested entirely on circumstantial—indeed, inferential—grounds.[50] And herein lay the dilemma of the enforcement of the commercial regulations, for the attempt to bolster the government position by testimonial evidence foundered on the rock of New England prejudice. Specifically, the problem was that nearly all persons on whom the government depended for direct testimony were hostile and uncooperative witnesses, either because they were interested parties or because they sympathized more with sectional needs than with national interest. Without such testimonial evidence, ships' papers, specious though they might be, possessed a controlling preponderance, and government contentions, as District Attorney George Blake and government collectors knew well, remained distressingly unsubstantial.[51]

By the time the case appeared before Story sitting at circuit in Boston in May 1816, the war was over. But even more for that reason, the whole gamut of political, personal, and legal pressures came into focus to try his mettle. The case pitted national authority against the perceived interest of Story's section. At stake were sums of "immense magnitude," estimated by H. G. Otis to be "upward of $100,000" and by George Blake, then attorney general for Massachusetts, at $140,000 or $150,000.[52] To complicate the matter, counsel for the defense were H. G. Otis, the lion of New England Federalism who had abetted Story's defection from Jeffersonian Republicanism, and William Prescott, who had befriended him as a beleaguered young attorney. Because of the ambiguity of the evidence Story had the option of choosing, and because he was *the* circuit judge his choice would be apparent to all. A path was readily available that, to use Story's earlier words, "without a great sacrifice of what the world would deem equity, might make me a very popular Judge of Court at this moment."[53]

That path he courageously forsook. Boldly employing the discretion that the case allowed, he declared that "in no case whatever is the court absolutely concluded by the original evidence. It is at liberty to entertain doubts extrinsic of such evidence, and to be satisfied of the verity of the transaction by proofs drawn beyond the mere formal papers and attestations of the parties." On the key question of the motion for further proof (entered by the captors in the district court, refused there, and brought on appeal before the circuit court), Story shifted the burden to the potential offender of national authority. "In cases of reasonable doubt" and where the conduct of the captors seems "fair, and is not tainted with illegality," the court would admit further proof. But where the position of the captors "does not admit of a fair explanation," further proof would be denied. On the basis, then, of "doubts" extrinsic to the "original evidence" (namely, the knowledge of the "strong temptations to illicit intercourse" and the frequent surrender to those temptations), Story held that the position of the captors did not admit of a fair explanation. Their motion for further proof was accordingly overruled, and the district court's condemnation of the prize to the government was affirmed.[54]

The bitterness and vituperation Story prophesied quickly appeared, delivered by none other than H. G. Otis, who assuredly spoke for a large number of his commercial friends:

> Upon the appeal [he wrote to Harper, who had been retained to handle the case before the Supreme Court], the motion for further proof was renewed—But Judge Story ordered the argument to proceed upon the merits, reserving the question of further proof to be decided as he should, after the hearing, think fit—It was argued accordingly and the Counsel for the Captors pleased themselves that Jupiter nodded assent to all their positions—Never upon the evidence was a sorrier case—But to our utter astonishment, when he promulged his decree it came forth as you will see, a most elaborate tissue of suspicions, proceeding upon the curious and avowed ground that the Court is not bound by evidence, but may be governed by its own conscience.[55]

Not only, thought Otis, was the ground taken by Story "curious," but his motives in taking it were most questionable. "In truth," Otis bitterly added, "we have no doubt that this learned Judge *after the hearing in Court*, permitted himself to be influenced by *out of doors* suggestions and suspicions originating in ignorance and in envy." Indeed, "in summing up the cause against the Captors, the argument, astuteness, jealousy and ingenuity of the Judge, left the same quality of the Counsel in total eclipse." Otis's disgust at Story's behavior on circuit was exceeded only by his apprehension "that he will now feel himself pledged to support his opinion, so as to influence his Colleagues [on the Supreme Court], some of whom to the astonishment and mortification of their best friends in this quarter are considered as giving him the pavé in all causes of this description."[56]

Otis, it turned out, was wrong about the final disposition of the case, which went against Story on appeal. But he was right about the "pavé." Story was his own man, not only on circuit but on the full court as well.

3. An Independent Judge on the Supreme Court

Otis had some reason to be apprehensive about Story's influence on the Court in Washington. The judicial system was organized not only so that the justice on circuit represented the Court to the section but so that he represented the section, with its special legal problems, to the Court. Story was appointed in part because of his expertise in admiralty and maritime law, the legal staple of New England; the plethora of legal problems dealing with prize law and neutrality that came with the war put an additional premium on his specialty. He was supposed to pull his load and he did. "We are stuffed with all sorts of complicated questions, particularly of Prize Law," Story wrote to Fay at the end of the 1812 term, "in respect to which I was obliged to take a decided part. As usual, the old maxim was verified—*Juniores ad labores*. I worked very hard, and my brethren were so kind as to place confidence in my researches."[57]

Indeed they did. Story's opinion-writing load increased from a modest two out of forty in 1812 (including *per curiam* opinions and one-sentence dispositions of cases), to six of forty-three in 1813, twelve of forty-four in 1814, seven of thirty-seven in 1815, and nine of thirty-nine in 1816, including in that year his great effort in *Martin* v. *Hunter's Lessee*. This total does not count Story's dissents or his opinions on circuit. Seventeen of Story's majority opinions for the Court during this four-year period were in admiralty law, and it was in this area that he first established his scholarly credentials with his brethren. When the chief justice ended his conference on one occasion by remarking that "brother Story, here . . . can give us the cases from the Twelve Tables down to the latest reports," he was not merely trying to put his colleague at ease. Judging by the increasing number of requests for his advice about admiralty and maritime law, Story was already the scholar in residence.[58]

That Story was respected by his brethren does not mean, however, that he was always in agreement with them or they with him, whatever the myth of a monolithic Marshall Court might suggest. Even in appeals from his own circuit like *Bothnea. Janstoff*, Story did not always sweep his colleagues away. The chief justice himself took on Story in that case, arguing that when fraud is imputed, both parties have full liberty "to adduce further proof on every point in the case."[59] Upon reargument on the basis of the additional evidence, Justice Johnson and the majority reversed Story's circuit decree, which had put the burden of proof on the defendant, by holding that in the absence of conclusive evidence of fraud, the Court "must pronounce in favor of innocence."[60] Story's refusal to enter an opinion indicated his willingness to stand by his circuit opinion. And *Bothnea* was only one of Story's several disagreements with the Court. From 1812 through 1816 he issued seven dissents (three of them unwritten)—more than any other justice on the Court during this period, including Johnson, and more than were entered during the first eleven years of the Marshall Court.

What seems clear from this record of dissent, in addition to the fact that Story was stubbornly independent, is that the scientific lawyer had become the scientific judge. Once he had taken a position on the basis of a scholarly investigation of authorities he stuck with it. At the same time he was determined to use wartime cases to strengthen the authority of the national government—this against the inclinations of some of his less jingoistic associates, including the chief justice. Indeed, while Story struggled against New England dissidents, Marshall continued a cordial correspondence with them. They, in turn, or some of them at least, went so far as to consider Marshall a suitable peace candidate in place of Clinton in 1812.[61]

Story's zeal for the war crept into the *Bothnea* opinion, as we have seen. It figured more strongly in *Brown* v. *U.S.* (1814), which separated him from Marshall and the rest of the Court over the question of wartime executive powers. The specific question turned on the power of the president to order a seizure of enemy property in the absence of federal statutory authorization. In reversing Story's circuit decision, the majority of the Court, speaking through Marshall, held that the exercise of executive power in regard to the confiscation of enemy property is not a matter of judicial construction and must necessarily be based on an act of Congress. Story's dissent, which revealed his intense concern for the energetic prosecution of the war, was grounded on the doctrine of implied power he had adumbrated in the case of *U.S.* v. *Sears* in regard to the enforcement of the embargo. "I think," he declared in reference to the president, that "he must, as an incident of the office, have a right to employ all the usual and customary means acknowledged in war. . . ." On him rests the duty to execute the law and preserve the sovereignty of the nation. "The best manner of annoying, injuring and pressing the enemy, must from the nature of things, vary under different circumstances; and the executive is responsible to the nation for the faithful discharge of his duty, under the changes of hostilities."[62]

Story's argument for a sweeping discretionary executive power in time of war was the first in a line of decisions leading to *U.S.* v. *Curtiss-Wright Export Corporation* (1936), in which Justice George Sutherland held that the powers to declare and to wage war were "necessary concomitants of nationality" and would exist even "if they had never been mentioned in the Constitution."[63] Story had in fact used almost identical words in expounding his theory of implied powers in his *Brown* dissent, and they applied as he spelled them out not only to executive powers but to congressional as well. Story's reasoning focused on the words in article I, section 8, clause 11, of the Constitution following the phrase "to declare war." He denied the contention that the explicit grant of power to Congress to issue letters of marque and reprisal, *ex vi terminorum*, eliminated that power as a corollary to be inferred from the power to declare war. Indeed, he said, "if the constitution had been silent as to letters of marque and capture, it would not have narrowed the authority of Congress." Such powers in fact "are ordinary and necessary incidents to the power of declaring war."[64]

This reasoning Story elevated to the status of a general rule of construction, adding a coda on the legal meaning of the Preamble of the Constitution that carried his broad constructionism far beyond John Marshall's wildest claims. "In truth," continued Story, "it is by no means unfrequent in the constitution to add clauses of a special nature to general powers which embrace them, and to provide affirmatively for general powers, without meaning thereby to negative the existence of power of a more general nature." And then referring to the Preamble: "The power to provide 'for the common defense and general welfare,' could hardly be doubted to include the power to 'borrow money': the power 'to coin money,' to include the power 'to make rules for the government and regulation' thereof."[65]

If accepted fully and in its broadest sense, Story's theory of construction would have gone far toward destroying the principle of limited and enumerated powers.[66] As it stood it was a direct precursor to the Court's doctrine of implied powers announced in *McCulloch* v. *Maryland* four years later. Even more pertinent to that great decision was Story's circuit decision in *U.S.* v. *Bainbridge* (1816), as it involved congressional rather than executive authority. The question, which again grew out of the wartime demands on constitutional power, was whether Congress by virtue of the constitutional grant "to provide and maintain a navy" had authority to pass a law permitting the enlistment of minors in the navy without the consent of their parents. It was an issue dear to Story's heart and directly connected to the war effort and "national policy"; about it he had not the slightest doubt. "It has been justly observed, in a work of the very best authority," he wrote in reference to Madison's *Federalist* 44, in words similar to Hamilton's famous report of 1791 regarding the First Bank of the United States, and in anticipation of Marshall's in *McCulloch*, "that no maxim is more clearly established in law, or in reason, than that wherever the end is required, the means are authorized. Whenever a general power to do a thing is given, every particular power necessary for doing it is included."[67]

Story's expansive interpretation of implied powers in the *Sears, Brown*, and *Bainbridge* opinions (the one he would apply to judicial power in *Martin* v. *Hunter's Lessee*) lays bare his approach to the whole question of federal power: He looked beyond the cases to the doctrine, beyond the moment to the future. This concern for a long-range national interest also governed his approach to American neutral rights as he spelled it out in *The Nereide* (1815). Again he parted company with the chief justice and the Court.

The issue in that case, as Marshall summed it up in his opinion, was whether "the conduct of Manuel Pinto . . . had impressed a hostile character on his property . . . laden on board of the Nereide," thus making it subject to capture and condemnation as lawful prize.[68] Pinto was a citizen of Argentina, a neutral power during the war between the United States and Great Britain. In 1813 he chartered a heavily armed merchant ship, the *Nereide*, belonging to British subjects, for a voyage from London to Buenos Aires and back with the express stipulation in the charter party that the ship sail under the protection of a British convoy. On the first leg of the voyage the *Nereide* was accidentally separated from the convoy, and while attempting to return to it was taken captive by an American privateer after an unsuccessful resistance. The vessel was taken to New York, where Pinto's property was condemned as lawful prize. The Court confronted the case on appeal and Story confronted the Court. At issue was a question of international law with long-range policy implications concerning American national interests in time of war—at least as Story saw the matter.

Marshall's opinion for the Court, following his great effort in *The Exchange* v. *McFadden* two years earlier,[69] struck a blow for neutral rights. Reversing the decree of condemnation by Judge William W. Van Ness below (which Story thought was "unanswerable"), the chief justice ruled that the right of a neutral to place goods on a belligerent vessel without sacrificing their neutral character was "universally recognized as the original rule of the law of nations."[70] Neither by the terms of the charter party nor by his conduct on the voyage did Pinto sacrifice the rights accorded to neutrals by international law.

Marshall's argument that neutral rights take precedence over belligerent rights, which was the gist of the Court's decision, appeared to be sound policy. Certainly it was attuned to the period of the Napoleonic Wars, when American economic interest was tied to neutral rights. It was also congenial to the sentiments of New England and close in spirit to ideas championed earlier by Story himself. The practical problem as Story now perceived it, however, was that the United States was a belligerent, not a neutral. Story's opinion looked immediately to the realities of war— to the fact that a diminution of neutral trade with Britain would weaken its war effort against the United States. It looked also to the future when American public and private ships would dominate the high seas, a position he had in fact been working to achieve since his stint in Congress in 1808–9. Story's dissent, then (drawn up, he recalled, "in a very full manner"), proposed nothing less than a radical shift in American policy.[71] This it did, not by contending that law follows policy, but by arguing as he would do throughout his career that *correct* legal doctrine was good policy. Belligerent rights, not neutral rights, was good policy.

It was also good law. Story conceded the general principle that "neutral goods may be lawfully put on board of an enemy ship without being prize of war,"[72] but found it incomplete and inconclusive. That doctrine alone, as asserted by the majority, subordinated belligerent to neutral rights. Story, following English law and Lord Stowell, chose to treat them as interdependent—an act of doctrinal daring that surprised British legal authorities and laid the foundation for an international legal friendship between Story and Lord Stowell, to whom he turned for support.[73] Story's position, quite simply, was that neutral rights were contingent on neutral duties, one of which was to maintain "a perfect impartiality as to all the belligerents" and another of which was "to submit to search." Pinto violated both principles, Story argued, in a tone that made clear his disgust with what he thought was wrongheaded law and weak-kneed policy. For a neutral to "charter an armed ship, and victual and man her with an enemy crew" and sail under the protection of an enemy convoy, was to surrender the rights of neutrality. Such conduct, Story concluded, "is utterly irreconcilable with the good faith of a friend, and unites all the qualities of the most odious hostility."[74]

Correct principle was the issue for Story in *Nereide* (and he never changed his mind on the correctness of his position).[75] But if one judges from that opinion and others of his wartime decisions, principle and policy were not separable. Story's principled adjudication, in plain terms, supported the war effort. In a pragmatic vein, it also looked forward, as did his stand on wartime executive powers, to national economic and military maturity. By urging these points on an unwilling Court, Story made himself the Court's strongest spokesman for martial power. Again, it was clear that Story's devotion to the Court and his affection for the chief justice did not mean intellectual subservience to either.

4. All Power to the Federal Courts

Story's plans for national grandeur as expressed to Nathaniel Williams in 1815—which included a standing army, a "permanent navy," national military and naval schools, and a national bank—depended on executive initiative and congressional power.[76] And such power his opinions sought to supply. But Story was also concerned with federal judicial power—doubly so, in fact, because in addition to being national institutions themselves, the federal courts were instruments for the consolidation of power in the other branches of the national government. Story's blueprint for America turned, to put it another way, on the full realization of national potential created by the Constitution, which in turn depended on the consolidation of the power of the federal courts.

Here there was much work to be done. The Founding Fathers did not settle the powers of the Supreme Court and the federal judiciary, partly for reasons of political expedience, partly because they were not omniscient, and partly because they were confused.[77] Much seemingly settled, moreover, was not beyond debate. Articles III and VI of the Constitution armed the Supreme Court with a "stately jurisdiction," to be sure, and put it at the center of American government. How, when, and with what finality the Court would use its power of judicial review, however, was not clear and had not been settled conclusively even by *Marbury* v. *Madison*.

Two specific and crucial jurisdictional matters were also unsettled, both of which were of immediate concern to Story. The first problem was that the constitutional and federal cases placed under the jurisdiction of the federal courts by article III could by the Judiciary Act of 1789 be heard in the first instance by state courts. Only through writ of error as provided by section 25 of that act could the Supreme Court reach the cases it was authorized to hear, and section 25 could be repealed or modified by a mere act of Congress. Equally precarious and uncertain was the status of the common law in the federal courts. The framers did not "embosom" the common law in the Constitution, as Julius Goebel, Jr., put it, for both ideological and practical reasons, the former being that it was antithetical to republican principles and the latter being that the common law in America had fragmented along state lines.[78] Yet the federal judiciary under the Constitution was infused with the common law. American lawyers and judges, like Story, had been schooled in its principles and methods. Each of the new states, whose laws the Supreme Court was by section 34 of the Judiciary Act of 1789 bound to follow in diversity cases, made the common law the foundation of its jurisprudence. The Process Act of 1789, which as a supplement to the federal Judiciary Act of that year set forth the processes by which the federal courts would operate, was shot through with common-law practice and terminology.[79] The Constitution itself could not be fully understood without reference to the common law.

To leave the common law out of American constitutional law was impossible, then. But how much to put in was uncertain. The debate would focus on the question of the common-law jurisdiction of the federal courts: whether they had a general common-law jurisdiction, or a common-law jurisdiction in criminal cases only; or whether they had neither, in which case the common law would serve merely as a general guide to the meaning of constitutional phraseology, if even that. These questions and others relating to the federal courts (and state judiciaries as well) became the subject of searching and heated partisan debate in the first decades of the new nation and were at times, as Story's Massachusetts experience made clear, the touchstone of party division and the focal point of ideological arguments over the meaning of republican government.[80]

As Madison's new Republican justice, Story was drawn into the vortex of this ideological storm. Or rather, he charged into it headlong of his own accord. Ten years as lawyer-scholar in Massachusetts (not to mention his encounter with antijudicial Republican hatchet men in Congress) persuaded him of the need for a stronger judiciary. That formative experience, now joined with self-interest, inspired the new justice to address the unsettled questions of federal judicial power with a plan that was as breathtaking in scope as it was audacious in execution. In an integrated and masterfully executed campaign, Story sought to secure a common-law jurisdiction for the federal courts, consolidate judicial review over state court decisions, and secure full constitutional powers for the federal judiciary. Again, it was the War of 1812 that called him into action. And again the young justice pitted himself against John Marshall and his other friends on the Court—not to mention the president who appointed him, along with most of his former Republican associates. Only a small part of Story's plan was realized. But taken in its objectives and interconnected strategies, it has no parallel in American judicial history.

Story staged his offensive for a reformed judicial system initially from his circuit court, a procedure that made sense because there he could pursue his scholarly researches without stint, speak his juristic mind without compromise. His reform effort began, in fact, with the circuit court itself, which he inherited from William Cushing in a state "quite unpropitious." The court lacked regular and well-known rules of procedure (because of his predecessor's casual style); the bar lacked discipline (for the same reason); and the docket was burdened with continuances (particularly of embargo and nonintercourse cases).[81]

The new justice started from scratch. One of his first acts, following the model reform in Massachusetts, was to introduce printed circuit reports, the sine qua non of principled adjudication and scientific practice. As reporter he hired his friend and former law-office student John Gallison.[82] William Smith Shaw, whom Story treated with every respect, stayed on as clerk of the Boston circuit, a position that by arrangement with John Davis he held jointly with the clerkship of the federal district court for Massachusetts. With the active cooperation of John Davis and the willing compliance of other, less-talented bench mates, and with the circuit court at Boston as a model of excellence, Story was in a position to strike a blow for basic reforms in practice and doctrine. Long-winded lawyers (whose indulgence by the Court *in banc* annoyed Story) were cut short; old pros, used to having their way with Cushing, were held to the mark; young lawyers were encouraged.[83] All were brought into mutual harmony and inspired to an excellence that made Story's circuit one of the most productive in the Court's history.[84]

And, thanks to Story's agile mind and quick pen, his court was also one of the most efficient. First the docket had to be swept clean. Cushing had permitted large numbers of common-law cases, including jury cases, to come before him on appeal from the district court. Story stopped the practice in *U.S.* v. *Wonson* (1812), which held that no appeals lay from the district to the circuit court except admiralty and maritime cases and those only on points of law by writ of error. Jury trials on appeal were abolished outright, a step that immediately struck 130 backlogged cases from the docket.[85] Armed with the authority to establish rules of practice without reference to state procedures (also established in *Wonson*) and the discretion allowed by the federal Process Act of 1790, Story then introduced a set of comprehensive rules for proceeding in prize cases (and later in equity cases), which he carefully circulated among federal district judges with whom he sat on circuit.[86] His learning, his tact and patience, and his willingness to do a lion's share of the circuit work brought out the best in them, too, establishing a "reciprocal communication" that vitalized the first circuit.

From a reformed court, Story was ready to reach out for an expanded federal common-law jurisdiction. The issue appeared in two widely disparate cases on circuit in 1812 and 1813. The first, *Van Reimsdyk* v. *Kane*, which came up at the November 1812 term of the Rhode Island circuit, seemed remote from the common-law question, as it dealt mainly with equity and conflict of laws. Van Reimsdyk was a Dutch merchant living in Java; the defendants were Rhode Island merchants who, through their agent, drew a bill of exchange on the plaintiff that was subsequently dishonored. Defense council pleaded a discharge under the Rhode Island bankruptcy law. Story rejected the argument and instead ruled that a contract made abroad to be performed abroad was governed by conflict principles.[87] What gave the case precedential importance was Story's reading of section 34 of the Judiciary Act of 1789, which bound the Supreme Court to the "laws" of the state in diversity-of-citizenship cases. By permitting federal courts to consult private international law in such cases, Story left the door open for a broad exercise of judicial discretion in the area of commercial law—a door he would open even wider thirty years later in *Swift* v. *Tyson*.[88]

It must not, of course, be inferred from *Van Reimsdyk* that Story was pushing for a *general* common-law jurisdiction for the federal judiciary. But Story no doubt did consider the common-law powers that might be inferred from the Constitution of 1787, from the federal Process Acts, and from the fact that state jurisprudence was rooted in the common law.[89] Assuredly, he knew of the efforts of the Ellsworth Court to claim a federal criminal common-law jurisdiction, and his own wartime experience on the New England circuit convinced him that these early efforts were firmly rooted in good policy.

The barrier was *U.S.* v. *Hudson and Goodwin* (1812), in which decision the Marshall Court clearly denied the existence of a federal criminal common law.[90] The decision was doubly ironic in that it stemmed from an indictment at common law for libel brought with the compliance of President Jefferson (who had been the chief opponent of federal common law)[91] against Federalist printers Hudson and Goodwin (whose acquittal now depended on a denial of common-law jurisdiction, which the Federalist party had heretofore championed). Because there was no federal statute setting out the crime of federal libel (Hudson and Goodwin's Connecticut *Courant* had charged the president and Congress with having secretly voted two million dollars as a bribe to urge Bonaparte to transfer the Louisiana Territory to Spain), the indictment rested entirely on the common law. The sole question, as Justice Johnson put it, was "whether the circuit courts of the United States can exercise a common law jurisdiction in criminal cases."[92]

A majority composed of both Federalists and Jeffersonians on the Court denied jurisdiction. Speaking for this majority, William Johnson declared that no criminal common-law jurisdiction had ever existed (a claim that was not quite true) or could exist. He conceded that a body politic had to be able to preserve itself by being able to punish attacks against its sovereignty, but such a principle was not unique to the common law and the appropriateness of the end did not justify the means. The only ground on which a federal common law might be claimed, reasoned Johnson, in a straightforward reliance on the states' rights assumption that all federal powers were concessions from the states, was through the doctrine of implied powers—which in good Jeffersonian style he refused to countenance.[93]

Story disagreed but remained silent; therefore, given Washington's absence, only a bare majority of the Court decided this crucial issue, and this without argument of counsel. Included in the majority was Chief Justice Marshall, who, though he did not agree with Johnson's states' rights reasoning, had already made up his mind that the federal criminal law was a matter for legislative codification.[94]

The Court's reasoning, as Story perceived, was as fragile as its majority. The Constitution did not settle the matter in "favor of the negative," as Johnson phrased it. Moreover, in his report on the judiciary system communicated to the House of Representatives, 31 December 1790, Attorney General Edmund Randolph was, on practical grounds, unwilling to rule out a limited common-law jurisdiction, particularly in light of the embryonic status of federal statutes.[95]

Federal courts were more positive still, and on at least four occasions before 1812 they had tried defendants indicted for nonstatutory criminal offenses.[96] Johnson was correct in suggesting that these cases were inconclusive, as all were circuit court decisions and not binding on the full Court. In one of the four (*Henfield*), moreover, the indictment rested on a treaty, and in another (*Worrall*) on international law as well as the common law. In these cases the court divided between district judge Richard Peters, who favored the common-law jurisdiction, and Justice Chase, who opposed it. In *Williams' Case* the issue of jurisdiction was not directly before the Court, though it was necessarily inferred in Chief Justice Oliver Ellsworth's opinion (which, however, was not concurred in by district judge Richard Law). To be sure, there was no precedential momentum in favor of a federal criminal common law before 1812, but neither was there, as Johnson simplistically asserted in *Hudson*, a "general acquiescence of legal men" against it.[97] There were judges and lawyers of learning and ability on both sides. And in no instance had the matter been fully argued or explored systematically by the full bench.

What confronted the Court in 1812, then, was not a clear mandate against the common law but a handle for it, if they chose to grasp it. That they chose not to do so had as much to do with political considerations as law. Certainly no other issue of that period was more explosive. Party lines between Federalists and Republicans were (thanks to the French Revolution and the predominance of foreign policy issues) drawn along pro-British/pro-French lines. The common law was a natural and inevitable focal point of these differences: Federalists liked it because it was a part of the English constitutional system, which they admired; Republicans distrusted it for that very reason. Above all, federal common-law jurisdiction meant a strengthened federal judiciary, which stood for aristocracy and nationalism, all causes that Federalists favored and Republicans opposed. Federalists liked the common law because they trusted judges more than legislators; with Republicans the reverse was true. Nor did it matter to Republicans that the issue was criminal law only. Indeed, it was the criminal side of the common law, with Federalist prosecutions under the Alien-Sedition Acts fresh in mind, that frightened them most.

Not all Republicans were against the common law, of course, nor were all equally moved by the ideological issues involved. The many who were, however, saw the common-law question as part of the great battle between John Marshall and Thomas Jefferson and between an aristocratic Supreme Court and a democratic Congress. At stake was republican government itself: the way it should make law. Because it pitted the legislators against the judges, the struggle for a federal criminal common law was the opening battle in the great nineteenth-century war over codification. In 1812 the legislature and the executive, controlled by the Republican party, held the upper hand, as Johnson's decision frankly conceded. It was the first of his political-minded decisions that would offend the legal science of Story. As for John Marshall, he was no more fond of butting his head against a brick wall in 1812 than he would be ten years later. Nor were his colleagues—excepting one.

A proclivity for scholarship, the zeal of youth, a touch of that "ambitious self-possession" he found descending upon him—all tempted Story to reopen the question, which a majority of his colleagues wanted closed. But what moved him most of all were the practical consequences of not undoing the *Hudson* interdict. Sitting judges like Story and district judge Richard Peters in Pennsylvania were, to borrow the words of the latter, "witnesses of the shameful Prostration of the Criminal Code of the United States."[98] The criminal code, to quote Story on the same point, was "grossly and barbarously defective,"[99] which is simply to say that Congress had not yet provided a comprehensive or even adequate definition of crimes against the government. As Peters complained, even those "enumerated" crimes were imperfectly defined, so that enforcement was precarious if not impossible. The "Honour of the Nation, & the Interest of Commerce" are at stake, cried Peters.[100] "The Courts are crippled," echoed Story, "offenders, conspirators, and traitors are enabled to carry on their purposes almost without check."[101] And Story meant the word "traitor" literally. New England secession was a constant threat and wholesale law defiance a present reality. In time of war, as Story pointed out in his charge to the grand jury in 1812, the practice and spirit of defying law threatened both national sovereignty and social order itself.

Story realized as early as 1808 that the most efficient and least controversial solution to the problem was for Congress to amend the federal criminal code. And his first response to *Hudson* was to urge that body to "give the Judicial Courts of the United States power to punish all crimes and offenses against the Government, as at common law."[102] In 1812 he actually drew up a "sketch" of an improved criminal code that he forwarded to Attorney General William Pinkney and in subsequent years to Senator David Daggett from Connecticut. That Congress failed to act confirmed Story in his low opinion of legislative government.[103] "It is truly melancholy," he wrote Williams in disgust, "that Congress will exhaust themselves so much in mere political discussions, and remain so unjustifiably negligent of the great concerns of the public. They seem to have forgotten that such a thing as an internal police or organization is necessary, to protect the Government and execute the laws." It was his firm conviction that "many members imagine that the laws will execute themselves."[104] On the codification question it was law versus politics all over again.

Even as Story pressed Congress for action he opened the judicial front in behalf of a federal criminal common law. To be sure, he administered law on the first circuit according to the Court's decision in *Hudson*, as his charges to grand juries in 1812 indicate.[105] But he believed that the decision, "however broad in its language,"[106] had not settled the question. Given the narrow majority, the lack of arguments by counsel, and the superficial nature of Johnson's opinion, he had a point.

He put that point forcefully at the October 1813 term of the circuit court in Boston in *U.S.* v. *Coolidge*. It raised the same general question as *Hudson*: whether, as Story stated it, "the circuit court of the United States has jurisdiction to punish offenses against the United States, which have not been specifically defined, and a specific punishment affixed, by some statute of the United States." But the *Coolidge* case also differed significantly from *Hudson* and thus permited Story to devise a legal stratagem designed to circumvent the earlier precedent. First, the *Coolidge* case— "an indictment against Cornelius Coolidge for forcibly rescuing a prize"— was factually neutral. Unlike the common-law libel in *Hudson*, which pitted Federalists against Republicans, the issues in *Coolidge* were only remotely political. More important still were the legal distinctions: *Hudson* turned nakedly on the existence of a federal criminal common law; *Coolidge* was a question of prize law coming under article III, section 2, of the Constitution, which extended federal judicial power "to all cases of admiralty and maritime Jurisdiction," and section 9 of the Judiciary Act of 1789, which located exclusive jurisdiction in prize cases in the federal courts. The issue in *Coolidge*, then, was not whether the circuit court had jurisdiction, but how and in what manner it should exercise a jurisdiction that it unquestionably had—that is to say, its admiralty and maritime jurisdiction. As Story saw it, "the whole difficulty and obscurity of the subject has arisen from losing sight of the distinction." [107]

Refocused with this crucial distinction in mind, the issue was not "whether the United States as a sovereign power, had entirely adopted the common law," but whether the "rules of the common law" shall define the "nature and extent" of authority bestowed by the Constitution and determine "the mode, in which it shall be exercised." Story contended that the common law "is appealed to for construction and interpretation" of the Constitution. [108] His argument was forceful precisely because it was not original. Story repeated what Attorney General Randolph said in 1790: State and federal judges and lawyers in the course of their business acted regularly on the same assumption (even those opposed to the common law). Who could deny that a Constitution framed by men trained in the common law should be interpreted by reference to that law? And who could deny that the common law gave meaning to such constitutional phrases as "trial by jury," "law and equity," or "writ of habeas corpus"— or "treason" (as Story pointed out in his charge to the grand jury in 1812) or "admiralty and maritime" (the issue in *Coolidge*).

Building on this obvious rule of construction, Story's logic was compelling: Jurisdiction over "admiralty and maritime" cases was vested exclusively in federal courts by the Constitution. Using the common law (meaning here the "whole system of English jurisprudence") [109] as the interpretive guide, it followed, first, that prize cases were a part of admiralty and maritime law; and second, that the forcible rescue of prize vessels was a recognized criminal offense at prize law under admiralty and maritime jurisdiction. Even though there was no statute making forceful rescue a federal crime, there was one—chapter 20, paragraph 11, of the Judiciary

Act of 1789—which provided that circuit courts "shall have exclusive cognizance of all crimes and offenses cognizable under the authority of the United States. . . ."[110]

Forceful rescue of prize, it would seem clear, was one such crime. But Story went further, applying to the federal statute the axiom of construction that he applied to the Constitution. Read this way, paragraph 11 of chapter 20 included not only forcible rescue but "without pretending to enumerate them in detail . . . all offences against the sovereignty, the public rights, the public justice, the public peace, the public trade, and the public police of the United States."[111] Here in fact was a list of offenses seemingly proscribed by *Hudson*.

Story's *Coolidge* opinion offered both a narrow and a broad argument for the common law and in either case provided more discretionary power for federal judges. That power, Story assured opponents, was not dangerous, because in exercising it judges would be bound by clear and fixed rules, by the science of the common law. As he put it, "upon any other supposition the judicial power of the United States would be left, in its exercise, to the mere arbitrary pleasure of the judges, to an uncontrollable and undefined discretion." Legal science, it would seem, justified judicial power.[112]

Story's position was bold, even "rash," as he admitted when he promised humbly to "submit, with utmost cheerfulness, to the judgment of my brethren," whose "superior learning and ability will save the public from injury by my error."[113] His brethren in fact did not agree, and when *Coolidge* reached them on appeal in 1816 they summarily reversed it on the basis of *Hudson*.[114] Story did "submit" or at least moderated his objections, as in *U.S.* v. *Bevans* (1818), where the Court, with Marshall speaking, again refused a common-law jurisdiction over crimes.[115] But the *Hudson* doctrine was no more convincing to him in 1816 than it was in 1812. Moreover, judicial self-abnegation was not his style; he acquiesced, as he put it, only because of "a delicacy in respect to the Chief Justice."[116] He did allow himself to write a separate opinion in *Bevans*, however, reaffirming his own position; on request he sent it to reporter Henry Wheaton, along with a remark that the chief justice's opinion was not up to snuff and a specific instruction not to make his own public.

Story had lost the first battle for a federal common law, though as we shall see not the war. Looking more to the twentieth century than the nineteenth and perhaps more to democracy than republicanism, the Court opted for a legislative solution. It was a small consolation for a scientific common lawyer like Story that when Congress finally got around to amending the federal criminal code in 1825, it was he who drafted the bill.

Still, his effort had not been entirely fruitless. Out of his *Coolidge* opinion came a rule of construction—that the common law was the authoritative key to constitutional meaning—which figured in his and the Court's interpretation of the Constitution. The implications of that rule for judicial authority Story soon demonstrated in the great maritime insurance case of *De Lovio* v. *Boit.*[117] By interpreting the grant of "admiralty and maritime" jurisdiction in article III of the Constitution according to English law and legal history, Story laid the broad foundation of federal admiralty jurisdiction. He not only made use of the *Coolidge* principle in *De Lovio* but added to it the corollary that recourse to the "universal" principles of admiralty law where appropriate was an equally valid means of constitutional interpretation: echoes of *Reimsdyk* v. *Kane,* shades of *Swift* v. *Tyson.* It is not surprising that Henry Wheaton, in his argument in *U.S.* v. *Bevans,* should refer to *De Lovio* as a "blaze of luminous reasoning" and use it to support an enlarged criminal common-law jurisdiction for the federal courts.[118]

5. A Court for the New Nation: *Martin* v. *Hunter's Lessee*

For a brief moment in 1816, Story may have been tempted to leave the Supreme Court. William Pinkney, on his way to Russia as minister, "pressed" Story "in the most friendly manner" to take his Baltimore practice, which was worth twenty thousand dollars a year, or more than three times what Story was making on the Court.[119] Story said no, partly because he was unwilling to uproot his family and partly because he hated the thought of "quitting old friends." But the undisguisable fact was that he liked judging, even if it did keep him "poor." And waiting for him, even while he was pondering the riches of Baltimore, was *Martin* v. *Hunter's Lessee,* in which the states' rights machine of Virginia challenged the whole structure of federal judicial authority.[120] Because he had delivered the decision in the preliminary case of *Fairfax's Devisee* v. *Hunter's Lessee* (1813)[121] and because Marshall disqualified himself owing to personal interest, Story was sure to be called upon.

Martin would be not only his first but his most important constitutional opinion. What Marshall did for judicial review in *Marbury,* Story would now do for the appellate power of the Court. The result was hardly less important. The litigation that ended with Story's ringing exposition of federal judicial authority in 1816 began during the American Revolution in a dispute over some 300,000 acres of rich timber and tobacco land in the Northern Neck of Virginia owned by Thomas Lord Fairfax, a citizen of Virginia.[122] On his death in December 1781, Lord Fairfax devised his land to his nephew, the Reverend Denny Martin (an English citizen who had never resided in Virginia), with the stipulation that he change his name to Fairfax, which he did. On 17 May 1793 Denny Fairfax agreed to sell 160,000 acres of his Virginia lands to a syndicate of Virginia speculators that included the future chief justice, his brother James M. Marshall, and his brother-in-law Rawleigh Colston.

The question was whether the speculators had really bought anything or, more correctly, whether the heirs of Thomas Lord Fairfax legally had anything to sell. The state of Virginia thought not. Acting under various confiscation acts passed during the Revolution against Tory lands, the state had issued a land patent to one David Hunter for 788 acres of land claimed by Denny Fairfax (and his heir and brother, Philip Martin) and later sold to speculators. After gathering momentum for twenty years in the courts of Virginia, the issues came to this: The state of Virginia (which litigated in the name of Hunter's Lessee) claimed under the state confiscation acts and under Virginia common law, which it contended prohibited alienation of land to foreigners. The speculators (behind the name of Martin on the record) claimed that the state confiscation acts violated the treaties of 1783 and 1794 with Great Britain and argued, even more fundamentally, that Virginia's confiscatory proceedings, by omitting an inquest of office, were illegal according to the common and statute law of the state.

When the Virginia court of appeals upheld the state in 1810,[123] James Marshall, for the speculators, sued out a writ of error under section 25 of the Judiciary Act of 1789 that brought the case (now *Fairfax's Devisee* v. *Hunter's Lessee*) before the Supreme Court. With Marshall and Todd absent and over Johnson's dissent, Story for the rest of the Court reversed the decision below, ruling that the federal treaties nullified the confiscation acts; in addition, the Court ruled that Virginia law allowed alienation of land to foreigners. The Virginia Court of Appeals not only refused to obey the Supreme Court but denied the constitutionality of section 25, under which the case had been brought. This denial brought on another writ of error to the Supreme Court and set the stage for *Martin*.

Story may well have been itching for a fight. His exhaustive arguments in *Fairfax's Devisee* appeared to overreach themselves, and the cocksure tone of his opinion, especially when he ventured to tell the Virginia court what Virginia law was all about, was provocative. His actual holding on the superiority of treaty over state law and his ruling on the legal inadequacy of state confiscation procedures, however, were solidly grounded in authority. Virginia, in fact, frustrated by years of contention with the Marshall Court, yearned for a showdown quite as much as Story, and there was little, short of abject surrender, that he or the Court could have done to avoid one.[124] *Martin*, in fact, was Virginia's Hartford Convention. The issue was no longer land but the role of the federal courts in the national government—indeed, the constitutional foundations of the government itself. The denial of the Court's jurisdiction under section 25 was the calculated decision by the states' rights forces of Virginia, not just Spencer Roane and the court of appeals but Thomas Ritchie of the Richmond *Enquirer*, the leaders of the Richmond Junto that controlled the state legislature, and Thomas Jefferson himself.[125]

The denial of section 25, even without Roane's states' rights harangue, unfurled the battle flag. Many cases given to the federal judiciary by article III of the Constitution had been lodged, in the first instance, in the courts of the states. If section 25, which allowed appeal by writ of error in such cases from the highest courts of the states to the Supreme Court, were unconstitutional, then the Supreme Court, with almost no original jurisdiction, would not be able to reach a large portion of its constitutionally granted jurisdiction. Consequently, the decisions of the state courts on the constitutional questions within their purview would be final and inevitably contradictory. Uniform national law and the powers of the Supreme Court were on the line. The issue equaled if it did not surpass that in *Marbury*: It looked back to the Virginia and Kentucky Resolutions, from which Roane drew his arguments, and forward to the great struggle of the 1820s and beyond that to the Civil War. Story was in the vanguard of history: a new Elisha indeed.

Such was his tone. Speaking for the Court, the junior justice chastised the state of Virginia for following the constitutional doctrines just announced by his own state at the Hartford Convention. Fusing together law, logic, policy, he made the case for appellate jurisdiction that was, as Chancellor James Kent later put it, "unanswerable and conclusive." [126] Because some constitutional questions (given to the federal courts by article III of the Constitution) could be heard in state courts, Story argued, it was imperative that those state court decisions be reviewable by the Supreme Court if there were to be such a thing as uniform federal law. Anything less would be a direct violation of the Constitution itself. It was a doubtful course, he added, to argue that the Supreme Court should not have the final power of review over federal questions because it might abuse that power. Here Story referred to the arguments of counsel for Virginia (his friends R. G. Harper and Samuel Dexter, no less). Whatever the intent of the framers, they urged moderation, judicial self-restraint: a *political* decision, that is to say. "The taper of judicial discord may become the torch of civil war," warned Dexter presciently, "and though the breath of a judge can extinguish the first, the wisdom of the statesman may not quench the latter." [127]

Justice Johnson listened and believed, making Dexter's reasoning a part of his concurrence. And, indeed, a full, conclusive disquisition on federal judicial power was not required. The practical necessity and constitutional logic of section 25 were apparent. On that essential point there appeared to be little judicial leeway short of abandoning standard axioms of constitutional and statutory construction and surrendering the Court's clear powers. The times did not require such a concession; nor did anyone on the Court, even Justice Johnson, who was most sympathetic to Virginia, advocate such a course. Conceivably Story might have let the obvious speak for itself; this at the least is what Dexter and Harper urged the Court to do and what Johnson did do in his concurring opinion.

But Story was not impressed by pleas for restraint or by his colleague's unscientific, political-minded approach to constitutional law. The question as he saw it was power, not liberty; not the fine-sounding phrases of the Declaration but the bold and clear mandate of the Constitution. "From the very nature of things," he said without hesitation, "the absolute right of decision, in the last resort, must rest somewhere. . . ."[128] The framers had spoken, and constitutional truth ought not to be diluted by compromise and political tinkering. His job was to make law and not merely to decide cases; he would not hold back.

This much was clear from his opening statement on the nature of constitutional union, which he aimed directly at Virginia states' rightists and those of the Hartford Convention as well. "The Constitution of the United States was ordained and established," he declared, "not by the states in their sovereign capacities, but emphatically, as the preamble of the constitution declared, by 'the people of the United States.'" Sovereignty belonged to the people, then, and contrary to Judge William Fleming of the Virginia court of appeals, they had spoken through their constitution to create a truly national government. That government operated not only directly on the people irrespective of state boundaries—a common interpretive theme of the *Federalist* and John Marshall's constitutional decisions—but directly on the states themselves.[129]

Story conceded that the national government could "claim no powers which are not granted to it by the constitution." Still, the document must be approached in the spirit in which it was created, as he proceeded to make clear: The Constitution, he declared in words strikingly similar to Marshall's in *McCulloch* v. *Maryland* three years later, was "not intended to provide merely for the exigencies of a few years, but was to endure through a long lapse of ages, the events of which were locked up in the inscrutable purposes of Providence." Consequently, the document was expressed in "general language," so that it might be adjusted by a "reasonable construction" to the "exigencies of the future."[130]

It was reasonable, then, contrary to the contentions of Virginia, that Congress should pass section 25. The rule was, said Story, repeating the position taken in *Brown* v. *U.S.* and for a second time anticipating Marshall in the bank case, that "where a power is expressly given in general terms, it is not to be restrained to particular cases" but must be left to the legislature "from time to time, to adopt its own means to effectuate legitimate objects, and to mold and model the exercise of its powers, as its own wisdom and public interest should require."[131] Implied powers applied to article III as well as article I, section 8, to judicial as well as congressional powers. In both cases the benefit of the doubt went to the national government.

Surely now enough was said: The power of Congress to pass section 25 was established beyond reasonable doubt. But there was a problem, at least for Story, who had little faith in congressional government. By arming Congress with broad powers of interpretation, was not the Court putting itself in jeopardy? Congress could act, but what if it chose not to? What, in regard to section 25, if it chose to take back what it had given (as it nearly did a few years later)?

Story dealt with that contingency. Not only was section 25 constitutional, he argued, as an implied power from article III, but that article operated with "obligatory force." Congress "could not, without a violation of its duty, have refused to carry it into operation" by passing section 25. When article III said "the judicial power of the United States *shall* be vested" it was a mandate to Congress from which there was no escape. "The judicial power must therefore," he continued, giving the words a precision and finality that Johnson refused to give them, "be vested in some court, by Congress: and to suppose that it was not an obligation binding on them, but might, at their pleasure, be omitted or declined, is to suppose, that, under the sanction of the constitution they might defeat the constitution itself; a construction which would lead to such a result cannot be sound."[132]

Even this was not the end of it. Not only *must* Congress pass section 25, but it *must* do what it did temporarily in the Judiciary Act of 1801 (and permanently in 1875)—that is, vest in the federal courts all the powers given them by article III of the Constitution. This was the ultimate objective of Story's decision in *Coolidge*, of his draft legislation to Congress, of his opinion in *De Lovio*. *Martin* was not merely an answer to Virginia, then; it was Story's ultimatum to Congress for the enactment of a comprehensive plan of federal judicial power.

And this plan also included his answer to that vexing question of the common law which seemed to have been laid to rest by the Court in *Coolidge*. There may have been no federal criminal common law, but there was a common law, nevertheless—that is, a body of fundamental rules and principles held in common by the states of the Union. In the exercise of its appellate jurisdiction the Supreme Court—again by necessary implication—had to have final power to interpret these principles. This was the premise of Story's decision in *Fairfax*, where he reversed the Virginia court of appeals on a point of Virginia common law. The right to do so was unavoidably part and parcel of the appellate power under section 25 as Story defined it in *Martin*. As in *Van Reimsdyk*, *Coolidge*, and *De Lovio*, there was no danger of abusing this interpretive power, for the common law, like maritime law and international law, was a science. Or rather, it might under Story's guidance become one, provided the Supreme Court was armed with the power of final review.

In a few years, Story would blame Andrew Jackson for the fall of the

American republic. In February 1815 he had to congratulate him for saving it. Story's ebullient letter to Nat Williams, wherein he laid out his scheme of national institutions and announced his intention to maximize the powers of the federal courts, came three weeks after the *National Intelligencer* announced General Jackson's "ALMOST INCREDIBLE VICTORY" over the British at New Orleans. A few short months before, the capital lay in ruins, Baltimore was under British guns, and the eastern seaboard of the nation was under threat of possible invasion. As British arms besieged the nation from the outside, the Federalists gathered at Hartford to issue a series of states' rights resolutions that avoided the substance of disloyalty by conceding to its spirit. In Richmond the Junto put on its own states' rights display, which, though it was less noisy, was even more threatening. Coming in the midst of such gloomy proceedings, the victory at New Orleans and the Treaty of Ghent that followed it seemed providential. Americans thanked God and themselves in an outpouring of national pride and cultural nationalism never before experienced by the young nation.

Story's *Martin* opinion—indeed, the plan for a reformed federal judiciary of which it was a part, as well as his theory of judicial statesmanship— must be seen as part of this war-inspired nationalism. Timing was the key to success. Ten years earlier the Court's claim to power in *Martin* would have encountered widespread opposition; ten years later it would have run headlong into the aroused forces of states' rights and a politically minded Congress that would have resented and resisted being told what it *had* to do. But in 1816 Story's talk about the "whole people," his plan to strengthen the national government by enlarging the powers of the federal courts, struck a popular chord.

Virginia was not persuaded, to be sure. What it thought was clear from the Richmond *Enquirer* of Saturday, 13 April 1816, which printed Johnson's concurrence in *Martin* without a single word on Story's majority opinion. Brilliant constitutional arguments, it would seem, even when backed by a majority of the Supreme Court of the United States, rarely translate directly into history, and Story's bold effort must be judged in part by what it failed to do. But if his victory was not totally conclusive, it was impressive nonetheless. Because his arguments comported so well with the spirit of the age, they were allowed to stand; because they stood they could be turned to for sustenance in future crises of the American people. These would not be long in coming.

Martin was Story's constitutional tour de force, possibly, as one scholar claimed, "the ablest and most impressive piece of constitutional analysis to be found in the Supreme Court's reports."[133] Unquestionably it raised the young justice to the front ranks of the Court. He was now not just an expert in commercial and maritime law but, along with Marshall, an authority on the Constitution. The chief justice, in fact, according to Story, "concurred in every word of it"[134]—a statement that raises the question whether some of the words were Marshall's. Given the intimacy of the Court and Story's respect for the chief, as well as Marshall's personal knowledge of the litigation at the state level, it is likely that Marshall was consulted even though he had disqualified himself. Clearly Story's talk of the people's Constitution echoes Marshall in *Marbury*, just as the doctrine of implied powers put forward in *Martin* prefigures *McCulloch* v. *Maryland*.

Still, there is no real evidence that Marshall dictated to his young colleague or that he wrote substantial parts of the opinion. Nor did he have to, because the basic ideas in *Martin* were not original. The theory of constitutional union, which Story would later make the basis of his *Commentaries on the Constitution*, had been stock-in-trade since the ratification debates and the *Federalist*. Implied power was as much Story's idea as Marshall's if one judges from the former's opinions in *Brown* and *Bainbridge*; and in fact it was more Hamilton's than it was either of theirs. Neither did Story have to be lectured on nationalism or on the need for a stronger judiciary. As for exhaustive scholarship and lucid and expansive exposition, these were already his hallmark. And they were the key to the greatness of Story's constitutional analysis in *Martin*. Judicial opinions are great not simply because of the law they declare, which is almost always diluted and modified in its implementation, but because of the reasoning they embody. Story's opinion, like Marshall's great efforts, was a state paper.

This point brings up Story's theory of judging, the notions of judicial statecraft that underlie such great opinions as *De Lovio* and *Martin*. Legal scholars, trained to trace the development of doctrine, are perhaps tempted to attribute more prescience to opinions than they deserve. Judges, like most people, are better at looking backward (or at least sideways) than into the future. Mostly they work with the materials at hand, the pressures of the moment, leaving to future courts and judges the job of extracting what is usable from what they do and say. For the early Supreme Court—indeed, for most of judicial history until the revolutionary extension of discretionary jurisdiction in the twentieth century—this was particularly true. The Marshall Court could not select or refuse to hear cases legally brought; justices could not control the timing of their decisions except within narrow limits. The opposite polarities of chance and obligation confined the range of judicial statesmanship.

Chance, the luck of the draw, the rules of the game, operated on Story's judicial strategy as it did on his colleagues'. But it is also true that he more than any of his colleagues, including even John Marshall in some respects, escaped the confines of accident and impermanence. He did so because of his juristic approach to judging, his scholarly approach to opinion writing. On circuit, on the full bench, earlier as a practicing lawyer and legal reformer in Massachusetts, and later as a professor and legal publicist at

Harvard Law School—in all these roles, from the force of training and the inclination of his mind, Story approached the law comprehensively and architectonically. That is to say, he consciously sought to put each rule, each case, in the fullest context of authority: to define by elimination, support by analogue, expand by extrapolation. As a Supreme Court justice he was a scientific lawyer in the best tradition of the early nineteenth century.

The mutually reinforcing, complementary interconnectedness of Story's opinions, then, was not accidental. Thus, the Court's decision in *Hudson* in 1812 prepared him for *Coolidge* in 1813, which permitted him to speak then and later on the question of the federal common law. *Fairfax* in 1813 set the stage for *Martin* in 1816, which was the basis of Marshall's opinion in *Cohens* v. *Virginia* in 1821. The same sequential pattern also connects *Terrett* v. *Taylor* in 1815 and *Dartmouth College* v. *Woodward* in 1819. He anticipated the need for *De Lovio* in 1812 and had the opinion ready by the time it came up (as we shall see). *Van Reimsdyk* in 1812 led consistently through a long line of decisions to *Swift* v. *Tyson* in 1842.

More important than tactical connections in these early cases was a reinforcing doctrinal unity that at the risk of being anachronistic might be called strategy. In his struggle for the common law, for example, he moved simultaneously on the legislative and judicial fronts. On the latter, in addition to outright argument for a federal criminal common law, he worked through conflict theory (as in *Van Reimsdyk*), under the rubric of admiralty and prize (as in *Coolidge*), by the way of appellate jurisdiction under section 25 (as in *Fairfax* and *Martin*). The doctrine of peremptory obligation announced in the latter was forecast in *Coolidge* and *De Lovio*. The implied-power doctrine announced specifically in regard to executive power in *Brown* v. *U.S.* was fortified in *Bainbridge* and (as Justice Johnson and John Taylor of Caroline County clearly discerned to their dismay) infused his argument for federal judicial power in *Martin*.

Whether Story literally believed that law predated cases, that deciding was discovering, is doubtful. At any rate he never had time for such legal metaphysics. The interconnected nature of his opinions does, however, attest to his belief in law as science. Deciding, judging, was an occasion for the exploration and exposition of the legal system. Holism was the key. Rules were systematically connected to principles. The common law was connected to constitutional law, and both were informed by the civil law— a process that should be informed by comparative law (as in *Van Reimsdyk*) and legal history (as in *De Lovio*).

And finally, legal doctrine refined and clarified in this way would be tested for its practical use, whether in fighting a war or creating a favorable environment for American business. To move from principle to system and back to the real world was to dwell, as Story's son put it, "'in the gladsome light of jurisprudence.'"[135] This is what Charles Sumner referred to when he said that Justice Story was a jurist, what Story himself meant when he talked about the "universal empire of judicial reason"[136] and when he declared to James Kent that "the Courts of the United States offer a scene for very enlarged and extensive examinations of the principles of jurisprudence."[137]

Implicit in Story's notion of judge as jurist, in his theory of judging, was a vision of the Court at the vital center of republican government. Just as Madison predicted judges would do in *Federalist 51*, Story took the Court for his bailiwick, his turf, his window on the world. And more: Story not only identified with the Court but identified the Court with himself—with his vision of law, his own theory of scientific judging. Story could not tolerate the uncertainty and the untidiness of the Constitution as it left the hands of the framers, American private law as it stood poised confusedly between England and the United States. Most assuredly he did not like the haphazard modifications in American law that popular opinion and the political branches of government threatened to make.

For Story the judge as for Story the lawyer, it was the science of the law pitted against the art of politics. The Court for Story was an instrument of clarification, a force for rationality. It followed that justices individually and the Court collectively should stand firm. In the judicial dog days of the 1820s, when retrenchment and compromise were the order of the day, this perfectionist view of the law, of the Court, of himself, would encourage Story to hold the line; it would also plunge him into excessive gloom and on occasion distance him from John Marshall. In the days of Chief Justice Roger Taney, Story's juristic idealism made him the bearer of constant dejection, the self-appointed champion of the "old law"—and at the same time the most important spokesman for legal reform in America.

During the "golden age" of the Marshall Court, that remarkable period of creativity from the end of the War of 1812 to the outbreak of rampant states' rights in the mid-1820s, Story's theory and style fit perfectly (so perfectly, in fact, that he was encouraged to believe in the eternal correctness of his ideas). His expansive approach to judicial power seemed not only desirable but realizable, as the other branches of government were in disrepair and government itself, without the organizing force of parties, was in the doldrums. Story's nationalism—the powers he would give the Court and those the Court would then give to Congress—was in tune with postwar sentiment. His cry for national institutions was commensurate with the dream of national greatness. American public and private law, raw and unformed as both were, awaited the clarification Story promised. Finally, American businessmen, anxious to exploit the new continent now open to them, waited on this re-formed law. Story's legal science, as we shall now see, was rooted in the realities of American economic history.

Chapter 4

Judge-made Policy and Economic Progress

THE REPUBLIC, REPOSING ON THE LAURELS OF A GLORIOUS WAR, GATHERS THE RICH HARVEST OF AN HONORABLE PEACE. Everywhere the sound of the axe is heard opening the forest to the sun, and claiming for agriculture the range of the buffalo.—Our cities grow and towns rise up as by magic; commerce expands her proud sails in safety, and the "striped bunting" floats with majesty over every sea. The busy hum of ten thousand wheels fills our seaports, and the sound of the spindle and the loom succeeds the yell of the savage or the screech of the night owl in the late wilderness of the interior.
> Niles' Weekly Register,
> 2 September 1815

It is obvious, that the law must fashion itself to the wants, and in some sort to the spirit of the age. Its stubborn rules, if they are not broken down, must bend to the demands of society.
> Joseph Story,
> *North American Review*, 1825

The Marshall Court spoke to the great constitutional issues of the golden age in Augustan rhetoric, in language bristling with moral imperatives and historical finality. The nationalist doctrines of *Martin v. Hunter's Lessee* (1816), *McCulloch v. Maryland* (1819), *Cohens v. Virginia* (1821), and *Gibbons v. Ogden* (1824) were part of our history, self-evident, universally understood—doctrines that "the good sense of the public has pronounced," the "people have declared," and "America has chosen."[1] Two interrelated consequences followed: By identifying with the Constitution, the Supreme Court worked to establish itself as the oracle of national law. Secondly, the Court's grand exposition transformed the Constitution from a "noble" but precarious "experiment" in republican government to the final source of republican principles to which all parties turned for legitimation.

Pronouncements of constitutional principle, however, no matter how persuasively rendered, do not fully explain the work of the Marshall Court, any more than writs of action explain the life of the common law. Each of the public lawmaking decisions of the Court was rooted in conflict between private economic interests and argued, without benefit of government counsel, by private lawyers. Behind the exposition of constitutional doctrine lay questions of power: To whom did it belong; how and for what purpose might it be used? The Court's law, in short, was inseparable from politics and economics—and finally from the consuming struggle between North and South over the direction of American history. The Marshall Court's constitutional nationalism carried with it a vision of American capitalism that put the Court in the eye of the political storm.

What was true of the Marshall Court was true also of its great scholar. Without denying the life of Story's mind or doubting his genuine commitment to principle and symmetry in the law, one can see from the beginning that he preferred the workaday wisdom of the common law to abstract reasoning and Platonic system building. His law took its character and spirit from the practical needs of real people and more specifically from the needs of the business community and the imperatives of the market as he saw them operate in New England. This was true of Story's constitutional law as well as his private law; indeed, in his American plan there was no disjunction between the two. Power was deployed in the federal system by the Court with an eye to unleashing the economic energies of individuals; those energies in turn would be shaped and guided by private law. Law-liberated self-interest operating across state lines, as much as any nationalist pronouncements from the Court, would strengthen American union.

And it would strengthen republican morality as well, as Story saw it. True to his residual Puritanism and his romantic vision of revolutionary service, he perceived legal-economic modernization as a moral struggle. But there were profound problems entailed in yoking law to capitalism (and judges to businessmen). Could a legal system fashioned in the spirit of revolutionary purity meet the needs of the new commercial manufacturing age? Would legal science scuttle itself in search of relevance? Would the impersonal force of the marketplace take only what it needed from Story's legal system and leave moral principle and judicial integrity to fend for themselves? Would communal self-interest so basic to republican thinking be swallowed up by uncontrolled economic individualism?

Story addressed these questions of economic progress and republican morality no less than did Andrew Jackson[2]—not in high-flown theory or in moral pronouncements about the law (although there were plenty of the latter) but in the design and substance of his legal system. The full scope of his effort to stimulate economic progress through law and make it moral at the same time would be apparent only after the assumption of his duties as Dane Professor at Harvard Law School and the publication of his legal commentaries. But already in the 1820s, as he struggled with questions of corporations, riparian law, patents and copyrights, banking and seamen's law, the outline began to take shape. Behind Story's opinions was a vision of economic man and a plan for economic progress. At the center of this

American plan, shaping and guiding the process, were American common lawyers and judges.

Story, this is to argue, perceived the duties of judging in terms of revolutionary statesmanship. Consistency of purpose and largeness of vision characterized his opinions, in small and great cases alike. As for the latter: The true comparison is not so much with modern Supreme Court decisions, perhaps, as with contemporary state papers such as Secretary of State J. Q. Adams's great treatise on weights and measures (1821) or Alexander Hamilton's brilliant memorandum on the constitutionality of the First Bank of the United States (1791). To judge for Story was to govern, and judge-made economic policy as he aimed to make it was uniquely compatible with republican society as he perceived it.

1. Capitalism and Pragmatic Law New England Style

New England was for Story what Virginia was for Thomas Jefferson, a window on America. Like his great enemy, Story hypostatized what he saw around him into a cultural norm to which the law had to fashion itself. And what he saw in Marblehead, Salem, and Boston, what he saw when he twice-yearly traveled the New England circuit and heard the humble and the mighty make their demands on the law, was a society dedicated to commerce and manufacturing.

He saw and empathized. Commerce and enterprise were second nature to him, part of the unquestioned values instilled by time, place, and family. His mother was the daughter of a merchant-shipper who descended from a line of ambitious, property-grubbing folk. From the beginning his father's family pursued the main chance. His brother William was a Boston entrepreneur—a "merchant," not a mere "Mr." His brothers-in-law and best friends, Stephen and Joseph White, were sea captains turned shippers. The Republican party he served so zealously as a young man was the party of aspiring, upwardly mobile entrepreneurs, and he served them also. Before Story took his seat on the Court he organized a bank and a marine insurance company, served as lobbyist for leading New England land speculators, and acted as their counsel before the U.S. Supreme Court. On more than one occasion as lawyer-legislator he championed New England commercial interests, and as a justice of the Supreme Court he continued to move confidently among the commercial and manufacturing leaders of his section: the Jacksons and the Lees of Newburyport, Thomas H. Perkins, Peter C. Brooks, Abbott and Amos Lawrence, H. G. Otis, and the Cabots, to mention only the famous figures.

Story was tied to this group by personal affection, common institutional affiliation (centering around Harvard University), and common politics (after he repudiated his early radicalism).[3] But the basis of the relationship was shared values in the culture of commerce: the almost religious belief in the civilizing impact of property when placed in the hands of entrepreneurial statesmen. What John Locke said about the fusion of individualism and property in his *Second Treatise* made sense to Story as he looked at his friends in the business community. So too did Paley's *Principles of Moral Philosophy*, a favorite of Harvard students, which argued that commerce was a part of the moral universe of natural law. Thus could Story understand his future colleague Justice William Johnson's language in *Fletcher* v. *Peck* when he said that property circulates "as the blood" through the body.[4] Thus would Story agree with his friend Francis Lieber when he proclaimed that "man yearns to see his individuality represented in the acts of his exertion—in property,"[5] and with Chancellor Kent, who declared that property is "inherent in the human breast," put there by God "to lift" men "from sloth" and to stimulate them to display "the various and exalted powers of the human mind."[6]

Property, it would seem, was not finally a piece of real estate, a bill of exchange, a ship at sea, but a transforming force in human history. People manipulated property because it was natural to do so. Their collective efforts, as Adam Smith argued, constituted the best approximation of the public good. Commerce was to New Englanders what cultivating God's earth was to Jefferson's yeoman: the source of civilization itself. Nowhere was the point more honestly stated than by Story's friend and circuit bench mate in Boston, federal district judge John Davis. After upholding the constitutionality of Jefferson's embargo in *U.S.* v. *The William* (1808), Judge Davis praised what the act (or rather President Jefferson) threatened to destroy. "Commerce," he declared in celebratory prose that foreshadowed Hunt's *Merchants Magazine* by thirty years, "merits all the eulogy, which we have so eloquently pronounced, at the bar. It is the welcome attendant of civilized man, in all his various stations. It is the nurse of arts; the genial friend of liberty, justice and order; the source of national wealth and greatness; the promoter of generous affection and enlarged philanthropy. Connecting seas, flowing rivers, and capacious havens, equally with the fertile bosom of the earth, suggest, to the reflecting mind, the purposes of beneficent Deity, relative to the destination and employments of man."[7]

Like Judge Davis, Story rarely missed a chance to praise commerce and property. Thus, in his article on maritime law in the *North American Review* in 1818, he declared that the "spirit of commerce" (along with "ambition and enterprise, the love of wealth") would impart "life and intelligence to the body politic" and "comforts and enjoyments" to all classes of people, and in general foster "the best interests of humanity."[8] He returned to the same theme in his speech in the Massachusetts convention of 1820 in defense of the property requirement as the basis of apportionment for the senate. Property, pursued honestly and morally, was, he assured the delegates, "the source of comforts of every kind, and dispenses its blessings in every form."[9] To the federal grand juries on the New England circuit the same year, he promised that commerce and enterprise could eliminate the age-old distinctions between rich and poor, obliterate class lines, unify the diverse economic interests of the country, and create the foundation of a free and enduring union.[10]

If commerce could do so much, if it were so much a part of national culture, how could the law not serve it? It should and did.[11] Without fanfare or theorizing, Story operated regularly on the practical principle— one that Oliver Wendell Holmes, Jr., rediscovered in his *Common Law* (1881) and that modern legal historians have begun to explore—that law must serve the needs of society. Law was, of course, no substitute for the creative individual who fought, won, and lost in the marketplace. Neither did law serve all economic groups equally, though plain folk were by no means eliminated from consideration. Women got little, to be sure, and slaves nothing but enslavement. The law responded best to those with the most to ask from it and those who could offer the highest legal retainers, which is to say that shippers got more than common seamen, corporations more than individuals, the rich more than the poor, commerce more than agriculture, and the North more than the South.

For Americans who had property and wanted more, then, the law was at their service, though they often had to fight one another (in court and out) to get it. What they wanted and most often got was not a restraining but a helping hand. Law, it was assumed, should release and maximize individual energy and promote individual economic goals. No one wrote a treatise saying all this because it was commonly understood (and because treatise writers, among whom was Story, were so busy making law work that they had no time to theorize about what they were doing). In any case, the method of the common law itself made it immensely adaptable to the practical, economic requirements of the early republic. Indeed, Story got the message from his first teacher, Samuel Sewall, who told him that the lawyer's job was to make English law serve American needs. And Story's colleagues on the Supreme Court learned the same lesson whether they came from Virginia, Kentucky, New York, South Carolina, or Ohio. As successful practicing lawyers, they had, like Story, been immersed in the economic life of their states and sections. Debates on the Court might reveal a continuing sectional bias, but there was a common faith in enterprise and a shared belief that law should help people help themselves.

This practical bias put a premium on Story's black-letter scholarship, his juristic approach to the law. It is true that his insistent legal science sometimes offended colleagues (Henry Baldwin and John Catron and perhaps even William Johnson) who did not appreciate being lectured on the nature of their judicial duties. Certainly not all of his brethren agreed with (or even fully understood) his grand scheme for American law. But Story's Yankee practicality was a common idiom. The "most striking characteristic of our age," he declared enthusiastically to the Boston Mechanical Institute in 1829 at the opening of its annual lecture series, was "the superior attachment to practical science over merely speculative science." For him there would be no "endless inquiries into mind, and spirit, and essences, and forms, and categories, and syllogisms."[12] Forget Plato and Descartes; give him Bacon and his science, Fulton and his steamboat. Give him the common law.

American legal science, true to the spirit of the age, was applied science. The practical objective, as important as it was simple, was to devise rules of business that were technically sufficient, organized systematically, administered uniformly and fairly, and known to businessmen. This law-fashioned rational economic environment was, as Story understood, one of the great aims of the Constitution itself.[13] The legal reform movement in Massachusetts in the early nineteenth century, of which he was a leader, looked to the same goal. Law journals of the age called for uniformity through legal science.[14] Statesmen like James Madison and Alexander Hamilton recognized the need, as did sitting judges like Theophilus Parsons and legal publicists like Stephen DuPonceau, Nathan Dane, and James Kent.[15] So did practicing businessmen such as Boston banker Thomas Haven and their lawyers; Daniel Webster put the matter plainly to Story on behalf of New England capitalists: "It is a great object to settle the concerns of the community, so that one may know what to depend on."[16]

Story was determined to make the law oblige, but there were major obstacles to be overcome, as he explained to the Suffolk Bar Association in 1821.[17] The first was the federal system itself, which confounded uniformity by permitting state law to go its own way. The second was confusion among lawmakers about substantive legal rules, which was a necessary consequence of the transitional state of American legal development. Almost from the moment Story began the practice of law he addressed these issues, and this is what gave his work its juristic cast. His scholarly style of practice, as well as his early publications, aimed to salvage clear rules from the chaos of uncertain authority. His championship of equity in Massachusetts was an effort to enlarge the reservoir of settled law—not just for women, children, and lunatics (the traditional beneficiaries of chancery) but for American entrepreneurs as well.[18] Judicial independence and lawyerly competence, which he worked to establish in Massachusetts, would facilitate the efficient and fair administration of justice. The Supreme Court, of course, offered Story the best forum for establishing legal uniformity, provided the Court could establish its authority at the apex of an integrated system of federal courts armed with ample powers:

thus his struggle for a federal common-law jurisdiction; his blow for an integrated federal judicial system in *Martin*; his opinions in *Van Reimsdyk* and *Coolidge*, which drew respectively on conflict theory and on the common law to assure uniform judicial construction. To strengthen the federal courts and regularize the process of adjudication, in short, was to enhance the potential for the kind of law American business needed; it was to accelerate the "tendency" toward the goal of a national system of contract and credit set forth in Story's *Commentaries on the Constitution*.[19]

Indeed, Story's scholarly style of judging was in part a response to the practical needs of American business. Copious references in his opinions to the civil law, to the maritime codes of the Mediterranean, to the great Continental jurists of the sixteenth and seventeenth centuries, to Stowell and Mansfield, were not simply exercises in pedantry or efforts to intimidate his colleagues (though they may at times have had that effect). On circuit Story mingled regularly with the working people of his section and if Justice Smith Thompson's estimation was correct, he knew their business and trades as well as they did.[20] What they sought in litigation on circuit and at Washington were rules of social conduct. Story's scholarship provided them with a reservoir of such rules—tried and tested by experience, confirmed by cross-cultural comparison—from which they might choose. The "people" spoke; Story responded and with the help of the lawyers fashioned principles to live and work by.

Take, as an example of this community lawmaking process, the October 1815 term of Story's circuit held in Boston for the district of Massachusetts. Story delivered fourteen opinions addressed to a cross section of the New England community: to rich and poor, to entrepreneurs, shippers, merchants, common seamen, and public officials—including judges and lawyers, present and future. Much of what he said was plainly administrative, which is to say that he applied law rather than created it, but it was important nonetheless. The clarification of federal commercial and customs regulations, for example, was crucial if enforcing officials were to know their rights and duties and if shipowners were to know what to count on.[21] Five of the fourteen opinions dealt with prize law: Story laid out the rules by which prize money was distributed (by written agreement among the parties and, lacking that, by the procedures set forth in the prize act of 1812); identified the proof necessary to establish legal right of capture (which to the great relief of New England privateers was more liberal than the proof necessary for condemnation); and explained the form in which it must be presented.[22] Owners, captains, and crewmen knew where they stood and thus learned, if they listened carefully, that the whole range of mercantile contracts would be interpreted "liberally" according to the intent of the parties and the realities of seafaring life.

Such was the explicit message in *Brown* v. *Jones*,[23] a suit by a common seaman for wages denied for alleged desertion. Seaman Brown's problem was an occasion for the judge to lay down the principles governing the construction of shipping articles (the contract that defines seamen's rights, duties, and compensation for voyages). Working from an analogy to marine insurance policies, Story held owners and captains to strict accounting. Ships' masters could not add additional intermediate voyages without relieving seamen of their obligation to complete their side of the contract. Loosely drawn mercantile contracts were not, at least on the New England circuit, to be instruments for exploiting the common sailor.

Customs collectors had their rights and duties, too, spelled out in *Ex parte Marquand*.[24] So did wharfingers, and the judge explained in *Ex parte Lewis* that admiralty law allowed them a lien on the proceeds of a foreign vessel libeled on a bottomry bond and sold. They were forewarned that if they signed personal contracts with the owners of ships at their wharfs, they would sacrifice a priority of claim over the bottomry interest in such proceedings. Whether they did business by specific contract or according to the general rules of admiralty law was their choice; the main point was that the consequences of what they did were now clear.[25] This was the practical impact of *Peisch* v. *Dickson*, too, in which Story established rules for the construction of contracts between factors and principles, the working relationship of which was basic to commercial-mercantile operations. As in *Van Reimsdyk* v. *Kane*, Story drew on conflict doctrine to show that factors had the security of person as well as goods for all advancements made on them.[26]

It is clear from Story's circuit opinions that he knew the detailed workings of the business community, that he drew regularly in his decisions on the "usages of trade." Occasionally, however, even he was baffled, perhaps because business practice itself was unsettled regarding matters before the court. In such cases, and there were two in the 1815 term, Story consulted the expertise of a special jury of informed merchants impaneled from the business community.[27] Impaneling mercantile juries was a practice that in Massachusetts went back to the seventeenth century and forward to the nineteenth, when the process was regularized by statute.[28] Whether Story borrowed the practice from the state court or from Lord Mansfield, who made frequent use of special juries in his commercial cases, is not clear. But in either case it brought Story and his court into a close working relationship with the local business community.[29]

Lawyers also figured prominently in this symbiotic relationship between Story's court and the business community in ways that enhanced his influence. Among the lawyers whom Story knew well and who argued before him in Boston during the 1815 term were Samuel Dexter (whose arguments at the bar he cut short), William Prescott (a lifelong friend from his Salem youth), Daniel Webster (his future ally and confidant in conservatism), and Thomas Selfridge, Thomas Welsh, and George Blake from lawyering days in Essex County. The circuit bar was a companionable yet competitive group of men with shared interests and a common outlook. For these lawyers and their clients—established merchants alongside widow Harvey and seaman Brown—Story's circuit court was a forum where order, rationality, and practical good sense prevailed. Nowhere in the federal system, not even in the democratic representative branches, was the exercise of power so intimately connected with the people on whom and for whom it operated.

Nowhere, either, was Story's use of power to facilitate commercial development more clear, or the fusion of scholarship, practicality, and long-range economic calculation in Story's judging more obvious. Take *De Lovio* v. *Boit* from the October 1815 term of Story's circuit court in Boston. The case was a libel brought in the federal district court on an insurance policy that a group of Boston businessmen had written on a Spanish vessel sailing out of Havana to ply the foreign slave trade. The sole question was whether federal courts had jurisdiction over such maritime contracts. The insurers, who refused to pay for loss owing to capture, said no. District judge John Davis agreed at the September 1815 term of his court, and the case went on appeal to Story's circuit court in Boston sitting for the October term.[30] At issue was the question of uniform commercial law for New England and the nation.

Story sensed the magnitude of the issue. In fact, he had begun to prepare his opinion after the lawyers' arguments before Judge Davis in June and before the judge's final ruling (timing which strongly suggests that Davis and Story consulted on legal strategy). "I shall deliver on this occasion," he wrote to Supreme Court reporter Wheaton on 5 September, in reference to the pending *De Lovio* case, "a very elaborate opinion upon the whole Admiralty jurisdiction as well as over torts and contracts, and shall review all the common law decisions on this subject, and examine the original rights of the Admiralty before and since the Statutes of Richard II."[31] The outcome of his research was never in doubt. Three years before *De Lovio* and after less than a year on the Court, he had concluded that the jurisdiction of the admiralty "rightfully extends over every maritime contract and tort." The "more its jurisdiction is known," he added, "the more it will be courted."[32] Thanks to Judge Davis's convenient denial of federal jurisdiction—a ruling in which he assuredly did not believe, as it would have cut drastically into the powers of his own court—Story had an opportunity to speak. With American commerce on the rise and nationalism in ascendancy, the time was ripe for a definitive pronouncement.

The challenge was to make a convincing case for a broad interpretation of the grant of "admiralty and maritime" jurisdiction to the federal courts in article III, section 2, of the Constitution. Unfortunately, the framers left no conclusive statement on that grant, and section 9 of the Federal Judiciary Act of 1789, saving "to suitors, in all cases [within admiralty and maritime jurisdiction], the right of a common law remedy, where the common law is competent to give it,"[33] detracted from the conclusion he wanted to reach, as did the pattern of state judicial intrusion into admiralty matters. Story's approach to the ambiguity of the constitutional language was, following his own axiom of construction laid down in *Coolidge*, to turn to English law. But there were difficulties in this course, too, because the broad authority of the early admiralty court in England—what Story wanted to transpose to the federal courts—had been drastically truncated by the encroachment of the common-law courts under Sir Edward Coke.

Story was undaunted. In fact, the prospect of slaying a legal giant like Coke and making some law in the process was obviously something he enjoyed. In an essay of eighty double-column pages, Story reconsidered the statutes from the reigns of the first two King Richards, which had been adduced as the basis for restricting the jurisdiction of the Court of Admiralty, and generally reassessed the entire position of the common-law courts vis-à-vis the admiralty courts over several centuries. Coke was "inconsistent and contradictory," palpably and plainly wrong. By Story's reckoning the correct interpretation of English law and history left to the admiralty cognizance of "all maritime contracts, and all torts, injuries and offences, upon the high seas, and in ports as far as the tide ebbs and flows."[34]

Here then, in the "ancient and original jurisdiction, inherent in the admiralty of England by virtue of its general organization" (which corresponded to the jurisdiction of the British admiralty courts at the time of the American Revolution), was the key to the meaning of "admiralty and maritime" in the Constitution. By going back to the early origins of admiralty, Story was able to emphasize the international character of admiralty law, a point he drove home, first, by tracing its origins in England back to the *Consoldat del Mare*, to admiralty practice in the ancient maritime courts of the Mediterranean and those on the Continent, and, second, by distinguishing between "admiralty" and "maritime" as used in the Constitution. Story's argument made centuries of legal experience of the Western world available to the judges of the new republic. Scholarship could be creative and practical. Indeed, Story concluded his *De Lovio* opinion on a frankly instrumentalist note. A broad admiralty jurisdiction for the federal courts, he confessed, came not just from "juridical logic" but from considerations of "national policy," from the "advantages resulting to the commerce and navigation of the United States, from a uniformity of rules and decisions in all maritime questions. . . ."[35]

Story was pleased, having, he confessed immodestly, "never pronounced an opinion in which I was more entirely satisfied." He was pleased, too, and surprised to find that his decision was "rather popular among the merchants." Among the "underwriters of Boston," as well, there was "great satisfaction."[36] He should not have been surprised, because uniform commercial law, made without the interference of juries and according to accepted commercial usage and convenience, was what the mercantile community wanted or, more accurately perhaps, could be persuaded to want. For in truth, the *De Lovio* opinion, dazzling as it was, was an incomplete victory. The decision did not oust state courts from jurisdiction over maritime contracts in general or marine insurance questions in particular. Moreover, the jurisdictional point, to Story's disappointment, was blunted by the failure of the parties to appeal the decision to the Supreme Court, where an affirmation would have given his opinion national standing. Indeed, not until 1870 did the Supreme Court accept *De Lovio*.[37]

Still, that opinion was law on the New England circuit, which meant that Story had created a forum for the settlement of maritime contract disputes that businessmen could now choose over state courts. Merchants and insurers would, of course, choose whatever court (and judge) appeared to offer them immediate advantage; when expediency dictated they even contested the jurisdiction of Story's court. *De Lovio*, then, did not guarantee a unified body of maritime contract law, but it did give Story a hand in its creation: Witness, for example, his creative fusion of actuarial precision into marine insurance law.[38] Any attempt to modify and modernize existing legal rules was bound to generate opposition, and Story's did just that. But he firmly believed that he understood the long-run interests of the business community better than businessmen themselves, and he was convinced that given a chance he could convince them. A mastery of black letter gave him a reservoir of refined and tested legal principles on which to draw, and his deep understanding of the operation of New England business told him how to pick, choose, and create.

In short, Story was bent on making his circuit court the dominant forum for the administration of principled commercial law for his section. From New England—Story's legal city on a hill—the word of law would spread. *De Lovio* was part of this grand plan, and as an instrument of conversion, it transcended its formal limitations. "This case is a very remarkable one," wrote David Hoffman in his influential *Course on Legal Study*, "being in truth, a learned and elaborate essay on admiralty jurisdiction, and one of the most elementary and luminous views of the subject extant. This great opinion ought to be thoroughly studied by those who aim at solid attainments in this department of the law."[39]

2. Judge Story and the Rise of the American Business Corporation: *Dartmouth College* v. *Woodward*

It is not surprising that the Marshall Court addressed the issue of national economic development, because the Constitution did the same thing. In fact, most of the Court's decisions, in both public and private law, were rooted in economic conflict. The arguments before the Court from which it drew its law were made in behalf of economically self-interested individuals or groups by lawyers deeply immersed in the business world. The justices themselves came from that same world and, like Story, maintained contact with it by riding circuit. Capitalism was the common currency of the Court's decisions. Those decisions, especially in the great constitutional cases from 1819 to 1824, constituted a coherent legal effort to promote economic growth. The prime objective of this judge-made economic policy was the creation of a national market where goods and credit circulated freely without state interference—an economic "E Pluribus Unum," as Webster called it in his *Gibbons* argument, that was "complete, entire and uniform."[40]

The twin pillars of this national commercial edifice were *McCulloch* v. *Maryland* (1819) and *Gibbons* v. *Ogden* (1824). *McCulloch* upheld the constitutionality of the Second Bank of the United States, which was not only the greatest financial monopoly of the age but a central regulatory agency designed to ensure a uniform national system of currency and credit. The implied-power doctrine that legalized the bank could also be employed by Congress to create a system of federally sponsored internal improvements to bind the nation (and the market) together, and Marshall specifically invited Congress to act. *Gibbons* struck an equally profound blow for a national market by a sweeping interpretation of federal power over interstate commerce that, if it did not automatically exclude state legislation, certainly permitted Congress to claim supremacy if it so desired. States were restrained in other areas, too, where they might interfere with property rights and the freedom of national economic maneuver. The contract clause of the Constitution, readied for this liberating chore by *Fletcher* v. *Peck* (1810), provided the constitutional wherewithal. In *Sturgis* v. *Crowninshield* (1819) the Court prohibited state bankruptcy laws that altered the obligation of retrospective contracts,[41] thus encouraging Congress to pass a uniform national bankruptcy law—which in fact Story, at that very moment, had drafted for their consideration. Speculators in the national land market were also encouraged by *Green* v. *Biddle* (1823), in which the Court, again using the contract clause, struck down Kentucky claimant laws which provided that no claimant of Kentucky lands under Virginia title could take land until he had reimbursed the original settler for his improvements on it.[42]

Marshall spoke for the majority in most of these key cases, in *McCulloch*, *Sturgis*, and *Gibbons*. Story's contributions, except for *Green* v. *Biddle*, for which he wrote the first of the Court's two opinions,[43] were lost in the secrecy of conference. But there is no doubt that he wholeheartedly supported the Court's plan for a national market, and there is some evidence, in those cases in which he did not speak, that he worked in the collective give-and-take of the Court's deliberations to give the decisions their nationalist cast. Implied powers, as noted, had long been his stock-in-trade and state legislative interference with property his bête noire. Judicial division over the scope of the *Sturgis* ruling in *Ogden* v. *Saunders* (1827)[44]—whether the contract clause prohibited not only retrospective state bankruptcy laws but prospective ones as well if they altered the substance of the contract—brought Story forth in support of Marshall's extreme nationalist position. Story led the nationalizing way in *Green* v. *Biddle* by holding that the contract clause of the Constitution applied to agreements between states, a position for which there was no conclusive authority. Though his role in *Gibbons* is not clear, it is possible that he may have helped Marshall write his great opinion.[45] But whether he did so or not, there is no doubt that he supported it with a vengeance, arguing for an expansive construction of federal commerce power perhaps greater than even Marshall envisaged.[46]

That Story was the most uncompromising constitutional nationalist on a nationalist Court seems clear. More difficult is the explanation of his preference. His nationalism did not, it is safe to say, stem from a slavish imitation of John Marshall. As already noted, he and the chief justice arrived at their respective positions from their own unique experiences and with more than a little difference on substantive points along the way. Was it, then, because Story was intellectually inclined, in the interest of system and symmetry, to push doctrine to its logical conclusion? He *was* so inclined (and did so with jurisdiction in *Martin* and elsewhere, with implied power, and with his exclusivist gloss on the commerce power). On the other hand, he resisted the Platonic approach to law and left the notion of an impeccably logical Constitution to his great enemy, John C. Calhoun. Perhaps, then, Story's constitutional doctrines followed the priorities of the Federalists, for there is no doubt that he had come to embrace Federalist political-economic principles, especially as spelled out by Alexander Hamilton.

One must admit that legal logic and Federalist politics played a part, that Marshall's support encouraged, even if it did not originate, Story's constitutional nationalism. One must consider, too, the crucial fact that Story loved national union for its own sake, and feared for its future at the hands of states' rightists. Yet beneath all these factors and basic to them was Story's practical-minded New England experience. Story was a constitutional nationalist because he wanted to encourage the development of a national market. He wanted a national market because New England merchants (whose opinions he respected) called for it and because the manufacturing revolution in New England (which Story appreciated) required it. It must not be forgotten (because Story did not forget it) that he was New England's representative on the Supreme Court. Nowhere was this more clear than in the legal development of the American business corporation, and nowhere was the effectiveness of the Marshall-Story collaboration more telling and the complementarity of public and private law in Story's legal universe more apparent.

The form of business organization that carried New England and the nation into the new economic age was the corporation.[47] The corporate device, an association of individuals for the accomplishment of private goals, ran far back in Western history, to the medieval guilds and religious organizations. It was well known in England and the colonies, but it was used almost exclusively for religious and political purposes as distinct from productive enterprise. By the end of the eighteenth century, American states had chartered 310 corporations, but only 8 of those were employed to produce goods. By 1830, however, 600 of the 1,900 corporations in New England alone were productive in function.[48]

Several factors worked to make the corporate form attractive to entrepreneurs like the Lowells, Lawrences, Jacksons, and Lees:[49] It facilitated the accumulation of capital from a broad base, especially after the perfection of the principle of limited liability, and this was crucial in a country without consolidated class wealth. While generating the capital necessary for large-scale undertakings, the corporation permitted centralized management, which fit neatly into the New England commercial heritage of economic individualism and single-family control. Finally, as Tocqueville would later observe,[50] the corporation was an ideal instrument by which government could perform its obligation to promote private enterprise. For the state to work through an aristocracy to undertake large-scale projects was impossible, because there was no unified class through which to work; for government to bestow special privileges on select individuals ran counter to egalitarian sentiment. For government itself to take on economic enterprise too big for private capitalists was impractical, given the embryonic state of public administration and the multiplicity of undertakings; also, too much government might threaten democracy. The solution, which satisfied both expediency and ideology, was for the government to arm associations of private individuals with a portion of its sovereign power so that they could accomplish collectively what they wanted but could not do privately.

To enumerate the characteristics of the business corporation and document its role in economic growth, however, is to run ahead of history. The American business corporation, except for the general corporate form that it inherited from England, had to be created by American lawmakers responding to the needs of American businessmen. Most of this creative process occurred at the state level. State legislatures brought the corporation into existence as a legal creature, and state courts filled in the interstices of statute law, clarifying in hundreds of decisions such things as the rules of internal governance, the transfer of stock, the responsibility of corporate agents, the liability of stockholders for corporate debts and of the corporation itself for torts. Available in state courts, too, against corporations exceeding charter powers or abusing them, were the prerogative writs of mandamus and ultra vires.

In these areas and others as well, the Supreme Court took a back seat to state legislatures and state judiciaries, though the Court could (through its diversity-of-citizenship jurisdiction, its broad power in law and equity, and its self-proclaimed jurisdiction over corporations) influence the direction of private corporation law. It was as interpreter of the Constitution and as the arbiter between state and nation that the Court touched most directly on corporate development. Most important, the contract clause in article I, section 10, permitted the Court to define the relationship between the corporation and the state legislature that created it. In defining this relationship the Court sponsored the corporation as a system of power and conditioned its entry into the ideology of free enterprise. It was here that Story made his mark.

The occasion was *Dartmouth College* v. *Woodward* (1819), which concerned the public character of the corporation and the role it would play in American history:[51] Would the corporate device take its legal character from the individuals who constituted it? If so, it would fall heir to the rights of private property so solicitously protected by American law, leaving the legislature only limited authority over the corporations it created. Or was the corporation public in character, on the premise that such a grant of power could be justified only if it were? If public in nature the corporation might be subject to legislative regulation in the public interest. Much was at stake. If the business corporation were subject to legislative regulation, then investors might be reluctant to buy stock. But if private capital were protected absolutely, the new concentration of economic and political power might subvert the public interest. The issue, in short, was whether American law (and American ideology) would treat the business corporation as the individual entrepreneur writ large or as a revolutionary new social force.

The *College* case, on the face of it, seemed remotely related, if at all, to this great question. It originated in 1816 as an educational issue when the Republican-controlled New Hampshire legislature passed a law revising the charter of Dartmouth College by increasing the number of trustees and making the new ones appointees of the Republican governor. This change sought to transform the college into a state university under state control. Counsel for Dartmouth argued before the New Hampshire Supreme Court that the state statute violated the New Hampshire Constitution and also, because the college charter was a contract, the contract clause of the federal Constitution. These legal bars to state regulation, all parties agreed, could be called into action only if Dartmouth College were a *private* corporation. Despite the forceful argument by college counsel on this point, the state court was not persuaded. Chief Justice William Richardson's opinion conceded that a charter was a contract that might come within the protecting perimeter of article I, section 10, but went on to hold that Dartmouth was *not* a private corporation but a public one. Thus the contract clause did not apply.[52] This decision was brought to the Supreme Court by a writ of error, was argued in 1818, and was decided at the opening of the 1819 term. Chief Justice Marshall delivered the majority decision; Washington and Story entered separate concurring opinions; and Duvall registered a silent dissent.

Because the case came on a writ of error, it turned on the constitutional question whether Dartmouth's charter was a contract protected against state impairment by the contract clause of the Constitution. That a charter was a contract, Marshall asserted, was a proposition so obvious that "it can require no argument"—a rather audacious assumption, as there was no clear precedent either in English or in American law to support it. Having established the "true" construction of the Constitution in the abstract, Marshall's problem was to apply it to the case at hand. Here the determining issue was the status of Dartmouth College. If by its charter it were a "civil institution"—that is, if it were a public corporation—then the state had a right to control it, even to the point of amending its charter. If, on the other hand, Dartmouth were a "private eleemosynary institution," endowed with the capacity to take property bestowed by individuals on the faith of its charter, then the state had no general right of regulation but was controlled entirely by the terms of the charter.[53]

Marshall's treatment of the corporation question suited the constitutional resolution he wanted to reach, which is to say that he avoided any sweeping doctrinal pronouncements about corporations. Conveniently ignoring his own statement in *Head* v. *Providence Insurance Co.*—that the corporation is the "mere creature of the act to which it owes its existence"[54]—he maintained that the character of corporations "does not grow out of their incorporation, but out of the manner in which they are formed, and the objects for which they are created."[55] By this rule, Dartmouth was an eleemosynary institution entitled by its private character to the protection of the contract clause.

Story's concurrence appears somewhat anomalous. The opinion of the majority was a conclusive victory for the party he favored, and he agreed fully with the path of legal reasoning laid out by the chief justice; it was a path that he had in fact helped chart as a lawyer in *Fletcher* v. *Peck* and one he would widen and expand as a justice in *Green* v. *Biddle*. His objective in concurring, then, was not to suggest an alternate legal route to the Court's conclusion but, it would appear, to open the majority opinion to the broadest possible construction.[56]

Story understood the radical lawmaking potential of the *College* case. He had followed it from its inception in New Hampshire, not as an impartial observer but as an active partisan of the college (which later gave him an honorary degree) and a confidant and adviser of its chief counsel, Daniel Webster.[57] Story had been one of those "few friends" who, after the argument in 1818, had received copies of Webster's brief with instructions to "send them to each of such Judges as you think proper. . . ."[58] More important, Story advised Webster on the strategy of litigation. Coming to the Supreme Court as it did on a writ of error to the New Hampshire Supreme Court, the case was confined to the federal question whether the New Hampshire law regulating the college corporation was repugnant to the federal Constitution. Story, as well as Webster, wanted to put the case on a broader ground, one that would permit the Supreme Court to consider not only the contract clause but the whole range of legal limitations on state regulation of corporate property that had been discussed before the New Hampshire court. To achieve this end, Webster, with the encouragement of Story, entered three separate actions of ejectment in Story's circuit court at Portsmouth, New Hampshire, in the spring 1818 term.[59] Though nominally to test the title to disputed lands that the college had leased to private individuals, these "cognate cases," as they were called, turned on the legality of the New Hampshire act that transformed Dartmouth College into a university. Because they came under diversity-of-citizenship jurisdiction, the circuit court and the Supreme Court on appeal could consider all the legal arguments against state regulation of corporate charters. To get the cases before the Supreme Court of the United States as quickly as possible, Story assured Webster that they would be sent up "in the most convenient manner,"[60] presumably by a pro forma division between Story and the federal district judge sitting with him at circuit.

Marshall's opinion so completely vindicated the college that the cognate strategy proved unnecessary, but Story still felt the need for a broader treatment of the subject. His *Dartmouth* opinion, in short, was less a concurrence to the majority opinion than an exegesis on it, one that allowed, at least in part, the expansive interpretation denied him by the failure of the "cognate" strategy. Story believed that the general inquiry "into the nature, rights, and duties of aggregate corporations at common law" was essential to the settlement of the College cause.[61] Here was the missing link in Marshall's narrower argument. And from this broad approach came Story's doctrine of public and private corporations, which was the crucial bridge from private eleemosynary educational institutions to the American business corporation.

Marshall gave Story the opening he needed for an expansive interpretation by relying on Story's opinion in *Terrett* v. *Taylor* (1815), a case involving Virginia's attempt to divest the Anglican church of some of its property located within the state. In negating state confiscatory legislation, Story divided corporations into two general types: public and private. Public corporations were those such as towns and counties "which existed only for public purposes"; thus the "legislature may under proper limitations . . . change, modify, enlarge or restrain them. . . ." Private corporations were those not "public" and presumably stood on different ground. Here the legislature could not "without the consent or default of the corporators" take property vested by the corporate charter. In this matter, he concluded for the majority, "we think ourselves standing upon the principles of natural justice, upon the fundamental laws of every free government, upon the spirit and letter of the constitution of the United States, and upon the decisions of the most respectable judicial tribunals. . . ."[62]

Story's pioneering opinion in *Terrett* was relied on by counsel at both the state and the Supreme Court levels, and Marshall cited it without elaboration to establish the private character of Dartmouth College. But the public-private dichotomy needed to be expanded more fully if it were to encompass business corporations as well as private colleges. There was, however, an obstacle to be overcome. The commonwealth tradition, which was strong in the states, held that corporations by their very nature were public; special privilege, it was assumed, would not be given to private individuals except to accomplish some public objective.[63] As Judge Francis Locke put it in *Trustees of the University of North Carolina* v. *Foy* (one of the few state cases to deal with the problem), "it seems difficult to conceive of a corporation established for merely private purposes. In every institution of that kind the ground of the establishment is some public good or purpose to be promoted."[64]

To define corporations by their function, by their impact on society, then, would be to admit they were both public and private, thus opening up the possibility of state regulation. The way out—and here Story drew on Marshall's majority opinion to complete the formulation of the public-private doctrine begun in *Terrett*—was to define corporations by the nature of their endowments and not their functions. Private corporations, he ruled, were corporations whose capital stock was private, a definition that clearly encompassed the new business corporation. To make the connection unmistakable, Story gave as examples of such private corporations "a bank, whose stock is owned by private persons, . . . insurance, canal, bridge, and turnpike companies." In all of these cases, the corporations were private, "as if the franchise were vested in a single person."[65] It followed—and here Story's reasoning from the common law tied in with the chief justice's exposition of the Constitution—that the charters of private corporations, because they were private, were protected against state alteration by article I, section 10, of the Constitution.

The distinction between public and private corporations was not new with the *Dartmouth College* case; nor, contrary to the impression given by Story's concurring opinion, was it an established doctrine in American law. Story had adumbrated the doctrine in *Terrett* v. *Taylor*, as we have seen, and antedating *Terrett* there were a few inconclusive state court decisions that groped obliquely toward the public-private doctrine.[66] The case most generally cited as ancient authority and the one relied on by Story was Lord Chief Justice Holt's 1694 opinion in *Philips* v. *Bury*.[67] Confusion abounded, however, because *Philips* v. *Bury* predated the modern business corporation, and Lord Holt's opinion was limited strictly to the issue of visitation as applied to charitable institutions.[68] Certainly American judges had come to no agreement on the meaning and applicability of Holt's ruling. In fact, some, like Marshall in the *Providence Insurance Co.* case or Locke in *Trustees of the University of North Carolina* v. *Foy*, pushed corporation law away from the public-private dichotomy.

What Story did—and his effort reveals the creative potential of the common-law tradition as well as his own brilliant capacity for improvisation—was to weld scattered English and American precedents together into a clear and symmetrical legal doctrine. Absent from his formulation was the doctrinal ambiguity that stemmed from the confused nature of the corporation itself, the ambiguity that had forced Judge Locke to deny altogether the possibility of a "merely private" corporation.

The confusion, as Story seems to have perceived it, came when one looked to the actual function of the corporation, to its role and impact on society. Conceivably, the definition of public and private might have followed function, as Judge Richardson's decision in fact did.[69] Such a functional approach to corporations would have invited American lawmakers to consider the public nature of private corporate property. Had they done so, a foundation might have been laid in the antebellum period for Chief Justice Morrison Waite's 1877 ruling in *Munn* v. *Illinois* that private property "affected with a public interest" is subject to state regulation.[70] For the Court to determine what part of the corporation was "public" and thus subject to legislative control and what was "private" and hence free from control would have plunged the Court into a morass of imprecision. This would not have been "legal science" as Story knew it, and it would in addition have made corporate stocks less attractive to investors. Story avoided the dilemma by abandoning the functional definition altogether and defining private corporations according to their foundation. On the one hand, this definition blinded the law to certain realities of corporate power; on the other hand, it recognized that the corporation was moving from the public arena to the private, from hospitals and charities to businesses and manufacturing concerns. Story's doctrine, for all of its tendencies toward abstract legal principle, was a practical response to a major aspect of corporate development.

Story's opinion also worked to influence that development, though it should be noted that the legal force of his concurrence was formally circumscribed. Justice Washington, in fact, specifically warned against applying the entire *Dartmouth College* ruling to "any other case than the one immediately before" the Court. Duvall dissented altogether, and Johnson concurred "for reasons stated by the Chief Justice." Only Livingston specifically mentioned his agreement with Story.[71] Still, Story's opinion melded so harmoniously with Marshall's that it appeared less a radical interpretation by one justice than a logical and inevitable consequence of the Court's reasoning. The result was to enhance the authority of Marshall's opinion, a symbiosis that could hardly have been accidental. The chief justice did not make any doctrinal statements about private corporations, nor did he supply common-law authorities for his argument that Dartmouth College was a private institution. Story did both, and on this point he had, according to his later statement in *Allen* v. *McKean*, "the approbation of the court."[72] By laying a common-law foundation under Marshall's constitutional ruling, Story added authority to it.

More important, Story's concurrence worked to broaden the scope of the Court's decision. Marshall's opinion focused appropriately on Dartmouth College as a private eleemosynary institution, and in a strict precedential sense the case pertained only to private educational institutions. But the *Dartmouth* ruling also applied to business corporations, as Marshall and others must surely have appreciated.[73] It was Story, however, who built the most explicit bridge from eleemosynary educational institutions to business corporations. Unlike the chief justice, Story did not limit his discussion of corporations to the case at hand but expounded on corporations in general. If there were doubt about the applicability of his doctrine to business as well as educational corporations, it was removed when he supplied specific examples of private corporations. He repeated this point with emphasis in *Allen* v. *McKean*.

Even more impressive (albeit indirect) evidence of the practical impact of Story's opinion and the *College* decision was the spectacular growth of business corporations in New England during the post-*Dartmouth* decade. Manufacturing corporations had been around before the Court's decision in 1819, of course, and there were still potential barriers to incorporation in the decade that followed (such as the absence of limited liability in Massachusetts). Nevertheless, the corporation became a major force in the transformation of New England manufacturing. Incorporations were sought with new enthusiasm throughout the 1820s and 1830s; in Massachusetts there were eighteen in 1828 alone and almost as many in 1829. It was during the 1820s that Boston-based capital transformed the Merrimack Valley and turned peaceful farms into "miles of mills," as one observer put it. And this is not to mention the flow of money into other New

England manufacturing corporations.[74] In the eight years between 1822 and 1830, according to one contemporary source, over $5.5 million was invested in the Merrimack area alone, and one textile corporation, the Merrimack Company, was capitalized at the unprecedented sum of $2 million.[75] The *American Jurist*, which praised the revolution in corporation law and Story's contribution to it, boasted that the investment in manufacturing corporations in 1830 exceeded the $30 million invested in banks and insurance companies.[76]

The *Dartmouth College* decision, fortified by Story's concurring opinion, played a crucial role in the transformation of the corporation from an association of individuals vested with a portion of sovereignty designed to accomplish a public service to an association whose corporate status was a promotional device employed by the state to facilitate the pursuit of private goals by private individuals. Public good did not go unreckoned in this new dispensation. But it was assumed, in the mode of Adam Smith, that the public good was most closely approximated when the state permitted—indeed, encouraged—individuals to pursue their own economic endeavours, bound only by contracts of their own making. Story never went quite so far as Daniel Webster, who argued that the corporation was a citizen entitled to the rights of comity provided by article IV, section 1, of the Constitution.[77] But he did help the corporation make its entry into American law and ideology as another enterprising individual and thus the beneficiary of the formidable protection against state regulation that Anglo-American law bestowed on individual property rights. In the process— and this is the truly radical aspect of the *College* decision (the one that Story unsuccessfully defended in the *Charles River Bridge* case)—state legislatures were reduced to the status of contracting individuals. Public contracts (those in which the state was a party and in which public welfare was on the line) were to be interpreted just like private contracts: by the courts according to the common law.

It was logical that the corporation should take on some of the attributes of the individuals who constituted it. The process of bestowing personality on the corporate form had ancient roots in Western law, and American judges continued the process almost without questioning it. Marshall showed the way in *Bank of the U.S.* v. *Deveaux*, which dealt with the right of a corporation to sue in federal courts. A corporation was an invisible, artificial creation of the law, admitted the chief justice, but it was also the individuals who composed it, and those individuals had rights that attached to the aggregate.[78] Among the rights that the corporation had in common with individual citizens was the right, under the diversity-of-citizenship clause of the Judiciary Act of 1789,[79] to sue in federal courts. But if the individual citizen's right to sue could be extended to the corporation, why not other individual rights? Why not extend the right to hold and freely use property as well? This is precisely what the Court did in its *Dartmouth College* decision.

Marshall's identification of the corporation with the individual lay buried in the technical discussion of beneficiary rights. Story's doctrine of public and private corporations, however, went straight to the point and made clear the nature of the legal and cultural shift under way. Where the foundation was private, so too was the corporation, just "as if the franchise were vested in a single individual."[80] However, had the Court chosen to determine whether a corporation was public or private by its function in society, and Story himself conceded the point, it would have been forced to conclude with Justice Locke of North Carolina that most private corporations have a public dimension. To that extent they would be subject to some state regulation. Story's method of determining whether a corporation was private or public circumvented the logic of a functional definition. He ignored the mixture of private and public in the corporation and hypostatized each into a symmetrical and self-contained category. Private corporations divested of their public character were identified more readily with the individual entrepreneur, a metamorphosis that was the cultural essence of the new business corporation. It was, as Willard Hurst expressed it, "the most potent single instrument which the law put at the disposal of private decision makers."[81]

Story's voice was a powerful one in this transformation of the corporation. The clarity and simplicity of the public-private dichotomy made his doctrine a convenient metaphor in the ongoing argument about corporations, and his status as a great legal scholar gave it a compelling legitimacy. Almost immediately, his theory of public and private corporations entered the current of legal discourse. Story's argument, including his phraseology and examples, was presented as established law in James Kent's *Commentaries on American Law*, the most influential treatise on American law to appear in the nineteenth century.[82] Moreover, Story's definition was accepted as the starting point for reasoning about corporations by Joseph K. Angell and Samuel Ames in their *Treatise on the Law of Private Corporations Aggregate*, the standard work on corporate law for the period.[83] With such advertisement, the doctrine quickly found its way into lawyers' briefs, judicial opinions, and legal periodicals. To be sure, there was bitter resistance to Story's thesis and its conservative, nonregulatory implications, but the very passion of the opposition was testimony to the growing momentum of the doctrine[84] and of Story's reputation as *the* expert on corporations.

Joseph Hopkinson made the latter point to Story himself shortly after Story's decision in *Allen v. McKean*, in which the principles of *Dartmouth College* were spread out with new authority and clarity. As Hopkinson put it: "A couple of pious old ladies were discussing the respective merit of several Clergymen by whose preaching and praying they had been edified. They agreed upon the superiority of Mr. A—— for a fast day; of Mr. B—— for a funeral sermon and of Mr. C—— for a charity discourse. But, said one of them, 'Give me Mr. D—— for a drought'. Now I say, Give me Judge Story for a Constitutional, corporation question."[85] Many who thought about the matter agreed—except, of course, Andrew Jackson and his friends.

3. Balancing Old Law and New Property: Judge-made Economic Policy

In the culture of the old republic, property, individualism, and liberty were locked in a covalent system of bonding. And it followed as a non-debatable proposition that American law should serve American capitalism, whether in building a body of uniform commercial law, or in forging a national market, or in creating a new corporate form of business organization. There were, however, severe tensions in this integrative culture as the country moved rapidly away from the corporate traditionalism of the colonial period to the market-oriented nineteenth century. For lawmakers who would make law serve the new age the resulting questions were unavoidable. Was it possible, for example, to release the creative energy of property without generating a conflict between various kinds of property: static as against dynamic, agrarian as against commercial as against manufacturing? And how could lawmakers assign priorities to these conflicting property interests without violating the basic legal value of absolute ownership? One side's property would be diminished and with it the moral authority of the law as the guardian of property. Put in more general terms, the question was whether the free market would produce free men—or free some men at the social cost of oppressing others. Perhaps the law would have to control as well as liberate the American businessman. And if so, how much? Which law? Would the market regulate itself? Or individuals themselves? Should the states intervene? Or the nation? The legislatures or the courts? Which, and what mixture?

For Story, whose juristic system (following the systematic model of Blackstone) sought to integrate law and culture, the dilemma was especially intense.[86] The problem was that he enthusiastically embraced all of the contradictory forces. The free market and economic individualism, in the style of Adam Smith, he accepted without question. He was a true believer in the transforming and civilizing forces of commerce and was willing to put the law at the service of the dynamic entrepreneurs who pioneered the commercial revolution. To this end he was a legal reformer and modernizer. But he also believed deeply in the sanctity of property and the moral values of traditional society as he experienced them in New England and Massachusetts. His plan for social-economic progress most assuredly carried with it a conservative, organic concept of community interest. There was no conflict, however: Story was convinced that American law might liberate and energize economic man and at the same time preserve property and keep the individual within the bounds of community well-being.

To perform this feat, the law itself had to be moral and scientific. Thus did Story the jurist confront Story the instrumentalist: A symmetrical, principled, architectonic system of law was not just intellectually satisfying for him, though it was that; it was also, practically speaking, indispensable to moral economic progress. Law must serve the marketplace without being overwhelmed by it. By Story's reckoning only judges trained in the science of the common law could guarantee that this would happen. As a Supreme Court justice, he aimed to show the way as he grappled with the legal problems generated by the economic revolution, questions on such workaday subjects as patents and copyrights, milldams, corporations, and seamen's wages.

American patent and copyright law revealed many of the tensions between law and capitalism in the early republic. Perhaps in no other area was the Lockean definition of property more literally accurate: that property is what one mixes one's labor with. Here too was a new, nonrealty kind of property closely associated with the new economic age, which laid claim to absolute rights of ownership. As Oliver Evans put it rhetorically in his suit against several flour millers in *Evans* v. *Ellicott*, are not "the rights of patentees, inventors of useful improvements . . . as whole, sole, and exclusively their mental property . . . *for their limited time*," as the property rights in "their mills, houses or lands? . . ."[87] Here again law seemed obliged to lend a promotive hand, for whatever encouraged technology and the creation and dissemination of ideas furthered progress. Indeed, American patent and copyright law was put on a frankly promotional basis by article I, section 8, clause 8, of the Constitution itself, which said that Congress shall have the power "to promote the Progress of Science and useful Arts, by securing for limited Times to Authors and Inventors the exclusive Right to their respective Writings and Discoveries."

Patent and copyright not only embodied the dominant Smithian theme that individual property rights and the national interest were synonymous, but carried with them the tensions in that concept. To grant a limited monopoly for inventions or literary productions, to make them private property, that is, would invite socially useful activity by rewarding it generously. But a too liberal construction of monopoly privilege could discourage further innovation and in the area of ideas work to restrict the "diffusion of useful knowledge," which all agreed was basic to the existence of a virtuous and informed republican citizenry.

The problem facing judges like Story in the area of patent law, then, was to strike a balance between promotion and restraint: to apply principles not fully formed to American technology in the throes of unprecedented growth. Neither the Constitution nor the several congressional statutes passed in pursuance to it offered much guidance, except to make it clear that law was expected to serve the national interest by encouraging invention. English patent statutes, after which those of the United States were modeled, offered some assistance to American judges, to be sure, as did English case law. Story took ample notice of both. But English law generally was not greatly in advance of American law, because both waited on the same forces of modernization. English decisions also varied greatly from one judge to the next and oscillated widely between liberal and conservative poles of construction. On the whole, however, English judges viewed patents as contracts between the inventor and society and accordingly drew, for both method and principles, from the more strict contract law rather than the more flexible rules of equity. English patent law also retained the outmoded idea that only a "manufacture" was patentable, that methods or ideas were not. Neither, for the most part, were mere improvements on existing inventions.

The antipatent bias of English principles was more congenial to the corporate eighteenth century than the radical nineteenth; in the United States it comported with neither the growing emphasis on economic individualism nor the explosion of invention during the period of rapid technological development. American circumstances pressed American lawmakers to liberalize English law to fit American needs. Until the creation of the patent office in 1836, and after as well, this burden of innovation—of sorting out the complex and contradictory claims of rival inventors, of balancing individual property rights in inventions (and writing) against the public interest—fell to the courts. This situation pleased Story and put his system of applied legal science to the test of relevance.[88]

Story grappled with patent law in some forty opinions rendered throughout his long tenure on the Court. Neither in these opinions nor in his anonymous note on patents, which appeared in Wheaton's reports in 1818, nor in his *Commentaries on the Constitution* did he deal theoretically or comprehensively with the subject.[89] He had no doubt, however, that the law should serve the public by encouraging invention.[90] He also accepted without question the notion that invention and writing were species of property. The need was clear. The problem was how, given the sporadic and fragmentary format of case law, to fashion a body of rules that was clear enough for judges to follow and that also recognized both property rights (themselves conflicting) and community interest—all without the guidance of settled precedent.

Story's first inclination (as revealed both in his early decisions and in his note on patents in Wheaton's reports) was to follow English precedents, particularly those narrowly conceived decisions that required formal definition and that resisted patents for method.[91] Story did not explain his preference for this confining approach. To draw on English authority was habitual for him, of course. More important, perhaps, was his concern for "scientific" adjudication in an area that was by its nature fraught with subjectivity and complexity and that, in some instances, to use Story's own expression, bordered on "metaphysics." Reliance on English principles supplied at least some measure of exactitude, especially those which (in the spirit of special pleading) demanded formal definition. Story also achieved precision by narrowing the range of questions to a judicially manageable scope (often at the expense of inventors). This was the case with his holding, following the statute of 1793, that an invention, to be patentable, must be "useful" and must also be a genuine "*exercise of inventive powers*," not merely a frivolous exercise or "the mere change of one known mechanical equivalent for another."[92]

Story never abandoned his determination to inject precision into patent law, but he did—following the lead of Marshall, Baldwin, and Livingston and the advice of Webster—modify his early strictness in favor of a more liberal and pragmatic approach. The change came first on circuit in *Ames* v. *Howard* (1833), in which he abandoned "over nice" construction in favor of a broad interpretation.[93] In *Blanchard* v. *Sprague* (1839) he took another large step in the liberal direction by permitting "method" to be patented, though he disguised the shift by associating method with a specific machine.[94] The following year, in *Wyeth* v. *Stone*, he moved still closer to the liberal position, this time by modifying his insistence on strict and precise definition.[95] In these cases and others Story did what Webster suggested in 1829: He moved away from undue reliance on English law in the direction of an American patent law that would favor inventors and, following the spirit of the Constitution, serve national interest by promoting technological progress. Again, legal science encouraged by Yankee enterprise merged with instrumentalism. Though he arrived at the liberal position somewhat hesitantly and with the helpful prodding of his friends on and off the Court, Story's authority (along with his copious exposition of doctrine) was of immense importance in giving legitimacy to the new position. Fairly or not, he was identified by contemporaries as the pioneer in the liberalization of American patent law.[96]

In copyright law Story also confronted the tension among private property, public interest, and republican values. No one seriously doubted that literary production was property worthy of the protection and encouragement of the law. But republican society, with its goal of an active and informed citizenry, put a premium on the dissemination of ideas. Story fully agreed but as an author also knew firsthand the beneficial effect of private property in literary production.[97] In the great copyright case of *Wheaton* v.

Peters (1834)—at considerable personal cost—he was forced to choose between private property and public interest.[98] That he chose the latter reveals what remained implicit in his patent decisions: that community interest was more than rhetorical window dressing. Just as clear was his personal integrity as a judge.

The *Wheaton* case originated with the decision of Supreme Court reporter Richard Peters to publish and sell six volumes of *Condensed Reports of Cases in the Supreme Court of the United States*, which contained cases from the volumes of the previous reporter, Henry Wheaton. Claiming a coyright for his reports under both the common law and the copyright act of 1790, Wheaton asked for a permanent injunction against the publication of Peters's volumes as an infringement of his copyright in the twelve volumes of reports he had brought out. Judge Joseph Hopkinson, on circuit, in the absence of Justice Baldwin, ruled against Wheaton on the grounds that there was no federal common law of copyright; that English law on the subject had not in fact been adopted by the states separately; and, indeed, that English law on the subject itself was inchoate. Most important, Hopkinson ruled that Wheaton, by failing to deliver a copy of his books to the secretary of state within six months of their publication, violated the fourth section of the copyright act, thus nullifying his claim under it.[99] Wheaton's appeal came before the Supreme Court during the January term, 1834.

Precedents in copyright law, as in patents, were virtually nonexistent, and the issues were complex and delicate. Court reporters were reimbursed for their difficult and important work only from the returns realized on the sale of the reports (though Wheaton had persuaded Congress to grant him an additional thousand dollars per year). His complaint (in which he was joined by his predecessor, William Cranch) that Peters's cheaper edition would deprive him of his main source of compensation for twelve years' labor rang true. On the other hand, a cheaper edition of the Court's reports (Peters's *Condensed Reports* sold for $25, as against Wheaton's $180) was much needed if lawyers were to have access to the Court's decisions, as all agreed was necessary for the development of scientific law. Story had, in fact, encouraged Peters's project with just this goal in mind.[100] Wheaton's contention, moreover, that decisions of the highest court in the land were the private property, even for a limited period of time, of the person who reported those decisions highlighted the conflict between private property and public interest.

The Court divided four to two (Justice Johnson being absent for the entire term) against Wheaton. All the justices agreed that Supreme Court opinions were not private property. There was, said John McLean, who wrote the majority opinion, no federal common law on the subject; nor had Pennsylvania incorporated English copyright law into its common law.

Copyright, then, was a monopoly grant that had no existence except as defined by statute—which principle became the foundation of American copyright law. Because copyright was a monopoly and because public interest was involved in any extension of the privilege, the terms of the grant had to be adhered to strictly if the author were to enjoy the benefits thereof —essentially the position Hopkinson had taken below.[101] Challenging this interpretation were the dissents of Justices Smith Thompson and Henry Baldwin, who contended that Wheaton, as a matter of equity and morality, had a common-law right to the fruits of his labor. The dissenters, no less than the majority, saw that a question of public interest was involved, but they reasoned that the best way to further it was to protect private property.[102] Wheaton in the meantime had to be satisfied with the acknowledgment by the majority that the reporter's notes (as distinct from the words of the justices) were copyrightable. The order to remand the case back to the circuit on a retrial of the facts concerning whether Wheaton had complied with the requirements of the 1790 statute was a concession of sorts, too, but as Story pointed out to Peters, there was no real possibility of a reversal.[103]

As a close friend of both Wheaton and Peters, Story had hoped to keep the issue between them private.[104] His decision to support the majority was, therefore, a painful and difficult one, for it meant certainly a recriminatory end to a close friendship and productive working relationship with Wheaton going back to Wheaton's days as reporter and extending to his scholarly efforts in international law. Wheaton expected Story's support, not unreasonably in light of their friendship and of Story's efforts in behalf of a federal common law, his concern for private property, and his latitudinous interpretation of the powers of Congress, all of which points were cited by lawyers for Wheaton. Wheaton therefore felt repudiated and deceived by Story's failure to support him. Indeed, he accused Story of having influenced Hopkinson's circuit decision against him with the promise to support it fully should the question come before the Supreme Court (though in fact Story had not expected the matter to go that far).[105] Wheaton also claimed that Story misrepresented the case to Marshall, who, without consulting the issues himself, relied on "his prevaricating brother" on account of his reputed friendship with Wheaton.[106]

Story had been instrumental in securing Hopkinson's appointment to the federal bench only several years earlier, and there is no doubt that his opinion carried great weight with Hopkinson. But there is no evidence among numerous extant letters between the two that Story made any effort to influence Hopkinson, and his high regard for Hopkinson's abilities would, in fact, have made such interference unlikely. Wheaton might more appropriately have been troubled by Story's relationship with Peters, had he known about it. Story had been the prime mover in securing the reporter's job for Peters. Their relationship, as revealed by their letters, was extremely frank and cordial. More important, Story encouraged Peters in his scheme to bring out the *Condensed Reports* and facilitated their sale once they were published. Such patronage was not unique for Story; indeed, he had encouraged and helped Wheaton no less generously. Certainly there is no evidence linking Story's commitment to the project to his legal position in the case. But in light of his long friendship with both men and his prior commitment to Peters's project, a withdrawal from the case would have been in order. Certainly it would have been an easy escape from a painful dilemma.

That Story refused the easy way, that he was willing to ruin a cherished friendship, that he was not persuaded even by his own arguments cited by counsel to change his mind, says much about his conception of judicial duties. His action, more than rhetoric, speaks directly to his deep concern that the public interest not be sacrificed by an excessive and extravagant extension of the rights of private property. For more than two decades Story had worked to expand the power of the federal courts, to integrate the federal judiciary into a single system capable of unifying American law. His whole life was devoted to spreading the word of law. Peters's *Condensed Reports* was a means to this end. The Court's decisions, if they were to guide republican society, must be part of the public domain.

Behind Story's efforts in such cases as *Wheaton*, in his decisions in admiralty, patent, and corporation law, is an unspoken premise (and one that for political reasons was destined to remain inferential): Story assigned courts in general and the Supreme Court of the United States above all others a central role in economic rule making. Judges working in the common-law mode, more than legislators and politicians (and the two increasingly merged in Story's perception), were uniquely qualified to lead the old republic into the new economic age. This was a heavy burden of statesmanship, given the magnitude of social and economic change and the inchoate structure of American law. Undaunted, Story willingly put judges in the front line of policy making with the promise that judge-made law would be relevant and, at the same time, true to the basic morality of property rights on which it rested. It was exactly this issue that Story himself grappled with for all to see on the New England circuit as he attempted to harmonize inherited doctrines of riparian law with the new uses of land ushered in by the growth of water-powered textile manufacturing. At stake was his vision of moral, economic progress through judge-made law.

American law at the beginning of the nineteenth century, following English law before Mansfield, was rooted in real property, which of all branches of the law was most given to concepts of absolute ownership and most oriented to preindustrial economic life and aristocratic social order.

Land law followed land use, however, and American circumstances doomed the aristocratic features of the old law. Primogeniture and entail, already on their way out in the colonial period, were dealt killing blows by the American Revolution as partible inheritance in fee became the dominant mode. Nor was landed wealth locked up in other unproductive uses, a theme celebrated by both James Sullivan (whose *History of Land Titles in Massachusetts*, written in 1801, was considered authoritative) and Story, who echoed him.[107] Gone was the English doctrine of mortmain and on its way out was the common-law doctrine of waste, which discouraged enterprise by holding tenants liable for any basic alteration in the condition of their holdings. These developments in private law were complemented by those in public land policy, which increasingly responded to the pressure to turn the public domain over to speculators—and ultimately to plain people.

With the rest of the legal and business community, Story praised this liberalization of land law and saw it as a reflection of a society committed to individual enterprise, in which wealth was fluid, individuals were mobile, and permanent classes were nonexistent. What he did not and could not abandon in the old law, what was to him the moral nexus between that law and the individualism of the new age, was the principle that existing property rights were sacred. The refusal to extend monopoly privileges unduly (as in patent and copyright law) was one thing; ownership established and vested by existing law was another. Security of property rights, including the right to deploy property freely and enjoy fully the fruits of one's deployment, was the foundation of the whole dynamic moral structure of free enterprise and of free government itself.[108] It was a dilemma, then, that this principle should be challenged by the very forces of individual enterprise Story praised and worked to unleash. The conflict was unavoidable in *Tyler* v. *Wilkinson* (1827), which pitted the old doctrines of absolute ownership against the demands of a new class of dynamic businessmen.[109]

The *Tyler* case, which Story encountered at the June 1827 term of the Rhode Island circuit, originated in a dispute over the use of water in the Pawtucket River near the border of Massachusetts and Rhode Island. The plaintiffs owned a dam called the "lower dam" and some of the adjacent mills run by the water it raised. The defendants owned Sargents Trench, which was a canal dug several rods above the lower dam and which ran water around the lower dam and back into the river again some ten rods below. Originally built for the passage of fish, the trench had long since been employed to turn textile mills. Water diverted by the trench, especially in times of low water, brought down the level of the lower dam and interfered with the operation of its mills.

The controlling principle of the old law was the doctrine of natural use, which held that owners of riparian land were entitled to equal use of the water in its natural course: Any use of water by owners of riparian property that injured other owners either by depriving them of water or by tortiously injuring adjoining land was actionable under the common-law doctrine of nuisance. Accordingly, the plaintiffs in equity claimed that the owners of the trench and the upper dam fraudulently combined injuriously to appropriate and use the water, to which they were not entitled by ancient usage and old law. The plaintiffs asked Story's court to establish their legal right to the natural flow of water and requested an injunction preventing further injury. The issue, as Professor Horwitz aptly points out, was not whether law would protect property, but rather what *kind* of property it would favor.[110]

Story's "classically transitional" opinion opened with a reaffirmation of the traditional principles of riparian rights, only recently refurbished in J. Angell's influential *Law of Watercourses* (1824):[111] Owners of riparian property, the rule went, have an equal right to use the water flowing over its natural course, without diminution or obstruction; "no proprietor has a right to use water to the prejudice of another." No sooner had Story stated the rule, however, than he drew back from the antidevelopment consequences that its application would bring. "When I speak of this common right," he said, "I do not mean to be understood, as holding the doctrine, that there can be no diminution whatsoever, and no obstruction or impediment whatsoever, by a riparian proprietor, in the use of the water as it flows; for that would be to deny any valuable use of it." Here as elsewhere, he continued, the law "acts with a reasonable reference to public convenience and general good, and it is not betrayed into a narrow strictness, subversive of common sense, nor into an extravagant looseness, which would destroy private rights."[112]

As in patent and copyright law, the problem was to strike a balance. To meet the challenge, Story introduced—or created, to be more exact—the rule of "reasonable use," which he hoped would serve as the guideline in this transitional area of economic development. Making up law, as Story did with the idea of reasonable use, was not so much a problem in the common-law method, which worked with boldness in the area of penumbra. But there *was* a problem (and a prophetic departure) in that the law that Story created was as much ad hoc process as principle—shades of *Cooley* v. *Board of Wardens* (1851), of *Standard Oil Co. of New Jersey* v. *U.S.* (1911), of *Palko* v. *Connecticut* (1937), of Justice Stone's footnote 4 in *U.S.* v. *Carolene Products Co.* (1938).[113] Story's reasonable use anticipated these modern cases in that it was not a fixed rule but a vague guide to ongoing adjudication, an act of faith that some solution could be devised case by case that would preserve property rights, satisfy riparian owners, and still encourage economic progress.

The difficulty with Story's rule came with its application. It was "unreasonable," he was sure, for owners of the lower dam to claim exclusive use of the water, leaving to the trench owners and owners of the upper dam only waste privileges—that is, what they did not use—except if such a claim were backed by "the most irresistable facts." So much for the unreasonable, but what was reasonable? The common sense of businessmen, it would seem, as interpreted by Judge Story: "Men who build mills and invest valuable capital in them [i.e., the owners of the trench and the upper dam], cannot be presumed, without the most conclusive evidence, to give their deliberate assent to the acceptance of such ruinous conditions." The "most conclusive evidence" of such surrender would be (and here Story reverted to the common law, which he had suspended to create the reasonable-use rule) either mutual agreement or prescription by prior use (for a period of twenty years). Because the proprietors could muster proof of neither, Story ruled "that the trench owners have an absolute right to the quantity of water which has usually flowed therein, without any adverse right of the plaintiffs to interrupt that flow in dry seasons, when there is a deficiency of water." On the other hand, "the trench owners have no right to increase that flow: and whatever may be the mills or uses, to which they apply it, they are limited to the accustomed quantity, and may not exceed it."[114] From here on it was a question of fact, which, according to the procedures at equity, Story referred to a master to ascertain.

What had Story attempted? Accomplished? The concept of reasonable use was an attempt to escape the antidevelopment implications of the natural-flow doctrine—an effort to loosen the hold of absolutist principles of the common law without surrendering them, in order to facilitate the productive use of property (providing, of course, that the owners who claimed under it were entrepreneurs who wanted to maximize the use of their property). Prior rights could, however, shield static property and retard economic development. The logic of economic growth was for the law to favor outright dynamic over static property, but this is exactly the unconditional choice that Story refused to make.

This refusal pitted Story, at least obliquely, against the strong developmental current of American riparian law. Many states, including New York, Massachusetts, and most of the other New England states, passed milldam acts that circumvented both the natural-flow principle and the prior-rights corollary; state courts including those of Massachusetts followed the legislative lead in a frankly instrumentalist vein. Despite variation from state to state, state law tended to give preference to dynamic capital, to milldam owners at the expense of farmers whose lands were flooded by the dams. Injunctions to prevent damage by flooding, which had been the main weapon of static capital, were no longer available to aggrieved riparian property owners. Damages were sometimes denied them altogether, if flooding could be shown to have increased the value of their property. More important, damages were reduced to yearly assessments that the injured parties had to accept.[115] That property which offered the most in production got the most from the law; static property owners helped defray the social costs of economic modernization.

Story's *Tyler* opinion was an alternative to this hardheaded, market-oriented legal model for economic growth. He was unwilling to give up the legal (and moral) principle of the old law that protected property rights; most assuredly he was not prepared to defer to state legislatures or to state courts who did give up this principle. Story's answer to legislative fiat—to the statutory amendment of the common law—was to invoke a creative application of the old common-law principles by judges (like himself) who understood the old law and appreciated its moral force but who could bend it to the needs of the new businessmen.[116] *Tyler*, backed by Story's prestige, held out the promise that principled law, morality, and economic progress were mutually compatible. Americans could have their cake and eat it too, providing the right chefs baked it.

4. Laissez Faire—But Not Quite: Judges as Guardians of Economic Morality

"At this moment, especially in our country," observed Charles Sumner in a speech to the Mercantile Library Association of Boston on 13 November 1854, "the merchant, more than any other character, stands in the very boots of the feudal chief. Of all pursuits or relations his is now the most extensive and formidable, making all others its tributaries, and bending at times even the lawyer and clergyman to be its dependent stipendiaries."[117] For "merchant" read businessman, entrepreneur, manufacturer, or "stockbroker" (following Emerson).[118] The senator from Massachusetts was talking about an economic-based social revolution that raised the American businessman to a position of conspicuous power. But what about lawyers as "dependent stipendiaries"? Could it be that in unleashing the dynamic entrepreneur and clothing him in corporate armor, lawyers and judges had become his servants? And what about Story, Sumner's friend and former teacher at the Harvard Law School? Was Story possibly one of the dependent "lawyers" Sumner had in mind? For all of his talk about community interest and the morality of the law, was Story a closet champion of laissez faire—the notion, that is to say, that the state and its law should promote capitalism but not regulate it in the interest of the commonwealth?

One thing is immediately clear: In the area of political economics, thought and action were inseparable. Neither Story nor his colleagues on the Court (nor his contemporaries in general) theorized about laissez faire, either for or against it. Story and the Court spoke with their actions, however, and what they said, as we have seen, was that law ought to promote and maximize individual economic creativity. Marshall spoke for the majority most often, but there is no doubt that Story supported the Court's plan for national capitalism, and there is some evidence (even in those cases where he did not speak) that he worked in the collective give-and-take of judicial conference to spur on the majority to its national capitalist conclusions. The implied-powers doctrine of *McCulloch*, as previously noted, had long been his stock-in-trade and state legislative interference with property his bête noire. It was Story's concurrence in *Dartmouth* that forged the most explicit link to private business corporations. And though his role in *Gibbons* is unclear, it is possible that he may have helped Marshall write the opinion, and there is no doubt that he struggled consistently to salvage the maximum economic nationalism from it.[119] In the contract cases Story was on the extreme nationalist wing: from *Fletcher*, in which he argued the contract principle; to *Dartmouth*, in which he expanded it; to *Green v. Biddle* (1823), in which he stretched it to extreme lengths by arguing that the agreement between Virginia and Kentucky making the latter a sovereign state was a contract within article I, section 10.[120]

Looking at Story's constant advocacy of constitutional nationalism, one might come to either of two contradictory conclusions: With the post-1937 Supreme Court in mind, one might argue that Story's support of congressional authority was meant to underwrite a vast apparatus of national regulation. The obverse side of constitutional nationalism was state delimitation. Looking at Story's consistent efforts here (his exclusivist interpretation of the commerce power and his contract clause decisions, for example) might lead one to believe that he wanted no regulation at all.

In fact, neither conclusion will stand. The first is furthest from the truth. Congress, as the general statute book makes clear, simply had not yet emerged as the agent of economic regulation; it would not do so for another half century or more. Neither Story nor his contemporaries on and off the Court reasoned beyond this accepted experience. Story, in fact, was quite explicit on the limited scope of national regulation. What he said about the power of Congress to regulate corporations goes to the heart of the matter. "I confess," he wrote to Daniel Webster in 1840, discussing whether corporations should be included in the proposed national bankruptcy bill, "that I feel no small doubt, whether Congress can regulate State Corporations by any other law than the State laws. A State Corporation is entitled to just such rights and powers, as the charter gives it, and I do not well see where Congress can get the power to alter or control them, or to suspend or extinguish them."[121]

The possession of power by the national government clearly did not, for Story (or for the Marshall Court either)[122] imply its use for regulation. Indeed, the great nationalist had a surprisingly truncated notion of what national government should actually do. "The powers of the general government will be, and indeed must be," he wrote in his *Commentaries on the Constitution*, "principally employed upon external objects such as war, peace, negotiations with foreign powers, and foreign commerce. In its internal operations it can touch but few objects, except to introduce regulations beneficial to commerce, intercourse, and other relations between the States, and to lay taxes for the common good."[123] Government (and law), in short, must adjust itself to the nature of republican society, which for Story, as he put it to the Boston mechanics in 1829, was "equality of social condition"—the assumption that Tocqueville made the basis of his great work and that he may have borrowed from Story.[124] The "character" and "circumstances" of the Americans, contended Story, "afford a wider range for talent and inquiry, than in any other country." There were no confining divisions of labor to make men into "mere machines"; there were no rigid classes, no "barriers against the advance of talent from one department of life to another." Republican government had to preserve this unique equality of life, to help individuals take advantage of their rare opportunity to improve themselves:[125] thus the preference for promotional efforts; thus the "mildness of government," the "absence of all laws regulating trade and obstructing local competition."[126]

But was not this the practical essence of laissez faire: a promotional, nonregulatory state pure and simple? The answer is yes but with significant qualifications. To depict Story as an advocate of laissez faire is to say that he believed, with John Locke and Adam Smith, in the miraculous possibilities of economic individualism. This he did. His own family history contained the message; so did his lawyering in Salem (with the Crowninshield family as a case in point). On circuit he observed and marveled at the productive energy of New England working folk; he also mingled on intimate terms with those who rose to the top. He was a great admirer of John Lowell, and his model capitalist was none other than Amos Lawrence.[127] For the law to help the likes of Amos Lawrence (or Nicholas Biddle, another of his friends) was for Story to help the working people of America.

An elitist Story was, but his elitism did not follow rigid class lines. He was acutely aware, to put it another way, that not every manufacturer was Amos Lawrence or every banker Nicholas Biddle. As a Unitarian and a rationalist, Story saw the good in people; as a practicing lawyer and judge he had learned firsthand that people do evil; as a Federalist of the old school he believed that law might capitalize on people's good moments to institutionalize the good in them. It did not follow, then, that because Story worked to liberate the American entrepreneur that he intended to give him carte blanche. Too much weight can be given to those dramatic constitutional decisions which curbed the power of the states. Important though they were, they still left intact much of the states' regulatory apparatus, which in the nineteenth century was considerable.[128] As a politician, a former state legislator, and a lawyer and judge, Story could not have been blind to this role of state government in the economic life of the people, a role that included not only promotion but regulation through licensing and outright regulation of prices, wages, hours, and quality of goods. More important still were state-sponsored internal improvements that not only promoted but also guided and channeled economic development. The police power doctrines recognized by the Marshall Court left much of this state regulatory structure in place. And even in the crucial area of corporate regulation, Story and Marshall conceded state legislative authority to act. It was, in fact, Story's concurrence in the *College* case that announced the reserve-power doctrine, which gave state legislatures the power to regulate the corporations they created by reserving such power in the charter. Also, neither Story nor any other justice questioned the authority of state courts to issue writs of quo warranto or ultra vires against corporations that misused or exceeded authority granted in the charter.

A half dozen Supreme Court decisions, in short, did not suddenly obliterate the tradition of state mercantilism. Even so, it was not mainly to state legislative government that Story turned to contain and regulate economic energy. Rather than to statutes passed by politicians, Story turned to the common law administered by judges and lawyers. This judicial bias was, as we have seen, the hidden premise of his choice of profession; it was the specific message of his opinion in *Tyler* and the constant motif of his decisions in patent and copyright. The duty of a Supreme Court justice, particularly as he rode circuit, was not just to create great principles but to engage in the daily administration of rules that would ensure that the economic process would be orderly, rational, and fair and equitable as well. All this brings us to Story's reliance on contract law, public and private, as the essence of judicial regulation and the key to republican economic morality.

The early nineteenth-century United States was the golden age of contract because it was the age of individualism and free will. In economics as in religion (which moved toward Universalism) and politics (which moved toward democracy), it was assumed that people were free to choose and that the public interest was best served when people who were free agents pursued their own self-interest. The "will theory" of contract law followed the logic of a free-will culture, which followed the radical individualism of American society in the nineteenth century.[129] Contract was the preeminent instrument of individual action, from which it followed that social morality depended on the enforcement of contracts. Thus could one Rockdale, Pennsylvania, businessman define contractual probity as "inherent in masculinity" and point to his loins when asked for references concerning his dependability. This is why a Rockdale textile manufacturer could refer to contractual honesty as a virtue given him by a "kind heavenly father." These Rockdale businessmen almost certainly had never read James Kent, William Paley, William Blackstone, Gulian C. Verplanck, or other expounders of contract. In all likelihood they had not studied the contract decisions of the Supreme Court. Yet, with the Court, with the great entrepreneurs of Boston and New York, with reigning intellectuals like Francis Lieber, they agreed on the centrality of contract, which was, as one scholar put it, both an "ego ideal and a theory of society."[130] Thus was Story speaking the langauge of his age when he declared that contractual morality was "the idea of justice implanted in the human mind," which "every state" must enforce,[131] or when he said even more explicitly, in his *Commentaries on the Constitution*, that the obligation of contract was "to be measured, neither by moral law alone, nor by universal law alone, nor by the laws of society alone, but by a combination of the three. . . ."[132]

To enforce the obligation of contracts was to regulate, and such enforcement was in Story's mind the special province of judicial government. Only judges, applying tested principles of the common law, could determine which parties were capable of contracting—those, that is, who were fully cognizant of the promises they made and independent enough to accept responsibility for compliance. Beyond this it was the duty of the courts to enforce the intent of the parties as expressed in contract and, in doubtful cases, to ascertain by rule of law what their intent was. In short, the courts were responsible for monitoring the contractual process; it was a process of regulation that belied the simple meaning of laissez faire but that at the same time bore a unique compatibility with it.

Take, as an example of the regulatory dimension, the unexplored area of seamen's contracts (especially those dealing with wages), a significant area because merchant seamen constituted the basic labor force of commercial seagoing America. Story knew the plight of working seamen intimately: From his Marblehead experience and from his lawyering in Salem, where seamen's wage cases were a constant professional staple,[133] he understood that the imperative of shipboard discipline gave captains and masters an excuse for abusive authority that made common sailors, handicapped further by their youth and ignorance, less-than-equal parties to contracts. Knowing their reputation for "rashness, thoughtlessness and improvidence" and their vulnerability to unscrupulous masters, captains, and owners, Story made them the special wards of judicial protection.[134]

Story was confined in cases of seamen's wages by the accepted principle of admiralty and maritime law (reaffirmed in the United States by the statute of 1790) that "freight was the mother of wages"—a principle that made seamen's wages, unlike labor contracts on land, highly contingent and subject to much uncertainty and abuse.[135] Admiralty law, on the other hand, permitted the judge considerable discretion (often without jury limitation), and Story's commanding scholarship and circuit reputation added to his scope of action. Judging from the series of eighteen opinions on seamen's wages handed down on circuit between 1814 and 1845, Story uniformly used this discretion to expand the rights of seamen. Employers were held to more demanding evidentiary standards in cases detracting from seamen's wages.[136] Seamen's procedural rights and remedies against masters, captains, and owners were expanded.[137] Most important, Story borrowed from equity (which admiralty resembled in his eyes) to enlarge the substantive contractual rights of seamen against unscrupulous masters who used the vagueness of shipping articles to exploit their employees. As Story put it in *Harden* v. *Gordon* (1823), "If there is any undue inequality in terms, and disproportion in the bargain, any sacrifice of rights on one side which are not compensated by extraordinary benefits on the other, the judicial interpretation of the transaction, is that the bargain is unjust and unreasonable, that advantage has been taken of the situation of the weaker party, and that pro tanto the bargain ought to be set aside as inequitable."[138]

Paralleling judicial reform in contracts were Story's efforts to abolish flogging and other harsh punishments that traditionally had been unquestioned but that worked to diminish the seaman's general status as a free bargaining agent. Portions of the Crimes Act of 1825, which Story drafted, addressed this question, and the acts of 1835 and 1842, also drafted by him, tackled the problem directly.[139]

Richard Henry Dana, Jr., Story's co-worker in behalf of seamen's rights, summed up Story's lifetime of work. "In his Circuit, which is the greatest maritime district of our country," wrote Dana to Story's son, "he has developed and built up, by his decisions, a system of legal principles and rules of practice securing to seamen the prompt payment of their wages, medicines and care in sickness, good treatment in performance of duty, and protecting them against unreasonable forfeitures, discharges in foreign ports, imprisonments, and advantages taken of them in their contract, not only creditable to his humanity, but founded in truest and largest reasons of public policy."[140] Story's legal experience on the New England circuit also found its way into national law when the occasion permitted, as it did in the great case of *Sheppard* v. *Taylor* (1831)[141] and in standard legal treatises, where it reached the profession at large.[142] Indeed, between the statute of 1790 and the great reform of seamen's law in the act of 1872 (in which the principle of contractual parity finally replaced the principle that "freight is the mother of wages"),[143] Story was the great humanizing influence on this branch of contract law.

In putting the Court on the side of common seamen, Story restrained captains and owners. Never was it more true, as Story himself put it to would-be lawyers at Harvard Law School, that "the oppressor may belong to the very circle of society in which we love to move. . . ."[144] And what was true for seamen's contracts was no less true for corporations. Indeed, even as Story was working to fashion the corporation into a practical instrument of business, he was laying the foundations of corporate fiduciary law.[145] Only one year after assuming his duties on the Court, in *Bank of Columbia* v. *Patterson's Adm'r.* (1813), Story departed from existing authorities to rule that corporations were liable for contracts not under corporate seal made by their authorized agents, a principle that made the corporate device at once more flexible and more accountable.[146] In *Bank of U.S.* v. *Dandridge* (1827), Story extended the principle further to cover obligations entered into by cashiers of banking corporations.[147] Both cases in effect established contractual duties by construction and implication, that is, by the implied-powers approach for which he was attacked so vehemently in the *Charles River Bridge* case and, in fact, the one that informed *Brown* v. *U.S.* and *Martin* v. *Hunter.*

Story also worked to hold corporations to a strict performance of contracts made with private parties. In *Wild* v. *Bank of Passamaquoddy* (1825) on circuit, he held that the cashier of a bank was prima facie the agent of the corporation with the authority to endorse its notes and otherwise manage its money in the ordinary course of business. Any restrictions on such authority without notice would not be binding on third parties—an extension of responsibility that was essential to the business operations of the bank as well as protective of those who did business with it.[148] His pioneering decision in *Wood* v. *Dummer* (1824) extended corporate contractual liability, too, by holding, as in a *cestui qui* trust, that stockholders were liable for corporate debts to the extent of the funds they received on the liquidation of the corporation.[149] To reach this decision Story borrowed creatively from equity and the old law and countered head on state decisions permitting stockholders to escape their equitable obligations. He stood his ground again in *Mumma* v. *Potomac Co.* in 1834 (the year he extended the *Dartmouth College* principle in *Allen* v. *McKean*), this time by holding that a corporation's contract survived its dissolution and that the capital stock of a dissolved corporation became a trust fund for the satisfaction of debts against the corporation.[150] Clearly the analogy of the corporation to the individual cut both ways with Story. As the editors of the *American Jurist* approvingly noticed in commenting on *Wood* v. *Dummer*: "If persons who trust these institutions are as well protected as if they trusted individuals," which was the burden of Story's opinion, "it is all that they can demand."[151]

It ought not to be imagined that Story's judge-imposed rules of business contradicted his promotional objectives. For him no less than for Benjamin

Franklin or Amos Lawrence or Obadiah Brown or John Crozier of Rockdale, morality was good for business. To hold legislatures morally and legally accountable for their promises to corporations was to provide a stable, dependable environment essential to the efficient deployment of capital. For the law to force corporations to keep their promises, and stand by the transactions of their agents, to oblige them to pay their debts, was to mold them into efficient business institutions. To prevent shippers from exploiting their labor forces was to save them from their own greed. Law, as Theodore Parker aptly put it, would "in private affairs take the place of conscience."[152]

Laissez faire was not yet the central issue. Individual enterprise set in the context of a vast and rich continent was the starting point. Law would unleash the individual when possible, restrain him when necessary. In both regards, judges rather than professional politicians and legislators should take the lead. The bench and bar, in Story's system, were not "dependent stipendiaries" to businessmen but equal partners in unleashing the forces of commerce, which would in turn strengthen the bonds of Union and raise the tone of civilization. It was a strategy that went back to the Constitutional Convention; it was the constant theme of the *Federalist Papers*. Madison and Gallatin saw the point no less than Hamilton. So did Henry Clay with his American Plan and Daniel Webster with his Whig program of economic nationalism. National journals preached the gospel of commerce and national union, as did small-town orators like Asa Child and prominent capitalists like Abbott Lawrence, who claimed that a "Rail Road from New England to Georgia would do more to harmonize the feelings of the whole country, than any amendments that can be offered or adopted to the Constitution."[153] Story's belief that what helped the textile capitalists of Boston helped the Republic was not hypocrisy or sham or conspiracy but a widely shared assumption of early national culture.

Chapter 5

New England Conservative as Constitutional Nationalist

We have all at risk . . . and we must always keep on board the ship of state, not only a competent crew to work the ship, but the most cautious and skillful, as well as the truest of the best.
Story on Daniel Webster, 1834

In the present crisis of our public affairs, it seems to me very important that every citizen should be in possession of sound views of the early & true friends of the Constitution.
Story to Willard Phillips,
27 January 1833

The chaotic period from the Panic of 1819 to the inauguration of Andrew Jackson or, more broadly, the quarter century following the War of 1812 constitutes a major watershed in American history. This period was simultaneously the end of the colonial age and the beginning of the modern one. The old regime did not, of course, collapse "all at once and nothing first," like the deacon's "one hoss shay." It vanished instead like smallclothes, silver shoe buckles, and wigs: incrementally, that is to say, with the generation that wore them. Gradualness did not ease the pain, however; nor did the advantages that change offered entirely assuage the fear of it. Indeed, change itself was not the main point so much as the intensified consciousness of it. Much that had held the early Republic together disappeared with the Treaty of Ghent. Gone most notably was the threat to national survival that had hung over the Republic since its birth. The challenge from a hostile world, be it England or France, kept alive the tradition of the American Revolution just as foreign policy issues conditioned the rhetoric and ideology of parties and postponed their confrontation with the pressing issues of modernization. If national indepenence was the goal of the American Revolution, then the Revolution ended with the Treaty of Ghent. The United States became a member in full standing of the family of nations, and the American people were free to exploit the new continent and define their national character.

Americans faced not just the continent, however; they faced themselves. What they painfully discovered was that they were fundamentally divided. The Panic of 1819 and the Missouri debates of 1820–21 drove home the message. In the midst of America's first national depression, public attention shifted to tariffs, banks, and internal improvements, then to the disputed election of 1824 and the nature of the American political system.

Above all, or rather beneath all, was slavery. Debates over these issues revealed how far Americans North and South and West had diverged as they worked out the logic of their geographical, demographic, and historical differences. The spirit of compromise, nourished by the Revolution (which made constitutional union possible), dissipated in the new struggle for political power. It was the 1790s all over again in that the American Revolution, that is, republican government and society—indeed, the character of American civilization—appeared to be at issue.

In this passionate struggle over American culture, Story was witness and actor, principal and agent. Visions of apocalypse were not new to him, of course, but now in the form of the rejuvenated forces of states' rights and democracy (in Massachusetts as well as Virginia) they took on a frightening tangibility. Out of his fear, which was intensified by personal tragedy and by a growing awareness of mortality, came a sense of renewed zeal for the *true* republic. For inspiration and guidance in this unsettled age of cultural warfare, Story, like Jefferson and Calhoun, turned to his own state and section, to New England. In this step he was joined by a like-minded, newly arisen tribe of conservatives who (partly in self-defense and partly in self-pride) defined American civilization by reference to sectional institutions and values.

These men aimed not only to preserve the Union under the Constitution but to make the nation over in the image of New England. In their battle plan New England history (written selectively), New England institutions (purged of colonial irrelevancy and Federalist excess), and New England virtue (regenerated) would rescue America from Southern states' rights democracy and the corrupting genius of Thomas Jefferson. This vision called Story to the barricades, and as he joined the conservative counterrevolution of the 1820s, he urged others to follow him. Out of this revolution, as the climax of his efforts, came his three-volume *Commentaries on the Constitution* (1833). It was Story's answer to Thomas Jefferson and the Virginia school, Calhoun and the disunionists of South Carolina. It was conservative, New England wisdom turned into constitutional history, the unfurling of the constitutional banner under which the armies of the North would finally march.

1. Autobiography, Republican History, and New England Conservatism

In many ways the 1820s, his own middle years, were the happiest of Story's life. His position as the Court's scholar in residence was firmly established, even though the dynamics of that institution shifted after 1823 with the appearance of new justices and new issues. In New England

Story made peace with the old Federalists, made new friends on and off the circuit, and worked successfully at making himself quite indispensable. Word of his accomplishments, circulated by such admirers as J. Evelyn Dennison, M.P., and Lord Stowell, justice of England's High Court of Admiralty, reached England too, so that the fame Story sought so assiduously seemed within reach. Most important, these were good years for Story's family. He and Sarah had lost four children in the eight years following 1811, but for the dozen years between the death of Caroline in 1819 and that of Louisa in 1831 they were spared that crushing grief. Louisa, their last child, was born in 1821 and survived the first dangerous years, while Mary (born in 1817) and William (1819) grew healthy and strong. Like his own father, Story was solicitous, tenderhearted, and full of spontaneous affection—and copious advice about good handwriting, the joys of learning French, and the "wonderful discoveries" of chemistry.[1]

Happy though they were for Story, these middle years also witnessed a deepening introspection, a growing sense of mortality—"a more sobered view of life," as he put it to his daughter Mary.[2] He became increasingly fearful for Sarah's health, which was especially fragile after the loss of her children and which after the death of Louisa in 1831 ended in permanent invalidism.[3] Story's own health was deteriorating too, a deterioration hurried on by his stubborn refusal to do much about it. He was fifty the year Andrew Jackson took office, and both events carried intimations of decline. Comparing the Gilbert Stuart portrait of Story in 1819 (see the frontispiece) with Chester Harding's in 1828 (see p. 72) reveals little evidence of decline, to be sure. And there is nothing in either to forecast the almost tragic visage in the daguerreotype taken shortly before his death (reproduced on p. 378). Still, the increasing complaints of exhaustion, prolonged bouts of influenza, several attacks of the "sick head ache," and a whole winter in 1826 with "no health" suggest that his chronic dyspepsia since the age of thirty-two was taking its toll.[4] Story's Washington physician prescribed an austere diet: small quantities of food and no fruits or vegetables or sweets. He was allowed no tobacco, a prohibition that gave him no problem, and only a medicinal touch of brandy and water; this latter restriction Story, with some help from his friends, translated into a regular glass or two of wine, usually watered. Story ignored the doctor's prescription of regular exercise when work got in the way, as it always seemed to do. Unfortunately, recreation for him was talking, not walking.

If the judge, as he was most often called in New England, could put aside his own health, he could not ignore the departure of youth and the passing of time. The death of old friends and family brought home the message. His wife's sister, Hester, died, and then Mrs. Daniel Webster, whom both he and Sarah mourned, and in 1823 his "beloved" brother Lieutenant Horace Cullen Story. More saddening still was the death by consumption in 1827 of his favorite sister and friend, Harriet, the wife of Stephen White.[5] "Tuneful themes," themes of youth, he wrote in "Lines for a Lady's Album," had been touched "by the sober wand of truth." Memory had a new provenance and softened "the soul to a gentler mood."[6]

Memory when it goes public becomes history, which is to say that again Story's own life paralleled national history. His introspective, retrospective inclinations sensitized him to the middle years of the Republic, to the demise of an age. The death of Jefferson and John Adams on 4 July 1826, the fiftieth anniversary of independence, warned Story and the nation that the old order was passing, but for him there were reminders closer to heart and home, not just old friends and classmates but New England heroes and statesmen from the days of the Revolution. Gone, he remembered sadly, were "Kit" Gore (Webster's teacher and friend), the irascible but kindly "Colonel" Pickering, and Judge Isaac Parker, whose friendship had transcended party animosity. Friends and compatriots outside New England were dying too: William Pinkney in 1822 and, on the Court, Brockholst Livington in 1823, Thomas Todd in 1826, and Robert Trimble, who replaced Todd, in 1828. Death hit the brethren again the next year with the passing of Bushrod Washington. "Wise, impartial, and honest," a "learned judge," "a real lover of the Constitution," Washington was Story's best friend on the Court after the chief justice. The "departure of such a man," lamented Story, meant the severing of ties with an earlier, glorious age.[7]

Story had been contemplating the lessons of that age for a decade, and they were much on his mind when he attended the inauguration of Andrew Jackson on 2 March 1829 and listened to the new president's plans for the future. The balmy southwest wind and clear sunshine that graced the occasion brought him no warmth. Following the election he thought about the significance of turning over the Republic to a military hero unschooled in the science of government. He commiserated with his old friend John Quincy Adams about the fickleness and ingratitude of the electorate, the hollowness of public service, and the decline of public virtue. The inauguration crowd, which he later described as "the highest and most polished down to the most vulgar and gross in the nation," was so boisterous that he could barely hear the address. What he did hear was thinly veiled criticism of John Quincy Adams and a promise to remove "obnoxious" government officials.[8] Jackson's words filled him with disgust and foreboding. When the president went on to kill the Second Bank of the United States, destroy the Cherokee nation in defiance of a Supreme Court decision, scrap national economic planning, and consolidate party government by implementing the spoils system—when Jacksonian Democracy unveiled itself—Story was not surprised, only saddened. He had already concluded, on inauguration day, that "the reign of King 'Mob,'" was triumphant.[9]

But why and how had the democratic "Mob" replaced the virtuous citizenry of the old republic? What was the root of the problem, the source of the crisis? Possibly the republican system itself, against which Story measured events and people, was less symmetrical, less unified, and more given to vagary and conflict than he allowed.[10] In fact, the great issues of liberty and power, democracy and aristocracy, had never been resolved. The question, therefore, was not so much what the true nature of republicanism was as who would settle the issue so that the Constitution and the nation might grapple with the new age. One could reason from the principle of popular sovereignty, attached as it was to the practice of representative government, that the people themselves should rule directly. On the other hand, the framers who set forth the doctrine of popular sovereignty distrusted the people and placed elaborate barriers between them and the actual power to govern.[11] The sovereign people spoke only in constitutional convention where, as it turned out, the aristocrats gathered to speak for them. The "continental elite" who met at Philadelphia hoped that government under the new Constitution, fortified by patterns of eighteenth-century deference, would continue to be run by men of experience, trained in history and the science of government.

Aristocracy and democracy, then, like the other compromises of the Constitution, lay in a state of unresolved tension, held together by the spirit of sacrifice and tolerance called forth by the idealism of the revolutionary experience. Jackson's election and the emergence of King Mob signified that the fragile republican balance had come undone, that the democratic potential in the Constitution had escaped the confines imposed by eighteenth-century conservatives. The "people," called into action by a newly organized political party and mobilized by a charismatic leader, had taken to heart the principle of popular sovereignty. They laid claim to the Constitution, which the old Federalists—and the new conservatives of the 1820s—claimed was their own to guard and interpret.

Had Story been more detached, he might have viewed this change as part of the natural history of republicanism, the inevitable consequence, as Ortega y Gasset would later argue, of the demographic revolution of the nineteenth century in which the masses by sheer force of numbers claimed cultural dominance.[12] But he was more an actor in history than a student of it. Although he conceded that the Constitution was a product of compromise, he had no doubt that it rested on firm principles institutionalized by statesmen and tested by experience. Nor was the problem academic. Ignorant or, worse, evil men threatened to undo the Revolution. It was not just the Jacksonians in the South and new West but the Democrats of Massachusetts and New England; it was states' rights madness sponsored by Virginia; it was party hacks and political demagogues wherever they were. And most of all, worst of all, behind all, was Thomas Jefferson.

The idea that Jefferson had turned the Revolution from its true course was hardly a new notion, of course. This was precisely what Arthur Walter and William Smith Shaw had argued; it was what John Marshall always believed; and it was the received wisdom, not to say the dominant obsession, of Federalist New England. What rekindled anti-Jefferson passion in New England and brought it home with new force to Story was the posthumous publication of Jefferson's *Memoirs* in 1829, edited by his grandson and literary executor, Thomas Jefferson Randolph.[13] The work was brought out in large part to redeem Jefferson's reputation from the assaults of his political enemies, and in fact the great man reached out from his grave to flail them with his version of American history. New England conservatives, who were busy writing their own account, were outraged. For Story, who figured uncomplimentarily in them, the publication of the *Memoirs* was a disaster of greater potential harm even than the calamitous election of Jackson. "Have you seen Mr. Jefferson's *Works*?" he inquired urgently of his friend Fay. "If not, sit down at once and read his fourth volume. It is the most precious melange of all sorts of scandals you ever read. It will elevate your opinion of his talents, but lower him in point of principle and morals not a little."[14] To Joseph Hopkinson he was even more candid about his disgust with Jefferson's "gross attack upon the public men of his day," "his attacks upon Christianity," "his unrelenting hatred of Hamilton, & his tirades against the Federalists."[15]

Story's distress is not hard to understand: Jefferson attacked his most cherished principles, his most revered heroes. Casting aside Burkean wisdom, Jefferson argued (in his famous letter to John W. Eppes of 24 June 1813) that "the earth belonged to the living, not to the dead."[16] Blackstone was "uncanonized" and the "chaos of law lore" reviled.[17] New England was downplayed and Massachusetts relegated to "degradation."[18] The Federalists were "dealt with in terms of unmeasured harshness," not only Hamilton but Pickering and Adams as well. Even Washington, whose "firm tone of mind" was "sensibly impaired by age," was pictured as the dupe of Federalist schemers.[19]

Closer to the bone yet was Jefferson's unqualified attack on the Marshall Court. Randolph edited out much of his grandfather's personal feelings about the chief justice, probably because of their virulence, but Jefferson's antijudicial sentiment was nonetheless in plain sight. The Marshall Court had hardly taken form before Jefferson branded it a Federalist "battery" from which the "works of republicanism are to be beaten down and erased."[20] The authority of *Marbury* was impugned, and charges of gross partiality were leveled against Marshall for his conduct in the Burr treason trial.[21] *McCulloch* and *Cohens* were assailed for their consolidating tendencies and for making the Constitution into "a mere thing of wax" that the justices "twist and shape into any form they please."[22] There for all to see was Jefferson's support of Spencer Roane's attack on the Court; there was Jefferson's censure of Marshall for "travelling out of his case to pre-scribe what the law would be in a moot case," his urgent plea to Justice Johnson to resist Marshall's domination of the Court by open dissent.[23] To top it off, Story, whose name was misspelled to boot, was singled out as the renegade "pseudo-republican" who single-handedly forced the repeal of the embargo.[24]

The publication of the *Memoirs* was an invitation to Story to do what he was already inclined to do and what New England had done for years: to hate Thomas Jefferson with a consuming passion. Even during his "radical" days as a Jeffersonian Republican, he had been less than enthusiastic about the president, and during the embargo crisis coolness turned to distrust. Now, with a little help from Marshall, Story was willing to blame the crisis of the 1820s on the "great Lamb of the mountains," as the chief justice named Jefferson.[25] Almost everything about the man was offensive—his vanity, his penchant for theorizing, his fluctuating principles, his love of power—but two things rankled above all else. The first was Jefferson's unqualified hatred of the Supreme Court, which for Story was tanta-mount to an attack on the Constitution itself. Connected with his anti-judicial bias and making it more dangerous was Jefferson's championship of political party. There is no extant evidence that Story heard about the new justification of political parties that emanated from Martin Van Buren's Albany Regency (a manifesto that justified professional politicians by equating service to party with love of country).[26] But he sensed the argument accurately enough and traced it to Jefferson, the arch-political demagogue.

Party, as it had been earlier, was again the bane of Story's existence, the source of his anxiety and despair about the future of the Republic. It was party that defeated President Adams's rational plan for national greatness and party that elected Andrew Jackson. Story had no personal animus to-ward the new president—in fact, knew little about him. But clearly he was not Washington, or Monroe, or Adams. He sensed that the general's success turned on slogans ("the corrupt bargain" allegation) and compro-mise (as in the new political axis between New York and Virginia Demo-crats engineered by Van Buren). Indeed, before the worst was known, Story had prophesied it. "The truth is," he wrote despondently and pre-sciently to the Reverend John Brazer on 4 February 1827 (after watching the politicians manipulate the tariff issue and defeat the Panama mission), "that the next election for the Presidency is the absorbing topic, and it is truly distressing to see how much legislation takes its color from this in-gredient." Worse still, it was not a passing or accidental thing. "I confess it is a source of melancholy and grave reflection to me, not on account of the success or failure of any candidate, but on account of the future destiny of the country, this will always be a subject of contest every few years, and that of course all the intermediate periods will be passed in efforts and excitements to defeat or aid particular candidates. A more distressing state of things could hardly occur in any republic, and least of all, in a federative republic." Henceforth, he predicted, there will be "bitter and permanent local factions," and the nation will be governed by "sacrifice and artifice." More and more he was convinced, along with Marshall, "that the Presidency is the ticklish part of our constitution. Perhaps it will prove its overthrow."[27] The judge's much-quoted observation that Jackson's election signified the reign of King Mob was more than rhetorical flourish.

Was it too late? Could the tide be turned? For all his forebodings, Story was not immobilized; he had a battle plan. He would call forth the Supreme Court to resist what party politicians had wrought. And he would meet the enemy on his own ground. Against the vacillating, short-range politics of "artifice" would stand the science of government as it was conceived by the founders. To negate the fanciful speculations of a Jefferson, Story would call on experience and history, on the ideas of Edmund Burke, whose philosophy assumed a new relevance for him and the age.[28] National interest would have to take priority over states' rights, and natural-rights ideology would have to give way to natural law. To accomplish these great objectives, virtuous leaders would be galvanized into action: Statesmen who stood above party, like Adams and Webster, would confront politicos the likes of Jefferson and Jackson. New statesmen in the image of the old ones, old truths newly refurbished, history made relevant—these things constituted the substance of Story's battle plan. The problem was not to resist historical change but to gain control of it. What Story really called for, what he worked openly and behind the scenes to create out of the chaos of the 1820s, was a conservative counterrevolution in behalf of the old republic.

To head this movement, at the helm of the conservative ship of state, Story wanted "the most cautious and skillful, as well as the truest of the best," as he put it in his anonymous encomium to Daniel Webster in the *New England Magazine*.[29] And who were these "men of talent," "men of virtue," the "truest of true" (references to which permeate Story's writings and dot the literary landscape of antebellum New England)? Rarely did anyone say exactly, and there was little need to. Soldiers of the new conservatism knew who they were. They were all those repelled by the assertive egalitarian tendencies of the 1820s; they shared a perception of New England's past glory and special mission and a view of themselves as an endangered species. New England conservatives were those who feared they had something to lose. It was a matter of "family," as one of them later put it, and family stood for tradition and a record of public service. "Four or five generations of gentlemen and gentlewomen" would do nicely, suggested Oliver Wendell Holmes, Sr., the "autocrat of the breakfast table," with a governor or two thrown in along the way, or a member of Congress, or a couple of doctors of divinity, and of course a long line of Harvard graduates.[30]

The "wise and the good" also tended to be rich or at least associated with wealth. Where the money came from—whether from real estate, commerce, banking, insurance, mercantile activity, or manufacturing—did not matter so long as the wealth was secure and honorable. Nor was it entirely clear whether status and family enhanced wealth or whether wealth bought status. What was clear was that Massachusetts in the 1820s, with Boston as its hub, developed a caste of first families who were connected by frequent intermarriage and constant interaction, who commanded immense economic power (most conspicuously, those connected with the newly founded Boston Association of textile manufacturers), who ran Harvard and most of Boston's churches, schools, and charitable institutions.[31] It was this group that Miles Coverdale sought out for conservative wisdom in Hawthorne's *Blithedale Romance*: "conservatives, the writers of 'The North American Review,' the merchants, the politicians, the Cambridge men, and all those respectable old blockheads who still, in this intangibility and mistiness of affairs, kept a death-grip on one or two ideas which had not come into vogue since yesterday morning."[32] In the 1820s they were not yet "old blockheads" but a natural and as yet inchoate elite. Story looked for them to unite in order to smash party and turn back the forces of states' rights democracy. Under their leadership New England might recapture its primacy in the Union. He put it bluntly to Webster in the early summer of 1827: "If the *national* Men do not now lay in New England a broad ground for a union among the best of all the old parties, it will be because there is a contagious Madness. Never was there a more golden opportunity."[33]

2. Joining the Wise and Good

Story not only joined Massachusetts conservatives but wished to lead them in asserting the "true spirit of New England," which he firmly believed would defeat the "Idols of party."[34] In the crucial area of constitutional law, he would speak for them to the American people. At the outset of the 1820s, however, he had as yet to establish his conservative credentials with the still-ruling Federalist establishment.[35] They remembered his early radicalism and recalled his stern enforcement of the much-hated national commercial regulations. Without commanding wealth and family name, Story had to prove his dedication and his value to the conservative cause.[36] By any reasonable criteria there should have been no problem. He had after all been true to real Federalism or, as he liked to say, to the party of Washington and Adams. He never doubted—the sure touchstone of conservative principle—that Hamilton was a great statesman. Never had he claimed that honor for Jefferson, even when he was a Jeffersonian. True, he had been a party man, but he had never hesitated to break ranks when principle or New England interests were involved. Because those interests were on the line once again, Federalists were prompted to invite him into the family. All that was needed was an occasion for him to display his conservative orthodoxy, and this came in the Massachusetts constitutional convention of 1820.

Before then, however, Story had begun to win over the opposition and open lines of communication. He had no compunction at humbling himself, either, as is clear from his confession of early errors to Harrison Gray Otis, the arbiter of Boston orthodoxy. "At the time when I first turned my thought to political subjects in the ardour of early youth," he wrote to Otis in December 1818, after waxing enthusiastic over the latter's manly efforts in the Senate, "I well remember that the sedition law was my great aversion. With the impetuosity & desire of independence so common to zealous young men, I believed it to be unconstitutional. I have now grown wiser in this, & I hope in many other respects; & for many years have entertained no more doubt of the constitutional power of Congress to enact that law, than any other in the Statute book. My present opinion has been forced upon me by reflection, by legal analogy, & by calm deliberation." Perhaps a little astonished if not embarrassed by this self-revelation, Story quickly went on to say, "You may smile at my confession, which I hope you will not call, as Mr. Randolph on another occasion did, 'a precious confession.'" But then he went on more forcefully: "The truth is & it ought not to be disguised, that many opinions are taken up & supported at the moment, which at a distance of time, when the passions of the day have subsided, no longer meet our approbation. He who lives a long life & never changes his opinions may value himself upon his consistency; but can scarcely be complimented for his wisdom. Experience cures us of many of our theories; & the results of measures often convince us against our will that we have seen them erroneously in the beginning."[37]

Whether Story's olive branch to Otis was the cause of his rapid ascension among the wise, good, and rich or merely an indication that he had already arrived and had only to be initiated is not certain. But clearly they welcomed him into their company, where he talked openly of "high conservatism"—so high, in fact, that it appeared to some to approach treason.[38] Among those in whom he could confide were the great and powerful of Massachusetts. He was a personal acquaintance of the Jacksons and Lees of Newburyport and Boston, of Colonel Thorndike and the "Merrimac Men," all of whom were leading capitalists of New England.[39] He dined with P. C. Brooks, reputedly the richest man in Massachusetts, and he was the patron of Brooks's son-in-law, Edward Everett, who proved to be one of the most articulate and active of the new conservatives.[40] Story had lawyered for the Appletons, and the Lawrence brothers were his confidants.[41] Otis was now numbered among his personal friends, as was George Ticknor, whose intellectual star was in the ascendancy. Even more productive was his working relationship and lifelong friendship with Josiah Quincy, Jr., whom Story supported for the presidency of Harvard in 1829 and who in turn used his power as president to support Story at Harvard Law School. Even Timothy Pickering, the historical curator of high Federalism, joined in welcoming Story aboard.[42]

Most revealing, perhaps, was his new friendship with John Lowell, probably the most revered of the Federalist worthies. When Story publicly defended Lowell from political calumny, the old man took him to his heart—and into the inner sanctum of respectability. Men might differ honestly on party principles, noted Lowell in his letter of thanks to Story, but honor bound them together, providing they were honorable men to start with.[43] Story was. The old wounds were healed, the old war forgotten in the new one to be waged. Lowell's was the letter that Otis, had he been more generous, might have written in 1818 in response to Story's supplication. It was a sure passport to the inner sanctum, one that Lowell explicitly invited Story to mention when convenient. Story's reply, if it was not fawning, was the ultimate in deference.[44] When Massachusetts Democrats like Attorney General Andrew Dunlap complained of Story's defection from Republicanism, when the *Boston Patriot* called public attention to Story's political apostasy, they had a point.[45]

Story's association with New England conservatives was a working alliance, not a social circle or a debating club. Its structure was informal, almost familial; in purpose it was determined and deliberate. Story was no mere figurehead. Judicial ethics or not, he became a force to reckon with. Witness, for example, his growing influence at Harvard, which, newly vitalized in the 1820s, became the intellectual nerve center of conservative ideas.[46] He was appointed to the board of overseers in 1818 (itself a signal of social status) and became a member of the corporation in 1827 (the only person to occupy both positions). In 1829 he became Dane Professor and head of the Law School. Before that, however, he took a leading part in reforming the university along with Nathaniel Bowditch (who replaced John Lowell as treasurer and business manager of the corporation) and George Ticknor (who aimed to modernize Harvard's curriculum). The object was nothing less than to make Harvard an instrument for the moral and intellectual salvation of the Republic.

Story's efforts at Harvard pleased New England conservatives. So also did his stand against the international slave trade and against the extension of slavery into the new West. He understood that judicial office required him to stand aloof from politically explosive issues, especially those like slavery which were bound sooner or later to come before the Court. He felt strongly, on the other hand, that public office did not disfranchise him as a private citizen or silence him on issues of public morality.[47] Accordingly, he spoke out forcefully against slavery at the Salem town meeting of 10 December 1819. In a speech reported approvingly in the *Salem Gazette*, he argued against any compromise that would extend slavery into Missouri or any new state on the ground that such an extension would violate the Constitution and the "principles of our free government."[48] Story also drafted the resolution, passed by the meeting and sent to Congress, that condemned slavery as a moral and political evil and that declared it "constitutional and expedient to prohibit the introduction of it into such States as may be hereafter established in any territory of the United States. . . ."[49] Story's antislavery memorial was so effective that Daniel Webster asked him to produce another for the Boston meeting, because "your facility in writing enables you to draw it up much quicker, as well as better, than any of us."[50]

Indignation against slavery and against the aggressive behavior of the South that lay behind it spilled over into Story's charges to circuit grand juries in 1819 and 1820. After the Missouri debates, Story would reluctantly agree to the compromise arranged by Henry Clay and others under the impression that the preservation of the Union required it; he was also a believer in a gradual, peaceful solution to the slavery problem. But he not only condemned the international slave trade in his charges—fought against it, as he put it to Jeremiah Mason, "*pugnis et calcibus*"—but attacked slavery itself.[51] From the charges, which were printed and circulated throughout New England, there was a direct line to his circuit opinion in *U.S.* v. *La Jeune Eugenie* (1822), which ventured far beyond existing international law to condemn the foreign slave trade as "unnecessary, unjust, and inhuman" and "repugnant to the general principles of justice and humanity."[52]

Antislavery in New England was not without its ambiguities and contradictions; nor was Story's opposition to slavery. Federalists, after all, had championed the Constitution of 1787, which legalized the "peculiar institution." And New England attacks on slavery could never entirely escape the charge of hypocrisy, because that section, though it had no slaves, had not a few shippers who profited from the slave trade. Antislavery in New England was also inextricably bound up with a paranoiac fear of the South and a fanatic hatred of Jefferson, both of which biases Story abundantly shared. There is some evidence, in fact, that Federalist attacks on slavery in the early 1820s looked to the establishment of a Northern antislavery party as a means of recovering from the debacle of the Hartford Convention.[53] Such a party would not take shape for another thirty years (too late to rescue the Federalists but useful to Northern Whigs whose raison d'être had evaporated). But there is no doubt that New England conservatives in the 1820s made the slavery issue an anvil on which they hammered out a sectional self-consciousness and a unique vision of New England destiny. There is no doubt, either, that Supreme Court justice Story's willingness to speak out, when judicial ethics might have justified silence, enhanced his status among the elite and worked to broaden their (and his) base of support.

Above all, however, it was the Massachusetts constitutional convention of 1820 that provided Story the opportunity to demonstrate his conservatism—and for Massachusetts conservatives to savor the fruits of organization. The convention was important enough for Story to take leave of his Rhode Island circuit, which he did with the permission of the Rhode Island bar.[54] Except for one week when ill health, his own and his children's, forced him to go home, he was in constant attendance during the two months the Convention was in session. What he learned during that period was the power of like-minded, well-placed conservatives, a force above party and, in Story's mind, against it. His position of authority among these men came as a result of his ranking position as Supreme Court justice. Hardly less important was the fact that he knew and was known by most of the powerful delegations from Suffolk and Essex counties. There were former Harvard classmates like Joseph Tuckerman, Samuel Wells, Leverett Saltonstall, and even his closest friend, Samuel Fay. Present was his brother-in-law Stephen White. Lawyers were in great abundance, of course, among them professional associates of Story's like Isaac Parker (chief justice of the state supreme court), Judge Charles Jackson of Boston, and his colleague on the circuit bench, federal district judge John Davis. In this group also were George Blake, his dear friend William Prescott, and his future patron Nathan Dane. And of course there was Daniel Webster, whom Story thought acquired a "noble reputation" for his leadership, one that would, with luck, carry him to the presidency.[55]

There side by side were young and old, former friends as well as former political enemies, veterans and arrivistes. Presiding over all (as George Washington presided over the convention at Philadelphia in 1787) was former president John Adams. What brought them together was the need to revise the state constitution of 1780 in light of Maine's separation. What galvanized them into a working coalition of conservatives were democratic ("radical," Story called them) demands for change that became the main agenda when the convention gathered in Boston in December 1820.

Most alarming to conservatives were democratic efforts to cut off state support for Harvard, the demand for the total disestablishment of the Congregational church, the plan to alter the basis of apportionment of the state senate from property to population (and thus to make both branches of the legislature popular), and the proposal (which frightened Story most) to alter the state constitution so as to permit the legislature to reduce judicial salaries. The battle lines were clearly drawn: At issue was nothing less than the constitution of 1780 and the entire structure of sound government erected on it—and not incidentally the continued dominance in Massachusetts politics of the commercial seaboard.[56] On one side, as Story saw it, was "a pretty strong body of radicals" supported by an even more potent class of men who were "lovers of the people, alias the lovers of popularity." Opposing them was "a strong body of sound, reflective intelligent men," firm in their patriotism and dedication to principle but also decidedly in the minority.[57] Their job, as Story described it to Bushrod Washington, was as crucial as it was difficult: "to support good principles of government & to fence in our old Institutions—religious, civil, & political—against reformers of all sorts."[58] Clearly the convention was a rehearsal for the nineteenth century.

The conservatives, Story conceded, "were for the most part on the defensive," and they failed in their own reforms, such as restructuring the state house of representatives. But they defeated the radical proposals, either on the floor of the convention or in the popular referendum that followed the convention. On the judiciary issue and Harvard College they were "triumphant."[59] Their overall success was due to several factors.[60] The disorganization of the reformers and their lack of leadership put them at a disadvantage and offset their numerical superiority. Though small in number, the conservatives were unified and knew clearly what they wanted. Taking advantage of the unwieldy size of the convention, they immediately gained control of the key committees, where they blunted the reforms before they gained momentum. The oratorical talents and expertise of men like Webster and Story could not be duplicated on the radical side; the latter also suffered from a lack of access to channels of communication, which were dominated by conservatives. Finally, there was no great ground swell of reform sentiment among the people, at least none that could be forged into a coordinated movement for constitutional restructuring.

The sparseness of the official journal of the convention and the hit-or-miss newspaper coverage of the daily proceedings make it difficult to reconstruct Story's role with any precision, particularly as he did not make notes of his own speeches. Even his decisive speech in behalf of the independent judiciary—by his own account, his greatest effort—was not reported, though it was reputed to have saved the judiciary from legislative emasculation.[61] Totally unrecoverable, too, are his efforts behind the scenes, though he tantalized historians with the assurance that he acted with Webster "in every important measure."[62] His elaborate speech defending the property apportionment of the senate has survived, however, and it captures the thoroughly conservative principles that guided him at the convention and thereafter as well.

The speech can be taken at several levels: On the practical political level it aimed to preserve the position of prominence held in the state legislature by the commercial classes of the eastern counties, the group most favored by basing senate apportionment on wealth rather than numbers. That practical concern, which of course Story could not mention (except privately to his friends), carried with it a principle that went back to Harrington's *Oceana* and forward through Locke and Burke to the framers: namely, that property was the foundation of the social order, basic to republican citizenship and inseparably connected with liberty.

Permeating Story's speech, too, at a more general level, was the fear that the masses, cut off from their past, ignorant of the science of government, and susceptible to the blandishments of demagogues, might with their new power destroy the republican fabric while trying to improve it. "The truth is that we have yet much to learn as to the nature of free governments," Story wrote to Marshall after the convention adjourned.[63] What Story learned from his experience at the convention was that Burke's conservative philosophy of change and his theory of leadership might be a corrective to the tyranny of the majority, a majority that insisted on translating popular sovereignty into the actual power to govern. Law must channel the democratic impulse. Men of wisdom and virtue, men above party, must make the law. The goal of American conservatism was not to resist change but to control it.

New England conservatives, Story was convinced from their victory in 1821, were equal to the task. Those men, in turn, learned that converted democrats had their uses. "Judge Story has been a most faithful & able champion of every right thing from beginning to end," declared Judge Parker to Harrison Gray Otis, whose idea it was to introduce "leading democrats" into the convention, "and really deserved that his former political errors should be entirely forgotten."[64] Story, as Webster observed, had greatly enhanced his reputation among the wise and good and was now a full member.[65] John Lowell's letter of admission, generous as it was, was recognition of work well done. As to *why* Story defected to neo-Federalism, no one proffered an explanation unless it was Isaac Parker, who observed to Webster that "there is no better remedy for democratic itching than a high judicial steam pressure."[66]

3. Supreme Court Justice as Conservative Activist

While Story, Webster, and company were fighting radical innovation and headstrong democracy at home, Massachusetts and New England men in Congress were doing battle in the Missouri debates over the extension of slavery in the Louisiana Purchase territory. At stake, it appeared to many, was not only the political power of Massachusetts and other New England states in the federal union but the very character of American institutions. Massachusetts no less than Southern seaboard states like Virginia and South Carolina (though for somewhat different reasons) feared decline as new western states entered the Union. The fear in New England went at least as far back as Federalist opposition to Jefferson's purchase of the Louisiana territory—the very territory over which battle lines were drawn in the 1820s. The crisis mounted after the War of 1812 with the admission of four new western states between 1816 and 1819 and the prospect of more to come. The fear was not only that slavery might find its way into the new West but, with the three-fifths clause of the Constitution in operation, that Southern power and political democracy Virginia style would gain ascendancy.

With this pervasive fear in mind, the Massachusetts convention of 1820–21 and the ground swell of antislavery sentiment in the Northeast appear to be the first battles in the sectional war and, as one scholar aptly put it, a "rehearsal for Whiggery."[67] Fear compelled the self-appointed saviors of New England to distill conservative wisdom from New England history, rally the section to its own best tradition, and, of course, consolidate conservative leadership. New England, thus refreshed and marching behind sectional wise men, would regain its rightful role in the councils of the government and save the Republic and the Constitution from the democratic ravings and states' rights theorizing of Southern slaveholders. Simplistic and reductionist it surely was, and highly emotional. But Story and others viewed the cultural landscape of the 1820s in precisely this way. Ironically, it was on this sectional perception of American history that Story would erect his great edifice of constitutional nationalism.

Success required the mobilization of the elite who would fashion the program of conservative activism and carry the word to the people. But there were problems here, among the most important of which was a strong and well-placed phalanx of old Federalists who looked resolutely backward to the good old days. But the good old days were, in fact, not that idyllic. Massachusetts Federalists since the time of John Adams had a record of division over substantive policy matters and political tactics, not to mention generational conflicts and personality clashes (as between the Adamses, father and son, and Timothy Pickering and the high Federalists).[68] Hanging over their heads as the most serious obstacle to recovery in the 1820s was the specter of the Hartford Convention, which their enemies used to brand the whole party as provincial and disloyal. Before conservatives in Massachusetts and New England could mobilize, Massachusetts Federalists would have to heal their internal divisions (most noticeably that between John Quincy Adams and the party), erase the stigma of the Hartford Convention, and shrug off the habiliments of doom and gloom left by the likes of Fisher Ames. From the troubled history of

Federalism they would have to salvage a unified philosophy of governance and adjust it to a society in rapid transformation in which banks, corporations, and tariffs, rather than war and peace, were the key issues. This they would have to do without becoming a political party outright and in such a way as to convince the people, whom they did not really trust, and the rest of the country, which did not trust them.

Story's total contribution to the solution of these problems cannot be fully known. It is lost in the privacy of strategy conferences, in burned letters, and in his obvious reluctance to come out in the open with activities that would readily be perceived as partisan and unjudicial. Enough is known, however, to verify the importance of his role. He hit the speakers' trail in behalf of New England virtue and as we shall see was the great spokesman for constitutional law and order New England style. He also used his considerable influence, at the risk of public rebuke, to patch up internecine Federalist quarrels, rally conservatives, place them in power, and get their ideas to the people. Most particularly, he worked closely with Daniel Webster (as he admittedly did in the Massachusetts convention and secretly had done in the *Dartmouth College* case) on the grand strategy of "amalgamation." Indeed, knowledgeable politicians like Rudolph Bunner and Gulian Verplanck of New York concluded that John Quincy Adams was in "the arms of Webster—Story—of the eastern Federalists rising up with new names and most of their old prejudices. . . ."[69]

Getting Federalists back into power was not an easy chore.[70] Although they were still strong on the state level, at least in Massachusetts, they had increasingly been proscribed from national office after the demise of the national party in 1816. The objective of amalgamation was to bring them back. The plan was to get John Quincy Adams elected in 1824 and re-elected in 1828 and then to persuade him to appoint Federalists (many of whom were critics of him and his father) to positions of national importance. Webster, who had used his influence in the disputed election of 1824 to give Adams the presidency, was to be the key broker in this process, as well as the main beneficiary. Not only would New England men— and with them Federalist principles—return to politics, but Webster would become the logical heir apparent to the presidency when Adams laid down the mantle in 1832.

Unfortunately, the success of this scheme turned on President John Quincy Adams. It was one thing to be antiparty, as he assuredly was, another to be self-righteously above politics and oblivious of political reality, as he also was. Then there was Adams's implacable hatred of the old Federalists and their contempt for him. This mutual animosity surfaced with a new virulence in 1824 with the publication by Timothy Pickering of *A Review of the Correspondence between the Honorable John Adams, Late President of the United States, and the Late William Cunningham*, which impugned the elder Adams for his resistance to high Federalism and the younger for his cowardly defection from the Federalist party. The ensuing argument, which J. Q. Adams entered with passionate zeal, led unavoidably to a heated debate over the Hartford Convention, which Adams condemned as disunionist.

Open warfare among the truest of the best over the very issue that had to be expunged from New England history called Story into action as peacemaker. His efforts were private and discreet, as he understood the dangers of dabbling openly in politics. From Marshall's appointment to the Court in 1801 and even before, there had been a barrage of criticism from the Jeffersonians about the Federalist bias of the judiciary. Within living memory one Supreme Court justice had been impeached on just such political grounds. As a leading consolidationist on the Court, Story was already suspect, especially among former political allies, who looked upon him as a defector. John Marshall, having taken some early lumps himself, subtly and humorously cautioned his friend to lie low.[71] Story agreed, at least in principle. As a justice he was, as he confessed to General Dearborn following his participation in the state convention, "obliged to avoid political writings." But, he added, "I intend to state to all our friends, my views in the most decided manner."[72] Those views—formulated by digesting copious quantities of current political writing (including several newspapers each day) and by consultation with leading politicians—followed the contours of New England interest. Like Webster, who was his chief informant, Story came late to the protective tariff, but he was an early supporter of Clay's American Plan and the program of planned national promotive legislation put forward by Adams that included federally sponsored internal improvements, a national bank, and a national bankruptcy act (which Story had already drafted and which Webster urged Congress to adopt). These would be the policy foundations of the Whig party, to which Story would later profess loyalty, but in the 1820s, they were, at least in Story's mind, principles above party. As he put it: "I seem to myself simply to have stood still in my political belief, while parties have revolved around me; so that, although of the same opinions now as ever, I find my name has changed from Democrat to Whig, but I know not how or why."[73]

Whether Story could support men and measures in the 1820s without supporting party was questionable even if he did so in the name of principle. The effort brought him close to, if it did not take him over, the precipice of judicial impropriety, even by the more lax professional standards of the early nineteenth century. That he took the chance is a measure of his conviction that a turning point in history was at hand—that, as he said, "all was at risk."[74] He acted, too, on the conviction, so dear to Hamilton, that men should march in front of events. Those men, Story passionately believed, should be men above party trained in the science of government, and to that end he mounted a one-man campaign to mobilize conservative statesmen.

Had Story done no more than lend his name to the cause of New England conservatism, he would have served it well. Models were crucial in the competition for public support, and as a Supreme Court justice Story was ideal. He was in plain fact the kind of statesman he admired, that is to say, a talented, dedicated public servant with a known record of independence from party. His position on the Supreme Court, even while it involved him in an ethical dilemma, gave him not only great prestige but real power, including a most useful source of patronage. His circuit duties, as we have seen, put him at the center of New England society. Story was a logical peacemaker among warring politicians, then, and a natural model for aspiring statesmen. Some, like young Edward Everett—conservative orator, publicist, politician, and future president of Harvard—openly relied on Story's support and encouragement.[75] There were undoubtedly many more young men like Sam Whitcomb, Jr., who emulated the great man without having met him.[76]

Story was not just a model for sound statesmen; he actively recruited and supported them. His most telling efforts took place at Harvard Law School, but his position on the Court gave him opportunities that he used freely. He was, for example, able to retain his old Harvard classmate (and newfound conservative ally) William Smith Shaw as clerk of the circuit court. As reporters on the first circuit he hired John Gallison (his former law-office student); Charles Sumner (whom he groomed to replace him at Harvard Law School and, he hoped, on the Supreme Court itself); and his own son, William (who seemed destined to follow in his father's conservative legal footsteps). It was Story's influence more than any other, perhaps, that accounted for the appointment of Richard Peters to the Supreme Court reportership when Henry Wheaton resigned in 1827. Story aided and encouraged Peters in his work and shared with him a deeply rooted and frankly expressed conservatism.[77]

Story treated his reporters as professional colleagues in the cause of scientific law and comrades in the dissemination of conservative truth through legal science. This was true, too, of his colleagues at the Law School, Asahel Stearns, who died in 1833, and Simon Greenleaf, who replaced him. Greenleaf had throughout the 1820s, in fact, been the beneficiary of Story's friendship and supportive attention.[78] In this respect he was one of a large group of promising legal statesmen and educators that included David Hoffman, Willard Phillips, Timothy Walker, Charles Sumner, George Hillard, Peleg Chandler, and Richard H. Dana, Jr. Story's helping hand was extended in plain friendship, but also in the conviction that good law disseminated by good men was the foundation and the salvation of republican society. This belief motivated Story's strenuous and successful effort to place Joseph Hopkinson on the federal District Court for the Eastern District of Pennsylvania.[79] It was behind his effort to make Jeremiah Mason of New Hampshire a federal circuit judge, which failed when circuit reforms sponsored by Webster (again with Story's advice) faltered. Mason, one of New England's greatest common lawyers and one of those "sound" conservatives whose company Story liked to keep, had to settle for branch director of Biddle's Second Bank of the United States in Portsmouth, New Hampshire, an appointment that Story in all likelihood supported.

And on it goes. There are numerous patronage letters among the scattered Story manuscripts. Most of them were requests for Story's support in soliciting political office of one sort or another, some important, others not. Story's replies are not generally available, but the constant flow of requests and Story's well-known generosity in helping friends suggest that he often responded favorably. There can be no doubt that he did so with an eye to putting men of talent and conservative principles into public service.

There was nothing improper about his recruiting efforts, though his extraordinary support of Hopkinson, Mason, and Peters appeared excessive to some. Of more questionable propriety was his collaboration with Webster, first as co-worker in the amalgamation strategy and then as private political and legal consultant. Story's primary role in amalgamation, aside from general planning sessions with Webster (to which Bunner referred in his previously quoted letter to Verplanck), was in the effort to make peace between President Adams and the old Federalists in Massachusetts. The need to reelect Adams in 1828 alone should have been sufficient to heal the breach, but the sparks of controversy kindled by the Cunningham correspondence in 1824 had burst into flames, only to be fanned hotter by gleeful Virginia Democrats. Adams's response to the slurs on himself and his father was to charge his accusers publicly with secessionist tendencies. At this point William Giles—Adams's old nemesis from Virginia—who had been quoted in the Cunningham correspondence as the source of the charge that Massachusetts Federalists had plotted disunion during the embargo crisis, revealed that John Quincy Adams himself had been his source. Adams could not resist this Democratic bait. In defense of his earlier statement, he now contended that such a Federalist plot had in fact existed; his contention then gave Giles the chance to claim that Adams exposed the plot to further his own political ambition—which was pretty much what Timothy Pickering had been saying all along. When leading New England Federalists demanded that Adams prove his charges or withdraw them, the fat was in the fire.[80]

Indeed, the fire was probably burning out of control when Story attempted to stamp it out. But even if 1828 was lost (and that was not certain) there remained the need for unity, if not love, among New England conservatives. Story was suited to encourage it. He was above low politics; he had a reputation for fairness and objectivity and a personality that was warm and generous. He had himself put aside past quarrels and had made peace with the old Federalists, the very ones (like H. G. Otis, William Prescott, Timothy Pickering, Israel Thorndike, and Isaac Parker) who now demanded an accounting from Adams. Story, moreover, was one of the few people whom Adams trusted and respected. They had fought the embargo struggle on the same side and both had paid a price: Story by gaining the enmity of Jefferson and fellow Republicans and Adams by alienating the high Federalists. Story agreed with Adams's scheme for national planning (for which the Marshall Court's constitutional decisions had laid the legal foundation), and he admired Adams for his support of the Supreme Court. They joined in a deep-seated suspicion of Southern expansion, and they were of one mind, too, on the evil of political parties.

It was with a sense of shared experience and values, then, that Adams turned to Story for consolation after the bitter defeat in 1828. He also asked Story to read and criticize his reply to New England Federalists, his final accounting, so to speak. When Story obliged he must surely have realized that this was the last chance to bring the warring parties together. His letter was a model of tact. He tried to assuage the president's offended pride, lower his high dudgeon, assure him that his reputation was safe. In short, he did everything but warn Adams outright that a further reply was destructive, that it played into the hands of the enemy.[81] Adams backed off, but mutual bitterness and distrust smoldered on. Keeping Federalists from setting the historical record straight was like asking Timothy Pickering to put the Hartford Convention behind him, which was like holding back a hurricane tide off Sewall's Point.

Amalgamation died (if it ever lived) with Jackson's victory in 1828, along with the hope that a nonparty man might occupy the presidency. The crusade to place New England conservatives in government, of course, continued. For his part, Story fought the battle from Harvard Law School, in continued private patronage efforts, and, most conspicuously, in furthering the career of Daniel Webster, who emerged from the 1820s as the great hope of conservative New England. The working alliance between Story and Webster was as natural as it was singular.[82] Both men aspired to true greatness; both framed their ambition in terms of the Revolution and tied it to the rising fortunes of the Republic. Yet both were New Englanders who would guide that Republic with New England wisdom and policy. They were thrown together by common commitment to the law, by regular associations as judge and lawyer both in Washington and in New England. Their personalities meshed as did their genius. Friendship, a common profession, shared aspirations, and joint fears informed their working alliance, which both perceived to be a last-ditch struggle for republicanism. The full scope of this relationship is lost to historians in confidential consultations, in private conversations over Madeira in the libraries of the wise and good, and in the Story letters Webster destroyed.[83] Still, enough remains to mark the alliance as one of the most extraordinary in American law and politics.

Story was an artesian well of legal information, a boon for lawyers who practiced before him (as William Wirt once observed), for those who knew him, and indeed even for those who did not but were bold enough to write for help. Such requests for information and advice peppered his correspondence, and these came from the famous as well as the obscure, from neophytes and veterans, from state and federal judges, and even from Chief Justice Marshall. More than anyone else, however, Webster "was in the habit of drawing" from Story's "deep and copious well of legal knowledge," as Theodore Parker put it.[84] Story skirmished in aid of Webster "upon the Enemy's out posts" in the Massachusetts convention.[85] Thereafter he stood ready to supply what help he could discreetly give—as, for example, in implementing Webster's amalgamation scheme. On more than one occasion, too, Story served as political speech writer, "the Jupiter Fluvius from whom Mr. Webster often sought to elicit peculiar thunder," as Parker again quaintly put it.[86] In all likelihood the two men consulted about Webster's reply to Senator Robert Y. Hayne (which Story looked on as "a vindication of New England"),[87] and there can be little doubt that Story responded to Webster's request for constitutional arguments to answer Jackson's veto of the bank: "Give me in a letter of three pages a close & conclusive confutation, in your way, of all its nonsense in this particular," Webster begged. "It will take you less than half an hour."[88] Among Story's letters to Webster, in addition, was a detailed legal and political argument against the president's power of removal of the deposits from the Bank of the United States and on the illegality of depositing public funds in state banks, an argument that made its way into the senator's speech in reply to Jackson's protest against his censure by the Senate.[89] As secretary of state Webster continued to consult Story: in regard to knotty problems of international law and on key sections of the treaty being negotiated with England over the disputed boundary between Maine and Canada.[90]

There was nothing improper in Story's supporting Webster in his negotiations with England, though the latter garnered some laurels in the process that were not entirely his. It was also accepted practice that Webster should rely on Story's drafting ability, as he did in joint efforts to secure a national bankruptcy act and reform the criminal code. More questionable was Story's political advice to Webster, as, for example, when he told him "very frankly" to run for the Senate. Highly questionable was Story's helpful hand in the *Dartmouth College* case, wherein he advised Webster on the strategy of litigation, agreed beforehand to facilitate that strategy by sending up the cognate cases on a pro forma division, and circulated Webster's argument among his professional friends with an imprimatur of approval.[91]

What contemporaries thought of the Webster-Story collaboration cannot be discerned because few were aware of it at all, and none realized its full scope. What Story and Webster thought is even more inaccessible, although Webster's refusal to make public Story's letters speaks forcefully to the point. Webster, one of the great "users" of the age, clearly benefited the most from having at his beck and call such a great legal mind. But Story also profited from the alliance, because it gave him inside information and access to the highest circles of political power both in New England and in Washington, as well as a ready outlet for his cherished political ideas and legislative projects. If he helped Webster rise to power, so much the better.

Story, to put the matter plainly, was willing to play politics in order to kill political parties. Contradictory it certainly was, but no more so than were American politicians of the previous three decades who berated parties while organizing them.[92] As early as 1820 Story marked Webster as a future president[93] and, at the same time, a man above party; a statesman, not a politician. This antiparty theme was the underlying message of his "Statesmen—Their Rareness and Importance: Daniel Webster," published anonymously in the *New England Magazine* in August 1834, in time to boost Webster for the coming presidential contest. This campaign biography—along with his eulogies of departed comrades in the law, with his moving testimony to the statesmanship of John Marshall,[94] with his patronage efforts—was part of Story's effort to educate the masses about the distinction between statesmen and politicians.

4. New England Sectionalist: Constitutional Nationalist

Not many listened to Story and his friends, and they plainly failed to turn back the Democratic course of American politics. New England conservatives, to be sure, did gain a beachhead in enemy territory. Harrison Gray Otis and Josiah Quincy, Jr., governed Boston for most of the 1820s, and the latter particularly demonstrated the compatibility of conservative leadership and democratic politics. Edward Everett, with Story's encouragement, went to Congress and served as governor of the state before he was overwhelmed by the Democratic tide. In such men as Nathaniel Silsbee, Abbott Lawrence, Nathan Appleton, Leverett Saltonstall, and Robert C. Winthrop (all of whom were close friends of Story), Massachusetts kept conservatives in national office; and of course Senator Daniel Webster continued until his death in 1852 as a formidable champion of New England capitalism. Webster failed to capture the presidency, however, though he spent his lifetime trying and in the process turned himself more and more into the kind of political animal that both he and Story condemned. The Whig party that Webster presumed to lead, moreover, hesitated between old-fashioned elitism and politics in the style of Martin Van Buren.[95] Consequently, it died aborning, leaving the field to Democrats or to conservatives who, in order to gain power, behaved democratically.

The democratization of the American polity would turn Story increasingly to judges and lawyers as the conservative counterweight to the tyranny of the majority, as we shall soon see. But New England conservatives, qua conservatives, had not yet given up in the 1820s and 1830s. Before they capitulated to hard cider and log cabins, before Webster gave way to William Henry Harrison in 1840, they had a point to make. In a surge of speechifying, preaching, and writing generated by anxiety, conservative intellectuals—probing the history of New England and the role of New England in the Revolution—stated the case for New England wisdom. New England, in short, was behaving like the Old South, and Massachusetts, like Virginia, was leading the way. Paranoia founded in real social and economic differences compelled each section to justify itself and define nationalism in its own terms, and therefore each expropriated the tradition of the Revolution as its source of legitimacy. To call the Northern effort in the 1820s cultural propaganda or conscious myth making is to reduce the complexities of cultural dialogue and to take the meaning out of myth, which, as Ernst Cassirer taught us long ago, functions only when it is believed. New England intellectuals—whether historians like George Bancroft, orators like Edward Everett, chroniclers like Timothy Dwight, or lawmakers like Joseph Story—believed deeply. Sincerity and not a little truth infused the sectional vision of the good life that they fashioned and disseminated to meet the challenge of the 1820s. Against Jefferson's republic of independent yeomen they pitted a commercial utopia made moral by an infusion of New England values. Story's program for moral economic progress through law, as already noted, fitted perfectly into this romantic mold.

New England messianism was of course not new. It went back to John Winthrop's *Arbella* sermon and to Cotton Mather's *Magnalia Christi Americana* (which Story consulted for his speech on the Puritans over the objections of his wife, who found Mather "incorrigibly dull & credulous"),[96] and forward to the cultural jeremiads of high Federalists frightened into action by the French Revolution abroad and the Jeffersonian one at home. But never had sectionalism been so broadly and purposefully defined and so voluminously articulated as in the 1820s.[97] The occasion was a series of bicentennial celebrations of the founding of New England towns—from Plymouth in 1819 (which called forth Daniel Webster) to

Salem in 1829 (where Story did the oratorical honors). In the ten years between were other bicentennial settlement celebrations, numerous patriotic moments, and political crises that invited New England to explore its past, define its character, and assess its future in the Union. When Tocqueville claimed in the 1830s that "the civilization of New England has been like a beacon lit upon a hill, which, after it has diffused its warmth immediately around it, also tinges the distant horizon with its glow," he captured the heuristic message of the previous decade.[98] Emerson made the point in his journal when he noted that "about 1820, the Channing, Webster, and Everett era began, and we have been bookish and poetical and cogitative since."[99]

New England conservative intellectuals in the 1820s did what they did best: talked and wrote in self-praise. Webster, who saw the issue in 1815, led the way: first with his "Discourse Delivered at Plymouth" (December 1820) and later with, among others, an even more glorious outpouring at Bunker Hill (where he talked in 1825 to an estimated group of one hundred thousand). Culminating a decade of speechmaking was, of course, his great debate with Senator Hayne of South Carolina, in which he lifted up New England while putting down Southern states' rights. Spurred on by his desire to emulate Webster, Edward Everett entered the fray in 1824 with his speech in praise of New England life at Plymouth (which Story called a "triumph").[100] Two years later, in "American Constitutions," he pronounced a conservative benediction on the deaths of Jefferson and Adams on 4 July 1826.[101] Story's friend and Harvard classmate William Ellery Channing took up the chant in his 1830 election-day sermon to Governor Levi Lincoln and the Massachusetts legislature. In it he tied together the tradition of New England religion (which Story had begun to explore) with New England commercial ideology, a theme that would gain momentum before its culmination in the Civil War.[102] In this genre of New England writ large Josiah Quincy, Jr.'s, "An address to the Citizens of Boston" should also be listed.[103] And this is only a sampling. From platforms and pulpits across New England, in election-day sermons, in local celebrations of patriotic events, more modest orators picked up the themes set forth by the conservative speechifiers.[104]

Equally impressive was the incredible outpouring of printed works in the 1820s on New England biography, history, and culture. Many of the speeches were printed and circulated in pamphlet form, as were a spate of original essays on New England. Some (including Story's) appeared in leading sectional periodicals of general circulation like Everett's *North American Review* (begun in 1815) and the *New England Magazine* (begun by Joseph T. Buckingham and his son Edwin in 1831). Among the first of several large works on New England to be published in the 1820s was William Tudor's *Letters on the Eastern States*, which, to Story's great delight,[105] appeared in serial form in the *Boston Daily Advertiser* before it was printed as a book in 1821. In 1820 appeared the third edition of *A Compendious History of New England* and the next year the first volume of Timothy Dwight's impressive four-volume *Travels in New England and New York*. Dozens of lesser efforts complemented these grand oeuvres, and this is not to mention numerous studies of New England heroes. The dominant theme of this avalanche of print was the uniqueness of New Englanders: their special enterprise, the transforming miracle of their commerce, their love of order, and their genius for self-government. It was Whig history, what New England's great historian George Bancroft (again with Story's aid and encouragement) would extract from the American colonial period.[106]

Story was an enthusiast for New England uplift. He deeply loved the American nation, but he got his ideas of what *kind* of nation it was and should be from family, home, schooling, friends. The vision was personal, as intense as his own experience of living. Accordingly, he made marriage and family the cornerstones of republican society, and they were all the more precious because of their fragility.[107] Religion sustained by the close-knit family was also part of Story's good republican society. Since his conversion at Harvard College he had been, as he confessed, a "decided Unitarian"—the religious persuasion that neatly fused New England's social elite with the Massachusetts intellectual establishment.[108] He attended church regularly, even when in Washington, where along with John Quincy Adams he went to hear the Reverend Mr. Little, and he served several terms as president of the American Unitarian Association. Unitarianism for him was a belief in "the divine mission of Christ, the credibility and authenticity of the Bible, the miracles wrought by our Saviour & his apostles & the efficacy of his precepts to lead men to salvation."[109] Like other Christians, he believed in the "divine authority" of the Scriptures; unlike them he disbelieved in the Trinity. But he believed that Christ was the son of God, "that he was a special messenger of God" who came to teach God's word. He disliked "cant & formal ordinances" and preferred "unaffected piety & above all religious charity."[110]

Story's Unitarianism, in short, was quintessentially New England; it fitted him like a glove and permeated his thinking about law and society. Its liberal view of salvation appealed to his romantic idealism, which he never, even with his growing antipathy to political democracy, shrugged off. Its decorum fitted his deep concern for social order, which he increasingly feared for in the 1820s. Unitarian emphasis on a learned clergy—on ministers who would "think & speak for themselves, & expound truth with a clear and manly frankness"—corresponded with his faith in the articulate "speaking aristocracy."[111] Reason was balanced with faith. Life in this world was addressed; life in the next assured. It was a faith he turned to when his children died; it was a reservoir of public values suitable to the crisis of the 1820s.

Story drew on those ideas publicly in 1828 in his speech on the founding of Salem, which, along with the efforts of Everett and Webster, ranks with the best of New England exclusivist oratory.[112] In the Salem address he distilled what was vital from New England Calvinism, a familiar undertaking of New England Renaissance writers like Emerson, Thoreau, and Hawthorne. More to the point, he captured the essential fusion between religious morality and the genius of New England enterprise and New England social order. His was a Burkean vision of New England, with its deep religious traditions; its hardy, moral people; its small towns and busy seaports; its great metropolis and noble university. It was this sectional vision of the good society that Story saw from the slopes of the Mount Auburn Cemetery as he dedicated New England ground to New England people.[113] Like Burke, Story celebrated "prejudice"; the prejudice of New England was for liberty.

New England propagandists laid special claim on the American Revolution, a claim that justified them in imposing New England ways on the rest of the nation. Indeed, New England resembled the nation at large, with its ocean; its mountains, plains, and rivers; its capital; its history. Geography as well as history invited New England conservatives to impose their filiopietistic version of republican society on the American people. To this end, Story and his friends worked to salvage what was best and wisest, most enduring and most universally applicable, from New England history. New England religion purged of intolerance (as in Story's Salem speech), New England Federalism purged of provincialism, New England history purged of misconstruction, would bolster the American republic of liberty. New England commerce and manufacturing would sinew liberty with power. And presiding over all was the Constitution. But it, too, had to be cleansed of democratic gloss and rescued from the misconstructions of states' rights theorists.

5. Liberty and Union through Law: New England History and Story's *Commentaries on the Constitution*

Looking back over American history through the critical eyes of his hero Thomas Jefferson, Vernon Parrington fell upon Story's *Commentaries on the Constitution*, begun in 1829 and finished in 1833. That work, Parrington concluded, with a touch of the disdain he lavished on Cotton Mather, was "steeped" in the spirit of the common law: Blackstone distilled by Story. Its "bias" was "Tory"; its backbone "the work of Hamilton and Marshall supplemented by a host of decisions by Federalist Judges."

It was loaded history, "crabbed and narrow legalism," nothing but a "new-modeled Federalism, adapted to changing conditions" (a charge Story would surely have taken as a compliment). Parrington did concede that the work contained "a common-sense realistic political philosophy" and admitted, ruefully to be sure, that it was the "triumph of the lawyer over the historian and political philosopher"—"the beginning of the lawyer's custodianship of the fundamental law."[114] Story, it would seem, was as influential as he was partisan.

Parrington's tone was mean, his praise grudging, his argument unsupported by evidence. But his view that Story's work was part of the New England effort to undo Jefferson's hold on America was exactly on target. Story's *Commentaries* grew out of his lectures as Dane Professor at Harvard Law School, a position he assumed in 1829. The book did not escape entirely the academic, lecture format from which it sprang. But Harvard Law School was itself a combatant in the great struggle for constitutional nationalism and New England conservatism. Its students were to be cadre in the struggle for true principles, legal statesmen to counter professional politicians. The *Commentaries* were ammunition for these shock troops of conservatism. The work was not only the most influential statement of constitutional nationalism made in the nineteenth century; it was also the climax and most telling achievement of the New England conservative counterrevolution of the 1820s.

Story the commentator was Story the teacher was Story the New England conservative nationalist who for ten years had been fighting at the barricades. Armageddon, he firmly believed, was at hand as he wrote his *Commentaries*. This work was, as Parrington said, infused with the spirit of the common law, but it sprang from an anxiety-ridden sectional self-awareness that went back at least to the embargo crisis when he and Bacon first grasped the sectional realities of American politics. Story praised Southern statesmen, to be sure, lawyers like Hugh Legaré of South Carolina and politicians like Henry Clay and even John Calhoun during his nationalist phase. Washington and Marshall, Southerners both, were his heroes and model statesmen. It was Southern thinking encouraged by New England timidity that he feared.[115] Convinced that Virginia was bullying and bluffing its way to national dominance, he urged New England to rise to its own and the nation's defense. By 1828 the issue had "come to the sheer point, whether the South shall govern the East, now & forever."[116]

The battleground in this sectional struggle, it was clear, would be the law and the Constitution. The Southern attack on the Marshall Court—led by Virginia, spurred on by Jefferson—made that clear by the early 1820s, if not sooner. What drove home that message for Story with special intensity and what broadened the judicial issue into a broad-gauge argument over the relationship of society and law was Jefferson's assertion that Christianity was not a part of the common law. Jefferson's long-held views on the matter were made public in 1824 when his letter to John Cartwright, the English radical, was published in the *Boston Daily Advertiser*. Jefferson not only vehemently denied that Christianity was part of the common law but traced the notion to an alleged mistranslation in Sir Henry Finch's *Common Law* (1613). It was in fact not an accident, alleged Jefferson, but a "Judicial forgery," part of "a conspiracy . . . between Church and State," and he dared any lawyer to prove differently.[117]

He had baited the bear in his own den. Edward Everett called Story's attention to Jefferson's letter: Both agreed that it was malicious and that it had to be answered.[118] Already in *Terrett* v. *Taylor* in 1815, Story had confronted the rising forces of secularism by nullifying Virginia's statute confiscating Episcopal property within the state.[119] At the Massachusetts constitutional convention he and other conservatives had successfully fought back the disestablishment movement in their own state. Story did not believe that the state could impose religion on its citizens.[120] Neither should it favor one sect over another (and in Massachusetts he worked to deny privileged status to Congregationalists). Like his father he was a champion of religious toleration, a point he made abundantly clear in his speech "History and Influence of the Puritans" on 18 September 1828.

But he also believed—and it was a central tenet of New England conservative ideology—that states should "foster and encourage the Christian religion generally, as a matter of sound policy as well as of revealed truth."[121] Like Burke and Lyman Beecher (who was working at this time to form a political party based on Christianity), Story had concluded that religion was the foundation of a stable, moral society. This was the Burkean gist of his argument with Jefferson, which he carried on in his inaugural address as Dane Professor in 1829, in the *American Jurist* of April 1833, and indirectly in the blasphemy trial of Abner Kneeland in the Massachusetts Supreme Court, where the prosecution based its case against Kneeland on Story's scholarship.[122] It was not that the state should make Abner Kneeland believe in Christianity but that the state, through the common law, had to protect Christianity and Christian society from him. As in laissez faire economics, the state should promote the religious beliefs of individuals, for, no less than property rights, they were the foundation of republican social order. Nowhere was the matter more plainly and forcibly put than in Story's letter to the Reverend Jasper Adams, whose sermon on the desirability of governmental support of Christianity was widely circulated. "My own private judgment has long been (& every day's experience more & more confirms me in it) that government cannot exist without an alliance with Religion *to some extent*, & that Christianity is indispensable to the true interests & solid foundation of all government." As for Jefferson's "egregious error" on the matter and the equally dogmatic statements of his friend Dr. Thomas Cooper: "It is due to truth, & to the purity of the law, to unmask their fallacies." [123]

If religion imparted morality to the law, it was clear that the law had to stand forth in defense of religion and civilization. By 1829, when Story began his *Commentaries on the Constitution*, there was a crisis in both. Jefferson's *Memoirs*, which vilified the Marshall Court and further attacked the common law, had hit the press; Andrew Jackson was in office; and the states' rights contagion spawned by Virginia had spread to South Carolina, where John C. Calhoun translated Jeffersonian theory into a plan of action, a plan that with some modification Senator Hayne would announce to the nation in his famous debate with Webster in January 1830. By November 1832, when Story's *Commentaries* were going to press, South Carolina, acting on Calhoun's theory, met in state convention to nullify the tariffs of 1828 and 1832. Secession and war seemed the next step as Senator Hayne, now Colonel Hayne, assumed command of state troops with the promise to defend the interests of South Carolina against all comers. "Words," as Story observed, "have in the soberest sense, become things." [124]

So had they also for him. However "technical" or "legalistic" his *Commentaries* appear to modern critics like Parrington, they were meant for action. Constitutional law, as Edward Everett noted in the *North American Review*, had left the schoolroom and the lawyer's study to "become— as it were—an element of real life." With Story, the "Constitution had been obliged to leave its temple and come down from the forum, and traverse the streets." [125] Let us admit that the *Commentaries* were biased toward nationalism and concede that Story's history was one-sided and in some respects as metaphysical as the states' rights school he criticized for its metaphysics—as when it made sovereignty unequivocally descend on the American people in 1776. Yes, the work is flawed by a lack of symmetry and by an excessively florid style. By modern standards it looks like a great beached whale; but in the nineteenth century it swam majestically in the raging seas of constitutional disputation.

Story shaped his book to do the job at hand, leaving structure to follow function and aesthetics and the niceties of style to fend for themselves. He went for the jugular of states' rights ideology and theory, which he treated openly as the work of selfish, shortsighted, and ignorant men. Against them he mobilized history as rewritten by New Englanders and law, the very marrow of his life. Two major strands of Southern states' rights arguments felt the brunt of his attack: The first to take shape, the corrupt well from which Southern contagion flowed, was the theory of dual sovereignty developed mainly by the Virginia school. [126] Among its ablest theoreticians were John Taylor of Caroline County (whose idea that there could be "new views" of the Constitution drove Story into a Burkean rage)[127] and St. George Tucker (whose comments on the Constitution in his 1803 edition of Blackstone's *Commentaries* drew Story's particular wrath). Spencer Roane was Story's main judicial antagonist until his death in 1822; Thomas Ritchie, with his Richmond *Enquirer*, was the key journalist for the Virginia school, as John Randolph was its principal orator. Behind them all, urging them on in their Union-destroying work, Story firmly believed, was Thomas Jefferson, the source not only of the democratic heresy but of the states' rights one as well. Alongside Jefferson and the Richmond Junto, amplifying and expanding their doctrines, were the South Carolina nullifiers, the product of a decade of economic decline and racist paranoia.[128] Calhoun was their main theorist, Hayne their famous orator, and the South Carolina legislature their most forceful advocate.

Story knew the Virginia school all too well for its unrelenting assault on the Marshall Court. More idealistic, egalitarian, and political than their Southern friends, the Virginians emphasized dual sovereignty and hypothesized a limited national government circumscribed by an unassailable body of state power, which they claimed was being subverted by judicial sapping and mining. Calhoun supplied the specific remedy for their grievance. Emphasis on dual sovereignty was dropped and the theory put forth that sovereignty was indivisible and that it resided from the moment of independence in the states. From this assumption came the corollary that the Constitution was a compact among sovereign states. Nullification was simply the method by which states as parties to the constitutional contract sought to renegotiate it. Nullification of a federal law by a state put all parties on notice that one party believed that the terms of the contract were being violated (by an act of Congress or by a decision of the Supreme Court). The other states might clarify the matter by constitutional amendment (a process that would give one-fourth the states plus one a veto), in which case the state that nullified the law could either rejoin the compact or, if it rejected the amendment, withdraw from the Union.

Virginia and South Carolina states' rights were distinguishable, and within each group there were further variants. But even before antebellum history merged them, they shared a common ground. Both talked theory but rested on the realities of economic and social self-interest. Both challenged the authority of the Supreme Court in general and the work of the Marshall Court specifically. Both threatened the authority of the national government, which in Story's mind was the sine qua non of republican government. Story, along with Marshall, understood the distinctions between Jefferson and Calhoun, but he lumped them together as enemies of the republic and constructed his *Commentaries* to eradicate both the Virginia ideal that the Constitution was a collection of rights and the South Carolina notion that it was a compact among sovereign states—

simultaneously and once and for all. This he did in a span of eighteen months, in the midst of his yearly stint on the Court and his harried circuit treks, while he grieved his daughter's death and his wife's growing invalidism, while he finished his *Commentaries on Bailments* (published in 1832) and began teaching at the Law School. Three massive volumes, a half million words, to put American history back on the right track. Shades of Cotton Mather!

Story's *Commentaries*—dedicated to John Marshall and adorned on its title page with quotations from Cicero and Burke to set the tone—was divided into three books. The first and second, devoted respectively to the colonial background of the Constitution and the revolutionary and confederation periods, were mainly historical. Book 3 mixed history and law to treat the origins and nature of the Constitution itself, and argued forcefully that the Supreme Court was the final expounder of it. Following this discussion, as the main body of the work and its most unique part, was a section-by-section, clause-by-clause analysis of the document based mainly on court cases, a reservoir of "correct" constitutional principles for lawyers and judges.

The history in book 1 drew eclectically from an impressive range of primary sources and secondary works in colonial history. With a tone of scholarly detachment but with unmistakable didactic purpose, Story treated American colonial history as it bore on the question of states' rights. The Burkean message, looking forward to the Constitution, was that American government was the cumulative product of historical growth and not, as Southern theorists inferred, an abstract and static body of natural rights.[129] Rights there were in Story's scheme of government, but they belonged to individuals and not states, and they were embedded in the tradition of the common law as it developed in colonial America. Story's argument, which followed Burke in fusing the common-law tradition with the natural-law ideas of the eighteenth century,[130] turned on his theory of the adoption of the common law. Contrary to some accounts, Story did not deny variation in the legal superstructure from colony to colony, variations according to local and regional usage. He did insist, in direct opposition to Jefferson, however, on the uniformity of the "general foundation"—the permeating spirit of the common law, the universality of basic principles. Refuting Blackstone, he argued that the "uniform doctrine in America ever since the settlement of the colonies," the "universal principle," is that "the common law is our birth right and our inheritance, and that our ancestors brought hither with them upon their emigration all of it which was applicable to their situation." Modified to suit American circumstances, then, the common law "has become the guardian of our political and civil rights; it has protected our infant liberties, it has watched over our maturer growth, it has expanded with our wants, it has nurtured that spirit of independence which checked the first approaches of arbitrary power, it has enabled us to triumph in the midst of difficulties and dangers threatening our political existence; and, by the goodness of God, we are now enjoying, under its bold and manly principles, the blessings of a free, independent, and united government." "Liberty under law," "Liberty *and* Union": The nation was nurtured by history and experience distilled in the common law.[131]

These themes, following the strategy of New England conservatism, marched forth against the visionary, speculative demagoguery of Jefferson and company. If law was the foundation of liberty and union, then lawyers were assured a central role in American government. Story's call for conservative leadership by the "*professional* intelligence of the Country," as he phrased it later to Richard Peters,[132] was unmistakable. But his hardest blows fell on the main claims of the states' rightists: that the states were sovereign, that the Constitution was a compact among sovereign states. Story's legal history of colonial America dropped both birds. If the American colonies were bound by English law (as the charters said they were) and accepted it as their birthright, if they gave their allegiance to the crown, they could not be sovereign precursors to sovereign states. And further, if national government was rooted in the shared experience of colonial Americans, an experience that transcended colonial boundaries, it was not a mere body of rights created by formal compact agreed upon by sovereign states and dissolvable at their pleasure. Armed with history, Story was ready in books 2 and 3 for the major assault on the twin evils of dual sovereignty and compact theory.

The definition and location of sovereignty in the American federal system was, as Story correctly perceived, the foundation on which all else rested. Accepted wisdom held that sovereignty lay with the people, but what that meant for the actual deployment of power within the federal system was not clear. On this subject the framers had not spoken clearly (and what they did say was not yet available to contemporaries). Intent, moreover, was always viewed from the standpoint of state and local self-interest. By the 1820s perceived self-interest had driven Virginia theorists, who had once been advocates of dual federalism, to a flat-out assertion of state sovereignty. And from Taylor, St. George Tucker, Roane, and Jefferson, from the Virginia-Kentucky Resolutions of 1798 and the Virginia Resolution of 1799, Calhoun distilled the pure doctrine of state sovereignty along with the means of implementing it. Sovereignty by his lights was indivisible; by his version of revolutionary history it descended on the states at the time of the break with England, and they never thereafter relinquished it. For Calhoun the sovereignty of the people meant the sovereignty of the people in their respective states, and it followed in his theory that these people might, acting in organic convention, nullify an act of the national government or, if they chose, withdraw their allegiance from the constitutional contract altogether.

The appeal of Calhoun's theory lay in its close logic and absolute assuredness, but those qualities came by raising constitutional theory to the level of metaphysics, where truth could be disjoined from consequences. Calhoun the constitutional logician was a perfect foil for Story the constitutional common lawyer. Story's strategy—drawing freely on volume 9 of Nathan Dane's *Abridgment of American Law* and John Quincy Adams's Fourth of July address, both of which appeared in 1829, on the works of James Wilson, and unabashedly on the *Federalist Papers*[133]—was to bring theory down to earth, to hold Southern thinking up to common sense, experience, and long-range self-interest. "Sovereignty," he began, is "used in different ways." In the "largest sense," it meant the "absolute right to govern" and obtained by "the very act of civil and political association" by which "each citizen subjects himself to the authority of the whole; and the authority of all over each member essentially belongs to the body politic." There is, he continued, a "far more limited sense" to sovereignty, one used "to designate such political powers as in the actual organization of the particular state or nation."[134] In this commonsense Aristotelian view of the matter, Story paved the way for his contention that sovereignty in the United States was divisible, had in actuality been divided between the state and the central government. It followed that the real problem was to ascertain the manner in which conflict between state and national authority would be settled, a question that would lead Story finally to his climactic exposition of judicial power.

Before that tack, however, he turned full sail into Calhoun's contention that upon independence undivided sovereignty devolved on the states. Sovereignty taken in the absolute sense, he declared, citing Wilson and Madison for support (and becoming almost as metaphysical as Calhoun in the process), lay not with the states but with the whole American people. In book 1 he had already established that the colonies were not "in the most large and general sense, independent, or sovereign communities," because they were "under and subjected to the crown." It followed not only as a "practical fact" but as a "legal and constitutional one" that when the colonies severed their allegiance to the crown, sovereignty fell to the whole American people and not the states. "From the moment of the Declaration of Independence . . . the united colonies must be considered as being a nation *de facto*, having a general government over it, created and acting by the general consent of the people of all the colonies." Story did not deny that the states retained sovereignty under the Articles—a concession to both historical fact and Southern theory. But that sovereignty was in the "limited sense already alluded to" (the one that Chief Justice Marshall conceded in *Gibbons* v. *Ogden*). This strategic concession relieved Story of the impossible obligation of denying state dominance during the confederation period. He was now free to catalogue the central government's devastating weakness during the confederation period (without conceding Calhoun's argument about state sovereignty) and to establish the easily demonstrable need for a stronger central government.[135] Theory (that all power resided in the whole people) and history (that the confederation was feckless) were in place for his refutation of the central operating idea of states' rights: that the Constitution was a compact among sovereign states.

"Whether the Constitution is a contract or not," thought Story, was "a very ill question in itself." But Calhoun's answer was "the leading ground, upon which all the Enemies of the Constitution in the South & West plan the overthrow of the Constitution."[136] Story felt "compelled" to confront the issue. He launched the assault in a short chapter called "Origin and Adoption of the Constitution," in which he assumed (and celebrated) the fact that he had previously asserted (but had not yet proved): that the whole people, possessed of sovereignty bestowed on them by independence, created the Constitution. That creation was a "still more glorious triumph in the cause of national liberty than even that which separated us from the mother country." What appeared here to be harmless rhetoric was in fact a compelling point. For if the Constitution was the completion of the Revolution, then those who would weaken it were by definition beyond the pale of revolutionary patriotism. Contract theory was untenable, then, because it broke the seamless web of revolutionary history. It was wrong on all other counts, too. In the first place, compact was not mentioned by the framers, "is nowhere found upon the face of the Constitution." Nor can it be intimated from any of its clauses. Beyond that the language is plainly against the notion. The separate states did not contract, but the "people of the United States" *did* "ordain and establish this Constitution." Contracts or compacts are *not* "ordained" and "established"; governments *are*. So is supreme law, which is what article VI calls the Constitution. Here in their own words was the "design of the framers." Such was the understanding of the ratifying conventions, too, as was clear from the use of the word "ratify," as well as from the instruments of ratification and from the acknowledgment even of the opponents of ratification.[137]

Most compelling of all, the framers—in contrast to the "artificial," "visionary" speculations of states' rightists—made sense. Their Constitution was supported by history and experience, the wisdom of Burke rather than the skepticism of Hume. The seeds of the Constitution lay buried in the common-law heritage of the colonial period and germinated with the realization that the government under the Articles was inadequate to the needs of the people. At work here, as in the common law, was a deep-seated process of accumulating wisdom. Carried far enough, it might have led Story to the theory of the organic state, but he stopped short.[138] The Republic, finally, was not the American "folk"; it was not a Platonic and indestructible idea laid up in heaven, or even a reflection of the natural law (which Story believed in). On the contrary, constitutional government was the work of real men, still-fragile wisdom salvaged from the chaos of history by experience. Wise and good men made the Constitution; foolish ones could destroy it. Then came the killing shot: In plain fact, Calhoun's dazzling logic, despite his promise that nullification was constitutional, led unavoidably to the chaos, confusion, and debility of the confederation years. This fear had been the driving force at the Constitutional Convention, the persuasion behind the *Federalist Papers*, the key to ratification. No matter how adorned it was with legal learning, it was an argument people could understand. So at least Story and his friends hoped.

Story may have given up on democracy but not on the American people. Reason and common sense could still reach them and must, for the "Constitution is responsible to the people."[139] They might not be able to govern directly, but they could distinguish between fools and statesmen—which point brought him to the Supreme Court and judicial power. It was a posthumous shootout with his old enemy Jefferson, a point-by-point refutation of his modern adherents, an appeal to the American people for their support of an institution that lacked all the trappings of democracy. What went for wisdom here was not so much what the framers fashioned (for if they planned judicial review they also left it in limbo) as what the Supreme Court under Chief Justice Marshall had wrought. Story's dedication of his work to Marshall was not just a heartfelt tribute to his friend but a testimony to his permeating influence on American public law. Whatever else the *Commentaries* did, they set forth the chief justice as the great statesman of the early republic.

Story's message and Marshall's was that the Supreme Court and not the states must be the final arbiter of the Constitution. If the Constitution created the Court, the Court preserved the Constitution, so that finally the two appear almost indistinguishable. Every argument previously mustered against states' rights in general was now made to support the authority of the Supreme Court and, indeed, the work of the Marshall Court. From the idea of popular sovereignty (which Story like the founders used to undercut state sovereignty) came the Court's democratic credentials: The sovereign people spoke only in organic convention, and when they spoke at Philadelphia, they created a judiciary coequal with the other, more democratic branches. To admit that sovereignty had to be divided between state and nation also led to the necessity of judicial authority, a point made in *Martin* v. *Hunter* and *Cohens* v. *Virginia*. No state—whether by its courts (as in the Virginia scheme of things) or by a special convention (as in the South Carolina plan)—can stand in final judgment on the Constitution without destroying it. The Supreme Court alone is equipped to apply the generalities of the Constitution to the specifics of life, to uphold it as supreme law. History and experience, again, and logic and the wording of the Constitution establish this central truth: Power must reside somewhere.

Having established the Court as the guardian and final interpreter of the Constitution, Story was obliged to demonstrate that it would not abuse its power as Jefferson and his followers charged it had done. Story's answer was to show that the justices were bound by "some fixed standard" of construction.[140] Chapter 5, book 3, entitled "Rules of Interpretation," undertook this difficult chore, and it was the first in a long tradition of scholarly efforts to establish workable objective norms of constitutional adjudication. Story turned for aid to such ancient authorities as Matthew Bacon's *Abridgment* and the works of Domat, Ayliffe, and Vattel, and to more recent English commentators like Rutherford, Wooddeson, and Blackstone. For American constitutional law, however, there was little specific guidance except for a few numbers of the *Federalist Papers* and the brief remarks of an occasional early commentator on the Constitution like William Rawle. Story consulted these sources, especially the *Federalist*, but he relied primarily on the decisions of the Marshall Court itself, on the great cases of *Martin* v. *Hunter, Cohens* v. *Virginia, Gibbons* v. *Ogden, Ogden* v. *Saunders, Sturgis* v. *Crowninshield.* Above all he turned to *McCulloch* v. *Maryland,* whose broad, creative conception of construction he transformed into a universal principle of constitutional interpretation.

From his sources Story extracted nineteen rules in all, some general, others specific, but all of them set forth with admirable clarity. The assumption was that the Constitution was not always clear, that the intent of the framers was not always manifest, that judges must judge. The objectivity that would neutralize judicial power would come not from a Newtonian constitution but from uniform rules of construction now made plain for working lawyers and sitting judges. The claim was that the Marshall Court had judged by principle, not whim; the promise was that the Court, bound by scientific rules of construction, would continue to be above politics. Permeating the whole argument was the spirit of *McCulloch,* whose bold nationalism ran back directly to Hamilton and the old Federalists. Marshall's opinion was as vital to the Court as it was to Congress, for not only did it arm the latter with implied powers but it charged the former with preserving a living Constitution. Judging, it would appear, then, was a part of the elite tradition of eighteenth-century governance. In the spirit of that tradition, Story ended chapter 5 with "an admonition to all those who are called upon to frame or to interpret a constitution." Using Burke's "Letter to the Sheriffs of Bristol in 1777" as his text, he concluded that "the business of those who are called to administer it [the Constitution] is to rule, and not to wrangle. It would be a poor compensation that one had triumphed in a dispute whilst we had lost an empire; that we had frittered down a power, and at the same time had destroyed the Republic." [141]

Story's "Rules of Interpretation" distilled all that preceded it: History embodied in the Constitution was translated into guidelines for statesmen. Nowhere—on either side of the constitutional debate or in any of the previous commentaries on the Constitution—had there been a section-by-section, clause-by-clause analysis of the document itself. Here now was such a work backed by the authority of the Supreme Court's reigning scholar. In a real sense constitutional history became constitutional law, for again it was the decisions of the Court that became the foundation of interpretation. Copious quotations from the Court's decisions, along with other relevant documents, moreover, made the *Commentaries* not only a work of analysis but a collection of documents ready for further citation, an important feature in an age when law libraries were limited. All this is to say that Story's *Commentaries* were the logical successor to the *Federalist Papers*, as well as the forerunner of the annotated *Constitution of the United States of America* assembled by the legislative reference service of the Library of Congress under the direction of Edward Corwin. [142] That great collective work was over a century away. Story had done it single-handedly in eighteen months. Parrington saw the point: With Story's *Commentaries* began the lawyer's monopoly of American constitutional law. The framers may not have planned it that way; Story did.

The response to the *Commentaries* marked them at once as the leading nationalist work on the Constitution, a position of authority that remained unchallenged throughout the nineteenth century (indeed, until the appearance of William Crosskey's *Politics and the Constitution* in 1953). Southern criticism, as Marshall had predicted, [143] was vociferous, but in the deep South Story got a hearing. Thus could Charles C. Jones, Jr., from Liberty County, Georgia—himself a graduate of Harvard Law School—praise the great jurisprudential accomplishments of Story and Marshall, and this in the midst of debates over Kansas and Nebraska in Washington and abolitionist riots in Boston. [144] Story's work on the Constitution was in fact used at the Citadel in Charleston until 1850, when it was finally replaced by Calhoun's works. [145] By then Southern theorists—beginning with Abel Upshur and Nathaniel Beverly Tucker before the war, and continuing after it with works by John Randolph, Henry St. George Tucker, Albert Taylor Bledsoe, Bernard J. Sage, and the greatest of them all, Alexander Stephens—had taken the field. [146] That Story was the focal point of Southern animus only testified to his prominence as *the* authority on the Constitution.

The reception of his *Commentaries* in the North and among "constitutional men" (as Story called those who agreed with him) [147] was enthusiastic and almost entirely uncritical. Marshall, who had spurred on his friend and promised in advance that he would "not be among the growlers,"[148] was full of praise. "It would give your orthodox Nullifyer [*sic*] a fever," he assured Story, "to read the heresies of your commentaries. A whole school might be infected by the atmosphere if a single copy would be placed on one of the shelves of a book case."[149] Marshall was delighted, too, that Story was coming out with an abridgment that would reach a wider audience with constitutional truth.[150] Webster, who used the ideas in the *Commentaries* against Hayne even before they were published, agreed with Marshall. James Kent dipped into the volumes immediately and thought them marked by "ardent, rapid and thorough & profound research, & sound, orthodox, elevated & accurate Principles." Story's learning and "comprehensiveness," he generously concluded, threw "all my little brief & narrow Sketches into the Shade."[151] Revised editions of Kent's own great work cited Story frequently and praised his decision to make the *Federalist Papers* the "basis" of his commentaries.[152] Judge Joseph Hopkinson, who received the first copy from the press with a request from Story that he review it for the *American Quarterly Review*, thought "the book must be not only read, but closely studied, to learn how much valuable matter it contains."[153] Jared Sparks, the historian and future president of Harvard, believed "no other work could in any degree supply its place."[154]

Reviews of the *Commentaries* were equally laudatory, and more important, they advertised the work and spread Story's fame. Hopkinson in the *American Quarterly Review* summarized the key themes of the *Commentaries* and praised his friend as the one man ideally equipped and placed to speak with authority.[155] The *American Jurist*, the new legal periodical emanating from Boston and run by Story's friends and admirers, thought that the work was so commanding that "it will be scarcely possible that any question henceforth arising on the subject should be superficially treated, either in legislative debate, or forensic argument."[156] The *American Monthly Review* likened Story's *Commentaries* to Blackstone's, and the *North American Review* not only praised the book lavishly but summarized its main points at length, promising that it would put an end "to the controversies, which agitate the country." In the hands of a new generation of "young men" this exegesis of constitutional "Scripture" would be the scourge of "party" and the instrument of salvation.[157] Citations in other legal commentaries of the antebellum period, such as those of Kent, Timothy Walker, and George T. Curtis, also helped to make Story's ideas legal and intellectual tender for the whole country. Indeed, its reception in England, Scotland, Germany, and France—with translations into French and Spanish and Portuguese—gave the work and its author a truly international status.[158]

What counted by Story's own standard of success, however, was whether the *Commentaries* actually educated, whether they mattered in the war of ideas. Although the evidence is impressionistic, there is little doubt that Story's book was *the* reference for lawyers and judges for the rest of the century.[159] The full work, updated and annotated by such scholars as Thomas M. Cooley, went through five American editions and was still in print at the turn of the century. Judges cited it with increasing regularity, too; indeed, one authority counted no less than forty-two separate cases in which the Supreme Court itself cited the *Commentaries*.[160] The work also had a wide general readership. Actual sales records are not available, but the appearance of several abridged editions speaks to its popularity. In April 1833 there appeared an abridged edition for college and high school students, containing "in compressed form the leading doctrines" of the larger work. The *Constitutional Class Book*, which was still more basic and aimed this time at "the higher classes of the common school" appeared the following year. A final abridgment, called *A Familiar Exposition of the Constitution* (1840), was suited for the general reader, the republican citizen who "should be in possession of sound views of the early & true friends of the Constitution."[161]

The commanding position of the *Commentaries* is attributable to several factors. Timing was fundamental, and Story presented his ideas on the Constitution when they were most needed. That he spoke for a broad-based conservative movement already under way is also important, for the movement provided ready-made channels for the dissemination of his ideas. Most important in this regard was Harvard Law School, where Story's *Commentaries* became the standard text. For the rest of the century Harvard law students circulated Story's constitutional ideas and some-times the *Commentaries* themselves to various parts of the country. No other American commentator had such a marketing system.

Circumstances and institutions favored Story, but it must be conceded that he sensed the potential and shaped his work to exploit it. He was a master propagandist who was among the first law publicists in the United States to grasp completely the converting possibilities of the new print culture. His ideas were not only timely—and that in itself was a matter of deliberate choice and a function of his genius as a writer—but carefully fashioned to address his readers, or rather, the several distinct classes of them. All else was subordinate to the educational chore at hand: His style (while ornate) was also clear and logical; his arguments (while learned and scholarly at one level) were finally plain and commonsensical; the structure of his work was distinctly functional. Fortunately, too, Story's work lacked competitors, at least any with the ready-made stature of a Supreme Court justice who could claim with much truth to have been present at the creation.

Moreover, and most important, perhaps, Story's work was persuasive because he drew deeply from the mainstream of revolutionary history and thus captured the high ground of patriotism from his states' rights critics. His constitutional nationalism, as we have seen, was rooted in sectional self-interest and permeated with New England conservative ideas. But he transcended mere sectionalism—or, more precisely, successfully fused it with American nationalism and harnessed it to the future greatness of the country. The old Federalist truths that Story salvaged from New England provincialism and enriched with incomparable legal learning became the constitutional foundation of Whiggism in the 1830s and 1840s and, after the ideological shift of the 1850s, of Lincoln Republicanism. Giving Calhoun, the Tuckers, and Stephens their due, still the fact remains that Story's version of the Constitution was validated by the Civil War. Story's *Commentaries* lasted in part simply because they were on the winning side of history. But surely, to some extent, Story's side won because he was on it.

Chapter 6

The New Court and the "Last of the Old Race of Judges"

On you will rest the hopes, and I do believe it—well founded hopes of all who look for the preservation of the Supreme Court in its wisdom and its just power.
Richard Peters to Joseph Story,
13 December 1836

John Marshall died on Monday, 6 July 1835. Story had feared the worst for four years, had tried to steel himself against the inevitable. Even so he was crushed. "Great, good, excellent man," he cried out when all hope was lost. "I shall never see his like again: His gentleness, his affectionateness, his glorious virtues, his unblemished life, his exalted talents, leave him without rival or a peer."[1] In his eulogy on the chief justice delivered to the Suffolk bar, Story had trouble deciding what most to praise, whether his unblemished "moral character" or "the principles, which governed his life and conduct" or his "intellectual" qualities and professional eminence.[2] He praised them all with heartfelt effusiveness in a speech that was at once a eulogy and a jeremiad. The chief justice, his gentle, modest friend, was also the old Federalist and the representative republican (which for Story were one and the same). Marshall grasped as none other the balance between liberty and order, embodied the conservative, constructive wisdom of the Revolution. In an age of speculation, demagoguery, and growing "intangibility and mistiness of affairs," to use Hawthorne's phrase,[3] he stood as a beacon of truth. As chief justice he combined moral character, wisdom, and love of principle with a razor-sharp legal mind. It was not that he excelled in black-letter scholarship (Story admitted that he did not) but that he brought legal scholarship to the practical task of governance, where he mixed it with an incomparable genius for seeing the real issues, for logical analysis combined with a style that turned logic into eloquence.

Above all, and all others, he was the master of constitutional law. In this "his peculiar triumph," he stood confessedly without rival, whether we regard his thorough knowledge of our civil and political history, his admirable powers of illustration and generalization, his scrupulous integrity and exactness in interpretation, or his consummate skill in molding his own genius into its elements, as if they had constituted the exclusive study of his life. His proudest epitaph may be written in a single line: "Here lies the Expounder of the Constitution of the United States." Even if the Constitution itself should perish, as Story honestly feared it might in 1835, Marshall's "glorious judgments will still remain to instruct mankind, until liberty shall cease to be a blessing, and the science of jurisprudence shall vanish from the catalogue of human pursuits."[4]

Story's grief is understandable. No one outside his immediate family had so much influenced his life and career. At their first meeting nearly thirty years before, Story had been awed by the greatness Marshall carried so modestly, charmed by his personality, which was as different from his own as the Blue Ridge Mountains were from rocky Marblehead. It was Marshall who introduced Story to the Court, eased his matriculation. With his gentle good humor he softened the young puritan's austere ways. Deep friendship followed mutual respect. Both men were highly moral, both affectionate family men who shared the frustration of absent families, the sorrow of sick wives and lost children. Each in his own way was a romantic.[5]

And both were legal scientists as the age understood that term. Their legal minds were unique, to be sure. There was in fact a grain of truth in the contemporary quip that Marshall decided the case while Story found the law. Marshall preferred to head for the "open sea" in his constitutional opinions, while Story moved methodically from "headland to headland," that is to say, from authority to authority. They often parted company, too, on matters of judicial strategy, in that Marshall preferred caution and moderation, Story purity. But for all their differences they arrived at a common ground: a shared vision, rooted in a common perception of the American Revolution, of a Burkean Constitution under the special guardianship of the Supreme Court.

Story grieved in 1835 not just for his friend, then, but for their beleaguered common cause. In his early eulogy to Washington he had owned the republican covenant; in his eulogy to Marshall he renewed it. With the chief justice gone, Story saw himself, as he put it to Harriet Martineau, as "the last of the old race of Judges."[6] It was not just that Jacksonian Democracy was hostile to the doctrines of the Marshall Court, but also that the evil forces of politics now threatened to invade the temple itself. The Supreme Court, which he and Marshall counted on to restrain the tumultuous and impatient majority and subdue party government, seemed more and more to be controlled by those very forces. Surrounded increasingly by Jacksonian colleagues, faced with unprecedented demand for change, Story was driven to fight chaos with scholarly authority, to speak out stridently for the legal version of republicanism that he shared with his departed friend. The 1837 term of the Court indicated that his version of republican law was doomed. His defeat also shows the price of victory and depicts the Supreme Court in its first confrontation with the classic dilemma of adjudication: the need to adjust old law to new history while preserving the semblance of legal continuity on which judicial authority must rest.

1. A Judicial Strategy for Hard Times: The 1820s Again

Marshall's death in 1835 is a convenient bench mark in the Court's history, the end of a chain reaction set in motion by the Court's audacious assertion of power in *Martin* v. *Hunter's Lessee* in 1816 and *Cohens* v. *Virginia* in 1821 and the creative use of that power in the three great policy-making decisions of the 1819 term: *Sturgis*, *McCulloch*, and *Dartmouth College*. These decisions cut substantially into state power in bankruptcy, taxation, and corporate regulation. Collectively they struck a blow for national capitalism, for businessmen, that is, whose interests depended on a stable national currency and the free flow of goods and credit across state lines. Congressional power was established on the broadest base (implied powers in *McCulloch* and the supremacy of enumerated powers in *Gibbons*) and made available for national promotional legislation (a national bank, a protective tariff, and federally sponsored internal improvements).

It could be argued that this nationalist, capitalist construction of the Constitution only followed the general intent of the framers. Story's *Commentaries*, as we have seen, argued precisely that, and he was probably correct.[7] But intent as a controlling aspect of constitutional construction has its problems. The framers (whose intent we can approximate) were not the ratifiers (whose intent is all but impossible to fathom), yet both must be consulted. More important still, neither the framers nor the ratifiers spoke for or controlled the feelings and needs of the American people as they moved into the nineteenth century; and they had to be heard. The fact is that before the meaning of the key clauses of the Constitution had been firmly settled, a powerful states' rights movement presuming to speak for a sizable portion of the American people took the field. It was rooted in perceived self-interest and nourished by the uncertainty of the Constitution on the precise demarcation between state and central power. The Marshall Court might stand on the authority of the framers and might speak with Olympian certainty when it struck down state laws. But Jefferson, Taylor, Roane, and company stood for a new reality: that continued Union under the Constitution depended on self-interest. They perceived, too, that the Court had taken sides in the ongoing struggle among diverse interest groups to define the Constitution. The Marshall Court, just like New England conservatives, was tidying up history. The government of strict and enumerated powers, which had originally attracted states' rights forces to the Constitution, had now become a government of power, adequate, as Marshall put it in the bank decision, to the "various *crises* of human affairs."[8] With the Marshall Court, the center of constitutional gravity had shifted, and the change had taken place not through formal amendment but through judicial construction. Judicial review was built into the Constitution, to be sure: by the wording of the document and the juxtaposition of articles III and VI, as well as by state precedents and the general understanding of the age. But judicial government as Marshall and his colleagues employed it had not been understood or foreseen. The policy-making decisions that clustered around *McCulloch* changed that situation. For the first time in American history, as William Wirt noted in 1823, the positive policy-making potential of the Supreme Court was clearly recognized.[9] It was perfectly logical that the political attack on the Court should have come with its institutional maturation.

And come it did, with a vengeance that outdistanced previous criticism of the Court and prefigured subsequent attacks against it as well. The justices had, of course, suffered political opposition before—as soon, indeed, as they took strong stands on important issues. *Chisholm* v. *Georgia* (1792) called down the wrath of Georgia and set in motion forces that led to the Eleventh Amendment. *Marbury* v. *Madison* (1803) mobilized Republican politicians against the Court, though less because of the doctrine of judicial review than because of Marshall's audacious lecture to President Jefferson on the rule of law. Pennsylvania openly defied the Court in *U.S.* v. *Peters* (1809) until newly elected President Madison put a stop to the protest. New Jersey never did acknowledge the Court's decision in *New Jersey* v. *Wilson* (1812), which extended a tax exemption granted to Indian land to subsequent private purchasers. Georgia was less successful in resisting *Fletcher* v. *Peck* (1810), but the opinion called forth the powerful Tertium Quid faction of the Republican party to do battle against judicial usurpation.

Anti-Court sentiment there had been, then, but not an anti-Court movement. Opposition focused on particular decisions rather than on the Court as an institution; for the most part criticism was confined to the state whose ox the Court gored. Republicans after 1800, fueled by Jefferson's excessive hatred of the chief justice, had generally been the most persistent critics of the judiciary. But the Republican party, itself inchoate and divided, had not taken a unified stand against the Court, thanks in large part to the pro-Court moderates in its ranks.[10] Neither was there a coherent anti-Court theory, perhaps because the Republican party had every logical reason to look to the Court to implement its doctrine of limited government and strict construction. To win Republican support, all the Court needed to do after laying claim to judicial review in *Marbury* was to strike down acts of Congress based on a broad nationalist construction of constitutional power. What it did, instead, was to nullify state laws (as in *Fletcher*,

Martin, and *Dartmouth College*) and uphold congressional acts with an expansive gloss on constitutional nationalism (as in *McCulloch*).

Virginia, recently sensitized to the new power of the Court by the *Fairfax* decision (1813), *Terrett* v. *Taylor* (1815), *Town of Pawlet* v. *Clark* (1815), and *Martin* v. *Hunter's Lessee* (1816), which were all Story's opinions, got the message and led the charge against judicial usurpation. Its position made sense. Virginia was the home base of states' rights, the domain of longtime Court haters like John Randolph, John Taylor, Spencer Roane, and Thomas Jefferson. Virginia politicians saw the challenge of *McCulloch* and projected it fully against the political-economic realities of the nineteenth century. Those realities, driven home by the Panic of 1819 and the Missouri debates in 1820, were that the Southern states were doomed to minority political status in the Union, that the institution of slavery lay at the mercy of a Northern political power increasingly inimical to it. Marshall's implied-powers doctrine simply armed the Northern majority with the power to interfere with slavery and to enact Clay's American Plan, which now appeared to be not a national but a Northern policy exacted at the expense of the South. Virginia was aggrieved, and the danger, as Story saw it, was that she "might combine the temporary interests of other States with her own, & by espousing their quarrels & assuming to be their champion, lead them astray. . . ."[11]

Such a movement needed a cause célèbre, an occasion to set forth a persuasive states' rights case against the Court. *McCulloch* was that cause. By destroying a strict interpretation of enumerated powers in that decision, Marshall obliterated the best defense of a minority section. Whereas the Court might have been the friend of the South, it had become a threatening enemy, and this is precisely what John Taylor of Caroline County, Virginia, argued in his attack on the *McCulloch* decision in *Construction Construed and Constitutions Vindicated* (1820). *Tyranny Unmasked* two years later and *New Views of the Constitution of the United States* in 1823 (which called forth Story's tirade against the presumption of "new views") completed his intellectual assault on national mercantilism and government by judiciary.[12]

Anti-Court theory, broadened and intensified by the growing codification movement at the state level, turned quickly into anti-Court politics, which threatened to turn into a movement. Virginia was stung again in 1821 when the *Cohens* decision reaffirmed the Court's appellate power under section 25 and reduced the effectiveness of the Eleventh Amendment as a barrier to suits against the states. Story's opinion in *Green* v. *Biddle* the same year—which ironically favored Virginia land speculators at the expense of Kentucky—brought the latter state more firmly into the Court-hating orbit. Animosity was inflamed in Ohio by *Osborn* v. *Bank of the U.S.* (1824), which reaffirmed the much-hated doctrines of *McCulloch* and cut further into the Eleventh Amendment by holding that an officer of the state was suable even if the state itself were not.[13] At the same term, New York was put in its place (and the power of Congress further enlarged) by *Gibbons* v. *Ogden*. By the end of the 1825 term, the Court in fact had declared unconstitutional the acts not only of Kentucky, Maryland, New York, and Virginia but of New Jersey, New Hampshire, Ohio, Pennsylvania, and Vermont as well.[14] Judicial rulings on slaves and Indians would soon bring South Carolina and Georgia into the movement— indeed, to the forefront of it.

Each state fashioned its own weapon against the Court, designed especially to suit its particular grievance. Anti-Court resolutions emanated from the legislatures of Virginia, Kentucky, and Ohio, and in Pennsylvania Chief Justice John Bannister Gibson struck a telling intellectual blow against judicial review in *Eakin* v. *Raub* (1825).[15] South Carolina blatantly ignored Justice Johnson's 1822 circuit decision striking down the Negro seamen's law. Kentucky resisted *Green* v. *Biddle*; Ohio mobilized against *Osborn*; and later, of course, Georgia with the help of Andrew Jackson openly refused to obey the Court's decision in the Cherokee Indian case of Corn Tassel.[16]

Even more threatening was the possibility of concerted state action in Congress. Anti-Court rhetoric was a common political theme throughout the 1820s, and judicial reform (as in the effort to expand the circuits in 1826) foundered on political considerations. There was constant talk of removal of justices as well; one critic even suggested a constitutional amendment providing for removal by the president upon the advice of two-thirds of both houses. Specific anti-Court measures ran the gamut. On the mild side was the proposal prompted by *Green* v. *Biddle* that no constitutional question be decided except by a majority of the whole Court—a requirement that Marshall, in fact, informally implemented after 1823. More extreme was the demand that all justices concur in any decision when the validity of state or congressional acts was at issue. Yet another variant, put forth by future Supreme Court justice Philip Barbour, required a minimum five of seven majority in all constitutional questions. Among the most inventive and radical was the suggestion introduced in the New York legislature in 1833 for the creation of a new supreme court to police the old one, a court made up of twenty-five judges, twenty-four of whom were to be the chief justices of the states.[17] Equally farfetched, and even more contrary to the Constitution, was the proposal to make the Senate the final appellate tribunal in all cases involving the constitutionality of state laws.

The most serious threats to the Court, because the most realizable, were the repeal of section 25 of the Judiciary Act of 1789 and nullification. Repeal could be accomplished by a simple majority in Congress and would, in a single blow, destroy the Court's appellate jurisdiction over constitutional questions (many of which were decided in the first instance by state courts). Nullification, as Colonel Hayne made painfully clear in his debate with Webster in January 1830, was a deliberate effort to remove constitutional questions involving federal power from the Supreme Court and put them in the hands of the states.[18] In either instance the Court was on the line. John C. Calhoun put it bluntly: "The question is in truth between the people & the Supreme Court. We contend, that the great conservative principle of our system is in the people of the States, as parties to the Constitutional compact, and our opponents that it is in the Supreme Court. This is the sum total of the whole difference. . . ."[19]

Willy-nilly at first and then progressively and relentlessly, the Supreme Court became the central protagonist in the great political struggle to define the federal union, in the debate over democracy and aristocracy—indeed, over the meaning of republican government itself. Story watched apprehensively, fearfully. Of all the portentous happenings of the 1820s this was the gravest. Hardly a letter passed between him and Marshall and other intimate correspondents during this decade that did not curse the Court's enemies and bemoan its declining power and prestige. Anxiety escalated with mounting pressure on the Court. In his calmer moments Story realized that states' rightists were divided among themselves and reasoned that most of the Court-curbing measures would fail.[20] But the general direction of things was ominous. Court haters now had a specific program, a theoretical underpinning, a regional base of operations, and powerful statesmen to champion and legitimize their cause. Nor could presidents be counted on to support the Court or put qualified men on it, as both Marshall and Story knew.[21] On the matter of appointments even friends were befuddled, as when Rufus Choate suggested that Martin Van Buren would be an ideal replacement for Bushrod Washington because of his prudence. Party and demagoguery had corrupted the people themselves, so that the only firm friends of the judiciary were the wise and the good and the elevated in society, but they were a beleaguered minority. The Court lay vulnerable if not to nullification then to the repeal of section 25; without the Court the Constitution was lost.

What should be done? Story had already called on conservatives to defend the Court. In his *Commentaries* he gave them the constitutional truth to disseminate to the people should they listen. But the odds for success were not good; in any case educational measures would take time. Meanwhile the justices would have to help themselves. And that was the rub. Story agreed with Hamilton in *Federalist* 78: "The truth is and cannot be disguised, even from vulgar observation," he confessed to Mason, "that the Judiciary in our country is essentially feeble, and must always be open to attack from all quarters. It will perpetually thwart the wishes and the views of demagogues, and it can have no places to give and no patronage to draw around it close defenders."[22]

If the Court was vulnerable, if it could not take the offensive against its enemies, then did it not have to bend its law to the political and economic realities of the new age? Common sense strongly suggested that a tactical retreat from the high nationalism and Olympian style of the golden age was in order. Wholesale reversals were, of course, out of the question. There was no way, either, in the pre-1925 days before certiorari jurisdiction, that the Court could escape sensitive cases, for, as Story put it in his *Commentaries*, it "has no more right to decline the exercise of jurisdiction which it is given, than to usurp that which is not given."[23] Still, the Court could back off, as indeed it had done even in its short history. *Chisholm* v. *Georgia*, as far back as 1793, had dramatized the dangers of a direct confrontation with sovereign states. Chase's impeachment, even if unsuccessful, had its lessons, and in the matter of federal criminal common law the justices had learned something of the virtue of a timely retreat. Indeed, as we now know, the Court had not been "monolithic" even at the peak of its power.[24] *Sturgis* v. *Crowninshield*, the companion of such bold decisions as *Dartmouth College* and *McCulloch*, for example, was a precedent if not in judicial backtracking then certainly in judicial compromise. Obfuscation had its uses. The Court if it chose could also decide cases narrowly and on nonconstitutional grounds when possible, an approach that Judge John Bannister Gibson forcefully pressed on the Marshall Court in *Eakin* v. *Raub* (1825). Even a flat-out reversal now and then was not unknown and was, in fact, a technique already built into American jurisprudence.[25]

Accommodation, whether deliberate or the result of division on the Court, was bound to come. The process began in 1823 when Smith Thompson, who replaced Brockholst Livingston, brought with him not only an independent mind but some mildly revisionist notions of states' rights (which he learned, ironically, from his judicial services with Story's friend James Kent). Robert Trimble replaced Thomas Todd in 1826 and was himself replaced three years later by John McLean of Ohio. McLean would in time drop his Jacksonian biases and become one of Story's staunchest allies and closest personal friends. Still, rapid turnover of justices loosened institutional cement and doctrinal regularity. Both gave way even more in 1830 when Henry Baldwin of Pennsylvania replaced Bushrod Washington, whose personal and doctrinal compatibility with Marshall and Story had been a stabilizing constant on the "old Court," as it increasingly came to be called.

Even more unsettling changes were soon to come, but already the direction of things was clear. New sections were to be represented more and old law less. A new generation of justices was making its appearance, and unlike the old, it was not rooted in the unifying experience of the Revolution. New justices not only brought new policy preferences to reflect the growing diversity of American society but brought a more pragmatic approach to lawmaking. Democratic and states' rights ideas that raged at the Court's door in the past henceforth would get a hearing in its councils, not simply because the new justices believed in accommodating tactics but because they believed in the truth of their perceptions. Marshall's dominance of the Court, which had rested on common values and a shared intellectual world of law, was bound to decline. And Thomas Jefferson was determined to hurry the process along, as when he pressured Justice Johnson to "throw himself in every case on God and his country" and write his own separate opinions, dissents if necessary, so that Marshall's hold on the Court might be broken.[26] Johnson did just that, entering nine concurring and eighteen dissenting opinions from 1825 to 1835, and many of these on important constitutional issues.[27]

The new justices soon came to accept division as normal. It was not that they voted as a bloc against the doctrines of the old Marshall Court but rather that they felt free to go their own way and did. The great principles of *McCulloch*, *Gibbons*, and *Dartmouth College* were not overturned, to be sure, but the Court increasingly refused to expand on them, and on more than one occasion found maneuvering room in what once appeared to be immovable constitutional truth. Changes in the area of commerce would come mainly during the chief justiceship of Roger Taney, but there were Marshallian intimations of things to come. Even *Gibbons* contained ambiguities, as Marshall made clear when he hedged on the exclusive nature of the commerce power and as Johnson showed in his concurrence.[28] In *Brown* v. *Maryland* (1827) the chief justice himself curtailed the applicability of *Gibbons* by distinguishing between goods in the original package (which Congress under the commerce clause could regulate) and those in retail (which it could not).[29] Further diminution of the exclusivist potential of *Gibbons* came two years later in *Willson* v. *The Blackbird Creek Marsh Co.* when the Court refused to void a Delaware law authorizing a bridge over a navigable stream on the ground that Congress had not yet acted.

Growing division in contract clause cases was even more noticeable. *Green* v. *Biddle* (1823) was the last contract case to be rendered in the aggressive mode of *Fletcher* and *Dartmouth College*, and that was done without benefit of a quorum, by a majority of only three, and over the bitter dissent of William Johnson.[30] The Court's "retreat and atonement,"[31] as the *United States Magazine and Democratic Review* later called it, was even more obvious in *Ogden* v. *Saunders* (1827), in which Johnson, in a majority bolstered by the Court's new members, upheld a state bankruptcy law that applied to contracts made after its passage.[32] For the first time in twenty-six years the chief justice dissented on a constitutional issue; Story and Duvall from the old Court joined him. Marshall himself gave way to the new age two years later in *Providence Bank* v. *Billings*, in which, abandoning the logic of *Dartmouth College*, he held for the Court that a Rhode Island banking corporation could not establish immunity from state taxes by reasoning inferentially from its charter.[33] Even in the area of state paper money, where the mandate of article I, section 10, was clearest, orthodoxy was losing ground. When the chief justice could muster only a majority of four to strike down a Missouri law creating interest-bearing certificates backed by state property and receivable for state taxes, it was clear that an erosion of contractual sanctity was under way.[34]

Marshall was painfully distressed as he complained to Story of the "revolutionary spirit which displayed itself in our circle."[35] But the truth was that he himself had made concessions behind which were two considerations. First of these was his own "temperance," as Jeremiah Mason called it,[36] that practical good sense and down-home logic which characterized his personality, his lawyering, and his judging. He understood what the times allowed and what the traffic would bear. He believed in legal science but, unlike Story, tempered it with discretion and prudence. In his own words (spoken after a circuit decision in which he circumvented the explosive issue of slavery), he was not "fond of butting against a wall in sport."[37]

More than that, John Marshall was Chief Justice Marshall, *primus inter pares*, the leader of the whole Court. From the beginning of his tenure he recognized that judicial unity meant authority and prestige. But he also understood that the work of the Court was collective. And collectivity took on a new meaning in the 1820s, so that unyielding perfectionism and doctrinal purity would isolate him from the Court he was required to lead. The harmony of the early Court was beyond recapture, and even a semblance of it called for restraint and moderation. When the great principles of the golden years were at stake (as in *Ogden* v. *Saunders*), Marshall would stand firm, but beyond that (as in *Blackbird Creek* and *Billings*) he was willing to maneuver. In short, his strategy was to lead when he could, bend when he had to. His goal, judging from the last ten years of his Court, was to consolidate previous gains and save the Court from its enemies.

Story generally saw eye to eye with his old friend on these matters. Indeed, the worse things got, the more indispensable did Marshall appear to be: "When he is gone, what are we to do?" he exclaimed to Peters on the eve of nullification.[38] Yet Story came at the law and approached the Court's crisis with his own, not Marshall's, reckoning. Unlike the chief justice, he had no institutional obligation to harmonize; life tenure gave him the freedom to save the Court and the law with his own medicine. His prescription was more legal science, not less; his strategy was not to accommodate the "new" constitutional ideas of his colleagues but to educate them to his. He saw the approaching dilemma early on and talked it over with "sound lawyers" and conservative friends. One of them, Jeremiah Mason (New England's greatest common lawyer, declared Webster), put the matter decisively to him and for him as the Court headed for a showdown with Virginia and Kentucky. "The Supreme Court has no choice of courses to be pursued," declared Mason. "The straightforward course is the only one that can be followed. It may be with as much temperance as the Chief Justice pleases, and no man ever excelled him in the exercise of that virtue. But any vacillation or retracting, which might be set down to the score of the present noisy threats, would be not only inconsistent with a due regard to personal character, but in their consequences, destructive of the best interests of the nation." [39]

Story really needed no prompting. His "personal character," as Mason put it, was on the line; so too was a view of the Supreme Court that he had nourished for at least a dozen years and a view of the law that went back even further. Story was the legal scientist in residence, his own man, and, more than that, New England's representative on the Court. And New England, as Story perceived it anyway, demanded that he do battle. He would answer falsehood with truth. "For the Judges of the Supreme Court," he pledged to Mason, "there is but one course to pursue. That is, to do their duty firmly and honestly, according to their best judgments. We should poorly deserve our place, and should want common honesty, if we shrink at the threats or the injuries of public men. For one, though I have no wish to be a martyr, I trust in God I shall never be so base as to submit to intimidation, come when it may. I believe the Court will be resolute, and will be driven from its course, only when driven from the seat of Justice." [40]

The time of testing was at hand. Mason's admonition to hold the line came within months of Jefferson's equally urgent plea to Johnson to undo the old Court. We do not know what went on in conference, but it is likely that the Story-Johnson polarity set the course of many a discussion. Certainly Story's commitment to doctrinal purity was a force to reckon with. Marshall must surely have seen the advantage, too. If there were new justices to be educated, who could better do it than Story? And if compromises were to be struck, it was well to have Story the conservative to balance off Johnson the Jeffersonian. Indeed, one wonders whether Marshall did not at times encourage Story to take the uncompromising stance that he as chief justice could not afford to take. Assuredly, Marshall's letters whetted his friend's passion for apocalypse, which intensified throughout the decade. Anxiety brought out the didact in him; it also forced him to think constructively and systematically about the Court and its law. The result would be embodied in his *Commentaries on the Constitution* and most particularly in chapter 5, "Rules of Interpretation." Before that work, however, and before even the worst of the crisis, Story was on his way to becoming the most unyielding justice on the Court, the self-planted bench mark of the old legal orthodoxy.

This did not mean that he shut his eyes to the vulnerability of the Court. He was, in fact, willing to maneuver the Court to safe ground as long as the modification could be made within the confines of principled adjudication and without the permanent surrender of the fundamental policy goals he believed essential to national welfare. Take, for example, the marvelously symbolic *Steamboat Thomas Jefferson* (1825).[41] This case, the first jurisdictional concession of the decade, was a libel for wages earned on a voyage by the steamship *Thomas Jefferson* from Shippinport, Kentucky, up the Missouri River and back, several hundred miles from the sea. The issue was whether such a case fell within the "maritime" jurisdiction of the federal courts. Opposition to such jurisdiction in Kentucky (fresh from its rebuke in *Green* v. *Biddle*) and Ohio (smarting after *Osborn* v. *Bank of the U.S.*)[42] was formidable. Kentucky courts had in fact denied jurisdiction, and in 1822 Senator Richard Johnson introduced a bill, which passed the Senate but failed in the House, that would have limited the jurisdiction of federal courts in such cases to the ebb and flow of the tide.[43]

Story's summary opinion of four paragraphs set just that limit. Federal jurisdiction, he declared, was not maintainable "upon acknowledged principles of law," because the service upon which wages were due was not "substantially performed, or to be performed, upon the sea or upon waters within the ebb and flow of the tide" (the standard demarcation of admiralty and maritime authority in English law). If there resulted an "inconvenience" to commerce, Story added, it ought to be removed not by the Court but by Congress acting under its authority to regulate foreign and interstate commerce—this from the justice who, according to legend, would declare admiralty jurisdiction over a cob in a bucket of water if someone happened to bring one into his Court.[44]

Why would Story, the great advocate of judicial power, and the self-proclaimed champion of federal admiralty jurisdiction,[45] lead the Court in repudiating its authority over the entire system of inland lakes and rivers at exactly the time when steamboat commerce on them necessitated uniformity? Was this not clear proof that he had traded principle for expediency? In fact, he had not, at least not by his scientific reckoning. The decision, as Story knew, was without question a timely act of self-abnegation. It was made, moreover, with the approval of William Johnson, who, as Story recounted, was "hostile" to admiralty jurisdiction and "watched with jealousy" while the issue was debated.[46] John Marshall, it would appear, looked on the decision as a compromise of principle: Story pointed out that Marshall favored an even broader federal admiralty jurisdiction than he did.[47]

Story admitted, too, that when "reasoning *diverse intuitu*" in earlier opinions, he seemed to have favored a "broader doctrine."[48] But he also insisted in both personal correspondence and subsequent opinions that his *Jefferson* opinion was good law and perfectly compatible with the principles he had laid out himself a decade earlier in *De Lovio* v. *Boit*. In that great effort, Story had laid the foundation of American admiralty law by transplanting his version of English admiralty law, which included the tidewater principle. In *De Lovio* legal science worked to achieve the broad policy goals that Story wanted. In *Jefferson* he demonstrated a willingness to stick by "science" when it pinched as well as when it comforted.

Story's discomfort, if he had any, was eased by the knowledge that the decision relieved political pressure on the Court and by the fact that the concessions made were less than they appeared and entirely correctable. As Story was careful to point out, the tidewater principle asserted in *Jefferson*—that is to say, the application of "locality" as a determinant of jurisdiction—applied only to torts. "As to contracts, the jurisdiction depends on the fact of their being *maritime* contracts or not."[49] And even where Story surrendered jurisdiction, he provided a corrective by inviting Congress to expand the diminished jurisdiction by statute, a nationalist solution that states' rightists could hardly take comfort in. Twenty years later Story followed his own advice. At the request of the Senate Judiciary Committee and with the approval of the Court, he drafted an act based on the commerce power extending federal jurisdiction over inland waters to federally licensed vessels employed in interstate commerce.[50] In 1851 a Court known for its sympathy to states' rights totally repudiated Story's *Jefferson* ruling, with only radical states' rightist justice Peter Daniel defending Story![51]

If states' rightists enjoyed the irony of Story's "retreat" in *Jefferson*, they could have found little else in his judging in the 1820s to comfort them. In the sensitive area of slavery adjudication, as witness his circuit opinion in *La Jeune Eugenie* (1822), he was downright aggressive, although he did not dissent later when the Supreme Court reversed him. In those 1820s decisions where the Court held the line, Story was always there, and more often than not, he urged on the Court, even on the chief justice, the most extreme nationalist construction. Story fully supported Marshall in *Gibbons* v. *Ogden* and, as noted, may even have helped him write the opinion[52] It was Story, too (along with Webster, who argued the case), who subsequently worked to rescue an exclusivist interpretation of national commerce power from Marshall's less-than-clear language on that point. To be sure, Story did go along silently with the chief justice in the *Blackbird*

Creek decision, in which Marshall discovered a concurrent commerce power, but he returned to exclusivism in his dissent in *New York* v. *Miln* (1837) and brought it forward again as a constructive tool in *Prigg* v. *Pennsylvania* (1842).[53]

Story was even more resolute in contract clause litigation, as witness *Green* v. *Biddle*. As a close friend of Justice Todd, who confronted the case on circuit, Story knew full well the explosive nature of the issue. He knew that land titles were tied into conservative banking in Kentucky and that radical banking interests as well as the relief party would resist any decision undercutting state land law. He understood that the ultimate goal of Kentucky resistance to Virginia land law was repeal of the Agreement of 1791 wherein Virginia seemed to hold Kentucky in bondage as a second-class state.[54] With these things in mind, and with the certain conviction that an adverse decision would bring Kentucky into the anti-Court movement, Story handed down his ringing repudiation of Kentucky's claimant law. In the process he elevated the Agreement of 1791 to the rank of a contract protected by article I, section 10, and thus forestalled the movement toward repudiation.

This was bold stuff indeed, and risky, as Story himself well knew. For him, however, it was a matter of legal science, as he explained in September 1821 to his friends in the Suffolk County Bar Association. Kentucky not only threatened uniform land titles but had perverted both law and equity. The legislature, asserted Story, in its ignorance and arrogance had created an abstruse "local jurisprudence, built on artificial principles, singularly acute and metaphysical," and quite beyond the reach of the "lights of the common law."[55] The challenge was not merely to resist heresy but to root it out. Two years of abuse by Kentucky did not change his mind, either. "The Occupying Claimant Law has at last been definitely settled, after many struggles," he wrote after the Court's second *Green* decision in March 1823. "I see no reason to take back our opinion, though for one, I felt a solicitude to come to that result, if I could have done it according to my views of great principles. I could not change my opinion, and I have adhered to it."[56] For Story as for Bushrod Washington, it was a matter of "God and conscience."

Story stuck by "great principles" even when they did not carry the day, as in the bankruptcy-contract case of *Ogden* v. *Saunders* (1827). The question here was whether a New York bankruptcy law governing contracts made after its passage violated the contract clause as set forth in *Sturgis* in 1819. Divisions in the earlier case surfaced as a majority, bolstered by the new justices and led by William Johnson, held that prospective bankruptcy laws were constitutional. Story was aghast at the notion, expressed in Johnson's opinion, that "all contracts of men receive a relative, and not a positive interpretation," and that state legislatures held the final say about this new relative law.[57] He joined Marshall's forceful dissent, which reasserted their interpretation of the *Sturgis* precedent: that state laws, either prospective or retrospective, cannot alter the substance (as distinct from the remedy) of a contract. Three years later in *Craig* v. *Missouri* (1830), Marshall, this time for a precarious majority, reaffirmed the sanctity of contract against state paper money legislation.[58]

Story also agreed with the chief justice that the Court was participating in its own destruction.[59] And it was precisely this internal surrender that Story had worked to avoid. His strategy had not been unyielding, as we have seen. But the only case in which he took an active part in judicial retreat was the *Thomas Jefferson*, and that fell within the principles of admiralty law as he conceived them. Beyond that the most he did was to remain silent, as in *Blackbird Creek* (which contradicted Story's exclusivist interpretation of the commerce clause) and *Billings* (which retreated from the high ground taken in *Dartmouth College*). He held his peace, too, in *Hawkins et al.* v. *Barney's Lessee* (1831) when Johnson, for a unanimous Court, retreated from *Green* v. *Biddle* by upholding a Kentucky land law that permitted adverse holders to claim color of title after seven years' possession.[60]

Why Story refused to speak out in these cases is not clear. Deference to Marshall (who wrote the opinion in two of these cases) was assuredly a consideration, and in addition Story uniformly refused as a matter of principle to record his dissents, except in unusual circumstances.[61] The prospect of a solo dissent may well have appeared pointless if not counterproductive, too, though growing desperation would soon change his mind on this subject. In any case it should come as no surprise that his deviations from purity were modest. New England conservative wisdom from the 1820s was that evil had to be confronted with principle, and Story himself had more than once warned against "non-resistance and passive obedience," "indifference," "indolence," and "moderation."[62] "Masculine force" was the order of the day and in fact always had been when it came to the Court. When his own party had attacked the independent judiciary, Story, as a young legislator, had responded with two bills for salary increases and another to introduce equity jurisdiction. On the Supreme Court it was young Justice Story who struck out for a federal criminal common law against the rest of the Court and much of the nation. Equally aggressive, or "manly," as Story liked to put it, was his response to Virginia in *Fairfax*, *Martin*, and *Terrett*.

Behind this no-compromise jurisprudence was a naturally didactic personality fortified by plenty of self-assuredness, a lofty ambition, and an immense pride in the accomplishments of the Marshall Court and the plaudits of conservative New England. Beyond personal, institutional, and regional pride, however, was an enlightenment faith in reason that translated into the jurisprudential conviction that law was scientific. That conventional notion was a part of Story's legal upbringing, as it was of that of most other lawyers of the early national period. But the 1820s gave it new tangibility. From a way of looking at the law it became a way of judging. Timing was crucial to the transformation. Story's first dozen years on the Court, following the nation's preoccupation with foreign affairs, were given over to questions of prize and neutral rights, to admiralty and maritime law generally. It was precisely in this branch of law, as Story himself pointed out in his 1818 essay in the *North American Review*, that science—that is to say, regularity, uniformity, system—prevailed.[63] Maritime issues ceased rather abruptly to be dominant in the mid-1820s, but the lessons about the law that Story learned from them stood. Uniformity was no less important to domestic commerce and manufacturing than it had been to foreign commerce and questions of international law. And what was true for private law seemed generally applicable to constitutional law, despite the obvious differences. When Story held the line against compromise in the 1820s he struck a blow for the integrity of the law. His "Rules of Interpretation" may have, as Parrington claimed, justified the decisions of the Marshall Court; they also reflected Story's maturing vision of American legal science. In this vision, creativity would be circumscribed by principle, which is what he urged his colleagues to uphold.

2. Georgia and the Cherokee Indians: The Moral Dimension of Scientific Law

There was one other dimension to the concept of legal statesmanship that Story urged on his colleagues. Judicial firmness was not only scientific; it was moral. And morality was not a matter of sentiment or even passion, though he had plenty of that. In his intellectual universe, morality and legal science were interconnected not incidentally or metaphorically but specifically and concretely. This was the gist of his argument with Jefferson over Christianity and the common law, which opened into his larger belief that correct law was natural law, part of God's design for mankind.[64] If law was God's design, as the eighteenth century insisted, and if the Court was the defender of the law, then those who attacked the Court were enemies of morality. That was the practical nub of the matter for Justice Story as for Joseph Story, New England conservative.

The Court was, then, the guardian not just of the Constitution but of republican morality. But could the people be made to understand? Opposed to this goal were political parties and demagogues, Andrew Jackson (who in Story's mind inherited the mantle of evil from Jefferson) and Jacksonian Democracy. Still, public virtue was only down, not out. What the people needed was a great heuristic cause that would set forth the Court in its true moral-legal light: the counterweight to moral decay. Such in fact were the Georgia Indian cases of 1831 and 1832, though their outcome was far different from what Marshall and Story planned.

Greed and racism put Georgia on a collision course with the seventeen thousand Cherokees who occupied the eastern slope of the Smoky Mountains in the northern and western sections of the state.[65] Georgians wanted their land and in the 1820s turned to the state to get it. To defend themselves the Indians looked to the federal government and the Treaty of 1791, which guaranteed them possession of all lands not ceded. Operating on the premise that the Indians were holding back civilization, the federal government promised Georgia to facilitate Indian removal from the land within the state. This pledge became increasingly difficult to justify, however, when the Cherokees gave up their nomadic habits, turned to agriculture, perfected a written language, adopted a constitution, and converted to Christianity, all of which they did in the 1820s with official encouragement from Washington. Cherokee efforts won praise from many Northerners, especially in New England, but only goaded Georgians into intensifying the expropriation campaign, particularly after the discovery of gold on Indian land in 1828. The state had already declared sovereignty over Indian land in 1824, but in December 1829 it passed a series of draconian laws, activated by Governor George Gilmer on 3 July 1830, which in flat violation of treaty guarantees extended state control over the Cherokees and opened their lands for immediate public auction. President Jackson's annual message to Congress on 6 December 1830, promising a "happy consummation" of the policy of Indian removal, backed Georgia all the way. With the passage of the Indian Removal Act of 1830, which made Story "blush" for his country,[66] Congress closed all lines of redress for the Indians except the Supreme Court and the American people themselves.

With states' rights in ascendancy and the Court's authority on the wane, the prospects of judicial salvation were hardly encouraging. Indeed, in *Johnson* v. *M'Intosh* (1823), a case involving a large tract of Indian land in Illinois, the Court may have encouraged Georgia by ruling that title to lands in America vested by discovery in the British government fell to the United States at independence; the Indians held by occupation only.[67] Georgia might take help from the Supreme Court, but it was adamant that it would not brook interference in its designs on Cherokee land. Its determination was clear in the case of Corn Tassel, a Cherokee arrested for murder under the newly asserted authority of Georgia over Cherokee territory and executed in 1830 after "intemperate and indecorous proceedings" and in blatant disregard of a show cause citation issued by the Court.[68]

It was as a last desperate measure, then, that William Wirt as counsel for the Indians set in motion *Cherokee Nation* v. *Georgia* (1831).[69] Wirt asked the Court on its equity side to enjoin Georgia from exercising authority over the Cherokees on the ground that the act of 1829 asserting state control over the Indians violated the Treaty of 1791 with the Cherokee "nation." Just the fact that "a few savages" could sue and drag a sovereign state before the bar of the Supreme Court brought back memories of *Chisholm* and sent Georgians into a rage.[70] To have ruled for the Indians, moreover, would have been to acknowlege a sovereign Indian state under federal protection within the boundaries of the state, a principle that Georgia and most other states would have resisted by force. Marshall knew this full well, and he understood also that a decision for the Indians would fuel already red hot congressional efforts to curb judicial authority. With victory out of reach, the Court could aim only to avoid humiliating surrender; Marshall achieved this goal in a marvelous act of equivocation and judicial improvisation. The Cherokees, he said for the majority, were a "domestic dependent nation," a status that entitled them to the protection of federal treaties. But they were not a sovereign state capable of suing in the Supreme Court under original jurisdiction.[71] Smith Thompson's dissent, supported by Story, summarily dispensed with the jurisdictional barrier raised by the majority and went boldly for the Indians on the merits.

Behind Story's silent dissent was a passionate conviction that law and morality were and should be one. He was in the midst of his argument with Jefferson over Christianity and the common law. On the Court and off he was working to expand the scope of equity because it protected those unable to protect themselves. On circuit he had denounced slavery and the slave trade and put forth his court as the defender of the common seaman. Were not the Indians entitled to help as well? Story believed so. At his first encounter with Indians at Monroe's White House in 1822 he had been immensely impressed by their intelligence, grace, and natural dignity, qualities that he was unwilling to attribute to the democratic "Mob."[72] Like Marshall he sensed the desperate plight of the Southern tribes as they faced the prospect of displacement by land-greedy settlers. He was not hopeful that the destruction of Indian civilization could be stopped, but he felt that the effort should be made, especially by New England. He urged his son "to speak in defense of the poor Indians," and he did so himself in 1828 in his Salem speech "The History and Influence of the Puritans."[73] By praising the Puritans for their Indian policy, Story condemned Georgia for its and went on public record as a champion of Indian rights. In the same speech he also took a potshot at the *Johnson* v. *M'Intosh* ruling that Indians held their land by occupancy only. On the contrary, he declared unequivocally, they held not only by natural law and moral right but by municipal law as well. If New Englanders had not always respected those rights, he added in reference to Georgia and the Cherokees, at least when they failed to do so "they were not encouraged or justified by the government."[74]

It would appear that Story was girding himself and New England for a showdown with Georgia. Indeed, anticipating the issues in *Cherokee Nation*, he admitted that it was "impossible not to have some thought on the subject." He pledged "to keep my mind open as much as possible," and he was confident that the Court would proceed "cautiously, & deliberately"; that it would "act within the line of duty"; that the Justices, "whatever our private opinions as men," would "not be tempted to exceed our jurisdiction."[75] Despite his protestations of neutrality, it is a good guess that Story's calmness under stress came from his certainty that truth, morality, and law were one and the same and all on his side. Quite simply, as he put it in his notes on the argument, the Cherokees had "rights, liberty, property" that the Court was obliged to protect.[76] The case was "extraordinary," to be sure, and its "political & national character" raised a real danger of retaliation against the Court. But that did not matter either. The question, he promised Hopkinson, would be "met without fear or favour, if it is to be."[77] After the decision he was firmly convinced that he and Thompson "were right" and pleased that the entire decision would be published and presented to the people.[78]

But how could Story have been so certain of his law, so pleased with himself, given his dissent from the chief justice, his friend and constitutional mentor? They had not, of course, always agreed on judicial tactics, as we have seen, and even as the *Cherokee* case was being decided they appeared to be parting company in the *Charles River Bridge* case which was argued first in the 1831 term. It could be simply that disagreement in the *Cherokee Nation* case was minimal: that Marshall thought that the jurisdiction of the Court was not, by Story's own test, "*clear & unequivocal.*" It is also possible they did not disagree at all, that Story's and Thompson's dissents were part of an agreed-upon strategy. Clearly Marshall's sympathy for the Indians was "in perfect accordance" with Story's, as he confessed after reading the latter's speech on the Puritans; like Story he felt that the time had "unquestionably arrived" for bestowing "magnanimity and Justice" on them.[79] And Marshall no less than Story believed that the Supreme Court was the proper instrument to use. The chief justice may have denied jurisdiction in his *Cherokee Nation* opinion. But, in a remarkable *dictum*, he also invited the Indians to bring another case without jurisdictional problems and went so far as to suggest, in advance, that justice and presumably the Court as well would be on their side.[80] To make the point even more forcefully, he invited Thompson and Story to make their dissent public, as they were not originally inclined to do.[81] What appeared to be a retreat under fire was in fact a call to the colors. Scientific law, it would seem, had some play in the joints.

The Cherokees and their counsel got the signal. In 1832 they appealed to the Court the judgment of the Georgia Superior Court for Gwinnett County, which had convicted and sentenced to prison two Northern missionaries for residing in Cherokee territory without the license required by state law. This action originated *Worcester* v. *Georgia* (1832), the culmination of a decade of warfare between the Marshall Court and states' rightists, political parties, and executive power. Bound together with the fate of the Cherokee people was the supremacy of federal law, as well as the authority of the Supreme Court in the American system of government. So at any rate Story conceived it, and assuredly the gauntlet was down. South Carolina, where nullification was at its peak, had already warned the Court against additional nationalist decisions. Section 25, under which *Worcester* came forward, was under bitter attack in Congress, and a confrontation with Georgia (whose lawyers refused even to appear) was unavoidable. The justices could not escape on a point of jurisdiction, and neither could they look for support to Congress (where sectional politics ruled) or to the president (who would not, it was reported by Story's "authentic sources," enforce any decision against the state).[82]

In Story's apocalyptic mood it mattered not. What did count was that the chief justice, "in his best manner," rebuked the immoral and unconstitutional behavior of Georgia. Marshall was indeed at his best and boldest. The chief justice could have narrowed down the case to a conflict between the Georgia statute of 1830, under which the missionaries had been imprisoned, and the federal Treaty of 1791, and this was in fact what Justice John McLean did in his concurring opinion. Instead Marshall chose the broadest ground, including as his opening gambit an exploration of section 25, the relevance of which Georgia denied. Citing Story in *Martin*, Marshall found the Court's appellate authority unshakable. He took the occasion to remind Congress that it had bestowed the power in the first place and "imposed" on the Court the "duty" of exercising it. "This duty, however unpleasant, cannot be avoided," he declared, and added that "those who fill the judicial department have no discretion in selecting the subjects to be brought before them."[83]

Whether this was entirely true in light of the strategy pursued in *Cherokee Nation* is somewhat doubtful, but it was music to Story's ears anyway. And so was the powerful vindication of the rights of the Cherokees. Abjuring the narrow approach, Marshall recapitulated the whole history of treaty relations between the Cherokees and Great Britain and the United States. Not only was the state act of 1830 unconstitutional, but so were all of Georgia's statutes subversive of Cherokee rights. That beleaguered people were a "distinct, independent political" community whose "natural rights" and "undisputed" possession of the soil were protected by a treaty that was the supreme law of the land. The Cherokee nation was a "distinct community" over which "the laws of Georgia can have no force."[84] The New England missionaries were imprisoned under an unconstitutional law and were entitled to their freedom. "Thanks be to God," exulted Story, "the Court can wash their hands clean of the iniquity of oppressing the Indians and disregarding their rights." [85] The hard line he had urged on the Court for fifteen years seemed now to have triumphed. "The Court had done its duty," he concluded righteously. "Let the Nation now do theirs." [86]

The nation did *not* do its duty. The Court's mandate to the Superior Court for Gwinnett County, ordering it to reverse its decision, was deliberately ignored. Because of a statutory deficiency, the Supreme Court never issued a second mandate ordering the release of Worcester, who continued to languish in prison; President Jackson was thus relieved of the obligation to enforce the decision (which contrary to most opinion he was inclined to do). [87] While all this was *not* going on, Georgia, with congressional sanction and presidential support, moved ahead with its policy of Indian removal and extermination. The law might be moral and the Court's hands clean, but it did not matter much unless the American people cared, and as it turned out, they did not.

The American people, in fact, were consulted. Indeed, never before or since was a single decision of the Supreme Court so directly subjected to public approval. Never did the justices seem so dependent on the people, who, as Story said, "ought to be the firm friends of the Court," because it helped only them and not itself. [88] The Court had acted; the president had not: The fate of the Cherokees turned on the presidential election of 1832. It is not entirely fanciful to suppose that the Court, or at least Marshall and Story, had the election in mind all along, especially if one remembers the unusual strategy of litigation used to get from *Cherokee Nation* to *Worcester*. Clearly there was a remarkable unity among pro-Cherokee and anti-Jackson leaders. Clay and Webster, the main opponents of Jackson in the emerging Whig party, were also the leading congressional champions of the Cherokee cause. John Sergeant and William Wirt, chief counsel for the Indians before the Court, were prominent anti-Jackson men, Sergeant as in-house counsel for Biddle's bank, who worked to make Jackson's veto message an election issue, and Wirt as the anti-Jackson candidate for the anti-Masonic party. Jackson, of course, had to oblige and did so quite as his enemies anticipated. He joined Georgia against the Cherokees just as Story predicted he would and obliged Webster with an issue when he vetoed the bank recharter bill in July 1832. Banking and economic policy were the main issues of the campaign, as it turned out, but Indian policy added a significant moral dimension. At issue also was Jackson's view of the Court, for in both the banking and the Indian issues a Supreme Court decision was directly on the line. Story, who had been predicting Armageddon for at least a decade, was certain the time had come. "The crisis is approaching," he warned Hopkinson, "doubtless, in which it must be decided whether we have a Gover^t, or not; whether the powers of the U. States are merely such as the states choose to acquiesce in, or whether they are capable of being enforced *scopio egore*." The issue "must forever be recurring; & must be settled."[89]

The "people ought to be the firm friends of the Court," but they were not. Called on by conservative nationalists to repudiate the immoral, unconstitutional reign of King Andrew, the electorate instead returned the "Old Hero" to a second term. The bank was as good as dead, and so in a few years were most of the Cherokees. Story's faint but persistent hope that the American people might reassert their good sense and reclaim their virtue crashed on the rocks of electoral politics. Nor did it console him that the newly elected president, within the year, toasted the "federal Union" and threatened to hang those who would destroy it. New England might soften its opposition to Jackson; Clay might work to facilitate compromise; Webster might be persuaded that better days lay ahead; even Harvard might honor the newborn hero with an honorary degree. But Story could not rejoice. If Jackson was saving the Union he was also destroying the Republic: Gone or going was the national bank that the Court had done so much to sustain and with it rational, efficient, conservatively controlled economic growth. Jackson doomed the protective tariff, too, which Story had come to believe was essential to New England.[90] With deep sadness he watched the "extermination" of the Indians and the further repudiation of the Court's authority.[91] Behind this disgrace and the other calamities of the age as well were political parties. Far from being eliminated, as Story and Adams had hoped, they had become an essential part of the constitutional system itself. The message was clear: If the Union were to survive it would be at the expense of the Republic and on the basis of compromises facilitated by professional politicians.

Some of that new breed—for example, Martin Van Buren of the Albany Regency—might praise the new system. Others, like Webster and the stillborn Whigs, might embrace it reluctantly "because the good is before them & the evil is distant." Again Story held his gloomy ground. "Upon politics I am fixed," he declared in 1833. "The late compromise is a surrender of the Constitution, to which under no circum[stances] will I be either a party, or a quiet looker-on." The duty of "public men" was to resist, and in the lead had to be the "*professional* intelligence" of the country.[92] At the head of this intelligentsia, one assumes, were certain justices of the Supreme Court.

3. The *Charles River Bridge* Case and Republican Law: "A Solitary Relic of Former Doctrines"

Certain justices could be counted on to resist, indeed, but not all; and that was the problem as Story perceived it: The Court had come to reflect the very forces of chaos it was supposed to contain. The new appointments and changed doctrines of the 1820s were but a trickle in the mounting flood of change that Marshall's death symbolized. Between 1823 and 1830 three new justices were appointed, two by President Jackson. In the next half dozen years he got three more: William Johnson died in 1834 and was replaced in 1835 by James Wayne of Georgia, whose main accomplishment, it appeared to conservatives, was his stalwart support of Andrew Jackson. Roger Taney's confirmation as chief justice in 1836, along with Philip Barbour's appointment the same year and John Catron's and John McKinley's in 1837 (to fill vacancies created by the judicial reorganization act of that year), gave the Democrats a majority of six. Peter Daniel's last-minute appointment by Martin Van Buren in 1841 would leave only Story and Smith Thompson from the old Court.

It could not be assumed, of course, that the ideology of the appointing president automatically doomed the new justices to be states' rights ideologues; nor can it be assumed that Jackson himself was a root-and-branch enemy of the Supreme Court.[93] Still, the changed complexion of the brethren could not be disguised. The differences were significant and distasteful to many. The Whigs lamented the seven Democrats on the Court. The North, distrustful of the six justices from the South and new West, felt itself underrepresented. The new justices also lacked the common experience of the Revolution and the confederation that had rallied the Marshall Court to a common nationalism. Devotion to the Union and respect for the Court were not lacking, but the new justices were removed a generation from the Revolution and did not revere the miracle of the Constitution, understand the fragility of constitutional union, or hold to the idealism of republicanism, as had their predecessors. On the wane, too, with the explosion of case law and the rise of legal instrumentalism, was the orderly legal universe conjured up by Blackstone.

The generational differences, as they manifested themselves in increased division among the justices, caused Story to "despair" of the "future course," which seemed full of "darkness, & ominous conjectures."[94] There was, of course, an occasional ray of hope. One was his new colleague Smith Thompson, who held the line with Story in *Ogden* v. *Saunders* and in the Cherokee cases. Story helped him whenever he could. John McLean also proved to be a good friend despite his Jacksonian connections. With a little tutelage he became a sound judge, too, though he occasionally slipped from orthodoxy, as in *Craig* and *Briscoe* v. *Bank of Kentucky*. Troublesome even to his friends was his desire to be president, which goal he pursued tirelessly from the bench.

With the other justices and the Court collectively there were more serious problems. Henry Baldwin from Pennsylvania was initially acceptable to Marshall and Story, in part, no doubt, because he was not John

Bannister Gibson, whom conservatives feared would get the appointment. He quickly fell out with Story, however, who by the end of the 1831 term doubted "that a certain Gentleman will ever become conciliatory."[95] After a nervous breakdown in 1833 that caused him to miss that term of the Court, Baldwin became increasingly paranoid and thereafter spent most of his effort dissenting, criticizing his colleagues, and abusing reporter Peters for bias and incompetence. The inevitable break between Story and Baldwin came in 1837 with the publication in the appendix of the reports of the latter's *General View of the Constitution*, which condemned the broad nationalism of the Marshall Court as unfounded and usurpatory. He took particular pains to refute the thesis in Story's *Commentaries* that sovereignty devolved on the whole people after 1776, adding insult to injury by relying on Calhoun to make his point. Story was so indignant that such a work had been published in the reports that he even upbraided his old friend Peters for letting it happen. Still, he was not surprised, for he had long since concluded that the Court had fallen on "evil days," that he could never "expect to meet again on that Bench such men, as I have seen there"[96]—and this was before he had reckoned with John McKinley from Alabama, who in fifteen years on the Court would write only twenty-some opinions and none of them in important cases.

Judge for judge the new Court simply did not measure up to the old one; collectively, its élan and efficiency were falling victim to a new "revolutionary spirit," as Marshall complained to Story after *Craig*. The problem was not just the priorities of such new justices as Catron (who was able but intensely political) or Daniel (who was a rigid states' rights ideologue with a record of chronic dissent). Even the old-timers added to the malaise. William Johnson not only persisted in his Jeffersonian dissents but was habitually "wanting in punctuality" and before his death in 1834 had withdrawn into social and intellectual "solitude."[97] Gabriel Duvall was a "gentle," "urbane" colleague and a conscientious judge who generally voted with Marshall and Story, but he became embarrassingly deaf and increasingly distracted by ill health and personal grief.

Even the chief justice was slipping by the early 1830s. He could not shake the deep depression brought on by his beloved wife's death, and his own health declined rapidly after 1832, hurried on no doubt by his casual ways (Edward Everett, for example, saw him hurrying to Court on a cold damp day without coat or hat). Increasingly he grew careless of his appearance, too, so that he appeared in Court with egg on his chin ("What a sloven the great man is," said Wirt affectionately).[98] His mind remained clear to the end, and his presence on the Court was a solace and inspiration to Story, but even his venerable presence could not harmonize the justices. Divided, contentious, the Court gradually abandoned its habit of communal living; plagued by absenteeism, sickness, and incompetence, it fell increasingly behind in its docket. Story was not only distressed but bored, and he went to Washington, if one judges by his plaintive letters to his wife and friends, mainly to see John Marshall and longed for New England as soon as he arrived.

The appearance of Roger Taney as chief justice made life in Washington even more untenable for Story, at least temporarily. He had nothing personal against him, and indeed they would develop a relationship based on mutual respect, if not affection. Yet in 1837 Story knew that what his friends said was true: that if justice prevailed, that if talents, service, and dedication counted, then he, Story, would have assumed Marshall's mantle as chief justice. He professed indifference, and he knew that Marshall's successor would "have a most painful & discouraging duty."[99] But he wanted the job and had in fact performed it effectively during the difficult interim period between Marshall's death and Taney's assumption of duties. He liked the taste of power, was pleased with his mastery of the new responsibilities, encouraged that the Court was gaining on the docket, "perfectly satisfied" with his position and even with his "present brethren." Aspire he might, but he also knew down deep that Jackson would never put the "most dangerous man in the U. States" in the nation's highest judicial office. He resigned himself "without hope or anxiety" to being "*hors de combat.*"[100]

Still, Taney was hard for Story and his friends to accept, as almost anyone would have been following in Marshall's footsteps. It was not that he was a bad lawyer. Story, for one, acknowledged his "fine talents"[101] and shortly after the new term began even conceded that life on his Court might be tolerable, even harmonious.[102] Nevertheless, it boded ill that the new chief was so thoroughly Jacksonian. Taney had been a party leader in Maryland, for which service he was appointed U.S. attorney general. In that office he supported states' rights and slavery and opposed corporations, except the state banks of Maryland, which many thought that he liked too much.[103] Taney had also written part of the veto message that attacked the Court and had issued the death sentence to the Second Bank of the United States. As treasury secretary he executed the sentence (and as state banker profited from the death).

In every respect, then, including even the trousers he wore instead of smallclothes, Taney reflected the spirit of the changing age, which was exactly what made Story uneasy. His personal preference was to resign. Rumor had it that he might become president of a Massachusetts insurance company or even a candidate for vice-president, and in fact he did decline an offer of the chief justiceship of Massachusetts.[104] A real alternative, and one that tempted him greatly, was to return full time to Harvard Law School, where he could teach the kind of law he no longer found on the Supreme Court. This step would bring him home to New England

and his family. Sarah, who was now a permanent invalid, needed him more than ever, and his daughter Caroline's death in 1831 brought him closer still to Mary and William. Comforted and sustained by family and friends, nourished by New England, he might gain strength to fight back the nineteenth century, or at least endure it.

Instead of leaving he stayed. The time to resign, as he said to Mason in 1822, was when he was young enough to resume the practice of law.[105] Probably it was too late in 1837 for a return to the bar. But even more to the point, he really did not want to desert the Court. He had already given twenty-five years of his life to the institution, and moreover he had promised Marshall he would stay until the end. Indeed, his actions belied the persistent pessimism of his letters. There remained still a faint possibility that the American people, even after electing Jackson a second time, might be saved. Just possibly he, Story, as Richard Peters had prophesied, was the sole remaining pillar on which redemption rested.[106]

If Story fancied himself a judicial messiah who might save the Court and the Constitution, then 1837 was certainly the moment to speak words of fire. The bank was gone, the Indians were destroyed, and the country was staggering from the worst depression in its short history—God's warning, thought many, that Americans should change their ways. Martin Van Buren, who pledged to continue the policies of Jackson, was newly elected president, and a Jacksonian Court led by a Jacksonian chief justice was ready for business. Facing it on the 1837 docket, moreover, were three great constitutional cases each of which turned on a fundamental legal issue of the new age. *Briscoe* v. *Bank of the Commonwealth of Kentucky* reintroduced the question whether a state could issue paper money,[107] an issue presumably settled in *Craig* v. *Missouri* (1830) but resurrected again by the prospective demise of the Second Bank. *New York* v. *Miln*[108] forced the Court to draw the line between state and federal power over interstate commerce and confronted it with a reconsideration of *Gibbons* v. *Ogden*, whose meaning had been clouded by *Brown* v. *Maryland* (1827) and *Willson* v. *The Blackbird Creek Marsh Company* (1829). More fundamental than either was *Charles River Bridge* v. *Warren Bridge*, which pitted private property against the power of the state to regulate corporations in the interest of public welfare.[109] On the line at the same time was the legal model for economic growth as defined by the Marshall Court in the *Dartmouth College* case. Each of these cases had been argued before the Marshall Court, but illness and division among the justices had forced their postponement until the 1837 term. Now they awaited resolution according to the lights of a new age and a new Court.

Viewed in the perspective of history, the crisis of 1837 was but an example, albeit a dramatic one, of what the Court has always had to do: make old law fit new circumstances. For Story, however, it was a final showdown with forces that for the previous twenty years had threatened to obliterate the patient labors of the Marshall Court. The Kentucky banking case, indeed, raised questions that went back in Story's mind (as they had in Marshall's) to the Confederation period. The Bank of the Commonwealth of Kentucky was chartered as a private corporation, but its stock was owned solely by the state, its president and board of directors were appointed by the legislature, and its notes circulated as legal tender. The issue was whether these notes were bills of credit which states were prohibited from issuing by article I, section 10, of the Constitution. *Craig* v. *Missouri*, in which the Marshall Court defined bills of credit broadly and struck down a Missouri act making loan-office certificates legal tender, was clearly controlling, despite the efforts of counsel for Kentucky to distinguish the two cases. Three of the five justices who heard *Briscoe* in 1834, including Marshall and Story, were prepared to bring it within the scope of *Craig*, but the case was continued because the Court refused to decide cases coming under section 25 without the concurrence of at least four justices. The majority, bolstered by Jacksonian appointments and following Jacksonian states' rights priorities, now upheld the constitutionality of the Bank of the Commonwealth and its notes. McLean for the majority presumed to distinguish *Briscoe* from *Craig*, but it was clear that *stare decisis* was less important than the impending demise of Biddle's bank, which would make state banks the major source of money and credit. A decision against the Bank of the Commonwealth, said McLean candidly, would be "a fatal blow against the State banks, which have a capital of nearly four hundred millions of dollars, and which supply almost the entire circulating medium of the country."[110]

Story was unimpressed by the practical argument and distressed by the hypocritical bow to *stare decisis*. He entered a bitter, solitary, admonitory dissent. A "profound reverence and respect" for the dead chief justice, he said, and "an earnest desire to vindicate his memory from the imputation of rashness, or want of deep reflection," prompted him to speak out.[111] He rejected as speculative and metaphysical the argument that a bank totally owned and controlled by the state whose notes were money was not a state bank. Even the Court's argument from expediency seemed unconvincing to Story, because the case involved state-owned banks and left untouched the private banking structure of the states. If neither law nor economics justified the disruption of the *Craig* precedent, then the Court must have acted out of ignorance or politics or both.

The Court's decision in *New York* v. *Miln* seemed less cynical than in *Briscoe*, but its doctrinal confusion and disregard of the old law was equally distressing. *Miln*, like *Briscoe*, had been argued in 1834 but continued because of the absence of two justices and division among the rest. At issue was a New York law passed in 1824 requiring the masters of all vessels arriving at the port of New York from foreign countries or from other states to report the names, ages, occupations, and other data of all passengers and to take bond that none should become wards of the city. Because the law was designed to keep the city from being overwhelmed with indigents it was not prepared to care for, the state could argue that it was a police regulation designed to protect the health and welfare of its citizens, a power set out tentatively by Marshall himself in *Gibbons* and *Brown* v. *Maryland*. Clearly, however, the law touched interstate commerce, and the question was whether it was a legitimate exercise of police power or an intrusion into the power granted to Congress over foreign and interstate commerce.

Thanks to the ambiguity of the precedents, the Court had some discretionary leeway. By picking up on the doctrine mentioned but not established in *Gibbons* (that congressional power over interstate commerce was automatically exclusive of the states), it could have struck down the New York law. Story pressured it to do so, citing Marshall as his authority. Barbour's opinion for the Jacksonian majority cited *Gibbons* and *Brown*, too, but found there a state police power that he defined vaguely as state authority to legislate for the safety and general welfare of the people within its jurisdiction. Some such diminution of national authority was probably inevitable, given the demand for state legislative activity in the early nineteenth century. But Barbour's contention that police power was "unqualified and exclusive" went far beyond anything that precedent or practice could justify. It flatly contradicted Marshall's ruling in *Gibbons*, which gave priority to federal law in conflict with state statutes, and ignored both the Tenth Amendment and article VI of the Constitution by setting up an area of absolute state power beyond the confines of the Constitution and seemingly without reference to it. Not surprisingly, Barbour did not carry his colleagues along this radical path, and the best the majority could do was to uphold the New York regulation without saying why.[112]

Story might have taken some consolation that the Court rejected Barbour's extreme states' rights position. He might have been gratified that the majority struggled to work within precedent (something that many conservatives had doubted they would do), and possibly he might have attributed some of its confusion to the ambiguity of the old law itself. But he was not in an understanding mood. The mistaken construction of a clear precedent in *Miln* was every bit as disturbing to him as the frank repudiation of one in *Briscoe*. Certainly the massive confusion about the commerce clause comported ill with his notion of the Supreme Court as an instrument for the clarification of national law. As for that law, it was perfectly clear without further adjustment and manipulation, at least as Story laid it out. He admitted "in the most unhesitating manner" that states had the right to pass police legislation. But that power must comport with the document itself and not, as Barbour suggested, with some a priori source beyond it.[113] Constitutionally speaking, it was commerce power as rendered by the Court in *Gibbons* and *Brown*, not police power, that was controlling. Those cases established beyond any doubt that state laws that touched interstate commerce and that conflicted with congressional acts in the same area were unconstitutional. When Congress regulated immigrants, as it had for years, and when it regulated passenger ships, as it had in 1819, it foreclosed state laws of the kind passed by New York. Even without direct conflict, however, the New York law was unconstitutional because it violated the exclusive power of Congress under the commerce clause, which Story had only recently spelled out in his *Commentaries on the Constitution*.[114] No one listened. The Court's leading scholar stood alone with only the comfort of knowing that he had "the entire concurrence, upon the same grounds, of that great constitutional jurist, the late Mr. Chief Justice Marshall."[115]

Even that consolation was denied Story in *Charles River Bridge* v. *Warren Bridge*, the most far-reaching of the great cases of 1837 and Story's most revealing argument with the Taney Court.[116] The facts went back to 1785, when the Massachusetts legislature chartered the Charles River Bridge Company to build a bridge between Boston and Charlestown. For building the bridge and maintaining it the legislature granted the company the right to collect tolls for forty years, a privilege extended an additional thirty years in 1792 as compensation for the chartering of another bridge across the Charles. In 1828, while the toll rights of the old bridge were still in force, the legislature chartered the Warren Bridge Company and authorized it to build a toll-free bridge only a few yards from the old bridge. The question before the Court was whether the imprecisely worded old charter implicitly conferred a monopoly on the old bridge company, upon which the new bridge encroached, so that the new charter violated the contract clause of the Constitution as construed by the *Dartmouth College* decision.

On this technical and discretionary question of implication hinged many of the heated political-economic questions of the day that divided Whigs and Democrats. The battle of the bridges in the Massachusetts legislature was, in fact, a catalyst in the resurgence of party in the 1820s. John Skinner and the citizens of Charlestown who petitioned the legislature for the free bridge in 1823 branded their opponents as soulless aristocrats and avaricious monopolists and set themselves up as champions of the public interest. Denying the charges and accusing their accusers of demagoguery, the spokesmen for the old bridge emphasized the extensive turnover in their stock (which neutralized extravagant profits) and pointed to the large number of widows and orphans among stockholders (to detract attention from established capitalists like P. C. Brooks and Harrison Gray

Otis, who held large blocks of stock). As the political scenario emerged, then, it was democracy versus aristocracy. An added, distinctly Jacksonian motif pitted the state legislature, presumably the instrument of popular will, against the Supreme Court, with its record of aristocratic favoritism. Politics and law had become inseparable.

Beneath partisan bombast and high-flown legal talk about contract, laches, nuisance, and ferry rights were the great economic issues of the age upon which the parties were dividing. It was not just Harvard's annual annuity that was at stake or the property of the old bridge company, which in 1823 was valued at $280,000. Capitalism itself was at issue: what it meant and who would set economic policy. For Webster and Warren Dutton, counsel for the Charles River Bridge Company, it was faith in legislative promises that counted most. And for Story, too, who asked Greenleaf in the course of his argument whether a legislature might charter a railroad to be built within five rods of another railroad chartered by a previous legislature with "an express provision . . . that no other road should be granted during the duration of the charter." [117] Story must have been astonished when his friend replied that the second charter would stand. Webster and Dutton were, for they raised the specter of massive expropriation. It seemed clear: If the Court permitted state legislatures to go back on their promises to investors in corporations then no one would invest; progress would come to a standstill; entrepreneurial genius would be stifled and with it economic progress and national greatness.

Greenleaf and John Davis for the Warren people argued just the opposite. They, too, wanted economic growth and corporate expansion. But the real threat as they saw it was from a judicial decision that permitted established capital to entrench itself behind implied monopoly and thus forestall new corporate development. On the pinpoint of implied power, it would seem, teetered the future of the Republic. On this, at least, all agreed.

The chief justice spoke for the Jacksonian majority in an opinion that disconcerted his critics as much by its persuasiveness ("smooth and plausible," admitted Webster; clear and distinct, said Sumner) as it distressed them by its "cunning" manipulation of the old law. [118] Private property was still sacred and must, declared Taney, be "sacredly guarded." Corporate charters remained contracts under the protection of the Constitution. *Dartmouth College* was still in force, or so it seemed. But, continued Taney, "the community also have rights," and the "happiness and well-being of every citizen depends on their faithful preservation." And above all the rights of the public ought not to be surrendered on the shaky ground of inference. Such, said the chief justice, was the import of Marshall's decision in *Providence Bank* v. *Billings* in 1830. It was the guiding principle of the common law, too, where it was established that "any ambiguity in the terms of the contract, must operate against the adventurers and in favor of the public." Implied monopoly was bad economic policy, as well. "Modern science" would be throttled, transportation would be set back a century, if existing companies could barricade themselves behind implied charter rights—and in fact such cases were already pending. The Court ought not to set its judgment over against that of a sovereign legislature to enforce an economic policy that would hold back economic progress; certainly it ought not to do so by mere construction and inference.[119]

Taney's opinion followed Jacksonian priorities. It struck a blow for democratic capitalism; it was a timely concession to states' rights and legislative authority (and one that did not permanently detract from the authority of the Supreme Court). It was a practical response to the economic realities of the new age and, despite its instrumentalism, even presumed to respect the precedents of the Marshall Court. And it was, in Story's considered view, dead wrong on all counts. Most assuredly his view was "considered": painfully, exhaustively. He watched the cause gather momentum in Massachusetts not as a casual or impartial observer but as an insider, if not, indeed, as a potential victim. Among the chief stockholders in the Charles River Bridge Company were his friends and conservative compatriots. Harvard University, which stood to lose two hundred pounds annually, was his alma mater, and as an officer he had an obligation to protect the school's interests. Daniel Webster, Story's ally in the cause of conservative truth, was the spokesman for the old bridge before the legislature and chief counsel at the state and national levels (a fact that was not neutralized by the presence of Simon Greenleaf on the other side). The state supreme court judges who went for the old bridge in 1830 were Samuel Putnam (Story's old friend and teacher) and Isaac Parker (his new supporter in New England conservatism).

Story could hardly have been unbiased in the case, and he was not. Following it closely from its inception in 1823, he saw emerge all the evils he had been fighting on and off the Court for two decades. There for all to see was the pusillanimous Massachusetts legislature, which "has fallen into more common hands than in former times." There were brazen demagogues like state supreme court judge Marcus Morton, whom Story condemned for political behavior.[120] He saw flagrant expropriation of property supported by public passion stirred up by party agitation. Here, in short, in a single case was everything he detested and feared. His colleagues on the Court might be hesitant and confused when they heard the case in 1831. Not Story. By 21 December of that year he had finished "a very elaborate opinion extending over sixteen folio sheets," which he hoped would carry the Court, settle the law, and bring Massachusetts back to its senses.[121] New arguments in 1837 did not change his mind, nor did the six intervening years of Jacksonian misrule. He opened his dissent in 1837 with an assurance that he had "examined the case with the most anxious care and deliberation." He was "free to confess, that the opinion which I originally formed, after the first argument, is that which now has my most firm and unhesitating conviction."[122] His literally was a voice from the past.

The *Bridge* case was a romping field for legal scholarship, and Story romped through fifty-seven authority-laden pages. There was the ancient common law of ferries to be consulted (because the old bridge claimed that it inherited the monopoly rights that had been granted to the ferry it replaced and whose annual annuity to Harvard it assumed). The law of nuisance figured, too, as it had on the state level, and Story turned to it—inappropriately, say some, and even deceptively.[123] But the heart of the matter was the contract clause and the meaning of the charter given by the legislature to the Charles River Bridge Company in 1785. On that constitutional point alone the case was brought before the Supreme Court, and if nuisance law was applicable it was because the charter vested property in the old bridge. Story stated what was known and what was not: "No one doubts, that the charter is a contract and a grant," he said; the question was whether it should receive a "strict or liberal interpretation."[124]

In other words, did the charter give to the Charles River Bridge the exclusive right to collect tolls without having explicitly said so? Common law, "good sense," and "justice," which for Story were indistinguishable, all indicated that it did. Put yourself, he said, in the minds of the parties to the charter contract—for Story the proper way to discover contractual intent. The legislature speaking for the commonwealth wanted a bridge built across the Charles River, an undertaking that in 1785 was a risky one. The bridge company wanted to make a profit and was willing to put its money at risk. Its only recompense, because the bridge would ultimately revert to the state, was the right to collect tolls. If this right were not exclusive it would be, in fact, no right at all. Story put it plainly: Would any sensible businessman venture capital in a risky enterprise in which the sole profit was the right to collect tolls if the legislature reserved the right to destroy these tolls at any time by chartering an adjacent free bridge? Impossible. Even without explicitly saying so, the legislature recognized the company's exclusive right to take tolls, Story continued, because it was equipped with the common sense of businessmen. In the eyes of the law, the legislature was presumed to have bargained in good faith, and any doubt about its intent to grant exclusive tolls was removed by the compensation awarded to Harvard when the Charles River Bridge destroyed the old ferry and by the thirty-year extension of the original charter to the old bridge company in 1792 as compensation for chartering another bridge across the Charles, which might have diminished the old company's tolls. And when the exclusive right was given, "the law giveth, impliedly, whatever is for the taking and enjoying the same."[125] If a new bridge was necessary, then the property rights of the old might be taken by eminent domain provided that adequate compensation was given. Without such compensation the legislature had plainly and simply confiscated property, and by 1837 this was clearly what had happened. Such action—and here Story followed Webster's and Dutton's arguments and confronted Taney's theory of economic growth head on—would retard investment and bring economic development to an abrupt halt by destroying the reliability of corporate charters.

Story's opinion and Taney's received a distinctly partisan reception, in itself a signal that the Court was entering the modern age. Democrats saw the Court's decision as the dawn of a great new epoch. Story's opinion they either ignored or condemned; the editor of the Boston *Advocate*, for example, thought his effort "better suited to the dark days of Dudley and Empson than to this age and this country."[126] Charles J. Ingersoll even singled him out during the debates at the Pennsylvania constitutional convention of 1838 as the arch-villain who had corrupted both Marshall and his Court.[127] For most conservatives, on the other hand, Story was a hero slain with the words of true law and sound policy on his lips. Whig journals like the *North American Review* defended Story and the old law, and Whig politicians sensed the congeniality between his law and their policy.

Among the legal profession there was more diversity of opinion. Story acknowledged as much. But he was certain "that a very large proportion of all our ablest lawyers" supported his dissent, and especially those "at the head of the profession in America, as men of learning & exalted talents."[128] Preeminent among the latter was Chancellor Kent, who had "*re*-perused the *Charles River Bridge* case, & with increased disgust," as he put it to Story. "It abandons or overthrows a great Principle of constitutional Morality & I think goes to destroy the Security & Value of legislative Franchises. It injures the moral Sense of the Community & destroys the *Sanctity of Contracts*." And if the legislature can "quibble away" their promises, so soon will the people. "Now we sadly realize that we are to be under the reign of little Men—a pigmy race & that the sages of the last age are extinguished." But one giant remained, who with "accustomed learning, vigor, & warmth, & force" had "vindicated the Principles & authority of the old settled law."[129] Among those who agreed were Jeremiah Mason, William Prescott, and, of course, Daniel Webster. No doubt they would have heartily concurred with Charles Sumner when he wrote to Story regarding the *Bridge* case that "nobody in our country, or in the world, could have written your opinion but *yourself. Aut Morus, aut Diabolus*. It will stand in our books as an overtopping landmark of professional learning & science."[130]

Indisputably Story's dissent was a monument of scholarship. But was it relevant to the new age? Had the great man read black letter right and history wrong? Certainly a shift in constitutional law had taken shape. But the period following 1837 was a period of unparalleled economic growth, not one of economic disaster, as Story had so direly prophesied. Capitalists showed a remarkable talent for adjusting to the new dispensation, and so, moreover, did the Supreme Court itself, consistently refusing after 1837 to extend corporate charter rights by implication.[131] Nor did concessions to state legislative authority disrupt the balance of power within the federal sytem. Although the Court did put itself on the side of dynamic capital, the threat to property did not unhinge society or even destroy established wealth. Even *Dartmouth College* still stood, so that corporate contracts were safe from legislative interference provided only that the contract was explicit. Perhaps the chief justice had taken a few liberties with the common law, but had he not deftly preserved at least the semblance of legal continuity, and with that the reputation and relevance of the Supreme Court? Certainly its authority to decide had not been diminished, nor would it be under Taney.

Possibly, then, Story's dissent had been too much colored by personal bias. It was, after all, written during those painfully sad days when he was grappling with the sickness of his wife and the death of his young daughter. Maybe Marshall's illness and the mounting attack on the Court from nullifiers and states' rightists had infused Story's scholarship with excessive pessimism. Some of his friends appear to have thought so: At least they seem not to have been persuaded that the future of the Republic rested on the fate of the Charles River Bridge Company. Charles Sumner, who praised Story's learning so fully, who felt "irresistably carried away by the rushing current" of Story's argument,[132] had originally not been convinced by it and even worked to make "Warren men" of Story's students at Harvard Law School. Simon Greenleaf, Story's dear friend and colleague at the Law School, obviously took the other side, and Harvard University itself, which let one of its professors argue against the pecuniary interest of the institution, must not have felt that *all* was at stake. Judge Joseph Hopkinson, for whom Story had the deepest respect and affection, was inclined to favor the new bridge, and even that unyielding conservative Richard Peters thought Story was too apocalyptic.[133] One scholar has argued persuasively that even John Marshall did not support Story when the case was first argued.[134] Worn down, depressed by a sense of his own irrelevance and the mortality of republican government, Story may have overstated his case and imposed on the law too much of his own sense of Götterdämmerung.

Admitting as much, Story's dissent still needs to be taken seriously as policy and law. The problem is to avoid anachronism, to discount history written by the winners—not an easy task, seeing that Story's own predictions proved so mistaken. Corporate expansion did not cease as a result of the majority opinion. If anything, the Court's concessions to dynamic entrepreneurs propelled the country into the takeoff stage of economic growth, and with a healthy broadening of the economic base.

Yet it does not follow, because Story's prophecy was mistaken, that his own plan for controlled economic growth was unworkable, that it would have forestalled corporate expansion by fortifying existing corporations with monopoly protection. There can be little doubt that Story's dissent, had it become law, would have worked to slow down and restrain corporate growth. In a real sense that was his intention. But it does not follow that his dissent would have precluded considerable economic advancement. Even in the area of most obvious applicability, that of bridge building, Story's opinion offered no absolute monopoly protection to existing corporations. First, an implied grant of exclusive rights, even if successfully claimed, would last only for the period of time set by legislative discretion. (The Charles River Bridge, for example, would have reverted to the state in 1855.) And if existing charters were subject to monopolistic interpretations, future ones could explicitly prevent such favored treatment if the legislature so willed. Nor would Story's position have precluded the building of other bridges, even during the period of the grant, and such bridges had, in fact, been built across the Charles. Whether an existing bridge could claim monopoly rights against a new bridge depended on the extent to which the second bridge damaged the revenue of the existing one, a matter that was necessarily a matter of degree and of fact—a question, in short, for a future court to decide. Story made clear, both in his manuscript notes on the argument and in his opinion, that the Court's decision was limited strictly to the case at hand and was "not to decide the principle for all cases. . . ."[135] The case at hand was unique; his ruling put no dead hand on future courts.

If Story's concession to the old bridge company did not rule out new bridges, then how can we be so certain that it would have curtailed the growth of railroad corporations? The fact that existing canal and turnpike companies tried to stop railroads by arguing implied monopoly does not prove the whole point. It is one thing to argue that a charter to a canal corporation would by implication preclude parallel canals (for the duration of the grant), quite another to claim that such a charter would automatically prevent railroads from building alongside canals. The point is that future courts could distinguish between canals and railroads in such matters as function and termini, and Story's emphasis on the limited scope of the *Bridge* ruling invited them to do so. Certainly the touchstones of common sense and business acumen by which the common law presumed to read the minds of contracting parties would not apply so irresistibly as in the *Bridge* case. And, most important, legislatures (knowing that they would be legally bound by their promises) would surely see that future charters avoided implied monopoly in areas of new technology. In any case outright taking was always possible as long as fair compensation was rewarded, and this was really all that Story and the old bridge company asked for.[136]

Whether Story's economic plan would have worked cannot be known; at least it deserves a "Scotch verdict." One thing is clear: It was perfectly consistent with his whole scheme of capitalism made moral and responsible through principled law. No jurist of his time was more sold on the virtues of capitalism than Story, none more concerned that it be virtuous. Economic expansion was taken to be the goal of American law both public and private. The issue was how fast and at what price—or rather, at whose expense. On these issues Story, like Nicholas Biddle, was a conservative. Change again was not the issue. Indeed, unlike Jefferson's liberalism, which would have conserved an agrarian republic, Story's conservatism (like Hamilton's) would have transformed it. It was just that the transformation should proceed according to the measured cadence marked out by conservative statesmen at the head of whom were justices of the Supreme Court.

All this brings us back to Story's passionate argument with Chief Justice Taney and the *Bridge* majority. Excessive though his reaction may have been, Story correctly sensed that a significant shift in public law had taken place, which is to say that he and Taney differed sharply not just over means but over fundamentals. At issue first of all was *Dartmouth College* v. *Woodward*. Taney's opinion paid deference to it and left it standing. But, as Story perceived, its meaning had been altered. Story's position in *Dartmouth*, as previously noted, was that grants and charters within the meaning of article I, section 10, were to be interpreted according to the private law of contract. Common law and constitutional law, mutually reinforcing, met on the common ground of legal science. Taney refused to be bound by this logic. His opinion did not overrule *Dartmouth*, but neither did it merely refuse to extend it by implication. By talking royal grants instead of private contract, Taney's opinion simply ignored *Dartmouth College* altogether, or short-circuited it, as Story tried to tell the Court and the nation.

To explore the subtle differences between Story and Taney over *Dartmouth College* is to touch on the shift in legal culture that the Taney Court signified. The shift was gradual, to be sure, more so than Story's jeremiad would suggest. But Taney's expedient use of law to achieve practical economic results was a victory for instrumentalism; that is to say, it revealed a preference for policy results over doctrinal purity. Instrumentalism, in this general sense, of course, had never been absent: not from the common law and certainly not from the constitutional law of the Marshall Court. The measured and moderate course of economic growth during this earlier period, however (being mainly commercial rather than manufacturing), permitted legal principles to mature gradually and to reflect prevailing social values in the process. The Taney Court, faced with accelerated economic change, was not allowed that luxury. Given the choice between preserving the coherence of the earlier period and harmonizing law with new economic forces, it chose the latter.

Story wanted to eat his legal cake and have it too. He did not ignore, had never ignored, the instrumental policy-making dimension of the law. Indeed, he disagreed openly with Taney over what sound policy was. But the source of his discontent and the focus of his dissent were the disjunction between law and morality that Taney's instrumentalism produced. Here it is hard to argue with him. There is no doubt that the Court's opinion destroyed the private property of the stockholders in the old bridge, though the state finally awarded a token compensation of $25,000.00. For the several annual payments it would have received, Harvard got only $3,333.30 and permission to receive the original annuity for the remainder of the existence of the bridge corporation.[137] (The people, incidentally, got two state-owned bridges, both of which collected tolls!) The private property of one group had been taken to pay for the economic convenience of another. And private property in Story's scheme of things was inseparable from liberty. The new Court had not just condoned outright expropriation but had destroyed, to quote Kent, "a great Principle of constitutional Morality" and had undercut the whole "moral Sense of the Community."[138]

It was contract that connected the "Sense of the Community" to the law, contract that put legal science on the side of morality, not to say Christianity. For Story as for many of his contemporaries, it went to the heart of republican society. By contract the American Puritans established their individual and collective relationships to their God, bound themselves together in churches and civil communities. From colonial religious and political experience, from the English legal heritage, from the influence of John Locke, contract entered the fabric of American social practice and political thought. It was made to justify the Revolution, and with Lockean theory, it stood ready to explain how a nation of free, rational, individual men could transform itself into a collective, sovereign people, and how that people could live together harmoniously. Contract, that is to say, followed inexorably from the rise of American individualism.

As a disciple of Burke, Story could not be a total Lockean, of course. He did not go so far with contract as to deny the organic, historical origins of the American Constitution, and he challenged those like Calhoun who did. Neither was he an individualist at the expense of the *res publica*. But he believed in American individualism and understood fully the social and economic logic of contract and how it depended on law. Contract law was the permeating theme of his great commentaries on commercial law.

Through the contract clause and the judicial decisions thereon, it became during the antebellum period one of the basic doctrines of American constitutional law. Contract, as Kent testified, was the essence of "constitutional Morality."

When in the *Bridge* dissent Story applied the law of private contract to governmental economic activities, he was, then, following the syntactic imperative of culture to integrate and harmonize: Private law became public law; common law infused constitutional law; private morality became synonymous with public, republican morality. Story may have been unable to appreciate individualism (read democracy) in American politics, but in economics the rational, moral individual was his basic unit of calculation. People were sensible enough to know their own interests, rational enough to deploy their property through contract, moral enough to abide by the consequences of their agreements—or at least through law they might be made moral enough.

And what worked for individuals also worked for legislatures, as he said both in *Dartmouth College* and in his *Bridge* dissent. He did not deny that the legislature might enter into the individualistic economic process. Indeed, he assumed, as did the age, that it would do so in order to stimulate individual activity and promote the public welfare (as when it chartered the Charles River Bridge Company). But once the legislature entered the economic arena through grants and charters, it was governed by the law that applied to individuals, that is, by private contract law. "Our legislatures neither have, nor affect to have, any royal prerogatives," he declared, referring to Taney's mistaken analogy of a legislative charter to a royal grant. The Massachusetts legislature, he continued, with states' rights arguments as the target, had no claim to sovereignty whatsoever. Only the people were sovereign, he pushed on, applying Federalist constitutional theory to the states; and the people in their sovereign capacity spoke only in their constitutions. "What solid ground is there to say, that the words of a grant, in the mouth of a citizen, shall mean one thing, and in the mouth of the legislature mean another thing?"[139]

Here is where law merged with morality; where Taney missed the point. By shifting the argument from contract to royal grant, Taney had argued for a double standard, one in which "public welfare" was an external value beyond the marketplace that the legislature might call on to justify its actions. But, as Kent pointed out to Story, if the "legislature can quibble away . . . its contracts with Impunity, the People will be sure to follow."[140] Story could not have agreed more fully. Legal principles in his historical scheme of jurisprudence grew incrementally out of communal values and experience. Principles of justice were the cement that held society together in moral harmony. Natural-law thinking that integrated law with economics and with politics in one interconnected moral order had given way to mere expediency. As Story said in his manuscript notes on the arguments in the *Bridge* case, "the only question here is of sheer power."[141] Rather than impose moral principle on economic change, American law following the Taney Court was taking its character from the amoral chaos of the marketplace and the immoral promptings of politicians.

Story was pessimistic because he sensed that the unified republican culture of which law was a part was coming undone. It was the purpose of his dissent, if not to fight back the tide of change, then at least to speak for the "old law" and the old Republic. In that simpler intellectual world law was scientific; legal science was moral and practical at the same time. Private law and public law were governed by the same principles, and both together released individual energy—and at the same time made it responsible to the common good.

Law was the cement of republicanism. And if law in a republic was so complex, so delicate, if legal science was so demanding, it followed for Story that lawyers and judges, not professional politicians and legislators, should be entrusted with lawmaking. It was by now a hoary cause with Story. And therein lay his final argument with Taney in the *Bridge* case, for the chief justice conceded too much authority to the legislature and the professional politicians who ruled there. By arguing that there was some principle of public welfare beyond the operation of the buyer-seller contractual process and by conceding that the legislature had some special prerogative to voice that principle, Taney came dangerously close to the ultimate democratic heresy, the very one presumably stamped out by republican constitutional theory: that the legislature itself and not the people was sovereign. Story glimpsed the emerging will theory of law, the cutting edge of legal positivism, and did not like what he saw.

Finally, in Taney's concession to legislative power was a demonstrated unwillingness to exercise the responsibilities that Story placed on the Supreme Court. At rock bottom their disagreement was a matter of scholarship. Perhaps, as some have suggested, Story himself played a bit too freely with "science," as when he oscillated imprecisely from nuisance to contract and back to nuisance in his argument. But he saw only the mote in his brother's eye. That Taney should misread the authorities on royal grants was one thing, but not to consult them was another, and to misconstrue the entire legal framework of the case was worse still. Either Taney was cynical or he was incompetent. Story did not say which, but it is a good guess that he agreed with Webster that the new chief justice's performance, however plausible, was ultimately "cunning and jesuitical."[142] But whether cynical or inept, the result was the same, and the same one as was manifest in *Briscoe* and *Miln*: By abandoning scientific standards of adjudication the Court launched itself on the turbulent sea of judicial subjectivism. Without scholarship, political bias would hold sway. Rather than controlling politics and party, Taney and the majority now invited them into the temple. Tragic enough it would have been if the Court had gone to defeat doing its "moral duty" (as in the *Cherokee* cases). But to surrender without battle was ignominy. What Story had feared for twenty years and labored to avoid had come to pass. The Court, it seemed, was done for, and with it the constitutional republic.

Marble Statue of Joseph Story, by William Wetmore Story.
Courtesy Harvard Law School Art Collection.

Chapter 7

Harvard Law School and the Salvation of the Republic

If I do not live otherwise to posterity, I shall at all events live in my children in the law. While that endures I am content to be known through my pupils.
      Story to Charles Sumner,
      10 February 1836

Harvard University; may it long continue a central luminary of general science and legal learning, at which members shall annually light their torches and go forth, to illuminate the cities and villages, and tribunals of the land, with the gladsome light of jurisprudence.
      Toast, ca. 1845

The *Bridge* decision convinced Story that the Goths and Vandals had sacked the Court itself, final proof that Jacksonian Democracy was not a passing fever but a chronic, if not fatal, contagion. To be sure, Story, like Holmes later, seemed inclined to exaggerate the hostility of the universe in order to ennoble the struggle against it, the better to rally the faithful to battle. But there is no reason to doubt that he believed fully that American history was on a downward-spiraling course. Yet despite the constant cries of despair and gloom, in the face of declining health and urgent warnings from doctor and friends, Story kept to his schedule of unremitting labor. As much as he liked his national and international reputation he could not bask in it; passivity was temperamentally out of the question, and so was stoic resignation.

What kept him going in the midst of such dark ruminations is, like most questions of human behavior, a complex matter. The sheer chemistry of an active mind, ingrained habits of work, ambition, refreshing visits with family and friends—all helped keep him at his post. But there can be little doubt that the astonishing productivity of Story's last twenty-five years was due in large part to the Law School of Harvard University and the remarkable reforms in American legal education and law that were taking place there under his leadership. Quite plainly he loved his "foster Children," as he called his students, and one of them, who had seen him both in Cambridge and Washington, noticed that "he seems never to have been happier except when at the Law School. . . ."[1] As Story himself put it in the midst of a busy term in 1832, "I really long for a visit to the old Lecture Room, and to sit down in the old chair, and to hear without languor."[2] Harvard Law was for him an oasis of excellence and hope in the desert of Jacksonian mediocrity and decline. By the late spring of 1844 he had decided to resign from the Court effective in August 1845 and, as he put it to his old friend James Kent, "devote the residue of my life and energies to the Law School exclusively."[3] The lack of camaraderie (underscored by the firing of reporter Peters during Story's absence) and mounting evidence that the Court was politicized, along with the conviction that if he stayed, he would be in a perpetual minority of the court, promoted the final painful decision. Above all, there was hope in education. Like the old Federalists who tolerated Jefferson because they thought a virtuous people might rise up and throw him out, Story found strength in the conviction that the American people might be reeducated to true republicanism.

Story's faith in education was characteristic of an age that believed in individualism and free will. His family preached the message; his early years at Harvard verified it. Throughout his long career—in such varied roles as member of the Salem school committee, correspondent with Joseph Lancaster, patron of the Smithsonian Institution, and overseer and member of the Corporation of Harvard University[4]—he manifested a faith in education. Indeed, if one believes his rhetoric on the subject, Story the conservative joined the perfectionist movement of the age. The "diffusion of knowledge" was one of the great characteristics of the age, along with the "progress of the spirit of free inquiry." Education was part of the American tradition, "the truest glory of our forefathers"—especially those of New England. Learning and knowledge "should not only confer power, but should also confer happiness." Education was the business of the Republic, then; and "what is the business of education, but to fit men [and, he added, women too] to accomplish their duties and their destiny?"[5] Behind Story's great opinions in *Dartmouth College* and *Allen v. McKean*, which laid the legal foundation of private education in America, was a vision of republican progress.

A liberal faith in progress through education, however, was tempered with a conservative vision of social order. Indeed, the educational reorganization of Harvard and the rejuvenation of the Law School, which must be viewed as interconnected phenomena, grew directly out of the revolution of New England conservatism in the 1820s. Whether through public libraries, mechanic institutes, or new periodicals, New England's elite recognized that they had to broaden their base of influence, and none more than Story. He was sure of the truth, convinced that the word could be spread, and possessed of a natural didacticism that matched his patriotic self-image. Talking, writing, arguing, fighting with words—these were his métier. Behind the judge and the legal scholar was Story the teacher. All this is to say that Story's acceptance of the Dane Professorship in 1829 was not a radical turn of career but an extension of educational work already begun. What Harvard Law School permitted him—which was what other institutions and voluntary associations did in the nineteenth century—was to do more effectively through institutional channels what he wanted to do as an individual. What he wanted was to teach scientific law and to make American law scientific, to reform the legal profession and through law and lawyers save the republic from political parties, professional politicians, and demagogues. The American people might yet be saved from their backsliding ways; conservative wisdom might contain democratic excess; and Story might live "to posterity," as he put it.[6]

1. The Founder's Vision

At the Harvard Phi Beta Kappa dinner on 17 July 1851, ex-president Josiah Quincy, Jr., delivered an extemporaneous and "feeling eulogy" on his departed friend Story, pronouncing him "the real founder of the Law School."[7] And so he was if any one man could claim the honor. True, law at Harvard dated from 1815, when the corporation appointed Isaac Parker Royall Professor of Law, and a full-time law school began two years later in 1817 with the appointment of Asahel Stearns as resident instructor. As chief justice of the state's highest court, Parker appeared to be the ideal man to deliver lectures on law to Harvard seniors, which was his main responsibility. But he was, as later gossip had it, "a good-natured, lazy lawyer" who became "a good-natured, lazy judge,"[8] and his desultory and superficial lectures did little to kindle interest in legal science. Stearns, on the other hand, worked assiduously at his many chores—as teacher, adviser, librarian, and administrator—but he was plodding, narrow in focus, and generally out of touch with the changes in and needs of American law. With only one student in 1828, with a faltering commitment from the corporation, law at Harvard desperately needed an infusion of money and dynamic and imaginative leadership. This the collaboration of Nathan Dane and Story promised.

They were called into action by a crisis in legal education that threatened to balkanize the profession and fragment American law, exactly at the time when unity in both seemed crucial. The root problem was the apprenticeship system, which, despite the appearance of proprietary law schools and university law lectureships, was still the dominant mode of legal education (and would remain so for the rest of the century). Apprenticeship training made sense to eighteenth-century Americans, of course, because law schools were nonexistent (until Litchfield in 1784) and accessibility to the English Inns of Court was reserved to a privileged few. The co-optative character of law-office training also fit nicely with the prevailing notions of the legal profession as a conservative, even Anglicized, elite. Most important, perhaps, the legal apprentice unavoidably learned local law, which suited the local and regional structure of most economic activity.

What worked for the eighteenth century, however, was increasingly dysfunctional in the nineteenth. Expanding national and international markets called for a breadth of law knowledge that most law offices could not supply because most lawyers themselves had not mastered the new legal "science" and because they could not afford the growing corpus of law reports and treatises necessary to learn it. Local bar associations, which set educational standards through their control of admission, were not inclined to face the problem and in any case could hardly be expected to advocate changes that would undercut their control of the profession.

Dane and Story turned instead to Harvard University and its fledgling law school as their instruments of reform. Harvard offered the potential of resources adequate for the study of national law as well as the prospect of institutional prestige and continuity. Moreover, its imprimatur on educational innovation in the law would work to overcome the resistance of local bar groups in Massachusetts and New England, many of whose members were loyal Harvard alumni. The problem was to convert the corporation, a challenge made somewhat easier, one must assume, by the dominance of lawyers and merchants among its membership and by Story's presence among them as the expert in residence. In any case, Dane's strategy was irresistible: offer money.

Sometime in 1828, possibly earlier, Dane decided to use the profits from his popular *General Abridgment and Digest of American Law* to endow a professorship that would in effect create a law school, and he began earnest consultation with Story about the plan in the fall.[9] Dane wanted Story to occupy the new chair—indeed, made his bequest contingent on Story's acceptance. Story accepted the job with some reluctance (as his son recounted) and a number of very specific stipulations. Leaving Salem was extremely painful, not only on his account but on Sarah's, too. He would have preferred a nonresident professorship, but Dane's bequest wisely prohibited such an arrangement. Story made his acceptance contingent on being able to sell his Salem property for at least seven thousand dollars (four thousand less than it cost him). He also extracted the promise from the corporation that a house on university property would be made available on reasonable terms, and one on the corner of Brattle and Hilliard streets was in fact found. He asked for a modest one-thousand-dollar annual salary, for which he agreed "to take a general superintendence of the Law School, that is to visit it, & examine the Students occasionally, & to lecture to them *orally* on the topics connected with the Dane Professorship from time to time in a familiar way." His efforts, he insisted, should be complemented by those of at least one permanent professor in residence who could be relied on for "the *drill* duty, & a constant attention to the Students." In addition to superintending, lecturing, and generally aiding the students "by occasional explanations & excitements," Story agreed to publish his written lectures—provided this and all else could be "so arranged as not to interfere with my judicial duties, which are & ever must be with me of paramount obligation & interest." [10]

Even with this escape clause, the new job was a monumental undertaking. On the other hand, it permitted Story to do what he was already inclined to do and what he was convinced needed to be done. It was, in addition, the natural outgrowth of his friendship with Dane and his growing involvement in the affairs of Harvard. The Story-Dane relationship went back to Essex County days. Despite political differences, they were drawn together in the tightly knit professional community by a mutual love of the law. Story admired Dane's "manly" constitutional nationalism and came to revere him as one of the great statesmen of the Revolution. Dane, like many other Federalists, saw Story as a young man of genius and energy who might, once he quit his Jeffersonian ways, carry forward the tradition of creative conservatism. Their collaboration in the reform of the Law School, which in all likelihood began before 1828, grew naturally out of this mutual admiration and out of the jointly held conviction driven home by the crisis of the 1820s that scientific law and a reformed legal profession would be decisive weapons in the conservative counterrevolution.

Story's decision to assume leadership of the Law School was also a consequence of his deepening involvement in the governance of the university. As both overseer and member of the corporation and as a leader in the "Salem administration" that reputedly ran the school in the 1820s, Story had been a champion of educational and administrative reform. A revitalized Harvard, it was felt, would be the institutional basis of conservative educational efforts; so also would a revitalized Law School. Working in tandem, both would be strengthened. It was, in fact, the Law School's close working relationship with Harvard University that propelled it into the front rank of the nineteenth-century law schools not only in America but in England, too. [11] University affiliation, as advertisements in the *American Jurist* indicated, brought to the Law School a much-needed stature, which enhanced enrollments and provided a liberalizing environment for professional training. [12] More than that, it guaranteed financial outlays adequate to support a first-rate staff and a library equipped with materials for the study of national jurisprudence, materials that competing law schools without institutional connections simply could not provide.

The remarkable working relationship between the Law School and the university was attributable in no small part to the cooperation of Story and

Josiah Quincy, Jr. The two men had crossed political swords in the early nineteenth century, but mutual respect blossomed into friendship during the 1820s. Quincy, like Story, was a forward-looking conservative who wanted to bury past grievances and form a common front against the enemy, a member also of the group that instigated reform at Harvard in 1824. Story himself observed that as mayor of Boston, Quincy demonstrated the possibilities of enlightened conservative leadership.[13] Such a man was the logical replacement for President John Kirkland, who retired in 1828 under fire from the reformers. Story had initially hoped that George Ticknor, one of the leading critics of the old administration, would get the job. But he was unacceptable to the overseers, and Quincy's defeat for reelection as mayor in 1828 made him available. Story now worked assiduously behind the scenes for Quincy, who upon his appointment was brought into the consultations about the Law School. The harmonious union of legal and liberal education was assured.[14] Strengthening each other, Harvard University and the Law School would bolster conservative efforts to reassert the role of New England in the affairs of the nation as a counterforce against Southernism, states' rights, and political parties.

What special role law and lawyers would play in this great effort, how they would prepare themselves to meet the challenge, was the subject of Story's inaugural address as Dane Professor, delivered 25 August 1829 to the gathered worthies of Harvard and Massachusetts. His speech bowed to the past, addressed the future, and radiated commitment. Lavish praise was bestowed on Dane, the "American Viner" (a reference to Charles Viner, the jurist who endowed the chair of law at Oxford occupied with such distinction by Sir William Blackstone). Dane, along with Ames, Dexter, Pinkney, and Marshall, was put forth as a model for the young men who would study at the Law School. Those young men who aspired were forewarned, too: Harvard Law School would be no place for gentlemen of "gay and ardent temperament," no place for idle learning or the "mere pursuit of pleasure or curiosity." Story ruled out pettifogging and promised a legal profession full "of transcendent dignity" that would offer deserving votaries "the brightest rewards of human ambition, opulence, fame, public honors."[15]

Story himself, it is obvious, was to be, along with Dane and the rest, a living model of this republican lawyer: If Dane was the American Viner then he, Story, would be the American Blackstone. He could not, of course, say so out loud, but the parallel became obvious when he sketched out the duties that the endowment obliged him to perform. He was to "deliver lectures upon the Law of Nature, the Law of Nations, Maritime and Commercial Law, Equity Law, and, lastly, the Constitutional law of the United States"—branches of jurisprudence intimately connected with "the best interests of civilized society." The objective was not to exhaust the vast field, but to "illustrate by examples, rather than exhaust by analysis," to "conduct the inquirer to the vestibule of the temple of jurisprudence; and leave to his future curiosity the survey of its magnificent halls, its decorated columns, its splendid porticos, its harmonized order, its massive walls, its varied crypts, its lofty domes, its 'ever-during gates, on golden hinges moving.'"[16] From these lectures would come a series of scholarly commentaries that would do for American law what Blackstone's did for English law: order and restate the law as it was and chart the course of its future development.

Story's rhetoric, with its walls, crypts, domes and "'ever-during gates,'" creaked with conservatism. Jurisprudence at Harvard, it might appear, would be chiseled in marble. And Story's reference to Blackstone carried overtones of the same theme. To order, systematize, and teach American law in the Blackstonian mode in the early nineteenth century, as Story promised to do, given the accelerated pace of legal change, seemed unavoidably to pit conservative scholarship against radical reality. Still, it would be a mistake to overemphasize Story's and Harvard's jurisprudential conservatism (not to be confused with the political conservatism that the law was intended to serve). Harvard's taught law might be instructed by ancient learning and refined by comparative jurisprudence. But the law at Harvard, as Story made emphatically clear, was to be American law suited to the needs of the American people in the nineteenth century. Inherited principles, as Story learned from Samuel Sewall, would have to be not only transplanted but transformed. A people caught up in an economic revolution needed reformed law that accommodated the needs of business. Above all, this law would have to be divested of its local and sectional idiosyncrasies and made accessible to the whole people. If the law at Harvard were truly to be American law, then it would, by definition, have to be functional and progressive. His conservative rhetoric notwithstanding, Story pledged that it would be.

But the question remained: What would be the guiding spirit of this reformed American law, the theory and method by which the many parts were made one? To the surprise of none—at least none who had read his *Martin* or *De Lovio* opinions, or his legal essays in the *North American Review*—Story declared that it was "the common law, in its largest extent, that the Law of this University proposed to expound."[17]

The message was simple enough, but the meaning was complex, for the common law as Story saw it had many facets and might be taken on legal, political, or philosophical levels. In one sense, the common law was "the collection of principles, which constitute the basis of the administration of justice in England, in contradistinction to the maxims of the Roman code." At the same time, it was judge-made law as opposed to statute law, and as such was derived from the unwritten "customs and usages . . . from immemorial practise." Indeed, "even judicial decisions are deemed but the formal promulgations of rules antecedently existing, and obtain all their value from their supposed conformity to those rules."[18] Story apparently saw no contradiction between a "collection of principles" and "customs and usages from immemorial practise"—how the former reflected a rationalism that the latter negated.

If Sir Matthew Hale and Blackstone could exist side by side in Story's eclectic system, Christian morality could join them without contradiction.[19] Here Story harked back to his recent argument with Jefferson, as would Simon Greenleaf in his inaugural discourse as Royall Professor. At the most cosmic level the common law was more than a body of principles, more than ancient usage bound to English history. It was a profound and universal exploration of moral and philosophical truth, the basis of which was Christianity—"notwithstanding the specious objection of one of our most distinguished statesmen." It followed (and here Story returned to the problem of leadership in his model commonwealth, the theme of conservatives in the 1820s) that the study of law would not only train the rational mind but teach the one who studied it "to build his reputation upon the soundest morals, the deepest principles, and the most exalted purity of life and character." The moral quality of the common law would, then, give the profession its "transcendent dignity," which in turn would repel the "sharp and cunning pettifogger," the "retailer of lawsuits," the "canter about forms," the "caviller upon words," and, as Burke put it, "the ministers of municipal litigation and the fomenters of the war of village vexation."[20]

By dwelling so heavily on principles of the common law and its Christian morality, Story seemed in danger of doing what he counseled against: engaging in speculation and metaphysics. In fact, he admitted frankly that "from its nature and objects, the common law, above all others, employs a most severe and scrutinizing logic," that "in some of its branches it is compelled to deal with metaphysical subtleties and abstractions" that "belong to the depths of intellectual philosophy."[21] But there were no disembodied principles in Story's version of the common law, no "bodiless cherubs" fluttering about, as Holmes quaintly put it.[22] Story launched the law at Harvard on a nonspeculative course, one that A. V. Dicey found in 1900 still to be its main characteristic.[23] Commonsense practicality rescued the American common law from the precipice of metaphysics just as it saved American philosophy from excessive idealism. The obligation of the common law to deal with cases and controversies among real people and parties forced it to grapple "with substances, instead of shadows, with men's business, and rights, and inheritances, and not with entities and notions. . . ." The common law is rooted in common sense. And "common sense has at all times powerfully countered the tendency to undue speculation in the common law, and silently brought back its votaries to that which is the end of all true logic, the just application of principles to the actual concerns of life." So in addition to being a body of principles, a collection of customs and usages beyond memory, and a moral code, the common law was the "instrument of administering public and private justice"; the "code, by which rights are ascertained, and wrongs redressed"; a system "by which contracts are interpreted, and property secured, and the institutions, which add strength to government, and solid happiness to domestic life, are firmly guarded." In all of its dimensions, it was the "birthright and inheritance" of "our ancestors," the foundation of "the jurisprudence of all the English colonies . . . , the ornament of every state within this republic." It was "the law of liberty," which republicanism transposed into liberty under law.[24]

The common sense of the common law, its concern with "men's business," rescued it not only from metaphysics but from a static, fixed, almost Newtonian quality that Story's emphasis on principle seemed to impart and that would have flatly contradicted the promise that law at Harvard would be American law. By tying the law to the needs of real people in the "actual concerns of life," especially in nineteenth-century America, Story assured that his legal system (and his conservatism, too) would accommodate historical change. History, in turn, would inform law.

Legal history, in fact, figured prominently in Story's plan for Harvard law, as it did in his opinions and legal essays; that history (witness, for example, his opinion in *De Lovio* or his essays "The Growth of the Commercial Law" and "The Progress of Jurisprudence")[25] emphasized legal change, adjustment, and growth. If the English common law was not static, then even less so would be American common law, for the changing principles of inherited law would have to accommodate American circumstances themselves undergoing rapid transformation. Like Hale's system of law (his *History of the Common Law* would be on the Harvard reading list), Story's would be open-ended, not static or fixed, but a growing, flexible, living law—a process. Law must, he said, "be forever in progress; and no limits can be assigned to its principles or improvements." Echoing Marshall in *McCulloch* v. *Maryland* he added: The "true glory" of the law is "that it is flexible, and constantly expanding with the exigencies of society." He concluded, "It moves onward into the path of perfection, but never arrives at the ultimate point."[26] And with growth and adjustment came the potential for creativity, the product of the interaction of inherited and mature legal systems with a society in the midst of rapid change and in need of technical and sophisticated law. Here, as Roscoe Pound observed, were the ingredients of the classic era of American judicial creativity.

The challenge at Harvard was, then, to teach law not as a body of fixed principles to be memorized but as a system and method of adjusting old rules to changing circumstances or, if necessary, of making new rules from old materials. Law would be science, not revelation. This was the foundation block of Harvard Law School as it had been the central goal of American jurisprudence since the Revolution. Legal science at Harvard, Story explained, would in its method and outlook most clearly resemble "the natural sciences, where new discoveries continually lead the way to new, and sometimes astonishing results."[27]

Story never explored the analogy between natural and legal science, but the parallels were there to see (and were explored at length by Quincy in his dedication address).[28] The experiential, the discrete, and the empirical in science were paralleled in law by the case-controversy orientation. Story searched the old books for cases and rules with no less enthusiasm than the naturalist employed in hunting down the skeletons of mastodons, and for much the same reason: to organize and arrange them. The duty of the legal scientist, like that of the natural scientist, was to order, arrange, and systematize, to establish the relationship between and among the minute and the discrete. The forte of Blackstone, no less than of Lamarck, was bringing order from apparent chaos. And progress in jurisprudence, judging from Story's forays into legal history, rested exactly on that syncretic ability. The great periods in English law for him (and for Quincy as well) were those in which such rationalization took place. Story's legal heroes were those who performed the systematizing and rationalizing function most effectively: Hale's *History* was a pioneering attempt to make sense out of the common law; under Bacon "the business of chancery assumed a regular course. . . ." The "venerable Plowden" brought order and exactness to the cases. In equity it was Lord Hardwicke who combined "the scattered fragments into a scientific system"; Eldon continued the work so that together they made equity the equal to common law in its scientific order and regularity.[29]

In the common law itself, the great systematizer was Blackstone, but Story reserved his greatest accolades for Lord Mansfield, who even more than Blackstone was Story's own model. Mansfield did what Story aimed to do: Onto the body of the common law he grafted the "enlightened and liberal rules" of commercial law, which he drew from every age and all nations. Mansfield did what the legal scientist should do: adjust old law to new circumstances; balance change with stability. He reduced the "many doctrines of the law to systematical accuracy by rejecting anomalies, refining and limiting their application by the test of general reasoning."[30] Balancing practical experience, common sense, and logic with the "philosophizing spirit," he moved the law toward "a more comprehensive argumentation and more perfect generalization." In Mansfield one sees, as Story put it to one of his students, how law "rises from a trade to a science."[31] Story wanted Harvard to do the same for American law.

Story's system, which was shamelessly eclectic, was also bold in its com-

prehensiveness and original in the combination of its various interconnected parts, in the balance struck between old and new, between change
and stability. The methodology and philosophy of the English common
law, which included equity law, too, would be the starting point of legal
reasoning in the United States. But its principles would be, as in fact they
had been in the past, refined and tested by use of the legal experience of
the whole Western world, by comparative analytical jurisprudence. Comparative jurisprudence and legal history would, that is to say, not stand
apart as separate specialties but be integral parts of the process of legal
reasoning itself and thus of legal education.[32] The final product of scientific
reasoning would be a system of law that would be moral, philosophical,
rational, and scientific and at the same time a practical tool for the American people, who wanted to get on with the nineteenth century. Harvard
Law would reform American law, but the wisdom of the past, Burke's "ancient constitution," would be respected. The element of change in American history, its inexorability, was acknowledged, but it would be safely in
the hands of lawyers made conservative by the law.

On the duty of conservatives and the conservative function of legal reform Story was explicit and emphatic in his address. The corruption of the
republican system of liberty under law, he declared (drawing on the legal
theories of the founders and reiterating the conservative jeremiads of the
1820s), would come from the perversion of the principles of popular sovereignty, from popular government run amok: "Our government is emphatically a government of the people, in all its departments. It purports to
be a government of law, and not of men; and yet, beyond all others, it is
subject to the control and influence of public opinion." Tyranny could
come from many quarters, Story acknowledged, but it was from the people
that the dangers were most to be feared. It mattered little whether the
people were urged on "by a spirit of innovation, or popular delusion, or
state necessity (as it is falsely called), it is still power, irresponsible power
against right. . . . At such times, the majority prevail by mere numbers,
and not by force of judgment; *numerantur, non ponderantur.*" The danger
was compounded by the fact that "our government . . . opens the widest
field for talents and exertion to every rank of life." Imbibing the Jacksonian theory of officeholding, some men assume that they are "born legislators; that no qualification beyond plain sense and common honesty are
necessary for the management of the intricate machine of government;
and, above all, of that most delicate and interesting of all machines, a republican government."[33]

What Story traced here was the ungluing of the republican synthesis,
the failure of conservative strategy to contain the forces of democracy that
were built into the American system of government.[34] To reverse the decline, Story turned to the common law in the broadest sense. Its spirit per-

meated the Constitution itself, and its principles might be made to guide Americans in their private relations—a rational alternative to the rule of force or the rash, innovative political process. Guided by its method and philosophy, Americans might confront the dramatic changes of the nineteenth century with the wisdom of the past.

Change was not the issue, nor could it be in a country so engulfed in change; again, the question was who should control it. The founders had counted (as in Madison's *Federalist* 10) on the selection of virtuous and patriotic men of talent. Popular suffrage, it was hopefully assumed, would sustain eighteenth-century deference, but that wishful notion was blasted by the rise of party and the professional politician. Story intended Harvard Law School to address this crisis of leadership. Lawyers trained in the science of the law would be the nucleus of a new class of statesmen, "the great professional men of the age," as one young convert put it.[35] Their conservative wisdom would be assured by the law they practiced. Because they were essential to the operation of American society, lawyers were not beholden to the fickle electorate. In an increasingly individualistic society, law, not tradition, was becoming the main social cement. Commanding the technique of social action made the lawyer a mediator in the affairs of the American people.[36] Law was, then, a system of social decision making to rival that of politics. Given their choice, Story was convinced, the American people would choose the rational environment of the courtroom to the smoke-filled rooms of the new politicos and the chaos of the legislative chambers. As in 1798, it was "Rise, united, Harvard's band." The legal profession, led by Harvard-trained lawyers, would be "placed, as it were, upon the outpost of defence, as a public sentinel, to watch the approach of danger, and sound the alarm when oppression is at hand." Against "public opinion . . . drugged into stupid indifference" or captivated by "arts of intrigue," against the "shouts of the multitude," the clamor of the public press, they would stand undaunted. If lawyers rose to the challenge they might "achieve a glorious triumph for truth, and justice, and the law"—and for the republic.[37]

2. Judge as Teacher

"Our success thus far exceeds our expectations," exulted Story after assessing the status of the school in the fall of 1829.[38] Things had fallen into place. Isaac Parker had bowed out gracefully, and Story's urging and quick action by the corporation had secured John Hooker Ashmun as Royall Professor and resident instructor to replace Asahel Stearns (who left with a bitter blast at Harvard's ingratitude for his services). Though only twenty-nine, Ashmun had established himself as a leading lawyer in

Northampton, where he was the head and mainstay of the Northampton Law School. "Solid rather than brilliant," Story remembered him; he brought teaching experience, "sagacity, perspicacity and strength" to Cambridge.[39] With the help of a few students who came from Northampton with Ashmun, the fall class of 1829 numbered 28, a healthy increase over the previous year, though most of the students came from close by.[40] Enrollments continued to improve, too, enough to elicit the bullish pronouncement from one student in 1834 that Harvard had assembled "the largest collection of young men that ever met at one place in America for the study of the law."[41] A further inducement to students who intended to practice locally was held out the following year when the Massachusetts legislature passed a law admitting graduates of the Law School into practice without the customary apprenticeship training. At the same time a vigorous national advertising campaign succeeded in attracting students outside New England. Fifteen states were represented in a student body of 62 in 1837–38, and students from twenty-one states attended in 1840–41. During Story's last year there were 156 students from twenty-one states, a roster that marked Harvard's as the largest and most cosmopolitan law school in the nation.[42]

Students at the Law School were distinguished not only by their national makeup but by their educational level and intellectual and professional tone. The Law School required no entrance exam, but a selection process operated, nonetheless, one that tended to favor the sons of the middle and upper-middle classes, where literateness and ambition were most easily nourished. The *American Jurist* emphasized to its readers in 1832 that legal education at Harvard cost "less than it would in a private office in one of our large towns."[43] Still, excluding board, room, and travel, the cost of two years at Cambridge was $100 per year,[44] a figure that (multiply by 10 for the modern dollar) worked to exclude sons of cash-short farmers and most working families. It was assumed, moreover, that Harvard law students were grounded in the classics, and so college graduates were favored. Originally, in fact, it was required that students with a B.A. take three years, whereas those without were to take five, the hope being that an additional two years would permit them to make up their deficiency by reading and attending regular classes at the college. The requirement was dropped by the corporation in 1834 as too restrictive, and thereafter all students, regardless of previous education, were graduated from the Law School after attending eighteen months.[45] Still, the fact remained that of the 956 students who were graduated from the Law School during the Story period, 632, or about 66 percent, were college graduates. In a population where less than 1 percent were college graduates and where many had not completed even secondary school, Harvard law students stood out as a privileged group.

Harvard College, itself in the process of an educational reformation,[46] added a liberal tone to the Law School too—in part because of its propinquity and even more from the fact that of the 632 college graduates who entered the Law School during the Story years, 227 came from Harvard College.[47] It is not surprising, either, to find among Harvard law students many sons of New England's economic and intellectual establishment, from families such as the Otises, Lowells, Abbots, Appletons, Crowninshields, Russells, Minots, Duttons, Hoars, Jacksons, D'Wolfes, Holmeses, and Danas. There was also a rather sizable number of sons and grandsons of lawyers and judges, a fact that boded well for the professional orientation of the new school. That there were among this group several students whose fathers were friends or colleagues of Story's suggests that his influence in bringing students was considerable. Three of Story's colleagues on the Supreme Court, John McLean, Thomas Todd, and Henry Baldwin, sent their sons, as did two associates on the circuit court, district judges Peleg Sprague and John Pitman. Ralph French, with whom Story had practiced law in Salem, sent his boy; so did C. P. Sumner, Story's Harvard friend. Also present were the sons of Joseph Tuckerman, Story's roommate at Harvard, and of Nicholas Devereaux and Nathaniel Bowditch, friends from Salem days.

These young men, like those from established families, brought with them a general tradition of literacy and, more important, an ambition to excel and a desire to serve their country. Nor, it should be said, was this republican ambition the exclusive property of an elite class; witness among the lesser-known students of Harvard such names as Rufus King Cage, George Washington Juston, John Jay Hyde, William Wirt Meredith, and Benjamin Franklin Howard, not to mention Lorenzo de Medici Sweat, Napoleon B. Bradford, James Napoleon Harding, or Napoleon Bonapart Mitchell.

Not every student took to the law, of course. Oliver Wendell Holmes, Sr., was put off by the drudgery of it all and "deserted to the enemy," as it was entered in the record book, referring to his decision to study medicine.[48] Others, like James Russell Lowell, stuck it out but without real interest and abandoned it later; others simply dropped out and disappeared. But student recollections and notes and diaries radiate a sense of common commitment. Indeed, the mere fact that they gave up the convenience of local law-office apprenticeship (which in most cases would have been more readily accessible) to attend Harvard was a sign that they planned to do something with their lives. Story's and Greenleaf's lectures on noble ambition, though they elicited knowing smiles, did not fall on deaf ears.

With a dependably large body of able and eager students, and the promise of solvency that came with numbers, Story pressed for a new building and an expanded library. Thanks to five thousand dollars more from Dane (secured by a discreetly importuning letter from Quincy), the new quarters were dedicated 24 September 1832.[49] Building a library, located on the first floor of Dane Hall, as the new building was called, took somewhat longer. Story had been cautious on the new building, not wanting to be premature or to spend too much on bricks and mortar (the very advice he was to give to the Smithsonian Institution later).[50] Books were another matter. Having already taken the lead in building a law collection at the Library of Congress, he was able to move with dispatch at the Law School.[51] If Harvard was to achieve "a decided superiority over every other Institution of like nature," he wrote Quincy on 3 November 1829, "it is indispensable, that the Students should have ready access to an ample Law library, which shall of itself afford a complete apparatus for study and consultation." Things were so bad, Story reported, that "the Students are compelled to resort to my own private library for almost all their practical inquiries in the course of their Studies. From six to twelve of them are constantly engaged in examining the Reports, and studying in the room in which it is lodged." Story, after consultation with Greenleaf, enclosed a list of desiderata that included, among other things, a complete run of both English and American reports. The latter, he added significantly, "are equally important with the former, for we have students from various parts of the Union; and may expect them all. We have now students from Georgia, So. Carolina, North Carolina, Virginia, Maryland, and from various states in New England."[52]

Story's plea for action was supported the following winter by a report from the Visiting Commitee of Overseers, which urgently recommended "a complete American Library." Story contributed to the effort by selling his own extensive series of reports and elementary treatises to the corporation. "The money," he added, "I do not want, and shall be quite content to let it lay on interest in the hands of the corporation taking a memorandum of the amount, as long as they choose."[53] In addition to parting with his own library at less than cost, Story used his influence to attract other collections, the most impressive of which was that belonging to Samuel Livermore, Story's friend from Essex County days—some four hundred volumes of European, Spanish, and Roman jurisprudence.[54] Story's other well-placed friends also contributed at his urging: Justice McLean was asked for his copies of the "printed Record of this Term" for the library.[55] Thaddeus Romeyn Beck sent Story volumes on medical jurisprudence that found their way into the library, as did Francis G. Lowell's German law books and George Joseph Bell's on the law of Scotland.[56] From Joseph Hopkinson he got Wallace's circuit reports; from Judge François X. Martin the reports of Louisiana; from his Salem friend Leverett Saltonstall a donation of Hindu laws.[57] At regular intervals he and Greenleaf sent requests to the corporation for reports, treatises, and related law works, and at the same time they brought law works in the university library into the Law School.[58] In 1836, thanks to Greenleaf's effort, Harvard's Law School regularly got "all statutes of other States than in the State Library."[59]

By Story's death the Harvard law library had nearly ten thousand volumes, which, thanks to the steady efforts of Charles Sumner and other student law librarians, were increasingly better organized and accessible. The library was not, perhaps, as one booster immodestly suggested, the greatest in the world, but it was easily the finest in America and in terms of its overall balance one of the best anywhere.[60] Harvard Law could now teach the kind of legal science Story advocated; and his prediction to Quincy had come true: that a great library would give the Law School in the view of the students and the general public "a decided superiority over every other Institution of like nature."[61]

Story cannot, of course, receive sole credit for the success of Harvard Law School. The vision and planning he shared with Dane and to a lesser extent Quincy, the execution with his colleagues Ashmun and Simon Greenleaf. Timing favored the venture, too, though Story and others must be credited with seizing the day. It was not accidental that Harvard made its debut as a national law school in the decade in which railroads proved feasible, in which steamboats became commonplace, in which the corporation consolidated itself as a new force in business. The vast outpouring of case law (Story counted two hundred volumes of American reports in his inaugural address) in twenty years and the explosion of treatise literature reflected the impact of economic growth and the rise of a national market system. The growth in the quantity of law, together with the pressure of a national market economy, made a national law school teaching scientific law both necessary and possible. Law-office education, though it remained the most common kind of legal training in the nineteenth century, lacked the resources to teach national law. Private academies, too—such as those in Philadelphia (run by Stephen DuPonceau), Northampton, New Haven, and Albany, and even finally Tapping Reeve's Litchfield Law School—fell by the wayside for want of library and staff. What became clear and what Story, Dane, and Quincy saw clearly was that legal education needed institutional affiliation: The union of Harvard Law School and Harvard University was the key to greatness. Not only would resources for law teaching be enriched, but the law would be taught, to quote James Bradley Thayer, "as other great sciences are studied and taught at the Universities, as deeply, by like methods, and with as thorough a concentration and lifelong development of all the powers of a learned and studious faculty."[62]

Story the educator was fortunate to be where he was when he was. But Harvard and the age were lucky to have him, for his "brilliant talents, enlightened zeal and indefatigable exertions," as Lemuel Shaw would later observe in his report to the corporation, were the sine qua non of success.[63]

The Dane Chair was, as Story himself noted, "created expressly for me. . . ."[64] Story saw what was needed, what could be done. Despite his staggering obligations on the Court and his already overburdened life, he continued to lead the venture. His presence secured for Harvard Dane's endowment to which he added one of his own by virtue of the fact that his salary of a thousand dollars per annum (which he refused to have augmented) was far below what his reputation warranted. The money and interest saved over the years, as Story pointed out in his will, made him the largest single benefactor of the law school during its formative period.[65] Story was also deeply involved in the administration of the school, and because of his stature, his generosity, and his position as overseer and member of the corporation, he was in a position to champion the interests of the Law School. In this regard his alliance with President Quincy was crucial. The two men shared a love of New England, a distrust for democracy, and a vision of duty and honor. Story championed Quincy for Harvard's presidency, and as president Quincy championed the Law School. With Quincy in the presidency Story's word counted almost as much at Harvard as it did in the circuit court across the Charles.

To Story's contributions as planner, benefactor, and administrator must be added his presence in the lecture room on he second floor of Dane Hall. As professor, Story was the life and soul of the Law School. His national and international reputation as a jurist would come after, and to some extent because of, his affiliation with the Law School, but he was well known for his work on the Supreme Court by 1829—for his trenchant scholarship, his consistent championship of national commercial law, and his nationalist interpretation of the Constitution. He gave Harvard Law School what none of its competitors had, a Supreme Court justice and nationally recognized scholar in the classroom. His presence there was a promise of scholarly excellence and a walking advertisement that the law at Harvard would be both scientific and national in scope. He was the model statesman-lawyer that the school hoped to produce.

What made Story so effective in that role was his ability to draw students to him. William Mathews, who entered Harvard Law School in 1836, was pleasantly surprised, as no doubt were many others. He had heard of Story's reputation before arriving and expected to find a "severe and stern" man with an "awe-inspiring countenance in every hue and lineament of which justice was legibly written, and whose whole demeanor manifested a fearful amount of stiffness, starch, and dignity"—"a walking Coke upon Littleton." What he saw was "a sunny smiling face which bespoke of a heart full of kindness," a "counsellor, philosopher," who could be a "friend to all of his pupils . . . without the slightest forfeiture of self-respect." Greatness was made accessible and was indeed the constant motif of legal education at Harvard. Story, as Mathews remembered, was "especially fond . . . of describing the great men of other days."[66] Sometimes he brought famous statesmen to his class, like Daniel Webster and Lord Morpeth, who were using the Harvard library in their consultations on the Webster-Ashburton Treaty, or ex-president John Quincy Adams, who managed to doze off during the lecture. But the main inspiration was the judge himself. When he returned from Washington students crowded around him. When he walked briskly into the lecture room for his two o'clock class, put down his white hat, and put on his spectacles, the students were with him, his younger brothers in the law.

Story clearly relished his teaching duties and, indeed, as he confessed to Ashmun, would "rather work at the Law School" than in Washington,[67] a preference that increased in proportion to the Court's growing Jacksonian character. The burden of teaching, which would have been full-time work for most men, was possible because of Story's natural talent: his didactic inclinations, his immense store of learning and lore at instant recall, and his gift for quick writing and extemporaneous speaking. Moreover, Story the teacher was doing what Story the judge and scholar had been doing for years, which is to say that law at Harvard under Story was taught as a brand of legal science that aimed at a uniform rational system of American jurisprudence.

The method of teaching, following Story's own judicial style, rested on two pillars: comparative law and legal history. Drawing on foreign law for American principle, testing American needs against inherited principles, was built into the fabric of American legal growth. What Story did at Harvard, with its admirable collection in comparative law, was to do more thoroughly what scientific lawyers had been doing for half a century. Legal history also grew naturally out of the common-law method. It was for Story as for Mansfield not ornamental or incidental. And rather than being separate from the "real" law courses, as in most modern law schools, it was built into each as an integral part of the process of legal reasoning. How it worked has been seen in Story's *De Lovio* opinion, in which his historical analysis of English admiralty was translated into a rule on the scope of federal admiralty jurisdiction. Legal history accommodated Story's belief in the changing nature of law and at the same time permitted him, as a good conservative, to emphasize the continuity of evolving principle. History, in short, was a method of critical analysis, a tool of legal reform.

Nowhere did Story put the matter so plainly as in his *Equity Jurisprudence* (1836). The brief history of English equity in his treatise, Story informed his readers, was not inserted "to gratify those, whose curiosity may lead them to indulge in antiquarian inquiries." History, "if not indispensible," was important for several reasons. Not only would it reveal "the nature and limits" of equity jurisdiction, history would also "explain, as well as limit, the anomalies, which do confessedly exist in the system" as the results of "accidental" or "political" circumstances, or "ignorance, or perversity or mistake in the Judges," or a variety of other factors that only historical inquiry would reveal. "Such a knowledge will enable us to prepare the way for the gradual improvement, as well of the science itself, as of the system of its operations." Legal reform, "to be safe, must be slowly and cautiously introduced, and thoroughly examined." History was "philosophy, teaching by example; and to no subject is this remark more applicable than to law, which is emphatically the science of human experience."[68]

Legal history and comparative jurisprudence, along with a "severe and scrutinizing logic," would move the legal system toward symmetry and universality, and the final product would be tested against the requirements of American society. At Harvard as on the Supreme Court there would be no place for "closet speculation" made "in the silence of the monastery, or in the seclusion of private life."[69] There could be no disjunction between rationality and common sense. Learning, like judging, must bend with the experience of the real world.

But how, in fact, should students blend philosophy, history, and logic with experience? The starting point at the Law School was treatise literature—both the old and the new, including the specialized variety that made its appearance in England and America in the first three decades of the nineteenth century. There were two "courses" of reading: The "regular," over which there would be "stated and frequent examination," was required of all students; the "parallel" course was supplemental reading to be consulted according to the students' interest and "leisure."[70] These two courses of reading were in turn broken down into personalty, commercial and maritime law, real property, equity, crown law, civil law, the law of nations, and constitutional law—that is, into the main subjects to be dealt with throughout the eighteen-month period of study. The standard texts for the whole course of study (and these were furnished the students until the cost of doing so became prohibitive) were Blackstone's and Kent's commentaries and Richard Wooddeson's *Elements of Jurisprudence* (1783), supplemented by Hale's *History of the Common Law* and James Sullivan's lectures. On personalty students read from the abridgments of Bacon and Dane, Chitty on contracts, and Starkie and Phillipps on evidence; in commercial and maritime law there were, in addition to Bacon and Dane again, Abbott on shipping, Paley on agency, and Marshall on insurance. In studying real property, students were spared Littleton's *Tenures* but still confronted Coke on Littleton, along with Fearne on contingent remainders, Preston on estates, and Stearns on real actions. Equity reading was sparse until Story's own volumes appeared, but students made do with Barton's *Suit in Equity*, Cooper's pleadings, and Maddock's chancery. Story's *Commentaries on the Constitution* became the standard text on constitutional law, but it was supplemented by *The Federalist Papers* and William Rawle's commentaries. Select cases and/or assignments from the reports themselves were part of the reading in each of the areas, too, and along with supplemental reading provided the raw material from which students would draw up their commonplace books (do-it-yourself law manuals that were a holdover from the old apprenticeship system).[71]

The problem that fell heavily on the classroom instructor was to salvage principles out of what were essentially raw data drawn from a distressingly broad and diffuse collection of sources, ancient and modern, American and foreign. Students were, of course, expected to grapple on their own, but Harvard offered distinct advantages over the often solitary and unassisted struggles of law-office students.[72] Talking law among themselves was, then as now, an efficacious habit, and a number of informal debating clubs among the law students gave a regularity and focus to this device of self-education. Text reading, too, was chosen with an eye to its systematizing impact. Blackstone's *Commentaries* remained the "unrivalled" text book,[73] the *one* book to master, as Webster and others testified, not only for system but, as Story advised his students, for felicity and style. Still, Blackstone wrote about English, not American, law, and because he stopped roughly in 1750 he omitted Mansfield's infusion of commercial law as well as important later developments in equity. Kent's *Commentaries* and Dane's *Abridgment* provided the beginning of a systematic understanding of American law. But Kent was "indistinct in his outlines," as Sumner politely suggested,[74] or downright "vague," as Rutherford Hayes later complained.[75] Dane, though helpful, was more encyclopedic than systematic and analytical. Story's treatises, when they entered the reading list, would speak more to American needs and give less random and irrelevant citation of precedent.[76] But even with more relevant texts the job of making sense out of such a mass of reading—some three hundred pages per week, according to one student[77]—fell to the classroom: to lectures, recitations, and moot courts.

Fortified by readings assigned in advance according to class (senior, middle, and junior), students met with faculty three times a week throughout the term.[78] The teacher examined students on their reading in a version of the old practice of "recitation" made flexible to accommodate the style of the teacher and the peculiarities of legal subject matter. Recitation and examination were to be punctuated, as the subject matter dictated, with more-or-less formal lectures that in the case of the Dane Professorship were to be the basis of written treatises. In fact, Story did *not* write his lectures to be made into books, except possibly in constitutional law;[79] nor did he as a rule write his lectures at all, or use his published books for his lectures. His great fund of legal learning at instant recall and his talent for extemporizing made written lectures unnecessary, even if he had had time to write them, as he did not. His passion for monologue, moreover, tended to blur the distinction between recitation and lecture, so that recitations often turned into disquisitions and lectures into rambling and informal commentaries on legal history and famous men as well as the day's lesson. Judging from student notes, there were frequent digressions on the subject of professional ethics and advice on how lawyers might serve their "age and country," illustrated by "higher wrought eulogies" on great jurists, past and present.[80]

If Story's lectures were not quite lectures, neither (to the relief of some of his students) were recitations quite recitations. "Where do I begin today?" he might start off. "Ah! Mr. L——, I believe you *dodged out* yesterday just before I reached you, so we'll begin with you."[81] When the laughter ceased, Story would get down to business with a general comment on the subject assigned in the readings, "sketching broadly the principles applicable to it."[82] Questioning followed, though Story could be, as students quickly discovered, easily diverted. At any rate, their answers often called forth "full and free commentary," as his son put it, or a "running commentary," as Sumner recalled, which omitted "nothing which can throw light upon the path of the poor student."[83] Reluctant students who listened to stories of "familiar or even mundane daily occurrences" found that they were drawn into "the midst of a legal discussion," and in the process the text was left behind. Story often swamped recitations with his own talk, but the students were privileged to see a great legal mind in action. When the judge was at his best they witnessed how legal history, comparative jurisprudence, and practical good sense would be translated into legal principles for the American people. "Like the Chinese juggler, he planted the seed and made it grow before the eyes of his pupils into a tree."[84]

That "tree," if the image might stand for the taught law at Harvard, was rooted firmly in the necessities of the real world, as well as the practical need to master the day-by-day aspects of practice. A good number of Harvard law students, in fact, either had studied in a law office or would do so after attending classes in Cambridge, and one of the aims of law at Harvard was in fact to improve apprenticeship education. Students were also urged to attend local courts, and at least once Story's circuit court was held in the library of Dane Hall. Many students were also involved in the exciting issues of the day—a "great stir" every few weeks, as one student put it, to keep them from the "blues." Among the happenings were "college rebellions, Texas meetings, Whig notifying meetings, . . . a great state temperance celebration, [a] State Abolition Convention; and some faint attempts . . . to excite enthusiasm for the nominees of the Loco-foco convention. . . ."[85] Story also drew freely on his own personal experience and opinion in order to make the law live for his students. The nullification crisis of the early 1830s, for example, called forth a running denunciation of states' rights and a plea for correct constitutional principles—that is, those enunciated in his *Commentaries on the Constitution*. Ten years later he was still on the same theme, delivering a powerful attack on the Southern states' rightists and the Northern abolitionists, both of whom he thought were making the union into a "rope of sand." Tariff, banks, internal improvements, and public lands, too, were discussed, and with finality, for Story viewed those issues as definitively settled.[86]

Legal education at Harvard was given a practical cast, also, by the attention given cases, a logical consequence of the common-law foundation of the curriculum. The formal case method, in which legal principles are expounded through leading cases (usually English) cited in sequence, was an innovation of C. C. Langdell in the 1870s. But the ground was laid in the Story period. At the very least it ought not to be assumed that Story and his colleagues relied exclusively and uncritically on legal treatises. Treatises did figure prominently in the course of study, as noted above, but the treatise approach was blunted by actual classroom teaching. Moreover, it was not necessarily at odds with case-law teaching. Story's own commentaries gave considerable attention to cases,[87] and in fact he was alert to the danger of too much reliance on treatise learning. As early as 1821 he warned "young men of the age" against confining "their reading too much to elementary treatises."[88] On the other hand there was no worship of "great" cases as the ultimate embodiment of the law's verities, as in the full-blown case method. If one believes the description of legal science in the *American Jurist*, principles would illuminate cases as much as cases would embody principle.[89] Cases were nonetheless the building blocks of legal science, and the "reports," as Story put it, were "the true depositories of the law."[90] One of his first actions as Dane Professor, in fact, was to press Quincy for "the entire circle of *Reports*." These, he said, and not "Text Books" were the "primary want," the most "urgent" need, and he wanted both English and American reports in both law and equity. On the American side the goal was to acquire the reports of all the states, "for we have students from various parts of the Union."[91] Reading from the reports or "Select Cases" was required, too, in each of the areas of law studied at Harvard,[92] and cases figured in classroom work as well. Students in Greenleaf's classes, at least after 1838, were assigned cases from the reports "such as would likely come before one in an office," and one of Story's great skills as a teacher was "putting cases."[93]

Cases also figured prominently in Harvard's moot court. Mooting, an ancient tradition of the English Inns of Court, was standard procedure at many of the private law academies in America and had been a part of Harvard's program from the beginning. Under Story, however, the technique was perfected and given new emphasis. Originally only one moot court was held each week, but the response was so good that the number, which included jury trials, was increased to two and sometimes three weekly.[94]

Students had two or three weeks to prepare their arguments, and cases were assigned "in rotation, according to their standing,—those in the two younger classes taking the part of junior counsel, and those in the more advanced studies acting as leaders." In addition to being an ingenious device for unifying the students, it provided a focal point of the learning experience and some drama and excitement as well. Here, as one student put it, "the law is fully spread out, reports ransacked for old cases, opinions, maxims, dictums, and statutes are all marshalled to give strength and force to the contending parties."[95] Learning, in short, was brought into focus on the case; principle translated into practice; legal and applied science fused.

Story was at his best in the moot court, opening with a sonorous "Gentlemen, this is the High Court of Errors and Appeals from all other courts in the world."[96] His moot assignments (of which he had amassed several hundred by his death) tended to be cases in commercial law, agency, and equity, and in many instances they were actual cases that had been or were to be argued before him either in Washington or on circuit. "He entered into them," his son recalled, "with the same zest and gusto as if they had been real,—nay, even with more unfeigned satisfaction." He took copious notes on student arguments, put demanding questions to student lawyers, and "delivered elaborate oral judgments."[97] The students caught his enthusiasm. Sensing the unique privilege of arguing before a justice of the Supreme Court, they approached their chores with earnestness and zeal. Story's moots were, in fact, festive occasions, and great student performances became part of a growing tradition of excellence. Story spurred participants on with lavish praise, declaring their arguments in many instances to be the equal of those at the federal bar.

Story doted on his students; they gave him affection and respect. It must not be assumed, however, that because he was the most famous of Harvard's law teachers that he was the teaching mainstay of the Law School. Judicial duties kept him occupied a good deal of every term, and though he pulled his load when in residence, he was able as a sometime teacher to escape much of the tedium and drudgery of the daily teaching and administrative duties that Ashmun and Greenleaf bore so patiently. And each man had his own teaching style. Story "was always ready and profuse in his instructions, anxiously seeking out all the difficulties which perplexed the student and anticipating his wants, leaving no stone unturned by which the rugged paths of the law might be made smoother and the steep ascents be more easily passed." Ashmun on the other hand "left the student more to himself throwing out hints which might excite his attention—cheering as the glimpses of a distant light to a benighted traveller—which but, nevertheless, did not supercede labor on his part." Ashmun taught with "the clenched fist," Story with "the open palm."[98]

Simon Greenleaf, it would seem, fell somewhere in between, but in any case, he was a man to reckon with. He assumed his duties as Royall Professor in 1834, by which time he had established himself as one of the leading lawyers in Maine and a legal scholar of some promise.[99] Story met Greenleaf on his northern circuit and soon struck up with him a deep friendship that after 1819 turned into a working relationship of the kind Story established with many leading lawyers.[100] The judge was greatly impressed by Greenleaf's work as reporter for the Maine Supreme Court (1820–32) and aided and encouraged him in the writing and publication of his first book, *A Collection of Cases Overruled, Doubted, or Limited in Their Application* (1821).[101] Story thought so highly of Greenleaf that he considered him for Supreme Court reporter to replace Henry Wheaton.[102] The place finally went to Richard Peters, but it was clear by 1826 that Story hoped to enlist Greenleaf in some phase of the struggle for the good society that was under way in New England.[103] Ashmun's death on 1 April 1833 provided the opportunity. Greenleaf's personal compatibility with Story, as well as his combination of scholarship and practical experience at the bar, made him the logical candidate to replace Ashmun. Story's recommendation to the corporation carried the day, or, as he frankly predicted to Greenleaf, had "a decisive weight."[104] Greenleaf decided to "obey the call," as he put it. He expressed some doubts about his ability but accepted enthusiastically, "trusting to the ardent desire for further improvement, & to the distinguished advantage, of exploring the deeper recesses of 'our favorite science' at *such* a place & under *such* a master."[105]

Greenleaf was a pillar of the Law School until his retirement on 10 June 1848. He refused an appointment to the Supreme Judicial Court of Massachusetts (a position that Story had earlier urged him to decline)[106] and kept at his scholarship until his death in 1853. "Old Green," as his students called him among themselves, was a man of unshakable integrity, unmistakable dignity, and an unswerving devotion to the Law School and its students. But his life there was not always easy. The success of the school in attracting new students, as Story acknowledged, simply meant more work for Greenleaf, who as senior professor in residence carried the routine burdens of teaching and administration.[107] Greenleaf was allowed freedom to practice law by the corporation, and he did so in both the state and the federal courts in Boston. But he was, to his dismay, required to reside in Cambridge, though in 1842 the corporation finally permitted him to move across the Charles.[108]

Greenleaf, for all his devotion to the Law School, was his own man. He felt free, also, to disagree with Story, as his argument for the Warren Bridge Company in 1837 indicates. Story's gracious acceptance of their disagreement attests to the durability of their friendship.[109] The judge was distressed by the implications of Greenleaf's argument and the Court's opinion, as we have seen, but he also conceded that his colleague's performance "has given essential aid to the Law Institution, as I predicted it would."[110]

The fact is that the two men worked together with extraordinary harmony and efficiency. A happy commingling of personalities, values, and talents was the key. But no small part of success was attributable to Story's sensitivity to Greenleaf's position: to the heavy burden he bore, to his modest salary, to the fact that he, Story, unfairly though unavoidably tended to get most of the laurels. Greenleaf was regularly consulted on Law School business—personnel, building, library, teaching, and student problems—and correspondence to the corporation regularly went forward over the signatures of both men. Story constantly reminded Greenleaf of his indispensability and of their mutual commitment. Equality was the guiding principle of their relationship, and nowhere was Story more explicit on this point than in acknowledging Greenleaf's dedication to him of his new work on *Evidence*, the first volume of which appeared in 1842.[111] "You & I have equally laboured in the same good cause in the Law School," wrote Story in a way that attested to his own tact and sensitivity as well as to the virtues of his colleague, "with equal zeal, & equal success. We have shared the toils together, & if we have earned a just title to public confidence & respect, you are every way entitled to an equal share with myself, nay in some respects to more." It was, Story continued, Greenleaf's "learning," his "devotion" to the school, his "untiring industry," his "integrity of purpose and action," that made for success and that kept Story himself from backsliding and despair. Story saw, too, what the sources confirm, that the tone and spirit of the Law School was set by his unique symbiotic association with Greenleaf. "What I dwell on with peculiar delight [as Story put it] is the consciousness, that we have never been rivals, but in working together, that we have gone hand in hand throughout; that not a cloud has ever passed over our mutual intercourse; & that we have lived as Brothers should live; & I trust in God, that we shall die such."[112] Greenleaf was equally frank in expressing his respect and affection for Story, from his letter of acceptance in 1833 to his commemorative discourse on his dead friend in 1845.[113]

Greenleaf and Story may have been equally committed to teaching the law as a science, but their styles of doing so were radically different—and mutually fortifying. Where Story was "vivid and impulsive," Greenleaf was cautious and exacting, though like Story he had a "singular felicity of expression" and an "untroubled stream of thought" that was hard to resist.[114] He was also a tough-minded lawyer and a bear in the classroom. If Story's forte, as one student suggested, was in lecturing and "communicating information," Greenleaf's was in "questioning." "Indolent students, who had skimmed over the lesson, dreaded his scrutiny, for they knew that an examination by him was a literal *weighing* of their knowledge."[115] Another student noted in his diary that Greenleaf "keeps the subject constantly in view, never stepping out of his way for the purposes of his own experience." Story's fondness for "digression," "high-wrought eulogies," and "arguments from his own experience," on the other hand, was well known.[116]

Such digressions could add charm and immediacy to lectures. They could also become distractions, as they may in fact have been during his last years, when he labored under the pressure of unfinished work and ill health. One who thought so was Henry C. Dorr, the brother of Thomas Dorr of Rhode Island, whose movement Story would later work to put down. The judge was "very busy in making a book on partnership," wrote Dorr, "so that he is seldom visible except at recitation. I think he shows manifest signs of old age. He talks more than he did two years ago, and is full of endless repetitions on the same thing, dwelling on what needs no explanation, till everybody is thoroughly tired of listening to him." Dorr concluded that he was "by no means so practical an instructor as prof Greenleaf" and thought he "might omit, with great profit to his audience, many of his stories about himself and his brethren on the Supreme Court."[117]

To pit Greenleaf against Story, however, is to miss the complementarity of their differences, the unique contributions of both, and the harmony of their working relationship. As teachers, "Story prepared the soil, and Greenleaf sowed the seed," and both chores were essential to success.[118] Story's style could be fairly criticized, but it was pretty much what he agreed to in 1829. Moreover, he stayed in the classroom in the face of rapidly declining health and a work load that would have sunk most men. As a teacher he was a model of excellence and a source of inspiration for Harvard's young lawyers. Not all agreed with his version of conservatism, as we shall soon see, but there were few who did not take away a sense of affection and gratitude. "His pupils in all parts of America," wrote one of them, "whatever may be their occupation or residence, or whatever the lapse of time, will rise up, as one man, and call him blessed. . . . We felt that he was our father in the law, our elder brother, the patriarch of a common family. We felt as if we were a privileged class, privileged to pursue the study of a great science, to practice in time in the cause and courts of justice before men, where success must follow labor and merit,—where we had only to deserve, and we could put forth the hand and pluck the fruit."[119]

3. Harvard Lawyers as Tocqueville's Legal Aristocracy

"If you were to ask me where the American aristocracy is found," wrote Tocqueville in *Democracy in America* (1835), "I have no hesitation in answering that it is not among the rich, who have no common link uniting them. It is at the bar or the bench that the American aristocracy is found."

Lawyers' training, their special knowledge, their intellectual bent and unique fiduciary function—their professional identity, that is to say—gave them a corporate character that set them apart from their fellow citizens, identified them as a "party," a "body," a "power," a "privileged intellectual class." On the other hand, because they commanded the tools and the language of social action, they were indispensable to the people, inevitable "arbiters between citizens." Without giving up their sense of identity or their conservative inclinations, they domesticated themselves to American democracy, accommodated themselves "flexibly to the exigencies of the moment," let themselves "be carried along unresistingly by every movement of the body social. . . ." But if they joined the ranks of American society and served the needs of the American people, they also worked to restrain the impulse of democracy, to mitigate the tyranny of the majority, which always threatened to destroy the republic. "When the American people let themselves get intoxicated by their passions or carried away by their ideas," Tocqueville argued, "the lawyers apply an almost invisible brake which slows them down and halts them. Their aristocratic inclinations are secretly opposed to the instincts of democracy, their superstitious respect for all that is old to its love of novelty, their narrow views to its grandiose desires, their taste for formalities to its scorn of regulations, and their habit of advancing slowly to its impetuosity."[120]

Tocqueville's legal aristocracy replicated Story's conservative lawyer-statesman, the model lawyer whom Story promised to educate at Harvard Law School in 1829. This is not surprising, because the Frenchman took his ideas about the legal profession, and other things as well, from Story's writings and from conversations with New England conservatives who were of one mind with Story.[121] But before the legal profession could perform the conservative role prescribed by Story and described as fact by Tocqueville, it would have to reform itself, raise its standards of learning and ethics, purge itself of the democratic tendencies that increasingly afflicted it.[122] This is to say that legal education at Harvard spoke to a perceived crisis in the profession. Like the rest of American society, the legal profession felt the impact of democratization as the growing number of increasingly specialized lawyers simply outran the ability of elite bar associations to maintain unity and control. The great danger, as Story saw it, was that the profession, just as it gained access to power, would be "split up into distinct provincial bars" and become devoted to "mere state jurisprudence," which by definition could not be legal science.[123] Harvard Law School would have to do on a national scale what elite bar associations once did on the local level: maintain standards, promote unity, and instill social responsibility. The hope was, as the *American Jurist* put it, that "Cambridge, like ancient far-famed Beryius, would become the great nursery of statesmen, legislators, and judges, and deserve, by way of eminence, the title of '*civitas legum*.'"[124] Judge Peter Thacher, in his address to the Suffolk bar in March 1831, was even more specific. "Go through the cities and villages of our country," he advised his audience; "what place is so barren, what village so small, in which is not found its lawyer, as well as its pastor? We mingle with the people in all their concerns, at home and abroad, in public and private, in the field and on the exchange. The influence of the profession is not confined to the administration of justice; it is felt in all the concerns of life and government."[125]

Story trained lawyers to shape history. He did not live to see the full fruits of his efforts in this regard, because the professional impact and social influence of his students lasted through the century. But he had reason to be confident, if Lemuel Shaw's April 1845 report to the corporation on the Law School was accurate. Harvard under Story had become an "American law school." Shaw saw there "a union of educated young men, engaged together in a course of liberal professional studies, men who afterwards distribute over all the United States, may be expected to have conspicuous and influential places in society, and may be looked to as a means of Union and harmony tending to the advancement of the common and general interest of the whole people."[126]

Harvard was in fact a national law school, as Shaw proclaimed, not only because national law was taught there or because its students came from the whole nation but because on graduation they dispersed "over all the United States." Many stayed in New England—some 398 out of the 863 whose destinations can be established or reasonably inferred, of which 236 located in Massachusetts, with a heavy concentration in the Boston region. But this is not surprising, given the predominantly New England origins of the student body.[127] What is significant is the large number (probably over half) who carried their Harvard law learning outside New England. Where they settled was influenced by many factors—family, connections, preference, accident—but it would appear that as lawyers they gravitated to places where their professional services were in demand. New England and Massachusetts attracted many, not only because of family origins but because the mature and varied economic life of that section and state required lawyers. The case was similar with the 142 who went to the middle states (New York, New Jersey, Pennsylvania, Maryland, and Delaware) and the seemingly high proportion that ended up in the growing urban centers.[128] The Midwest got 83 (28 of whom went to Illinois) and the Far West 41 (with 21 going to California)—numbers that are roughly in proportion to the state of social and economic maturity in those areas. The South, which had its own peculiar needs for lawyers and few quality law schools to train them, took 152, the largest number of any section outside New England.

Most Harvard lawyers undoubtedly allied themselves with the dominant social and economic interest groups of these various regions. Southern lawyers from Harvard made law work for planters and businessmen of the old South, and some—Charles Du Bignon from Glynn County, Georgia; Samuel Parish Davis from Jones County, Georgia; and Julius St. Julien Pringle from South Carolina—became planters themselves. The large contingent of Harvard lawyers who settled in prominent commercial-industrial areas almost certainly put to use the commercial law that was the staple of Harvard Law School. Like Southern students who went back to plantations, many Northerners (at least 33 and probably more) affiliated themselves with commercial, mercantile, and industrial interests, of which banking and railroads were especially popular. That a number turned from law to business is not surprising, given the business orientation of Harvard's law curriculum and the express intention of Harvard Law School to train businessmen as well as practicing attorneys.

All this is to say that Harvard lawyers, like members of Tocqueville's American legal profession, accommodated themselves readily to the "body social"—or, more specifically, the middle and upper classes who needed the law and could pay lawyers to shape and mold it to fit their needs. Wherever they went, Story followed their "future advancement" with "unaffected interest," perhaps even too much interest, he confessed to one of them.[129] And he was especially active in behalf of young men who promised to fill the leadership role that he felt was so much needed: men like Richard H. Dana, Jr., who praised Story so lavishly; George Hillard ("my friend and pupil"); Timothy Walker, who with Story's encouragement carried the tradition of legal scholarship and Harvard's brand of legal education into the new West; or Senator Charles Sumner.[130]

No student was closer to Story, excepting his own son, than Sumner, and the remarkable relationship between the two reveals the depth of Story's commitment to his students and his charismatic impact on them. Story was solicitous of young Sumner, in part because of his long-standing friendship with his father, C. P. Sumner. But he also looked out for the sons of many others of his friends and acquaintances. What set Sumner apart in Story's mind, as Richard Dana, Jr., saw clearly, was that he "was acknowledged to be the best scholar in the school."[131] Sumner, on his part, viewed Story as the model for his own career as well as a parental substitute for a distant and rather ineffectual father,[132] a natural association in light of Story's own paternalistic style and the prevailing assumption that the Law School, like Harvard College, stood in loco parentis. Story made the earnest young man part of his own family, nurtured his interest in the law, introduced him to the great jurists of Europe and America, and got jobs for him as librarian and instructor at the Law School. His hope was that Sumner would one day succeed him as Dane Professor.

Story's concern and patronage were not, however, limited to the select few, though none were treated quite so royally as Sumner. Story was often there to greet returning students on alumni day and sometimes was the orator of the day. Former students, too, were always welcome in Washington and came in numbers, so many on one occasion that it seemed like a class reunion. Story stayed in touch with former students like Sumner and Peleg W. Chandler, who practiced in Boston. Traveling the New England circuit also kept him in contact with Harvard Law graduates practicing in the area and gave him the chance to continue in the role of mentor and adviser. Richard H. Dana, Jr., remembered one instance in Story's circuit court in Boston when, "during an interval in the argument: he stepped up to the Bench to inquire whether a motion was in order. . . . But this was not enough for him," recounted Dana. "He could not meet a pupil without a greeting. He moved from his seat, his face beamed with kindness, and he shook me by the hand in the most cordial manner, & then listened to my business." [133]

Story seems to have displayed the same cordial response when students wrote him, as they did in dozens of letters, wanting advice or letters of introduction or jobs or simply to report to their mentor some victory or some achievement. Story was cautious about patronage matters, or at least discreet,[134] though he used his influence liberally, especially in matters pertaining to the judiciary. When he did, a word or two did wonders, as Sumner (like Webster) acknowledged. He was always ready with advice, counsel, and encouragement to his students or letters of introduction to ease their way. "Wherever you may go," he said in one letter, after answering the question asked, "I shall travel in thought towards you, as one whose merit I ought not to forget." [135]

What comes through this simple statement, and others like it, is that teaching law for Story was not a job but a commitment, a part of his life's work—indeed, an extension of his personality. When Richard H. Dana, Jr., recalled Story as a "father in the law" to his students, an "elder brother, the patriarch of a common family," [136] he touched the central theme of Story's life and laid bare a conception of leadership that went back to the Revolution, to Marblehead, to Elisha Story the gentle patriarch, and to Joseph the eldest brother. Story and his students (and their notebooks tell the tale) were in it together as a "common family," and Greenleaf, too, and Ashmun (who lived, as he put it, among his students as "but the eldest boy upon the form").[137] Story spurred his children on to excellence, to serve truth and justice as he saw them; unabashedly he confessed that his "pride was connected to them, and their fame." [138] His own he entrusted to them.

Whether the motive was the public good or private satisfaction, Story's faith was well placed, for the young men of Harvard Law School did come to occupy "conspicuous and influential places in Society." Many gravitated into the world of letters and print, as might well be expected from an educated elite. Among them were Richard Henry Dana, Jr., whose *Two Years before the Mast* came out while he was still at Cambridge; James Russell Lowell, poet, essayist, and professor of letters at Harvard; and John Motley the historian. Less well known but distinguished in New England literary and intellectual circles were men like John Wingate Thornton (class of 1840), founder of the New England Historical and Genealogical Society and leader in two publishing companies; John Patch (1834), who edited the *Literary Museum* of Boston; and George S. Hillard (1832), editor of a journal revealingly named the *Christian Register and Jurist*. Benjamin Park (1831) was associated with the *New England Magazine* and half a dozen other magazines during his long career. There were a number of newspapermen, too, like Thomas Brewer, editor of the Boston *Atlas*; William John Buckminster, editor of the *Massachusetts Ploughman*; Caleb Buckingham, editor of the *Boston Courier* for many years; Nathan Hale, who joined his father in editing the *Boston Daily Advertiser*, and John Wentworth, editor of Chicago's first newspaper, the *Chicago Democrat*. And this is not to mention men like Charles W. Palfrey and others who edited small-town papers in various places across the country.

Harvard lawyers who went into publishing probably found only indirect use for their law, though they were well placed to influence popular attitudes about legal issues. Those who went into politics, on the other hand, benefited more directly from their training. Law, as Tocqueville observed, equipped politicians with the tools and language of public action, and the legal profession was, by its nature, flexible enough so that one could be, as many were, politician and lawyer at the same time. Story realized, perhaps from watching his friend Webster, that politics often detracted from professional excellence. He hoped, nonetheless, that his students would carry their legal learning and conservative values into the political arena (though he advised them to do so after the age of forty, when their legal careers were established).[139] Among the many Story students who rallied to the call were one president of the United States (Rutherford B. Hayes), six U.S. senators, nine congressmen, three members of the cabinet, and six foreign ministers or ambassadors. Three of Story's students were state governors; over fifty at some time in their public careers served in state legislatures (where Story felt that sound legal learning and conservative values were especially wanting); and several were members of state constitutional conventions. Many of these same men and many others of Story's students as well performed notable services in nonelective roles at the national, state, and community levels.

Story hoped that lawyers would become statesmen who would counter party demagogues: that his students who went into the South would spread the word about constitutional union, that those in business and commerce would use the wisdom of the law to check antiproperty, speculative adventurers like those who destroyed the Charles River Bridge. But his faith was mainly in lawyers qua lawyers, judges, and legal scholars. There is no way to measure the impact of day-to-day lawyering, but it is reasonable to assume that many Harvard Law students practiced the kind of "scientific" law they learned at Harvard.

Certainly there were among Story's students many competent lawyers and some distinguished ones, like William Whiting, patent specialist and solicitor for the War Department during the Civil War; George Ticknor Curtis; George Minot; Peleg W. Chandler; George S. Hillard; and Francis B. Crowninshield. And there were occasional great ones, like William Evarts and Benjamin R. Curtis, the latter of whom became associate justice of the Supreme Court in 1851. Harvard students were amply represented, too, in all levels of the American judicial establishment. There were two U.S. attorneys general, five federal district attorneys, several clerks, and other lesser officers. Six served on federal circuit and district courts. Thirty-nine can be identified for sure as judicial officers on the state level, among them five chief justices of state supreme courts and one justice of a territorial supreme court. At least two were court reporters for state courts, and many more were local judicial functionaries.

Others of Story's students emulated him more directly by going into legal scholarship and teaching. Nathaniel Holmes returned to Harvard Law School (1868–72) after practicing in Saint Louis, Missouri, and serving as judge of the state supreme court; Charles T. Russell taught at Boston University Law School; and Timothy Walker was the founder and principal teacher of the Cincinnati School of Law, the leading law school in the Midwest for many years. Walker also founded (with Story's encouragement) the widely read and influential *Western Law Journal*, and his *Introduction to American Law* (1837) rivaled some of Story's own treatises in popularity. Two of the most prominent legal journals of the antebellum period were founded and edited by Harvard law graduates. The first, *American Jurist and Law Magazine*, founded in 1829 and edited by Charles Sumner, Luther S. Cushing, and George S. Hillard, was jurisprudential in tone. The second, Peleg W. Chandler's *Monthly Law Reporter*, organized in 1838, was more practical in nature. Both were encouraged by Story and, as we shall see shortly, worked to spread the gospel of scientific law that Story taught at Harvard. Harvard students who became leaders of state and local bar associations undoubtedly did the same. One, Alexander R. Lawton, class of 1842, went on to found the American Bar Association and served as its president; a second, Thomas J. Semmes (1844), also served as president of the organization.

An incomplete listing of offices held and distinctions earned by Harvard law graduates cannot, of course, capture the collective impact of more than nine hundred law students, much less the complex way in which their careers touched their age. But the evidence seems to verify Story's hopes and Shaw's boast in 1845. Harvard lawyers had no monopoly on talent; they were not necessarily the best lawyers or in all cases even good ones. But collectively they ranked high in talent, and they had the most up-to-date and relevant legal education available in the United States and a remarkable record of achievement. Conceivably, their training and positions of power qualified them to be Tocqueville's legal aristocracy and Story's conservative corrective to American democracy.

But were they? No definite answer is possible, but there is sufficient reason to think that Harvard lawyers, like the legal profession in general, had less impact on American history than it had on them, that much of Story's grand plan for a cadre of conservative lawyer-statesmen went unrealized. His theory, like Tocqueville's, rested on the assumption that the study of law imparted conservative values and a common world view that would serve as a practical guide to the great and small issues of the day. Among Story's students were those who did in fact imbibe this conservative world view and act on it. But the pressures of social class and section took a toll of purity, just as did the simple need to make a living. Students from the South, despite Story's eloquent pleas for nationalism, did not forget their Southern ways even while they were in Cambridge, as periodic outbursts between them and Northern students indicate. Nor did Story convert all Northern students. Wendell Phillips had doubts from the beginning and quickly moved away from Story's self-righteous conservatism to support abolitionism, social reform, and radicalism. Henry Dorr was sharply critical, too, even before Story's action against his brother on the Rhode Island circuit gave him cause to criticize. The odds are that many students merely took the solid legal education and left behind Story's zealous philosophizing. Indeed, Story's own son, after a promising start as a lawyer and legal scholar, abandoned first the law and then his country. Story's favorite student, Charles Sumner, defected from conservative orthodoxy, first to the peace movement and then, after Story's death, to radical abolitionism. Others, despite Story's injunction, followed the same path.

The professional unity of Harvard lawyers and the American legal profession suffered as well from the pressures of working and living and practicing law in the real world. Story assumed, as did Tocqueville, that a common vision of legal science would unite the profession. But one senses that Story's intellectual world had receding relevance for working lawyers whose main business was to make law work for their clients.

It may be that lawyers who sat at Story's feet held out longer against the pressures of chaos and adhered more firmly to their belief in law as moral science than other lawyers; it is impossible to say. But it seems fair to surmise that the "balkanization" of the profession that Story feared, not the unity that he strove to create, was the order of the day. Most Harvard lawyers, like most American lawyers, took their clues to social action, if not ideological coloration, from the group, class, and section to which they belonged, from the clients and interests they served. Some were abolitionists; others were antiabolitionists. Some spoke for law and order against the mobs that attacked the abolitionists; others joined the mob or hooted it on. Lawyers as lawyers did not speak through a national bar association or with a single voice in the various and diverse local bar groups. Lawyers were firmly planted on both sides of the issues of slavery, Indians, corporations, tariffs, and banking. And on the great question of constitutional union, where Story urged them to take a stand, there was division, not unity. Harvard lawyers who went South pledged their faith to that section for the most part. The legal profession contributed its talents to extremists of both North and South. As the American nation rushed toward the precipice of war, neither Harvard-trained lawyers nor the profession as a whole set up barriers against the onrush of social violence or raised banners to rational, constitutional order. Indeed, if one were to venture a single generalization about lawyers in the antebellum period, including those taught by Story at Harvard, it would be pretty much the opposite of Tocqueville's: Rather than controlling American society, lawyers were the instruments of its radical transformation. Rather than controlling change, as Story hoped, they—like the majority justices on the Taney Court—were carried along by the forces they worked to unleash.

Harvard lawyers and the American legal profession could not turn back political democracy, replace the professional politician and the state legislatures with lawyer-statesmen and common-law courts, or save the nation from war. Still, there is the possibility that lawyers, if they did not control change, might have worked to set limits on it, simply by making the common law the language of social action and by offering the courts as rational forums for the debate of public policy. If they did, then Story did not fail entirely, for as I shall argue in the next chapter, he did more than any other American jurist to spread the word of the law. Indisputably, Harvard Law School under his leadership became the leading force in shaping American legal education, and with that the profession and to some extent the law itself.[140] The victory was Story's more than any man's. At no time, not even in the golden age of Langdell, did one man do so much to establish the character, tone, and direction of the school.

Chapter 8

Spreading the Word of Law: Codifier and Publicist

It is very clear that a great republic, in which there is room for talents; in which thoughts and actions are not restrained by religious or political despotism; in which education is encouraged, and moral character is esteemed; in which law rules, and not the sword; in which each one asserts his rights by law, and not by force; and in which there is representation, jury-trial, and a free press, is the natural field of law and equity; but to produce these in perfection, there must be a national *character. The rules of law and equity, in important matters, must be uniform, and pervade the whole nation.*
Nathan Dane, 1823

He is the Lope de Vega, or the Walter Scott of the Common Law.
Charles Sumner on Joseph Story, 1845

He has done more than any other English-speaking man in this century to make the law luminous and easy to understand.
Oliver Wendell Holmes on Joseph Story, 1886

When Nathan Dane saw that the American republic was "the natural field of law and equity,"[1] he grasped a profound and much-neglected truth about the relation of law and culture in the antebellum United States. American democrats resisted the common law for its elitism and conservatism, to be sure. Lawyers of all persuasions acknowledged its artificialities and irrelevancies. But the common law came to the United States anyway and, as John Bannister Gibson put it in his famous dissent in *Eakin* v. *Raub* (1825), entered "so essentially into the composition of our social institutions as to be inseparable from them."[2] Philosophical lawyers like Dane, Kent, and DuPonceau agreed. So too did Tocqueville, whose theory of the bench and bar as America's aristocracy rested on the same common-law premise. What all attested to—and the American people as well by their pervasive litigiousness—was that the common law was a system of social decision making suited to American conditions.

Story understood the congeniality of the common law and American republicanism as clearly as any man of his age. He saw, too, that while serving Americans, the common law might at the same time restrain their excessive democratic impulses. He also realized that before the common law could either serve or restrain effectively—indeed, before it could be fully transplanted—it would have to be reformed. The common law would not only have to be made relevant to American needs, it would have to be known to those who would make use of it. To spread the word of scientific law was the raison d'être of Harvard Law School. It was also the underlying objective of Story's monumental series of legal commentaries written as Dane Professor.

1. Conservative as Reformer: Codification "under the Forming Hand of the Judiciary"

That the conservative activist of the 1820s, the enemy of new views of constitutional law, self-proclaimed champion of the old law, and "last of the old race of judges" should also have been a leading legal reformer is a paradox worth resolving. The tension between conservatives and reformers was real, and both tended in the course of struggle to entrench themselves behind unyielding ideologies. Yet conservatism and reform were not mutually exclusive, as the dimension of social control in evangelical Protestantism, temperance, education, and prison reform (to mention only some movements) attests.[3] Story embodied the paradox: He feared change yet believed it to be inevitable (as American conservatives had to do). As reformers necessarily must, he thought change might be controlled and directed. And indeed, the mirror image of all his pessimism was his idealism about America: its culture, its literature, its government, its science, its future.[4] As for American law, his hopes were nothing short of audacious, providing of course that it might be shaped and formed by "sound" scientific lawyers.[5]

Story defined the process of conservative legal reform in his confrontation with the codification movement that gathered force in the United States following the War of 1812. Jeremy Bentham's famous letter to president-to-be James Madison in 1811 (and later his circular letter to the governors of the states),[6] offering to codify all of American law, set the debate in motion and drew the line between radical and conservative codification. The codification movement would have come without Bentham, however, because American law had developed to the point where clarification, refinement, and systemization were desperately needed. Several interrelated factors contributed to the crisis: The explosion of American case law alone was enough to raise the issue, as Story noted in 1835. "More than 150 volumes of reports are already published . . . ," he observed; "the danger . . . seems to be, not that we shall hereafter want able reports, but that we shall be overwhelmed with their number and variety."[7] If one counted both English and American reports along with the indexes, digests, and abridgments necessary to use them, as Timothy Walker did in 1844, the "records of the common law" would amount to a thousand volumes.[8] Just when the growing interstate nature of their practice demanded they do so, practicing lawyers found it impossible to master the basic sources of the law. Access to relevant, up-to-date law was further obstructed by the derivative nature of American jurisprudence; the problem of determining what parts of English law suited America was complicated by the rapid social and economic transformation of American society. If that were not enough, the American federal system permitted each state to fashion its own unique version of the common law. Unless something were done "to avert the fearful calamity," Story warned Suffolk County lawyers in 1821, the profession would be "buried alive, not in the catacombs, but in the labyrinths of the law."[9]

The problem was pressing; but were codes the solution? If so, could or should all of the common law be codified, as Bentham and his American champions insisted? If not all, then how much? And who was to say? On these and related questions concerning codification, Story worked his way to moderate ground between radical codifiers on the one hand and standpat common lawyers on the other. His first public statement on the matter, however—in the *North American Review* in 1817—contained grave reservations about the workability of any sort of code. "To a certain extent," he argued, "law must forever be subject to uncertainty and doubt, not from the obscurity and fluctuation of decisions, as the vulgar erroneously supposed, but from the endless complexity and variety of human actions." It followed that both statute and common law "must necessarily be general in their language, and incapable of a minute and perfect application to the *boundless* circumstances of life, which may modify, limit, or effect them." Story concluded briefly and without supporting argument that no code, "however extensive," could provide "for the infinite variety of distinctions, as to civil justice, arising from the imperfection of human language and foresight, from the conflict of opposing rights, from the effect of real or apparent hardships, and from those minute equities, which are often found in different scales, adding somewhat to the weight of each, but rarely forming an exact equipoise."[10]

"Utopian dreams of excellence" in the style of Bentham were clearly out of the question. But moderate codification was not, despite Story's pessimistic assessment in 1817. Story had already participated, along with Dane and William Prescott, in a revision of Massachusetts statutes.[11] This modest success and the growing fear that the chaos of unstructured and unknown law might overwhelm the profession shifted the burden of his argument from the difficulties of codification to the possibility, even necessity, of it. There was, he declared to the Suffolk bar in 1821 after he had sketched out the impending crisis facing them, "but one adequate remedy," and that was "a gradual digest, under legislative authority," of the settled portions of decisional law. The way must be paved "to a general code, which will present, in its positive and authoritative text, the most material rules, to guide the lawyer, the statesman, and the private citizen." [12]

If Story was a codifier in 1821 it was with serious reservations. Indeed, his speech to the Suffolk bar was, as one scholar has noted, the "earliest statement of the moderate position." [13] Picking up on his own objections to total codification made in 1817, he warned against the dangers of perfectionism: "We ought not to permit ourselves to indulge in the theoretical extravagance of some well-meaning philosophical jurists, who believe that all human concerns for the future can be provided for in a code, speaking a definite language. Sufficient for us will be the achievement, to reduce the past to order and certainty. . . ." More specifically, codification should be limited to those portions of the common law "which under the forming hand of the judiciary, shall from time to time acquire scientific accuracy." [14] Here in judicial control was the principle that would guide his action on Massachusetts codification in the 1830s and the one that would in another sense inform his commentaries on American commercial law.

What Story meant by moderate codification, the balance he struck between radical perfectionism and entrenched conservatism, was further clarified in his response to Henry Wheaton's letter requesting advice on the codification movement in New York. Story's suggestion, after reading Wheaton's revision of the committee's draft code, was to go beyond the "mere revision of the Statute Law" and codify the common law itself, or "at least the part which is most reduced to principles & is of daily extensive application." Such a code, he was quick to add, would not "render future legislation unnecessary, or . . . supercede the necessity of perpetual appeals to the courts of justice" (a phrase almost verbatim from his 1817 statement). [15] There was "no visionary expectation of a perfect, infallible, or universal system" behind his code, Story assured Wheaton—no Benthamite nonsense, that is to say. But, he continued, "I am in favour of a Code, because I think it may reduce to certainty, method, & exactness much of the law, already passed by judicial tribunals & thus give to the public the means, with a reasonable compass, of ascertaining their own rights & duties in many of the most interesting concerns of human life." In addition, "the labours & exhausting researches of the profession" would be greatly abridged. [16] The legislature might move, then, but only where the courts had reduced law to principle. This conservative process—adumbrated in 1817, announced in 1821, and repeated in private correspondence during the 1820s [17]—remained the essence of his theory of codification.

Story's ideas were maturing, but there were still unanswered questions of a theoretical and practical nature. What about the application of codified principles, for example? Would the courts, operating in the common-law mode, apply such principles to changing circumstances? Who would determine the respective roles of the courts and legislatures as the codification movement progressed? Who, indeed, would determine what principles would be codified in the first place? These were fundamental questions for conservatives, as Story well knew, because the 1820s and 1830s, which spawned codification movements, also generated states' rights, democracy, and a return to political parties. Increasingly, the bench and bar came under attack for alleged elitism, and legislative government was put up as a democratic counterpoise to the courts. Codification, which had originally appeared to be a necessary means of legal reform—the "one adequate remedy," as Story called it in 1821—appeared increasingly to be the first volley of a full-scale assault on judicial government, even the law itself. The question was whether even moderate reform was possible, seeing that it might open the floodgates of radicalism. As a champion of moderate codification, Story had to address the question.

Story's response came in his "Law, Legislation and Codes," one of his several anonymous essays published in Francis Lieber's *Encyclopaedia Americana* (1829–33), which, it should be noted, sold one hundred thousand copies.[18] Despite the potential of democratic excess, Story stuck to his position of moderate reform. In fact, his arguments were addressed less to Benthamite radicals, of whom there were few in America, than to stubborn common lawyers who resisted any reform at all. Story not only repeated his by then familiar warning against total codification but fortified his position with arguments from historical jurisprudence. Change, he assumed, was inevitable in law, but gradual change was the rule and history set the limits: "Law is gradually formed," he continued, "and must differ in different ages, according to different circumstances of society. . . ." Law "must vary according to the progress or regress of a nation . . . it can rarely settle comprehensive principles, and must, by degrees, thread its way through the intricacies of human actions. . . ." Because of the complexity and incremental nature of legal development, it followed that "no legislature can make a system half so just, or perfect, or harmonious, both from want of time, and experience, and opportunity of knowledge, as judges, who are successively called to administer justice, and gather light from the wisdom of their predecessors."[19]

So much for the conservative; what now of the reformer? Admitting the historical nature of legal change and the congeniality with it of the common law did not, Story argued, settle the debate over codification. For all of its virtues in accommodating legal change to fit the national character, the common law was not perfect or self-sufficient. No less than a legislative code, it was a "system of rules" that were often "fixed, certain, and invariable" and that could be "quite as unyielding as any code can be." Legislatures, on the other hand, though inept at making law, had the sovereign capacity and the responsibility for regulating "the general concerns of society." Where the courts spoke wisely if sometimes obscurely, the legislatures could speak clearly and with authority. Both had virtues; both disabilities. They contended against one another, but they also worked in tandem and harmoniously to create clear, scientific, and workable law. Witness, he said, the work of Justinian or Napoleon, or the New York Code of 1830, or the state statute law governing real estate, descent, and conveyance, as areas of effective collaboration.[20] The solution, he concluded, was not to assert the supremacy of positive law (as the Benthamites did) or the self-sufficiency of the common law (as did advocates of the status quo) but to define carefully and by the axioms of historical jurisprudence what each could do best.

The division of labor was this: The courts, proceeding by the familiar common-law method, were best at fashioning rules of law and of applying those rules to the infinite and changing circumstances of life. On the other hand, the case-by-case method that so aptly created principles (or discovered them, as the nineteenth century still had it) could also obscure them. The doctrines of the common law were often "scattered in different cases" and subject to varying interpretations, even in the hands of "lawyers of great research and accuracy." Some, such as those governing contingent remainders and executory devices, were so enmeshed in extended cases as to be beyond the comprehension of many lawyers, even with the aid of Fearne. The adversary nature of common-law proceedings often added to doctrinal confusion, too, because each side picked and chose its own doctrines, and even asserted false doctrine. Judicial *obiter dicta* also added to the confusion of lawyers in search of principle.[21]

What legislatures could do—and again Story expanded on the theme he had adumbrated in 1817—was not to create principles of law but to clarify and refine those which had been developed over time by the common-law courts. If the common-law rule was lost in an overgrowth of inaccessible cases, why should not the legislature state it clearly and save practicing lawyers the trouble and time and expense of searching it out? If the rule was "confessedly" uncertain, why should not the legislature "interfere" and "fix a rule, such as on the whole, stands upon better reasoning, and general analogies of the law?"[22] Codes in this way might contribute to the uniformity, regularity, and accessibility of American law.

At the same time, judicial authority would be preserved against undue legislative encroachment in two fundamental ways. First, judicial decisions over the years, drawing directly from the experience and needs of real people, would determine the rules that governed society, as in English legal history. Second, even after the principles developed by the courts were stated and clarified in a code, it would remain the duty of the courts to apply those principles to actual cases. The only problem would be to guarantee that they did so with objectivity and uniformity. To assure that they did and to answer democratic charges of uncontrolled judicial discretion Story set forth a list of twenty-one axioms of interpretation that resembled in abbreviated form the "Rules of Interpretation" set out in his *Commentaries on the Constitution*.[23] At one and the same time, Story testified to his faith in objective scientific law (and hardly a better example is to be found) and to his recognition that the common law under the impact of nineteenth-century change was falling away from that standard. Behind the moderate reformer was an anxious conservative.

Moderate codification, as Story conceived it, was intended to end the warfare between the courts and the legislatures. He conceded in good conservative fashion that the result might never be perfect, but he asked, "Because we cannot form a perfect system, does it follow that we are to do nothing? Because we cannot, without rashness, give certainty to all possible or probable details of jurisprudence, shall we leave every thing uncertain and open to controversy?" Conservative wisdom might encourage reform as well as oppose it. Moderate codification guided by conservative good sense, as in the partial codification movements in Virginia and New York, "may be useful, and, indeed, indispensable for the wants and improvements of society, in its progress from one stage to another. The question of more or less is a mere matter of expediency and policy."[24]

Story's essay, although it was unsigned, was known to be his.[25] Along with his previous public statements and extensive private advice, it consolidated his position as the leader of moderate reform and put him in the eye of the codification storm in Massachusetts.[26] The movement in that state came to a climax in January 1836 when Whig governor Edward Everett, in his first annual address, asked the legislature to consider the codification of the state's common law. The issue had been brewing for two decades, and Story had been involved from the beginning. Well before Bentham dramatized the issue, Story had turned to the legislature for support in his effort to introduce equity into Massachusetts. He was involved more successfully in the revision of state statute law, and his address to the Suffolk bar in 1821 had in effect put the issue of codification on the public agenda. Story was drawn to speak out, too, by the rise of Jacksonian Democracy in Massachusetts, which gave codification a distinctly ideological coloration. American Benthamites like Robert Rantoul, Jr., who mixed radical codification proposals with slashing attacks on lawyers and the common law, called forth the conservative reaction. In between was the *American Jurist*, edited by Story's friends, which advocated moderate reform and attempted to inject rationality into the increasingly politicized debate. In the context of the movement for the democratization of the law—intensified by the abolition of special pleading in 1836 and the pending decision in the *Bridge* case—Story's strictures on moderate reform took on new meaning. Governor Everett's appointment of Story to lead the state commission on codification was in fact designed to head it off, that is, to keep it safely in the hands of moderate conservatives.

Story accepted his friend's offer, but only "after a good deal of reflection" and "not without much hesitation"[27]—possibly even, as he later claimed, "very much against his will."[28] He had reason to hesitate. The political climate was ugly, and many of his closest friends (including Webster, Kent, and Hopkinson, to mention only some)[29] were either lukewarm or opposed to codification. On top of judicial and teaching responsibilities he assuredly did not need or want another job. What he did want, however, even more than moderate reform, which he still cherished, was to save the common law of Massachusetts from the gathering forces of radicalism and novel experimentation. "The present state of popular opinion here makes it necessary to do something on the subject," he wrote candidly to Wilkinson,[30] and that "something" was decidedly conservative. He "reluctantly accepted" the chairmanship of the special commission on codification, he admitted to fellow conservative George Ticknor, "from an anxious desire to moderate the movement, & to report a very qualified system of codification, principally though not exclusively, of our common civil law."[31]

To that end the first order of business was to place reliable conservatives on the "Common Law Commission" (as Everett revealingly called it).[32] Elite control of change had, of course, been a constant goal of American conservatives, and moderate codifiers like Timothy Walker realized that success depended on putting the matter in the hands of "the Marshalls, the Websters and the Storys of our land."[33] Story emphatically concurred. Indeed, elite control had been the unarticulated corollary to his moderate codification theory from the outset. And there is no doubt that he accepted the chairmanship with the understanding that he would be joined by men of sound principles and that he would play a major role in choosing them. Negotiations with Everett about the makeup of the commission had, in fact, begun even before his formal agreement to serve as chairman.[34] Story was amenable to Everett's suggestions, but in addition he recommended his colleague at the Law School, Simon Greenleaf, whose "views of Codification," he assured Everett, "are perfectly in coincidence with my own."[35] Story also informed Everett that he would take kindly to the appointment of Theophilus Parsons and Charles Sumner, neither of whom, as it turned out, was willing to serve.[36] Story suggested initially that the Jacksonian radical codifier, Robert Rantoul, Jr., be appointed "so as to avoid any possible suggestion of the scheme being a mere party measure."[37] But he changed his mind, most likely after consultation with Parsons,[38] for fear "that the radical character of his opinions might embarrass the prudent execution of the Commission."[39]

The final list of members—Simon Greenleaf, Theron Metcalf, Charles Forbes, and Luther Cushing—all had Story's approval: Greenleaf and he agreed on principles and tactics; Metcalf, who originally opposed any codification, had been converted to moderate reform by Story himself;[40] Forbes had been educated by, and was in full accordance with, Story's essay on codification in Lieber's *Encyclopaedia Americana*;[41] Cushing peddled the moderate line in the *American Jurist*, which he coedited. Here, then, was an intellectually congenial group representing the elite lawyers of Boston, Harvard Law School, the *American Jurist*, and the Supreme Court of the United States on circuit. To a man they agreed with Story on codification and deferred to his predominance on the commission.

Story was the sole author of the commission's report, which despite his "violent" bout of illness was ready for Everett by 24 December; Everett then submitted it to the legislature for its guidance.[42] The report, dated January 1837, opened with an eight-page summary of the common law in Massachusetts: its transplantation and development and guiding principles. Next was a specific plan for its reform and codification. Here without essential deviation Story followed the principles and arguments (and sometimes even the language) set forth in his essay in Lieber's *Encyclopaedia*. That is to say, he steered a course between the radicals, who demanded total codification, and the reactionaries, who wanted none. Once again he argued the impossibility of total codification while urging the practicality and expediency of a moderate approach that would clear up areas of confusion, enhance uniformity, and rescue working lawyers from drudgery and impending chaos. Specifically, the report recommended codification in only three areas: First was criminal law, a logical area, as of all branches of the law it should be the most certain and widely understood. For conservatives it was safest, too, because no property rights per se were involved. The second category was procedure and the law of evidence "as applicable both to civil and criminal proceedings,"[43] a rather surprising concession in light of Story's feeling that the abandonment of special pleading in 1836 was but another example of the "restless love of innovation."[44] The area was in desperate need of clarification, however, and again it was only remotely connected with property rights. Most important were those areas of commercial law already settled according to principle by the courts, particularly "commercial contracts" such as agency, bailments, guaranty and suretyship, bills of exchange, insurance, and partnership.[45]

In these specific areas where principle had been established the legislature might restate the law in positive form, tidy it up, eliminate meaningless technicality, and resolve conflict and confusion. Outside these areas, however, the common law of the state would remain in force, so that "everything not governed by the code is to be left precisely as it now is." The courts, moreover, would retain the right to apply the principles stated in the code to all prospective cases according to the method of the common law. Finally, to guarantee that all changes would be "strenuously and sedulously directed" and implemented "with a cautious and skillful hand, and with a deep sense of the delicacy of intermeddling with established principles," Story's report recommended the appointment of at least five commissioners "of high standing in the profession" to carry out the job.[46]

"We have not yet become votaries of the notions of Jeremy Bentham," Story assured Wilkinson, shortly after putting the report in the hands of the governor. And it would be hard to dispute that fact. Indeed, it is tempting to argue that Story, under the guise of reformer, had deliberately scuttled codification in Massachusetts. But that would be to ignore his record as spokesman for moderate codification. A more likely explanation is that, in attempting to apply his theory to actual problems, Story realized the unlikelihood of success. Talk of radical reform discouraged proponents of cautious, piecemeal action, and the elitist implications of his moderate plan were bound to raise democratic hackles. Given his pessimistic assessment of legislative government and the "speculative" tone of the age, he undoubtedly sensed the danger in inviting the legislature to do anything at all, lest it do too much. Certainly it must be conceded that Story's report, selectively read, gave plenty of ammunition to the forces for the status quo, who in fact won the day in Massachusetts. A commission was appointed by the legislature to codify the criminal law, as Story's report recommended. But it did not report until 1841, by which time support even for "safe" reform had evaporated. By 1844 the codification movement was dead in Massachusetts and for all practical purposes in other states as well.[47]

Story did not kill it, however, or at least he did not intentionally do so. Admittedly, he preferred no codification to the radical kind; and he came to doubt whether success was possible. But he put himself on record in 1836 for moderate codification and conservative reform, as he had done consistently since at least 1821. No statement, concluded one scholar, "in all the debates over codification in the United States . . . argued as logically, comprehensively and trenchantly for codes as Story did in this special report."[48] In light of the general trend away from codification across the nation during this period, it is doubtful if Story could have done more. Almost certainly he could not single-handedly have revived codification in Massachusetts.

Nor did he feel obliged to, for as always Story worked on a broad front, and the fact was that codification was not the only road to reform. In fact, Story gave up on codification after 1836 and concentrated full time on treatise writing, where improvements in the law could be made more surely, safely, and profitably. By late 1836, when his report on codification was in legislative hands, he had already written commentaries on four branches of American law. These volumes, along with those of his contemporaries, more than the conservative naysaying of his report, put the finishing touch to the codification movement.[49] On the other hand, Story's confrontation with codification greatly influenced his career as publicist. The codification struggle accentuated the need for immediate measures to order the chaos of American decisional law; it also clarified the limits of reform and defined those areas where it was possible. Story the publicist took over where Story the codifier left off. The constant premise of both was his long-held distrust of legislative competence and a preference for law made by judges.

2. Form Follows Function: Treatise Law as Applied Science

Part of his job as Dane Professor required Story "to prepare and deliver, and to revise for publication, a course of lectures" on five branches of American law,[50] which he set forth in his inaugural address as "the Law of Nature, the Law of Nations [i.e., international law], maritime and commercial Law, Equity and the Constitutional Law of the United States."[51] The law of nature, which he defined as the "philosophy of morals" behind all law (what we would call jurisprudence), was dropped from the list in keeping with the practical orientation of the Law School. The remaining subjects, Story sanguinely predicted, could be handled in "four goodly volumes."[52] Ultimately he wrote eleven hefty tomes on nine major areas of American law, not counting his early editions of Abbot and Chitty or the special student versions of his work on the Constitution. Except for the three volumes on the Constitution in 1833, all the works concerned private law and specifically commercial law. Directly commercial were *Bailments*, (1832), *Agency* (1839), *Partnership* (1841), and *Bills of Exchange* (1843) and its companion volume, *Promissory Notes* (1845). The four remaining volumes, which were not technically commercial law but which were indispensable to it, were *Conflict of Laws* (1834), *Equity Jurisprudence* in two volumes (1836), and *Equity Pleadings* (1838). While writing new volumes, Story was also seeing completed ones through the press and preparing new and often significantly enlarged editions of earlier works— all this in the span of sixteen years, in the midst of teaching and administrative duties at the Law School and increasingly heavy judicial obligations at Washington and on circuit, not to mention his codification efforts, his public speaking, his anonymous publications, and his ever-broadening role as adviser, patron, and drafter of legislation. With the assistance of

Little, Brown and Company (and its immediate predecessors, Charles Little and Company and Hilliard, Gray and Company), with whom he published exclusively, Story became a one-man West Publication Company.

His commentaries on the various branches of private law deserve an extended analysis that would put each in the context of nineteenth-century doctrinal developments. The problems addressed here are more limited: to ascertain their common technique and methodology as well as their underlying purposes and to see them as interrelated parts of Story's grand effort to create an American commercial common law suitable both to the needs of the new capitalism and to the values of old republicanism. But first, Story's legal publications ought to be viewed as part of the contemporaneous explosion of New England letters.

The main flowering of literature in New England, F. O. Matthiessen's "American Renaissance," came after Story's death, to be sure, and the formative phases of the movement—the challenge to Unitarian orthodoxy, Emerson's American Scholar and Divinity School addresses, and the first literary rumblings of Transcendentalism—he condemned by ignoring. Still, in the most practical sense his books, like theirs, were part of a publication revolution. Change accelerated after 1815 with the surge of popular periodicals and cheap newspapers and progressed rapidly with improvements in printing technology and the development of publishing companies designed to draw on the mass market that the transportation revolution made possible.[53] Many if not most of the writers, at least of fiction, resented their dependence on the popular readership and on the publishers who promised access to it. On this point Story the conservative was most progressive. He saw the mass market as a vehicle for spreading the word of law and grasped as fully as any publicist of the age the need to adjust his books to the audience he wanted to reach. His relationship with Little, Brown and its parent companies can only be pieced together inferentially from scattered extant correspondence, but there is no evidence of the subservient relationship of which American Renaissance fiction writers constantly complained.[54] The difference may well have been that law books, like history and biography and unlike fiction, had an identifiable and dependable market. That his volumes came out with the quasi-official imprimatur of Harvard University was yet a further advantage in marketing, and in fact there was a cordial relationship between Little, Brown and the university.[55] Story's congenial relationship with the company, however, stemmed mainly from the fact that he was an asset and could negotiate from strength. Given the inchoate state of the publishing industry in the 1830s and the need of most publishers, including Little, Brown, to expand their markets, it is reasonable to think that he had as much to offer them as they him. His exclusive contract, indeed, may well explain how the law department of the company (which was the province of C. C. Little) became one of the most important legal publishing operations before the Civil War. Success meant comfortable wealth for Story, too, and for his son. What his specific contractual arrangements with Little, Brown were cannot be said, but his share of the profits was undoubtedly generous.[56]

Story's financial success separated him from most other writers of the age, who struggled desperately for money and recognition. Still, he shared many cultural values with them, not the least of which was the aspiration to create an intellectual inheritance commensurate with national greatness. Emerson and his friends looked to an American literature; Story aimed to create a literature of American law. Like the members of the Concord school he ignored, he also drew on New England tradition; like them he argued about the lessons it taught. Indeed, Story the legal publicist fits readily into the pattern of cultural dialogue, as R. W. B. Lewis called it, between the "Party of Hope" (which would include Emerson, Thoreau, and Walt Whitman) and the "Party of Memory" (of which Hawthorne and Melville were the leading figures).[57] The principled law that Story expounded in his commentaries—that taught at Harvard Law School—no less than Hawthorne's literature worked to restrain the perfectionism and radical speculation that threatened the stability of the republican community.

Story wrote for national glory, then, and for conservative truth and personal fame, and for a handsome profit as well. But first and most directly he wrote in response to the pressing practical needs of the working lawyer who had to bring vast quantities of unorganized case and statute law to bear on the novel problems of a new age. This pressure had already set in motion a tradition of English treatise law. Story's treatises were in fact an extension of this tradition, just as they were part of the movement toward legal rationalization in America that generated printed reports and abridgments (like those of Nathan Dane), that led to revisions of state statute law, and that improved indexes and digests. Most specifically, however, Story's treatises grew out of, and grappled with problems left unresolved by, the abortive codification movement. Treatise writing for Story, like codifying, followed decisional law, which is to say that he abjured theorizing and proceeded only in those areas of the law where principle was most settled—as in commercial contracts generally, and agency, bailments, partnership, and bills and notes in particular.

Commercial law was Story's judicial specialty, of course, and the same qualities went into his treatises on the subject as went into his judicial decisions. But treatise writing as legal science had certain distinct advantages over judging, as well as over codification. Story the publicist, unlike Story the judge, was not limited in expounding principles by the facts before him, nor was he answerable to judicial colleagues for his statements of the law. Unlike codification, treatise law did not depend on the whims of politicians or the vagaries of legislative government. What successful treatise writing demanded, on the other hand, was little short of monumental. To do what he wanted to do, Story would have to master vast areas of law single-handedly, extract principles from hundreds of cases and the works of countless jurists, and present them in an idiom and form understandable to a wide variety of American lawyers. Scholarship, moreover, rather than the imprimatur of the legislature (as in codification), would be the key to authority and thus acceptance. In the largest sense the problem was pedagogical. Against this practical challenge his work as publicist ought in fairness to be measured.

Story's initial decision to publish separate volumes on select subjects rather than a comprehensive multivolume work in the style of Blackstone (and Kent) was well thought out and eminently practical. Kent in fact had already produced *the* great work in that genre, just as Dane had supplied *the* abridgment of American law. "The course now," as Dane himself put it to Story, was "to publish large law works on a few branches of the law. . . ."[58] Story noted the same trend when he wrote in the *North American Review* in 1817 that "there has been a larger number of treatises on the leading topics of the common law produced within the last half century, than in all the preceding time."[59] Such English works as Starkie on evidence and Chitty on pleading (noted by Dane in his letter to Story) and Jones's essay on bailments, Bayley's bills of exchange, Parke on insurance, and Redesdale on equity pleading (noted by Story) served as working models of the new type of treatise literature.

Separate volumes on specific subjects had functional advantages, too, which Story was quick to exploit. They were easier to organize and write. They could be got to press more quickly and revised more readily (and editorial revision was to the nineteenth-century treatise what the pocket supplement is to the twentieth-century lawbook). Rushing volumes into print (in 1842 he had three volumes upon different subjects in the press) would deprive Story of valuable prepublication criticism, the kind that so much benefited Blackstone,[60] and it also subjected him to the charge of "book-making."[61] But timely volumes were more imperative than definitive ones, and the need was to get specialized, up-to-date volumes to working lawyers, who could choose according to their needs without investing in a costly multivolume work that might be out of date by the time it was published. On the other hand, if lawyers chose to purchase all of Story's volumes, they would get a systematic overview, because the separate volumes were carefully interrelated and sequentially connected, as we shall shortly see.

Practicality and pedagogical considerations dictated the organization of the separate volumes, too. In addressing the practical needs of the profession Story drew consciously on the experience, the virtues and mistakes, of Continental and English jurists.[62] Though he saw his own books as part of this treatise tradition, he was also convinced that a new emphasis was needed. Continental jurists, he observed in the preface to his *Bailments*, the first of his commentaries, almost always "discuss every subject with an elaborate, theoretical fulness, and accuracy, and ascend to the elementary principles of each particular branch of the science." The English, on the other hand, "with few exceptions, write Practical Treatises, which contain little more than a collection of the principles laid down in adjudged cases, with scarcely an attempt to illustrate them by any general reasoning, or even to follow them out into collateral consequences." What America needed, he concluded, was a "union of the two plans."[63] With the Continental penchant for "general reasoning" about "elementary principles" he would combine the down-to-earth case orientation of English treatises. Through a mixture of the two, theoretical and speculative excesses of the former and the confusing chaos of the latter could be avoided. Legal science Story wanted, but *applied* legal science. Principle was the sine qua non of legal science; case reasoning kept principle practical. Balance was the desideratum in writing as well as teaching.

The search for system was a controlling theme of eighteenth-century science, of which the science of law as well as the science of government was a part. The Newtonian revolution of the seventeenth century set the tone of the eighteenth. The duty of legal scientists, like that of such great natural scientists as Blumenbach, Buffon, and Lamarck, was to discover regularity and symmetry in nature's confusion and complexity. Bringing rational order out of apparent chaos was, as Story saw it, the genius of Blackstone, the distinguishing mark of Mansfield's commercial law, of Hardwicke and Eldon in equity, and of Stowell in admiralty and maritime law; and in this tradition Story made the search for organizing principle the essence of his legal science. Such was the theme of his early unfinished manuscript "Digest of American Law"[64] and the motif of his early scholarship. It was the hallmark of his judicial opinions as well as the foundation of legal education at the Law School, of which the treatises were but an extension. Story grasped the simple but profound truth that principled law was practical law. If cases might be made to yield principles, then principles, once ascertained, might organize cases.[65] By cutting through the chaos of proliferating case law, principle might save American judges and lawyers from the threatened inundation. It followed that the function of Story's treatises was to ascertain those principles which were settled, to distinguish major principles from auxiliary ones, to arrange them according to the logic of the subject, and "to illustrate them by general reasoning" and follow them out to "collateral consequences."[66] Technique, structure, and tone followed function.

If principle was to be the means of clarifying case law, making it accessible and uniform, then the method of determining principle was of fundamental importance. Story's approach, as in his scheme of codification, was conservative. Given his command of the material and his well-known propensity for didacticism it would have been tempting simply to assert principles in their logical completeness and to manufacture those which could not be discovered. Text writing invited both perfectionism and authoritativeness, because the author, unlike the judge, was not answerable for his opinions. Personal lawmaking, too, could always be disguised in authorities, covered with a gloss of natural law (or the accepted practice of the mercantile community), or simply given as convenient policy, plain instrumentalism. Story referred to all of these in the pages of his commentaries but never as the controlling source of doctrine and never as a substitute for a scholarly canvassing of existing authorities. The duty of the commentator as Story practiced it was not to create but to discover principles, by the patient, thorough sifting and analysis of cases, treatises, and statutes.

His restraint made sense, given that he deliberately chose to write on commercial law, where principles, thanks to Mansfield and Continental judges and jurists, were mainly settled. "Occasionally," to be sure, as he admitted in his *Bailments*, he would avail himself "of the freedom belonging to a commentator to express a doubt, to deny a doctrine." But, he hastened to add, "rarely" would he do so, and only "when the point was purely speculative, or the common law authorities justified me in the suggestion."[67] As a practice, he also informed the reader when authorities were themselves confused or in conflict—for example, in the law of collision, the matter of gross negligence.[68] Sometimes in such instances he would throw his weight on one side or the other, though more often he would strike for common ground among contending authorities, as, for example, on the important subject of guaranty of promissory notes.[69] If the confusion was apparent, not real, he would generally settle the matter. Where conflicting authorities could not be harmonized, he did not hesitate to leave questions open for future clarification by the courts.[70] "It will probably be found in the future, as it has been in the past," he said in reference to a disputed point in equity, "that professional opinions will continue divided upon the subject, until it shall have undergone a more searching judicial examination, not upon authority merely, but upon principle."[71] System and principle were the goals, but they did not rule everywhere. Lawyers needed to distinguish the ideal from the real, to know when principle did not rule as well as when it did.

Story ranged widely in search of unifying principle. With the exception of *Conflict of Laws*, the staple of his commentaries was English and American (state and national) case law. Though he drew broadly from a vast field of decisional law, he had decided favorites. In equity the stars were Hardwicke and Eldon and on the American side his friend Kent, whose reputation was enhanced and internationalized by Story's citations.

At the center of a wide constellation of common-law judges cited, and holding them together with a principled analysis of commercial law, was Mansfield. Among American judges, Story favored those of the leading commercial states of Massachusetts, New York, and Pennsylvania, but reports of all the states were consulted and cited. The Supreme Court opinions, at Washington and on circuit, were cited and quoted frequently, too, including those from the New England circuit, without reference to authorship. Most of the English cases used came from the post-1760 period when English law and equity began to respond to the forces of commerce and manufacturing. American cases cited tended to be the most recent ones.

Where principles in the common law were obscure, Story frequently turned to the civil law for guidance and clarity, for that "general reasoning" which was the hallmark of legal science. He felt free to dip back into Roman law for illuminating principle or to uncover the roots of modern doctrine. More often he cited eighteenth- and nineteenth-century European jurists, especially those of France and Scotland, where the tradition of civil law was strong. He admitted that the "distinctions and speculations of civilians" seemed "remote from the practical doctrines of the common law," and they were not put forth as controlling authorities. On the other hand, the "free habits of the Civilians" permitted them "subtile distinctions," "refined speculation, and theoretical inquiries" not open to common lawyers. Though seemingly "remote from the practical doctrines of the common law, they may yet be of great utility in the investigation and illustration of elementary principles."[72]

Here in the style of Mansfield was a self-conscious, eclectic, practical-minded comparative jurisprudence in action.[73] Story was not, of course, the first to make use of non-English jurisprudence. Continental jurists like Vattel, Burlamanqui, and Grotius had been current in America for half a century or more, and new editions of those and other works continued to appear throughout the early nineteenth century. While drawing on foreign jurisprudence Story did not lose sight of the unique character of American jurisprudence, a theme expounded with special force in his anonymous essay "American Law" in *Kritische Zeitschrift für Rechtswissenschaft und Gesetzgebung des Auslandes* (1836).[74] But law in America, especially private commercial law, was for Story part of a Western legal tradition that went back to ancient Rome. What he said of American law regarding contracts and real property was true generally of commercial law in his system: that it was "disposed to avail itself of the best principles of commerce, which can be gathered from all foreign sources not excluding even the civil law." Using the method of comparative jurisprudence, American commercial law, with that of England, France, and Germany, might be decided "upon universal reasoning, and in the same manner."[75]

This emphasis on universality and rationality puts Story's commentaries in the tradition of the American Enlightenment—indeed, marks them as one of its most notable monuments. Commercial common law was not, however, on that account a vague, mystical creation, a "brooding omnipresence in the sky," as Holmes would later put it.[76] The comparative and historical techniques, as Story applied them, were demanding and rigorous, and the "universal reasoning" they ascertained was based, in good Burkean fashion, more on what was than on what should be. One might even be so bold as to argue that, through Story's brand of scholarship, he was in a meaningful sense really discovering law and not making it. At any rate, that was the unmistakable impression conveyed in his commentaries, and it added immensely to their authority and thus their acceptability.

So, too, did the clarity of his argument, for lawyers could not accept what they could not understand. A sense of priority—how much to say, how much to exclude—was basic, for, as he put it, "The business of commercial life will not stop, while lawyers plunge into folios of a thousand pages, to ascertain a possible shade of distinction in the construction of contracts."[77] The crabbed and arcane language, the kind he cried over in *Coke on Littleton*, would give way in Story's commentaries to simple, logical exposition. Organization followed naturally, too, from the need to communicate to a new tribe of democratic lawyers, not all of whom were trained at Harvard Law School. The pattern repeated consistently in all his commentaries was first to define the subject and then to trace its origins (as he did, for example, in the first three chapters of his *Commentaries on Bills of Exchange*). Next the argument would be developed according "to the order of the subject"[78] and with an eye to guiding principles; thus, in Bills of Exchange, he moved logically from competence of parties (chapter 4), to their rights and duties and obligations (5), to consideration (6), to the transfer of bills (7), to presentment (8), to proceedings for nonacceptance (9), to presentment for payment (10), to proceedings on nonpayment (11), to payments and other discharges of parties (12), and finally in the last two chapters to a brief survey of guaranty of bills and letters of credit and inland bills.

In each chapter the commentary moved from the simple to the complex, repeating key points at regular intervals so as not to lose the novitiate and always with principle and "constructive generalization," to use Mark Howe's phrase,[79] up front. Story's commentaries may have, as later critics claimed, lacked distinctive style, but his language was not the "wishy-washy . . . rattle-clap common English" depicted by Rufus Choate in one of his more choleric moods.[80] Story lacked the grace and elegance of Blackstone, but he also avoided the dense turgid quality of Kent (of which some students at the Law School complained). Story's text was straightforward, flowing, energetic—a legal plain style in the manner of the Puritan sermon and functionally suited to the chore at hand.

If Story was a pioneer in comparative and historical jurisprudence and in the creative use of civil law, it did not keep him from grounding his commentaries firmly in the common law and its case method of legal reasoning. Indeed, with the exception of *Conflict of Laws*, cases were the main vehicles for exposition and illustration. And they were drawn from a wide variety of jurisdictions and in quantity impressive enough to please even a Jerome Frank (who later criticized the case method for its narrow use of cases). He also sensed the importance of leading cases in clarifying doctrine and deliberately included extensive quotations from them to help lawyers who did not have access to relevant reports. In this sense Story's commentaries prefigured the great casebooks of Thayer, Ames, Beal, and others, and it is not surprising that his works found a place at Harvard Law School during the heyday of the case method.[81] Above all, Story's reliance on cases imparted a practical tone to his books. The principles he extracted from cases were not the "disembodied cherubs" that Holmes found fluttering about in most treatises, and nowhere were they distilled to abstract logic.

His mastery of case law, his comprehensive, eclectic scholarship, set him apart from all but a handful of American lawyers. But Story the commentator, like Story the judge, did what most common lawyers do as a matter of course: He distinguished, analogized, and extrapolated if necessary in search of consistent rules to guide social action. Story's method was not original, but he did it better than most and integrated it with comparative and historical modes of analysis. By preserving the common-law tone, Story gave his volumes a pragmatic cast, avoiding the dangers of speculation and theorizing that his reliance on civil law might otherwise have imparted. Principle balanced with practice is what comes through. Principle was what American lawyers needed; the common-law mode of reasoning was familiar and, as Story employed it, authoritative. Altogether, then, his commentaries were practical, understandable, and convincing.

3. Rounding Out the System of American Law: Equity Jurisprudence and Conflict of Laws

As a student of codification, Story came to understand the unsystematic tendencies of law in America: the centrifugal disruption of uniformity caused by federalism and the unevenness of doctrinal transplantation, both of which were exacerbated by the breakdown of professional unity. He turned treatise writer to remedy this chaos on the assumption that the parts of American law—state and national, decisional and statute, public and private—could be systematically related. These rationalizing plans rested on eighteenth-century intellectual premises, though to call him a Newtonian, given his accommodation of change and growth in the law, would be misleading. But he agreed with Blackstone (as well as Paley and Pope) that "parts unite / in one harmonious rule of right," that "countless wheels distinctly tend / by various laws to one great end."[82] Story's commentaries, like Blackstone's and Kent's, reflected, if not Newton, then the intellectual world he helped create. Writing to contain the nineteenth century with the eighteenth, Story assumed that beneath infinite variety and change, unity and order prevailed.

The systematic conception of American law, of which Story's commentaries were a part, was outlined most explicitly in his anonymous article "American Law" written in the summer of 1834 at the suggestion of Francis Lieber for publication in Carl Joseph Anton Mittermaier's German law journal, the *Kritische Zeitschrift für Rechtswissenschaft und Gesetzgebung des Auslandes.*[83] The essay, which appeared in Mittermaier's journal in 1836 (and in the Swedish *Juridiskt Arkif* the following year) points up the unity Story perceived in the diversity of American law and suggests the manner in which his various works on that subject were interconnected. To begin with, public and private law, though separate, were not functionally distinct. The Constitution provided the political and legal framework within which the common law would work, even though the latter was not "embosomed in the new system."[84] Commercial operations, as Story noted in his *Commentaries on the Constitution*, depended on political unity, on constitutional union; ties of union, on the other hand, would be strengthened by uniform private commercial law, which would enhance business relationships between citizens of different states, thus circumventing and finally diminishing state and regional particularism.

Story's volumes on commercial law, then, were connected in the larger scheme of things with Story's work on the Constitution. And what is more, the volumes on commercial law, though published seriatim, were themselves interconnected. Story turned to bailments as the subject of his first volume of commercial law, not only because of its immense practicality (seeing that the growth of a national market required the shipping and handling of goods by various parties remote from the original owners or producers) but because bailments were at the center of the entire system of commercial law. As he put it, the "law of Bailments lies at the foundation of many commercial contracts . . ."; it is preliminary to the "full discussion" of "many other important heads in our jurisprudence."[85] Agency, the second volume in Story's commercial-law series, was a logical extension of bailments and was itself "intimately connected" with the other "leading branches" of commercial jurisprudence. In turn, it led "by a very easy and natural transition, to the Law of Partnership . . . ,"[86] for "every Partner is an agent of the Partnership; and his rights, powers, duties, and obligations, are in many respects governed by the same rules and principles, as those of an agent."[87] Bills of exchange and promissory notes were closely connected and were, before Story, generally treated under a single head. Both, along with agency, bailments, and partnership, were parts of the general law of commercial contracts that was the heart of "the great System of Commercial Law" which Story mentioned in the dedication of his *Partnership* to his old teacher, Samuel Putnam, and upon which he founded his great opinion in *Swift* v. *Tyson*.[88] The subjects of equity and conflict of law would round out this system. The former, if it could be introduced into America, would fill in the gaps of the common law, supplement its procedures, soften its harshness. Conflict theory, if one could be formulated, would supply rules for deciding what to do when existing rules came into conflict because of American federalism.

One cannot fail to observe, explained Story in volume 2 of his *Equity Jurisprudence*, "to what an immeasurable extent" the system of equity reaches beyond "the prescribed bounds of the Common Law." If the common law was, as Story felt, full of "masculine vigor," then equity was feminine, a status that, according to nineteenth-century notions, gave it a special moral function. Indeed, Story was ecstatic about the quality of "remedial justice" that equity might impart. It provided "succor" to the distressed, assistance to the infirm, protection to the weak against the "cunning and profligate," "support of the purest morality," and "unflinching resistance to oppression and meditated wrong."[89] His commitment to equity did not, however, stem entirely from sentimental moralism or an intellectual fondness for legal symmetry. As early as 1808, when he drafted a bill introducing equity into Massachusetts, Story had concluded that American law *required* an infusion of equity. His rationale for incorporation, worked out essentially in 1808 and expanded in his article in the *North American Review* in 1820,[90] was made the foundation of his equity volumes, and it rested on solid legal and economic ground. Most compelling was the recognized fact of legal history that equity and common law, though separate branches of law, were historically integrated parts of a single system of administering justice. Even Robert Rantoul, Jr., that ardent critic of English law, had to concede that building American law on the English common law without bringing in equity would be cutting off the supply of useful and tested principle and truncating the American system of remedial justice.[91]

Fortunately for Story's plans for transplantation, English equity had moved from the loose, discretionary, and hotly contested jurisprudence of its early days to an accepted and mature body of principles. Fraud, trust, and accident had long been recognized as equity's "peculiar province," as Story put it in 1820.[92] And under Hardwicke, whose chancellorship ran from 1737 to 1756, clear and refined rules in those areas were worked out. Eldon, whose two terms ran from 1801 to 1806 and from 1807 to 1827, continued the process of refinement and moved on to establish a viable relationship between equity and commerce. The result was that Story could declare with confidence in 1820 that equity "as a science" was "quite as regular and exact in its principles and rules, as the common law; and, probably, as any other system of jurisprudence, established generally by positive enactments, or usages, or practical expositions, in any country, ancient or modern."[93]

These principles, adjusted to American circumstances, had begun to make their way into American law, thanks in large part to the efforts of Kent in New York and of William Johnson, who for many years reported his equity decisions. It was clear to Story, as it was to Kent, that certain aspects of English equity would be of "limited application"—such matters as the authority of the English chancellor to grant writs of scire facias to repeal patents, the English law of charities, the authority of the chancellor as *parens patriae*, and bills of specific performance.[94] But equity, purged of its irrelevances and armed with its unique rules of evidence and special mode of proceeding, could do what the common law could not. Equity, for example, could render the judgment for one party or the other, and it could, when the complexities of the case required it, adjudge "to a certain degree, in favor of both parties."[95] Through bills of discovery, its authority to bring all the parties (principal and auxiliary) before the court at once, its more flexible rules of evidence, and the wider judicial discretion it allowed, equity could often unravel the truth more readily than the common law. And through injunction, equity could prevent injustice from being done, where the common law could act only after the fact.[96] Injunctive relief could prevent costly and time-consuming litigation, and so could the complicated and unique doctrine of interpleading, which required multiple plaintiffs suing the same defendant in the same court for the same thing to settle the priority of their claims in their pleadings before the trial.

These special qualities gave equity dominance in matters of fraud, trust, and accident and made it the special protector of "lunatics, children, and women," as the phrase went. What Story, along with Kent, also saw, and what must be emphasized, was that the unique substantive and procedural qualities of equity were as valuable to American businessmen as they were to the weak and vulnerable. With the growing complexity of business organization and mercantile transactions, the incidence of fraud among merchants and between partners rose dramatically and thus increased the need for equity to untangle and settle it. Mortgages as much as wills raised equitable questions concerning fiduciary relationships and responsibilities. The settlement of questions of general average (the staple of maritime insurance) was facilitated by bringing all parties into court simultaneously. And this was just the beginning.[97] The business community and its lawyers had only to be assured that equity would not undercut title to property or obliterate or diminish contractual sanctity. Story promised just this when he insisted in his commentaries on a "strict equity" for America and one that "follows" the common law. This double-edged principle was a major facet of his transplantation strategy.[98]

Some strategy was needed, too, because American resistance to equity was deep-seated, mainly on the grounds that it was insidious and grasping in its jurisdiction and dangerously imprecise in its principles—and thus an instrument of judicial aggrandizement. The charges were not valid, and Story continued to insist that "there is not, at the present moment, a single department of the law, which is more completely fenced in by principle, or that is better limited by considerations of public convenience, both in doctrine and discipline, than equity."[99] Clearly, the problem was not with equity but with the nonscientific practice of it in America. To correct this difficulty Story undertook to clarify equity principles, which like those of the common law were often scattered among English and American reports and inaccessible to most lawyers. Jurisdiction would have to be clarified, too, if the "spectral dread"[100] of equity were to be allayed. And the refinements of equity pleading would have to be made understandable to working lawyers. Here Story had the advantage of Lord Redesdale's *Treatise on the Pleadings in Suits in the Court of Chancery* (1780), which was thorough and authoritative. But even with this help—and he drew from it unashamedly—the fact was that there was no real tradition of equity practice in the United States and no independent equity bar. The practice in the federal courts and in many state jurisdictions of conjoining equity and law was particularly debilitating. But even in states like New York, where chancery existed in separate courts, there was not a well-defined equity bar dedicated to the mastery of the subject. The growing tendency in many states to merge law and equity, which would ultimately obliterate the latter, hopelessly muddled both the principles and the practice of equity.

Before democratic opposition to equity could be allayed, then, Story would have to educate to the principles and practice of the science of equity a legal profession immersed, if not submerged, in the common law. How to proceed in the face of professional disunity and ignorance was the question. His answer—and it is the controlling assumption of his commentaries on equity and the key to their structure and organization—was that equity and law, though mutually supportive, should be administered in separate and distinct courts. Such a system, as Story must have known, made success contingent on state legislatures, which he did not trust. It also ran counter to the tendency in most states toward a fusion of law and equity.[101] Such a plan also lacked wide support among lawyers, some of whom felt threatened by equity and others of whom (like Mansfield) liked equity but trusted the common law to absorb what was useful in it.[102] Yet the advantages of a separate system of state equity courts, if it could be brought off, appeared considerable. State judges and lawyers would be permitted, would of necessity have, to master the principles and practice of equity. The status of equity practice in federal courts would be immensely enhanced because the equity cases coming into federal courts under diversity jurisdiction (the overwhelming majority of them) would be informed by scientific principles and practice. Legal reform would take a great leap forward, and so would the unity of federal and state courts and the uniformity of American law.[103]

Story's assumption that equity in America would be separate from the common law dictated the organizational structure of his *Commentaries on Equity Jurisprudence*. The challenge was to set forth equity as a distinct field of law and, at the same time, to connect it harmoniously with the common law. Consequently, the matter of jurisdiction was crucial, and here Story followed the "well known" eighteenth-century classification of auxiliary, concurrent, and exclusive formalized by Fonblanque's *Treatise of Equity* (1793).[104] Underlying the jurisdictional arrangement was the controlling assumption that equity complemented the common law by providing unique remedies and procedures. Equally important, equity would not encroach on the common law so as to weaken the fabric of contract. Story did, to be sure, save portions of the equitable doctrine of specific performance that potentially contradicted the tendency of American contract toward damage awards in cases of breach.[105] He allowed equity to order specific performance in contracts dealing with both real and personal property—providing justice required it. And that was a matter of judicial discretion, not legal right. Discretion, moreover, would be closely circumscribed. Specific performance would not ordinarily be applied when damages could be assessed accurately. And parties who asked for it "must show a strict compliance with the terms of the contract, or stand for relief upon some other real principle of equity."[106] Even in cases involving real property, where its use was greatest, defenses could be raised against it and statutory limits would also control the application of the specific performance principle.

Equity would not vitiate American contract law or reward the sloppy, slothful, irresponsible adventurer at the expense of "real business men." Story was explicit: The very "notion, that a court of equity is at liberty to dispense with a strict compliance with the terms of the contract, when no accident, mistake, or fraud, . . . had intervened to prevent an exact compliance . . . is so repugnant to a just conception of the obligation of contracts, and of the right of the parties to stand upon their own stipulations, . . . that one wonders, that such an extraordinary authority should have ever been assumed or tolerated."[107] And Story's *Equity Jurisprudence* was equally assuring. Indeed, that work contains his most forceful endorsement of the will theory of contract. "For Courts of Equity, as well as

Courts of law," he wrote, "act upon the ground, that every person, who is not, from his peculiar condition or circumstances, under disability, is entitled to dispose of his property in such manner and upon such terms, as he chooses; and whether his bargains are wise and discreet, or otherwise, profitable or unprofitable, are considerations, not for Courts of Justice, but for the party himself to deliberate upon." As for "inadequacy of consideration" as a limit on the freedom of contract: "The Common Law knows no such principle." Neither does "common sense." Nor is it a "distinct principle of relief in Equity." Harsh contracts, where there is no fraud, are the province of "conscience, and morals, and religion," not law.[108]

If Story seemed at pains to make equity sound like the common law, it was because he envisaged a system in which the two would work together but still remain separate and distinct. Given the stage of American legal development, his determination to separate them made much sense. For only by keeping equity distinct could he set forth its principles fully and clearly. And even if equity would be subsumed by the common law in America, it was important at the moment of transplantation that a clear statement of principle be made. Clarity was also enhanced by following a tripartite division of jurisdiction. Artificial it was. But given the scattered nature of equity principles, it was probably the only organizational device available to Story.[109] And within it he expounded the science of equity with the practical techniques of exposition employed so effectively in his other volumes on commercial law and the same infectious enthusiasm.

The result was that his works on equity had a lasting impact on American legal development, more so, Roscoe Pound has argued, than even his work on conflict.[110] His *Equity Pleadings* went through ten editions, though it was the most imitative and least creative of any of his commentaries.[111] *Equity Jurisprudence* was more original in design, and its wideranging scholarship was Story at his best. English cases supplied him with most of the material for generalization, but large doses of Kent gave an American tone to the work, which soon became standard in both England (with three editions, the last of which was in 1920) and the United States (with fourteen editions in all). Despite its popularity in this country, the book did not persuade American lawyers to create a separate system of equity, as Story had hoped. His plan for reform did not entirely fail, however, for the currency that he gave equity principles permitted their readier incorporation into the mainstream of American law. The result was a reformed common law the transplantation of which even Jacksonian America found hard to resist.

In yoking the common law and equity, Story aimed to enlarge the supply of tried and tested rules by which Americans might pursue their individual goals fairly, predictably, and efficiently. But even if the common law were accepted and equity brought in to supplement it, the uniform operation of scientific law was not assured. First, there was no guarantee that the laws governing persons and property in the United States would be recognized by foreign countries, and this was a serious problem in light of the growth of international commerce. Second, because American federalism permitted each state to have its own version of the common law (and equity), there was inevitable legal conflict and uncertainty among those who transacted business across state lines. Article IV, section 1, of the Constitution, which required that "full faith and credit shall be given in each State to the public acts, records, and judicial proceedings of every other State," appeared to address this problem. And theoretically the full faith and credit clause might "federalize the separate state legal systems," as Justice Robert Jackson once put it.[112] But neither Congress nor the federal courts had explored the unifying potential of that clause in Story's time, and he would scarcely recognize it in his *Conflicts*. Codification confronted the problem of domestic conflict, as did Story in his treatises. But codification was dead and the unifying impact of treatise education was long-range at best. The fact remained that no two states possessed identical law; the difference in many cases was substantial and, with the growth of interstate and international commerce, increasingly inconvenient. Indeed, in Story's opinion the "sanctity of contracts and the security of property" and even "domestic relations" were increasingly in jeopardy.[113] What was needed until universal scientific law obliterated state legal idiosyncracies was a set of rules for resolving the conflict of rules.

A theory of conflict was, then, the sine qua non of Story's system of American law, and he threw his "whole weight" into the subject, sensing, as he put it to his friend Peters (and correctly, as it turned out), that it would be his "best law work."[114] But the difficulties were enormous. He could consult a growing body of English case law on the subject, and American courts had already handed down some five hundred decisions dealing in one way or another with the issue.[115] But, unlike those in commercial law, cases in conflict did not cluster around accepted principles, and there was little to be got from English publicists, who barely recognized conflict as a legitimate subject of inquiry. Even Kent glossed over the subject in his four volumes, leaving Samuel Livermore, a New Orleans lawyer, as the only American authority before Story.[116] Livermore's *Dissertations on the Questions Which Arise from the Contrariety of the Positive Laws of Different States and Nations*, which appeared in 1828, was written as a rebuttal to an 1827 decision of the Louisiana Supreme Court in which case Livermore had argued and lost. The book, as William Leslie noted, was replete with a "rich and delicate intellectuality."[117] It was also fragmentary and, more to the point, argued in the tradition of the civil law for the universality of rights. Story consulted Livermore only to refute him, for he had already rejected universality of rights for the principle of national comity that rested on the foundation of the nation-state and state sovereignty. Comity was the principle that Judge Alexander Porter of the Louisiana Supreme Court used to defeat Livermore in *Saul* v. *His Creditors* (1827). Story cited that case approvingly in his own commentaries, but his preference came not from the authority of Judge Porter so much as from his recognition of the realities of American states' rights.

All of this is to argue that the comity principle in Story's *Conflict* grew directly out of the realities, or more specifically, the disabilities, of American federalism. What he needed to do was refine the theory and develop guiding principles for the various areas where conflict occurred and to fortify his work with authority enough to make it acceptable without the support of legislative fiat and in the face of the vast discretionary power that it bestowed on judges. Authority, Story presumed, would come from scholarship, which in his *Conflict* was nothing short of prodigious. He seemed as much at home in Roman law as in recent American and English cases, of which he cited more than fourteen hundred. For organizing ideas, however, he drew mainly on Belgian, Dutch, French, and Italian jurists of the seventeenth and eighteenth centuries. Missing only were the German scholars, except those in Latin translation.[118] Altogether he cited forty-seven treatise writers, but his primary authorities, according to his own reckoning, were "Roberburg, the Voets (father and son), Burgundus, Du Moulin (Milinaeus), Froland, Boullenois, Bouchier, and Huberus."[119] Boullenois was cited most often, though Huberus was probably the most directly influential. Story was, of course, not the first to use Continental jurists, but his authorities were not well known and were often inaccessible (even he could not consult the originals in some cases until later editions). No scholar anywhere had ever undertaken to study systematically the whole panorama of Western legal history—Roman, Continental, English, and American—in search of organizing themes and commonly acceptable principles. This he did, and he wrote the volume, too, in the nine months from April through December 1833 while teaching and riding circuit.[120]

His book was uniquely eclectic. Conflict theory as it was expounded by Continental civilians tended to divide law into three categories—personal, real, and mixed—each with separate principles. Story admired the "comprehensive philosophy" behind such theory. But he felt strongly that this traditional approach to the resolution of conflict of laws was too "theoretical" and "metaphysical" and had too much of "a purely local" character.[121] What he sought was a theory that was universal in application (that is, capable of organizing the various areas where conflict occurred) and suitable to the realities of both international conflict and the conflict among American states. Story settled on the principle of comity, which was rooted in state sovereignty; for authority and refinement he turned to the Dutch jurists of the seventeenth century and most particularly to Ulricus Huberus. "It is plain," reasoned Story, with one eye on Huberus and the other on American Federalism, "that the laws of one country can have no intrinsic force, *proprio vigore*, except within the territorial limits and jurisdiction of that country." Two corollary principles followed logically: First, if conflict theory was grounded in municipal law, then the rights vested by that law would be safeguarded. Second, if, as Story put it, no nation is bound by "morals" or "natural law" to give recognition to the laws of another, then each nation "must judge for itself what its true duty in the administration of justice in its domestic tribunals" is to be. In short, the principle of comity would control. And the rules of comity "which are to govern are those which arise from mutual interest and utility, from a sense of the inconveniences which would result from a contrary doctrine, and from a sort of moral necessity to do justice, in order that justice may be done to us in return." [122]

These principles laid down in chapters 1 and 2—sovereignty, with its corollaries of vested rights and comity—guided Story as he moved through the main heads of the subject. And in the organization of these, he moved consistently from principle to application. Following the two chapters on theory he explored the general areas of national domicile and capacity of persons. Then in consecutive order followed marriage and divorce; contracts; personal and real property; wills, testaments, succession, and distribution; foreign guardianship and administrations; jurisdiction and remedies; foreign judgment; penal laws and offenses; and evidence and proofs. His pattern of exposition, following that of his other treatises, was to set forth "elementary principles," support them by authority, and refine and illustrate them by reference to cases (the important ones of which were copiously extracted and checked for accuracy against the originals).[123] Theory necessarily occupied a more conspicuous place than in Story's other commentaries, and comparative jurisprudence was from the nature of the subject more controlling. Still, practicality dominated, and again extensive quotation from other jurists and cases made his book a surrogate for a casebook as well as a forerunner of later scholarly anthologies in conflict.

Glowing reviews at home and abroad, both in England and on the Continent, established *Conflict* as an instant classic. Mittermaier in Germany praised Story's masterful balance between practicality and scholarship, and France's leading authority on conflict, M. Foelix, was fully converted.[124] English lawyers and judges—among whom were Lord Erskine, Baron Parke, Lord Langdale, Justice Bosanquet, and Henry Roscoe—added to the current of compliments.[125] A whole branch of English and American law had been "forthwith systematized," as Albert Dicey would later put it.[126] Horace Gray agreed with Story's prediction and proclaimed

Conflict his "highest claim to reputation as a jurist." The work went through three editions before Story's death in 1845, and a hundred years after it appeared one scholar would "without question" acclaim it as "the most remarkable and outstanding work on conflict of law which had appeared since the thirteenth century in any country and in any language."[127]

Modern scholars have paid Story the supreme compliment of continuing to debate his ideas.[128] They have also criticized his scholarship as being indiscriminately eclectic, lacking in historical analysis, and wanting in scientific rigor. Some find the concept of "sovereignty" too "elusive" a foundation;[129] others condemn it as a defense of slavery.[130] Whether that charge is justified or not (and I argue later that it is not), one could still fault Story for not being more explicit in applying conflict theory derived from seventeenth-century Europe to the federal union in the nineteenth. It could also be maintained that Story's reliance on sovereignty introduced into his jurisprudence a positivistic note that was at odds with his concern for the eternal moral verities of natural law. And without a doubt the vagueness of comity placed great, perhaps excessive, discretionary authority in the hands of the judge, though here at least Story was perfectly consistent.

Let us admit that Story's *Conflict* was vulnerable on a number of these counts and others, too, perhaps. Still, like his other volumes on American law, it must in fairness be judged by its practical service to the profession and by its contribution to American law as it stood when Story wrote. Here the argument is compelling; indeed, many of the alleged shortcomings turn to advantages. It may well be that it was only because Story's theory was not overly refined that it was "so clearly explained, with so little mystification, that the plainest understanding comprehends it."[131] What might appear to be indiscriminate use of sources, it could be argued, was not only unavoidable but a necessary element of establishing authority, as well as providing a practical reference tool for American practitioners. As for the principle of sovereignty, to make it the starting point of American conflict law made as much sense for a young nation only recently free from colonial bondage as it did for the Dutch republic of the seventeenth century only recently freed from the dominance of Spain. Certainly the sovereignty of nation-states was a fact of law in the nineteenth century no less than it was a fact of politics. And this was as true when dealing with the settlement of conflict among the states of the federal union as it was when adjusting conflict between the United States and foreign nations. The states' rights dimension of Story's domestic conflict theory, in any case, does not contradict his constitutional nationalism, for the federal Constitution continued supreme and controlling even if its full faith and credit provision remained largely unexplored. Here as elsewhere he grounded theory on reality.

Finally, it should be said that Story's theory of conflict did not pose an irresolvable contradiction between municipal sovereignty and natural law. It is true that his celebration of the "peculiar genius of municipal law" appears to retreat from the Enlightenment universalism that his legal system aimed to establish. But the contradiction largely disappears when it is recalled that conflict theory was but one part of his overall jurisprudential system. To admit conflict between sovereign states pursuing their own self-interest, moreover, is not to deny the larger area of agreement, particularly on commercial-law principles. If conflict theory conceded the imperfections of universal legal science, it did not keep Story from looking forward to the day when exclusivism in the law would give way to universality. His hope was that "comity of nations would be but another name for the justice of nations."[132]

He also hoped that his *Conflict* would be "attractive to the Jurists of the Common Law."[133] So it is not surprising that the practical spirit of the common law was firmly maintained: in the abundance of cases and the prevalence of case reasoning; in the moderation of theory; in the non-perfectionist, practical quality of argument and illustration. The common-law tradition asserted itself, also, in the principle of judicial supremacy, which Story's theory of comity furthered. Judicial control was in fact the essence of Story's conflict theory, no less than it was in his scheme of codification. For if convenience, self-interest, and policy considerations were, as he declared, the standards by which foreign laws would be permitted to operate, it was inevitable that the courts should say when policy came into play and what it was. As much as anything, it was this large area of judicial discretion which distinguished Story's theory from preceding ideas;[134] it also supplied a flexibility that compensated for theoretical imprecision and that assured continued relevance.[135] After all the theorizing was done, it was the bench and the bar working with foreign materials and comparative jurisprudence—but in the tradition of the common law—that would supply the community with workable and uniform rules of action.

4. Toward a Paradigm of American Law

Story's commentaries called forth critics and carpers. Among the latter was William Kent, who had replaced Story at Harvard Law School on the latter's death and who was troubled by his failure to fill Story's shoes; he privately accused his predecessor of having sunk "into mere *book-making*." (Story's *Agency* he found to be "diffuse to shallowness," a "pretty poor affair.")[136] Timothy Walker may have had his old mentor in mind when he criticized "giving long abstracts of cases" as a means of "making or amplifying law books."[137] Charles C. Jones, Jr., of Liberty County, Georgia, was even more explicit. "Judge Story's writings are daily growing, in the estimation of many of us, of less and less repute," he wrote to his parents on

13 June 1854. "The truth is, he wrote *too* rapidly, and consequently without sufficient care and consideration." Young Jones was not entirely pleased with Story's format, either: "He is most profuse also in quotation from every source. I have heard it remarked by persons who are well informed on the subject that Justice Story has been known to embody an entire English treatise in one of his works, that in others the amount of original matter contributed would not constitute one fourth of the volume." A little more "deliberation and succinctness" in the style of Professor Greenleaf would have helped, thought Jones,[138] and later generations of Harvard law students and their professors seemed to agree. They too turned on the founder for the "looseness" of his scholarship, as Brandeis put it;[139] and finally they ignored him.

But adulation was the order of the day while Story lived. Continental jurists turned to his works for instruction; English lawyers and judges, citing him in their briefs and opinions, praised their newly found "Giant Son."[140] Latin America would soon join the chorus of acclaim: Witness the verbatim adoption of *Conflict* in the Argentinian Civil Code of 1853, not to mention the Spanish edition of his *Commentaries on the Constitution* published in Buenos Aires in 1881.[141] At home he was celebrated as the "American Blackstone" (an honor Story rightly reserved for Kent) or "Justinian" (Holdsworth would later suggest Littleton as more appropriate). Fellow members of the professional elite like Hopkinson, Webster, and Kent gladly claimed him for America. Leading law journals gave his commentaries extended coverage (and free advertising), and even lay journals like the *American Quarterly Review* reviewed his works under the impression that Story's legal scholarship was the people's business and their salvation.[142]

Most important, practicing lawyers paid him their highest compliment: They bought his books and read them. Collectively, his eight works on private law went through seventy-one editions, so that many of his volumes were in circulation for a half-century after their first publication. With good reason, Charles Sumner dubbed him the "Walter Scott of the Common Law,"[143] which is to say (as Holmes did in fact say) that Story did "more than any other English-speaking man in this century to make the law luminous and easy to understand."[144] And this was basically what Mr. Charles Jones, Jr., concluded, too. "For my part," he added after having recited the prevailing litany of criticism against Story, "I do by no means agree with those who speak so slightingly of his productions. I have read several of them, always with great pleasure, and I hope with profit." He was sure in his young man's wisdom that Story and Marshall "accomplished more for the advancement and improvement of American jurisprudence than any persons who preceded or have followed them."[145] And he was right.

Why this remarkable educational coup? Being there at the right time is part of the explanation, though timing for Story (as for Marshall) was itself a matter of knowledge and a measure of critical insight. Story also mastered the tools at hand (the mature legal inheritance of the Western world, no less) and saw the needs of the moment (a uniform commercial common law for American capitalists). This is not to claim that Story fully understood the direction of American legal history, and it is even less to argue that he had control of it. Here irony abounds. The unique moment in American legal history—the complementarity of needs and sources to fill them—encouraged Story in his audacious search for an American law. The same moment frustrated his effort because the pace and scope of legal change was already too great for one man, even Story, to master; thus the "looseness" complained of later and the "simple philosophizing" that irritated critics. Holmes was right: No man of Story's age "or of the succeeding generation could have stated the law in a form that deserved to abide, because neither his nor the succeeding generation possessed or could have possessed the historical knowledge, had made or could have made the analyses of principles, which are necessary before the cardinal doctrines of the law can be known and understood in their precise contours and in their innermost meanings." [146] Clearly, by the late nineteenth century no one lawyer would attempt "to occupy the entire field of the common law." Treatise writing would become the province of legal specialists and system making a collective effort. [147]

Incomplete Story's commentaries were (he was just embarking on admiralty and maritime law at the time of his death) and imperfect. Yet taken as a whole, his treatises stand as the last great one-man effort to synthesize American law. They came at exactly that moment when the law had outrun the capacity of existing aids (digests and abridgments) to make sense of it and before codification was feasible. Doctrinal maturity was sufficiently advanced to permit a treatise statement of the law, yet not so complex as to discourage the effort. Story exploited the potential of the moment brilliantly. He knew what was needed and what was acceptable. He grasped the fact, so clear retrospectively, that American law, given the direction of American history, would have to be fashioned from inherited materials. Story's comparative-law methodology was shaped to fit that fact. By accommodating comparative law to the common law, he perfected a treatise format that made sense to American lawyers. The method was also appropriately conservative, for it undertook to systematize and clarify doctrine without creating it out of whole cloth. The process of organizing, sorting, and refining was not only suitable to Story's own scholarly inclinations but suitable for treatises in which bold doctrinal creativity would have been pointless and probably counterproductive. What American law needed before it moved on to an even more disorganizing period of growth was to consolidate the changes and adjustments it had already made. In the conservative spirit of the 1820s, yet with a reformer's vision of the future, Story put in place a substantial foundation upon which future change might build.

Story not only fashioned what was needed but, equally important, gained acceptance for what he created. No mean feat it was. Treatises, unlike legislative codification, had no extrinsic authority; they succeeded only by their ability to persuade—and that was not easy in a country increasingly divided along political, sectional, economic, and ideological lines. Story's position and reputation gave his work a unique sort of legitimacy to counter that pluralism. As a justice of the Supreme Court, as the representative of national law on the New England circuit, Story got a hearing that no other American jurist then or since could match. His professorship at the Law School added further to his scholarly credentials, and his students were a ready-made network for the national distribution of his publications (a significant advantage when bookselling was still done essentially door-to-door and when national marketing devices were in their infancy). But most of all, authority came from the books themselves, their design, their substance. At the price of being "loose," even "simple," Story's treatises were understandable. And Story's mixture of comparative law, legal history, and common-law methods radiated authority and grounded American law in the legal history of the Western world, without sacrificing its utilitarian, pragmatic character. The moral tone that Story mixed with his practical, applied legal science was useful in assuring opponents that law and lawyers were friends of republican virtue. Moral, practical, scientific: It was working law for working lawyers.

There is, of course, no scientific way to measure the impact of Story's writings on the American legal mind. Many lawyers undoubtedly knew little about Story; even those who knew his work imposed their own necessities on it. Perhaps there were more than a few country lawyers like G. T. M. Davis who lost cases for citing highfalutin "Down-East law books" like Story's.[148] But the evidence, such as it is, suggests strongly that Story's commentaries worked significantly to create a paradigm of American law in the sense in which Thomas Kuhn used the term to describe the process of doing and thinking science. The definitional ingredients of Kuhn's model were certainly present:[149] Story's comparative common-law method provided the community of American lawyers (or at least a crucial portion of them) with a "disciplinary matrix." Principles illustrated by cases fortified by comparative analysis provided them with "shared examples" of the science. In Story's mode of legal reasoning were their "symbolic generalizations"; in his books, as well as his teaching and judging, he preached—indeed, symbolized—the "shared commitment" of professionals. Here, in short, was "the entire constellation of beliefs, values, techniques" that might make American lawyers into a community of legal scientists. This is the foundation beneath Holmes's claim that Story did "more than any other English-speaking man in this century to make the law luminous and easy to understand."

The vitality of the paradigm that Story helped shape lay in the harmony between the common-law spirit that permeated it and the dominant values of American society. Story's commentaries did not, of course, speak to the enslaved, the poor and propertyless. But to the property-owning middle and upper classes and to the venturesome entrepreneurs who defined cultural values, the groups who had most use for law and access to lawyers, Story's grand scheme of commercial law provided a system for the efficient deployment of individual creative energies. Through agents, partners, and corporations, throughout the network of commercial relationships, the individual will could extend itself without diminution of authority, efficiency, or responsibility. Law was put to the service of the will in an age of free will. The authority of the state lay behind the common law, of course, but governmental intervention never contradicted American capitalism as long as it helped capitalists. More to the point, governmental authority as it was transmitted through the courts and the common law seemed especially suitable to an age that liked liberty no less than it needed active government. Codifiers like Rantoul and William Sampson might argue that legislative codes were the American way, but the common law that Story's commentaries strengthened bore a correspondence to the American social and ideological landscape that the hatred of things English and a widespread distrust of lawyers could not obscure. If his system implied that judges were to be policy-makers, that was precisely what he had in mind, as we shall presently see.

Chapter 9

Commerce, Commercial Law, and National Union

There is freedom from restraint, and an habitual eagerness to expand our law, which favor every attempt to build up commercial doctrines upon the most liberal foundation.
Story on American commercial law, 1825

Trade is in its nature consolidating, because it will not recognize arbitrary geographical lines; it is creative of such strong common interests, wherever it once connects people in relations with one another, that local jealousies, and all narrow notions of exclusive independence, vanish before it.
Merchants' Magazine on commerce, July 1839

Read Story's workaday correspondence with Brockholst Livingston and Bushrod Washington as they compare circuit decisions in search of mutual clarification and uniformity; study his detailed essay-letters on the legal problems that troubled Chief Justice Prentiss Mellen of the Maine Supreme Court;[1] read the scholarly exposition of English legal history in *De Lovio*; watch him grapple with new doctrines in *Dartmouth College* and defend old ones in the *Bridge* case; remember his enthusiastic rendition of legal science at Harvard Law School and the tour de force of legal scholarship in his treatises. Here and elsewhere the message is the same: He was a lawyer's lawyer who was massively absorbed and fully at home in what he was doing. Living so much for and in the world of law could give it a life of its own. Story knew and relished this life of ideas. Hardly less than later legal realists who criticized him he also knew that the law, whatever might be its intellectual attributes, was rooted in history and social necessity. As he put it to the readers of the *North American Review*, the "law must fashion itself to the wants, and in some sort to the spirit of the age."[2] In the same article and elsewhere he went on to say with total approval that commerce was the historical force to which American law must adjust.

Just how the intellectual life of the law and the practical world of business were related Story never spelled out. What he did say about law and commerce often tended toward high-flown rhetoric, if not propaganda, and was quite devoid of anthropological curiosity. But Story practiced pointedly what he talked about so romantically. He knew from practice that law did not "fashion itself," as he put it, but was fashioned by lawyers, judges, legislators, politicians, and even the people. The commercial wants to which these groups adjusted law were not abstract verities written in the clouds but instead the practical calculations of businessmen who needed law to help them mobilize resources, expand markets, and maximize profits. To say that law must adjust to commerce was, then, to posit a relationship among judges and lawyers and the mercantile community that begs for clarification.[3]

Story's position on the Supreme Court, of course, brought with it appellate responsibilities that encouraged a philosophical approach to judging, one that invited him to follow his own "scientific" turn of mind. But a Supreme Court justice in the antebellum period dealt regularly with a wide range of common-law questions. Indeed, as Story himself put it, "The general mass of business, which employs the supreme court, consists of private controversies respecting property, or personal rights and contracts."[4] On circuit, moreover, Story was thrust even more directly into a world whose values and institutions were shaped by men of business: the Jacksons and Lees, the Appletons, Grays, Crowninshields, and Lawrences, and more modest versions thereof. The forces of shipping, trade, and manufacturing unleashed and directed by entrepreneurs like these were sweeping New England and the nation into the modern age, and American law with them. Story, who aimed to channel American history through law, was swept along as well. He went willingly because he believed with many others in the nineteenth century that commerce, civilization, and national union went hand in hand and because he was under the illusion that law, or rather, lawyers and judges, might control the forces of capitalism they worked to unleash. As a commercial judge, then, Story was part of a political tradition that went back to the Constitution of 1787 and forward through Hamilton and Marshall to Webster, to Clay and the American Plan, and to Abbott Lawrence and the Cotton Whigs. To facilitate national commerce through uniform commercial law was to strengthen constitutional union. To do so, Story believed, would make statesmen out of judges.

1. The Politicization of the Supreme Court: Story's Last Years

Story agreed with Chief Justice Marshall as early as 1831 that a "revolutionary spirit" had invaded the Supreme Court, and nothing that happened thereafter changed his mind. The 1837 term confirmed the worst. From then on until his death in 1845 his letters exuded an almost paranoiac gloom. He was "a solitary relic of former doctrines,"[5] the "only survivor of the old Court," standing alone as in a Thomas Cole landscape "among the ruins with monuments of the past."⁶ And on went the dirge: The Republic was drifting, "the vital principles of the Constitution are uprooted and disregarded," the Court was on its last legs.⁷

It was, then, with a sense of liberation that he decided to resign effective "in the early Autumn" of 1845 and, as he said to Kent, "devote the residue of my life and energies to the Law School."⁸ He had postponed the decision because he knew that Tyler would appoint no one "of the School of Story and Kent."⁹ But now personal reasons supervened. Plainly he was overcommitted, and he desired more time with Sarah, whose invalidism made her progressively more vulnerable to his long absences at Washington and on the circuit. His own health was precarious, too, especially after prolonged illness in late 1842 and early 1843, and waiting for him were the volumes on admiralty and maritime law that would complete his great work on commercial jurisprudence.

To resign made practical sense. But why the unrelieved pessimism about the Supreme Court, especially in light of the leading role he continued to play in its councils? Indeed, excepting the 1837 term, Story was not the solitary dissenter he perceived himself as being, at least not in any literal sense. The Court was badly divided, to be sure, but Story stood with the majority much of the time and in most of the important cases. Indeed, he spoke for the Court no less than fifty-six times during the period from 1838 until his death (despite his absence during the 1843 term) and entered only seven dissents and two separate opinions. In the critical area of slavery adjudication he was, as I shall argue shortly, the mainstay of judicial moderation. That he spoke for the majority in such explosive slave cases as *U.S. v. Amistad* and *Prigg v. Pennsylvania* was an unmistakable sign of his continued stature.

Story should have been cheered, too, by the Taney Court's favorable treatment of American capitalists, both the agrarian and the commercial varieties. The Court's leading decisions favoring large speculators in the land market came after Story's death, but when they came (as in *Cervantes v. U.S.* [1854], *Fremont v. U.S.* [1854], and *Arguello v. U.S.* [1855]), it was the spirit and the law of *Fletcher v. Peck* that prevailed.¹⁰ Corporate capitalism did not go unattended, either, despite the bitter resentment of the radical agrarians on the Court. Here the Taney Court left its own mark, to be sure. It was police power rather than exclusivism that the majority saved from Marshall's opinion in *Gibbons*. Taney's *Bridge* decision continued to guide the Court in corporate contract questions, too, and *Briscoe v. Bank of Kentucky* was allowed to stand.

But these changes could be seen as practical if not inevitable adjustments to a new age in which states' rights was a fact of life and national economic planning impossible in the face of an economy fast splintering along sectional lines. The fact was that corporate growth and economic expansion continued full force despite their setback in the Panic of 1837, and the Taney Court went along. Taney himself made it clear in *Bronson* v. *Kinzie* (1843) that state relief laws which impaired substantive contract rights would not be tolerated.[11] It was the chief justice, too, who spoke for the Court in *Bank of Augusta* v. *Earle* (1839), which raised the question whether corporations chartered in one state could do business in another.[12] In good Jacksonian fashion, Taney conceded that state legislatures might prohibit foreign corporations from doing business in the state, but he went on to say that in the absence of such legislation the right of corporations to operate across state lines was assumed. Hardly less important to corporate growth was the Court's decision in *Louisville, Cincinnati, and Charleston Railroad* v. *Letson* (1844), which held that, for purposes of jurisdiction, corporations could be considered citizens of the states in which they were chartered.[13] To Story's great satisfaction *Letson* removed the increasingly unworkable fiction created by Marshall in *Bank of the U.S.* v. *Deveaux* and assured corporations continued access to federal courts.[14]

Change was balanced with continuity, then, even without considering Story's victories for free enterprise and national commerce in the *Vidal* will case and *Swift* v. *Tyson*. The changes, moreover, had been made with a minimum of doctrinal disruption. Unworkable precedents from the Marshall period had been abandoned, to be sure, but only when circumstances demanded it and then without vindictiveness or sweeping doctrinal exegesis. Above all, the great constitutional decisions of the earlier period still stood: *Martin* v. *Hunter* and *Cohens* v. *Virginia* and of course *Marbury* v. *Madison* on judicial power; *McCulloch* and *Gibbons* on the authority of Congress; and even *Dartmouth College* v. *Woodward* on the sanctity of corporate contracts. Instead of knocking down the Marshall Court, the Taney Court had stood on its shoulders. And while adjusting law to the new age it had developed a distinctive and appropriate judicial style: Divided the Court had become, of necessity, but more democratic, less grandiose in its assumption of authority, less Augustan in style, more willing to admit its errors and acknowledge its limitations. And for all of this, the Court had not surrendered its power to decide, even in those areas where it retreated from absolutism, as in corporate contracts and commerce. The spirit of John Marshall had not for all the dire prophecies been exorcised.

Why, then, Story's "utter despondence," his tendency to dwell on exaggerated change and ignore continuity? Why the refusal to concede the inevitability (if not the necessity) of doctrinal adjustments? Why his unwillingness to celebrate the Court's survival? Story's relationship with his colleagues was no doubt partly to blame. He had come on the Court at an unusual moment. His first eleven years, from 1812 to 1823, were the most stable in the Court's history and probably the most peaceful. Communal living, shared values of the revolutionary age (which seemed especially relevant during and after the War of 1812), the absence of party division outside and the soothing presence of John Marshall inside submerged differences among the justices and harnessed them to a common cause. Story could not help but see the early Marshall Court as the model.[15] But the circumstances of that period were impossible to duplicate, just as its camaraderie was unrecoverable.

To be sure, Story did not want for companionship on the new Court. Justice Thompson was a good if not intimate friend from the old days and one, moreover, who agreed basically with Story's views on the Constitution. He did not board regularly with Story, however, because he often brought his young wife with him to Washington for the Court's annual session. After the Court gradually abandoned its practice of communal living in the 1830s, Story generally roomed with John McLean from Ohio.[16] With his Jacksonian political past and his unabating passion for the presidency, McLean seemed at first glance an unlikely companion, but he recognized Story's genius and "loved" him "as a very dear brother."[17] Story respected McLean, too, forgave him his past politics, and accepted his new ambitions with the assurance that "few things in life would gratify me so much as to see you in the President's chair."[18] As a Northerner and a nationalist, McLean shared common doctrinal ground with Story and would carry on many of Story's constitutional preferences after his death (particularly the exclusivist view of the commerce clause). Both men were antislavery, though McLean was more favorable to antislavery radicalism than his conservative friend. That distinction did not disrupt their deepening friendship, however, which was cemented for Story by McLean's deep respect for the Court and the law.

This common professional bond was also the key to Story's good working relationship with the chief justice, a relationship that in time broadened into mutual respect, if not affection. Story's misgivings were slow to disappear and occasionally recurred. But Taney's opinions in cases like *Bronson* (where his respect for contracts and private property was manifest), *Bank of Augusta* (where he reversed McKinley's radical circuit decision, which frightened Story), and *Holmes* v. *Jennison* (which Story thought was "masterly")[19] eased his memory of the 1837 term. Taney was not only a first-rate lawyer but increasingly appeared to Story an indispensable ally against the threatening radicalism of the agrarian ideologues on the Court. Taney seems to have appreciated Story for the same reason. He also sensed Story's uneasiness with some of the new justices and attempted to assuage it. Above all, he saw Story's greatness as an essential ingredient in the efficient and authoritative operation of the Court. Story's absence during the 1843 term drove home the point. Two years later the chief justice wrote to Peters what he truly believed, that Story's loss to the

Court "was irreparable, utterly irreparable in this generation, for there is nobody equal to him."[20]

If Story was indispensable to the Court and if the Court was not feckless, why, to return to the question, did he dwell so despondently on the Court's new ways and its changed law? The answer lies perhaps in the simple fact that for all the continuity, the shift Story perceived was real and significant. Part of the difference between the Marshall and Taney Courts lay in the murky area of small-group dynamics: in the amorphous realm of personality and legal talent; in the mind-set of the justices; and in the way they fit or did not fit into the Court's collective operation. In the matter of legal ability, comparisons with the Marshall Court suggest some slippage among the Taney justices. The chief justice was a distinguished lawyer, as even his enemies had to concede, and his style of leadership fitted the new age well. But he was no Marshall and he was not a "leading mind," the absence of which on the Court troubled Webster and his friends.[21] Smith Thompson was an independent and conscientious judge and a pleasant colleague. But he was a cut below Brockholst Livingston, whom he replaced, and made more concessions to the states (in commerce, bankruptcy, and currency matters) than pleased Story. McLean, on the other hand, was sound doctrinally (despite his *Briscoe* opinion) and decidedly more able than his predecessor, Robert Trimble. Barbour was also a step up in ability from Duvall, whom he replaced in 1836, and despite his states' rights, proslavery persuasion was thought by Story to be a "perspicacious, close, and vigorous" judge and a colleague of dedication and integrity.[22] Story could not say the same about Barbour's successor, Peter Daniel, whose rigid states' rights ideology drove him into chronic dissent that not only divided the Court but also increased the work load for the other justices.

John Catron and John McKinley came on the Court in 1837 to fill the vacancies created by the judicial act of that year. The former was canny, feisty, and very political, but he was also a solid, hardworking judge. McKinley worked hard enough but was out of his depth, and in fifteen years on the Court he wrote not one important opinion. James Wayne, who replaced William Johnson in 1835, was more effective than McKinley but decidedly of less stature than the man whose seat he filled. He was, moreover, as one scholar has noted, full of "political energies," which unfortunately he applied "in the councils of the Court."[23] He was a moderate Jacksonian who loved the Union, opposed the protective tariff and the national bank, favored Indian removal, and accommodated slavery as a fact of life. Story probably accepted him as a possible convert to judicial moderation.

Of all Story's colleagues, Henry Baldwin proved to be the most disruptive, and in this respect he was the very opposite of the gentle, competent, and cooperative Bushrod Washington, whose alliance with Story and

Marshall had done so much to stabilize the Marshall Court. Baldwin's mental condition continued to deteriorate after his breakdown in 1833, so that he withdrew increasingly into isolation, general obstructionism, and pointless dissent. He was particularly critical of Story, resenting his learning and attacking his opinions, it will be recalled, in his *General View* (1837), which to Story's disgust Peters had printed in the appendixes of the Supreme Court reports. That favor did not keep Baldwin from charging Peters with favoritism and incompetence, a charge that further disrupted the work of the Court and finally drew in Story as Peters's defender. The climax came in 1843, when a cabal of Baldwin, Catron, Daniel, and Wayne—a majority of the seven justices present that term—summarily replaced Peters with Benjamin C. Howard (whom McLean thought "will certainly make a capital Reporter if he canvasses as well as our brother Wayne, with whom he was educated").[24] Peters's time may indeed have come, and even Story had some reservations about his friend, but the peremptory dismissal without so much as a note to the absent Story was unethical and deeply wounding, and it brought the Court itself into "odium."[25]

More than that, the reporter episode was indicative of the politicization and institutional breakdown of the Court, which not even the astute leadership of Taney could contain or disguise. How the earlier Court had worked so harmoniously is still not entirely explicable. There had always been disagreement and irascible personalities. Perhaps it was the sheer force of Marshall's charisma that kept things in check or possibly the luck of the judicial mix: the intellectual complementarity of Marshall and Story, of Story and Livingston, and the strength of the Marshall-Story-Washington axis that permitted the Court to incorporate the crusty independence of William Johnson with little disruption. Maybe it was the shared values of the Revolution and the common intellectual world provided by the taught tradition of the common law that made the Marshall Court cohere.

But whatever the mysterious quality was, the Taney Court had less of it. What troubled Story and what measured the difference between the old Court and the new was not just doctrine but the method by which the Court went about its work. Story saw the change, as we have already noted, in the *Bridge* case, when he complained about the majority's abuse of scholarship. And the complaint was predictive, whether one turned to the chaos of commerce clause litigation, or to the undefined notion of police power, or to the increasingly volatile nature of slavery adjudication. In none of these areas did Story's "Rules of Interpretation" make sense. It is hard to imagine, indeed, that any comparable collection of "scientific" axioms of construction could have been salvaged from the work of the Taney Court—certainly none that would have pleased Story.

The disorganizing force that increasingly permeated the deliberations of the Taney Court was politics or, more broadly, political ideology. Jeffersonian critics of the Marshall Court's consolidating policies made the point in the 1820s; now conservative critics of the Taney Court, like those writing in the *American Jurist* in April 1838, came to the same conclusion: "In regard to the subject of constitutional jurisprudence," went the argument in response to the Court's great decisions of the 1837 term, "it is well known, that the power, exercised by the courts of the United States, in controlling the legislation of congress and of the several States, in certain cases, and the jurisdiction conferred upon those courts to the exclusion of the state courts, in reference to certain persons and subjects, have introduced a political element into the functions of the federal judiciary. . . ." This element had led, in turn, to "divisions of our jurists and statesmen into two opposing sects or schools . . . the one of a more strict, and the other of a more liberal interpretation of the constitution. The liberal school (if we may venture so to speak), after a long and brilliant career, is at present without a doubt yielding ground to its rival." Then to the basic point: "The conflicting principles, which lie at the foundation of the doctrines of these opposing schools, are so far political in their character, and so identical with those, which have always divided and still divide our thinking men into two great political sects, more or less corresponding with the political parties of the day, that it is not probable the struggle between them will ever be terminated, though the subjects with which they may at any particular time be connected, may cease to have any interest in the public mind."[26]

What the *Jurist* said was prophetic; it was also pretty much what Story had implied in his three dissents in 1837 and what prompted his constant complaints in private correspondence about the corrupting influence of party. The Court had not escaped. What value judgment one attached to that fact of course varied. What threw Story into the darkest gloom Justice Catron found to be perfectly normal, as we shall see. Even the *American Jurist*, by promising neutrality between the two schools of judicial interpretation, calmly accepted judicial politics as inevitable. But good, bad, or inevitable, politicization of the judicial process had taken a leap forward, a fact that manifested itself in several ways, some institutional and some legal, some subtle and others obvious. Among the latter was the party nature of the appointment process under Jackson and Van Buren. Andrew Jackson did not introduce the idea that appointees to the high Court should agree with the appointing president, any more than he introduced the spoils system into American politics. Presidents from Washington on consulted the political principles of their judicial nominees along with such qualities as general ability, geographical location, and legal specialty. John Adams expected political consequences from his appointment of John Marshall just as Jefferson did from his appointment of William Johnson.

Yet there was a subtle but important difference regarding the Supreme

Court appointments of Jackson and Van Buren. Judicial appointments before Jackson may have been political, but government through party had not yet been accepted as legitimate, even by politicians.[27] Justices who came to the Court during the so-called second American party system brought new attitudes with them. Most, including Chief Justice Taney, had been active party men and accepted the then fashionable notion that party was not only necessary but a positive good. At the very least Story's new brethren did not agree with him that political parties were antithetical to the Court, the Constitution, and republican government. And that was the whole point: Story's attitude about law and politics and the relation between them was rooted in an eighteenth-century version of republican statesmanship that his new colleagues, even McLean, did not fully share or even understand.

Whether accepting political parties as a necessary good *caused* Jacksonian justices to behave more like politicians than their predecessors is hard to say. But the fact is, as Story perceived (and Catron frankly admitted), they did.[28] Evidence of the Court's politicization might include McLean's active pursuit of the presidency. Less well known but no less revealing was the unjudicial behavior of others of Story's brethren. With no trace of compunction, for example, Catron exchanged political gossip and offered political advice to his friends, among whom were Democratic presidents Jackson, Polk, and Buchanan. More than once he passed on information about pending cases and otherwise babbled about the supposedly secret deliberations of the Court. Peter Daniel carried on a frank political correspondence with Martin Van Buren after joining the Court, and Barbour and McKinley likewise maintained their political connections. Wayne, too, was "essentially political minded" and had the dubious distinction of introducing the political practice of caucusing into the "councils of the Court." Even Taney willingly rendered advice to Presidents Jackson, Polk, and Buchanan, beyond what the chief justice might legitimately offer as spokesman for the Court in matters pertaining to the judiciary.[29]

Story would have been outraged had he known of this Democratic politicking, even if it did not come to much. But since the *Dartmouth College* case Story himself, as we have seen, had been the active political confidant of Daniel Webster and other conservatives, including President John Quincy Adams. Story continued to draft important congressional legislation, too, not only on judicial matters such as the admiralty jurisdiction of the federal courts and seamen's rights but in politically sensitive areas like bankruptcy. Story's political activities were not always narrowly partisan, but his support of the Whig party, openly acknowledged to Henry Clay and others, leads one to believe that he continued to give active support to Webster and other conservative politicians. Story would, of course, argue that Webster was a statesman, not a politician, and that the Whigs were not really a political party—and on both scores he had a point. But it is nevertheless a testimony to the permeating quality of party spirit that the most vociferous antiparty man on the Court was one of the most politically active.

It was symptomatic of the new age that parties themselves took notice of the political importance of the Court, as, for example, when they killed judicial reorganization in the 1820s or when Whigs and Democrats fought over the appointment of Taney to the Supreme Court in 1835. In fact, the Marshall Court had been one of the key issues on which the emerging party system had cut its ideological teeth in the 1820s. Party lines on the judicial issue did not always thereafter remain so clearly drawn, but the Court was a constant subject of political debate until the Civil War. It was natural in this situation that presidents in their appointments should be conscious not only of political principles but of party affiliation. More important, the justices became increasingly aware of the political implications of their decisions. Too sharp a line can be drawn between the Taney Court and its predecessor in this matter, certainly. From the beginning, justices of the Supreme Court reflected the social, economic, and legal interests of the states and sections from which they came, and given the nature of circuit responsibilities, they were expected to do so.[30] But the Jacksonian justices brought with them a much more sharply defined and insistent sense of sectionalism. Nor was the imperative to make law follow state and sectional interest counteracted by shared revolutionary values or a shared legal universe. Blackstone's elegant science of law was further away; a freewheeling, economically responsive instrumentalism closer at hand. It was not that suddenly a new kind of functionalism pervaded judicial deliberations. But a subtle shift in American law, from Enlightenment notions of legal science to instrumentalism, invited the justices to do what instinct inclined them to do anyway: shape law to fit the social-economic needs of their sections.

While the Taney Court increasingly divided along sectional lines, it also declined in efficiency. The problem began during Marshall's last years, when absences and death put the Court behind in its docket. The appointment of new justices did not solve the problem, either, and may even have exacerbated it. Story, at least, thought so. The Court "made very slow progress," he observed at the end of the 1838 term, "and did less in the same period than I ever knew. The addition to our numbers has most sensibly affected our facility as well as rapidity for doing business. 'Many men of many minds' require a great deal of discussion to compel them to come to definite results; and we found ourselves often involved in long and very tedious debates."[31] And not only was the Court talking more, working harder, and getting less done, but the work load was embarrassingly lopsided. From 1837 through 1845 (excluding the 1843 term, which Story missed) the Court decided 318 cases. Story spoke for the majority in 60 (or about 19 percent) of those, whereas Baldwin, Daniel, and McKinley wrote only a handful of run-of-the-mill opinions.[32] The disparity of the work load appears even more conspicuous when it is recalled that several of the justices did not bother to publish their circuit opinions. When the chief justice wrote Story to say how much he missed him on his right hand in the 1843 term, he was not only trying to soothe his colleague's hurt feelings about the Peters affair but telling the plain truth. Story's failure to be placated is also understandable when one puts all the factors together. To be insulted by a politically minded court engaged in a secret political caucus while he was flat on his back was bad enough, but to be doing the work of those that put him down was too much.

Not only was the Court doing less of what it was supposed to do, but what it did it did less well—measured at least by the standards of judicial performance Story brought from the Marshall Court. He knew, of course, that the Marshall Court was not perfectly united, but still the great decisions of the golden age were spoken in one voice and presented as the great state papers that they were.[33] It was a style exactly commensurate with Story's vision of judges as statesmen and of law as a science that could be rendered in clear, authoritative fashion. The Taney Court, as Story saw it, fell drastically away from that model, as the personality conflicts, the sectional ideologies of the justices, conference wrangles, and perpetual division made their way into the printed pages of the reports. Judicial dissent and the pervasive habit of writing separate opinions threatened to carry the Court back to the pre-Marshall days of seriatim opinions. Equally ominous was the fact that division seemed to have more to do with social and economic—that is to say, sectional—ideology than law. Dissents often seemed to be gestures of despair and nostalgia, Story's as well as those of radical agrarian conservatives whose laments had little effect on the development of legal doctrine.

Frequent and bitter division on the Court detracted from its capacity to educate and lead. What was worse in this regard for Story, and most telling about the politicization of the judicial process, was the manner in which the Court put together its majority opinions. Story's preference for judicial over legislative government had always rested on the presumed rationality of the common-law process. But increasingly judicial decisions resembled legislation: Justices caucused, they compromised, they considered constituencies, and their decisions commonly settled cases without clarifying principle. Indeed, settled doctrine was often unsettled. Here the 1837 term was predictive, much as Story feared. The *Bridge* decision left *Dartmouth College* on the books, but the meaning of that precedent had been substantially altered. And though the Court did consistently follow its new ruling, it also failed largely to convince—except perhaps that the Court was willing to manipulate law to achieve policy results. The *Miln* decision, as already noted, launched the Court on a path of doctrinal chaos as justices struggled over exclusive versus concurrent versions of the com-

merce power and tried at the same to make a place for the emerging concept of police power (which as Taney perceived was merely a convenient
way of circumventing a constitutional clarification of the commerce clause).
Story stuck by his exclusivist interpretation of *Gibbons* but persuaded, besides his friend McLean, only Wayne, an addition that could hardly have
provided much comfort. Even more threatening to Story's common-law
version of legal science was the fact that lawyers and justices frequently
cited the same precedents to prove opposing points. This, as we shall see,
was particularly a problem in the great debate over slavery and the Constitution, and indeed it was in the realm of slavery adjudication more than
any other that legal doctrine gave way to political expediency.

How the Court's increased politicization was evaluated varied greatly.
Catron, one of the most eminent practitioners of the new style, made his
position clear in his observation to Andrew Jackson that division on the
Supreme Court was just as natural as in the Senate, and almost as common.[34] Perhaps the fact that the Court got on with the business of deciding
cases at all, given the personal and ideological divisions among the justices, was itself a minor miracle. But Story did not see it that way. He was
wrong, of course, to think that the Court was gone, but he correctly perceived that the Court was in the process of transformation. At best a kind
of pragmatism had invaded constitutional law—the inevitable consequence, it might be argued, of the political nature of the Constitution itself. Worse still, the justices were behaving like politicians and legislators.
Story thought the worst, and this opinion accounts for much of the intellectual anguish of his last years. It explains in part why he turned so enthusiastically to his students at the Law School, who believed, at least for a
while, that law was a science. It explains the energy poured so unstintingly
into his commentaries in the hope of fighting back the tide of legal phil-
istinism. It explains his preference on the Court for commercial law (as in
Swift), where principle could most likely prevail and where his own authority was greatest. Finally, it explains why he so gladly turned from the
cacophony of the Court's sessions in Washington to the New England circuit. There he aimed to demonstrate the meaning of scientific adjudication
and its relevance for American capitalism. As in the seventeenth century
and in the 1820s, New England would yet be "as a city upon a hill."

2. America's Mansfield: A Commercial Judge on the New England Circuit

"I have lost my confidence and hopes in the constitutional guardianship
and protection of the Supreme Court," wrote James Kent dejectedly to
Story after assessing the decisions of the 1837 term. The only consolation,

he went on to say, was "to get hold of another volume of Sumner [that is, Story's circuit decisions as reported by Charles Sumner] & there I am sure to find the law of the land expounded and enforced with the most extensive learning, the best taste, the loftiest morals, the most unshaken independence and freedom and the most attractive graces of style and eloquence."[35] Story's intentions, it must be said, ran along precisely those lines, even though he often complained about the arduous demands of circuit riding. He was required to hold two terms annually, the first running from May 1 through June 27 and the second from October 1 through November 27. He traveled a thousand miles each term, holding court in Massachusetts at Boston, in Maine alternately at Portland and Wiscasset, in Rhode Island alternately at Providence and Newport, and in New Hampshire alternately at Portsmouth and Exeter. Even during vacation he was pressed with circuit obligations. "The business in the terms does not give an accurate view of the real business of the Court," Story wrote to John Bailey on 8 December 1823. "Almost all of the questions of Law argued in terms are taken under advisement & examined & decided in Vacation. There are also many important cases, (usually equity causes) which are argued, & principally *in writing* . . . upon which I am obliged to spend a great deal of time in vacation."[36]

Relentless and exhausting it was, but Story loved it. New England was home, being close to Sarah was a mutual joy, and the children cherished his company. After graduating from Harvard, William had gone to the Law School (class of 1841) and then on to a practice in Boston and, apparently at least, to a life of legal scholarship. Mary Story married George Ticknor Curtis, a former student of her father's, so the Curtis family was there to welcome the judge back home. So were Story's students at the Law School, along with family and old friends from Salem. Story's schedule, it must be said, did not allow much time for socializing. He rose at seven in the summer, according to his son's account, and after a family breakfast and the daily newspapers, he returned to his study and there worked on his commentaries or composed circuit opinions. His only break was to lecture at the Law School, and pretty much his only exercise was the short walk over and back. After his lectures he returned again to his study, though sometimes, weather permitting, he took Sarah for a drive in the open chaise. After a simple dinner he returned again to his books, which he finally closed at around seven o'clock. Thereafter until he retired at ten or so he would enjoy his family or entertain friends and sometimes students from the Law School.[37]

All of this refreshed and sustained Story, and so in fact did circuit duties themselves. Circuit riding under any circumstances was rough work, but the New England circuit, as Kent correctly observed, was "the most pleasant in the U. States."[38] Certainly, as Kent recognized, the first circuit was one of the richest in lawmaking potential. Its people were literate, energetic, and enterprising; they were bound together by history and institutions (like Harvard College and Harvard Law School) and caught up in the first phases of the commercial, industrial, corporate revolution. Story mingled easily with these people, relished the direct contact, as trial judge, with lawyers and clients. He liked the give-and-take of the courtroom as well as the professional camaraderie that went with circuit duties. But most of all, perhaps, he appreciated circuit judging because—whereas in the full Court his "free judgments" were "modified, controlled & sometimes fettered by the necessary obedience to the opinions of my Brethren"—he was on circuit able "after full research & elaborate consideration" to exercise his "own free judgment."[39] He did, of course, ordinarily sit with the federal district judges in each district of his circuit, but he was the senior judge—a justice of the Supreme Court, not a judge of a circuit, as Daniel Webster observed—and could, providing he had the ability, become the dominant influence.[40] Story saw the opportunity. As he put it to Hopkinson, "if my fame shall happen to go down to posterity, my character as a Judge will be more fully & accurately seen in the opinions of the circuit Court than in the Supreme Court."[41]

Certainly the powers at his disposal as circuit judge were commensurate with his high hopes. In terms of jurisdiction alone, the circuit courts played a central role in the administration of federal law. They possessed original cognizance, concurrent with state courts, of all suits of a civil nature in common law or equity in which the matter in dispute exceeded five hundred dollars and the United States was a plaintiff, or an alien was a party, or the suit was between citizens of different states. With certain exceptions they also had exclusive cognizance over all serious crimes against the United States. And in addition they had appellate jurisdiction from all final decrees and judgments of the federal district courts in which the amount in controversy exceeded fifty dollars. In addition to being the major trial courts in the federal system, the circuit courts, because of their position in the federal judicial structure, were unique "representative" institutions as well. The traveling Supreme Court justices were, as James Bayard aptly noted, "an emanation" of the full Court in Washington, the living symbols in fact of national authority in an age when the central government was often a remote and tenuous entity.[42] On the other hand, the circuit judge was expected to represent local law on the full bench in Washington. The early circuits followed sectional lines; Supreme Court justices were appointed in part because of their mastery of the legal staple of their sections and were, paradoxically, allowed at Washington to sit in cases they had decided on circuit. As one contemporary authority put it, the circuit arrangement permitted justices "to mingle with those they serve, and to learn the manner, habits and feelings of the people, and acquire to an enlarged extent, the peculiar policy of the several states, their law and local institutions."[43]

There were, of course, limitations on the lawmaking power of the circuit courts. Their decisions were subject to review by the full bench. Unless affirmed by the Supreme Court, circuit decisions had no impact outside the jurisdiction of the court that made them. Even that impact, of course, was nullified by an adverse ruling above. The lawmaking potential of the circuit courts also varied from one circuit to the next according to such variables as the nature of litigation and the quality of the bar. And much obviously depended on the ability of the circuit justice himself: his ability as a trial judge, his mastery of the law, his understanding of the character and the special needs of his circuit. But, limited or not, the circuit courts of the early republic were the major trial courts in the federal system. As we shall see, their jurisdiction over suits between citizens of different states made them a primary forum for the growing class of capitalists doing business across state lines. In the great majority of cases, circuit decisions established law for the people of the circuit. If authoritatively rendered, they could influence both state and national law as well.

Success depended on Story's ability to inspire "respect and confidence," as Webster put it, and his ability to produce "a reciprocal communication through all branches of the judicial department."[44] Respect and confidence followed ability, however, which had to be demonstrated in the professional give-and-take of circuit judging. The first lawyers Story had to impress were those he sat with on the circuit bench in each of the districts of his court. The exact relationship between the justice and the district judge was nowhere fully specified and accordingly varied all the way from the third circuit, where district judge Hopkinson outshone the mentally unstable Justice Baldwin,[45] to the fourth, where the district judge, as his partner Justice Duvall complained, was so aggressive that he all but stopped the operation of the court.[46] By virtue of his authority, the Supreme Court justice was expected to lead, but the district judge was no silent partner. Consultation was accepted and agreement necessary as a protection against shoddy law and injustice.[47] District judges often decided cases to relieve an overloaded docket or in the absence of the justice, and in many of the remote western circuits did so as a regular thing.[48] An effective circuit court, then, depended on a harmonious working relationship between the justice and the district judge. The problem facing the circuit justice was the delicate one of leading without dominating.

By his exhaustive learning, infinite tact and patience, and unwearying industry, Story made himself *the* circuit judge. He did not do everything, of course. When the docket was overburdened, as it usually was on the first circuit, Story and his partner shared the load, sometimes holding court simultaneously in adjoining rooms. In emergencies and occasionally when only routine questions were on the docket, Story gratefully yielded the duties to the district judges. Almost certainly he consulted the special expertise of his fellow judges, as he must have done with Judge John Davis of the Massachusetts district, for example, who was one of the ablest admiralty judges in the country.[49] In his last years on the circuit, he frankly confessed that he meant "to stand upon a *fair division* of labors with the District Judges."[50]

But in fact Story shouldered the lion's share of the circuit burdens and responsibilities for the thirty-three years of his tenure. He handled the many administrative details that came in the daily operation of the court: questions from district judges, from officers of the court, from government's attorneys, from parties before the court.[51] He was constantly plagued with patronage matters regarding such circuit offices as clerk, marshal, and court reporter.[52] He kept a close eye on the publication of circuit opinions and assumed a major responsibility for establishing the working rules and prevailing mode of practice in his circuit. Story's main burden, however, was writing opinions. With the ready compliance of the district judges, he handled the important cases that came before the court. ("I had rather take 40 lashes," wrote district judge John Pitman of the Rhode Island district to Story, than try the *Warren Case* alone—unless Story would send "a note of the points raised in the former trial & your ruling thereon. . . .")[53] It was Story, too, who accepted the progressively burdensome responsibility of clearing the circuit docket each term. Only one year before his death he complained that the labors of his circuit fell "exclusively" on him.[54]

Story's controlling position on the circuit bench and his influence on the district judges with whom he sat is clear. District judge John Davis, Story's circuit companion from 1812 to 1841, pronounced him "everything that could be wished." His "eminent ability and unwearied industry," his "able decisions" and "learned labors," owned Davis, relieved "solicitude" about circuit duties and gave him "salutary aid in various departments of . . . official duty."[55] For district judges of more modest ability, the indebtedness must have been even greater. District judge Ashur Ware of Maine, who sat with Story for twenty years, thought him among the world's greatest jurists and paid eloquent tribute to his services on the circuit bench.[56] So did John Pitman: "No person with whom I have associated has exercised so great an influence upon the last half of my life as your lamented husband," he confessed to Story's widow; "I have lost the stay and staff of my age and one to whom I always went nor went in vain for advice and sympathy."[57] Story's influence apparently also reached Judges David Howell and Peleg Sprague.[58]

With authority on his own court secure, Story was in a position to influence the legal profession of his circuit, to engender within it that "reciprocal communication" of which Webster spoke. The potential was great, but so was the challenge, because the circuit judge's talents were there for the profession to see. Judicial weakness might demoralize the whole bar, as Justice McKinley's had on circuit in New Orleans,[59] or might surrender authority to some dominant lawyer like William Pinkney on the fourth circuit, who "like a slave driver" ran roughshod over Justice Duvall and Judge James Houston.[60] Judge Story had his work cut out for him in New England. The bar, with the profession of Suffolk and Essex counties in Massachusetts as the hub, was distinguished and proud. The old elite, including Harrison Gray Otis, William Prescott, Nathan Dane, George Blake, Jeremiah Mason, and Samuel Dexter, was still around. New arrivals like Daniel Webster and later Charles Sumner, Richard H. Dana, Jr., George Hillard, Rufus Choate, Peleg Chandler, and the Curtis brothers (George Ticknor and Benjamin Robbins) maintained the tradition. They were equipped and inclined to judge judges with critical eyes.

In establishing his authority with the circuit bar, Story had advantageous connections. He had studied law with two leaders of the Massachusetts profession, Samuel Sewall (later chief justice of the Supreme Judicial Court of Massachusetts) and Samuel Putnam (who became a justice on the same court), and won their esteem and lasting affection. During a decade of practice before the courts of Massachusetts (and occasionally New Hampshire) Story had argued against (and with) the leading men of the profession—Prescott, Dexter, Dane, Mason, Putnam, Blake, and Otis, to mention only some—and convinced them of his ability. His Harvard ties strengthened the professional ones, too, as they did for many lawyers in New England. Of the 294 members of the Suffolk County bar from 1781 to 1840, for example, no less than 182 were educated at Harvard. The network of associations was intricate: Story's colleague on the circuit bench, John Davis, for instance, was a classmate of Jeremiah Smith, the great judge of New Hampshire, and of Elijah Paine and Samuel Dexter, leading Massachusetts lawyers. Dexter, in turn, was Story's professional colleague before 1812 and one of the leaders of the circuit bar. Many of Story's own class of 1798 went into law, and some, like Leverett Saltonstall, C. P. Sumner (father of Charles and later sheriff of Suffolk County), and Stephen Longfellow, longtime leader of the Portland bar, maintained lifelong professional and personal ties with Story. Even family connections had professional overtones for Story. His father-in-law, William Wetmore, was a distinguished lawyer in Boston and a judge of the Court of Common Pleas. His brother-in-law and confidant, Samuel Fay, became a probate judge for Middlesex County. His daughter, Mary, married George Ticknor Curtis, an outstanding lawyer and the brother of Benjamin Robbins Curtis, who went on from a distinguished professional career to the Supreme Court of the United States. William Story was, through his father's influence, reporter for the first circuit from 1839 to 1845.

If many of the lawyers who argued before Story on circuit were former professional colleagues and friends, still more had been his students at Harvard Law School. Story's influence with the New England profession grew with the school.[61] Many of Story's students remained in New England to practice, and the best—like Peleg Chandler, George Hillard, Benjamin Robbins Curtis, George Ticknor Curtis, Rufus Choate, Ebenezer Hoar, Thomas Hopkinson, George Minot, Albert Nelson, Henry Paine, Daniel Richardson, and Charles Sumner—assumed leading roles in the profession. Almost invariably they carried with them a deep admiration and affection for Story, as we have seen.

What is more important, Story brought from the lecture room at Harvard to the circuit bench the same determination to *teach* correct law. The profession, it must be said, stood in need of help. The increasing complexity of American society in the early nineteenth century required the lawyer to master a corpus of law rapidly transcending state lines and growing in quantity and sophistication, without the help of well-established, nationally oriented law schools and with only primitive aids to legal research. At the same time, the rapid increase in the number of lawyers seriously threatened to undercut professional standards and break down "the sentiment of union and fraternity" of the bench and bar.[62] The problem was to reinvigorate professional élan and, as Story put it to Kent, "to preserve in the profession a steady spirit of original investigation & to unite a deep respect for authorities with an habitual inquiry into their consonance with principles."[63]

The circuit justice was well situated to teach. His perambulations were a source of communication among the bars of the various districts, and his visits were occasions for social and professional intercourse. Most important, through his conduct of the court the judge could condition the standards of practice and learning of the bar. Story used the potential to the utmost. Sometimes, as with the practice of equity, the educational chore was very specific. There were no separate courts of equity on the first circuit, and legal competence in this crucial area lagged badly. Acutely aware of his responsibility, Story deliberately modeled the practice of equity in his court after that of Chancellor Kent's distinguished chancery court in New York. In doing so, he hoped not only to "awaken the ardour of the bar" to chancery jurisprudence but to convince the profession to reform that system on the state level.[64]

Specific problems aside, Story conducted his court so as to instill that respect for authorities and that spirit of original inquiry which he thought so vital. The atmosphere of his courtroom was always friendly, urbane, and amicably competitive.[65] Yet he ran a tight ship. He disliked the "exceedingly prolix & tedious" argumentation before the Supreme Court and kept it at a minimum in his circuit. When a clear understanding of the issues or the law before the court demanded it, or when lawyers drifted away from the point, Story did not hesitate to interrupt (even great lawyers and personal friends like Samuel Dexter did not escape criticism).[66] On the other hand, as the circuit reports abundantly testify, he had a keen eye for excellence and generously complimented able arguments at the bar. To the young and inexperienced lawyer, he was especially gentle and encouraging. "He treated us," recalled Richard Dana, Jr., "as though he had our success at heart. He took care to interweave some compliment, if it was in the least degree deserved, and if our argument was on a false scent, from some ignorance of later decisions, or some error of application, he would bear it patiently, or try to give us the right direction, or the necessary information, in such a way as not only to save our feelings, but to save our credit with our clients and the spectators."[67]

Story's efforts to educate the profession were not confined to the circuit courtroom but overflowed into natural channels worn by personal and professional connections. Important leaders of the circuit bar like Charles P. Daveis of Portland and former Law School students practicing in New England like Charles Sumner, Peleg W. Chandler, and George Hillard relied on Story for advice and assistance. Government attorneys, marshals, clerks, reporters, district judges, and other legal officers of the circuit called constantly on Story's knowledge. So also did state judicial officers. Prentiss Mellen, chief justice of the Maine Supreme Court, for example, constantly bombarded Story with intricate legal queries. "As you and I are embarked in the common cause of Law," began Story in one of his responses, and in that spirit he answered Mellon in a series of letters that were themselves scholarly essays on knotty problems of the law.[68] The constant flow of letters requesting information from lawyers, laymen, friends, and strangers would suggest that Story rarely said no to an honest query on the law. For his personal friends and members of the professional elite, the evidence suggests that he did much more. In the case of Daniel Webster, as already noted, Story supplied answers to questions on private and constitutional law, gave tactical advice on litigation, drafted bills, wrote speeches, and gave political advice; in 1834, when conservative going was rough, he defended Webster's statesmanship.[69] Webster and many other lawyers on the New England circuit knew exactly what William Wirt meant when, with Story in mind, he wished "to Heaven that I had such an Oracle of the law in my neighborhood in the form of a Judge of the Supreme Court."[70]

Story's commanding mastery of the law carried him far, but the "representative" function of the circuit court required that he mingle with the people and learn their manners, habits, and feelings, that he fashion legal science to suit their special needs. Here Story was superb. His New England credentials, stamped in Marblehead, were impeccable; his love of the place and his pride in it were a matter of public record. Friendly, gregarious, sympathetic, he engaged the common folk whenever he got the chance—which, given two thousand miles of travel annually, was often. Story talked to the people formally in his opinions, of course. In his charges to the grand juries, impaneled in each district of the circuit, he spoke more directly. As we have noted, Story preferred a broad, general charge with a close explanation of the law, braced with a lecture on sound policy and republican morality. The broad charge suited Story's talents for teaching and his bent for didacticism. Meticulously he explained to the jurors the nature and meaning of the law they were charged to uphold: offenses against the nation, against public justice and right, against the police and public trade, against persons and property within the jurisdiction of the United States. Emphasis shifted with circumstances. When the passions of war were dangerously strong in 1812, Story warned against the "persecuting zeal of prerogative and the fury of popular faction" and dwelt heavily on the law of treason.[71] When Congress made the slave trade piracy in 1819, Story responded in his charge to the circuit in 1820 with a luminous discourse on the law of piracy and a passionate condemnation of the nature and evils of the trade. In the same charge he countered the spirit of disunion generated by the Missouri Debates with an encomium on constitutional union and American patriotism.[72] Running as themes through all his charges were warnings against the "secret vindictive policies of rulers, & the bold, misguided zeal of popular factions" and praise for an "enlightened and virtuous" citizenry.[73]

Backed by Story's reputation and circulated in the newspapers and sometimes in pamphlet form, these charges worked further to establish both the law of the section and Story's authoritative position as its expounder. On the circuit he became "Judge Story," not "Justice"; it was not a decline in authority but a measure of intimacy and pride of possession. He had become a New England institution, as is indicated by Sam Whitcomb, Jr.'s, recollection that he had been "taught to respect & love" Story "from youth," even though he had "never met him."[74]

If they revered him, he understood them. Indeed, anecdote had it that Story knew more about New England life than those who lived it. Justice Smith Thompson, according to Justice Todd, used to cite Story on circuit as an illustration of how "a truly great mind deems all knowledge important, and is ever on the alert to add to the general stock by observation as well as study." The rest of Todd's account is worth quoting for what it says about Story:

> While traveling in the interior on one of his circuits his carriage broke down, which made it necessary for him to employ the Blacksmith, harnessmaker and waggon-maker of the village to effect the proper repairs.

While they were at work Judge Story entered their shops, and conversed with them about their several trades in that easy off-hand way for which he was remarkable and which was perhaps the secret of his being able at all times to make uneducated people feel perfectly at home in his presence.

After he was gone these mechanics met, as usual in the Evening, at the village tavern to chat over the events of the day. I have had a customer of my own cloth, said the blacksmith—a man of singular skill and knowledge in the business. I got from him some valuable hints about shoeing horses, ironing [?] waggons &c. He understands the trade to perfection; though I should not judge he worked much himself, for his hands are as white and delicate as a woman's. He doubtless carries on a heavy business in one of the large cities.

You are mistaken, said the harnessmaker, he is of my cloth, as I can prove to you in a moment. He showed me a nine stitch which the English put in their harnesses, that gives a peculiar finish, and is much stronger than the ordinary one, with all practise I cannot stitch like that. He is a harness-maker without a doubt.

You are both wrong exclaimed the waggon maker. He is of my trade. Why, he is perfectly familiar with every branch of the business; and besides I saw him handle some of my tools in a way which convinced me that he had served a regular apprenticeship. I confess his hands don't look much as if he worked *none*. He has probably made his fortune in the business, and retired—But I know he is a waggon maker.

They agreed to refer the point in dispute to the landlord who then informed them that their customer was no less a personage than Judge Story.[75]

A mastery of the details of life, it would seem, was as much required on circuit as a mastery of the law. Cases involving blacksmiths and harness and wagon makers did not, to be sure, occupy much of Story's time. But he applied the same curiosity and sure knowledge of facts and concepts to commerce and manufacturing. Story learned by doing, or rather, by trying cases, and the hundreds of cases he tried touched almost every aspect of New England's economic life. His knowledge of the practice and needs of the business community, as we have seen, also came from personal, social, and professional connections. His mother was the daughter of a prominent Marblehead merchant, and his father moved among the commercial elite of Marblehead and Salem. One of his brothers was a substantial Boston merchant; another engaged in New England shipping. Two of his brothers-in-law and closest friends (Stephen White and William Fettyplace) were men of commerce. Among his early law clients were the great merchant shippers of Essex County. Advising the Grays, Ornes,

Appletons, and Crowninshields and serving as president of the Merchants' Bank of Salem brought him directly into the inner circles of business, as did his later association with the Lowells, Cabots, Jacksons, and Lees, with Harrison Gray Otis, P. C. Brooks, Nicholas Biddle, and Thomas Hansard Perkins ("the head of our commercial community," to whom Story dedicated his *Commentaries on the Law of Promissory Notes*). When Story celebrated the civilizing miracle of commerce (as he did explicitly in his public speeches and implicitly in his treatises on commercial law) he articulated cultural values that he had long since internalized. His work as a mercantile judge was not part of a conspiracy but rather part of that "aggressive and cohesive cultural pattern" which Max Lerner found existing between "business enterprise" and judicial power."[76]

The functional bridge between judges and businessmen on the first circuit was the common law itself. The common law, as the *American Jurist* put it, "we consider to be admirably adapted to the interests of a commercial people."[77] Story agreed and, indeed, from the beginning of his career, set up the common law as distinct from legislative law in its method of economic rule making. And it was appropriately distinct, for the common law fitted perfectly the needs of economic individualism as Story saw it operating. Common-law judging was, of course, a deployment of the power of the state. The English judges who, over the centuries, replaced local law with a law common to the whole kingdom did so in the name of royal authority; Story's authority on the first circuit derived in part from his national office. But Justice Story, as already observed, was Judge Story on the New England circuit. If he represented national authority, he served New England. Most important, the law he administered, at least as he himself conceived it, was law not only suited to the community of which he was a part but partly created by that community.[78] The common law was called into action not by the sovereign but by individuals. Sometimes Story was asked to interpret positive law, an act of the sovereign state, but much if not most of what he did was to settle disputes over contracts between individuals in which the sovereign state was only indirectly connected if at all. Sometimes the contract involved simple debt, but given the five-hundred-dollar (later two-thousand-dollar) cutoff for civil suits, contract questions generally involved significant transactions between businessmen from different states.

Whether the issue was a simple debt, a policy of insurance, or a bill of exchange, Story's responsibility was to effect the intent of the parties to the contract. It was this responsibility which took him into the general commercial law (where contract was the grand theme) and through that into the practice and usages of trade and commerce in New England. Here the social environment of circuit judging merged with the intellectual life of the common law. For the guiding assumption of commercial contracts, as the *American Jurist* made clear, was "interest": that the parties to the bargain knew what their own interests were and how best to effectuate them. "Hence," continued the *American Jurist*, "the rule of law must be founded upon the supposition, that the parties to a contract of sale will conduct themselves with that common and ordinary degree of prudence and discretion, which the generality of mankind are governed by in the common affairs and transactions of life."[79] Individual rationality and free will, it was assumed, provided the foundation of contract law. Story often made the same point himself and never more simply, perhaps, than in his *Commentaries on Promissory Notes* when he declared that "every contract presupposes, that it is founded in the free and voluntary consent of each of the parties, upon a valuable consideration, and after a deliberate knowledge of its character and obligation."[80]

Rules for the construction of contract, it followed, derive from actual contracts; contractual norms from the cumulative experience of merchants over the years as extracted by judges in actual cases. Thus it was that Story's friend John Pickering could say to the Boston Society for the Useful Diffusion of Knowledge in 1830 "that *our* commercial law should be founded upon well-settled commercial usage."[81] Thus could Story make the "usages of trade," the "course of trade," and "mercantile usage" the basis for the construction of mercantile contracts on his circuit. Commercial practice distilled into rules of law could be found in the decisions of commercial judges of various countries; and conflict theory permitted Story to apply those rules consistently. He also consulted local usage, while at the same time watching that it not be prematurely elevated to the level of principle.[82] Judging was for scholars, but it helped if one knew some wagon makers and textile manufacturers, too. The mode of action was settled: Judges working with businessmen and their lawyers might fashion economic rules of the game acceptable and advantageous to all. It was a process, as the *Merchants' Magazine* put it, in which "the evil influence of political difficulties . . . brooding over the markets" would not be felt.[83]

Story's circuit experience prepared him to suggest in *Swift* v. *Tyson* that judges *discovered* the principles of commercial law rather than making them. Such, of course, was not true in any literal sense (as Story himself suggested by the wording of his statement). But if judging on the New England circuit was any indication, outright judicial legislation was the exception, not the rule. Creativity came most obviously in cases of the "first impression," where the factual situation demanded an extrapolation from existing rules, or in cases where principle itself was confused. Thus in *Citizens' Bank* v. *Nantucket Steamboat Co.* (which Story tried on circuit in October 1811, one month *before* he was confirmed), he was asked for the first time to define common carriers for the purpose of assessing liability;

he did so broadly and by reference to the "usages and customs" of business.[84] Another instance when Story had occasion to strike out on his own was *Peters* v. *Warren Insurance Co.* (1838), in which the question was whether accidental collision was "a peril of the seas within the meaning of the common policy of insurance" and how in such cases damages were to be assessed.[85] There were no relevant American decisions on this important issue and only one recent English case, which Story contradicted in ruling that accidental collision was a peril of the seas for purposes of assessing losses. So authoritative had Story's decisions in the maritime insurance area become by this time that Lord Denman concluded that his ruling in *Peters* would "at least neutralize the effect of the English decision, and induce any of their courts to consider the question as an open one."[86]

Despite such cases, however, innovation was not as important a characteristic of Story's 743 reported circuit decisions as administration. Story's circuit court in this respect was a clearinghouse for rules of economic behavior. Cooperation, not conflict, was the essence of the matter. Litigation was, of course, framed in adversarial terms, and individual merchants were inclined to push the law to their own advantage. Occasionally, as the *Merchants' Magazine* pointed out, the courts had to expose "a rogue's true character" to the moral "gaze of the community," and so litigation became a source of character information for the business community.[87] The main point, however, as the *American Jurist* emphasized, was that the "mass of the country is well disposed, and will act fairly under equitable laws."[88] This was particularly true of the commercial community, which was "a class the members of which have little or no bitterness of feeling towards each other, but who submit to the courts of justice the determination of their rights, from a sincere desire to ascertain what they are."[89] To judge was to educate, then, and not just the legal profession but businessmen as well. "There is a large amount of legal knowledge daily required in the transactions of the merchant," declared the *Merchants' Magazine* on this point, "and which he should make a part of his business information and education. This consists in understanding the great leading principles which govern sales, agency, negotiable paper, suretyship, and the like."[90] These principles, observed the same publication earlier, "are simple themselves, and few in number; but in their application to the business of life, the details of cases vary so much—the circumstances of each are so different, and those differences are often of so minute a character, that a most distressing uncertainty hangs over many parts of the subject. . . ."[91]

What businessmen wanted from Story, then, was not so much the creation of new rules as the clarification and refinement of old ones and their fair application to the increasingly complex economic life of the section. *Pope et al.* v. *Nickerson*, one of Story's last opinions, might be taken as an example of his response: one of "the daily mine-run of the cases, unsorted, unselected," to use Karl Llewelyn's phrase.[92] In this case, an action of assumpsit, the schooner *Annawan* was, while bound from Malaga to Philadelphia, forced to put into Bermuda under stress of weather; there part of the cargo was sold for repairs and the balance raised on a bottomry bond on the vessel, freight, and cargo. After proceeding on its course, the ship was forced back to Bermuda a second time; this time the captain sold the vessel and more of the cargo before returning to Philadelphia, at which point the Philadelphia shippers sued the Boston owner for the whole cargo. Story was called to rule on the nature and extent of the liability of the owners for the various decisions of the master as he coped with disaster in Bermuda—whether the liability of the owner *in personam* was absolute or affected with the future fate of the ship on the return voyage; the contractual reach of a bottomry bond drawn up in Bermuda—all of which questions were interlaced with conflict of laws problems: The shippers lived in Philadelphia and the owner in Massachusetts; the contract for freight originated in Malaga and the bond in Bermuda. It was business as usual on the New England circuit.

There is no evidence that Story created any new rules in settling these questions. Yet his opinion, in addition to being reported in Chandler's *Law Reporter* and Hunt's *Merchants' Magazine*, two major commercial periodicals for the region, was cited as controlling in no less than thirty-five state and federal court decisions, and this is not to mention numerous references in lawyers' briefs.[93] It is a fair assumption that Story had given businessmen in Boston and Philadelphia, shipmasters and bondsmen, economic rules which they accepted as authoritative and on which they acted in the future course of business.

This is not to say that Story's word went unchallenged on the New England circuit. Indeed, to understand fully his efforts there, one must explore the resistance he encountered. Significantly, that opposition came primarily in the application of federal statutes, as witness his struggle to uphold federal commercial regulations during and after the War of 1812. Even more revealing of the vagaries and difficulties of circuit judging was his effort to provide a uniform interpretation of the federal Bankruptcy Act of 1841, which involved him in a three-year battle with Chief Justice Parker of the New Hampshire Supreme Court. Story had a personal stake in the matter because he worked with Webster in drafting the bankruptcy bill that became law in 1841.[94] As circuit justice he was also responsible for the administration and interpretation of the measure. By his own reckoning some five thousand bankruptcy actions were entered in his circuit.[95] Most of these were at the district court level, but the circuit court had concurrent jurisdiction over some issues, and in all cases decisions from the district courts could be appealed to the circuit court.

Story attempted to provide uniform and efficient guidelines for the administration of the act on his circuit, in part through off-the-bench correspondence and conversations with federal district judges and circuit lawyers. Mostly, however, he worked through his circuit opinions, the leading one of which was *Ex parte Foster* (1842).[96] And it was here, ultimately, that he crossed judicial swords with Parker. The struggle began inconspicuously in March 1841 when Foster petitioned the district court to be declared bankrupt under the 1841 act. The problem was that some of Foster's creditors (among whom was William Appleton, the brother of Story's friend Nathan Appleton) had already attached his property upon mesne process (i.e., in anticipation of the final judgment) in the Court of Common Pleas for Suffolk County under the Massachusetts Bankruptcy Act. Foster petitioned in equity for an injunction from Story against Appleton, which if granted would deny Appleton the privileged position secured by his attachment. Appleton, in short, would not be permitted to use the state courts and the state bankruptcy law to defeat the equitable distribution of assets provided for by the national Bankruptcy Act.

Story saw the case as a states' rights challenge to uniform federal law— except the troublemakers were not Thomas Jefferson and Virginia but William Appleton and Massachusetts. The difference did not deter him. He certified the case back to the district court with an order to issue the injunction, along with a scholarly argument that attachment upon mesne process was not only invalid under Massachusetts equity but did not give Appleton a "vested lien" in any case. Story's *obiter* on Massachusetts law was bound to ruffle local legal pride. So did his holding on the main question, that is, the extent to which an attachment upon mesne process under state law was maintainable under the Bankruptcy Act of 1841. For the district court to recognize such a process and permit it to go to judgment, reasoned Story, would be to validate the privileged claims of some creditors over others, a step that would plainly defeat the process of fair distribution provided for in the national act. Accordingly, he ordered the district court to enjoin the state bankruptcy proceedings. At the same time he laid it down "as a general principle" that federal district courts possess full equity powers in bankrupty matters. Indeed, Story asserted that Congress had given the federal courts a more "liberal jurisdiction" in this regard "than the Lord Chancellor, sitting in bankruptcy, was authorized to exercise."[97]

One day before delivering his *Foster* opinion, Story wrote to Senator John Berrien, reporting that the "Bankrupt Act works well. The Courts, at least in my circuit, are working through all the difficulties incident to the new system . . . and if Congress will let it alone for another year, and leave the Courts to adjust the machinery, probe the defects, and dispel some of the supposed embarrassments which must in all new systems arise in giving them practical operation, I am persuaded that the system will grow popular, and will be one of the most lasting benefits ever conferred upon our country."[98] These hopes, it turned out, were illusory in regard to both congressional support and the status of affairs on the first circuit. No sooner had the legislation gone into effect than Democrats, led by James Buchanan and others, attacked it as an example of Whig consolidationism and judicial aggrandizement. The forces of repeal won the day in March 1843.[99] Story was also challenged in his own fiefdom by New Hampshire's Parker, who undercut *Foster* by holding that an attachment upon a mesne process under state law was valid when made *before* federal bankruptcy proceedings had begun.[100]

Story fought back. His letter to Senator Berrien was an attempt to forestall repeal, as was his detailed report to Secretary of State Daniel Webster on the workings of the Bankruptcy Act in his circuit. In response to Parker's challenge on circuit he reasserted his broad construction of the 1841 act "with undoubting confidence" in *In re Bellows* (1844).[101] Parker shot back with another repudiation in *Kittredge* v. *Emerson* (1844)— a position reinforced by a resolution of the New Hampshire legislature defying the "unwarrantable and dangerous assumptions of the Circuit Court."[102] Story's final blast in the judicial battle came from the Supreme Court bench in *Ex parte City Bank of New Orleans* (1845), in which the Court had been asked to oust the federal district court in favor of state bankruptcy proceedings.[103] His opinion, as he declared to his son, went to "great pains" to reassert the principles of *Ex parte Foster* and the other "New Hampshire cases which have been so stoutly contested in the State courts."[104] His reasoned justification of the Bankruptcy Act and of the authority of the federal courts to administer it was backed by the whole Court except Baldwin, but by this time the act had already been repealed. Parker in the meantime, in defiance of Story's *New Orleans* opinion, had reasserted his position on mesne process and liens. In addition, he claimed state bankruptcy authority over mortgaged property.[105] Four years later a unanimous Supreme Court upheld him on the essential point that state courts retained jurisdiction over bankruptcy suits, including attachments upon mesne process, begun before the institution of proceedings in federal courts.[106]

So much for the limitations and frustrations of circuit judging. Not only had Story made enemies in New Hampshire, but the rumor was that "he was not liked much in Providence" either.[107] Even his closest friends and most ardent admirers could occasionally turn against him. Such happened in the case of Nichols and Couch, in which Story's lenient sentence of ship's officers convicted of cruelty to seamen was condemned by Richard H. Dana, Jr. (one of Story's favorite students), in the *American Jurist* (which generally praised the judge and circulated his ideas). In the process of criticizing Story, however, Dana testified to the permeating quality of his circuit influence. "The sentence upon Nichols and Couch," wrote Dana, "is already known far and wide among the masters, mates, seamen, land lords, and shipping masters of our city, and is the common topic in cabins and forcastles."[108] The point was clear: When the judge spoke, New England listened—and most of the time gladly heeded. It was finally a matter of intrinsic authority. It helped that Story was a Supreme Court justice on circuit, that he was *the* chief representative of national sovereignty in New England. But most of what Story did in New England was not a matter of sovereignty. The rules governing commercial maritime New England that Story laid down in his court were in no simple way the doings of government, any more than they were of Story's own making. His words were accepted as law because he made inherited legal principles serve the needs of business, which he understood as an insider. Story's circuit court had become a New England institution. As Richard Henry Dana, Jr., put it, it was New England's "good fortune" to have such a man presiding over "our chief maritime court."[109] George T. Curtis put the point even more conclusively as he contemplated the day when Story would not sit on the circuit bench. "It must be long before that public confidence follows the Court again, which now rested upon all its doing, if you retire from the Bench," he wrote to Story in 1844. "The public have been so long accustomed to know that a decision of yours is *the Law*, drawn from *all* its sources and resting on its broad foundations, so many of the commercial and professional classes have grown up under your administration, that whenever you retire, it will be seriously felt."[110]

3. Uniform Commercial Law and Constitutional Union: *Swift* v. *Tyson*

Story's effort in behalf of a national bankruptcy system says much about his responsiveness to economic modernization. In championing bankruptcy he recognized that the impersonal forces of the market could erode the moral obligation to repay debts in full. What he inferentially accepted in *Tyler* v. *Wilkinson* he here conceded outright: that property rights could not always be absolutely secure in the new economic age. That recognition did not prevent him from embracing the economic revolution that was under way. What he saw—and the perception helped harmonize the radical change he embraced and the conservative principles he cherished—was the congruence between the demands of the new economic individualism and the principles and method of the old law. Indeed, the interconnectedness between law and economic growth was pervasive and dynamic. New technology, encouraged by patent law, increased production, which necessitated expanded markets. Expanded markets called

forth economic specialization, as sedentary merchants turned into specialists in wholesaling, retailing, insurance, marketing, and financing.[111]
Specialization in turn called for the refinement and extension of old principles: thus, for example, Story's decisions in marine insurance; his effort
in his treatises on commercial law to make principles of contract law follow
business operations increasingly done indirectly at a distance by agents
through commercial paper; and his opinions in *Dartmouth College* and the
Bridge case, which applied private contract law to corporate charters. Corporations, created by the law, in turn permitted venturesome capitalists to
raise money enough to activate new technology to take advantage of new
interstate markets made possible by new transportation technology. Insurance companies encouraged such large-scale ventures, and a national
bankruptcy system, if it could be devised, would encourage to try again
those who had once tried and failed.

Private law and national capitalism, themselves interwoven, were also
connected with public law and constitutional politics. From the Revolution on, national government and national capitalism went hand in hand.
Those classes who did business on an interstate basis—whether they were
land speculators, bankers, manufacturers, or shippers—were the most vigorous champions of national government. And the more business was conducted across state lines in the nineteenth century, the more it confronted
the disabilities of the federal system and what, to the expansive energies of
commerce, appeared to be the artificiality of state boundaries. Commercial
law operating uniformly throughout the nation became the rallying cry
of pre–Civil War capitalists whose operations depended on the interstate
exchange of goods and credit. And what their self-interest required became, in the anthropomorphized cultural propaganda of the age, the sine
qua non of everything good and beautiful. As preached by the champions
of business, commerce brought wealth, leisure, education, art, refinement,
morals—civilization. Commerce also strengthened national union, harmonizing individualism and community as republican culture required.
"Trade is in its nature consolidating," reasoned the *Merchants' Magazine*
on this point, "because it will not recognize arbitrary geographical lines; it
is creative of such strong common interests, wherever it once connects
people in relations with one another, that local jealousies, and all narrow
notions of exclusive independence, vanish before it."[112]

Story was the great champion of uniform commercial law and all that
went with it. The necessity of uniform law was a lesson taught him
by New England capitalists; uniformity was the essence of legal science:
principle and practice merged. And by facilitating uniform commercial
law Story could not only serve his section but consolidate the Union
along commercial lines—the goal of Massachusetts conservatives since the
1820s. As a Supreme Court justice he was ideally placed to put his ideas

into practice. Indeed, of all the branches of government, the federal courts were best equipped to facilitate commercial rules that transcended state boundaries.[113] Part of this leverage came in public law, in construing the Constitution so as to limit state interruption of interstate business.[114] The authority of the federal courts to shape uniform private law was equally to the point. When the framers gave the federal judiciary jurisdiction over suits between citizens of different states, they made the federal courts the primary forum for the settlement of interstate disputes, almost all of which had to do with economic transactions. State judiciaries had concurrent jurisdiction over most such matters, but capitalists seeking to avoid the bias of local judges and juries obviously preferred federal courts as the most likely neutral forum. The crucial question was what law would be administered in that forum. Section 34 of the Judiciary Act of 1789 addressed the question when it provided "that the laws of the several states, except where the constitution, treaties or statutes of the United States shall otherwise require or provide, shall be regarded as rules of decision in trials of common law in the courts of the United States in cases where they apply."[115] But in what diversity cases did state "laws" control federal courts, or more precisely, in what ones did they not? Section 34 did not say for sure.

This brings us to Justice Story and the remarkable case of *Swift* v. *Tyson* (1842). In a brief opinion for a unanimous Court, Story distinguished between "state laws strictly local" and "general commercial law." The former consisted of "rights and titles to things having a permanent locality" (mainly real estate) and was evinced by state statutes and judicial constructions thereof. In these local matters federal courts were bound by state laws when trying diversity cases. But on questions of "general commercial law," that law "not at all dependent upon local statutes or local usages of a fixed and permanent operation," the Court was free to make up its own mind.[116] Clear enough it would appear, and apparently uncontroversial as well. On the construction of section 34, there was no disagreement among justices who frequently and bitterly divided on other matters. The decision was barely noticed by contemporary newspapers and periodicals,[117] and there was nothing in Story's own correspondence to suggest that his opinion was exceptional.

In fact, *Swift* was one of Story's most influential decisions and by all counts his most controversial. Opposition to the *Swift* doctrine, led by Justice Stephen Field, began on the Court itself and gathered momentum from the 1890s down to 1938, when Story's decision was abruptly overturned by Justice Louis Brandeis in *Erie Railroad Co.* v. *Tompkins*.[118] Law professors and legal scholars joined the debate, too, and still continue to argue.[119] About the only point of agreement among the disputants is that Story's reading of section 34 proved to be the staging ground for a massive assertion of federal judicial authority. Federal judges began to implement *Swift* immediately, with the general approval of state courts and legal commentators. But the major breakthrough came after the Civil War when the Supreme Court expanded the category of general commercial law created by *Swift* to include municipal bonds and torts. In the process, the distinction Story drew between general and local law was blurred, so that further intrusions of federal judge-made law were invited into areas once reserved to the states. Rather than creating a uniform body of commercial law, *Swift* had by the turn of the century given rise to two bodies of law, one federal and one state, with the latter varying from jurisdiction to jurisdiction.[120] The resulting choice of forum naturally drew into the federal courts those parties, many of whom were corporations, who wanted to escape state regulations and the limitations of local law. Story's opinion, which originated in the desire to establish a body of uniform commercial law beyond the reach of politics, had produced legal confusion, pitted state judiciaries against federal courts, and put the Supreme Court itself on the political firing line. That *Swift* should have been repudiated by Brandeis during the anti-Court heyday of the New Deal seems entirely appropriate, especially because the job of establishing uniform commercial law had again been taken up by codifiers, this time operating in the National Conference of Commissioners on Uniform State Laws and working through state legislatures.

Brandeis's opinion in *Erie* not only held *Swift* to be "unconstitutional" but repudiated the entire legal world from which Story had fashioned his opinion and, indeed, Story himself. Story's authority had been used to advance the *Swift* doctrine, and it was probably inevitable that critics of *Swift* should also criticize its author. Story did have his defenders on and off the Court, but the naysayers carried the day and the picture they painted of Story was increasingly unfavorable. Field's dissent in the railroad tort case of *Baltimore & Ohio Railroad* v. *Baugh* (1893) set the tone with a lingering wisp of Jacksonian malice. Not only was *Swift* a cover for judicial lawmaking, Field argued, it was plainly unconstitutional, despite "the great names which may be cited in favor of the doctrine"—that is to say, Story.[121] That Holmes was also critical was not surprising, given his growing impatience with judge-made law justified by theories of mechanical jurisprudence. Holmes did not repudiate *Swift* from the bench but privately condemned it as "pure usurpation grounded on a subtle fallacy." That fallacy was Story's notion that there was such a thing as a "general law," which Holmes mockingly depicted as "a brooding omnipresence in the sky."[122]

Holmes seems to have inspired the faculty at Harvard Law School and Harvard-trained legal scholars to turn on the founder. Among the Harvard men who found Story's *Swift* doctrine wanting were, in addition to

Holmes, John Chipman Gray, Joseph Henry Beale, Louis Brandeis, Felix Frankfurter, and Charles Warren. Warren did not accuse Story of being an ideologue sunk in false notions of legal metaphysics, the gravamen of criticism from legal positivists like Holmes, but he did call forth historical evidence purporting to prove that Story's construction of section 34 ran counter to the intentions of those who framed it.[123] The stage was set for Brandeis's repudiation of *Swift* as "unconstitutional" and his sweeping assumption that the "general commercial law" to which Story referred was mainly a creation of the judge's own mind. John Chipman Gray had in fact already made the point in 1909, with applause from Holmes.[124] "Among the causes which led to the decision in *Swift* v. *Tyson*," wrote Gray in his *Nature and Sources of the Law* (1909), "the chief seems to have been the character and position of Judge Story. He was then by far the oldest judge in commission on the bench; he was a man of great learning, and of a reputation for learning greater even than the learning itself; he was occupied at the time in writing a book on bills of exchange, which would, of itself, lead him to dogmatize on the subject; he had had great success in extending the jurisdiction of the Admiralty; he was fond of glittering generalities; and he was possessed by a restless vanity. All these things conspired to produce the result."[125]

Like other statesmen, judges cannot escape being judged by what they have wrought, but Gray not only presumed to judge but to explain. Explanations must be rooted in the history of the time, and Gray's was not; nor, would it appear, were those of Holmes and Brandeis. Viewed by what *preceded* it rather than what followed it, *Swift* appears quite *un*revolutionary. Such certainly is the inference to be drawn from the Court's unanimity on section 34. If Story's opinion did unconstitutionally invade the territory of state courts, surely states' rights radicals on the Court like Daniel would have protested; surely Baldwin, who distrusted Story and who had already attacked him for his consolidating doctrines, would have objected.[126] Story's authority on the Court, moreover, contrary to Gray's assertion, was not unassailable; indeed, his defeat in the reporter crisis occurred less than a year after his opinion on *Swift*. Other evidence also points to the nonusurpatory nature of the opinion: the silence of contemporary newspapers and periodicals and the ready acceptance of the opinion by state judges (some of whom were, as in the bankruptcy litigation, already vigorously challenging Story's authority). Especially telling was the noisy silence of New York state lawyers and judges. It is significant, too, that William Story, whose habit in his *Life and Letters* was to call attention to his father's memorable decisions, did not mention Swift as a breakthrough opinion. Neither, so far as can be ascertained, did Story himself.

The evidence strongly indicates, then, that *Swift* was generally compatible with the prevailing assumptions of law at the time it was given.

Indeed, this is precisely what makes the opinion so important for understanding Story. His opinion in *Swift* spoke for and to the age. To appreciate the point more fully we must divert at least briefly to the unusual (or perhaps not so unusual) commercial practices of two audacious plungers in Maine lands: Jarius Keith and Nathaniel Norton.

Keith and Norton wanted a tract of Maine land that English speculators put up for sale, but they had no ready cash. To circumvent that problem they agreed to sell what they did not yet own to a group of New York investors, using the money they got to finalize the purchase. In the course of this high-flying operation, they had occasion in 1836 to draw up a bill of exchange for $1,862.06, which was accepted in New York by George Tyson as payment for a second installment on the purchase of the Maine land. Keith and Norton endorsed this bill to Joseph Swift as payment for an antecedent debt. The Panic of 1837 brought down Keith's and Norton's house of paper and they went into bankruptcy. Tyson discovered that they did not own the land which they sold him and in payment for which he had accepted their bill of exchange. When Swift presented the bill to him, he refused payment, assuming not unrealistically that because Swift had done business with Keith and Norton, he was in fraudulent collusion with them. And the fact was that if Keith and Norton had presented the bill directly to Tyson, he could have used fraud as his defense for nonpayment. The question on the merits that ultimately confronted Story in *Swift* was whether that defense was also good against Swift.

The substantive issue in *Swift*, then, was not section 34 but the negotiability of bills of exchange.[127] Few issues were more central to the operations of American businessmen. Bills of exchange, historically, were created by merchants themselves as a means of facilitating commercial interchange in the face of specie shortage and government instability. A note drawn by one party and accepted by another, specifying an amount of money to be paid at a certain day, was in the hands of the drawer as good as specie—provided faith in the bill could be maintained as it circulated from party to party. This quality of negotiability depended on the perpetuation of an undiminished obligation to make good on the bill. Bills of exchange were, as Swift's lawyer emphasized in his argument before the Court, the major source of mercantile credit. They could be bought and sold and quite early in American history were treated as commodities themselves. And because they could be discounted by banks they were a crucial source of short-term business credit.[128] Their utility depended, however, on full negotiability, and this was the specific issue in *Swift*. If each bill carried with it the equities of the original parties, if payment could be defeated by circumstances that remote acceptors of the bill had no way of apprehending, then the faith necessary for full negotiability would be seriously diminished.

Except for a fluke in state decisional law the question of negotiability in *Swift* would not have presented an unusual or difficult problem. The tendency of commercial law in both England and America, following the needs of business, had been to maximize negotiability. Mansfield, who led the way, had ruled that bills of exchange accepted as payment for prior debts were bills in due course: that is to say, bills not encumbered by the equities that existed between the original parties. Not all state judges agreed, as was to be expected, given their vast disparity in experience and learning as well as the varying strength of commercial interests in their states.[129] Among the judges who did agree was Kent of New York. The problem was, however, that his decision in *Bay* v. *Coddington* (1821) gave the impression that bills taken in payment for antecedent debts under certain circumstances were not bills in due course and thus carried with them the equities existing between the original parties. There were no New York statutes on the subject, and subsequent *lower* state courts in New York picked up on the perceived exception in Kent's *Coddington* opinion.[130] Story took notice of the slippage but emphasized that the most current New York appellate decisions were returning to the correct, that is, the Mansfieldian, meaning of *Coddington*. But contrary precedents, even if not conclusive ones, could now be cited by Tyson's lawyers to bolster their client's defense for nonpayment, provided it could be established that the decision in the circuit court and before the Supreme Court was controlled by New York decisional law via section 34.

To reach the question of negotiability, Story first had to rule on the meaning of that section: whether and to what extent the Court was obliged to follow "the decisions of local tribunals" in diversity cases.[131] It was here, as we have seen, that Story distinguished between laws "strictly local," which the Court was bound to follow, and "general commercial law," where the Court could follow its own reasoning. The question is whether that holding was usurpation prompted by the "restless vanity" of the judge. External evidence, as already noted, points to the fact that Story's opinion was not revolutionary. So does the opinion itself when placed in historical context.[132] Story specifically addressed the question of usurpation in *Swift* when he declared his construction of section 34 consistent with "all the various cases, which have hitherto come before us for decision." Such a statement is striking in that, if it were untrue, it would certainly have drawn fire from states' rights dissenters. In fact, the division between local and general law as Story defined it in *Swift* was the product of a half century of judicial practice.[133] Story had also been entirely consistent in the matter; indeed, in one of his first important circuit opinions, *Van Reimsdyk* v. *Kane* (1812), he refused to be bound by a Rhode Island bankruptcy statute and turned instead to principles of general commercial law and conflict theory.[134] General commercial law was again held by

Story to be within the province of the federal courts in diversity cases in *Le Roy* v. *Crowninshield* (1820), this time in the area of commercial contracts.[135] Both *Van Reimsdyk* and *Le Roy* were cited approvingly in numerous cases, not only by federal courts but by state courts as well.

That state courts should have generally approved of Story's and the Supreme Court's reasoning on section 34 is worth noting. State judges may not always have agreed with Story or with other federal judges when they decided diversity cases by principles of conflict and general commercial law. But they did not deny that there were general principles of commercial law to be ascertained by consulting English and American cases and appropriate legal treatises. This approach was relevant to *Swift* as well, as Story took pains to make clear: The lower state courts whose decisions Tyson's lawyers relied on did not presume to be interpreting state law but argued (in Story's words) from "the general principles of commercial law," reasoning "as ourselves"—that is to say, as common lawyers. Story never ruled that they could not do so. New York judges were free to pursue their own reasoning about the principles of general commercial law, and the Supreme Court would attend to their arguments. On the other hand, the Court would not be bound in diversity cases by what state judges said about general commercial law.[136] To have been so bound in *Swift*, indeed, would have meant that decisions made at the nonappellate level of the state judiciary would have governed in mercantile transactions between New Yorkers and out-of-staters. The main point here is—and it undercuts the jurisprudential grounds on which Holmes criticized and Brandeis repudiated *Swift*—that both state and federal judges agreed on the existence of a general commercial law ascertainable by judicial analysis.[137] In this matter *Swift* rested on widely accepted jurisprudential assumptions of the age.

This is not to suggest that the intellectual life of antebellum law was perfectly placid or, for that matter, that *Swift* meshed perfectly into Story's own system. On the most practical, nonjurisprudential level, for example, one notes the tension between Story's constant rhetoric about the morality of the common law and the type of financial shenanigans that law sanctioned in *Swift* (though in fairness to Story, he never said that every contract was ethical). There was also a tension between the declaratory view of law in *Swift* (that judges discovered law but did not make it) and the embryonic legal realism of the age (that judges do make law and policy, too—and here one has only to listen to the charges of the Jeffersonians against the Marshall Court). As Professor Horwitz notes, Story's own theory of conflict conceded that law was rooted in the will of the sovereign.[138] A first impression of *Swift*, indeed, suggests that the judge-made general law that Story called forth there was at odds with the positive law sanctioned by a sovereign state. If there was a contradiction between Story in *Swift* and Story in *Conflict of Laws*, however, he did not have to resolve it.

The crucial point is that the Court's authority in *Swift* was made to rest not on general (that is, judge-made) law but on a congressional statute (section 34) passed to clarify rules of decision in cases of diversity jurisdiction as granted to the federal courts by article III of the Constitution. Conflict principles operated under the authority of positive law. This was not a limitation of importance in Europe, where conflict theory originated because there was no supra-state authority, but it was crucial to the United States, where the Constitution and federal statutes were supreme. Thus Congress *might* have acted under the full faith and credit clause of article IV, section 1, to create national rules of comity. What Story argued was that Congress *had* in fact acted in section 34 and that it intended that federal courts should apply the general commercial law in diversity cases.

Swift did not, then, set forth a theory of judge-made law in opposition to the laws of the sovereign states. Like the federal criminal common law in *Hudson*, the commercial common law in *Swift* rested on a positive law foundation. Moreover, the judge-made law that Story did refer to in *Swift* was obviously not the common law in toto but only general commercial law, which by the facts of the case was restricted further to the principles of contract governing commercial paper, and these only as they were applicable in diversity cases. What Story did, to put it another way, was to recognize that American federalism made two legal forums available to citizens who did business across state lines, one state and the other federal. By distinguishing between local and general law, Story attempted to clarify which law would apply to each.[139] If his decision benefited certain commercial classes—and there can be no doubt that it did—it was not because he perverted the intention of the framers in the matter of diversity jurisdiction but rather because he followed out their pre-commercial bias so relentlessly.

Story did in *Swift* in this respect, then, what he had been doing on circuit: He gave interstate merchants consistent economic rules that suited their own interests and that they had in part created. He ruled that a bill of exchange taken for a previous debt was a bill in due course that did not carry with it the equities belonging to the original parties. Such a holding, declared Story, "is for the benefit and convenience of the commercial world to give as wide an extent as practicable to the credit and circulation of negotiable paper. . . ." Not so to rule—which alternative Story considered—would have seriously devalued all bills of exchange in circulation that had been taken for antecedent debts and would have destroyed much of the banking credit as well, because "more than one half of all bank transactions in our country, as well as those of other countries, are of this nature."[140] Andrew Jackson pulled down a large part of the national credit structure when he destroyed the Second Bank; Story was not about to demolish what was left. It boiled down to the fact that plungers and kiters like Keith and Norton had to get more than they deserved so that honest businessmen like Amos Lawrence could get what they needed. As for people like George Tyson: next time they would know better the risk they were taking.

To show that *Swift* was grounded on statutory authority and rooted in the economic realities of antebellum America works to disprove the charge of aggrandizement that has been brought against Story. Certainly his opinion had little to do with judicial metaphysics. There still remains the possibility, however, that even if the general commercial law in *Swift* was not a "brooding omnipresence in the sky" it was an open-ended concept that invited federal judges to encroach on state common law in pursuit of what they thought was sound economic policy. The charge takes us back to a close reading of Story's opinion, to bills of exchange, to an age when legal science was not merely a "glittering generality." A careful reading of *Swift* reveals that Story's reference to "general commercial law" was made specifically in regard to contract principles governing commercial paper: to the "construction of ordinary contracts" and "other instruments of a commercial nature."[141] Contract law as applied to commercial paper was no small matter, certainly, but it was in the legal lexicon of Story's day well defined. Even Holmes conceded that had "Bradley, Harlan, et al." stuck to the matter "dealt with" by Story, "no great harm" would have resulted.[142] If there was no harm, there was no blank check: no blank check because the general principles governing commercial contracts were well settled.

In fact, Story cited two precedents by the Supreme Court itself to support his ruling on the negotiability of bills taken for antecedent debts: *Coolidge et al.* v. *Payson* (1817) and *Townsley* v. *Sumrall* (1829).[143] When he spoke in *Swift* of the principle being "so long and so well established, that it is laid up among the fundamentals of the law, and requires no authority or reasoning to be now brought in its support,"[144] he stood on solid ground. Kent made exactly the same point, and Story quoted him approvingly in his *Commentaries on Promissory Notes*: "'The law concerning negotiable paper, has at length become a science, which can be studied with infinite advantage in various codes, treatises, and judicial decisions; for, in them, every possible view of the doctrine, in all its branches, has been considered, its rules established, and its limitations accurately defined.'"[145] Story studied these codes, treatises, and judicial decisions in his commentaries on commercial law; indeed, he chose to write on that subject for the very reason that had caused him to single it out earlier for codification: Of all the areas of the law it was the most settled. Gray might look on Story's research as a source of vanity; Kent more correctly saw it as the accepted mode of legal reasoning in the antebellum period. Only by the positivist legal standards of a later period did legal principles derived from the common-law process brood in the sky.

The point is not to say that Story's opinion in *Swift* was passive or unimportant but rather to insist that he spoke in the legal idiom of his age. He spoke, moreover, at a rare moment of stasis in the relationship between law and economic history. The economic changes of the nineteenth century had vitalized the inherited legal world of the eighteenth without having yet overwhelmed it. The corporation had come into its own, but corporate monopoly had not yet made a mockery of economic individualism. Manufacturing had moved to the cutting edge of economic change, but the values and practices of an older commercial age were still in place, despite the rumblings of dissonance. The law of commercial contracts shaped in this earlier age of the common law was still relevant and meaningful. The common law as a system of judicial economic rule making was still a pervasive fact of life.

Swift did not create this world, but reflected it, which is to say that Story's opinion was more normative in character than radical. Story did in *Swift* what he had been doing all along, what he did incomparably well, and what the age accepted as legitimate. What happened to *Swift* after the Civil War happened not because Story had unconstitutionally aggrandized federal judicial authority in 1842 but because the economic world that Story's law presumed to direct exploded beyond the capacity of judges to master it. That they attempted to do so cannot be blamed on Story's vanity, even though his name was called on for authority. If there was vanity involved, it was the vanity of the common law itself. Story never backed off from the power that the common law gave to judges to shape social policy, and here *Swift* is of a piece with *Hudson, Martin*, and *De Lovio*. *Swift* also resembles those opinions in that the common-law authority claimed is not without limit. Had later judges attended more carefully to the limits Story imposed in *Swift*, they might not have leaped so boldly from bills of exchange to torts and beyond. Had Story lived, perhaps he would have made the limitations of that opinion clear. The real arrogance in that opinion, what invited aggression, to put it another way, may have been that Story assumed that common-law policy making would remain in the hands of judicial scholar-statesmen like himself—shades of the *Charles River Bridge* case. As it was, he was so closely intertwined with the opinion in *Swift* that to repudiate it was to repudiate him. Post–Civil War legal positivists and legal realists could not break the hold of the common law on the American legal mind without challenging its great champion, and this point may explain the outbreak of totemic cannibalism at Harvard Law School.

Story would have been hurt by the attack, no doubt, but he would not have been surprised at the assault on the common law. He had felt for a long time that it was besieged, from without by legislative government and political parties and from within by unscientific judges. Certainly he was acutely aware that the word of judges was no longer automatically accepted as the word of law. Indeed, at the very moment he reasserted the claim of judicial preeminence in commercial law, he saw judicial authority challenged in constitutional law. The issue was slavery, and the challengers were the abolitionists. In slavery litigation, the politicization of the judicial process would be most manifest: in *Groves* v. *Slaughter* (1841), *U.S.* v. *Amistad* (1841), and *Prigg* v. *Pennsylvania* (1842). Compared to those cases, *Swift* must have appeared to Story as an oasis of legal science.

Swift was also a timely blow for national union made in the spirit of the old Federalists and of the Constitution itself. National commerce unleashed by uniform commercial law, it was assumed, would strengthen the fabric of national union. Working for national commerce and national union outside the structure of sovereign states and beyond the selfishness of party, Story saw a phalanx of lawyers, judges, and businessmen of vision and energy. In *Swift*, individualism and community, the common law and the Constitution, were mutually supportive, just as republican theory said they should be.

Chapter 10

The Crisis of Conservative Constitutionalism

The national constitution is our last and our only security. United we stand, divided we fall. . . . The structure had been erected by architects of consummate skill and fidelity; its foundations are solid; its compartments are beautiful as well as useful; its arrangements are full of wisdom and order; and its defences are impregnable from without. It has been reared for immortality, if the work of man may justly aspire to such a title. It may, nevertheless, perish in an hour by the folly or corruption or negligence of its only keepers,— THE PEOPLE.
    Story, *Commentaries on the Constitution*

And finally what is that course, reckless & rampant spirit of abolitionism *to come to or to accomplish? It will soon have* you *in its maw (& begins already to nibble at you) for your Pens^a. & Maryland opinion, but it can't get at you to swallow you alive, & so you will escape the Whale's belly at present.*
    Ezekiel Bacon to Story, 8 May 1842

In great opinions like *Swift*, in his commentaries on American law, through his teaching at Harvard Law School, on circuit in New England, Story worked to unite the nation in the image of New England. It is ironic if not contradictory that he should have drawn back finally from the completion of the task, leaving it to the abolitionists to capture the high ground of anti-Southernism that he once held and to unleash forces that would finally impose the Northern cultural values he cherished on the entire nation. Temporarily, at least, Story found himself on the losing side of American history. The issue was slavery, or rather, abolition, or both. Together they challenged Story's constitutional system and the theory of conservative control that went with it. He did not live long enough to see the worst, but the damage wrought during his last years was immense and pervasive. The problem was that the Constitution that Story celebrated as the bulwark of republican liberty also legitimated human slavery. Once legalized it would not stay on the state level where the framers put it and Story hoped to keep it. Not only did slavery expand territorially and numerically, but in unexpected ways it insinuated itself into the fabric of national life, including the constitutional process itself. Slavery was behind the resurgence of radical states' rights in the 1820s; it was the hidden reason for Southern opposition to the nationalism of the Marshall Court. More than anything else it explained the doctrinal and constitutional fragmentation of the Supreme Court itself, which began in the last years of Marshall and accelerated under Taney until it climaxed in *Dred Scott*.

Finally, it was slavery that raised most pointedly the question of "THE PEOPLE" and their constitution. Statesmen of "consummate skill and fidelity" made the Constitution, as Story put it, but the people were its "only keepers."[1] Slavery called them into action. When Calhoun challenged the constitutional guardianship of the Supreme Court, he did so in the name of the people of the sovereign states who would speak their constitutional piece in state conventions. No less a radical challenge to the judge's Constitution came from the abolitionists, who demanded that the people claim *their* Constitution for freedom.

Story was caught between the extremes. He answered the states' rights challenge in the name of the founders, with the promise of objective judicial construction of a Constitution that protected slavery. But what could he say to quiet the challenge from abolitionists who took the Constitution seriously but interpreted it to mean freedom for all people? Irony confounded his reply. Story was prominent among those conservatives who called New England antislavery morality into being in the 1820s and who warned against Southern expansionism. The Constitution that he expounded in his *Commentaries* of 1833 was meant to arm New England against Southern doctrine. Now a determined, vocal, and growing movement in his own section—indeed, among his own students—challenged not only his interpretation but his authority. Story died before the full force of that challenge was felt, but he lived long enough to respond. At issue was the Union he worked to preserve, the moral structure of constitutional law to which he dedicated his life, and, indeed, the American Revolution as he presumed to understand it.

1. Whose Constitution Is It?
Justice Story versus the Abolitionists

Less than a year after the *Bridge* decision, an article appeared in William Lloyd Garrison's *Liberator* concerning Story's charge to the circuit grand jury in Boston on Friday, 19 October 1838. Story had condemned the slave trade in sweeping terms and praised the "glory and honor of this country, that she was the first among nations to aim at the suppression of this nefarious commerce. . . ." Essentially this was the charge given in 1819 and 1820, which made Story into something of a New England moral hero. The reporter for the *Liberator* was not similarly impressed.

"We could not but marvel," he commented bitterly, "that the cheeks of the Judge were not instantly suffused with crimson blushes of shame, at the utterance of such an idle and false panegyric. We were amazed, that a man so intelligent, so familiar with the facts of our national history, as himself—in full view of the present enslavement of one-sixth portion of all the inhabitants of the land—should venture to boast of what this country had done to abolish the African slave trade." The Constitution that Story celebrated as the foundation of rational liberty this abolitionist found to be a "wicked, fearful, bloody" bargain with slavery that no body of men, however wise and skillful, were competent to make. Their bargain with slavery "was null and void before God from the time it was made, and for the fulfillment of which this nation deserved, instead of a fulsome puff, the direst retribution of offended Heaven." So much for the opinion of the nation's leading constitutional scholar: "Shame and infamy! O, Judge S. thou art a bad STORY-teller!"[2]

To malign Judge Story in Boston was truly to beard the lion in his den. He was a New England institution. On circuit his word was literally law. He was indispensable to the business community. Many of the bar were his former students at the Law School, and most of them were friends and supporters. Not only was he a giant in the law, but he was a decent, moral man. And more to the point, he had spoken out consistently on and off the bench against slavery and the slave trade. His antislavery record is worth looking at because it was the other side of the proslavery Constitution which he expounded in the name of objective jurisprudence and for which he drew abolitionist fire.

Story's legal position and judicial strategy concerning slavery and antislavery, like much else in his constitutional jurisprudence, took shape in the 1820s—that is to say, before abolitionism upped the ante on proslave constitutionalism. Story could recognize the framers' concessions to slavery and still praise their work mainly because Congress, not the Court, bore the burden of maintaining the constitutional compromise. Indeed, the early Court dealt only indirectly with slavery. It is sobering to see John Marshall troubling over the common-law doctrine of hearsay evidence— for example, in *Queen* v. *Hepburn*—when a man's freedom is at stake.[3] But few questioned the morality of doing so, and when they did the answer was that the Court was only abiding by the basic constitutional principle governing slavery: that it was strictly a matter of municipal—that is to say, state—law.[4] Story no less than the other judges was sanitized by this principle; for example, in the admiralty case of *Emerson* v. *Howland*, where an owner sued to recover wages earned by a slave whom he had hired out, Story merely recognized the controlling force of Virginia law: "The owner of the slave has the most complete and perfect property in him. The slave may be sold or devised, or may pass by descent, in the same manner as other inheritable estate. He has no civil rights or privileges. He is incapable of making or discharging a contract; and the perpetual right to his services belongs exclusively to his owner."[5]

There is no evidence that Story cringed when he intoned the grim realities of Virginia's slave code. Any guilt, moreover, might well have been assuaged by his willingness to enlarge the area of freedom where the law allowed judicial discretion. The international slave trade was one such area. Story's passionate condemnation of the trade in his circuit charges, which the *Liberator* dismissed so abruptly in 1838, was in fact reflected in his decisions on both the circuit and the Supreme Court level. Story's strong antislavery feelings could be seen in his disposition of matters of evidence and proof, questions that allowed him judicial discretion and that abounded in slave-trade litigation.[6] Nowhere was he more expansive on those matters than in the circuit case of *U.S.* v. *La Jeune Eugenie* (1822).[7] That case also afforded him the rare opportunity to address the substantive issue of the slave trade itself, which opportunity he used with revealing dexterity.

The *Eugenie* originated in the act of 2 March 1807 outlawing the slave trade and authorizing the president to station American public ships along the African coast with orders to seize American vessels engaged in that trade after 1 June 1808. *La Jeune Eugenie* was captured by an American cruiser on suspicion of being an American slaver and libeled for violating the interdict of 1807 as well as "the general law of nations." The French claimant pleaded that *La Jeune Eugenie* was a French vessel which American ships could not stop and over which an American court of law possessed no jurisdiction, a claim pressed through diplomatic channels by the French government. Not to be deterred, Story promised to adhere "fearlessly and faithfully" to the law without seeking shelter "under the wings of executive authority."[8]

Story was boldly creative, or so at least it appeared. He did not rule on slavery itself and was not "permitted to deny" its legality because it was municipal law and part of the "domestic policy" of individual nations. But the slave trade was another matter. Story traced its origin and progress, and detailed its characteristic brutalities in graphic and passionate language. Such a trade, he concluded in a sweeping and much-quoted peroration, "is repugnant to the great principles of Christian duty, the dictates of natural religion, the obligations of good faith and morality, and the eternal maxims of social justice." It was impossible that the slave trade with all its inhumanity "can be consistent with any system of law, that purports to rest on the authority of reason or revelation. And it is sufficient to stamp any trade as interdicted by public law, where it can be justly affirmed, that it is repugnant to the general principles of justice and humanity."[9]

They were moving words, but what did they signify? At the very least they revealed Story's deep abhorrence of the slave trade and slavery. There is no doubt, either, that his opinion, like his charges to the grand jury, carried great authority in New England, where it was widely circulated. That such sentiments should emanate from the New England circuit spoke well of the strength of conservative propaganda in the 1820s. But did the opinion really count for much? Perhaps it was more rhetoric than substance, and this was the point indirectly made later by the *Liberator*. Possibly the *Eugenie* opinion had more to do with ideology than with law. Such, in fact, was the implication of the Supreme Court's decision in *The Antelope* (1825), which abruptly overruled Story. Marshall's opinion was simple and to the point: The slave trade was not contrary to international law because nations had not acted collectively to outlaw it.[10] Story entered no dissent.

Concerning the charge of puffery and the implications of irrelevance, several points need to be made. The first is that Story's opinion in *Eugenie* was not simply a judicial ukase equating international law with natural law. The case grew out of circuit responsibilities for the enforcement of laws against slave trading and called forth a considered statement of the law of evidence in such cases, a position consistent with other of Story's decisions and one that in this respect was not overruled by *The Antelope*. The initial question in *Eugenie* was whether it was legally American or French. It was flying French colors at the time of its seizure and subsequently proved to be carrying French papers; Story admitted that it seemed "documented as a French vessel," at least enough so to suffice "in ordinary times, under ordinary circumstances." But times and circumstances were not ordinary. Ten years of adjudicating trading-with-the-enemy cases had alerted him to the technique of "disguises and fraud," which he recognized as common to the slave trade as well. It is too much, he said, echoing not only the spirit but the words of *Bothnea and Jahnstoff*, "to ask a court of justice to shut its eyes against what is passing in the world, and to affect an ignorance, of what every man knows. . . ." What Story saw was that the vessel was American-built and had been divested of American title and naturalized by the French marine only two years before its capture. Such camouflage, said Story, could "be cheaply bought"; he was prompted to rule that "affirmative evidence" (at the very least a bill of sale) was necessary to prove that "the case had no admixture of American interests."[11]

Story not only modified the presumption of innocence in slave-trading cases but worked to modify maritime tort law regarding the right of search and seizure in order to procure convictions. The right of visitation and search on the high seas was the most effective way of penetrating the fraud of slavers sailing under false colors with fabricated papers. Story admitted that the right of visitation and search "can be exercised only in time of war, in virtue of a belligerent claim," but he insisted, following the tradition of prize law, that the right of visitation on the high seas existed independently of the right of search and seizure. He applied that right to the slave trade and went further to hold that such visitation, even if followed by seizure and even if finally unjustified, would not be tortious if the action were taken in good faith and under good presumption of guilt.[12]

Story's strictures on evidence and marine tort law make it clear that the *Eugenie* opinion, whatever else it might be, was a part of an ongoing effort on the first circuit to enforce the statutes against foreign slave trading. His principles would not perhaps have closed all the gaps in the enforcement of the law, but they certainly would have narrowed them—a point that is especially clear when Story's circuit decisions are compared to those of district judge Samuel Betts and Justice Samuel Nelson on the second circuit, where judicial laxness made the port of New York a haven for slave traders.[13]

If Story's ruling on evidence in *Eugenie* deserves to be taken seriously, so also does his position on natural law and universal morality. In isolation his statement seems moralistic if not moralizing, especially when contrasted with Marshall's hardheaded positivism in *The Antelope*. But the differences between the two men, as Robert Cover has suggested, were not that great.[14] Reading Story's sonorous statement on the immorality of the slave trade in the context of his scholarly argument reveals that the debate was less a confrontation between natural-law morality on the one hand and legal positivism on the other than an argument over the meaning and sources of positive law. Marshall emphasized the necessity of formal collective action. Story reasoned pragmatically from "sound sense and general policy," as he put it. The law of nations, he contended, "does not rest upon mere theory, but may be considered as modified by practice, or ascertained by the treaties of nations at different periods." Citing principles of neutrality law and the law of belligerents, Story also argued that universal agreement among nations was not requisite for the creation of a judicially enforceable rule. Legal doctrines, moreover, could be admitted even if they had not "received any public or general sanction."[15]

It might appear that Story was paving the way for a judicial lecture on morality. In fact, he was preparing to argue that the content of international law might be reasonably derived from the actual political and legal behavior of individual nations. Reasoning from national interdictions of the foreign slave trade (which included those of France, the United States, and Great Britain) and from the collective positions taken at Vienna, Aix-la-Chapelle, and London, Story concluded that the sense of Europe was against the legality of the trade. The United States had already made it piracy in May 1820 and was in the midst of negotiations with England aimed at giving the piracy principle international standing.[16] There was, as Marshall was to argue in *The Antelope*, no formal instrument of international law banning the slave trade. But "the traffic is vindicated by no nation, and is admitted by almost all commercial nations as incurably unjust and inhuman." Reasoning from widespread municipal action against the slave trade and the growing collective opposition to it, Story went on to consult the universal morality of natural law. But that law rested on a firm foundation of positive law and history. It was a position, he declared, that was "neither novel or alarming."[17] One is strongly tempted to agree.

Story, at any rate, never changed his mind on the correctness of his *Eugenie* doctrine, Marshall and *The Antelope* notwithstanding. He had a point here, too, though losers in law rarely get a hearing in history. Both decisions rested on the assumption that there was no positive international law governing the slave trade. Marshall's decision was therefore no less an instance of judicial lawmaking than was Story's, and perhaps was even more so. Story's, at least, was grounded firmly in positive law and history. Perhaps, too, Marshall's opinion was more politically motivated, for the fact is that his formal approach in *The Antelope* permitted him to circumvent a politically controversial decision. Here as elsewhere in the 1820s, the chief justice had an aversion to brick walls. Story, on the other hand, remained true to his no-retreat, no-compromise theory of adjudication. Clearly he agreed with Webster that "*there will be no avoiding the main question in the Young Eugenie*," even if it meant parting company with such authorities as John Marshall and Lord Stowell.[18]

Story's opinion was consistent in ways other than its no-compromise stance. In matters of evidence and proof, *Eugenie* paralleled other decisions on circuit and on the Supreme Court; and all were comparable and generally derivative from his experience with the trading-with-the-enemy cases that grew out of the War of 1812. *Eugenie* was typically heuristic, too. Like his circuit charges, it aimed at educating New England to its own best values. There can be little doubt, either, as Robert Cover has observed, that he hoped to shape the course of congressional debate on the international status of the slave trade, which bore on the negotiations between the United States and England on that issue.[19] His opinion also provided a backup position should such negotiations fail, provided, of course, that he could carry the Supreme Court, as he most assuredly set out to do. Story's position on the slave trade was also consistent with—indeed, inseparable from—his political opposition to the extension of slavery. In this as in other aspects of the law of slavery he followed the intentions, or rather, the hopes, of the framers, who believed that nonextension would doom the institution itself.[20]

Story seems not to have theorized about the long-run implications of nonextension, but his lifelong position speaks to the point. From his resolute position of nonextension, staked out first at the Salem town meeting in 1819, he never retreated. No other New England statesman in the

1820s was more fearful of Southern aggression or more determined to resist it. His fear and his determination, undiminished in the 1830s, burst forth again over the Texas question. He opposed annexation in 1837 and, despite his constitutional nationalism, supplied constitutional arguments against it that were used by Northern antislavery memorialists.[21] By the 1840s the issue had become an obsession with him, and he urged "all good men and true patriots" to wake up to the danger. Not only was the admission of Texas "grossly unconstitutional," but it would "give the South a most mischievous, if not a ruinous preponderance in the Union," an imbalance that in fact might well lead to "dissolution."[22] Polk's nomination in the summer of 1844 on a platform of expansion was a further blow and called forth a tirade against "the profligacy of public men, the low state of public morals—& the utter indifference of the people to all elevated virtue & even self respect." Indeed, he was prepared to admit that "the theory of our govt" was "a total failure."[23] Polk's election, which settled the annexation issue, led to yet another condemnation of "office-holders and office seekers, and corrupt demagogues." Even "Massachusetts men," it seemed, rejoiced that "their own state is to be reduced to perpetual bondage to the slave-holding states." So incensed was Story that he repudiated the unequal operation of the three-fifths clause of the Constitution—this despite the argument supporting the clause in his *Commentaries*. "We hug the chains," he concluded, "which we are assisting to form for ourselves."[24]

Story's record against slavery was clear. Before William Lloyd Garrison or Wendell Phillips had spoken out, he had taken a stand. Few men could claim such a consistent record of opposition to the slave trade. None had been so forceful in counteracting Southern constitutional theory or in condemning Southern expansionism. Why then, it must be asked, the bitter assault in the *Liberator*; why the demand that Story cringe and blush with shame?

To answer the question is to distinguish the antislavery position (which Story held) from abolitionism (which he condemned with a passion otherwise reserved for Thomas Jefferson and Andrew Jackson). Story was a gradualist on the question of emancipation. He condemned Southern aggression but showed no inclination to condemn individual Southerners who held slaves. He had no faith in colonization, but he was willing, as he confessed to Webster in 1822, "to give it a fair chance of success," if for no other reason than that it might "nourish a strong distaste for slavery among the more kind & benevolent men of the Southern States" who might be encouraged to accept "the ultimate emancipation of slaves."[25] Slavery would end because it would not be replenished by the foreign slave trade, because it would not be permitted to expand into new territories. The process would be peaceable, rational, gradual, and institutional, and this was precisely what the abolitionists opposed.

Their method, their raison d'être, if one believes Wendell Phillips, was to present the moral issue so that it could not be ignored or compromised.[26] Moral truth, by the canons of Christian perfectionism, was the burden of the individual conscience. Slavery was not an abstract wrong but a mortal sin whose existence damned those who tolerated it. On this there could be no compromise. Those who were not with the abolitionists were against them, even those who, like Story, were against slavery. To attack individuals, then, made perfect sense to the abolitionists, and to attack Story made special sense. Not only was he a gradualist and an institutionalist, but he was the highest federal officer in New England and the ultimate authority on the Constitution that gave institutional sanction to slavery. Between Story and the abolitionists, then, it was a question of the Constitution itself: What did it mean regarding slavery? And even more important, who would say what it meant, the judges or the people?"[27]

Story's position on both points was steadfast. Though he feared that the people would claim the Constitution, he argued that it should be in the care of "the professional intelligence of the country," that is to say, the lawyers and judges. This was the thrust of his *Commentaries on the Constitution*, and that work went on to say what lawyers and judges should think about slavery. Long before the publication of Madison's notes on the convention in 1840, which the abolitionists used to expose the bargain struck with slavery, Story made it clear that the slave provisions were part of the supreme law of the land. Slavery was a "matter of compromise and concession," which the framers made the sine qua non of union. Story was not at ease with the bargain that had been struck. He noted the "sacrifices of opinion and feeling" that the "eastern and middle States" made "to the peculiar interests of the south"; he acknowledged the Southern "prejudices" that necessitated Northern concessions. Wherever possible he minimized the damage done to freedom by those concessions, as, for example, when he spoke of the "glory" of the provision banning the foreign slave trade.[28]

Still, the grim reality of slavery had insinuated itself into American public law, and Story faced that fact unflinchingly. There for all to see was article IV, section 2, which required that persons "held to service or labor in one State, under the laws thereof, escaping into another . . . shall be delivered up on claim of the party to whom such service or labor may be due." This odious clause, Story admitted, "was introduced into the Constitution solely for the benefit of the slaveholding States, to enable them to reclaim their fugitive slaves who should have escaped into other States where slavery was not tolerated." He went even further to conclude that "these provisions for the arrest and removal of fugitives . . . contemplate summary ministerial proceedings and not the ordinary course of judicial investigation . . ."[29]—a position that not only read the hated Fugitive Slave Act of 1793 back into the Constitution but undercut arguments for jury trial in rendition cases.

Story dealt frankly with the moral compromises made in the interests of Union and never more so than in his discussion of the three-fifths clause of article I, section 2, paragraph 3, which provided that slaves were to be counted as three-fifths of freemen for purposes of taxation and representation. Here, as he recounted it, the argument was between those who looked on slaves as property and those who saw them as "persons as well as property." Story advised that the "federal Constitution should, therefore, view them in the mixed character of persons and property which was in fact their true character." This arrangement was a "real compromise" for "the common good" and was "entitled to great praise for its moderation, its aim of practical utility, and its tendency to satisfy the people that the Union framed by all, ought to be dear to all, by the privileges it confers as well as the blessings it secures." Story conceded that the compromise "had been complained of as a grievance"; in fact, it put the Constitution explicitly behind slavery. His advice, nonetheless, was that "he who wished well to his country will adhere steadily to it as a fundamental policy which extinguishes some of the most mischievous sources of all political divisions,—those founded on geographical positions and domestic institutions. . . . The wishes of every patriot ought now to be, *requiescat in pace*."[30]

There were other aspects of Story's constitutional system that bore less directly on the question of slavery, among which were a broad concern for property rights, an exclusivist interpretation of the commerce clause, and a generous view of congressional authority that had broad though unclear implications concerning federal authority over slavery in the territories.[31] One final aspect of the Constitution that carried implications for slavery was article IV, section 1, which required that full faith and credit be given by states to the acts, records, and judicial proceedings of other states. Among those "state acts" and "judicial proceedings," it would appear, would be either the slave laws of the Southern states or the laws of Northern states that extended freedom and varying degrees of civil and political equality to black people. The framers, however, did not speak to that point, and neither did Story; nor in fact were any slave cases brought under article IV, section 1.[32]

The status that free and slave states would accord each other's laws, however, was a question that could not be avoided, especially in cases in which slaves made their appearance in Northern states either as temporary residents or in transit with their masters. Story dealt with these matters in his treatise on *Conflict of Laws* published in 1834, one year after the publication of his work on the Constitution. That he did not, however, confront the issue of slavery head on may help to explain why his conflict principles could be cited subsequently (mostly after his death) both to further freedom and to restrain it.[33] Story in fact took a compromise position, as he did in his *Commentaries on the Constitution*, based frankly on the realities of power in the federal system. The starting point of his conflict theory, it will be recalled, was the principle of comity, which in turn was based on a recognition of the existence of sovereign states. Slavery existed by law in some of those states; freedom existed in others. The extent to which each recognized the other was entirely up to the judicial and legislative authorities of each state, which would in this as in other things determine the question finally on the basis of self-interest.

This was a position entirely compatible with a careful reading of Mansfield's opinion in *Somerset* v. *Stewart* (1772) as supplemented and clarified by Lord Stowell's decision in *The Slave Grace* (1827).[34] Neither case questioned the legality of slavery as a municipal institution. In the former, Mansfield ruled that the law by which a slave was held in his domicile does not have force in England. In the latter, Stowell held that a slave freed by residing in England resumed the status of slave upon return to her former domicile, where the law of slavery prevailed. How Story's conflict theory was intended to operate might reasonably be inferred from the fact that he accepted both *Somerset*, which he read in the least expansive sense, and *Grace*. Slavery existed as a fact of life and positive law; so did freedom. Sovereign states were under no obligation to recognize the law of other sovereign states. Thus could Chief Justice Lemuel Shaw free a Virginia slave brought by his master into the free state of Massachusetts in *Commonwealth* v. *Aves* (1836)—a decision that Story applauded.[35] Thus could lawyers in *Strader* v. *Graham* (1851) cite Story's *Conflict* to prove that slaves in Kentucky who resided temporarily in the free state of Ohio were slaves upon their return to Kentucky.[36] Story's comity principle was a two-edged sword: Sometimes it cut for freedom, sometimes for enslavement. But in any case—and it is a simple point of profound importance—it could operate only in those areas where the Constitution did not restrict state sovereignty regarding slavery, most noticeably, that is, in the obligation to return fugitives. Story's comity theory might be used by abolitionist lawyers like Salmon Chase to cut a swath of freedom. Still, they could not forgive him for making so clear the constitutional compromise struck with slavery.

On that question, indeed, the abolitionists had their own theory—or rather, theories, because abolitionist constitutional thought was often diffuse, contradictory, and shifting. Between 1830 and 1861 there were in fact several discernible constitutional positions, and all of them spelled trouble for Story.[37] On the left were the Garrisonians, whose constitutional ideas were articulated most forcefully by Alvan Stewart and Wendell Phillips. They recognized that the Constitution legitimated slavery, and they repudiated it, as the *Liberator* put it in 1838, as a "wicked, fearful, bloody" bargain and, as Garrison put it in 1844, as a "covenant with death," an "agreement with hell."[38] This group could turn to Story to prove their charge, and Phillips, one of Story's most promising students at the Law School (class of 1833), did just that. They advised free states to withdraw from the Union and Story to resign from the Court. As Phillips put it, with Story in mind, no doubt, "No oath of office, no obligation to the constitution of the United States can excuse an outrage on justice to humanity."[39]

Abolitionist constitutionalists who did not damn the Constitution and advise disunion and who were less personally abusive to Story presented him an even more difficult challenge. This group divided into moderates and radicals.[40] The moderates, who often drew on the small-government ideas of the states' rightists themselves, insisted, in opposition to the Garrisonians, that the Constitution had not established the legality of slavery in the states or anywhere else and, moreover, had no power to do so. Radicals like George W. F. Mellen, William Goodell, and Lysander Spooner went even further. Their Constitution not only did *not* support slavery but *did* support freedom, which by a mixture of arguments from natural law, colonial history, and a broad reading of *Somerset* they contended was the natural condition of mankind.

Radicals disagreed with moderates, but both constituted a powerful challenge to Story's orthodox view of the Constitution. What they agreed on—and here they could quote Story against himself—was that slavery had no legal standing except by the positive law of the slave states themselves. Rather than comity between slave and free states, as Story urged, they drew a battle line. What they insisted, and what they argued in state and federal courts, was that judges opt for freedom, that they employ the discretion that the law allowed (and a neutral or antislave Constitution sanctioned) to broaden the area of freedom. Spooner said in 1845 what abolitionists had said all along: To say that a judge must judge narrowly (must, that is, be bound by a slave Constitution) is to say that "he has no right to judge." Taking judicial statesmanship to the limit, he insisted that the judge was his own arbiter, that he was "bound only by his own convictions." To help inform those convictions Spooner supplied a special guide to constitutional construction. Here he had Story specifically in mind, for not only did he entitle his chapter "Rules of Interpretation" (after Story's chapter 5 in the *Commentaries on the Constitution*), but he went on, in a section called "Rules Cited for Slavery," to refute those of Story's principles of construction which stood in the way of freedom.[41] Spooner had derived not only a new constitutional morality but a new moral theory of judging—or rather, a theory of judging for judges who wanted to be moral.

Story's response to the abolitionists, whether Garrisonian perfectionists or moderate or radical constitutionalists, was to lump them in with Southern states' rightists and to condemn them all as fomenters of chaos. Social order was the root of the matter for Story, and in the largest sense it was a problem of demography. The population at the time of the Philadelphia convention was less than four million; by 1840 it was over seventeen million. The question was whether the vast new throng of Americans would be brought into the culture of the old Republic—or more precisely, how and under whose terms they would be brought in. The matriculation, according to Story, should be gradual and under the guidance of conservatives who would see to it that the values and institutions of the old republic would be dutifully preserved in the new age. What he saw around him, instead, was the inundation of tradition. The "predominant danger of our day," he told the alumni of Harvard in August 1842, with abolition in Boston and the Dorr Rebellion in Rhode Island as a backdrop for his warning, is "the tendency to ultraism of all sorts, and in all directions." Story was not referring only to "government and polity," or "the fundamental changes and even abolition of constitutions," or "the fluctuating innovations of ordinary legislation." Rather, he assailed the attitude of mind that put these things, along with literature and morals and all else, in jeopardy. He concluded that "the spirit of the age has broken loose from the strong ties, which have hitherto bound society together by the mutual cohesions and attractions of habits, manners, institutions, morals, and literature." Cut adrift from the experience and wisdom of the past, society was at the mercy of "a restless spirit of innovation and change—a fretful desire to provoke discussion of all sorts, under the pretext of free inquiry, or of comprehensive liberalism." And worse: "This movement is to be found not merely among illiterate and vain pretenders, but among the minds of the highest order, which are capable of giving fearful impulses to public opinion."[42]

Story spoke in the spirit of Metternich, whose ideas he felt should "in the present state of the world" be seriously attended to.[43] Searching for solid ground, he called for a return to "Grotius, and Puffendorf, and Vattel, and Burke, and Adam Smith, and the authors of the Federalist to enlighten our judgments, and purify our souls from debasing generalities."[44] Story spoke on the subject of literature, but there is no doubt that abolition was much on his mind, and within the year he lectured his students at the Law School on the dangerous abolitionists, "those mad men, who even now are ready to stand up in public assemblies, and in the name of conscience, liberty, or the rights of man, to boast that they are willing and ready to bid farewell to that Constitution under which we have lived and prospered for more than half a century, and which I trust may be transmitted, unimpaired, from generation to generation for many centuries to come."[45] Nor were the abolitionists the illiterate masses. Among them were the sons and daughters of Boston's finest families, Harvard's very own, and even lawyers of ability trained by Story himself (like Phillips and later Sumner and Richard Henry Dana, Jr., to mention only some). The only thing worse than a plain demagogue was an able and well-trained demagogue. Story feared the new movement precisely because its leaders could impart "fearful impulses to public opinion."

All this is to say that Story saw abolition as part of the whole centrifugal tendency of nineteenth-century history. Everywhere the masses, under the sway of demagogues, were chipping away the foundations of republicanism. The resurgence of political parties and the concomitant decline in the quality of public leadership were part of this phenomenon. Southern states' rights was another facet of democratic dementia, just as was Jefferson's defection from noblesse oblige. Reform was out of hand, too, though occasionally conservatives might keep it sane (as Story did in codification). The masses were out of control. He feared the new immigrants armed with the vote—indeed, was firmly convinced that they caused the Whig ticket to lose in New York and Pennsylvania in 1844.[46] Mob rule was part of the same problem. Story detected symptoms of the disease wherever he looked, whether it was Jackson's inauguration, the attack on the Ursuline Convent in Charlestown in 1834, the "shocking riots" in Philadelphia in the 1840s, or the Dorr Rebellion in Rhode Island. "I mourn over such occurrences," he wrote to Peters, "not merely for the misery they bring with them,—but for the proofs, which they afford, that religious Bigotry, & popular Delusions are as triumphant in the Mobs of Republics, as of Despotisms—without the means of suppressing them in the former. . . ."[47]

Into Story's dismal view of the "present state of our country" abolitionism fit neatly. He was "altogether opposed to the Abolitionist movement," not merely for its own sake but because it had "a tendency to aggravate every other difficulty."[48] It was an invitation to demagoguery. It agitated the already overheated political scene (as when abolitionists detracted from crucial Whig votes on the Texas issue in 1844).[49] Abolitionists called mobs into action against them and became mobs to defend themselves. They berated gradualism, ignored the lessons of conservatism, and approached institutions with arrogant disrespect rather than Burkean "reverence."

Above all, they threatened constitutional government and federal union. Story sensed what modern scholarship has confirmed: that beneath the varieties of abolition was a deep strain of Christian anarchism.[50] Whether they took sustenance from natural law, the Declaration of Independence, the teaching of Jesus, a radical reading of *Somerset*, or all together, the abolitionists carried their own version of the Constitution to the people. Whether they advocated ignoring it (as Garrison advised) or making it over (the message of Stewart and Spooner), the consequence was the same: to unsettle the constitutional compromise on slavery that in Story's mind was the last barrier against a dissolution of the Union.[51]

As in the *Bridge* case, the issue was one of legitimacy. "It is astonishing how easily men satisfy themselves that the Constitution is exactly what they wish it to be," Story complained to Greenleaf during the crisis over the admission of Texas.[52] That was the nub of the matter. Who were the abolitionists to invite the people to lay claim to the Constitution? By what right could they dictate law to judges who had studied Coke and Blackstone, pondered Burke, read history, and imbibed the wisdom of the *Federalist*; who knew the true meaning of the Constitution, or at any rate how and where to find it? For Story there could be but one set of "Rules of Interpretation." Two or more meant none at all. Without agreed-upon axioms of interpretation there would be no Constitution, and without it anarchy would prevail. He never lived to make this point to Lysander Spooner, but he said it in no uncertain terms to Thomas Dorr and his followers, who like the abolitionists presumed to know the true meaning of the Revolution.

2. Judge Story and the Dorr Rebellion: Social Justice and the Higher Morality of Law and Order

In the largest sense, Story's argument with the abolitionists turned on the meaning of popular sovereignty, which was a problem rooted in the American Revolution and embodied in the Constitution. The framers conceded that the people were sovereign, but the government they created was designed to be run by the elite. Abolitionism was a part of the ongoing struggle between those who would expand the democratic implications of popular sovereignty and those who would preserve conservative dominance. When the abolitionists challenged the judges' monopoly on the Constitution, they did so not only in the name of freedom but in the name of the people. Story heard the challenge. He did not answer the abolitionists directly on their interpretation of the American Revolution, but he did speak with unmistakable finality to Thomas Dorr and his pathetic band of rebels, who were for him indistinguishable from abolitionists, mobs, political parties, and other popular groups who presumed to claim sovereignty in the name of the Revolution. In answering them, he supplied a judicial remedy to social disorder that he complained was lacking in republics. In the process he made clear the historical and ideological backdrop against which his opinion in *Prigg* v. *Pennsylvania* must be projected.

Nowhere before the Civil War were the radical implications of popular sovereignty more fully drawn (and nowhere was the conservative suppression of them more complete) than in the abortive Dorr Rebellion.[53] This dramatic effort at reform from the bottom up in 1841 and 1842 was the climax of two decades or more of thwarted effort to liberalize the Charter of 1636, which without basic change still served as the constitution of Rhode Island. Radicals complained that the charter lacked a bill of rights and failed to provide an independent judiciary, but their most telling complaints concerned antiquated freehold suffrage and apportionment that disfranchised growing numbers of citizens in the expanding urban areas of the state. The continued unwillingness of the established government to reform itself led Thomas Dorr and his followers to bypass it entirely, elect a constitutional convention by universal manhood suffrage, and draw up a new constitution. The "People's Constitution," which reformed the judiciary and extended the vote to every male citizen over the age of twenty-one, was ratified in January 1842, and in April the new government, with Dorr as governor, met briefly to demand that the old charter government relinquish power.

The existing legislature, in the meantime, had outlawed the reform constitution; conservatives brought forth their own moderate reform constitution, which was accepted by the electorate in November 1842 and went into operation in May 1843. The Dorrites refused to recognize this new constitution, and when they threatened to resort to force in defense of their own legitimacy, the established government declared martial law and called out the militia to repel the threatened attack. Popular support for the Dorrites dwindled drastically after President Tyler promised to support the established government. Dorr's failure to capture the state arsenal at Providence in May 1842 and the bloodless rout of his followers at Chepachet the following June ended any real threat to the standing order. What remained to be dealt with, aside from the fate of Thomas Dorr himself and of a handful of plain people who stuck by him, were the radical ideas he used to justify his struggle for representative government in Rhode Island. Simply put, he believed that the American Revolution established a tradition of revolution. When the Declaration justified revolution against oppressive government, when the founders said the people were sovereign, Thomas Dorr believed them. And when the conservatives consistently refused to establish representative government in Rhode Island, he took them to task on American principles.

As a Supreme Court justice on circuit, charged with the maintenance of law and order, Story could hardly have been expected to sanction a popular uprising. Still, there were certain things about the Rhode Island situation that might have invited him to pursue a moderate, conciliatory course, especially in the early years of the struggle before both parties became intractable. The fact was that the old charter, in addition to being shockingly unrepresentative, had produced legislative dominance, had weakened the judiciary, and had in the process produced an indolent, ineffective political establishment—all of which Story should have condemned by his own standards of good government. Moreover, the Dorrites had effected their revolution by ballots, not bullets, and could claim with much truth that their free-suffrage constitution was more representative of the sovereign people than the old charter. Even when the reformers turned radical, their objective remained constitutional government, including among other reforms an independent judiciary.

Story saw no ambiguity in the Rhode Island situation, showed no signs of sympathy for the reformers, and made little effort to understand them. He agreed with Thomas Dorr on one thing only: that republican principles were at stake. Forty years before, Story had argued with William Smith Shaw and Arthur Walter, who attacked Jefferson's interpretation of the Revolution; now he agreed with them. The Dorr episode for Story was not just an illegitimate effort at constitution making. For him Dorr was but another demagogue and his followers (among whom conservatives feared were disproportionate numbers of "the foreign population") another mob.[54] They were peddling a perverted view of the American Revolution. The true principle was, as Story's friend and former student John Whipple put it, that the "Constitution annihilated the revolution."[55] For Story the American Revolution was designed to make further revolution unnecessary. Webster would make the point for him in *Luther v. Borden* (1849) when he argued that there could be no *right* of revolution, as Dorr had contended, but only revolution proved right by its success.[56] There was all the more reason to stamp out the brush fire in Rhode Island, for if Thomas Dorr could make over the constitution, so could William Lloyd Garrison. Story saw the danger and stated his remedy bluntly to Webster in April 1842 when he declared that "there cannot be any doubt that the whole proceedings of the so-called 'free suffrage' convention and the constitution makers are without law and against law." A violent confrontation of "the most serious consequences" was imminent, and "it is the duty of all good men to avert it."[57]

Averting confrontation meant suppressing reformers, even if it required enlisting the judiciary to do so. Behind-the-scene maneuvers began in January 1842 when federal district judge John Pitman, who was Story's contact man on the scene, warned Story of the growing "revolutionary movement." He also sent along a pamphlet he had written attacking the views of the reformers and requested an opinion on its constitutional arguments. He wondered, too, whether in publishing it he had become, as some charged, "a 'political judge.'"[58] Story's return letter praised Pitman's argument as "perfectly sound" and supported his extrajudicial efforts. "If ever there was a case that called upon a judge to write and speak openly and publicly," he declared, "it was the very case before you."[59]

Story also acted on his own advice, though not "openly and publicly." Conservative strategy in Rhode Island was to isolate Dorr and other leaders of reform from the people of Rhode Island by a combination of moderate suffrage reform and a show of force. It was in regard to the latter that

Pitman suggested to Story the need for "such cautionary measures" from the federal government "as may open the eyes of the deluded among us." His plan was that Story use his influence with Daniel Webster, then secretary of state in the Tyler administration, to achieve this objective.[60] Story responded with a letter advising Webster to ask Tyler to issue a preliminary proclamation "warning all persons not to attempt to carrry any measures into effect by military power, or by insurrectionary movements." The president should also "hold the militia in readiness to be called forth at the first moment where an insurrectionary movement shall exist." In fact, suggested Story, an order sending "two or three companies of regular R. I. Troops" to Newport, in readiness to act, might help make the point.[61]

Whether Story's letter turned the tide of presidential indecision is hard to determine, but Tyler did promise support to the conservatives in Rhode Island, and his support did undercut popular support for the reform constitution. In any case, Story continued to employ his own plan for law and order, which, as senior circuit justice for Rhode Island, he was able to bring into action. Part of his strategy was educational—for instance, his charge to the circuit grand jury at Newport on 15 June 1842, in which he warned radicals that the law of treason awaited them if they persisted in defying the established government. Whether it was appropriate for a federal judge to define Rhode Island's law of treason is a point of some dispute, and certainly the dangers of political abuses of the treason doctrine were great. Story had once warned New England grand juries against such abuses; now he saw no need for restraint. Indeed, the "alarming crisis" prompted him to declare that treason could be committed against the state as well as the national government, and under certain circumstances against both at once. "Levying war," moreover, included not only "a direct and positive intention entirely to subvert or overthrow the government" but also any overt attempt by force to "prevent the execution of any one or more general and public laws of the government, or to resist the exercise of any legitimate authority."[62] The net was broad enough to catch Dorrites or abolitionists—or members of almost any other protest movement that resisted the enforcement of law, whether or not it aimed to overthrow the government.

This judicial hard line was a potent weapon that the law-and-order party quickly put to use. Story's friend Whipple, who was a leader of that party, immediately requested a copy of his old teacher's "able charge" for printing and circulation. Story quickly supplied it.[63] And its impact was not academic, either, for Thomas Dorr had been arrested in October 1843 and indicted for treason. Chief Justice Joseph Durfee of the Rhode Island Supreme Court, before whom Dorr would be tried, turned to Story for encouragement and information. Durfee had been unable to hear Story's charge at the June circuit but had got a copy of it from Pitman. The chief justice "was gratified . . . afterwards to learn, that the part of it which defined treason, and distinguished between treason against the state and treason against the United States, was to be published." Durfee wanted to verify this point and others, because he did not want his forthcoming charge to the jury to "conflict with the opinions of the national tribunals."[64] And in fact the crucial issue in the state trial, and Dorr's main hope, was exactly the definition of treason against the state. Durfee deferred entirely to Story in the matter, as his own charge indicates.[65]

In the meantime a more meaningful and decisive debate was taking place in the circuit court of Joseph Story, one that would end finally in *Luther* v. *Borden* four years after Story's death. He was called into action in a case that grew out of the attempt to arrest Martin Luther for his active and possibly treasonable support of the Dorr government. Acting under a declaration of martial law, militia captain John Child and eight men broke into Luther's house in Warren, Rhode Island, in the early morning of 29 June 1842, in search of Luther. He had already fled, but they intimidated his hired man and aged mother and generally ransacked the house.[66] An action for trespass was brought against Luther Borden, who was one of the search party, at the November 1842 term of the circuit court in Providence, and a companion case charging personal trespass was entered in behalf of Rachel Luther. The actions were carefully coordinated and backed by the suffrage forces and ultimately by Dorr himself, in the hope that by challenging the right of the government to declare and act under martial law, the legitimacy of the People's Constitution and the radical principles of popular sovereignty would be established.

Story met the radicals head on when the case came to trial at the November 1843 circuit court in Newport. The defeat he inflicted on their legal strategy and ideology was every bit as humiliating as their rout at the battle of Chepachet. Benjamin Hallett, counsel for the Luthers in both cases, was prepared with an elaborate argument purporting to establish the legality of the Dorr uprising and the resulting People's Constitution. Story ruled from the bench, however, that all arguments to that point were irrelevant. The only issue before the Court was whether the men charged with trespassing had acted legally under the martial law declared by the legal government of Rhode Island. Presented with this ruling on evidence, the jury could only bring in a verdict of not guilty, and it obediently did so. With the agreement of the parties, Story then divided pro forma with Judge Pitman to send the case on to the Supreme Court. The Dorrites were denied a legal forum for their radical ideas, and the legality of both martial law and the existing conservative government was affirmed. Round one went to law and order.

The second *Luther* case brought even worse news for radicalism than had the first. By this time, Dorr had fled the state to avoid imprisonment, Martin Luther was serving a five-month jail sentence imposed by Judge Durfee, and the forces of law and order were in control throughout the state. The only legal issue now concerned the declaration of martial law by which they had consolidated control. Story handed the conservatives a conclusive victory on this point and at the same time revealed his utter contempt for radical theories of popular sovereignty, which Hallett again tried to press on the court. Story signaled the outcome when he opened court with an announcement that he would not have time for extended arguments, because he was obliged to return to Boston in two days to try a "case of great importance."[67] What was to have been the radicals' day in court was suddenly transformed into an incidental trial that could not be allowed to interfere with truly important business. Hallett's arguments were treated with the same dispatch. As in the first case, he wanted to challenge the legality of martial law in Rhode Island, or at least to argue that if it existed legally in some parts of the state, it did not do so in Warren, where the alleged trespass occurred. Story immediately cut him short, stating that the issue of martial law was not before the Court, but only the question whether it had been abused. Hallett persisted with the argument that martial law was "an arbitrary military act" and as such could apply "only where the troops were in the field." Story stopped him again with the curt observation that "as far as the questions of law were concerned, he was as ready to decide them now, as he would be at the end of the trial."[68]

What the Dorrites had hoped would be an occasion for them to vindicate the people's power to overthrow an unrepresentative government had suddenly turned into an opportunity for Story to elaborate a theory of martial law that would prohibit them from doing so. The law as Story laid it down was everything conservatives could have wanted. Rhode Island "is a sovereign State," he declared, "and must have the right to maintain her own sovereignty." The precedent was Shays's rebellion. When "a State finds its government, its existence as a State, as well as internal peace in danger," it may declare martial law. The power to do so was civil, not military, and the sole judge of whether to use that power was the state legislature. As for Hallett's contention that martial law could be limited to that part of the state where armies were in the field, the answer "in one word" was no. Here Story summoned his considerable prerogative as senior circuit justice. Among the "things which a court that has been for some length of time established should be presumed to know," he said, is that a state under martial law means the whole state: "every man, woman and child."[69]

Story's charge to the jury settled the legality of martial law in Rhode Island and left unresolved only the question whether it had been abused by the militiamen in the *Luther* case. His summary of facts and evidence for the jury left no doubt on this point, either. One juror, however, held out for one hundred dollars' damages out of sympathy for old Mrs. Luther. Story was forced to declare a mistrial, but he blunted that defeat and avoided a retrial by arranging a division between himself and Pitman on the bogus question whether the jury had the right to decide if the situation in Rhode Island in 1842 warranted a declaration of martial law.[70] Both *Luther* cases, then, went forward to the Supreme Court, one on appeal and the other on a writ of error stemming from the pro forma division between circuit judges.

No doubt Story expected a full vindication of his conservative doctrines by the Supreme Court, and perhaps he might have got it had he lived to defend his circuit action in conference. As it turned out, the decision in *Luther v. Borden* (1849) was at least a partial defeat for Story's position. At the circuit level, Story had called the shots. He had defined treason for the chief justice of Rhode Island. In the *Luther* cases he assumed for the federal courts the authority to determine which government in Rhode Island was legal. Not only did he define martial law, but he expounded the theory of unlimited legislative discretion in the matter. His rulings on evidence, which shaped the verdicts, pushed to the very limits of judicial discretion as well, although his action was perfectly consistent with his rulings in slave-trading cases and in those which arose under the embargo and nonintercourse laws.

Story's aggressive use of judicial authority did not please the Court, which was even more democratic than it had been and which, in any case, did not have to face the crisis in Rhode Island, long since settled. Taney, who spoke for the Court, made it perfectly clear that Story had no authority, as a federal circuit justice, to rule on the legality of the Rhode Island charter government or on the constitutionality of its act of martial law. On these matters, Story should have deferred to "the decision of state tribunals"—the very opposite, of course, of what he was inclined to do. The chief justice went on to say that when the national government acted in such cases—as it could under article IV, section 4, which guaranteed "republican" government to the states—the authority belonged to Congress, not the courts, because the question was political in nature.[71] The mere fact that Congress had admitted representatives and senators from Rhode Island had settled the question whether it was republican or not.[72] Story's judicial nationalism, then, was out of bounds, and if one believed Justice Levi Woodbury's dissent, so were his ruling on evidence and his broad doctrine of martial law. Such an unlimited concession of power to state legislatures, said Woodbury, was at odds with "all our social usages and political education, as well as our constitutional checks."[73]

Taney's ruling, it should be emphasized, was no victory for radicalism; indeed, if one overlooks the Court's criticism of Story's method, *Luther* could be interpreted as a vindication of his conservatism. There was, to be sure, a concession to state judicial authority that supplied a Jacksonian motif, as did Taney's preference for legislative action at the national level. Beyond that, however, conservatism swept the field. The guarantee clause, thanks to Taney's dictum, became a monument to the status quo. Conservative rule in Rhode Island was vindicated, martial law was upheld, and Hallett's arguments on republican ideology were dismissed no less abruptly than they had been by Story. The judge might have been a little distressed that Webster argued for judicial restraint in political questions, but he certainly would have approved his old colleague's version of the Revolution: how in that great event "conservatism was visible throughout."[74]

In any case, what happened at the Supreme Court level four years after Story died ought not to obscure what he carried off in 1843—that he helped defeat radical social change—or what that step said about his political-legal ideology. To say that the issue with him was a matter of law and order is to risk taking the passion as well as the ideological content out of his action. Story did, of course, strike a blow for social order, one that called into action all aspects of his authority as circuit justice, political and educational as well as legal. Never mind that the great nationalist resorted to arguments from state sovereignty; forget that he conceded unlimited discretion over martial law to state legislatures, though in every other respect he held them in contempt. The inconsistencies Story tolerated in his own jurisprudence speak only to the extent of his alarm.

What alarmed him was not just Thomas Dorr but what he had come to stand for. Social disorder among the masses had for Story become the great challenge to republican society. In this regard the Dorrites in Rhode Island were indistinguishable from the mobs that followed Jackson, those that rioted in Philadelphia, those that attacked the Ursuline Convent in Charlestown—all of which he had specifically denounced. Worst of all were the abolitionists against whom he was struggling in Massachusetts. If the radicals could make over Rhode Island's constitution in the name of the people, could not the abolitionists do the same with the federal Constitution? They had in fact claimed as much. The assertions of popular constitutionalists would have to be rooted out wherever they cropped up. For Story, then, law and order had become a form of higher morality rooted in the revolutionary experience. How deeply he believed this and how much he was willing to pay for his beliefs was clear in *Prigg* v. *Pennsylvania* (1842), which pressed on him quite a different concept of morality.

3. Yardstick Law and Fugitives from Slavery: Judge Story in the Belly of the Whale

When Story laid out the terms of the constitutional compromise on slavery in his *Commentaries*, when he set forth his rules of interpretation, he established guidelines for his own decisions on the slavery question. Patriots everywhere were urged to preserve the compromise, and judges as statesmen more than others. What was statesmanlike in 1787 or in 1833, however, was not necessarily so in 1842. Compromise carried with it the tacit understanding that both North and South would continue to benefit equally from the agreement. Neither believed that it had. After the bank decision, the Missouri debates, the revolts of Denmark Vesey and Nat Turner, the Southern states turned paranoiac and assertive. They demanded access to new territory, protection from abolitionist agitation, and a general show of good faith in the North, especially in the return of fugitive slaves.

The North responded with fear, anxiety, and moral aggression. What troubled the North was that slavery, rather than dying out, was expanding. In 1790 there were 697,624 slaves, in 1840 there were 2,487,355; and slave territory expanded just as dramatically.[75] In this light, Southern demands for equality appeared to be part of a conspiracy to dominate. Indeed, slavery was becoming a national institution and, if the South had its way, a constitutional one in the largest sense of the word. Such was the implication of the civil rights debates in the 1830s over the Southern effort to suppress freedom of petition and censor the mail. The appearance in 1840 of a third party dedicated entirely to the issue of slavery was another sign. Political parties, despite their inclination to suppress divisive issues, would have to take a stand (as Henry Clay would learn in 1844). Congressmen and senators would have to speak out (as Webster would tragically discover). So, too, would justices of the Supreme Court. When they did—as in the cases of *Groves* v. *Slaughter*, *Amistad*, and *Prigg* v. *Pennsylvania*, all in 1841 and 1842—they discovered that deference to judicial authority and tolerance for judicial error were all but gone. Abolitionist constitutional thought, if it had not swept the field, had at the very least established a "new morality" by which judges were to be judged.[76] To maintain the constitutional compromise on slavery in 1842, when the spirit that called it forth in 1787 had turned into hatred and fear, could make villains of heroes.

Groves v. *Slaughter* (1841) might well have served as a warning that slavery as a constitutional issue could not long be suppressed.[77] The Court was no stranger to slavery, of course. Diversity cases in Southern circuits regularly brought up state laws in which slavery was at issue, and some of those cases reached the Supreme Court. Even Story on the New England circuit was not immune from involvement, as we have noted already in *Emerson* v. *Howland*, which prompted him to recognize the slave law of Virginia. Occasionally a justice confronted the issue of slavery head on, as did Justice Johnson on circuit in *Elkison* v. *Deliesseline* (1823), in which he struck down a South Carolina law requiring the imprisonment of Negro seamen arriving in the port of Charleston as a violation of federal authority over foreign and interstate commerce.[78] There was not, it is safe to say, a single important case after 1819 in which the deployment of power in the federal system was at issue where slavery did not silently influence the deliberations of the justices. Indeed, slavery more than any single issue lay behind the doctrinal chaos and growing legal relativism against which Story railed. Still, the Marshall Court did not have to confront directly the constitutional issue of slavery or the domestic slave trade. Neither did the Taney Court until *Groves* v. *Slaughter* in 1841.

The litigation, instituted by Slaughter to recover payment of notes received for slaves sold by him in Mississippi in 1836, seemed to be a matter of state law, but constitutional issues were unavoidable. The purchasers of the slaves refused to pay Slaughter, arguing that the notes were void by the state constitution of 1832, which prohibited the importation of slaves for sale after 1 May 1833 (a provision aimed at maintaining the value of existing property in slaves). Even to hear the case in 1841 was risky; for the Court to rule on the question of Mississippi's regulation of commerce and its relation to the domestic slave trade would have plunged the Court into the political maelstrom.

The majority succeeded in circumventing the constitutional question by ruling that the Mississippi constitutional prohibition against the importation of slaves was inert in the absence of implementing legislation, of which there was none. But the strategy of quiescence was not entirely successful, in the first place because individual justices felt compelled to speak out. McLean, whose antislave sentiments pressed increasingly hard against his commitment to uphold the positive law of slavery, insisted on exploring the constitutional issue. This step, in turn, prompted Taney and Baldwin to do the same and, in fact, led the latter to suggest that slavery was protected by the due process clause of the Fifth Amendment[79]—the position Taney announced as law in *Dred Scott*. More devastating yet to the strategy of judicial circumvention, though less readily apparent, were the proslave implications of the majority's position. By *not* ruling on the constitutional conflict between the commerce power and the state constitution, that is, by ruling that the state prohibition was inoperative, the Court had in fact validated several million dollars' worth of notes held by slave traders. By unavoidable implication the Court sanctioned the slave trade itself.

Story was on the spot. To join the majority would be to countenance the domestic slave trade, which he hated, and to put blood money in slave traders' pockets. To explore fully the question of commerce power in relation to slaves, on the other hand, would unleash the furies on and off the court. Story's nonsolution was a silent dissent, which he later rationalized to Robert J. Walker, who argued the case for Slaughter. Story believed that the Mississippi constitutional provision prohibiting the sale of slaves was self-activating and that it was "a positive, present, operative prohibition of slaves." The notes of slave traders, accordingly, "were utterly void."[80] How Story could have tolerated state regulation of the slave trade is not immediately clear in light of his own sweeping view of national commerce power. But his willingness to do so indicated a desire to keep slavery local and himself out of hot water. That would no longer be possible in the *Amistad* case, two weeks later, which carried him and his colleagues further still toward the nationalization of the slavery issue.

No slave case before *Dred Scott* attracted so much national attention as *U.S.* v. *Amistad*,[81] although *Prigg* was more significant. Certainly none was so inviting to the abolitionists, whose argument that law should serve freedom, not slavery, was voiced passionately by the venerable John Quincy Adams. Standing proudly before the Supreme Court were forty-some Africans who claimed no more and no less than their freedom. They had been imprisoned on board the Spanish-owned *L'Amistad*, which cleared Havana in June 1839 for Puerto Principe. The Africans rose, killed the captain and some of the crew, and ordered those remaining to return them to Africa. Instead the crew surreptitiously guided the vessel into American waters, where it was discovered by the U.S. brig *Washington* off Montauk Point in Long Island Sound. The ship and the Africans aboard were libeled for salvage. The Spanish owners, reasoning from the Treaty of 1795, counterclaimed, with the support of the Spanish minister in Washington. At each step of the way from the district to the circuit court to the Supreme Court the issues gathered intensity. The question had, in fact, as Adams put it to the justices, become a contest between freedom and the immoral machinations of two great governments, an argument Story remembered as "extraordinary . . . for its power, its bitter sarcasm, & its dealing with topics far beyond the Record."[82] Northern opinion demanded freedom. For the South, anything short of a return of the slaves to their Spanish captors would be a threat and an affront. The burden of compromise took on dreadful tangibility.

Twenty years before, in *La Jeune Eugenie*, Story had explored the law's full potential for freedom and couched his conclusions in inspired rhetoric. Now, as spokesman for an increasingly divided Court, in a period of explosive sensibilities, he walked the razor's edge of legal precision. He came down firmly for freedom but based his decision on the narrowest possible ground. The question was not whether slavery in general was good, bad, moral, or legal but whether certain Spaniards owned certain Africans. His reasoning turned on the Treaty of 1795 with Spain, the nineteenth article of which provided for the return of "all ships and merchandize . . . which shall be rescued out of the hands of any pirates or robbers on high seas. . . ." Emphatically, but with painstaking exactness, Story excluded the *Amistad* from this provision and the *Amistad* Africans from being pirates and robbers. To be that they would have had to be slaves in the first place. They "are not slaves, but are kidnapped Africans, who, by the law of Spain itself, are entitled to their freedom, and were kidnapped and illegally carried to Cuba, and illegally detained and restrained. . . ." Story regretted the "dreadful acts" by which they were forced to regain their freedom, but these acts did not, as counsel for the Spaniards insisted, make them pirates. He also rejected the arguments of the U.S. government that the Court ought not to go beyond the ship's papers, which documented Spanish ownership of the Africans, and he did so most especially, he said, because "human life and human liberty are in issue, and constitute the very essence of the controversy." Here he sided briefly with Adams and New England. Indeed, he went even further with them to challenge, at least indirectly, the racist premises of American slave law. If the Negroes were not slaves but freemen, as he declared them to be, then the United States was "bound to respect their rights as much as those of Spanish subjects." Indeed, the question of "rights" should be decided not by treaty but by "the eternal principles of justice and international law."[83]

Echoes of *La Jeune Eugenie*—but echoes only. The case turned on a close reading of the law. Story had not shifted his moderate objective stance, nor had the Court altered its determination to give each section its due and to offend neither if possible. Ominously, however, that was no longer possible. Story's opinion did give something to both sections, but neither was entirely pleased. The North got freedom, but extremists preferred more of Adams's passion and less of Story's objectivity. The South was even more uneasy. Story's narrow ruling might have pleased Southerners, but they were too upset with the implications of what he did to rejoice at what he did not do. Story's talk about "eternal principles" of justice, harmless though it was, was bad enough, but his willingness to go behind the ship's papers could easily appear to be a discretionary act of bad faith. The result of it all, moreover, was to free slaves and weaken the principle of slave property, and perhaps even to countenance mutiny on slave ships. The question of slave property was clearly an issue. Southern pressure on the Polk administration eventually resulted in an award of fifty thousand dollars' damages to the Spanish government, which clearly undercut Story's decision.[84]

The South was less successful in nullifying Story in the matter of slave mutiny. In October 1841 slaves on the *Creole*, bound for New Orleans out of Hampton Roads, Virginia, mutinied and carried the vessel into the port of Nassau, where British officials freed the slaves. Story figured at least indirectly in their freedom. Not only was his theory of conflict cited as legal grounds for not returning the fugitives, but Story advised Secretary of State Daniel Webster that he had no legal grounds for requesting a return of the slaves—advice that Webster ignored.[85] Possibly, too, the *Amistad* opinion counted; at least the abolitionists believed that the slaves had "acted in accordance" with that decision.[86] Whether the abolitionists went so far as to praise Story himself is doubtful. In any case, after *Prigg* they damned him to hell.

"Masks of the law are of two kinds," according to John Noonan, Jr., "those imposed on others and those put on oneself."[87] Antebellum judges who confronted the question of slavery from the bench found these masks useful. Slaves were made to wear the mask of property. And as long as they did, they could be held in bondage; disposed of in wills; and sold, bartered, and torn from their families according to the technicalities of legal rules—all without raising questions of morality among the rest of society. Judges who thus dispensed with morality also wore masks, ones fashioned from a respect for positive law, canons of legal science, and dedication to judicial office. Story knew both kinds of masks. In *Prigg* v. *Pennsylvania* neither would shield him.[88] Abolitionist constitutionalists would rip off one mask; Margaret Morgan would refuse to put on the other.

Margaret Morgan was a slave, a piece of property under Maryland law, though she grew up in an atmosphere of virtual freedom. She was also a mother and a wife and a human being who wanted to live as a free woman with her husband in the free state of Pennsylvania.[89] She had lived there five years with her two children, who by the law of Pennsylvania were born free, when slave catcher Edward Prigg came to bring her back to her owner in Maryland. To reclaim Margaret, Prigg was required by the Pennsylvania personal liberty law of 1826 to get a certificate of removal issued by a state official, a process designed to protect free blacks from unlawful rendition. Upon being refused such a certificate, Prigg seized Margaret and her children against their will, whereupon he was indicted for kidnapping under the law of 1826. Extradition was opposed by Maryland for several years, but the desire of both states to settle the question of fugitive slaves prompted a joint decision to proceed with the case. An agreed-upon verdict of guilty by the trial court, upheld pro forma by the Supreme Court of Pennsylvania, sent the case to the federal Supreme Court, where it awaited Story and his colleagues in 1842. It was the personal liberty law of Pennsylvania against the federal Fugitive Slave Act of 1793, which Story had already declared to be constitutional in his *Commentaries on the Constitution*. The South had come for its pound of flesh and blood. As an advocate of the constitutional compromise of 1787, as the self-designated master of objective adjudication, Story felt obliged to give it to them—or not "it" but Margaret Morgan and her children.

If *Amistad* went to the North then *Prigg* went to the South, or so at least a plain reading of the opinion would indicate. Story's defense of the slaveholder's right to a return of escaped slaves bristled with imperatives: of rights and guarantees that are "positive," "unqualified," and "absolutely secured" and of "duties" on nonslaveholders "positively enjoined."[90] The constititional principles Story brought to bear were not new. He started with the principle stated in his own conflict theory, that slavery was a "mere municipal regulation, founded upon and limited to the range of territorial laws." This was Mansfield's position in *Somerset*, which he agreed with, and Shaw's in *Commonwealth* v. *Aves*, which for the first time was recognized by the Supreme Court. Story went on to reason that except for the positive guarantee in the rendition clause of the Constitution (article IV, section 2, clause 3), slaveowners would depend entirely on the comity of other states for the return of their property. It followed logically that the fugitive slave clause was "of the last importance to the safety and security of the southern States"—and the grounds on which they entered the Union.[91]

Story said in no uncertain terms what he had already said in his *Commentaries*, that the constitutional position on fugitive slaves "manifestly contemplates the existence of a positive, unqualified right on the part of the owner of the slave, which no State law or regulation can in any way qualify, regulate, control, or restrain." Here he relied on the theory of exclusivism (of which he was the Court's most consistent exponent) and his own reasoning in *Martin* v. *Hunter's Lessee* to complete the argument for slavery: Not only was the fugitive slave law constitutional (and the Court's own precedents were cited for additional authority); not only did Congress have the exclusive right to pass such a law; but by the imperative of the Constitution (as in *Martin*) it was obliged to pass legislation "to protect the right, to enforce delivery, and to secure the subsequent possession of the slave."[92] Congressional action dealt only with the remedy. The right of rendition rested in the Constitution itself, which clothed the slaveowner "with entire authority, in every State in the Union, to seize and recapture his slave. . . ." The only qualification on this absolute right—and here Story accommodated the doctrine of state police power—was that it be exercised "without any breach of peace or illegal violence."[93]

Here, in language all too plain for some, was an argument for the return of fugitive slaves anchored solidly in the Constitution and backed by the greatest living authority on American constitutional law. And on the immediate issues before it, the Court overwhelmingly agreed, a point Story took pains to emphasize.[94] All the justices, with the possible exception of John McLean, agreed that the Pennsylvania personal liberty law of 1826 interfered with the constitutional right of rendition and was unconstitutional and void. The act of 1793, although it was not directly before the Court, was constitutional (except that portion of it which required the cooperation of state officials).[95] Edward Prigg was not a kidnapper. Margaret Morgan and her children became slaves.

What the Court said and what the decision actually meant, however, were two different things. What it meant was not all that clear, as the confused response of contemporaries indicates. Opinion varied predictably.

Moderates praised Story for the impartiality and courage of his stand. Abolitionists condemned him on moral grounds, and Southern opinion seems generally to have been placated, at least until the South discovered that the North could use the opinion to expand the area of freedom. And how best to use the opinion soon divided abolitionists. What was most confusing—and is most relevant here—was Story's own view of the matter: what he seems to have said in the opinion and what he thought he had accomplished.[96]

What he intended, it might be insisted, must be inferred from the thrust of what he did, which, simply speaking, was to reaffirm the South's constitutional right to reclaim fugitives. The complication comes from what Story himself (and his son, too) thought he had accomplished. Upon his return to Massachusetts in the spring of 1842, he spoke of his opinion in *Prigg* "repeatedly and earnestly" to his family and friends as a "triumph of freedom."[97] The "triumph" came, as William Wetmore Story explained it, presumably speaking his father's mind, from the doctrine of exclusivism: "in establishing, contrary to the opinion of four of the Judges, that the extradition of fugitive slaves is exclusively within the jurisdiction of the Federal Government, and that the State Legislatures are prohibited from interfering even to assist in giving effect to the clause in the Constitution on this subject. . . ."[98]

Story's exposition of the exclusivist doctrine in *Prigg* was grounded on *Sturgis* v. *Crowninshield* (1819), in which Marshall argued that certain constitutional grants of power to Congress were meant to exclude state action entirely. The test for exclusivism was to be found in the words of the constitutional grant, as well as the "nature of the power" in question and "the true objects to be attained by it."[99] The nature of the fugitive slave clause (which Story argued was sweeping in the constitutional rights it bestowed), as well as the "true objects to be attained" (which boiled down to an efficient and uniform rendition of fugitive slaves throughout the Union), required that states not interfere. The Constitution, as Story put it, "does not point out any State functionaries or any State action to carry its provisions into effect. The States cannot, therefore, be compelled to enforce them [i.e., the rights bestowed on slaveholders concerning rendition]," and further, "it might well be deemed an unconstitutional exercise of the power of interpretation to insist that the States are bound to provide means to carry into effect the duties of the national government, nowhere delegated or entrusted to them by the Constitution." Once Congress acted, as it did in 1793, that action "must supersede all State legislation upon the same subject; and by necessary implication prohibit it. For, if Congress have a constitutional power to regulate a particular subject, and they do actually regulate it in a given manner, and in a certain form, it cannot be held that the State Legislatures have a right to interfere, and, as it were, by way of complement to the legislation of Congress, to prescribe additional regulations, and what they may deem auxiliary provisions for the same purpose."[100]

What, then, could states do and not do under Story's ruling? They could not, of course, pass legislation interfering with the constitutional right of masters to recover slaves. But neither could they be required to pass legislation implementing recovery, and if they did, it would probably be unconstitutional (excepting possibly police legislation passed merely in the interest of keeping the peace). Accordingly, Northern states would be relieved of any obligation to return fugitive slaves, and without state cooperation, slaves could not effectively be recovered—or so the argument for "freedom" went. And it was given credence by a series of acts passed by Northern states (beginning with Massachusetts in 1843) that prohibited state officials from aiding in the rendition of slaves.[101] These acts were justified by reference to Story's exclusivist ruling in *Prigg*, and as Southern opposition indicated, they did in fact interfere with the return of fugitive slaves. In this respect, it might be argued, *Prigg* reasserted the municipal nature of slavery and may even have encouraged extralegal opposition to the return of fugitives, just as *Brown* v. *Board of Education* contributed to radical protest in the name of constitutional law.

Was *Prigg*, then, for all of its strong language about the rights of slaveholders, really a triumph for freedom? Certainly that construction comports with Story's hatred of slavery, not to mention his sincere belief in Christian morals and his general sense of decency. Possibly *Prigg* was like *Amistad* or the *Creole* mutiny affair, in which the law permitted judges to discover what they wanted to find (in Story's case a loophole for freedom)[102] without openly violating their commitment to the Constitution and the tradition of objective adjudication.

To admit that *Prigg* furthered freedom need not commit one to the triumph-of-freedom argument or to the conclusion that Story set out with freedom as his main objective. In fact, there are serious problems with that conclusion, ones other than the suspicion that a biographer must have of an apologia written by a loving son of his father. Intent, in any case, must in the first instance be deduced from the opinion itself. Story was most forceful and majority support surest when he proclaimed the constitutional right of rendition, a right that was stated in sweeping terms and held to be self-executing. So comprehensive was Story's definition of that right, in fact, that he seems to have prohibited trial by jury in rendition cases (though admittedly that issue was not before the Court). The same would appear true of other common-law remedies against illegal imprisonment: the writ of habeas corpus and the writ de homine replegiando (which Charles Francis Adams and others specifically felt had been violated by *Prigg*).[103]

In this regard Story's failure to distinguish between state laws applying to fugitive slaves and those applying to free blacks was crucial. McLean argued compellingly along these lines,[104] and Story's own theory of conflict seemed to oblige him to presume that laws passed in free states like Pennsylvania were meant to be applied to free blacks, not to fugitives— and thus to except such laws from the interdict of his broad reading of the fugitive slave clause. If Story intended to make his opinion truly a triumph for freedom, he should have explored the matter. And what about his tantalizing reference to police power, which he would use to remove fugitive slaves in the name of order but not slave catchers, whose presence fomented disorder? There was also his willingness to extend the absolute right of return of fugitives to slaves in transit as well.[105] The fact that Northern state judges uniformly found a way around that dictum—and sometimes used Story's conflict theory as a corrective to his opinion— cannot remove the question why, when it was unnecessary to the decision, he made the statement in the first place.

Such questions about Story's opinion make one hesitate to call it a triumph and raise further speculations about what he thought he was doing. Still, it might be reasoned—and William Story suggested as much—that whatever proslavery concessions the opinion contained came only as unavoidable offshoots from the exclusivist doctrine whose main thrust carried the day for freedom. One must ascertain, then, whether exclusivism did carry the day for freedom, and the first aspect of that larger question is whether it carried the majority of the Court. The uncertainty here comes from the fact that only three justices (Wayne and McLean with Story) explicitly supported the concept. The position of two justices (Catron and McKinley) was not recorded on this matter or any other connected with this case, and in fact their names were not mentioned in the reports (though the manuscript records of the Supreme Court list them as present).[106] The position of Baldwin is also unclear. He wrote no opinion, merely indicating in a brief paragraph that he concurred in the judgment but "dissented from the principle laid down by the court as grounds for their opinion."[107] One would assume that among those "principles" with which he disagreed was Story's doctrine of exclusivism, particularly as he was on record against the consolidating tendencies of Marshall and Story. On the other hand, Wayne specifically included Baldwin among those who supported exclusivism.[108] Taney, Daniel, and Thompson came out specifically against the principle. What one does with the three uncertain votes is crucial. All three most likely did not go with Story. His son, in fact, who probably heard from his father on the matter, counted four dissenters.[109] It is difficult to believe that Baldwin supported Story on exclusivism in light of his states' rights jurisprudence and his general dislike of his colleague's conspicuous erudition. Catron and McKinley may have gone with Story to make a majority of five, but as Joseph Burke has noted, both were inclined to resist extreme nationalist positions and neither was especially deferential to Story.[110] It might be argued that Taney's careful refutation of the exclusivist doctrine is proof that Story had a majority support on that point, but the chief justice himself evinced doubt by the use of the phrase "as I understand the opinion of the court."[111]

The Court's ambiguity concerning exclusivism—the uncertain majority and the strong dissents—is symptomatic of the impact of slavery on constitutional adjudication. Indeed, the confusion in *Prigg* prefigures *Dred Scott*, but it does not in itself refute the argument about freedom. What the Court actually says often means less than what people think it means, or what lawyers and judges can make it mean. Northern state legislatures did make exclusivism work for them when they passed laws prohibiting state cooperation in the rendition of fugitives, just as state judges salvaged freedom from Story's *dictum* on the laws of slaves in transit.

To concede that exclusivism became law and that it worked to produce freedom is still not to resolve the problem, however. Exclusivism, like Story's theory of comity, was a two-edged sword. If it could cut for freedom when wielded by the North it could and did cut for slavery in the hands of the slaveholders. Even as a constitutional doctrine, exclusivism had two sides. William Story argued that it worked to reassert the municipal nature of slavery and his father's opinion did the same. But it also worked to nationalize slavery by reaffirming that rendition was a constitutional right operative in every state of the union. If the *states* in the North were relieved of rendition responsibilities, *citizens* of the Northern states who owed allegiance to the Constitution were not. And neither were federal judges, who were specifically mentioned by Story as obliged to aid in enforcement.[112]

What that concession meant came home to Story within the year when James Gray of Norfolk, Virginia, appeared before him on circuit in Boston to request a certificate authorizing him to reclaim his slave George Latimer. Gray encountered strong opposition from the abolitionists in Boston, who had petitioned Chief Justice Lemuel Shaw, author of *Commonwealth v. Aves*, for a writ of habeas corpus and later for a writ of personal replevin issued on the authority of the state's personal liberty law of 1837.[113] Lawyers for Latimer cited *Prigg* to show that proceedings against Latimer under authority of state and local officials were illegal. Shaw was unconvinced and went on to rule that Latimer was legally detained under the authority of the fugitive slave law of 1793 and the fugitive slave clause of the Constitution, and he cited *Prigg* for support. Shaw also used *Prigg* to dismiss the writ of personal replevin, arguing that the personal liberty law of 1837 was unconstitutional, as it clearly was by Story's reasoning. Shaw hated slavery but felt bound by his oath to the Constitution which, under *Prigg*, required the return of fugitives.

Story showed the same dedication to duty. When Gray appeared before him on Saturday, 5 November, Story acknowledged the owner's constitutional right to rendition and recognized the summary procedure established in the act of 1793, both of which he affirmed in *Prigg*. The only requirement before he issued the certificate of removal was that Gray produce a certificate of ownership; he was given two weeks to do so. In the meantime he remanded Latimer to the possession of Gray and stood ready to send him back into slavery. Story escaped that final decision because he fell ill. The illness, which kept him from the entire 1843 term of the Court, may in fact have been hastened by the agony of the decision that awaited him. But however much he suffered it was not enough to keep him from being publicly branded "SLAVE-CATCHER-IN-CHIEF FOR THE NEW ENGLAND STATES."[114]

In the Latimer affair *Prigg* had been cited on both sides, but it worked more for slavery than for freedom. To return to the triumph-of-freedom argument, it might be argued that by sanctioning state neutrality *Prigg* made rendition impracticable. In fact, the process became so complicated and the outcome so uncertain in the *Latimer* case that Gray finally took the four hundred dollars raised by abolitionists in Boston and went home without his slave. Rendition, it would appear, was a hollow right without the support of the state, which support had been undercut by *Prigg*. If this was the case in Boston, where federal judges were readily accessible, how much more difficult would rendition be in states like Ohio, where distance and communications made access next to impossible?

Had not *Prigg* entered history, willy-nilly, perhaps, but surely nonetheless, on the side of freedom after all? The best evidence for this conclusion is that the South, responding to the difficulties of reclaiming fugitives, now demanded a more stringent national fugitive slave act and got it in 1850. That act circumvented the difficulties posed by *Prigg* by creating a body of federal officials in each state armed with summary rendition authority and charged with administering the return of fugitive slaves.[115] That law was evidence that *Prigg* had worked for freedom, but the argument proves too much. Again *Prigg* cut for slavery, for in the brutal act of 1850 the nationalization of slavery in that decision bore its bitter fruit. If rendition was a constitutional right operative in every state, if Congress was obliged to provide a remedy adequate to that right, was not the logic of a national statute irresistible? *Prigg* set in motion forces that led directly to the act of 1850 and beyond it to *Dred Scott*, in which Taney made the definitive case for the national and constitutional character of slavery.

Story cannot be blamed for all the history that followed *Prigg*. But nothing he said in that opinion would have tempered the draconian provisions of the 1850 statute. What he did say to Senator Berrien of Georgia on the matter of fugitive slave legislation is even more to the point. Story and Berrien had collaborated on legislative matters, and in 1842 Story forwarded to him a draft of a bill for a more effective rendition of fugitive slaves. "In the MSS Bill, which I handed you," he wrote, "the provision was *general*, that *in all cases*, where by the Laws of the U. States, powers were conferred on State Magistrates, the same power might be exercised by Commissioners appointed by the Circuit Courts." This was precisely the administrative innovation introduced by the act of 1850. Story went on to say that the change was necessary because of *Prigg* and "might be done without creating the slightest sensation in Congress," because if it "were made general . . . it would then pass without observation." These suggestions were prompted, Story concluded, with nothing in mind except "to further a true administration of public Justice."[116]

All of this says that if one seeks to prove that *Prigg* was a triumph for freedom, the argument must fail. There is one other difficulty with the argument, one that goes to the heart of Story's intent. To believe that Story consciously designed his opinion to make freedom triumphant, one must believe that he deliberately introduced a doctrine that would vitiate the right of recapture that he had plainly stated in the most absolute terms, a right that he had also defined in his *Commentaries* and that, if intent means anything, the framers themselves had established. Had Story set out to write an opinion for freedom he would have had to recant his earlier admonition to all patriots to uphold the slavery compromise of 1787; he would have had to deliberately encourage *judicial* circumvention of positive law. Had he done this, he would have behaved exactly as abolitionist constitutionalists advised, and this was the last thing he wanted to do.

Indeed, Story's opinion was influenced more by his fear of abolition than by his desire to free fugitive slaves. Judging by the opinion itself (rather than what his son said that his father said about it), it is fair to assume that Story did not *set out* to write an opinion for freedom. Whether he had *any* grand strategy in mind is doubtful. Certainly he did not want the job of speaking for the majority, and it was pressed on him by his brethren with an eye, no doubt, to giving the Court's decision a full measure of authority. His strategy, if one can call it that, was simply to state the law as he believed it to be, and this was what his son also concluded that he had done.[117] Story said as much to Ezekiel Bacon shortly after he handed down the opinion and while it was being assailed in the Northern press. "I shall never hesitate to do my duty as a Judge, under the Constitution and laws of the United States," he wrote, "be the consequences what they may. That Constitution I have sworn to support, and I cannot forget or repudiate my solemn obligations at pleasure. You know full well that I have ever been opposed to slavery. But I take my standard of duty *as a Judge* from the Constitution."[118]

Story returned to *Prigg* and the theme of judicial responsibility in his speech to the students at Harvard Law School on 21 December 1843—"the most eloquent lecture I have ever heard," remembered one of them. He talked about the rendition clause of the Constitution, which "some people wish to evade, or are willing wholly to disregard." And he went on to say: "If one part of the country may disregard one part of the Constitution, another section may refuse to obey that part which seems to bear hard upon its interests, and thus the Union will become a 'mere rope of sand'; and the Constitution, worse than a dead letter, an apple of discord in our midst, a fruitful source of reproach, bitterness, and hatred, and in the end discord and civil war. . . ." [119]

What Story did in *Prigg*, as he put it to his students, was to obey his oath of office; he upheld the slavery compromise of 1787, which, if it meant anything at all, meant that slaveholders had a constitutional claim to escaped slaves. *Prigg*, it must be remembered, did not create this claim. But it did reaffirm it in no uncertain terms. If freedom came out of this reaffirmation it came in the long run from the fact that a "naked" statement of the law would set in motion a current of public opinion determined to change it. This is how Wendell Phillips perceived the issue and how the American people, or at least a majority of them, ultimately saw it, too, as the Civil War attests. [120]

Change by violence, war, and revolution was not what Story had in mind in 1842, however. *Prigg* put forth compromise, and held out something to both North and South, in the hope that the great body of republican citizens might be rallied to the tradition of constitutional law and order that was the republican way of solving problems. This is to say that like Lemuel Shaw, Daniel Webster, Henry Clay, or the early Lincoln, for that matter, Story was an old Whig. For better or worse, he went back to the American Revolution, which taught him to cherish the Constitution, for all of its imperfections, as the only safeguard against chaos and social disorder. Taken in this perspective (the way Story took it), *Prigg* was not simply a conflict between positive law on one side and morality on the other but a choice between two different standards of morality: one radical and individualistic, the other Burkean and conservative. That Story's Burkean solution in *Prigg* should have intensified the chaos it hoped to control is only further evidence that Northern conservatives had lost touch with, and control of, history in the years before the Civil War. The war, it must be remembered, however, was an occasion for the resurrection of conservative values as well as the return of conservatives to power. [121] If Story's ideas were out of phase in the 1850s they most assuredly were not in the 1860s and 1870s, when law and order Whig style reasserted themselves. Story's doctrine of martial law and his dream of a national commercial Utopia would bring him back into the mainstream of American history—at least partly.

Daguerreotype of Justice Joseph Story, by Mathew Brady (ca. 1844).
Courtesy Library of Congress.

Epilogue

Statesman of the Old Republic

May our successors in the profession look back upon our times, not without some tender recollections. May they cherish our memories with that gentle reverence which belongs to those who have labored earnestly, though it may be humbly, for the advancement of the law. . . . And thus may they be enabled to advance our jurisprudence to that degree of perfection, which shall make it a blessing and protection to our country, and excite the just admiration of mankind
    Joseph Story, 1821

Are you not thus statesmen while you are lawyers, and because you are lawyers?
    Rufus Choate, 1845

In the ordinary and low sense which we attach to the words "partisan" and "politician," a judge of the Supreme Court should be neither. But in the higher sense, in the proper sense, he is not in my judgment fitted for the position unless he is a party man, a constructive statesman, constantly keeping in mind his adherence to the principles and policies under which this nation has been built up and in accordance with which it must go on.
    Theodore Roosevelt, 1902

Story informed close friends of his decision to quit the Court in the winter of 1845. He planned to make the announcement official in the fall of that year after completing his circuit and clearing the docket for his successor. The Court had been the focus of his life for thirty-three years; to leave it was to admit defeat. But he saw no alternative: "I must be in a dead minority of the Court," he explained to Ezekiel Bacon, "with the painful alternative of either pressing an open dissent from the opinions of the Court, or, by my silence, seeming to acquiesce in them. The former course would lead the public, as well as my brethren, to believe that I was determined, as far as I might, to diminish the just influence of the Court, and might subject me to the imputation of being, from motives of mortified ambition, or political hostility, earnest to excite popular prejudices against the Court. The latter course would subject me to the opposite imputation, of having either abandoned my old principles, or of having, in sluggish indolence, ceased to care what doctrines prevailed." Neither alternative was acceptable, and he concluded sadly "that by remaining on the Bench I could accomplish no good, either for myself or for my country."[1]

Once made, the decision seems to have lifted a great burden from the judge's shoulders. As his son put it, he had passed "the grand climacteric" of life: "He and his constitution seemed to have undergone a change which bade fair to insure him at least ten more years of strong health."[2] Indeed, his prospects were promising. His work on *Promissory Notes* came out in the summer of 1845 amid much acclaim at home and abroad. That volume completed his work on the various aspects of commercial contracts and freed him to turn to admiralty and maritime law, the last portion of his grand survey of American jurisprudence. In addition, he had agreed "with pleasure" to do a biography of Chief Justice Marshall, "that great and good man."[3] All this he could do within earshot of Harvard's bells while spending time with Sarah and his children and grandchildren. And, of course, there were his "children in the law," as he called his students. To them he pledged "the residue of my life and energies."[4] The University was delighted at Story's decision to return full time to the Law School and immediately set about making appropriate adjustments in his salary.[5] Harvard Law School had never been more prosperous or its future more promising. There were 140 students, one of the largest classes ever and one of the most national in makeup. The library was now the best in the country and growing rapidly, and plans were under way for a new library building and lecture room. Above all, the sense of purpose was still strong. At the commencement celebration in July 1845, Story heard Rufus Choate tell the assembly of notables, old friends, and students what he himself had said at his inaugural sixteen years before: that Harvard lawyers should be statesmen *because* they were lawyers.[6] Story returned home that evening with a sweet sense of accomplishment and contentment. He was "lucky" to have lived such a full and happy life, he confessed to Sarah. Remembering their lost children, she wondered whether his life had really been that contented. He admitted the pain but added that it was eased by his trust in the ways of Providence and his belief that he would join his children in heaven. He was grateful for his own good fortune. "My fame," he admitted honestly, "and the praise that has been so kindly given me, have been a great delight. What right had I to expect the prosperity and success that I have met with in life?"[7]

Two months later, on 10 September, Story died. He had fallen ill again after a strenuous effort to complete his circuit, successful to the point of leaving his last opinion written up in his desk. He grew progressively weaker for eight days and, knowing that death was certain, bade a serene farewell to his family. His last words praised God.

Those who had joined him so joyously at the Harvard celebration in July returned to pay their last respects. After the memorial service in his home, they followed his body to Mount Auburn Cemetery. Lining the road on both sides inside the gate were his students from the Law School, who stood solemnly with doffed hats and "countenances of sorrow." At the graveside gathered, as Sumner recollected, "all in our community that is most distinguished in law, in learning, in literature, in station; the Judges of our Courts, the Professors of the University, surviving classmates of the deceased, and a thick cluster of friends." He was buried among his children.[8]

Sumner returned to Mount Auburn after the other mourners had gone. He walked by the grave of Story's classmate Channing, who had tried valiantly to teach republican religion just as Story had aimed to teach republican law. Buried nearby was Professor John Ashmun, whose services to the Law School had been praised so fulsomely by Story in 1833. Sumner also remembered a similarly brilliant New England autumn day in 1831 when his departed friend had consecrated the ground in which he now lay buried. On that day Story had praised the capacity of the "rural cemetery" not only to console the bereaved but to inspire the living: The "illustrious dead" of Mount Auburn, the "great, the good, and the wise" buried on its slopes, would exercise "an animating presence, for our example and glory."[9] Story was talking about Burkean community, about republican fame. And Sumner still believed them possible. As he mourned his friend and teacher he was consoled by the "thought of the pilgrims that would come from afar, through long successions of generations, to look upon the last home of the great Jurist. From all parts of our own country," he predicted, "from all the lands where law is taught as a great science, and where justice prevails, they shall come to seek the grave of their master."[10]

Sumner's prophecy seems extravagant to modern sensibilities, but it would be a mistake to attribute it solely to his romantic nature. What Sumner said of Story is what Story said of John Marshall in 1835—indeed, what as a young Fourth of July orator he said of Washington in 1800. Fame had a special meaning for those Americans whose lives were touched by the Revolution. With it went a vision of a republican community rooted in virtue, dedicated to the tradition of public service. From early manhood on Story aimed to rank among the statesmen of the Republic. Sumner accorded him that honor, and who could disagree? No jurist of his age had done so much so well. As Sumner put it, "He was in himself a whole triumvirate."[11]

If one admits (as Story himself did) that Marshall was *the* expounder of the Constitution, concedes that no single work of scholarship in the antebellum period equaled Kent's *Commentaries*, and acknowledges (as modern scholars are now doing) that much of the truly creative work in American private law was done on the state level by judges like Lemuel Shaw and John Bannister Gibson, none of these concessions detracts from the commanding position that Story assumed by virtue of the scope of his activities. One must add to his great constitutional opinions like *Martin*, *Dartmouth College*, and the *Charles River Bridge* the fact that Story's *Commentaries on the Constitution* synthesized the great decisions of the Marshall Court, passed them on to succeeding generations of lawyers, and translated them into rules of construction for future judges. What was true of constitutional law was even more true of private law. As Holmes put it, "He has done more than any other English-speaking man in this century to make the law luminous and easy to understand."[12] In legal education he led the century, too, being the first to explore the educative potential of a university-based law school teaching *national* law. And to this one must add the educative impact of his scholarly opinions, his commentaries, and even his work on circuit. If one calculates not only the magnitude of his separate accomplishments as judge, author, and teacher but the force that each gathered by being related to the other, and adds to that sum the happy correspondence between what Story did and what his age needed (and allowed), then one could argue that no other person in American legal history has occupied such a position of influence. Certainly the vast outpouring of testimony from lawyers and judges, bar associations, courts, and other public bodies across the land on his death indicates that contemporaries acknowledged this level of greatness.[13]

Story's treatment by subsequent generations, however, has been more problematic, although a case can be made that he has never been forgotten. Those who read William Wetmore Story's remarkable *Life and Letters* of his father, published in 1851, could not fail to see the judge's magnanimity and the marvelous range of his accomplishments. Touching evidence of Story's lasting presence appears, too, in unexpected places. His statue, done by his son, still presides over the entrance to Langdell Hall, so that the father continues to bless his "children in the law." There is a Story Street in Cambridge and one in the Bronx. On a stained-glass window in the Cathedral of Saint John the Divine in New York City, Story consorts on equal terms with Solon, Hammurabi, Bracton, Grotius, and his esteemed colleague John Marshall.[14]

Most important as evidence of Story's durability has been his continued relevance in the life of American law. His commentaries continued to sell well into the twentieth century, even if scholars grew dissatisfied with them. Story's theory of conflict of laws may not hold the high ground it occupied in the nineteenth century, but twentieth-century critics have had to grapple with it nonetheless.[15] No decision from the antebellum Supreme Court was more actively employed in the post–Civil War period than *Swift* v. *Tyson*, and even now a lively debate rages on whether it should be "exhumed."[16] Story's decisions on the fiduciary responsibilities of corporations also have a current relevance.[17] His concern for the sanctity of private property and the duty of law to guarantee it have never ceased to be appreciated.

Story, it would appear then, came out on the winning side of American history. True, his defense of the slavery provisions of the Constitution and his hatred of abolitionism jeopardized his standing with the generation of Northerners that fought the Civil War. His posthumous return to the mainstream, however, was not long in coming. Story's hatred of Southernism was much akin to Northern sentiment in the 1850s, and his willingness to fight just wars—a position expressed to Charles Sumner shortly before his death [18] and implied clearly in his doctrine of martial law as laid down during the Dorr uprising—brought his ideas into harmony with the Union war effort. The revitalization of Whiggery in 1877, based as it was on a fusion of national union and national capitalism, resonated with his Whig politics. And above all, Story's constitutional nationalism, expressed so unanswerably in *Martin* v. *Hunter* and so authoritatively in his *Commentaries*, became the order of the new day. Admittedly, the old judge could not have been reconciled to the dominance of political parties and party men in the modern age. On the other hand, he would surely have been gratified by the continued relevance of the common law to American society and the activist role of lawyers and judges in modern America.

It might appear, then, that Sumner was right, that Story the legal statesman had achieved lasting fame. In fact, he had not. The fame so fully bestowed on Story by his own age did not last much beyond it. If he was not entirely forgotten, neither by most counts was he placed in the Pantheon of great American statesmen, which honor more often than not went to political figures rather than jurists and scholars. Even more baffling was the fact that, contrary to Sumner's prophecy, devotees of the law "through long successions of generations" did *not* come to pay homage to their master. In Story's house of jurisprudence, it would seem, there were many rooms, and many proved comforting and useful to the modern age. But those who took lodging did so for the night, without much noticing the jurisprudential architecture of the building in which they resided and without understanding the cultural foundation on which the great edifice rested. Those who did glimpse Story's whole system of jurisprudence (most notably the judges and legal scholars who repudiated his opinion in *Swift*) found little to admire. Story's writings about legal science and the morality of law—indeed, his constant reference to *the* law—are likely to draw a snort or a yawn from modern law students. It is not surprising, of course, that Story's work should have been questioned by new generations of lawyers and judges. But it is noticeable that in this process of supersedence there were so few of those "tender recollections" which Story hoped future lawyers and judges would bestow on his labors, so few efforts among those who criticized him and borrowed from him to understand the great man in the full context of his own times.

Even at Harvard Law School, the judge's stature and relevancy declined with an uncharitable swiftness. One student who attended the Law School in 1852–53 recalled that, though Story's memory was "green," there was "a distinct anti-Story reaction" in Cambridge, especially in regard to his written works. Students particularly did not like "his copious citations from the unknown works of foreign jurists," and consequently the great collection of civil law that Story labored to bring to the library went unused.[19] Institutional gratitude was not entirely lacking, to be sure. In 1850 the Story Association, Harvard Law School's first alumni association, came into being, though it should be noted that the initiative was taken by former students of Story's who were distressed that the University itself had not yet acted.[20] A further and somewhat "tardy" acknowledgment of Story's services came in 1875 with the creation of the Story Professorship. Even these gestures seemed to lack conviction, however. The first official meeting of the Story Association in 1851 was given over to antiabolition harangues and a political defense of the fugitive slave act of 1850, so that Story's name was hardly mentioned—to the great dismay of Josiah Quincy. The first president of the Story Association was William Kent, the son of James Kent, who as professor at the Law School lived uncomfortably in Story's shadow and who privately denigrated his scholarship.[21] Ironically, the first occupant of the Story chair was John Chipman Gray, whose offhand remarks in his *Nature and Sources of the Law* (1909) did so much to popularize the notion that Story was sunk in vanity and jurisprudential metaphysics.

Criticizing the founder, in fact, seemed to be the fashion in the decades on either side of 1900. Already in 1886 Holmes could declare with finality that "Story's simple philosophizing had ceased to satisfy men's minds" and could estimate that "there are plenty of men nowadays not a hundredth part of Story's power who could write as good statements of the law as his, or better."[22] As telling as Holmes's criticism is the fact that Story was increasingly ignored. The first dozen volumes of the *Harvard Law Review,* founded in 1887, made surprisingly few references to his work, even when they would have seemed appropriate. Dean Langdell's case method might have been seen as building on the common-law methodology of instruction introduced by Story; it was billed instead as a radical break. So too was the realistic view of constitutional law that James Bradley Thayer announced in his pioneering essay "The Origin and Scope of the American Doctrine of Constitutional Law," published in the October 1893 issue of the *Harvard Law Review.* As for private law, it will be recalled that Gray, Holmes, and Brandeis played key roles in laying *Swift* to rest.

The new age, it was clear, was bent more on repudiating the antebellum world of law than on understanding it. And here in the struggle of a new jurisprudence to define itself one catches a glimpse of the reasons for Story's unceremonious decline, why he was acknowledged mainly while he was being rejected. It was not that Story was suddenly irrelevant, one must speculate, but that he persisted in seeming relevant. As Grant Gilmore suggested, "The extraordinary achievement of the first half century of law may well have contributed to the excesses of the following half century."[23] Because so much that Story wrought lasted into the late nineteenth century, he could be held responsible, at least symbolically, for its excesses. In the age of corporate abuse, Story's defense of corporations seemed positively sinister, as did his suspicion of state regulation. Because he appreciated Amos Lawrence so much it could be concluded that he would have approved equally of John D. Rockefeller and J. P. Morgan. Story's celebration of property rights appeared to bolster the forces of social injustice, just as his expansive view of judicial authority seemed to lead directly to the unparalleled conservative activism of the late nineteenth-century Supreme Court. Story's version of legal science and principled adjudication could easily be seen as a primitive version of rule formalism and mechanical jurisprudence. In short, those who wanted social reform through reformed law, who wanted to break the bond between law and corporate conservatism, found themselves pitted against, if not Judge Story, then at least the legal world he helped make.

The question begged is whether Story's jurisprudence really did contribute significantly to the conservative legal establishment of the late nineteenth century. To deny the connection would be pointless, but Story's legal system must be judged by standards not of a later age but of his own. There is, however, one aspect of Story's thought that may have invited later misuse, this being the almost total absence in his jurisprudence of self-critical perspective. Skepticism was not one of his intellectual qualities; speculation was positively anathema; and the anthropological curiosity that permeates Holmes's *Common Law* was not even hinted at. Certitudes bristled at every turn. This pervasive quality of assuredness, it might be argued, obliterated the concessions to change that Story did at points make; it may have, perhaps unfairly, imparted to his jurisprudence a static quality that invited ossification. Judges and lawyers, the main keepers of Story's fame, had to diminish it to get on with the work of adjusting law to real life as their profession required them to do. Those who found something in Story's jurisprudence to use did most to keep his reputation alive. That Pound found the most—this being his (and Story's) deep faith that legal science could produce socially relevant law—may explain why he of all the early twentieth-century legal activists came closest to understanding Story as a man of his own age.[24]

Bits and pieces of Story's law will undoubtedly continue to be salvaged from the wreckage of his jurisprudence. But his system as a whole, like Humpty Dumpty, can never be put together again. It must be understood as the creation of a unique moment in American history or, more precisely, as the singular commingling of history and biography. The American Revolution inspired its children to be great; Story was located in time and place so as to receive the full force of the Enlightenment message; his natural genius made greatness possible. If he was passionately confident in what he did, it was because the age invited such faith in the works of reason; if there was a unity to his life's work, it was in no small part because the culture of the early republic was itself integrated.

This is not to deny the tensions that lay beneath the surface. The new West beckoned, but Europe was still close, closer in some ways than in the age of modern technology. The deferential society of the eighteenth century had given way to the democratic tendencies of the new republic only grudgingly; a final accommodation remained to be worked out. Nationalism was as yet a thin veneer covering localism. State and sectional self-interest lay close to the surface of American reality and threatened, both in the North and in the South, to turn into self-conscious sectionalism and sectional nationalism. The republican notion that private interest and community welfare could be complementary had not yet been put to the practical test by ordinary men and women coping with the drudgery and insecurity of daily life. What kept the possibility alive, what held together the other polarities of republican culture, was the living memory of the Revolution. To those like Story whose lives it touched the Revolution was a miracle, a sign of God's grace, a reminder of the covenant. Beneath the umbrella of revolutionary idealism, Americans convinced themselves that individual, class, state, and sectional interests might be harnessed to the chariot of republican greatness. With Washington as his model Story set out to realize the promise of the American Enlightenment, to make the Revolution permanent.

What strikes modern tastes in Story's writings and speeches as bombast, what elicited from even his own students a tolerant smile, is the key to understanding. Lawyers and judges should be statesmen. Law was an instrument of revolutionary purpose, a means of fulfilling Story's obligation to God, the fathers of his country, his own father. History encouraged Story the jurist to be audacious; and how else can one understand his insatiable ambition, his unrelenting labor, the vast scope of his jurisprudence? Even the absence of self-criticism in Story's system is largely attributable to the age, which, perhaps because it was so anxious, dealt in absolutes so easily. Story was so busy thinking about how law might be harnessed to the needs of a republican people that he had no time or inclination to think about thinking. Jurisprudential self-consciousness was a luxury reserved for a later age, an age when growing complexity generated skepticism (and curiosity) and swamped easy answers in intellectual relativism.

In contrast, Story's age and Story's law were shot through with a faith in the creative force of human reason. If Blackstone represented the first surge of Enlightenment thought in the law, then Story was the crest of the wave. Both imposed a rational structure on diverse, chaotic, and increasingly complex materials by the sheer force of their organizing genius. And both did so without surrendering a belief in the morality of rationality. With Thomas Jefferson, Story shared the fundamental belief that mankind could be studied scientifically, that the complex problems of human government would yield to the science of government of which legal science was but a part. Story's system of American law was grounded in the rationalism of the eighteenth century. Many years ago Carl Becker taught us how idealistic, how romantic, this new "heavenly city" was. But that was no problem. Story's age allowed him to be a rationalist and a romantic at the same time. It was precisely because he aspired to so much for his country and for the law that he fell prey to gloom and despondency.

If Story's idealism was rooted in enlightened reason, so also was the superstructure of his jurisprudence. The revolutionary age encouraged American statesmen to think systematically and comprehensively. Such was the thrust of the prevailing method of the natural sciences, which set the intellectual tone for the age. Systematic thinking was possible, moreover, because knowledge was yet manageable and society in America comparatively simple and homogeneous. Specialization had not yet fractured the intellectual universe; thus, politics was inseparable from economics and both were connected to morality and ethics. Above all, perhaps, American statesmen were invited to think comprehensively because they assumed that they were "building for the ages." Story was a "philosophical" lawyer, a "juristic" judge, for the reason that John Adams was a president, a political thinker and writer, and a student of history all at the same time: because early national culture contained a syntactic imperative to unify and harmonize.

Story's legal system tended consistently toward integration. Public and private law, the common law, and the Constitution were seen interconnectedly as part of the larger world of legal science. Equity and the common law, though separate, were complementary. Conflict of laws made a science of cacophony. Commercial law, of which contract was the essence, rested on the same assumption as did republican government: that people were rational creatures who, with the aid of law and institutions, might control their own destinies. Story accepted the premises of John Locke and Adam Smith that individual enterprise and community well-being were inseparably connected. But that acceptance did not keep him from being one of the most dedicated Burkeans of his age. Story would unleash the creative energies of individuals through commercial and constitutional law on the assumption that national union would thereby be strengthened. He applied the private law of contract to the public law of corporations without hesitation. There was no contradiction, either, between governmental paternalism and free enterprise. The market economy that Story strengthened at every turn would, he assumed, not lose its beneficent character as long as scientific lawyers held sway.

One stands in amazement at the bold systematizing of Story's law—and at what he assumed law could do, what republican lawyers and judges were expected to do. Law was for Story what religion was for Jonathan Edwards: the mind, heart, and soul, the binding cement, of a community dedicated to individualism. Like the authors of the *Federalist*, Story saw law as the instrument by which men institutionalized their rational moments as a bulwark against their foolishness, passions, and selfishness. That lawyers and judges would have a special role to play in republican culture followed logically. Story saw this potential for judicial governance and realized that lawyers and judges might shape the course of history. To be a teacher, an author, and a judge was to be a statesman as the American Enlightenment defined the term.

By the standards of the revolutionary age, Story had a right to expect fame for his efforts—the republican immortality that Sumner was so sure would be his. But fame (in contrast to notoriety) is a function of a community united in purposes, values, and beliefs. The republican community brought into being by the American Revolution was a victim of the nineteenth century despite the victory of nationalism (and perhaps, as Carl Becker suggested, because of it). Story the nationalist, who seemed so clearly on the winning side of history, was at least in one profound sense a loser. Such was his own perception of things (as it was also John Marshall's). Story was not only an actor in American history but a witness of it. What he witnessed and recounted, in the pervasive gloom of his private correspondence, was the growing strength of centrifugal forces that eroded the foundations of republican community. Story saw these forces not as inevitable consequences of demography or economics or social history but as a decline in morality, human backsliding from the ideals of the Revolution. He addressed the perceived transformation of the old republic not so much intellectually as emotionally.

Perhaps for this reason he failed to question the intellectual and historical premises on which he operated. Instead he tightened the knot of interconnectedness in his system and reasserted the unified vision of republican law with even more assurance. Faith mixed with fear accounted for what he did not see in his age, what he did not fully consider. He did not, for example, sufficiently explore the ethics of his working alliance with Daniel Webster (though surely he was shocked to hear from Sumner and must have known earlier that Webster was on the payroll of New England capitalists).[25] He was not inclined to scrutinize closely the relationship between nationalism and sectionalism, to consider the possibility that New

England nationalism stemmed, no less than Southern sectionalism, from self-interest—or that the Constitution itself might in the last analysis rest on the same foundation.

He did not fully appreciate the revolution in social and economic power that came with the business corporation, though some of his contemporaries did, including some of his colleagues on the Supreme Court. He saw individuals down in their fortunes and he contributed generously to alleviate their condition, but there is no evidence that he was troubled by the enormous and frightening gap between rich and poor in the cities of Jacksonian America.[26] By insisting with the conservatives of the age that equality was the main condition of American society, he failed to consider the possibility that the law he fashioned so effectively to serve the likes of New England businessmen might be inapplicable to other Americans or even threatening to them. The growing inequality of American society, the subtle emergence of class lines, could undermine contractual freedom. Legislatures rather than judges might have to address social injustice that the free market produced. Story caught no intimation of such developments. Finally, by opposing abolitionism, he paid a price that proved the sincerity of his nationalism and of his faith that law would bring order and justice. But he did not perceive that abolitionist constitutionalism, which culminated in the Civil War amendments, might be the cutting edge of a new admixture of morality and law, that in a segmented and unequal society lawmakers might have to choose social justice over legal science and perhaps even property rights.

To recount what Story did not see is not to blame him. To be sure, some of his contemporaries grappled more boldly than he with the mounting problem of social dislocation. Perhaps the tensions in his own legal system—as in *Tyler* v. *Wilkinson*, for example, or the *Bridge* case, or in his decisions relating to slavery—should have prompted him to inquire and question. Still, the historical writing on the wall was not clear, especially not, one feels, when read from a New England perspective. It is unlikely, moreover, that Story could have built so well had he doubted more. In any case, what he did when faced with the unhinging forces of nineteenth-century history was to struggle valiantly to complete his magnificent edifice of law that rested on the foundation of an earlier age. That he did so helps explain why the greatest of early nineteenth-century legal reformers should also have been a pioneer American conservative. Modern conservatives bent on resurrecting states' rights and weakening the Supreme Court will not find much comfort in Story's judicial nationalism. Nor will conservative pundits who mobilize the learning of the Western world to prove that plumbers are corrupt and grape pickers overpaid. But as James McClellan has so persuasively shown, Story's contributions to American conservatism were formidable. Resistance to change, he saw, could not be the focal point for conservatism in a country where change was endemic. Who controlled change was the issue, and no conservative of his age or ours worked so comprehensively to put the "right" men in control. Elitist Story was, but his elitism was based on merit, service, and ability, not inherited privilege. His doubts about popular government, moreover, never turned to cynicism and withdrawal. As long as Story lived, he struggled to make American society rational, equitable, and moral. Perhaps his faith in the American people ought to be measured not by what he said about them but by what he did for them.

Story's conservatism, then, ought not to obscure his creative impact on American law. Unlike Burke, who defended institutions as the embodiment of human wisdom and morality, Story was forced to create institutions that lived up to the ideals of a society conceived in revolution. Conservative law was harnessed to the goal of radical creativity, and the historical moment allowed the polarity to stand. Because the law was limited in scope and embryonic in character, Story could master it and presume to shape and mold it. But he did his shaping at a time when the social, economic, and demographic foundation on which his legal system rested was rapidly shifting. The age that encouraged Story to build nobly doomed his noble system to impermanence. No doubt Holmes was correct that no man of Story's generation, including Story himself, "could have stated the law in a form that deserved to abide."[27] But no man *except* one of Story's generation would have been tempted to try. In this respect, Story saw himself accurately: He was, truly, "the last of the old race of judges."

Story was right, too, about the American Revolution, against which he judged men and measures. For all its impact, it was a profoundly perishable moment. He never lived to see the last gasp of republican aspiration, but those inspired by that earlier age who lived beyond the Civil War often found themselves beyond the pale.[28] George Ticknor, with whom Story had worked to build greatness for Harvard, New England, and the nation, fell silent in the years after the war, his energies spent, his learning wrapped tight around him to keep out the chill blast of irrelevance. Longfellow, who in many ways was to American poetry what Story was to American law, was increasingly remembered, like Story himself, for his weaknesses rather than his strengths. And so it went. New England's men of learning and letters who labored confidently to define a national culture came themselves to seem quaintly provincial, unseated, or perhaps, like Henry Adams, degraded by a pervasive "democratic dogma." The new order wanted new heroes. Intellectuals in harmony with the new science were not prepared to admit their indebtedness to the old. So it was that Langdell's legal science replaced Story's with little generous remembrance and no acknowledgment of shared principles and common objectives.

In the despondency of his last years, Story sensed that he was doomed to be in perpetual dissent, not only from the majority of the Supreme Court but from the main current of American history. William Wetmore Story lived to see his father's fears come true, and in his own expatriation he spoke his father's disillusionment and his own distress at the ingratitude of his countrymen. In 1857 he gave up a promising career in law and legal scholarship, took up sculpting, and traded the "small potatoes" society of Boston and government by Presidents Pierce and Buchanan for the beauty and artistic freedom of Rome. In the father, romanticism and rationalism were fused: ambition with public service. With the son as with the new age, the harmony of the republican world was a fading memory. After Gettysburg and the Wilderness, glory seemed a hollow word; in the age of Grant, fame was a pointless quest.

Notes

Chapter One

1. Arthur M. Walter to William S. Shaw, 30 May 1803, William Smith Shaw Papers, Boston Athenaeum.

2. *Memoir of William Ellery Channing, with Extracts from His Correspondence and Manuscripts*, 3 vols. (Boston, 1848), 1:52.

3. Walter to Shaw, 1 July 1803, Shaw Papers.

4. Josiah Dwight to H. G. Otis, 16 March 1808, H. G Otis Papers, Massachusetts Historical Society, Boston (hereafter cited as MHS).

5. John R. Howe, "Republican Thought and the Political Violence of the 1790s," 19 *American Quarterly* (Summer 1967): 147–65.

6. Shaw to Walter, 6 January 1798, Shaw Papers.

7. See Erik H. Erikson, *Young Man Luther: A Study in Psychoanalysis and History* (New York, 1958). The passage cited as chapter epigraph is on pp. 253–54.

8. See especially "Ambiguities of the American Revolution," chap. 7 in Michael G. Kammen, *People of Paradox: An Inquiry concerning the Origins of American Civilization* (New York, 1973), pp. 225–49.

9. *Life and Letters of Joseph Story*, ed. William W. Story, 2 vols. (London, 1851), 1:2, 3 (hereafter cited as *LL*).

10. Perley Derby (drawing on James Savage) starts the Story family in America with Elisha, who allegedly arrived from England about 1700 with his sister Sarah ("Elisha Story of Boston and Some of His Descendants, Compiled by Perley Derby, with Additions by Frank A. Gardner, M.D.," 50 *Essex Institute Historical Collections* [1914]: 297–312; 51 [1915]: 41–52). Ruth Story and Devereaux Eddy argue convincingly that William Story of Ipswich was the first Story in America ("The Ancestry of Judge Joseph Story, Justice of the Supreme Court of the United States," 83 *Essex Institute Historical Collections* [January 1947]: 59–66). I have accepted their conclusions.

11. Story and Eddy, "Ancestry of Judge Story," pp. 60–61.

12. Will of Elisha Story, 30 September 1725, no. 5138, Registry of Probate, Suffolk County Court House, Boston.

13. For these real estate transactions see Annie H. Thwing, comp., "Inhabitants and Estates of the Town of Boston, 1630–1800 . . . ," 2 vols. (Boston, 1916), bound typescript in MHS.

14. For the litigation between Lydia and William along with the warrant from the probate settling the matter, see will of Elisha Story, 1725.

15. Thwing, "Inhabitants." See catalogue entry to Thwing's work at the MHS, under William Story, for 5 August 1762.

16. Documents concerning William Story are scarce possibly because his papers were burned by the Boston mob in August 1765. His forestalled career as place-seeker has been pieced together from the Thomas Hutchinson manuscripts at the MHS and other contemporary sources by G. B. Warden. I am grateful to him for making available to me, through the generous good offices of Mary Beth Norton, his "Preliminary Report: Benjamin Franklin and the Hutchinson Letters" (18 January 1971), from which my account is derived.

17. John Adams, *Diary and Autobiography of John Adams*, ed. L. H. Butterfield, associ-

ate eds., Leonard C. Faber and Wendell D. Garrett, 4 vols. (Cambridge, Mass., 1961), 2:45–46.

18. The account of the Whately letters is told in chap. 7 of Bernard Bailyn, *The Ordeal of Thomas Hutchinson* (Cambridge, Mass., 1974), pp. 221–73.

19. I have drawn heavily on the excellent summary of Marblehead's economic history in George A. Billias, *General John Glover and His Marblehead Mariners* (New York, 1960), pp. 17–27. Also see his *Elbridge Gerry: Founding Father and Republican Statesman* (New York, 1976), chap. 2.

20. See Billias, *Gerry*, pp. 37–39, for a succinct account.

21. Samuel Roads, Jr., *The History and Traditions of Marblehead* (Boston, 1880), p. 504.

22. Marblehead's revolutionary politics are treated in ibid., pp. 83–90, 123–57; Arthur M. Schlesinger, *The Colonial Merchants and the American Revolution, 1763–1776* (New York, 1918), pp. 60, 80, 184–85, 260, 314, 440–41, 479–80, 481–83; Billias, *Glover*, pp. 27–66; and Billias, *Gerry*, pp. 11–54.

23. Autobiographical letter to William Story (hereafter cited as "Autobiography"), 23 January 1831, in *The Miscellaneous Writings of Joseph Story . . .* , ed. William W. Story (Boston, 1852), p. 7 (hereafter cited as *MW*).

24. Roads, *History of Marblehead*, pp. 123–24.

25. *Salem Gazette*, 5 May 1801, as cited in Paul Goodman, *The Democratic-Republicans of Massachusetts: Politics in a Young Republic* (Cambridge, Mass., 1964), p. 116.

26. Roads, *History of Marblehead*, p. 125.

27. See Billias, *Glover*, for the exploits of General Glover and his men.

28. Journal of Edward Bowen, 23 January 1779, as quoted in Samuel Roads, Jr., *The Marblehead Manual* (Marblehead, Mass., 1883), p. 9.

29. S. B. Farmer to Mr. Beltram, Hartford, Conn., 11 March 1898, Pedrick Papers, Marblehead Historical Society, Marblehead, Mass.

30. Ibid.

31. *LL*, 1:14–16.

32. "Autobiography," pp. 3–4; *LL*, 1:9–12; Mary E. Phillips, *Reminiscences of William Wetmore Story* (Chicago, 1897), pp. 17–18. For confirming details of Elisha's participation in the Boston Tea Party see Joseph Story to B. B. Thatcher, 29 March 1836, Joseph Story Letters, Free Library, Philadelphia.

33. The relation between colonial and revolutionary thought has been explored by Perry Miller, Edmund Morgan, and Allan Heimert, among others, but see especially Nathan O. Hatch, *The Sacred Cause of Liberty: Republican Thought and the Millennium in Revolutionary New England* (New Haven, Conn., 1977).

34. On the centrality of family in education see Bernard Farber, *Guardians of Virtue: Salem Families in 1800* (New York, 1972), p. 172.

35. "Autobiography," pp. 6–8.

36. William Bentley, *The Diary of William Bentley, D.D., Pastor of the East Church, Salem, Massachusetts*, 4 vols. (Salem, Mass., 1905) 1:303.

37. Story to Richard H. Dana, Jr., 14 October 1840, *LL*, 2:343.

38. *LL*, 1:29–30; "Autobiography," p. 10.

39. Story to Edward Everett, 1 November 1832, Joseph Story Papers, MHS. This letter was also autobiographical in nature, as requested by Everett.

40. "Autobiography," p. 7.

41. Ibid., p. 10.

42. Ibid., pp. 5–6.

43. See p. 180 in Chapter 5. Useful insights on the role of family in education and socialization can be found in Bernard Bailyn, *Education in the Forming of American Society: Needs and Opportunities for Study* (Chapel Hill, N.C., 1960); Farber, *Guardians of Virtue*;

and Joseph F. Kett, *Rites of Passage: Adolescence in America, 1790 to the Present* (New York, 1977).

44. Story to W. W. Story, 10 February 1833, Charles Sumner Papers, Houghton Library, Harvard University, Cambridge, Mass. (also quoted in *LL*, 1:27).

45. Elisha Story's last will and testament is on deposit in the files of the Trial Court, Probate and Family Court Department, Essex Division, Essex County Court House, Salem, Mass. See Essex County Probate Docket, 1638–1840.

46. For the success ethic and the movement of young men into cities in the early nineteenth century, see Kett, *Rites of Passage*, chap. 4. Also helpful in understanding the role of the family in secular socialization is Rowland T. Berthoff, *An Unsettled People: Social Disorder in American History* (New York, 1971), pp. 204–17.

47. S. B. Farmer to Mr. Beltram, Hartford, Conn., 11 March 1898, Pedrick Papers.

48. For the historical context see "The 'Copartnership of Marriage,'" chap. 14 in Berthoff, *Unsettled People*, pp. 204–17.

49. *LL*, 1:15.

50. She was made sole executrix of his will (*LL*, 1:13).

51. "Autobiography," p. 3.

52. Ibid., p. 4.

53. Ibid.

54. "Epitaph on my Father—who died August 1805," Joseph Story Papers, microfilm, University of Texas, Austin (hereafter cited as Story Papers, UT).

55. See Farber, *Guardians of Virtue*, p. 187, on the growing moderation of family discipline.

56. Such deference prevailed among many families of the Federalist elite. James M. Banner, Jr., *To the Hartford Convention: The Federalists and the Origins of Party Politics in Massachusetts, 1789–1815* (New York, 1970), p. 55.

57. Story himself recognized an intermediate stage between childhood and adulthood that was unknown to an earlier age; "juvenescence," he called it (Story to W. W. Story, 10 February 1833, Sumner Papers).

58. As recounted by W. W. Story, *LL*, 1:25–26.

59. "Autobiography," p. 5.

60. For a concise discussion of the educational philosophy in *Emile*, see Victor G. Wexler, "'Made for Man's Delight': Rousseau as Antifeminist," 81 *American Historical Review* (April 1976): 266–91, especially 271–75.

61. *LL*, 1:75–76.

62. Maria Edgeworth and Richard L. Edgeworth, *The Practical Education*, 3 vols. (London, 1801).

63. Channing, *Memoir*, 1:35–36.

64. "Autobiography," pp. 8–9.

65. Joseph Story, *The Power of Solitude, a Poem in Two Parts* . . . (Salem, Mass., 1801).

66. Edward Young, *Night Thoughts on Life, Death and Immortality* . . . (London, 1777).

67. "Autobiography," p. 10.

68. George Wilson of Marblehead got the account directly from Hawkes, who was there (*LL*, 1:19–20).

69. See Jennifer Tebbe, "Print and American Culture," 32 *American Quarterly* (Bibliography issue, 1980): 259–79, for a general discussion of the subject.

70. His ordination sermon on the occasion of Daniel's call to the church at Marietta, Ohio, in 1798 is mentioned in Harriet S. Tapley, *Salem Imprints, 1768–1825: A History of the First Fifty Years of Printing in Salem, Massachusetts* . . . (Salem, Mass., 1927), p. 367. For his ebullient patriotism see Rev. Isaac Story, *A Discourse, Delivered February 15, 1795, at the Request of the Proprietors' Committee* . . . (Salem, Mass., 1795), and *A Sermon,*

396 | *Notes to pp. 19–26*

Preached February 19, 1795 . . . Being the Federal Thanksgiving . . . (Salem, Mass., 1795), no. 29571 in *Early American Imprints, 1639–1800,* ed. Clifford K. Shipton (microcard).

71. Isaac Story to William Story, 24 August 1797, Story Papers, Marblehead Historical Society.

72. Paul S. Boyer and Stephen Nissenbaum, *Salem Possessed: The Social Origins of Witchcraft* (Cambridge, Mass., 1974), p. 133.

73. *LL*, 1:22, 26–7.

74. Quoted in *LL*, 1:13.

75. Story to Edward Everett, 1 November 1832, Story Papers, MHS.

76. Kett, *Rites of Passage,* pp. 18–20.

77. Michael Walsh, *A New System of Mercantile Arithmetic . . .* (Newburyport, Mass., 1801).

78. Story to Everett, 1 November 1832, Story Papers, MHS.

79. Viscemius Knox, *Elegant Extracts; or, Useful and Entertaining Passages in Prose, Selected for the Improvement of Scholars at Classical and Other Schools in the Art of Speaking, in Reading, Thinking, Composing; and in the Conduct of Life* (London, ca. 1783). There were various editions in England and the United States of this standard anthology.

80. "Autobiography," p. 10.

81. For the episodes dealing with Harris and Story's early entrance into Harvard see ibid., pp. 11–12.

82. Ibid., p. 13.

83. Ibid., p. 14.

84. Edward Everett, "Biographical Memoir of Daniel Webster," in Daniel Webster, *The Writings and Speeches of Daniel Webster,* National Ed., 18 vols. (Boston, 1903), 1:15.

85. Story to W. F. Channing, [23 September] 1843, Channing, *Memoir,* 1:45.

86. Cleveland Amory, *The Proper Bostonians* (New York, 1947), p. 294.

87. Channing, *Memoir,* 1:60.

88. "Autobiography," pp. 15–16.

89. From the account of D. A. White of Salem, in Channing, *Memoir,* 1:58.

90. For education at Harvard during the late eighteenth century see Josiah Quincy, *The History of Harvard University,* 2 vols. (Cambridge, Mass., 1840), 2:258–83; Samuel E. Morison, *Three Centuries of Harvard, 1636–1936* (Cambridge, Mass., 1936), pp. 133–95; Richard Hofstadter, *Academic Freedom in the Age of the College* (New York, 1955), pp. 152–208; and Russel B. Nye, *The Cultural Life of the New Nation, 1776–1830* (New York, 1960), pp. 171–94.

91. Story to W. F. Channing, [23 September] 1843, Channing, *Memoir,* 1:49.

92. "Autobiography," p. 17.

93. *LL*, 1:59–60.

94. "Autobiography," p. 14.

95. Story to W. F. Channing, [23 September] 1843, Channing, *Memoir,* 1:46.

96. Morison, *Three Centuries of Harvard,* p. 184. On Rollin and ambition see John Adams to Benjamin Rush, September 1807, as quoted in *The Spur of Fame: Dialogues of John Adams and Benjamin Rush, 1805–1813,* ed. John Schutz and Douglass Adair (San Marino, Calif., 1966), pp. 94–95.

97. Hofstadter, *Academic Freedom,* p. 193.

98. Daniel Walker Howe, *The Unitarian Conscience: Harvard Moral Philosophy, 1805–1861* (Cambridge, Mass., 1970), p. 165.

99. John Marshall, *The Papers of John Marshall,* ed. Herbert A. Johnson (Chapel Hill, N.C., 1974), 1:334.

100. Frederick Rudolph, *The American College and University: A History* (New York: Vintage, 1965), p. 25.

101. Morison, *Three Centuries of Harvard*, p. 174.

102. Channing, *Memoir*, 1:47.

103. Story to W. F. Channing, [23 September 1843], Channing, *Memoir*, 1:45–50.

104. Story gave his composition to Woods for criticism, which chore the latter took with great seriousness (Leonard Woods to Story, 12 September 1796, Joseph Story Papers, microfilm, Clements Library, University of Michigan, Ann Arbor [hereafter cited as Story Papers, UM]).

105. Nye, *Cultural Life*, p. 35.

106. Channing, *Memoir*, 1:66.

107. Walter to Shaw, 3 September 1799, Shaw Papers.

108. Channing, *Memoir*, 1:54.

109. Walter to Shaw, 16 October 1802, Shaw Papers.

110. James Banner, Jr., notes the tendency of orthodox clerics in Massachusetts to take a dim view of the enterprising ethos, whereas Unitarians increasingly favored worldly success (*To the Hartford Convention*, p. 57 n. 8).

111. For a discussion of Story's mature Unitarian views see pp. 180–81.

112. Story's poem "Reason" was delivered at Commencement (*LL*, 1:58). "A few years afterwards," Story burned the poem, and noted that his "memory retains no traces of it" ("Autobiography," p. 17).

113. Joseph Story, "Life, Character, and Services of Chief Justice Marshall: A Discourse Pronounced on the 15th of October, 1835, at the Request of the Suffolk Bar," in *MW*, p. 641.

114. John Adams to George Wythe, 1776, *The Works of John Adams . . .*, ed. C. F. Adams, 10 vols. (Boston, 1850–56), 4:200.

115. This phrase, used many years later in his eulogy on Chief Justice Marshall, captures his own youthful sentiments (*MW*, p. 641).

116. Addison's play *Cato* was first performed in London on 14 April 1712. It was a great favorite among American college students and was even performed before Washington at Valley Forge in 1778 (Meyer Reinhold, *The Classick Pages: Classical Reading of Eighteenth-Century Americans* [University Park, Pa., 1975], pp. 147–51).

117. See Hatch, *Sacred Cause of Liberty*.

118. See I. Story, *A Discourse, Delivered February 15, 1795*, and *A Sermon, Preached February 19, 1795*.

119. Quincy, *History of Harvard*, 2:156.

120. Story's letter to W. F. Channing recaptures this self-generating intellectual life among Harvard students and their commitment to excellence during his stay there (Channing, *Memoir*, 1:45–50).

121. Ibid., pp. 49–50.

122. Ibid., pp. 70–72.

123. Story's ode was printed in the *Columbian Centinel*, 30 June 1798.

124. See, for example, Thomas Welsh to Joseph Story, 17(?) June 1799, Story Papers, UM; Story to William Williams, 12 January 1838, Story Papers, UT; and especially Nathaniel Lord to Arthur Walter, 20 May 1799, Shaw Papers.

125. Lord to Walter, 20 May 1799, Shaw Papers.

126. Story to S. P. P. Fay, 6 September 1798, *LL*, 1:71.

127. Michael Walsh to Story, 1794, Story Papers, UT.

128. A. B. [Walsh] to Story, 4 July 1797, ibid.

129. C. D. [Walsh] to Story, 5 July 1797, ibid.

130. Joseph Story, *An Eulogy on George Washington, Written at the Request of the Inhabitants of Marblehead and Delivered before Them on the Second Day of January, A.D. 1800* (Salem, Mass., 1800), pp. 15, 3, 10.

131. See Schutz and Adair, *Spur of Fame*, especially chap. 1.

Chapter Two

1. "Autobiography," p. 30. The first headnote to this chapter comes from this document, also p. 30. The second headnote is from *LL*, 1:310.
2. Erik H. Erikson, *Identity: Youth and Crisis* (New York, 1968), p. 241.
3. "Autobiography," p. 17.
4. Joseph Story, *A Selection of Pleadings in Civil Actions, Subsequent to the Declaration* . . . (Salem, Mass., 1805).
5. See Gerard W. Gawalt, *The Promise of Power: The Emergence of the Legal Profession in Massachusetts, 1760–1840* (Westport, Conn., 1979), for an excellent discussion of the whole subject.
6. Lord to Walter, 20 May 1799, Shaw Papers. Lord's letter, itself a paean to ambition, ends with a poem in praise of aspiration.
7. Ibid.
8. "Autobiography," p. 19.
9. See Story to S. P. P. Fay, 6 September 1798, *LL*, 1:75–76; Story to Fay, 6 January 1801, 15 April 1799, *LL*, 1:77, 80; Story to Thomas Welsh, 19 October 1799, *LL*, 1:81–83.
10. Story to Fay, 6 September 1798, *LL*, 1:71.
11. Samuel Sewall to Story, 12 February 1799, Story Papers, UM.
12. Blackstone's influence in America is discussed in chap. 10 of David A. Lockmiller's *Sir William Blackstone* (Chapel Hill, N.C., 1938), pp. 169–90; and in Dennis R. Nolan, "Sir William Blackstone and the New American Republic: A Study of Intellectual Impact," 51 *New York University Law Review* (November 1976): 731–68.
13. Sewall to Story, 12 February 1799, Story Papers, UM.
14. For an intellectual analysis of Blackstone's *Commentaries* see Daniel Boorstin, *The Mysterious Science of the Law* (Cambridge, Mass., 1941).
15. Lawyers such as William Pinkney and Theophilus Parsons saw Coke both as a test of prowess and as a key to success at the bar. For American lawyers on Coke see Charles Warren, *A History of the American Bar* (Cambridge, Mass., 1912), pp. 171–78.
16. "Autobiography," p. 20.
17. Sewall to Story, 3 April 1800, Story Papers, UM.
18. "Autobiography," p. 20.
19. Sewall to Story, 3 April 1800, Story Papers, UM.
20. Story to Fay, 6 January 1801, *LL*, 1:77.
21. Sewall to Story, 3 April 1800, Story Papers, UM.
22. Samuel Putnam to W. W. Story, 28 May 1846 (draft), Samuel Putnam Papers, Essex Institute, Salem, Mass.
23. I have relied heavily on the superb description in William Nelson, *Americanization of the Common Law: The Impact of Legal Change on Massachusetts Society, 1760–1830* (Cambridge, Mass., 1975), especially chap. 5.
24. Sewall to Story, 24 March 1800, Story Papers, UM.
25. Sewall to Story, 12 February 1799, Story Papers, UM.
26. Ibid.
27. Putnam to W. W. Story, 28 May 1846, Putnam Papers.
28. Sewall to Story, 12 February 1799, Story Papers, UM.
29. See especially the data on Massachusetts lawyers in Gawalt, *Promise of Power*, chap. 2.
30. "Autobiography," pp. 20–21. Charles Warren, *Jacobin and Junto* (Cambridge, Mass., 1931), p. 165, could discover only six Antifederalist lawyers as of January 1801.
31. The fusion of law and politics is apparent, for example, in Parsons's much-circulated

charge to the grand jury in 1806, especially the section printed in Theophilus Parsons, [Jr.,] *Memoir of Theophilus Parsons, Chief Justice of the Supreme Judicial Court of Massachusetts . . .* (Boston, 1859), pp. 201–5. Also see Banner, *To the Hartford Convention*, pp. 184–87, 291; and Linda K. Kerber, *Federalists in Dissent: Imagery and Ideology in Jeffersonian America* (Ithaca, N.Y., 1970), chap. 5. For further insight on law and politics in the early nineteenth century consult Richard E. Ellis, *The Jeffersonian Crisis: Courts and Politics in the Young Republic* (New York, 1971); Maxwell H. Bloomfield, *American Lawyers in a Changing Society, 1776–1876* (Cambridge, Mass., 1976), especially chap 2; and Gawalt, *Promise of Power*, chap. 3.

32. "Autobiography," p. 20.

33. William T. Whitney, Jr., "The Crowninshields of Salem, 1800–1808: A Study in the Politics of Commercial Growth," 94 *Essex Institute Historical Collections*, pt. 1 (January 1958): 1–36; pt. 2 (April 1958): 79–118.

34. Ibid., pt. 1, pp. 31–32.

35. As quoted in *LL*, 1:87–88.

36. Silvan Tompkins, "The Psychology of Commitment: The Constructive Role of Violence and Suffering for the Individual and for His Society," in *The Antislavery Vanguard: New Essays on the Abolitionists*, ed. Martin B. Duberman (Princeton, N.J., 1965), pp. 270–98.

37. Story to Fay, 28 February 1801, *LL*, 1:87.

38. Story to Capt. Ichabod Nichols, 24 March 1801, Story Papers, UT; Story to Fay, 28 February 1801, *LL*, 1:87.

39. Story to Fay, March 1801, Story Papers, UT.

40. Jacob Crowninshield to Capt. Richard Crowninshield, 24 November 1802, Crowninshield Papers, Peabody Museum, Salem, Mass.

41. Story to Nichols, 24 March 1801, Story Papers, UT

42. Story to Lydia Pierce, 28 November 1801, ibid.

43. *Salem Gazette*, 7 July 1801.

44. This letter, addressed "Dear Sir" and circulated by the Salem Republican committee, "John Hathorne, Chairman," was written by Story and most likely addressed to the Republican Town Committee of nearby Lynn.

45. Bentley, *Diary*, 2:455.

46. The episode, with a long excerpt from the *Gazette*, is recounted in Tapley, *Salem Imprints*, pp. 127–31. Also see Whitney, "The Crowninshields of Salem," p. 28 n. 97.

47. The charge and countercharge can be found in the *Register* for 28, 31 March 1803 and in the *Gazette* for 4, 5, 7 April 1803.

48. Story's beating is gleefully recounted in Shaw to Walter, 20 April 1803, Shaw Papers. Also see Bentley, *Diary*, 3:18.

49. "Your triumph in Massachusetts seems to be almost complete. One *grand effort* more in the Spring will put faction to sleep" (Jacob Crowninshield to the Reverend William Bentley, 26 November 1804, Crowninshield Papers).

50. "I never for a moment believed Mr. Jefferson to be an enemy to his country, nor to my mind has his conduct ever been substantially proved *criminal* in any degree" (Story to Nichols, 24 March 1801, Story Papers, UT); Story to Thomas Jefferson, 14 January 1806, Jefferson Papers, Coolidge Collection, MHS; G. W. Prescott to Story, 3 August 1803, Story Papers, UM.

51. See especially Story to the Honorable G. Duvall, 30 March 1803, *LL*, 1:102–4.

52. Joseph Story, *"An Oration," Pronounced at Salem, on the Fourth Day of July, in Commemoration of Our National Independence* (Salem, Mass., 1804).

53. William E. Channing, *The Works of William E. Channing, D.D.*, 11th complete ed., 6 vols. (Boston, 1849), 1:362.

54. Goodman, *Democratic-Republicans of Massachusetts*.

55. Jacob Crowninshield to Capt. Richard Crowninshield, 24 November 1802, Crowninshield Papers.

56. Henry Dearborn to Jefferson, 31 July 1802, Thomas Jefferson Papers, Library of Congress, Washington, D.C. (hereafter cited as LC); Daniel Brent to Jefferson, 7 September 1802, ibid.; Jacob Crowninshield to Richard Crowninshield, 14 April 1803, Crowninshield Papers.

57. Story to Duvall, 30 March 1803, *LL*, 1:102–4.

58. Artemas Sawyer to J. Russell, 11 September 1804, Shaw Papers.

59. Story to Duvall, 30 March 1803, *LL*, 1:102–4.

60. Ibid., p. 102.

61. Story to Nathaniel Williams, 6 June 1805, *LL*, 1:104–6.

62. Justice of the Peace Records of Thomas Bancroft, MSS, Essex Institute, Salem, Mass. Story argued six cases before Bancroft. Some were appealed to the Court of Common Pleas (hereafter cited as CCP), as was the practice before the courts were reformed.

63. Nelson, *Americanization of the Common Law*, pp. 15–16. For a discussion of the process of review, which generally included a jury trial concerning the facts, see Parsons, *Memoir*, p. 234.

64. Sewall to Story, 24 March 1800, Story Papers, UM; Fee Book, MS, Story Papers, New York Historical Society, New York, N.Y. Also see Gawalt, *Promise of Power*, pp. 91–92. For a general description of this system see Parsons, *Memoir*, pp. 192–93.

65. This is not to count two terms for 1805 for which the docket book is missing. CCP Docket Books, Essex County Court House, Salem, Mass.

66. Fee Book, Story Papers, New York Historical Society; "Autobiography," p. 22.

67. Story's name appears several times throughout the period in local newspapers as the administrator of estates. See *Salem Register*, 26 January, 9, 27 August 1804, 11 August 1806; *Essex Register*, 14 February 1810; and *Salem Gazette*, 21 April 1807. The indenture (in Story's handwriting) settling the boundary between the estates of William Story and John Pedrick, Jr., before the justice of the peace is at the Marblehead Historical Society.

68. Story's victory over Prescott in *Rust* v. *Low*, 6 Mass. 90, is recounted in *LL*, 1:116–18, and his encounter with Mason in the Superior Court of New Hampshire in "Autobiography," pp. 23–25.

69. Whitney, "The Crowninshields of Salem," describes the wide-ranging economic-political battles of the Crowninshield family.

70. For Story's debt-collecting efforts see Jacob Crowninshield to Richard Crowninshield, 13, 24 June, 30 July 1803, Crowninshield Papers. On his counsel concerning bankruptcy see Jacob Crowninshield to Richard Crowninshield, 29 January 1803, ibid.

71. This case, involving a debt on a bond, was argued at the November term of the Supreme Judicial Court held in Essex. Story won a prestigious victory over Dexter and Prescott. The "equity" was with Appleton, observed Judge Isaac Parker, but thanks to Story, the "authorities" were with Crowninshield (3 Mass. 443–75).

72. Story, Legal Form Book, MS, New York Historical Society, entry for 24 May 1805. For Story's service on the school committee see *Salem Register* 29 March 1804, 11 April 1805, 10 April 1806.

73. William Wirt to Peachey R. Gilmer, 9 August 1802, William Wirt Papers, LC.

74. Story to Fay, 6 January 1801, *LL*, 1:77.

75. Story to Jefferson, 14 January 1806, Story Papers, MHS. The poem was reviewed in 2 *Monthly Anthology* (June 1805): 379–82.

76. William Draper Lewis, ed., *Great American Lawyers* . . . , 8 vols. (Philadelphia, 1907–9), 3:132.

77. *MW*, p. 26.

78. Story to Fay, 8 October 1805, *LL*, 1:114–16.

79. Story to White, 28 May 1808, *LL*, 1:169–70.

80. Among the most compelling documents testifying to the watershed character of these events is his poem "My Former Days," 1805, Story Papers, UT.

81. Benjamin Waterhouse to Levi Woodbury, 9 February 1835, Levi Woodbury Papers, LC.

82. Richard Hofstadter, *The Idea of a Party System: The Rise of Legitimate Opposition in the United States, 1780–1840* (Berkeley and Los Angeles, 1969), explores this theme.

83. For an insightful discussion of the inchoate nature of early national political parties see Ronald P. Formisano, "Deferential Participant Politics: The Early Republic's Political Culture, 1789–1840," 68 *American Political Science Review* (June 1974): 473–87.

84. Story's legislative career has to be pieced together from scattered references in newspapers. See, for example, *Boston Gazette*, 26 March 1807; *Columbian Centinel*, 11, 21 June 1806, 28 February 1807; *Democrat*, 11, 16 June 1808; *New England Palladium*, 6, 13 June 1806, 25 March 1808, 16 January 1812; and *Salem Register*, 16 May 1805, 7 April 1806, 17 January, 14 May 1807. Also see Mass. Legislative Documents, 1798–1809, A, State Archives, Boston.

85. As early as 1803 the Crowninshields were looking to break the Federalist monopoly on state banking (see Jacob Crowninshield to Nathaniel Silsbee, 15 December 1803, Crowninshield Papers). Story was called upon to support a state bank bill sponsored by Benjamin Crowninshield, Jr., in 1808 (Mass. Legislative Documents, 1798–1809, A; *Columbian Centinel*, 27 January 1808). The Merchants Bank of Salem, with a capital of $300,000, was chartered in June 1811. Story was not listed among the incorporators for obvious reasons, but his clients, George Crowninshield, Jr., and John Crowninshield, were (Gustavus Myers, *History of the Supreme Court of the United States* [Chicago, 1925], pp. 267–69). The Crowninshields also chartered the Salem India Wharf Corporation in 1809 (ibid.).

86. For Story's position as manager of the impeachment, see C. P. Sumner to Story, 28 July (?) 1807, Joseph Story Papers, LC. The disputed election is discussed in Edward Stanwood, "The Massachusetts Election in 1806," 20 *Proceedings of the Massachusetts Historical Society*, 2d ser. (1906, 1907): 12–19.

87. Joseph Story, "Address on Resigning the Speaker's Chair, Delivered in the House of Representatives of Massachusetts, January 17, 1812," in *MW*, pp. 64–65.

88. Again see Stanwood, "The Massachusetts Election in 1806."

89. *Columbian Centinel*, 11 June 1806; *New England Palladium*, 13 June 1806.

90. *Boston Gazette*, 26 March 1807.

91. Bentley, *Diary*, 3:412.

92. Antilawyer sentiment is discussed in Bloomfield, *American Lawyers*, chap. 2; and Gawalt, *Promise of Power*, chaps. 13 and 14.

93. Theodore Sedgwick to Story, 9 December 1807, Story Papers, LC.

94. See Report of Judiciary Bill by committee of Wheaton, Upham, Story, Bangs, Perry, doc. 5881 A, State Archives; Sedgwick to Story, 27 January, 9 December 1807, Story Papers, LC; and Sewall to Story, 29 January 1806, Story Papers, UM.

95. [J. Story], Act Establishing J. Court of Chancery, 16 January 1808, Report of the Judiciary Committee, doc. 6413, State Archives. Story discusses this report and quotes extensively from it in his "Chancery Jurisdiction," in *MW*, pp. 172–76. An interesting contemporary discussion is found in Erastus Worthington, *An Essay on the Establishment of a Chancery Jurisdiction in Massachusetts* . . . (Boston, 1810).

96. Isaac Parker to Story, 8 June 1805, 31 May 1806, Story Papers, UM; Parsons to Story, 8 June 1806, ibid. A manuscript copy of Story's committee report containing

the Salary Act of 1806 can be found in the State Archives; the report is printed in *MW*, pp. 58–62. For Story's account see his letter to Edward Everett, 1 November 1832, *LL*, 1:134–35.

97. Story to Everett, 1 November 1832, *LL*, 1:134–35.

98. Adams to Ezekiel Bacon, 17 November 1808, as quoted in Charles Warren, *The Supreme Court in United States History*, new rev. ed., 2 vols. (Boston, 1926), 1:341–2.

99. H. G. Otis to Robert G. Harper, 19 April 1807, Otis Papers.

100. George Cabot to Timothy Pickering, 28 January 1808, Henry C. Lodge, *Life and Letters of George Cabot* (Boston, 1877), p. 377.

101. Bentley, *Diary*, 3:346.

102. Ibid., 3:361.

103. The most penetrating account of the complex politics of the embargo is Burton Spivak, *Jefferson's English Crisis: Commerce, Embargo, and the Republican Revolution* (Charlottesville, Va., 1979). Also useful are Louis M. Sears, *Jefferson and the Embargo* (Durham, N.C., 1927); and Henry Adams, *History of the United States of America*, 9 vols. (New York, 1889–91), 4:152–453.

104. Jefferson to Henry Dearborn, 16 July 1810, *The Works of Thomas Jefferson*, Federal Ed., 12 vols. (New York, 1904–5), 11:398–99.

105. Story to Jacob Crowninshield, 17 December 1805, Crowninshield Papers.

106. Joseph Story, "Infringements of the Neutral Trade of the United States," in *MW*, pp. 43–57.

107. Bentley, *Diary*, 3:212; Putnam to Pickering, 29 January 1806, Timothy Pickering Papers, MHS; Fisher Ames to Pickering, 27 November 1805, ibid.

108. Story, "Infringements," p. 53.

109. *Democrat*, 11 June 1808.

110. Putnam to Pickering, 9 November 1808, Pickering Papers.

111. Story to Stephen White, 24 December 1808, *LL*, 1:191; Story to Joseph White, Jr., 31 December 1808, *LL*, 1:172–73.

112. *Annals of Congress: Debates of the House*, 10th Cong., 2d sess., 1808–9, pp. 942, 1091.

113. Story to Fay, 9 January 1809, *LL*, 1:177–83. Story said he had "always" thought this to be the case; this statement was incorrect, as his 28 February 1808 letter to William Fettyplace shows (*LL*, 1:165).

114. Story did, however, also work to soften some of the harsher aspects of the new legislation. See *New England Palladium*, 13 January 1809.

115. Story asked for and got almost daily reports of local opinion concerning the embargo and related matters. Among his most reliable informants were Joseph White, Jr., and Stephen White, merchants and shippers of Salem and Story's brothers-in-law. Story also received frank opinions from Samuel Fay, C. P. Sumner, and other friends.

116. For Bacon's discussion of the struggle after Story left, see Ezekiel Bacon to Story, 22 January, 5, 15, 26 February 1809, Story Papers, LC. Story revealed his willingness to compromise in his letter to Fay of 9 January 1809, *LL*, 1:177–83. There is no evidence that he changed his mind later.

117. At the Salem town meeting of 26 October, Story fought back a petition asking for the repeal of the embargo. He did not want to commit himself until he had "documents in the Cabinet which would be communicated to Congress early in the ensuing session, and which are necessary in forming an opinion of the expediency of raising the Embargo . . ." (*Democrat*, 21 November 1808). Bentley thought Story "too vacillating" (*Diary*, 3:390).

118. See, for example, among the several letters from Bacon keeping Story informed, that of 5 February 1809, Story Papers, LC.

119. Story to Jacob Crowninshield, 17 December 1805, Crowninshield Papers.

120. Story to Crowninshield, 4 January 1806, ibid.

121. Joseph Story, *Address before the Regimental Officers at Salem, July 4, 1808* (Salem, Mass., [1808?]).

122. "Mr Story has come out most decidedly in favor of the immediate creation of a respectable Navy," reported the *New England Palladium*, 17 January 1809. "From that moment he has lost every particle of weight which he possessed with the southern members. It is possible that they might have overlooked the frequent instances of independence which he has formerly manifested in the Legislature of Massachusetts, and even what they call his *'Yazooism*,' had he imposed upon himself a perfect silence upon that subject, but his inclination for a Navy is with them a sin not to be forgiven." For some of Story's various efforts in behalf of a respectable navy see "Memorial Relative to British Aggression . . . ," in *MW*, p. 56; and see *Independent Chronicle*, 18 January 1808, for his advocacy of a strong navy while in the Massachusetts house. He took a similar position in the debate over the Wheaton Resolutions (*Columbian Centinel*, 28 May 1808). For his efforts in Congress see *Annals of Congress: Debates of the House*, 1808–9, pp. 906, 907, 976–77, 1078, 1079, 1095.

123. Story to Fay, 9 January 1809, Story Papers, UT. This letter clearly sets forth Story's position on the embargo problem and states his misgivings about America's response as well as about the disabilities of Congress and political parties.

124. Story to Edward Cutts, 30 January 1809, Story Papers, MHS.

125. Hofstadter, *Idea of a Party System*, especially chaps. 1–3.

126. Information is taken from CCP Docket Books and from Records, CCP Volume, March–June 1809, Essex County Court House.

127. From 6 Mass. (1809) Story argued *Fowler et al.* v. *Bott* 63; *Commonwealth* v. *Warren* 72; *Commonwealth* v. *Warren and Johnson* 74; *Rust* v. *Low et al.* 90; *Cook* v. *Essex Fire and Marine Insurance Co.* 122; *Wheatland* v. *Gray* 124; *Whitteridge* v. *Norris* 125; and *Commonwealth* v. *Thompson* 134.

128. Story argued six cases at the November term of the Supreme Judicial Court in Essex even though he was then a sitting justice of the U.S. Supreme Court. These no doubt were cases previously docketed.

129. *The Case of John Tucker*, 8 Mass. 286–87 (1811).

130. *Essex Turnpike Corp.* v. *Collins*, 8 Mass. 292–99 (1811).

131. Professor Hiller Zobel has organized the case files of the federal district court cases at the Federal Archives and Records Center, Waltham, Mass., by subject matter for the years of Story's practice. In the December term of 1809 alone, nineteen writs were served against violators of the embargo (see folder marked Embargo Violations). Twenty cases were tried under embargo laws in 1810.

132. District Court Docket and Minute Book, vols. 1–4 (1789–1811), Federal Archives and Records Center, Waltham, Mass.

133. Circuit Court Docket, vols. 2–3 (June 1804–May 1812), ibid.

134. Morgan D. Dowd, "Justice Joseph Story and the Politics of Appointment," 9 *American Journal of Legal History* (October 1965): 274.

135. Among the works I have drawn on for an understanding of law and economic growth are Morton Horwitz, *The Transformation of American Law, 1780–1860* (Cambridge, Mass., 1977); and Oscar Handlin and Mary Handlin, *Commonwealth: A Study of the Role of Government in the American Economy: Massachusetts, 1774–1861* (New York, 1947). Also useful are Nelson, *Americanization of the Common Law*, and Parsons, *Memoir*, which concentrate on the legal culture of Massachusetts, and Francis W. Gregory, *Nathan Appleton: Merchant and Entrepreneur, 1779–1861* (Charlottesville, Va., 1975), which traces economic change through the career of a leading businessman.

136. Joseph Locke to Nathan Dane, 18 March 1809, Nathan Dane Papers, MHS. Story

apparently called Locke's testimony before referees into question; Locke in turn accused Story of being "illiberal" and "imprudent" and charged him with "mutilating evidence."

137. Samuel Putnam to W. W. Story, 28 May 1846, Putnam Papers.

138. Charles Sumner, "The Scholar, the Jurist, the Artist, the Philanthropist," in *The Works of Charles Sumner*, 15 vols. (Boston, 1870–73), 1:264.

139. Review of Story's *Selection of Pleadings*, 2 *Monthly Anthology* (September 1805): 483.

140. Story's publisher noted in 1806 that the first printing of his *Pleadings* was nearly gone (B. B. Macanulty to E. Butler, 21 November 1806, B. B. Macanulty Letter-books, 1802–7, Essex Institute, Salem, Mass.). Macanulty said elsewhere, "There never has been a book published in this part of the country so much approved of as the *Pleading*" (Macanulty to P. Byrne, 20 May 1805, ibid.). At five dollars per volume, Story must have done quite well.

141. *American Precedents* was collected mainly from the manuscripts of Chief Justice Parsons (Parsons, *Memoir*, p. 221).

142. Leverett Saltonstall wrote his father in 1805 in desperate need of English reports from which to study the arcane technique. A lawyer, he said, "must not only follow the old course—take the prescribed remedy, but must apply this in *exact form*. An error *of a word* for want of a book by a young practitioner may occasion a loss of more money and reputation th^n any library is worth" (draft, 1805, Leverett Saltonstall Papers, MHS).

143. Directly connected with practice was his digest "supplementary to Comyns's and on the same plan, containing the doctrines laid down by the courts, and the important writers on jurisprudence in England and America." Law business and legal scholarship forced him to abandon the project, but he had covered insurance, admiralty, and prize (MSS digest, 3 vols., Treasure Room, Harvard Law School; also see *LL*, 1:119–20).

144. *Kilham* v. *Ward*, 2 Mass. 236.

145. 3 Mass. 443.

146. William Minot to Saltonstall, 6 November 1807, Saltonstall Papers.

147. 6 Mass. 90. Story's victory over Mason is recounted in "Autobiography," pp. 23–25.

148. 6 Mass. 63.

149. 6 *Monthly Anthology* (February 1809): 84.

150. The most complete account of the politics of Story's appointment is Dowd, "Story and the Politics of Appointment."

151. "Autobiography," p. 35.

152. See Bacon to Story, 19 September, 8 October 1810, Story Papers, LC.

153. Jefferson to Gideon Granger, 22 October 1810, Gideon and Francis Granger Papers, LC; Jefferson to James Madison, 15 October 1810, Jefferson, *Works*, 11:150–52.

154. Story to Nathaniel Williams, 30 November 1811, *LL*, 1:200–201; also see Story to Fay, 24 February 1812, *LL*, 1:215–17.

155. Bentley, *Diary*, 4:69.

156. Josiah Quincy, Jr., *Figures of the Past from the Leaves of Old Journals* (Boston, 1883), p. 158.

157. *Columbian Centinel*, 23 November 1811.

Chapter Three

1. *MW*, p. 65.

2. Story to Fay, 16 February 1808, *LL*, 1:161–64.

3. "Verses on the Death of Caroline," *LL*, 1:209–10.

4. For Story's early visit to the Supreme Court and his impressions of future colleagues see Story to Fay, 16, 25 February 1808, *LL*, 1:161–64, 166–68.

5. Story to Sarah Story, 5 March 1812, *LL*, 1:217–18.

6. For his evaluation of the bar see Story to Fay, 16 February 1808, *LL*, 1:161–64.

7. Story to Williams, 16 February 1812, *LL*, 1:213–15. The *Holland Land Company* case was *Fitzsimmons et al.* v. *Ogden et al.*, 7 Cranch 2 (1812).

8. 7 Cranch 115 (1812).

9. Story to Fay, 24 February 1812, *LL*, 1:215–17.

10. 7 Cranch 156 (1812).

11. James Sterling Young, *The Washington Community, 1800–1828* (New York, 1966). Unfortunately, Young does not deal with the Court in any detail.

12. Story to Williams, 16 February 1812, *LL*, 1:213–15.

13. Story to Fay, 24 February 1812, *LL*, 1:215–17.

14. Joseph Story, "Sketch of the Character of John Todd," in *MW*, p. 70.

15. Donald G. Morgan, *Justice William Johnson, The First Dissenter: The Career and Constitutional Philosophy of a Jeffersonian Judge* (Columbia, S.C., 1954), treats his career with great precision.

16. In compiling the comparative data on the justices, I have consulted the entries in the *Dictionary of American Biography* and Leon Friedman and Fred L. Israel, eds., *The Justices of the United States Supreme Court, 1789–1969: Their Lives and Major Opinions*, 4 vols. (New York, 1969): vol. 1.

17. See Julius Goebel, Jr., "The Common Law and the Constitution," in *Chief Justice Marshall: A Reappraisal*, ed. W. Melville Jones (Ithaca, N.Y., 1956).

18. Marshall makes the point himself in his anonymous essay published in the Philadelphia *Union*, 24 April 1819, and reprinted in *John Marshall's Defense of McCulloch v. Maryland*, ed. Gerald Gunther (Stanford, Calif., 1969), pp. 80–81. See also Donald M. Roper's "Judicial Unanimity and the Marshall Court: A Road to Reappraisal," 9 *American Journal of Legal History* (April 1965): 118–34.

19. On the representative function of the Supreme Court justices on circuit see R. Kent Newmyer, "Justice Joseph Story on Circuit and a Neglected Phase of American Legal History," 14 *American Journal of Legal History* (April 1970): 112–35.

20. The appearance of vol. 2 of the *Oliver Wendell Holmes Devise History of the Supreme Court* has done much to close this gap in legal historiography. See especially pt. 2 of George Haskins and Herbert Johnson, *Foundations of Power: John Marshall, 1801–15* (New York, 1981), which appeared after this chapter was written.

21. A good treatment of Federalist antiwar activities can be found in Adams, *History of the United States*, 6:399–405.

22. 12 Wheaton 19 (1827).

23. Adams, *History of the United States*, 6:401–2.

24. Story to Williams, 8 October 1812, *LL*, 1:243.

25. Story to Williams, 24 August 1812, *LL*, 1:228–30.

26. Story to Williams, 3 August 1813, *LL*, 1:246–48.

27. For an example of Parsons's broad-gauged charge, see Parsons, *Memoir*, pp. 201–5. Story probably heard this charge, given in 1806; it was reprinted in 14 *American Jurist and Law Magazine* (hereafter cited as *American Jurist*) (July 1835): 26–39.

28. Story to Fay, 13 February 1808, *LL*, 1:157–59.

29. Joseph Story, "Charge to Grand Jury, 1812," Story Papers, UT.

30. For the distinction see Charles G. Haines, *The Role of the Supreme Court in American Government and Politics, 1789–1835* (New York, 1960), pp. 285–86.

31. Story, "Charge to Grand Jury, 1812."

32. Ibid.

33. Ibid.

34. Homer S. Cummings and Carl McFarland, *Federal Justice: Chapters in the History of Justice and the Federal Executive* (New York, 1937), p. 70. For their discussion of federal

embargo legislation and wartime illegal trade, see pp. 67–77. See also Donald R. Hickey, "American Trade Restrictions during the War of 1812," 68 *Journal of American History* (December 1981): 517–38.

35. The point was established in *U.S.* v. *La Vengence*, 3 Dallas 297 (1796), and reasserted in *The Aurora*, 7 Cranch 382 (1813). Also consult Cummings and McFarland, *Federal Justice*, pp. 70–71.

36. *The Orono*, 18 Fed. Cas. 830. (No. 10,585) (C.C.D. Mass. 1812).

37. *Boston Repertory*, 31 May 1808, cited in Warren, *Supreme Court*, 1:418.

38. For example, see *The Ploughboy*, 19 Fed. Cas. 885 (No. 11,230) (C.C.D. Mass. 1812); *The Short Staple and Cargo*, 22 Fed. Cas. 23 (No. 12,813) (C.C.D. Mass. 1812); *The Argo and Appurtenances*, 1 Fed. Cas. 1100 (No. 516) (C.C.D. Mass. 1812); *U.S.* v. *The Mars*, 26 Fed. Cas. 1166 (No. 15,723) (C.C.D. Mass. 1812).

39. 3 Fed. Cas. 811 (No. 1,608) (C.C.D. Mass. 1812); 27 Fed. Cas. 1006 (No. 16,247) (C.C.D. Mass. 1812).

40. 27 Fed. Cas. 1010.

41. *The Falmouth*, 8 Fed. Cas. 981 (No. 4,631) (C.C.D. Mass. 1812); also see *U.S.* v. *Mann*, 26 Fed. Cas. 1153 (No. 15,717) (C.C.D. N.H. 1812).

42. 27 Fed. Cas. 1010.

43. 20 Fed. Cas. 300 (No. 11,576) (C.C.D. Mass. 1812).

44. 14 Fed. Cas. 27, 29, 31 (No. 7,575) (C.C.D. Mass. 1813).

45. 3 Fed. Cas. 962 (No. 1,686) (C.C.D. Mass. 1814). This case is spelled differently in the reports of each stage of litigation, and those spellings sometimes differ from the ones employed in the depositions and correspondence relating to the case. The spelling here is determined by the source used.

46. Ibid., 962–64.

47. H. G. Otis to R. G. Harper, 2 December 1815, Robert G. Harper Papers, LC.

48. *The Bothnea and Jahnstoff*, 2 Wheaton 177 (1817).

49. The grounds for government suspicions were stated by Story (*The Bothnea. Janstoff*, 3 Fed. Cas. 964–67). Indeed, H. G. Otis thought that the judge did a more thorough job of presenting the government's case than did the government's counsel (Otis to Harper, 2 December 1815, Harper Papers).

50. Henry Warren, one of the collectors involved in the case, expressed the dilemma very concisely. "Indeed from the nature of the case," he wrote to Richard Rush, "I could not expect to be very successful in these enquiries, because the fraud which I supposed and still suppose to exist in the case was to be inferred from the conduct and evidence of the captors" (16 January 1817, Papers of the Attorney General, Massachusetts, Box 1 [1813–41], National Archives).

51. Something of the frankly suspicious frame of mind developed by law enforcement officials as they dealt with constant attempts to break the law can be seen in the correspondence of the period. See William Preble to William Wirt, March 1818, 1 February 1820, Papers of the Attorney General, Massachusetts, Box 1 (1813–41); Henry Warren to Richard Rush, 16 January 1817, ibid.; George Blake to William Pinkney, 23 January 1814, ibid.

52. Otis to Harper, 2 December 1815, Harper Papers; see Blake's notes on *Malcomb et al. of the Privateer Washington* v. *U.S.*, Papers of the Attorney General, Massachusetts, Box 1 (1813–41).

53. Story to Williams, 3 August 1813, *LL*, 1:246–48.

54. *The Bothnea. Janstoff*, 3 Fed. Cas. 966–67. It is instructive to note that Story was more generous in permitting evidence beyond the ship's papers when such evidence worked *against* those engaged in illegal trade. See his opinion in *The Liverpool Packet*, 15 Fed. Cas. 641 (No. 8,406) (C.C.D. Mass. 1813).

55. Otis to Harper, 2 December 1815, Harper Papers.
56. Ibid.
57. Story to Fay, 24 April 1814, *LL*, 1:261.
58. William Plumer, Jr., *Life of William Plumer* . . . (Boston, 1857), as quoted in Gerald T. Dunne, *Justice Joseph Story and the Rise of the Supreme Court* (New York, 1970), p. 91. For a sample of Marshall's queries to Story on admiralty and maritime matters and Story's obliging response, see John Marshall to Story, 13 July 1819, Story Papers, MHS, and Story to Marshall, 26 July 1819, John Marshall Papers, College of William and Mary, Williamsburg, Va. For subsequent letters in which Marshall draws on Story's learning in matters of commercial law see Marshall to Story, 15 June, 13 July 1821, 2 July, 9 December 1823, and Story to Marshall, 27 June 1821, Story Papers, MHS.
59. *The George, Bothnea, and Janstoff*, 1 Wheaton 414 (1816).
60. *The Bothnea and Jahnstoff*, 2 Wheaton 177.
61. See Albert J. Beveridge, *The Life of John Marshall*, 4 vols. (Boston, 1919), 4:1–3, 30–41.
62. 8 Cranch 110, 128–29, 149.
63. 299 U.S. 318.
64. *Brown* v. *U.S.*, 8 Cranch 151.
65. Ibid.
66. For a critique of Story's theory of the general welfare clause see Henry St. George Tucker, "Judge Story's Position on the So-Called General Welfare Clause," 13 *American Bar Association Journal* (July–August 1927): 363–68, 465–69.
67. 24 Fed. Cas. 950 (No. 14,497) (C.C.D. Mass. 1816).
68. *The Nereide*, 9 Cranch 413 (1815).
69. 7 Cranch 116 (1812). In this decision Marshall exempted all public ships of friendly nations from the jurisdiction of American courts. See Warren, *Supreme Court*, 1:424–26. For Story on Van Ness's opinion see his letter to Henry Wheaton, 5 September 1815, *LL*, 1:266–69.
70. 9 Cranch 425.
71. Story to Wheaton, 5 September 1815, *LL*, 1:266–69.
72. 9 Cranch 437.
73. This remarkable international friendship can be traced in the Story-Stowell letters in *LL* and in the Story Papers, UT.
74. 9 Cranch 438, 454–55.
75. Story to Wheaton, 5 September 1815, *LL*, 1:266–69.
76. Story to Williams, 22 February 1815, *LL*, 1:253–54. To this list of national institutions Story later added a "national newspaper" (Story to Henry Wheaton, 13 December 1815, *LL*, 1:270–72).
77. Julius Goebel, Jr., treats the problem of uncertainty in his *Antecedents and Beginnings to 1801*, vol. 1 of the *Holmes Devise History of the Supreme Court* (New York, 1971). William W. Crosskey essentially denies that there is a problem (*Politics and the Constitution in the History of the United States*, 2 vols. [Chicago, 1953]).
78. Goebel, *Antecedents*, pp. 229–30.
79. Goebel devotes an entire chapter to the process acts (ibid., chap. 12).
80. This is the theme of Ellis, *The Jeffersonian Crisis*, and figures also in Warren, *Supreme Court*; Crosskey, *Politics and the Constitution*; Gawalt, *Promise of Power*; and Bloomfield, *American Lawyers*.
81. *LL*, 1:221. Story speaks of Cushing's "protracted infirmity" and the "unpropitious" state of the circuit court docket in "Autobiography," p. 35.
82. For Gallison's statement about his volumes and his duties as reporter, see 30 Fed. Cas. 1272–73 (Appendix).

83. Story writes of his dislike of "prolix and tedious" arguments in his letter to Fay, 24 February 1812, Story Papers, UT. On his confrontation with Dexter over legal authority see Abraham Payne, *Reminiscences of the Rhode Island Bar* (Providence, R.I., 1885), pp. 240–41.

84. Story's role on circuit is spelled out more fully in Newmyer, "Story on Circuit," pp. 112–35.

85. *U.S. v. Wonson*, 28 Fed. Cas. 745 (No. 16,750) (C.C.D. Mass. 1812). Also see *LL*, 1:221.

86. Thomas Burgess to William Smith Shaw, 21 August 1812, Shaw Papers; in this letter Burgess requests a copy of Story's rules in prize cases for Judge David Barnes. Simon Greenleaf printed Story's circuit rules in his *Collection of Cases Overruled, Doubted, or Limited in Their Application, Taken from American and English Reports* (Portland, Maine, 1821).

87. 28 Fed. Cas. 1062 (No. 16,871) (C.C.D. R.I. 1812).

88. 16 Peters 1 (1842).

89. Crosskey mobilizes impressive evidence to show that the Constitutional Convention intended the common law, to the extent that it was applicable, to be the "standing law of America" *(Politics and the Constitution, 1:620–25).*

90. 7 Cranch 32. My discussion of this case and others concerning the federal criminal common law has profited from the scholarship of Professor Kathryn Preyer, whose paper on the subject, "Joseph Story, the Supreme Court and the Question of a Federal Common Law Jurisdiction over Crimes," was delivered at the Organization of American Historians meeting, Los Angeles, April 1970.

91. Leonard Levy, *Jefferson and Civil Liberties: The Darker Side* (Cambridge, Mass., 1963), pp. 61–66.

92. 7 Cranch 32.

93. 7 Cranch 33–34.

94. See his circuit opinion in *Livingston v. Jefferson*, 1 Brockenbraugh 211 (1811).

95. See *American State Papers: Miscellaneous*, 1:21–36, especially 25.

96. The cases are *U.S. v. Smith*, 27 Fed. Cas. 1147 (No. 16,323) (C.C.D. Mass. 1792); *Henfield's Case*, 11 Fed. Cas. 1099 (No. 6,360) (C.C.D. Pa. 1793); *U.S. v. Worrall*, 28 Fed. Cas. 774 (No. 16,766) (C.C.D. Pa. 1798); and *Williams' Case*, 29 Fed. Cas. 1330 (No. 17,708) (C.C.D. Conn. 1799). Because federal district court decisions were not generally reported, no generalization about the status of the common law there can be made.

97. *U.S. v. Hudson and Goodwin*, 7 Cranch 32.

98. Richard Peters to Timothy Pickering, 16 April 1816, Pickering Papers.

99. Story to Nathaniel Willams, 27 May 1813, *LL*, 1:244–45.

100. Peters to Pickering, 16 April 1816, Pickering Papers.

101. Story to Williams, 27 May 1813, *LL*, 1:244–45.

102. Story to Williams, 8 October 1812, *LL*, 1:243.

103. It was moved in the House of Representatives in 1813 that inquiry be made "into the expediency of providing by law for the more effective punishment of crimes against the United States . . ." (*Annals of Congress: Debates of the House*, 13th Cong., 1st sess., 1813–14, p. 805). No further action was taken. In 1816 Story sent a bill for the extension of federal criminal jurisdiction to William Pinkney with an argument supporting it. The bill had the approval of all of the justices except Johnson, who disagreed with section 11, which granted a general common-law jurisdiction over crimes. Story's manuscript is printed at length in *LL*, 1:293–301. For his correspondence to Senator David Daggett from Connecticut on the same subject see Story to Daggett, 3, 24 November, 31 December 1818, Joseph Story Papers, Yale University Library, New Haven, Conn.

104. Story to Williams, 27 May 1813, *LL*, 1:244–45.

105. Story, "Charge to Grand Jury, 1812." Story went so far, in keeping up a front to the lay public, as to declare "that few if any injuries to the public or to individuals remain without ample redress."

106. *U.S.* v. *Coolidge*, 25 Fed. Cas. 621 (No. 14,857) (C.C.D. Mass. 1813).

107. 25 Fed. Cas. 619 (No. 14,857) (C.C.D. Mass. 1813).

108. Ibid.

109. Ibid., 620.

110. 1 *U.S. Statutes at Large* 78.

111. *U.S.* v. *Coolidge*, 25 Fed. Cas. 620 (No. 14,857).

112. Stephen DuPonceau recapitulates many of Story's arguments in his *Dissertation on the Nature and Extent of the Jurisdiction of the Courts of the United States . . .* (Philadelphia, 1824), including, with much elaboration, the idea that the common law was a science that shaped and restrained judicial abuse of power.

113. 25 Fed. Cas. 621.

114. *U.S.* v. *Coolidge*, 1 Wheaton 415.

115. 3 Wheaton 336.

116. Story to Henry Wheaton, 10 April 1818, *LL*, 1:305.

117. 7 Fed. Cas. 418 (No. 3,776) (C.C.D. Mass. 1815).

118. *U.S.* v. *Bevans*, 3 Wheaton 335–56, 359.

119. Story to Stephen White, 26 February 1816, *LL*, 1:278–79.

120. 1 Wheaton 304 (1816).

121. 7 Cranch 603.

122. *Fairfax's Devisee* v. *Hunter's Lessee*, 7 Cranch 603–17. A very useful analysis of the complicated litigation at the state level can be found in John F. Treon, "*Martin* v. *Hunter's Lessee*: A Case History" (Ph.D. diss., University of Virginia, 1970), chaps. 1–3.

123. *Hunter* v. *Fairfax's Devisee*, 1 Munford 218 (Va. 1810).

124. Treon, "*Martin* v. *Hunter's Lessee*."

125. Ibid., chap. 5.

126. James Kent, *Commentaries on American Law* (Philadelphia, 1826–30), 12th ed., ed. O. W. Holmes, Jr., 4 vols. (Boston, 1873), 1:321; all references are to this 12th ed.

127. 1 Wheaton 320.

128. Ibid., 344–45.

129. Ibid., 375, 379.

130. Ibid., 322.

131. Ibid., 326.

132. Ibid., 328, 326.

133. Crosskey, *Politics and the Constitution*, 2:811.

134. Story to George Ticknor, 22 January 1831, *LL*, 2:48–49. For a discussion of the problems of authorship see Dunne, *Story*, pp. 135–36.

135. *LL*, 1:310.

136. *MW*, p. 215.

137. Story to James Kent, 15 August 1820, *LL*, 1:379–80.

Chapter Four

1. *McCulloch* v. *Maryland*, 4 Wheaton 418, 432 (1819); *Cohens* v. *Virginia*, 6 Wheaton 414 (1821).

2. For the theme of republican restoration in Jacksonian Democracy see Marvin Meyers, *The Jacksonian Persuasion: Politics and Belief* (New York, 1960), especially chap. 2.

3. See Chapter 5, section 2.

4. 6 Cranch 143.

5. Lieber is quoted in Joseph Dorfman, *The Economic Mind in American Civilization*, 5 vols. (New York, 1946–59), 2:869.

6. Kent, *Commentaries on American Law*, 2:319.

7. *U.S.* v. *The William*, 28 Fed. Cas. 623 (No. 16,700) (Fed. Dist. Court, Mass. 1808).

8. Joseph Story, "Literature of Maritime Law," a review of Frederick J. Jacobsen's *The Laws of the Sea . . .* , reprinted in *MW*, p. 93.

9. Joseph Story, "Speech on the Apportionment of Senators, Delivered in the Convention of Massachusetts, Assembled to Amend the Constitution, in November 1820," in *MW*, p. 183.

10. "A Charge to the Grand Jury, First Delivered in the Circuit Court of the United States, for the Judicial District of Maine, at Its First Session in Portland, May 8, 1820," in *MW*, pp. 122–47. See especially pp. 122–27.

11. The literature on the subject of law and economic growth is rich. Among those works most useful to me have been Handlin and Handlin, *Commonwealth*; Louis Hartz, *Economic Policy and Democratic Thought: Pennsylvania, 1776–1860* (Cambridge, Mass., 1948); Frederick K. Hendrich, "The Development of American Laissez Faire: A General View of the Age of Washington," 3 *Journal of Economic History*, supp. (December 1943): 51–54; Robert A. Lively, "The American System: A Review Article," 29 *Business History Review* (March 1955): 81–96; J. Willard Hurst, *Law and the Conditions of Freedom in the Nineteenth-Century United States* (Madison, Wis., 1956); Horwitz, *Transformation of American Law*; and Harry N. Scheiber, "Property Law, Expropriation, and Resource Allocation by Government: The United States, 1789–1910," 33 *Journal of Economic History* (March 1973): 232–51.

12. Joseph Story, "Developments of Science and Mechanical Art," in *MW*, p. 478; his preference for the practical approach to matters of government can be seen in his praise of Francis Lieber's work on the state (Story to Lieber, 15 August 1837, *LL*, 2:278–79).

13. Story's discussion of the practical benefits of the Constitution permeates his *Commentaries on the Constitution of the United States . . .* , 3 vols. (Boston, 1833), 5th ed., ed. Melville Bigelow, 2 vols. (Boston, 1891); all references are to this 5th ed. See, for example, his chapter on the Preamble, chap. 6, bk. 3.

14. See, for example, 1 *American Law Journal* (January 1808): vi; and "Provincial and Colonial Laws," 3 *American Jurist* (January 1830): 115–21, especially 115.

15. See, for example, Madison to Martin Van Buren, 28 April 1826, McGregor-Madison Papers, folder no. 4888, McGregor Library, University of Virginia, Charlottesville; Madison to Peter S. DuPonceau, May (?) 1821, Stephen DuPonceau Papers, letterbook 1777–1839, Historical Society of Pennsylvania, Philadelphia; Nathan Dane to Daniel Webster, 20 August 1829, Daniel Webster Papers, New Hampshire Historical Society, Concord; and 1 *American Law Journal* (January 1808): vi. Other statements on the need for uniform law abound in printed and manuscript sources.

16. Webster to Story, 10 April 1824, Webster, *Writings*, 17:348–49. For a fascinating statement of mercantile dependence on courts for "fixed principles" and "useful landmarks for the merchant" see Thomas Haven to Francis [Joseph?] Hopkinson, 9 March 1836, Joseph Hopkinson Papers, Historical Society of Pennsylvania.

17. Legal uniformity is the grand theme of Story's speech, "Progress of Jurisprudence," delivered 4 September 1821 and reprinted in *MW*, pp. 198–241.

18. For Story's reference to equity and economics see his "Chancery Jurisdiction," in *MW*, pp. 163–64.

19. Story, *Commentaries on the Constitution*, 2:494, sec. 1694.

20. As reported by Justice Thomas Todd, n.d., Story Papers, UT.

21. See, for example, *U.S.* v. *Hayward*, 26 Fed. Cas. 240 (No. 15,336) (C.C.D. Mass. 1815); *The Margaretta*, 16 Fed. Cas. 719 (No. 9,072) (C.C.D. Mass. 1815); *Ex parte*

Marquand, 16 Fed. Cas. 776 (No. 9,100) (C.C.D. Mass. 1815); and *U.S.* v. *Farnsworth,* 25 Fed. Cas. 1048 (No. 15,072) (C.C.D. Mass. 1815).

22. *The London Packet,* 15 Fed. Cas. 799 (No. 8,474) (C.C.D. Mass. 1815); *The George,* 10 Fed. Cas. 201 (No. 5,328) (C.C.D. Mass. 1815); *San Jose Indiano,* 21 Fed. Cas. 403 (No. 12,324) (C.C.D. Mass. 1815); *The Dash,* 7 Fed. Cas. 2 (No. 3,584) (C.C.D. Mass. 1815).

23. 4 Fed. Cas. 404 (No. 2,017) (C.C.D. Mass. 1815).

24. 16 Fed. Cas. 776 (No. 9,100)

25. 15 Fed. Cas. 451 (No. 8,310) (C.C.D. Mass. 1815).

26. *Peisch* v. *Dickson,* 19 Fed. Cas. 123 (No. 10,911) (C.C.D. Mass. 1815).

27. The two cases were *Harvey* v. *Richards,* 11 Fed. Cas. 746 (No. 6,183) (C.C.D. Mass. 1815), and *Peisch* v. *Dickson,* 19 Fed. Cas. 123 (No. 10,911). In *Harvey* the jury was impaneled with consent of the parties to determine an issue of fact in a contested will. In *Peisch* the issue concerned the construction of a contract between a factor and his principal.

28. See note and comments in 19 Fed. Cas. 125 (No. 10,911).

29. Mansfield's use of special juries is treated in C. H. S. Fifoot, *Lord Mansfield* (Oxford, 1936), pp. 105–15. For the American practice see Horwitz, *Transformation of American Law,* pp. 155–59.

30. The manuscript record of Judge Davis's decree is in the *De Lovio* case file at the Federal Archives and Record Center, Waltham, Mass., along with other documents, including a copy of the controverted insurance policy. My thanks to Dan Ewald for his careful research in these documents.

31. Story to Wheaton, 5 September 1815, *LL,* 1:266–69.

32. Story to Nathaniel Williams, 24 August 1812, *LL,* 1:228–30.

33. 1 *U.S. Statutes at Large* 76–77.

34. *De Lovio* v. *Boit,* 7 Fed. Cas. 441 (No. 3,776).

35. Ibid., 443.

36. Story to Williams, 3 December 1815, *LL,* 1:269–70.

37. *Insurance Co.* v. *Dunham,* 78 U.S. 1 (1870). Also see Horwitz, *Transformation of American Law,* pp. 251–52. Horwitz's evaluation of the *De Lovio* opinion has been immensely useful to me, as has that of Alfred S. Konefsky and Andrew J. King in their editing of *The Papers of Daniel Webster: Legal Papers,* 2 vols. (Hanover, N.H., 1982), 2:474–82.

38. Konefsky and King, *Webster: Legal Papers,* 2:476–82.

39. David Hoffman, *A Course on Legal Study,* 2d ed., 2 vols. (Baltimore, 1836), as quoted in 7 Fed. Cas. 418 (No. 3,776).

40. *Gibbons* v. *Ogden,* 9 Wheaton 14 (1824).

41. 4 Wheaton 122.

42. 8 Wheaton 1.

43. Ibid., 11–18. Story's decree was deferred, and so Henry Clay was permitted to appear as *amicus curiae* for the Kentucky claimants. The Court's second decision, written by Washington, reaffirmed Story.

44. 12 Wheaton 213.

45. Warren, *Supreme Court,* 1:608.

46. 12 Wheaton 213. Senator Charles Sumner made the point in a Senate speech of 14 February 1865 on a "Bill to Regulate Commerce among the Several States," when he cited Story's opinion in *U.S.* v. *Coombs,* 12 Peters 72 (1838), for an expansive construction of *Gibbons* (Sumner, *Works,* 9:246–47). Story's broad construction of *Gibbons,* following Webster's argument, was also clear in his dissent in *New York* v. *Miln,* 11 Peters 102 (1837).

47. For the development of the business corporation in New England, with an emphasis

on legal doctrine, see E. Merrick Dodd, *American Business Corporations until 1860, with Special Reference to Massachusetts* (Cambridge, Mass., 1954). For the corporation in the larger historical context see Handlin and Handlin, *Commonwealth*; and Hartz, *Economic Policy and Democratic Thought*. Still useful is Guy S. Callender, "The Early Transportation and Banking Enterprises of the States in Relation to the Growth of Corporations," 17 *Quarterly Journal of Economics* (November 1902): 111–62.

48. Dodd, *American Business Corporations*, p. 11.

49. Contemporaries understood the function of the corporation; for example, see "Corporations," 4 *American Jurist* (October 1830): 298–308.

50. His discussion is found in chap. 5, book 2, *Democracy in America*, ed. Phillips Bradley, trans. Henry Reeve, 2 vols. (New York: Vintage, 1959), 2:114–18.

51. 4 Wheaton 518. The *College* case has been discussed in many places. One of the most useful recent works, especially concerning the tangled legal and political background, is Francis N. Stites, *Private Interest and Public Gain: The Dartmouth College Case* (Amherst, Mass., 1972). Useful as a supplement to general works on the Court is Bruce A. Campbell, "Law and Experience in the Early Republic: The Evolution of the Dartmouth College Doctrine, 1780–1819" (Ph.D. diss., Michigan State University, 1973).

52. The case at the state level is found in Timothy Farrar, *Report of the Case of the Trustees of Dartmouth College against William H. Woodward* (Portsmouth, N.H., 1819). For arguments of counsel on the public-private question, see pp. 40–48.

53. 4 Wheaton 627–30.

54. 2 Cranch 127 (1804).

55. 4 Wheaton 630.

56. This point is spelled out more fully in R. Kent Newmyer, "Justice Joseph Story's Doctrine of 'Public and Private Corporations' and the Rise of the American Business Corporation," 25 *DePaul Law Review* (Summer 1976): 825–41.

57. See R. Kent Newmyer. "Daniel Webster as Tocqueville's Lawyer: The *Dartmouth College* Case Again," 11 *American Journal of Legal History* (April 1967): 127–47.

58. Webster to Story, 9 September 1818, Webster, *Writings*, 17:287.

59. For a detailed discussion see Stites, *Private Interest and Public Gain*, chap. 8; and Maurice G. Baxter, "Should the Dartmouth College Case Have Been Reargued?" 33 *New England Quarterly* (March 1960): 19–36.

60. Daniel Webster to Jeremiah Mason, 23 April 1818, Webster, *Writings*, 17:281.

61. *Dartmouth College v. Woodward*, 4 Wheaton 667 (1819).

62. 9 Cranch 43, 49.

63. This commonwealth theme is explored in Handlin and Handlin, *Commonwealth*, especially chap. 5.

64. 1 Murphy 88–89 (N.C. 1805). I wish to thank Gary L. Broder for his helpful research into the background of the public-private dichotomy in English and American law.

65. 4 Wheaton 668.

66. In addition to the *Foy* case, see *Waring v. Catawba Corp.*, 2 Bay 109 (S.C. 1797); *Commonwealth v. St. Patrick Benevolent Soc'y*, 2 Binn. 441 (Pa. 1810); and *State ex rel Kilbourne v. Tudor*, 5 Day 329 (Conn. 1812).

67. 91 English Rep. 900 (1 Lord Ray 5) (1694).

68. *Philips v. Bury* raised the question of the power of the Court of King's Bench to review the action of a visitor of Exeter College. Lord Holt ruled that private charitable corporations, i.e., those founded by private persons, are subject to the governance (visitation, in this case) of those who create them. Holt's ruling, as E. M. Dodd pointed out, was meant to distinguish between "ecclesiastical and eleemosynary foundations" and "corporations merely lay constituted for civil purposes." To see Holt's opinion as the foundation of the modern doctrine of public and private corporations would be to wrench it from the

context of seventeenth-century legal history. See Dodd, *American Business Corporations*, pp. 17–18.

69. *Dartmouth College* v. *Woodward*, 65 New Hamp. 624–43 (1817).

70. 94 U.S. 113, 125–26 (1877). This case arose when the Illinois legislature, in response to farmer protests, imposed maximum charges for grain storage. Elevator owners claimed that such a regulation deprived them of private property without due process of law under the Fourteenth Amendment. Over the powerful dissent of Justice Stephen Field, the Supreme Court sustained the law, holding that private property affected with public interest is subject to state regulation.

71. 4 Wheaton 659, 666.

72. 1 Fed. Cas. 489, 496 (No. 229) (C.C.D. Me. 1833).

73. For a discussion of this general issue see Campbell, "Law and Experience in the Early Republic," especially chaps. 4 and 8.

74. See Dodd, *American Business Corporations*, p. 379 and n. 7.

75. 10 *Merchants' Magazine and Commercial Review* (hereafter cited as *Merchants' Magazine*) (May 1844): 426–27.

76. "Corporations," p. 300.

77. See his argument in *Bank of Augusta* v. *Earle*, 13 Peters 551–53 (1839).

78. 5 Cranch 61, 86 (1809).

79. 1 *U.S. Statutes at Large* 78.

80. 4 Wheaton 668–69.

81. Hurst, *Law and Conditions of Freedom*, p. 15.

82. Kent, *Commentaries on American Law*, 2:276.

83. Joseph K. Angell and Samuel Ames, *A Treatise on the Law of Private Corporations Aggregate* (Boston, 1832), pp. 8–9.

84. Powerful opposition to Story and the Supreme Court's pro-corporate views was voiced during the Pennsylvania constitutional convention of 1837. See Hartz, *Economic Policy and Democratic Thought*, pp. 243–53. The *United States Magazine and Democratic Review*, January 1839, pp. 99–144, captures the passion of the anticorporate, anti-Court forces. Corporations are singled out as gross violators of American egalitarian principles, and the Supreme Court, particularly in the *College* decision, is lambasted for its expansion of corporate privilege. Story is named as the culprit who led the Court, including Chief Justice Marshall, down the primrose path of corporate favoritism (ibid., p. 120).

85. Joseph Hopkinson to Story, 1 August 1833, Story Papers, UT.

86. Duncan Kennedy's discussion of Blackstone raises intriguing questions about the collision of Blackstone's system with the chaos of American legal history. See his "Structure of Blackstone's Commentaries," 28 *Buffalo Law Review* (Spring 1979): 205–382.

87. Quoted in 9 *Niles' Weekly Register*, addendum (14 October 1815): 5.

88. I have drawn on Frank D. Prager's summary of English and American patent law and of Story's role as a patent judge. See his "Changing Views of Justice Story on the Construction of Patents," 4 *American Journal of Legal History* (January 1960): 1–21, and "The Influence of Mr. Justice Story on American Patent Law," 5 ibid. (July 1961): 254–64. Helpful, too, are Floyd L. Vaughan, *The United States Patent System: Legal and Economic Conflicts in American Patent History* (Norman, Okla., 1956); and Bruce W. Bugbee, *Genesis of American Patent and Copyright Law* (Washington, D.C., 1967).

89. Joseph Story, "On the Patent Laws," appendix, 3 Wheaton 12–29; Story, *Commentaries on the Constitution*, 2:83–85, secs. 1151–56.

90. For Story's celebration of American inventiveness, see especially his "Developments of Science and Mechanical Art," a discourse delivered to the Boston Mechanics' Institute in November 1829 and reprinted in *MW*, pp. 475–502.

91. Prager, "Changing Views of Justice Story," pp. 1–11.

92. Prager, "Influence of Story on Patent Law," pp. 262–63.

93. 1 Fed. Cas. 755 (No. 326) (C.C.D. Mass.). Prager, "Changing Views of Justice Story," pp. 11–19, treats Story's shift to a liberal interpretation.

94. 3 Fed. Cas. 648 (No. 1,518) (C.C.D. Mass.).

95. 30 Fed. Cas. 723 (No. 18,107) (C.C.D. Mass. 1840).

96. See especially the laudatory account of Willard Phillips, *The Law of Patents for Inventors* . . . (Boston, 1837), in 18 *American Jurist* (October 1837): 106, 107, 113.

97. For Story's paean to the "general diffusion of knowledge" see his speech "Characteristics of the Age" in *MW*, especially pp. 344ff.

98. 8 Peters 591.

99. Judge Hopkinson's opinion is printed in 8 Peters appendix (Lawyer's Edition). A full discussion of the case from Wheaton's point of view is found in Elizabeth F. Baker, *Henry Wheaton, 1785–1848* (Philadelphia, 1937), chap. 17.

100. Story to Richard Peters, 26 June 1828, Richard Peters Papers, Historical Society of Pennsylvania.

101. 8 Peters 658–60.

102. Ibid., 668–99.

103. Story to Peters, 6 June 1834, Peters Papers.

104. Story to Kent, 17 May 1834, *LL*, 2:181–82.

105. Wheaton to Mrs. Lyman, 22 May 1837, as quoted in Baker, *Wheaton*, p. 127.

106. Wheaton to Mrs. Lyman, 14 May 1837, as quoted in ibid., p. 131.

107. Story's praise of the democratization of American land law can be found in "Progress of Jurisprudence," p. 214.

108. See, for example, his impassioned statement in *Wilkinson* v. *Leland*, 2 Peters 657–58 (1829). On the right to deploy, his opinion in the Girard will case, *Vidal* v. *Philadelphia*, 2 Howard 127 (1844), is revealing.

109. 24 Fed. Cas. 472 (No. 14,312). (C.C.D. R.I.). The conflict between static and dynamic property, conceptualized by Hurst in *Law and Conditions of Freedom*, has been expanded by Stanley I. Kutler, *Privilege and Creative Destruction: The Charles River Bridge Case* (Philadelphia, 1971). My thinking on *Tyler* is particularly indebted to Horwitz, *Transformation of American Law*, chap. 2 and especially pp. 38–40. Thanks, too, go to John Juliano for the use of his research on *Tyler*.

110. Horwitz, *Transformation of American Law*, chap. 2, explores this theme.

111. Ibid., p. 39.

112. *Tyler* v. *Wilkinson*, 24 Fed. Cas. 474 (No. 14,312).

113. 12 Howard 299; 221 U.S. 1; 302 U.S. 319; 304 U.S. 144. The ad hoc character of reasonable use, as well as Story's reluctance to abandon old law, is clear in his opinion in *Webb* v. *Portland Manufacturing Co.*, 29 Fed. Cas. 506 (No. 17,322) (C.C.D. Me. 1838). In this case Story refused to make reasonable use controlling, returning instead to the unqualified natural-flow principle, which he strengthened by permitting action under it despite only token damages. *Tyler* was cited as authority.

114. 24 Fed. Cas. 475, 476 (No. 14,312).

115. For a discussion of judicial construction of the milldam acts see Horwitz, *Transformation of American Law*, pp. 47–54.

116. And Story in the codification controversy would further insist that the legislature should codify only those principles of the common law already settled by the courts. For a discussion of his position on codification see Chapter 8, section 1.

117. Sumner, "The Position and Duties of the Merchant," in *Works*, 3:488.

118. Perry Miller, *The American Transcendentalists: Their Prose and Poetry* (New York, 1957), p. 6.

119. See n. 46 to this chapter.

120. 8 Wheaton 10–17. Story's opinion was delivered in 1821 but is reported in 8 Wheaton, along with the Court's opinion by Justice Washington in 1823.

121. Story to Webster, 10 May 1840, *LL*, 2:330–32.

122. Robert K. Faulkner, *The Jurisprudence of John Marshall* (Princeton, N.J., 1968), is very good on this point.

123. Story, *Commentaries on the Constitution*, 1:383, sec. 513.

124. Story, "Developments of Science and Mechanical Art," pp. 475–502, especially 499–500.

125. Story makes this point to Francis Lieber in praising the latter's *Manual of Political Ethics* (Story to Lieber, 15 August 1837, *LL*, 2:278–79).

126. Story, "Developments of Science and Mechanical Art," pp. 499–500.

127. See, for example, Story to John Lowell, 20 November 1823, Story Papers, MHS; and Story to Amos Lawrence, "Saturday noon," *Extracts from the Diary and Correspondence of the Late Amos Lawrence* . . . ed. William Lawrence (Boston, 1855), pp. 179–80. Story corresponded on personal terms with T. H. Perkins, P. C. Brooks, and other prominent New England entrepreneurs as well.

128. This is the message of such works as Hartz, *Economic Policy and Democratic Thought*, and Handlin and Handlin, *Commonwealth*, though one ought to apply the corrective of Robert Lively's "The American System."

129. For a discussion of the will theory of contract see Horwitz, *Transformation of American Law*, pp. 22–26.

130. Contractual morality as a way of business and a societal value is discussed in Anthony F. C. Wallace, *Rockdale: The Growth of an American Village in the Early Industrial Revolution* (New York, 1978), pp. 18–22.

131. See Story's anonymous article on "Contract" in *Encyclopaedia Americana* . . . , ed. Francis Lieber (Philadelphia, 1829–33), new ed., 13 vols. (Philadelphia, 1846), 3:503; all references to this work are to the new ed.

132. Story, *Commentaries on the Constitution*, 2:249, sec. 1378.

133. Story to Richard H. Dana, Jr., 14 October 1840, *LL*, 2:343.

134. *Brown v. Lull*, 4 Fed. Cas. 407 (No. 2,018) (C.C.D. Mass. 1836).

135. I would particularly like to thank Bonnie Sarno (Vontell), whose honors thesis, "Justice Joseph Story and the Transformation of Seamen's Contract Law, 1790–1872" (University of Connecticut, 1981), was immensely helpful to me in understanding Story on seamen's wages.

136. *Cloutman v. Tunison*, 5 Fed. Cas. 1091 (No. 2,907) (C.C.D. Mass. 1833); *Coffin v. Jenkins*, 5 Fed. Cas. 1188 (No. 2,948) (C.C.D. Mass. 1844); *U.S. v. Gibert*, 25 Fed. Cas. 1287 (No. 15,204) (C.C.D. Mass. 1834); *Harden v. Gordon*, 11 Fed. Cas. 480 (No. 6,047) (C.C.D. Me. 1823); *Orne v. Townsend*, 18 Fed. Cas. 825 (No. 10,583) (C.C.D. Mass. 1827).

137. *Sheppard v. Taylor*, 5 Peters 675 (1831).

138. 11 Fed. Cas. 485 (No. 6,047).

139. For his legislative efforts see Story to Richard H. Dana, Jr., 9 July 1841, *LL*, 2:372–73; and Richard H. Dana, Jr., to William W. Story, 3 May 1851, *LL*, 2:373–74.

140. *LL*, 2:374.

141. 5 Peters 38.

142. Story's decisions provided basic doctrinal substance for the two most important treatises of the age (written, not coincidentally, by friends and former students): Richard H. Dana, Jr., *The Seamen's Friend, Containing a Treatise on Practical Seamanship* (Boston, 1841); and George Ticknor Curtis, *A Treatise on the Rights and Duties of Merchant Seamen* . . . (Boston, 1841). Kent's *Commentaries on American Law* also drew heavily on Story's circuit decisions.

143. 17 *U.S. Statutes at Large* 268.

144. Joseph Story, "Value and Importance of Legal Studies: A Discourse Pronounced at the Inauguration of the Author as Dane Professor of Law in Harvard University, August 25, 1829," in *MW*, p. 521.

145. For the impact of Story on modern corporate law in this respect see Gerald T. Dunne, "Justice Story and the Modern Corporation—A Closing Circle?" 17 *American Journal of Legal History* (July 1973): 262–70.

146. 7 Cranch 299.

147. 12 Wheaton 64.

148. 29 Fed. Cas. 1215 (No. 17,647) (C.C.D. Me.). Bushrod Washington was very approving of Story's opinion in this case. See Washington to Story, 1 February 1825, Story Papers, MHS.

149. 30 Fed. Cas. 435 (No. 17,944) (C.C.D. Me.)

150. 8 Peters 286.

151. "Manufacturing Corporations," 2 *American Jurist* (July 1829): 118.

152. Quoted in Miller, *Transcendentalists*, p. 356.

153. See, for example, 25 *Niles' Weekly Register* (8 November 1837): 147, or almost every issue of the *Merchants' Magazine*. Also see Asa Child, "An Oration, Delivered before the Citizens of Norwich, on the Anniversary of National Independence," 4 July 1838, as quoted in Merle E. Curti, *The Growth of American Thought*, 2d ed. (New York, 1943), p. 404; and Lawrence to Henry Clay, 26 March 1833, Henry Clay Papers, LC.

Chapter Five

1. See especially Story to Mary O. Story, 8 March 1829, 7, 20 February, 14 March 1830, 4 March 1833, Story Papers, UT; and Story to William Story, 10 February 1829, Story Papers, MHS.

2. Story to Mary O. Story, 4 March 1833, Story Papers, UT. "Nor Mind, nor Rank escapes the common doom," he wrote in 1827 in his poem "Reflections on Life"; "Youth feels the withering touch of slow disease" (ibid.).

3. Story to John G. Palfrey, 2 July 1835, John G. Palfrey Papers, Houghton Library, Harvard University. He wrote Palfrey that his wife could no longer go out in the evenings on account of her health. On 16 December 1836 he wrote to George Ticknor, "Mrs. Story has become a permanent Invalid & I can indulge no hope of any final relief. She has not been abroad except in a carriage for a year" (Story Papers, UT).

4. See, for example, Story to Stephen White, 19 March 1826, Story Papers, UT.

5. Story to Bushrod Washington, 4 July 1827, *LL*, 1:519.

6. *LL*, 1:443–44.

7. See Story's "Sketch" of Washington, in *MW*, pp. 808–11.

8. Story to Sarah Story, 7 March 1829, *LL*, 1:562–63.

9. Ibid.

10. A brilliant statement of the complexities of republicanism and the Revolution is Kammen's "Ambiguities of the American Revolution," chap. 7 in his *People of Paradox*.

11. See Gordon S. Wood, *Creation of the American Republic, 1776–1787* (Chapel Hill, N.C., 1969), for an astute discussion of the ideology and strategy of the framers.

12. José Ortega y Gasset, *The Revolt of the Masses*, 25th anniversary ed. (New York, 1957).

13. Thomas Jefferson, *Memoirs, Correspondence, and Private Papers of Thomas Jefferson, Late President of the United States, Now First Published from the Original Manuscripts*, ed. Thomas Jefferson Randolph, 4 vols. (London, 1829). For the publication and reception of

the *Memoirs* (including a fine discussion of Story's reaction to them) see Merrill D. Peterson, *The Jefferson Image in the American Mind* (New York, 1960), pp. 29–36.

14. Story to Fay, 15 February 1830, *LL*, 2:33.

15. Story to Joseph Hopkinson, 13 February 1830, Hopkinson Papers.

16. Jefferson, *Memoirs*, 4:200–205.

17. Jefferson to Judge John Tyler, 17 June 1812, ibid., pp. 182–84.

18. Jefferson to General Henry Dearborn, 17 March 1815, ibid., pp. 264–65.

19. See Jefferson's prefatory remarks to the "Anas," ibid., p. 463.

20. Jefferson to John Dickinson, 19 December 1801, ibid., 3:495–96.

21. Jefferson to George Hay, 2 June 1807, ibid., 4:76–77.

22. Jefferson to Spencer Roane, 6 September 1819, ibid., pp. 324–27.

23. Jefferson to Judge Johnson, 12 June 1823, ibid., pp. 377–84.

24. Jefferson to Dearborn, 16 July 1810, ibid., pp. 151–152.

25. Marshall to Story, 18 September 1820, John Marshall Papers, LC. For other Marshall letters to Story blasting Jefferson see 13 July, 18 September 1821, 25 December 1832, Story Papers, MHS. Bushrod Washington also joined in the attack: Washington to Story, 4 December 1821, ibid. Story expressed his total contempt for Jefferson in his letter to Hopkinson of 13 February 1830, Hopkinson Papers.

26. See Michael Wallace, "Changing Concepts of Party in the United States: New York, 1815–1828," 74 *American Historical Review* (December 1968): 453–91; and for a more general discussion, chap. 6 in Hofstadter, *Idea of a Party System*.

27. *LL*, 1:513–14. For Marshall's opinion see his letter to Story, 30 December 1827, Marshall Papers, College of William and Mary.

28. Story to Ticknor, 6 March 1828, *LL*, 1:536–37. Story added, "The time is not yet arrived, in which the best [of Burke] can be safely published."

29. [J. Story], "Statesmen—Their Rareness and Importance: Daniel Webster," 7 *New England Magazine* (August 1834): 92.

30. Amory, *Proper Bostonians*, p. 17. Useful in understanding elite society in Boston and Massachusetts before the Civil War are Frederic C. Jaher, "Boston Brahmins," in Jaher, ed., *The Age of Industrialism in America: Essays in Social Structure and Cultural Values* (New York, 1968); David B. Tyack, *George Ticknor and the Boston Brahmins* (Cambridge, Mass., 1967); Paul Goodman, "Ethics and Enterprise: The Values of the Boston Elite, 1800–1860," 18 *American Quarterly* (Fall 1966): 437–51; Ronald Story, "Class and Culture in Boston: The Athenaeum, 1807–1860," 27 *American Quarterly* (May 1975): 178–99; and S. E. Morison, *The Life and Letters of Harrison Gray Otis, Federalist, 1765–1848*, 2 vols. (Boston, 1913).

31. On Harvard University during the antebellum period see Howe, *Unitarian Conscience*; Ronald Story, *The Forging of an Aristocracy: Harvard and the Boston Upper Class, 1800–1870* (Middletown, Conn., 1980); and Morison, *Three Centuries of Harvard*. Tyack's *Ticknor* is also useful.

32. Nathaniel Hawthorne, *The Blithedale Romance*, vol. 8 of *The Complete Writings of Nathaniel Hawthorne*, Old Manse ed. (Boston, 1900), pp. 200–201.

33. Story to Webster, 10 June 1827, Story Papers, MHS.

34. Story to Robert Winthrop, 24 February 1840, ibid.

35. For an interpretation of New England Federalism after 1816 see Shaw Livermore, Jr., *The Twilight of Federalism: The Disintegration of the Federalist Party, 1815–1830* (Princeton, N.J., 1962).

36. Story is listed among the Boston elite not born to the purple in Tyack, *Ticknor*, p. 279 n. 52.

37. Story to Otis, 27 December 1818, Otis Papers.

38. The occasion was a dinner at Abbott Lawrence's in 1841 given for Lord Morpeth

(*Memoir and Letters of Charles Sumner*, ed. Edward L. Pierce, 4 vols. [Boston, 1877–93], 3:479). Also see Tyack, *Ticknor*, pp. 216–17.

39. R. Booth to Story, 22 April 1831, Story Papers, MHS.

40. Everett to Story, 13 April 1821, Story Papers, MHS.

41. For Story's high opinion of Abbott Lawrence see his letter to Edward Everett, 26 June 1843, *LL*, 2:447–48. See also Story to Amos Lawrence, "Saturday noon," Lawrence, *Diary*, pp. 179–80.

42. Colonel Pickering to Story, 22 August 1822, Story Papers, UT.

43. Lowell to Story, 14 November 1823, Sumner Papers.

44. Story to Lowell, 20 November 1823, Story Papers, MHS.

45. On 1 January 1824 Story received an apology from J. B. Davis, editor of the *Patriot*, and a promise prompted by the "solicitation of the Proprietors of that establishment" that it would not happen again (Story Papers, UT). On Story's apostasy see "Brutus" to Joseph Story, n.d. (draft), Andrew Dunlap Papers, vol. 14, Essex Institute, Salem, Mass.

46. R. Story, *Forging of an Aristocracy*.

47. Story to General H. A. S. Dearborn, 10 January 1822, Charles W. Upham, "Salem Witchcraft Illustrated with Portraits and Autographs, Ch. K. 1.40, Chamberlain Collection, Boston Public Library.

48. *LL*, 1:359–61.

49. *LL*, 1:360–61.

50. Webster to Story, 4 December 1819, Story Papers, MHS.

51. Story to Jeremiah Mason, 26 November 1819, *LL*, 1:366. His charge to the grand jury is quoted at length in *LL*, 1:336–47.

52. 29 Fed. Cas. 832 (No. 15,551) (C.C.D. Mass.), as quoted in *LL*, 1:350–51.

53. For a balanced discussion of Northern antislavery and sectional politics at the time of the Missouri debates see George Dangerfield, *The Awakening of American Nationalism, 1815–1828* (New York, 1965), pp. 119–24.

54. Story to Bushrod Washington, 13 January 1821, Story Papers, microfilm, New York Historical Society. From this letter it is clear that Story fully grasped the conservative nature of the convention.

55. Story to Jeremiah Mason, 21 January 1821, *LL*, 1:394–96.

56. Story to Marshall, 27 June 1821, Marshall Papers, College of William and Mary.

57. Ibid.

58. Story to Washington, 13 January 1821, Story Papers, New York Historical Society.

59. Story to Mason, 21 January 1821, *LL*, 1:394–96.

60. Samuel E. Morison's *History of the Constitution of Massachusetts* (Boston, 1917) has a useful account of the convention of 1820.

61. Story to Mr. Agg, 17 August 1827, Story Papers, MHS. See also "Autobiography," pp. 36–37.

62. Story to Agg, 17 August 1827, Story Papers, MHS.

63. Story to Marshall, 27 June 1821, Marshall Papers, College of William and Mary.

64. Judge Isaac Parker to H. G. Otis, 10 January 1821, Otis Papers.

65. Webster to Jeremiah Mason, 12 January 1821, *Memoir and Correspondence of Jeremiah Mason*, ed. G. S. Hillard (Cambridge, Mass., 1873), p. 258.

66. Parker to Webster, 19, 25 February 1825, as quoted in Livermore, *Twilight*, p. 190.

67. Howe, *Unitarian Conscience*, p. 206.

68. The generational conflict among Federalists is the central theme of David H. Fischer's *Revolution of American Conservatism: The Federalist Party in the Era of Jeffersonian Democracy* (New York, 1965). Intraparty divisions are also treated in Manning J. Dauer, *The Adams Federalists* (Baltimore, 1953); Banner, *To the Hartford Convention*; and Robert A. East, "Economic Development and New England Federalism, 1803–1814," 10 *New England Quarterly* (September 1937): 430–46.

69. Rudolph Bunner to Gulian Verplanck, 19 February 1823, Gulian C. Verplanck Papers, New York Historical Society. Another reference to the Story-Webster relationship is found in Nathaniel Silsbee to Jeremiah Mason, 25 February 1824, Ch. D. 7.44, Chamberlain Collection, Boston Public Library.

70. The comeback effort of the Federalists in the 1820s is the theme of Livermore's *Twilight*. Especially useful to me on the cultural resurgence of New England conservatives in the 1820s has been Harlow Sheidley, "Sectional Nationalism: Massachusetts Conservative Leadership and the Epic of New England, 1820–1836" (research paper, University of Connecticut, 1977).

71. Marshall to Story, 9 December 1823, Marshall Papers, LC.

72. Story to H. A. S. Dearborn, 10 January 1822, Upham, "Salem Witchcraft," Chamberlain Collection. Also see Story to Edward Everett, 4 August 1825, *LL*, 1:363–64.

73. Quoted in *LL*, 1:540.

74. Story, "Statesmen—Their Rareness and Importance: Daniel Webster," p. 92.

75. Among the many letters between Story and Everett, see the following as evidence of their mutual esteem and joint commitment to conservative activism: Story to Everett, 4 August 1825, 7 March 1820, 31 May 1831, *LL*, 1:363–64, 366–68, 2:94–95. Story's autobiographical letter to Everett, which appeared in 1 *New England Magazine* (December, 1832): 433–48, is found in Story Papers, MHS. Also see in this regard Story to Everett, 8 December 1832, Story Papers, MHS.

76. Samuel Whitcomb, Jr., to John McLean, 13 February 1844, John McLean Papers, LC.

77. Along with those to Joseph Hopkinson, Story's letters to Peters contain some of the frankest opinions about men and events, as well as about the business of the Supreme Court.

78. Story knew Greenleaf from his circuit travels in Maine. He praised Greenleaf's Maine reports and encouraged him in his legal scholarship (Story to Greenleaf, 25 December 1819, 28 May 1822, Story Papers, UT). See pp. 259–62.

79. On 4 March 1826 Story wrote Hopkinson "in the *strictest* confidence" on what he must do to get the nomination. On 23 February 1829 he informed Hopkinson of his confirmation (Hopkinson Papers). Also in these papers is Story's letter of 18 January 1827 to President Adams recommending Hopkinson.

80. Shaw Livermore recounts the amalgamation effort in *Twilight*. Harlow Sheidley sees the struggle in the larger context of New England conservatism in chap. 4 of her "Sectional Nationalism." I have drawn freely on both accounts, though neither deals fully with Story. Useful also is Samuel F. Bemis, *John Quincy Adams and the Union* (New York, 1956).

81. Story to Adams, 20 October 1829, *LL*, 2:13–17. For Story's running account of his new closeness to Adams see Story to Sarah Story, 26, 30 January, 21, 25 February 1829, Story Papers, UT.

82. I have dealt with this remarkable alliance in "A Note on the Whig Politics of Justice Joseph Story," 48 *Mississippi Valley Historical Review* (December 1961): 480–91. Webster's habit of harnessing talent for his own use is discussed in Newmyer, "Daniel Webster as Tocqueville's Lawyer."

83. Webster refused William Story's request for his father's letters, some of which Story had hoped to use for his *Life and Letters*. See *LL*, 2:408.

84. Theodore Parker, *Additional Speeches, Addresses, and Occasional Sermons*, 2 vols. (Boston, 1855), 1:170.

85. Story to Jeremiah Mason, 21 January 1821, *LL*, 1:394–96.

86. Parker, *Additional Speeches*, 1:170.

87. Story to Sarah Story, 29 January 1830, *LL*, 2:34.

88. Webster to Story, 21 July 1832, 14 *Proceedings of the Massachusetts Historical Society*, 2d ser. (1900–1901): 408–9.

89. Story to Webster, 25 December 1833, *LL*, 2:155–58.

90. See Newmyer, "Whig Politics of Story," p. 488.

91. Joseph E. Sprague tells of Story's political advice to Webster in his letter to Edward Everett, 20 May 1827, Edward Everett Papers, MHS. I discuss Story and Webster in the *College* case in "Whig Politics of Story," pp. 489–91; also see Baxter's excellent account in "Should the Dartmouth College Case Have Been Reargued?"

92. For an analysis of the antiparty theme in early national politics see Ronald P. Formisano, "Political Character, Antipartyism and the Second American Party System," 21 *American Quarterly* (Winter 1969): 683–709.

93. Story to Mason, 21 January 1821, *LL*, 1:394–96.

94. Story's eulogies of Samuel Dexter, William Pinkney, Justice Robert Trimble, Thomas A. Emmet, Justice Bushrod Washington, Isaac Parker, Justice Thomas Todd, Hugh S. Legaré, and Justice Philip P. Barbour were reprinted in *MW*, pp. 779–828. For his longer piece on Marshall, a speech originally delivered to the Suffolk Bar Association in 1835, see *MW*, pp. 639–97.

95. Lynn L. Marshall, "The Strange Stillbirth of the Whig Party," 72 *American Historical Review* (January 1967): 445–68.

96. Story refers to his wife's "disdain" for Mather in a letter to Judge Samuel Fay, 10 September 1828, *LL*, 1:551.

97. The idea of the 1820s as a cultural watershed in New England history has yet to be explored systematically. Vernon L. Parrington's "The Mind of New England," bk. 3 of his *Main Currents in American Thought: An Interpretation of American Literature from the Beginnings to 1920* (New York, 1927), is rich in suggestions.

98. Tocqueville, *Democracy in America*, 1:32.

99. Emerson, *Journals*, 7:339, as quoted in Parrington, *Main Currents*, p. 317. For Webster's remarkable (and prefiguring) statement on New England and the Union see Webster to Rev. (?) Washington, 11 January 1815, autograph file of Webster letters, Houghton Library, Harvard University.

100. Story to Everett, 4 January 1825, *LL*, 1:447–48.

101. *A Selection of Eulogies Pronounced in the Several States in Honor of Those Illustrious Patriots and Statesmen, John Adams and Thomas Jefferson* (Hartford, Conn., 1826).

102. William E. Channing, *A Sermon Preached at the Annual Election, May 26, 1830 . . .* (Boston, 1830).

103. Josiah Quincy, *An Address to the Citizens of Boston . . . [upon] the First Settlement of the City* (Boston, 1830).

104. My thanks to Harlow Sheidley for sharing with me her research in progress on the communication network and propaganda strategy of Massachusetts conservatives in the 1820s.

105. Story to Everett, 7 March 1820, *LL*, 1:366–68.

106. Story to George Bancroft, 28 April 1834, Story Papers, MHS.

107. For Story's argument on the centrality of marriage and the family in republican society see his "Natural Law," an unsigned article that appeared in Lieber, *Encyclopaedia Americana*, 9:150–58. This important and hard-to-get article is conveniently reprinted in James McClellan, *Joseph Story and the American Constitution: A Study in Political and Legal Thought with Selected Writings* (Norman, Okla., 1971), pp. 313–24; pp. 315–17 are particularly relevant.

108. See Howe's excellent treatment of this theme in *Unitarian Conscience*.

109. Story to William Williams, 6 March 1824, *LL*, 1:441–42. An interesting insight into Story's Unitarianism is found in his letter to Andrewes Norton, 28 December 1843, which praises Norton's disproof of the Trinity (Sumner Papers).

110. Story to Sarah Story, 23 February 1827, Story Papers, UT.

111. Ibid.

112. Joseph Story, "History and Influence of the Puritans: A Discourse Pronounced at the Request of the Essex Historical Society, September 18, 1828, in Commemoration of the First Settlement of Salem, Mass.," in *MW*, pp. 408–74.

113. "Consecration of the Cemetery at Mount Auburn: An Address Delivered at the Consecration of Mount Auburn, as a Cemetery, September 24, 1831," in *MW*, pp. 565–80.

114. Parrington, *Main Currents*, pp. 302–3.

115. Anti-Virginia and anti-Southern sentiments appear regularly in Story's writings after about 1820. See Story to Stephen White, 27 February 1820, *LL*, 1:361–63; Story to Everett, 7 March 1820, *LL*, 1:366–68; and Story to Jeremiah Mason, 25 June 1820, *LL*, 1:365.

116. Story to George Ticknor, 2 February 1828, *LL*, 1:534–36.

117. Jefferson to John Cartwright, 15 June 1824, as quoted in McClellan, *Story*, p. 118. McClellan treats the controversy between Story and Jefferson over the common law with admirable precision in ibid., chap. 3, "Christianity and the Common Law." Useful to me also has been Peterson, *Jefferson Image*, pp. 95–98.

118. Story to Everett, 15 September 1824, *LL*, 1:429–30.

119. 9 Cranch 43.

120. Story, *Commentaries on the Constitution*, 2:631, sec. 1876.

121. Ibid., 2:629, sec. 1873.

122. See Story, "Value and Importance of Legal Studies," in *MW*, p. 517; and J[oseph] S[tory], "Art. V—Christianity a Part of the Common Law," 9 *American Jurist* (April 1833): 346–48. Peterson's discussion is found in *Jefferson Image*, pp. 96–98.

123. Story to the Reverend Jasper Adams, 14 May 1833, Story Papers, UM. By putting the Adams letter in context, McClellan has shown its importance (*Story*, pp. 136–41).

124. Story to Hopkinson, 27 November 1833, Hopkinson Papers.

125. [Edward Everett], "Story's Constitutional Law," review, 37 *North American Review* (January 1834): 65–66.

126. For a fine summary treatment of Virginia constitutionalists see Elizabeth Kelly Bauer, *Commentaries on the Constitution, 1790–1860* (New York, 1952). I have relied heavily on her scholarship.

127. When Story met Taylor for the first time in the winter of 1824 he found him entirely admirable. "I scarcely recollect any person whom I have been so much struck with in so short an interview; & yet all our opinions upon the Gov. & constitution, & the politics of the nation are probably the most direct contradictions" (Story to Sarah Story, 29 February 1824, Story Papers, UT).

128. William W. Freehling, *Prelude to Civil War: The Nullification Controversy in South Carolina, 1816–1836* (New York, 1966).

129. The historical approach to legal development is stated explicitly in Story's *Commentaries on Equity Jurisprudence, As Administered in England and America*, 2 vols. (Boston, 1836), 1:59–61.

130. The natural-law dimension of Story's legal system is explored fully in McClellan, *Story*, especially chap. 2. The relation of the common law to Burke and conservatism is treated in J. G. A. Pocock, "Burke and the Ancient Constitution: A Problem in the History of Ideas," chap. 6 in his *Politics, Language and Time: Essays on Political Thought and History* (New York, 1971).

131. Story, *Commentaries on the Constitution*, 1:116, 109–110, 111, secs. 163, 156–57, 158.

132. Story to Peters, 24 April 1833, Peters Papers.

133. Story made no bones about his reliance either. "I am going on with Lectures on the

Constitution of the U.S., & hope in two years to complete them. I mean to embody in them the *whole substance* of the Federalist with all the earlier aids" (Story to Kent, 24 June 1831, Story Papers, MHS).

134. Story's discussion of sovereignty is found in *Commentaries on the Constitution*, 1:149–50, sec. 207.

135. Ibid., 1:151, 152, 157–58, secs. 208, 210, 215. See chaps. 2, 3, and 4 for his analysis of the confederation period.

136. Story to Hopkinson, 27 November 1833, Hopkinson Papers.

137. Story, *Commentaries on the Constitution*, 1:245, 252–58, secs. 340, 351–58.

138. Andrew McLaughlin, "Social Compact and Constitutional Construction," 5 *American Historical Review* (April 1900): 467–91.

139. Story, *Commentaries on the Constitution*, 1:304, sec. 397.

140. Ibid., p. 305, sec. 399.

141. Ibid., pp. 348–49, sec. 456.

142. The first edition of an annotated Constitution was issued in 1913 as S. Doc. 12. Subsequent enlargements and refinements led to Corwin's great work, the first edition of which appeared in 1953 officially listed as Doc. 170, 82d Cong., 2d sess.

143. Marshall to Story, 24 April 1833, Marshall Papers, LC.

144. Charles C. Jones, Jr., to the Reverend and Mrs. C. C. Jones, 13 June 1854, *Children of Pride: A True Story of Georgia and the Civil War*, ed. Robert M. Myers (New Haven, Conn., 1972), pp. 45–46.

145. John Hope Franklin, *The Militant South, 1800–1861* (Cambridge, Mass., 1956), p. 167.

146. Again Bauer's *Commentaries* has been indispensable.

147. Story to Hopkinson, 22 June 1832, Hopkinson Papers.

148. Marshall to Story, 22 September 1832, Story Papers, MHS.

149. Marshall to Story, 24 April 1833, ibid.

150. Marshall to Story, 3 June 1833, ibid.

151. Kent to Story, 16 April 1833, ibid.

152. Quoted in *LL*, 2:655.

153. See Story to Hopkinson, 30 March 1833, Hopkinson Papers; and Hopkinson to Story, 1 August 1833, Story Papers, UT.

154. Sparks to Story, 16 June 1834, Story Papers, LC.

155. 14 *American Quarterly Review* (December 1833): 329.

156. "Story's Commentaries—Vols. II and III," 10 *American Jurist* (July 1833): 147.

157. Everett, "Story's Constitutional Law," especially pp. 65–66.

158. William W. Story summarizes M. Paul Odet's review in *Revue des Deux Mondes* and Professor R. Mohl's in *Kritische Zeitschrift* and makes references to reviews in *Revue Etrangère, Law Review* (London), and *Edinburgh Law Journal* (*LL*, 2:655–56).

159. Bauer, *Commentaries*, p. 359.

160. Ibid., p. 353.

161. Story to Willard Phillips, 27 January 1833, Story Papers, MHS.

Chapter Six

1. Story to Peters, 19 June 1835, *LL*, 2:199–200.

2. *MW*, pp. 684–85.

3. Hawthorne, *Blithedale Romance*, p. 201.

4. *MW*, pp. 694, 696.

5. For Story on Marshall's romantic, sentimental qualities see *MW*, p. 680. Notice also in the frontispiece to this book, how Gilbert Stuart captures Story's Byronic qualities.

6. 7 April 1837, *LL*, 2:275–77.

7. Crosskey's *Politics and the Constitution* is the most extreme statement on the consolidating intentions of the framers. Although Crosskey's argument is excessive, his scholarship is massive and has yet to be refuted. Not surprisingly, Story was his hero.

8. *McCulloch* v. *Maryland*, 4 Wheaton 415 (1819).

9. Wirt to President Monroe, 5 May 1823, as quoted in Warren, *Supreme Court*, 1:589–91.

10. This is the theme of Ellis, *The Jeffersonian Crisis*.

11. Quoted in Gerald Gunther, "The Warren Court and the Marshall Court—Strategy in Constitutional Adjudication" (paper prepared for Claremont Seminar, January 1965), pp. 41–42.

12. Taylor's constitutional writings are discussed in Bauer, *Commentaries*. For a full study of Taylor see Robert E. Shalhope, *John Taylor of Caroline: Pastoral Republican* (Columbia, S.C., 1980).

13. 9 Wheaton 738.

14. Warren, *Supreme Court*, 1:653. For the political reaction to *Gibbons* see ibid., pp. 617–19.

15. 12 Sergeant & Rawle 330 (Pa.).

16. For Story's response to this insult see Story to Sarah Story, 28 January 1831, *LL*, 2:43–45. Warren, *Supreme Court*, chaps. 13 and 16, contains the best discussion of the anti-Court movement of the 1820s. I have relied on his account, especially 1:657, 663, 669, 717, 721.

17. Gunther, "The Warren Court and the Marshall Court," p. 22.

18. Senate debates on Foote resolution, *Register of Debates*, 21st Cong., 1st sess., 27 January 1830, pp. 87–92.

19. John C. Calhoun to Virgil Maxcy, 1 September 1831, Galloway, Maxcy, Markoe Papers, LC.

20. Mason to Story, 8 January 1822, Mason, *Memoir*, pp. 261–62; Story to Mason, 21 February 1822, ibid., p. 264; Story to Ticknor, 22 January 1831, *LL*, 2:48–49; Story to Sarah Story, 28 January 1831, *LL*, 2:43–45.

21. Marshall to Story, 2 July 1823, Story Papers, MHS.

22. Story to Mason, 10 January 1822, *LL*, 1:411–12.

23. 2:399, sec. 1576.

24. Roper, "Judicial Unanimity and the Marshall Court."

25. See for example, Greenleaf, *Cases Overruled, Doubted, or Limited*, a work known and approved by Story.

26. Jefferson to Johnson, 4 March 1823, Jefferson, *Works*, 12:277–80.

27. Morgan, *Johnson*, p. 185. Morgan's fine account of the internal division on the late Marshall Court is found in chap. 10.

28. 9 Wheaton 222–39.

29. 12 Wheaton 436–49.

30. 8 Wheaton 1. Warren notes, however, that the three absent judges agreed with the decision (*Supreme Court*, 1:640).

31. For a critical retrospective analysis of the Marshall Court (and especially of Story) see the *United States Magazine and Democratic Review*, January 1838, pp. 143–73; June 1840, pp. 497–515.

32. 12 Wheaton 213.

33. 4 Peters 514 (1830).

34. *Craig* v. *Missouri*, 4 Peters 410 (1830). For Marshall's gloomy assessment see Marshall to Story, 3 May 1831, Marshall Papers, LC; and Marshall to Story, 15 October 1830, Story Papers, MHS.

35. Marshall to Story, 3 May 1831, Marshall Papers, LC.

36. Mason to Story, 8 January 1822, Mason, *Memoir*, pp. 260–63.
37. Marshall to Story, 26 September 1823, Story Papers, MHS.
38. Story to Peters, 14 November 1831, Peters Papers.
39. Mason to Story, 8 January 1822, Mason, *Memoir*, pp. 260–63.
40. Story to Mason, 10 January 1822, *LL*, 1:411–12.
41. 10 Wheaton 428.
42. 9 Wheaton 738 (1824).
43. Warren tells the story in *Supreme Court*, 1:635.
44. "Note," 37 *American Law Review* (November–December 1903): 916.
45. See, for example, his statement to Hopkinson, 9 February 1835, Hopkinson Papers.
46. Story to Hopkinson, 3 January 1835, ibid.
47. Story to Hopkinson, 12 December 1833, ibid.
48. Story to Hopkinson, 22 December 1834, ibid.
49. Story to Hopkinson, 12 December 1833, ibid.
50. 5 *U.S. Statutes at Large* 726 (1845); "From Judicial Grant to Legislative Power: The Admiralty Clause in the Nineteenth Century," 67 *Harvard Law Review* (May 1954): 1214–37, especially 1222.
51. *Propeller Genesee Chief* v. *Fitzhugh*, 12 Howard 443 (1851).
52. See Warren, *Supreme Court*, 1:608–9, citing remarks from New York newspapers concerning Story's possible role in writing the opinion.
53. 11 Peters 102; 16 Peters 539.
54. For the issues in Kentucky at the state and lower federal court level see Sandra F. Van Burkleo, "Securing the Commonwealth: Law, Politics, and Finance in Kentucky, 1817–1832" (paper presented at the American Historical Association Meeting, Washington, D.C., 30 December 1980).
55. Story, "Progress of Jurisprudence," in *MW*, pp. 218–22.
56. Story to Todd, 14 March 1823, *LL*, 1:422–23. Todd missed the 1823 term on account of illness.
57. 12 Wheaton 282.
58. 4 Peters 410.
59. Marshall to Story, 15 October 1830, Story Papers, MHS.
60. 5 Peters 457.
61. Story's "usual practise," as noted in *Inglis* v. *Trustees of Sailor's Snug Harbor*, 3 Peters 145 (1830), was to submit "in silence to the decisions of my brethren, when I dissent from them."
62. See Story to John Hooker Ashmun, 30 January 1831, *LL*, 2:47–48; and Story to Stephen White, 25 February 1831, *LL*, 2:50.
63. Joseph Story, "Literature of Maritime Law," reprinted in *MW*, pp. 93–121.
64. Again, see his "Natural Law," in Lieber, *Encyclopaedia Americana*.
65. A fine general account of the struggles of the Cherokees is found in Dale Van Every, *Disinherited: The Lost Birthright of the American Indian* (New York, 1966). On the Cherokee litigation before the Supreme Court I have found Joseph C. Burke, "The Cherokee Cases: A Study in Law, Politics, and Morality," 21 *Stanford Law Review* (February 1969): 500–531, most useful.
66. Story to Sarah Story, 26 February 1832, *LL*, 2:84–85.
67. 8 Wheaton 543.
68. Story describes the case in a letter to his wife, 28 January 1831, *LL*, 2:43–45.
69. 5 Peters 1.
70. Georgia's reaction is recounted in Warren, *Supreme Court*, 1:732.
71. 5 Peters 17–19.
72. Story to Sarah Story, 10 February 1822, *LL*, 1:412–13.

73. Story to William Story, 10 February 1829, Story Papers, MHS.

74. *MW*, p. 462.

75. Story to Hopkinson, 10 February 1831, Hopkinson Papers.

76. Story, judging from his notes on the arguments, was particularly impressed with Wirt's contention that the case was not political only, but involved basic rights on which the Court was obliged to act (Story, "Memorandums of Arguments in the Supreme Court of the United States Beginning with the January Term, 1831, and Ending with the January Term, 1832," MS, Harvard Law School).

77. Story to Hopkinson, 10 February 1831, Hopkinson Papers.

78. Story to Peters, 24 June 1831, Peters Papers.

79. Marshall to Story, 29 October 1828, Marshall Papers, LC.

80. 5 Peters 15, 20.

81. Story to Peters, 17 May 1831, Peters Papers.

82. Story to Hopkinson, 12 March 1832, Hopkinson Papers.

83. *Worcester v. Georgia*, 6 Peters 541 (1832).

84. Ibid., 559, 561.

85. Story to Sarah Story, 4 March 1832, *LL*, 2:86–87.

86. Story to Ticknor, 8 March 1832, *LL*, 2:83–84.

87. See Warren, *Supreme Court*, 1:758–69.

88. Story to Hopkinson, 22 January 1831, Hopkinson Papers.

89. Story to Hopkinson, 12 March 1832, ibid.

90. Story to Peters, 24 April 1833, Peters Papers.

91. Story to W. W. Story, 21 February 1836, *LL*, 2:229.

92. Story to Peters, 24 April 1833, Peters Papers.

93. Charles Warren cautions against a simplistic judgment of Jackson in this regard, and so does Richard P. Longaker, "Andrew Jackson and the Judiciary," 71 *Political Science Quarterly* (September 1956): 341–64.

94. Story to Peters, 17 May 1831, Peters Papers.

95. Ibid.

96. Story to Peters, 18 August 1834, Peters Papers.

97. Story to Sarah Story, 16 January 1829, Story Papers, UT.

98. Wirt to Elizabeth Wirt, 1 February 1830. "The Chief Justice was badly shaved this morning," Wirt wrote, "and came into the court with a quantity of egg on his underlip & chin . . ." (William Wirt Papers, Box 16, Maryland Historical Society, Baltimore).

99. Story to Peters, 24 July 1835, Peters Papers.

100. Story to Simon Greenleaf, 9 February 1836, *LL*, 2:228; Story to Sarah Story, 27 January 1833, *LL*, 2:117–19; Story to Richard Peters, 24 July 1835, *LL*, 2:200–202; Story to John McLean, 12 October 1835, *LL*, 2:208–9.

101. Story to Fay, 8 March 1826, *LL*, 1:492–93.

102. Story to Sumner, 25 January 1837, *LL*, 2:265–67; Story to Greenleaf, 11 February 1837, *LL*, 2:267–68.

103. Taney's rather shady involvement in Maryland state banking is treated by David Grimsted in his essay "Robbing the Poor to Aid the Rich: The Bank of Maryland Swindle, 1833–1838" (unpublished paper).

104. Story to Peters, 25 October 1831, Peters Papers. For reference in the Camden, N.J., *Journal* to Story as a vice-presidential possibility in 1832 see draft essay by John McLean, in McLean Papers, vol. 4, no. 843–44.

105. Story to Mason, 10 January 1822, *LL*, 1:411–12.

106. Peters to Story, 13 December 1836, Joseph Story Papers, Essex Institute, Salem, Mass.

107. 11 Peters 257 (1837).

108. Ibid., 102.

109. Ibid., 420.

110. Ibid., 317.

111. Ibid., 350.

112. An extended discussion of the Court's decision in *Miln* is found in Carl B. Swisher, *The Taney Period, 1836–64*, vol. 5 of the *Holmes Devise History of the Supreme Court of the United States* (New York, 1974), pp. 360–65.

113. 11 Peters 157.

114. See bk. 3, chap. 15, especially secs. 1067–72.

115. 11 Peters 157.

116. Ibid., 420. Three general accounts of the *Bridge* case have been especially useful to me: Kutler, *Privilege and Creative Destruction*; Swisher, *Taney Period*, chap. 4; and Charles Warren, *History of the Harvard Law School and of Early Legal Conditions in America*, 3 vols. (New York, 1908), 1:chap. 24. I have drawn substantially on my own article, "Justice Joseph Story, the Charles River Bridge Case and the Crisis of Republicanism," 17 *American Journal of Legal History* (July 1973): 232–45.

117. 11 Peters 533.

118. Webster to Jeremiah Mason, 3 February 1837, from a copy sent by William Mitchell to Chief Justice Harlan F. Stone, filed with Stone to William Mitchell, 9 January 1945, as cited in Swisher, *Taney Period*, p. 17; Sumner to Story, 25 March 1837, Story Papers, MHS.

119. 11 Peters 544–53.

120. Story to Ashmun, 24 February 1831, Story Papers, MHS.

121. Story to Peters, 21 December 1831, Peters Papers.

122. 11 Peters 584.

123. See C. Lee Mangus, "Note: Justice Story's Doctrine of Judicial Supremacy and the Uncertain Search for a Neutral Principle in *The Charles River Bridge Case*," 53 *Indiana Law Journal*, no. 2 (1977–78): 346–48 n. 38.

124. 11 Peters 588.

125. Ibid., 608–9.

126. As quoted in Swisher, *Taney Period*, p. 90.

127. See Hartz, *Economic Policy and Democratic Thought*, p. 245.

128. Story to Peters, 12 May 1837, Peters Papers.

129. Kent to Story, 23 June 1837, *LL*, 2:270–71.

130. Sumner to Story, 25 March 1837, Story Papers, MHS.

131. The Handlins summarize the contrasting reactions to the *Bridge* decision in *Commonwealth*, pp. 212–17. The Court's treatment of corporate contract cases, in light of the decision, is lucidly discussed in Kutler, *Privilege and Creative Destruction*, especially chap. 10.

132. Sumner to Story, 25 March 1837, Story Papers, MHS.

133. Hopkinson to Story, 1 August 1833, Story Papers, UT. Reference to Peters's differences with Story on the "late Constitutional Decisions" is made in Story to Hopkinson, 3 March 1837, Hopkinson Papers.

134. Kutler, *Privilege and Creative Destruction*, pp. 172–79.

135. Story, "Memorandums of Arguments," p. 161.

136. My argument here and in what follows is taken in considerable part from my "Story, the Charles River Bridge Case and the Crisis of Republicanism."

137. Warren, *Law School*, 1:541–43.

138. Kent to Story, 23 June 1837, *LL*, 2:270–71.

139. 11 Peters 602.

140. Kent to Story, 23 June 1837, *LL*, 2:270–71.

141. Story, "Memorandums of Arguments," p. 151.
142. Webster to Mason, 3 February 1837, as cited in Swisher, *Taney Period*, p. 17.

Chapter Seven

1. Henry Moore to Sumner, 7 January 1833, quoted in Warren, *Law School*, 1:458. The "children in the law" quotation used as epigraph is also from Warren, 1:501. The toast given as the second epigraph is from the quinquennial folder of Justice Lemuel Shaw, Harvard University Archives.
2. Story to George Hillard, 7 March 1832, Story Papers, MHS.
3. Story to Kent, 10 June 1845, *LL*, 2:538–39.
4. Story to Dr. A. L. Peirson, 3 April 1823, Story Letters, Essex Institute, Salem, Mass.; Joseph Lancaster to Story, 29 September 1819, Story Papers, MHS; Story to W. C. Rives, 14 January 1845, W. C. Rives Papers, "J. Story" folder, LC. This last letter contains a broad statement of Story's approach to public education measures.
5. Story, "Characteristics of the Age," "History and Influence of the Puritans," "Developments of Science and Mechanical Art," and "Science of Government," all in *MW*, pp. 344–45, 455, 490, 634.
6. Story to Charles Sumner, 10 February 1836, as quoted in Warren, *Law School*, 1:501.
7. Richard Henry Dana, Jr., reports the speech (*The Journal of Richard Henry Dana, Jr.*, ed. Robert F. Lucid, 3 vols. [Cambridge, Mass., 1968], 2:439).
8. This was Story's characterization of his old friend, as reported by Rutherford Hayes in Charles R. Williams, *The Life of Rutherford Birchard Hayes, Nineteenth President of the United States*, 2 vols. (Boston, 1914), 1:36, entry of 27 November 1843.
9. Dane to Story, 6 September 1828, as quoted in Arthur E. Sutherland, *The Law at Harvard: A History of Ideas and Men, 1817–1967* (Cambridge, Mass., 1967), p. 92.
10. Story to ?, 19 May 1829, Story Papers, in Harvard College Papers, 2d ser., 1828–29, 3:239, Harvard University Archives. William Story's account of his father's acceptance is found in *LL*, 2:2–3.
11. William S. Holdsworth makes the point in *A History of English Law*, 16 vols. (London, 1922–66), 12:90.
12. 13 *American Jurist* (January 1835) notes on p. 108 in this regard: "It may not be known to all our readers at a distance, that this Institution is a branch of the University, at Cambridge."
13. Story to Quincy, 14 January 1829, Story Papers, New York Historical Society, contains Story's eloquent testimony to Quincy's statesmanship. Something of the continued working relationship of the two men can be glimpsed by the Story-Quincy letters in the Harvard College Papers. See especially the letter, in Story's handwriting, from Story, Samuel Straw, Charles G. Loring, James Walker, John A. Lowell, and Samuel A. Eliot to Josiah Quincy, 29 March 1845, on the latter's retirement (Harvard College Papers, 2d ser., 1843–45, 12:263–64). Quincy's career is treated in Robert A. McCaughey's superb *Josiah Quincy, 1772–1864: The Last Federalist* (Cambridge, Mass., 1974).
14. See Quincy's letter to W. W. Story, 20 August 1851, *LL*, 2:564. Quincy's enthusiastic support of the Law School, as well as his understanding of the problems facing American legal education, can be seen in his "Address on the Occasion of the Dedication of Dane Law College," 9 *American Jurist* (January 1833): 48–66. The cooperation of Dane, Story, and Quincy in the founding is treated in Sutherland, *Law at Harvard*, chap. 4; and Warren, *Law School*, 1:413–24.
15. Story, "Value and Importance of Legal Studies," in *MW*, pp. 516, 522.

16. Ibid., p. 533.

17. Ibid., p. 506.

18. Ibid., pp. 505–6.

19. On the relation of law, social philosophy, and morals see Pocock, "Burke and the Ancient Constitution: A Problem in the History of Ideas," chap. 6 in his *Politics, Language and Time*; Hale is discussed on pp. 216–24. On Blackstone in this regard see Boorstin, *Mysterious Science*.

20. Story, "Value and Importance of Legal Studies," pp. 517, 519.

21. Ibid., p. 508.

22. Oliver Wendell Holmes, *Collected Legal Papers* (New York, 1920), p. 42.

23. A. V. Dicey, "The Teaching of English Law at Harvard," 13 *Harvard Law Review* (January 1900): 422–40. The common law, argued Dicey, echoing Story, kept the teachers at the Law School "from the unreality and vagueness which are apt to infect speculative jurists . . ." (p. 429).

24. Story, "Value and Importance of Legal Studies," pp. 508–9, 504–6.

25. These essays are reprinted in *MW*, pp. 262–94, 198–241.

26. Story, "Value and Importance of Legal Studies," p. 526.

27. Ibid.

28. 9 *American Jurist* (January 1833): 52–58.

29. Story, "Progress of Jurisprudence," in *MW*, pp. 203–5.

30. Ibid., p. 207.

31. Story to Asa Aldis, 15 February 1832, Story Papers, Yale University Library.

32. The first course in the "history of early English common law, known as 'Points in Legal History,' was given by Professor James Barr Ames" in 1886 (1 *Harvard Law Review* [October 1887]: 145). As far as I can determine, this was the first formal course in legal history offered at Harvard Law School.

33. See Story, "Value and Importance of Legal Studies," pp. 511–23, for the more explicitly conservative portion of the address, and for the quotations, pp. 511, 512, 513, and 519.

34. This general theme is developed by Wood, *Creation of the American Republic*; and by Robert E. Shalhope, "Toward a Republican Synthesis: The Emergence of an Understanding of Republicanism in American Historiography," 29 *William and Mary Quarterly* (January 1972): 49–80.

35. Simon Yandes to Calvin Fletcher, 15 September 1838, *The Diary of Calvin Fletcher, Including Letters to and from Calvin Fletcher*, ed. Gayle Thornbrough and Dorothy L. Riker, 8 vols. to date (Indianapolis, 1972–), 2:37.

36. President Quincy spoke to this point, too, in his dedication speech (9 *American Jurist* [January 1833]: 62–63).

37. Story, "Value and Importance of Legal Studies," pp. 520–21.

38. Story to Hopkinson, 7 November 1829, Hopkinson Papers.

39. Joseph Story, "Eulogy on Professor Ashmun . . . ," 4 April 1833, in *MW*, p. 611.

40. See report on the Law School ordered by the overseers, drawn up by Charles Sumner, and presented in February 1849, in *LL*, 2:532; and Story to Quincy, 3 November 1829, Harvard College Papers.

41. Charles Sumner, as quoted in Warren, *Law School*, 1:488.

42. Ibid., 2:13, 34.

43. 8 *American Jurist* (October 1832): 489.

44. "The Law Institution of Harvard University," 4 *American Jurist* (July 1830): 218. Students were accommodated with rooms in college buildings and boarded in the commons at $1.75 per week.

45. Requirements in 1830 are described in ibid. Amended residence is mentioned in Sutherland, *Law at Harvard*, p. 104.

46. The transformation of Harvard University during this period is treated in R. Story, *Forging of an Aristocracy*; as well as in "The Augustan Age, 1806–1845," in Morison, *Three Centuries of Harvard*.

47. These figures and those following are based on biographical information on Harvard Law School graduates published in Warren, *Law School*, vol. 3. This information, it should be emphasized, is uneven and incomplete and yields only approximate generalizations.

48. Sutherland, *Law at Harvard*, p. 101.

49. Warren, *Law School*, 1:476.

50. Story to Ashmun, 11 January 1831, ibid., p. 469. "I would lay out as little money as possible in *mere bricks & mortar*," he advised W. C. Rives concerning the Smithsonian Institution (14 January 1845, Rives Papers).

51. For Story's efforts regarding the law collection at the Library of Congress see Joel R. Poinsett to Story, 24 May 1824, Story Papers, LC; and Marshall to Story, 2 August 1832, Story Papers, MHS.

52. Story to Quincy, 3 November 1829, Harvard College Papers.

53. Ibid.

54. Warren, *Law School*, 2:80.

55. Story to McLean, 9 February 1843, *LL*, 2:432.

56. Edward Wigglesworth to Story, 27 November 1832, Story Papers, MHS; Story to George Joseph Bell, 8 June 1839, Story Letters, Free Library, Philadelphia.

57. Story to Saltonstall, 7 October 1844, Story Papers, UT; Story to Hopkinson, 9 February 1835, Hopkinson Papers, HSPa.

58. See Story and Greenleaf's letter (in Story's hand), 8 May 1834, Harvard College Papers.

59. Warren, *Law School*, 2:81.

60. These exuberant claims were politely refuted in "A Catalogue of the Law Library of Harvard . . . ," 26 *American Jurist* (October 1841): 254–61. Greenleaf's claim to international greatness is found in Warren, *Law School*, 2:83.

61. Story to Quincy, 3 November 1829, Harvard College Papers.

62. James B. Thayer, "The Teaching of English Law at Universities," 9 *Harvard Law Review* (October 1895): 173.

63. Quoted in Warren, *Law School*, 2:38.

64. Story to Hopkinson, 15 August 1829, Hopkinson Papers.

65. The report of the special committee appointed by the overseers concluded that "Story must be regarded as the largest pecuniary benefactor of the Law School, and one of the largest pecuniary benefactors of the University" (quoted in *LL*, 2:534). See *LL*, 2:530–34.

66. William Mathews, "Recollections of Judge Story," 4 *Lakeside* (December 1870): 379–80.

67. Story to Ashmun, 1 March 1832, *LL*, 2:91–92.

68. Story, *Commentaries on Equity Jurisprudence*, 2:59–62. G. Edward White discusses Story's use of legal history in *Patterns of American Legal Thought* (Indianapolis, 1978), pp. 64–68.

69. Story, "Value and Importance of Legal Studies," pp. 508, 510.

70. "Law Institution of Harvard University," pp. 219–20, lists the required reading.

71. Sumner describes the practice in *Memoir*, 1:94.

72. The Law School made much of its advantages over straight law-office education. See, for example, Quincy's address on the dedication of Dane Law School, 9 *American Jurist* (January 1833): 60–64 especially.

73. Story, "Value and Importance of Legal Studies," p. 547.

74. Sumner, *Memoir*, 1:113.

75. Williams, *Life of Hayes*, 1:146.

76. Story's approach is spelled out in the preface to his *Commentaries on the Law of Bailments, with Illustrations from the Civil and Foreign Law* (Cambridge, Mass., 1832), 4th ed. (Boston, 1846), xiii; all references are to this 4th ed.

77. Fletcher, *Diary*, 2:37.

78. Sumner describes the system in his letter to Jonathan F. Stearns, 25 September 1831, Sumner, *Memoir*, 1:109.

79. He wrote to Ticknor on 10 March 1830 that he was "impatient for leisure to prepare some written lectures, for there is a terrible deficiency in good elementary books" (quoted in Warren, *Law School*, 1:444).

80. The impact of one such uplifting speech can be seen in Williams, *Life of Hayes*, 1:136–37, entry of 4 January 1844.

81. Mathews, "Recollections of Judge Story," p. 380.

82. William Story, who was a student at the Law School, describes his father's teaching technique in *LL*, 2:36.

83. Ibid.; Sumner, *Memoir*, 1:112.

84. *LL*, 2:37.

85. Williams, *Life of Hayes*, 1:153–54.

86. Ibid., pp. 131, 158–59.

87. For example, see the chapter entitled "Common Carrier" in his *Commentaries on Bailments*.

88. Story, "Progress of Jurisprudence," p. 207.

89. "Whether Law Is a Science?" 9 *American Jurist* (April 1833): 349–50 especially.

90. Story, "Progress of Jurisprudence," p. 207.

91. Story to Quincy, 3 November 1829, Harvard College Papers.

92. "Law Institution of Harvard University," pp. 219–20.

93. Richard H. Dana, Jr., describes Greenleaf's "new system of giving us cases" in his letter to his father, R. H. Dana, Sr., 27 November 1838, Richard H. Dana, Jr., Papers, MHS. Story's method of putting cases is discussed in *LL*, 2:36.

94. Warren, *Law School*, 2:chap. 27, contains a thorough account of mooting during Story's time. Also see *LL*, 2:52.

95. Williams, *Life of Hayes*, 1:117.

96. As recalled by Alexander Lawton and quoted in Warren, *Law School*, 2:70.

97. *LL*, 2:53.

98. "Sketches of the Law School at Cambridge," 13 *American Jurist* (January 1835): 114–15.

99. A brief biographical account of Greenleaf as well as a list of his principal publications is found in Harvard Law School Association, *The Centennial History of the Harvard Law School, 1817–1917* ([Cambridge, Mass.], 1918), pp. 215–19, 304–5.

100. A complete collection of Story's letters to Greenleaf (sixty-five in number, beginning in 1819 and two draft letters of Greenleaf to Story) was preserved by Greenleaf and is now on deposit in the Treasure Room, Harvard Law School Library (hereafter cited as Story Letters, HLS). I have profited much by my discussion of these letters with Professor Fred Konefsky of the faculty of law and jurisprudence, State University of New York at Buffalo.

101. For Story's high opinion of "Greenleaf's *Reports*" (as Story urged him to call them) see Story to Greenleaf, 7 July 1821, 25 May 1822, Story Letters, HLS. Story's encouragement of Greenleaf's scholarship can be seen in several letters, including Story to Greenleaf, 5 September, 11 November 1819, 9 June 1820, 6 January, 2 June 1821, ibid.

102. Story to Greenleaf, 10 October 1826, ibid.

103. Ibid.

104. Story to Greenleaf, 18 April 1833, Story Letters, HLS.

105. Greenleaf to Story, 27 April 1833, ibid.

106. Story to Greenleaf, 10 February 1842, ibid.

107. See Story to Greenleaf, 20 January 1838, ibid., for Story's solicitude about Greenleaf. The corporation, he told Greenleaf, ought "to remember the proverb of not riding a free horse to death."

108. Harvard Law School Association, *Centennial History*, pp. 217–18.

109. See Story to Greenleaf, 23 January 1837, a note of congratulation sent Greenleaf at the bar of the Supreme Court of the United States upon the completion of his argument in the *Bridge* case (Story Letters, HLS).

110. Story to Greenleaf, 20 January 1838, ibid.

111. Simon Greenleaf, *A Treatise on the Law of Evidence*, vol. 1 (Boston, 1842).

112. Story to Greenleaf, 6 January 1842, Story Letters, HLS.

113. Greenleaf to Story, 27 April 1833, ibid.; Greenleaf, *A Discourse Commemorative of the Life and Character of Joseph Story, 18th of September 1845* (Boston, 1845).

114. Theophilus Parsons in his eulogy on Greenleaf, "Address to the Students of Harvard Law School," 20 October 1853, as quoted in Warren, *Law School*, 1:483.

115. Mathews, "Recollections of Judge Story," p. 380.

116. Williams, *Life of Hayes*, 1:113.

117. Henry C. Dorr to Thomas Wilson Dorr, 28 May 1841, Thomas W. Dorr Collection, John Hay Library, Brown University, Providence, R.I. My thanks to Professor David Grimsted for bringing this letter to my attention.

118. Parsons, "Address to the Students," as quoted in Warren, *Law School*, 1:483.

119. Richard H. Dana, Jr., to W. W. Story, 3 May 1851, *LL*, 2:317–22.

120. Tocqueville, *Democracy in America*, ed. J. P. Mayer, trans. George Lawrence (New York, 1969), pp. 268, 264–65, 268–70. Regarding the legal profession, I have preferred Lawrence's translation to Reeve's, which is cited elsewhere.

121. See George W. Pierson, *Tocqueville in America*, abridged by D. C. Lunt (Garden City, N.Y., 1959), pp. 439–40, 442.

122. Bloomfield puts the early nineteenth-century democratization of the legal profession in historical perspective in *American Lawyers*, especially in chap. 5. Also see Gawalt, *Promise of Power*.

123. Joseph Story, *A Discourse on the Past History, Present State, and Future Prospects of the Law* (Edinburgh, 1835). This important essay was not reprinted in *MW* but can be found in McClellan, *Story*, pp. 325–49; see p. 340. Kermit Hall discusses the "localism" that "dominated the lower court appointment process in the ante-bellum era" in his "Social Backgrounds and Judicial Recruitment," 29 *Western Political Quarterly* (June 1976): 243–57.

124. 11 *American Jurist* (April 1834): 370.

125. Judge Thacher's "Address to the Suffolk Bar" is quoted in 5 *American Jurist* (April 1831): 398.

126. Quoted in Warren, *Law School*, 2:37.

127. These calculations and those following are based on the class lists printed in Warren, *Law School*, vol. 3. Although this information will yield rough conclusions about the demography of Harvard law students it is incomplete and inexact in many respects. In dealing with career patterns of Harvard Law School graduates, I have supplemented my own calculations based on Warren's list by reference to Harvard Law School Association, *Centennial History*, especially app. 7, which contains career information on Law School alumni by class.

128. Only a handful are clearly identifiable as rural, whereas a sizable number settled in urban areas; Boston, which attracted most, was followed by New York City, Chicago, and Philadelphia.

129. Story to Aldis, 15 February 1832, Story Papers, Yale University Library.

130. Story to Kent, 4 April 1831, Story Papers, MHS; Timothy Walker to Story, 10 April 1831, Story Papers, Essex Institute, Salem, Mass.: Story to Salmon P. Chase, 1 March 1834, Salmon P. Chase Papers, Historical Society of Pennsylvania.

131. Dana, *Journal*, 2:662.

132. Sumner's family life, as well as his relationship with Story and Harvard Law School, is treated in David H. Donald's *Charles Sumner and the Coming of the Civil War* (New York, 1961).

133. Dana, *Journal*, 1:321.

134. Story to David Hoffman, 9 January 1841, Appointment Files for State Department, National Archives. My thanks to Professor Maxwell Bloomfield for calling my attention to this letter.

135. Story to Aldis, 15 February 1832, Story Papers, Yale University Library.

136. Dana to W. W. Story, 3 May 1851, *LL*, 2:317–22. Indeed, students loved Story "as a father," as one of them, J. G. Marion, wrote to Sarah Story, 19 October 1845, Story Papers, UT.

137. Story, "Eulogy on Professor Ashmun," p. 606.

138. Story to Aldis, 15 February 1832, Story Letters, Yale University Library.

139. Williams, *Life of Hayes*, 1:37.

140. This subject is developed in Robert Stevens, *Law School: Legal Education in America from the 1850s to the 1980s*, Studies in Legal History (Chapel Hill, N.C., 1983). Unfortunately, this book did not appear in time for me to consult it.

Chapter Eight

1. Nathan Dane, Introduction to *A General Abridgment and Digest of American Law* . . . , 9 vols. (Boston, 1823–29), 1:xv. For Story's review of Dane's *Abridgment* see "Digests of the Common Law," in *MW*, pp. 379–407.

2. 12 Sergeant & Rawle 346.

3. For insightful discussions of conservatism in antebellum reform see Clifford S. Griffin, *Their Brothers' Keepers: Moral Stewardship in the United States, 1800–1865* (New Brunswick, N.J., 1960); Joseph R. Gusfield, *Symbolic Crusade: Status Politics and the American Temperance Movement* (Urbana, Ill., 1963); and Michael B. Katz, *The Irony of Early School Reform: Educational Innovation in Mid-Nineteenth Century Massachusetts* (Cambridge, Mass., 1968). The conservative face of American liberal ideology is explored in Louis Hartz, *The Liberal Tradition in America: An Interpretation of American Political Thought since the Revolution* (New York, 1955).

4. See, for example, his speeches "Developments of Science and Mechanical Art," "Influence of Scientific Studies," and "Literary Tendencies of the Times," all in *MW*, pp. 475–502, 740–78.

5. See his "Discourse on the Past History, Present State, and Future Prospects of the Law," in McClellan, *Story*, app. 2, pp. 325–49.

6. Jeremy Bentham to Madison, October 1811, *The Works of Jeremy Bentham*, compiled by John Bowring, 11 vols. (1838–43; reprint, New York, 1962), 4:453, 457, 459, 476–77. For Bentham's role in American codification and for the American movement in general I have found Charles M. Cook, *The American Codification Movement: A Study of Antebellum Legal Reform* (Westport, Conn., 1981), most useful.

7. Story, "Discourse on the Past History . . . of the Law," p. 334.

8. Timothy Walker, "Codification . . . ," 1 *Western Law Journal* (July 1844): 435.

9. Story, "Progress of Jurisprudence," in *MW*, p. 237.

10. Joseph Story, "A Course of Legal Study," reprinted in *MW*, pp. 70–71.

11. *The Charters and General Laws of the Colony and Province of Massachusetts Bay . . . Published by Order of the General Court* (Boston, 1814). Dane, Prescott, and Story were appointed a committee to supervise the work.

12. Story, "Progress of Jurisprudence," p. 237.

13. Cook, *American Codification*, p. 106.

14. Story, "Progress of Jurisprudence," pp. 238, 237.

15. Story, "Course of Legal Study," p. 71.

16. Story to Wheaton, 1 October 1825, Wheaton Papers. The Story-Wheaton exchange on codification is discussed by McClellan, *Story*, pp. 92–93.

17. Also note Story's advice to Thomas Grimké of South Carolina in a letter of 7 August 1827, as quoted in McClellan, *Story*, p. 94 n. 105.

18. Story's article was inserted at the last minute in response to "the interest now felt in law and legal reforms" and appeared as a coda to a translation from *Conversation-Lexikon* that dealt with legal philosophy and codification in Germany and France. Story's part of the piece is pp. 581–92 in vol. 7. For the circulation of Lieber's work, see McClellan, *Story*, p. 66 n. 22.

19. Story, "Law, Legislation and Codes," p. 588.

20. Ibid., pp. 588, 581, 591.

21. Ibid., pp. 591, 590.

22. Ibid.

23. Ibid., pp. 586, 583–85.

24. Ibid., p. 591.

25. C. E. Forbes to Story, 22 May 1836, Story Papers, MHS.

26. See Cook, *American Codification*, pp. 170–81, on the codification movement in Massachusetts.

27. Story to Everett, 17 March 1836, Story Papers, MHS.

28. Story to James J. Wilkinson, 26 December 1836, ibid.

29. For Webster's position see "Wheaton's Reports," reprinted from the *North American Review* in Cook, *American Codification*, p. 103; on Hopkinson see ibid., pp. 37–42.

30. Story to James J. Wilkinson, 26 December 1836, Story Papers, MHS.

31. Story to Ticknor, 16 December 1836, Story Papers, UT.

32. Everett to Story, 5 December 1836, Edward Everett Letterbook, Everett Papers, MHS.

33. Walker, "Codification," p. 436.

34. Story to Everett, 17 March 1836, Story Papers, MHS.

35. Ibid.

36. Parsons to Everett, 17 March 1836, Story Papers, MHS; Sumner is mentioned in Story's letter of 17 March 1836 to Everett, ibid.

37. Story to Everett, 17 March 1836, ibid.

38. Parsons to Everett, 17 March 1836, ibid.

39. Story to Everett, 22 March 1836, ibid.

40. Story to Everett, 4 April 1836, ibid.

41. C. E. Forbes to Story, 22 May 1836, ibid.

42. Story to Everett, 6, 24 December 1836, ibid.

43. Joseph Story, "Codification of the Common Law," in *MW*, pp. 715–16.

44. Story to Wilkinson, 26 December 1836, Story Papers, MHS.

45. Story, "Codification," pp. 730–31.

46. Ibid., pp. 718, 733.

47. Cook, *American Codification*, p. 181.

48. Ibid., p. 176.

49. Roscoe Pound, "The Place of Judge Story in the Making of American Law," 48 *American Law Review* (September 1914): 692.

50. Dane's letter describing the terms was laid before the board of the corporation by Story on 2 June 1829; it is quoted in Warren, *Law School*, 1:418–21.

51. *MW*, p. 533.

52. Story to Bushrod Washington, 13 August 1829, Story Papers, MHS.

53. The history of legal publishing in America has yet to be written. The revolution in American publishing is treated in Charles A. Madison, *Book Publishing in America* (New York, 1966); and Hellmut Lehmann-Haupt, *The Book in America: A History of the Making, the Selling, and the Collecting of Books in the United States* (New York, 1939). Suggestive discussions of the relationship between writers of literature and publishers in the early national period can be found in William Charvat, *Literary Publishing in America, 1790–1850* (Philadelphia, 1959); and Matthew J. Bruccoli, *The Profession of Authorship in America, 1800–1870: The Papers of William Charvat* ([Columbus, Ohio], 1968).

54. The changing relationship of author and publisher is discussed in Charvat, *Literary Publishing*, chap. 2.

55. See the suggestive letter of Little, Brown to Josiah Quincy, 24 September 1842, Harvard College Papers, 2d ser. (1842–43), 11:185–86.

56. Authors like Cooper whose works were in demand could command profits of 40 percent or more (Charvat, *Literary Publishing*, p. 54). Little, Brown business records are not extant for this early period. Something of the cooperative partnership between the company and Story can be inferred from C. C. Little and Co. to Story, 5 August 1839, Story Papers, MHS. Also see Story to Hillard, Gray and Co., 27 January 1833, Story Letters, Free Library, Philadelphia.

57. R. W. B. Lewis, *The American Adam: Innocence, Tragedy, and Tradition in the Nineteenth Century* (Chicago, 1955).

58. Dane to Story, 15 April 1834, Story Papers, UT.

59. Story, "Course of Legal Study," p. 76.

60. Holdsworth, *A History of English Law*, 12:720. Also see Story to J. G. Palfrey, 22 October 1842, Palfrey Papers.

61. William Kent to James Kent, 10 March 1847, Kent Papers.

62. Story, "Course of Legal Study," pp. 74–80.

63. Story, *Commentaries on Bailments*, p. xiii.

64. MS in the Treasure Room, Harvard Law School.

65. For Story's praise of principle and his expressed desire "to build our commercial law, as much as possible, upon principles absolutely universal in their application," see Story to Lord Stowell, 22 September 1828, *LL*, 1:557–61.

66. Story, *Commentaries on Bailments*, p. xiii.

67. Ibid.

68. Ibid., pp. 571, 608–9, sec. 609.

69. Joseph Story, *Commentaries on the Law of Promissory Notes* . . . (Boston, 1845), 3d ed. (Boston, 1851), chap. 10; all references are to this 3d ed. See also, for example, his discussion of the liability of agents in *Commentaries on the Law of Agency* . . . (Boston, 1839), pp. 279–80, sec. 278.

70. See Story, *Commentaries on Bailments*, pp. 571–72, sec. 570.

71. Story, *Commentaries on Equity Jurisprudence*, 1:359–60, sec. 365.

72. Story, *Commentaries on Bailments*, pp. 626–27, sec. 625.

73. For a discussion of Story as the pioneer of comparative jurisprudence in America, see Kurt H. Nadelmann, "Joseph Story's Sketch of American Law" (with a Foreword by Felix Frankfurter), 3 *American Journal of Comparative Law* (Winter 1954): 1–26.

74. Reprinted in ibid., with a discussion of the background and publication of the article.

75. Ibid., pp. 22, 24–25.

76. See his dissent in *Southern Pacific Company* v. *Jensen*, 244 U.S. 222 (1916).

77. *MW*, pp. 293–94.

78. Joseph Story, *Commentaries on the Law of Bills of Exchange* . . . (Boston, 1843), 2d ed. (Boston, 1847), p. 319, sec. 272.

79. Mark DeWolfe Howe, *Justice Oliver Wendell Holmes*, 2 vols. (Cambridge, Mass., 1957–63), 1:179.

80. Edward G. Parker, *Reminiscences of Rufus Choate, the Great American Advocate* (New York, 1860), p. 249.

81. Joseph Redlich, *The Common Law and the Case Method in American University Law Schools* (New York, 1914), p. 30.

82. From Blackstone's poem "The Lawyer's Farewell to His Muse," as quoted in Holdsworth, *History of English Law*, 12:704.

83. For a discussion of the publication and significance of this article see Nadelmann, "Story's Sketch of American Law," pp. 3–8.

84. Goebel, *Antecedents*, p. 229. Goebel discusses the failure of the framers to incorporate the common law formally into the constitutional arrangement (pp. 229–30).

85. Story, *Commentaries on Bailments*, p. 1, sec. 1.

86. Story, *Commentaries on Agency*, pp. 1, 40, secs. 1, 37.

87. Joseph Story, *Commentaries on the Law of Partnership* . . . (Boston, 1841), 3d ed. (Boston, 1850), p. 1, sec. 1.

88. Ibid., p. vii.

89. Story, *Commentaries on Equity Jurisprudence*, 2:732, 733, sec. 1517.

90. Story, "Chancery Jurisdiction," reprinted in *MW*, pp. 148–79. Large portions of the 1808 report were included in this 1820 essay. The early report is reprinted with a brief introduction in Gerald T. Dunne, "Joseph Story's First Writing on Equity," 14 *American Journal of Legal History* (January 1970): 76–81.

91. Robert Rantoul, Jr., *Memoirs, Speeches and Writings of Robert Rantoul, Jr.*, ed. Luther Hamilton (Boston, 1854), p. 282.

92. Story, "Chancery Jurisdiction," p. 174.

93. Story, *Commentaries on Equity Jurisprudence*, 1:33 n. 3.

94. Story, "Chancery Jurisdiction," pp. 155–63.

95. Ibid., pp. 164–65.

96. Story devoted an entire chapter to injunctions, *Commentaries on Equity Jurisprudence*, 2:154–227.

97. Story sets forth the advantages of equity in "Chancery Jurisdiction."

98. A very illuminating discussion of Story's approach to equity is Gary L. McDowell, "Joseph Story's 'Science' of Equity," *Supreme Court Review*, 1979, pp. 153–72.

99. Story, "Value and Importance of Legal Studies," in *MW*, p. 540.

100. Ibid.

101. Roscoe Pound, "The Decadence of Equity," 5 *Columbia Law Review* (January 1905): 20–35, discusses the course of American equity.

102. William S. Holdsworth, "Blackstone's Treatment of Equity," 43 *Harvard Law Review* (November 1929): 8.

103. Story, "Chancery Jurisdiction," especially pp. 170–72.

104. Holdsworth, "Blackstone's Treatment of Equity," p. 24.

105. The trend is traced in Horwitz, "The Triumph of Contract," in his *Transformation of American Law*. Story's *Equity* is discussed briefly on p. 184.

106. Story, "Chancery Jurisdiction," p. 159.

107. Ibid., pp. 158–59.

108. Story, *Commentaries on Equity Jurisprudence*, 1:249–51, secs. 245–47.

109. Sir William Holdsworth's discussion of the historical relationship of law and equity provides a useful perspective for understanding Story's strategy. See his "Blackstone's Treatment of Equity."

110. Pound discusses the impact of Story on American equity in "Story in the Making of American Law," pp. 694–95.

111. Story frankly acknowledged his heavy reliance on Redesdale and "his close almost servile obedience to authority" (*Commentaries on Equity Pleadings* . . . [Boston, 1838], p. viii).

112. Robert H. Jackson, "Full Faith and Credit—the Lawyer's Clause of the Constitution," in Association of American Law Schools, *Selected Readings on Conflict of Laws* (Saint Paul, Minn., 1956), pp. 241–42 (first published in 45 *Columbia Law Review* [1945]). Also see Elliott E. Cheatham, "Federal Control of Conflict of Law," in AALS, *Selected Readings*, p. 259 (first published in 6 *Vanderbilt Law Review* [1953]); and Hessel E. Yntema, "The Enforcement of Foreign Judgments in Anglo-American Law," in AALS, *Selected Readings*, pp. 376–403 (first published in 33 *Michigan Law Review* [1935]).

113. Joseph Story, *Commentaries on the Conflict of Laws* . . . (Boston, 1834), 6th ed., ed. Isaac Redfield (Boston, 1865), p. 7, sec. 4; all references are to this 6th ed. Story's grim assessment of the problem was quoted in 11 *American Jurist* (June 1835): 371. On the need for conflict theory see Judge Alexander Porter to Kent, 1 December 1831, James Kent Papers, LC; and the review of Story's work in 17 *American Quarterly Review* (June 1835): 303–18.

114. *LL*, 2:142; Story to Peters, 24 April 1833, *LL*, 2:140–41.

115. Ernest G. Lorenzen, "Story's Commentaries on the Conflict of Laws—One Hundred Years After," 48 *Harvard Law Review* (November 1934): 18.

116. Story noted the paucity of English sources in his *Commentaries on Conflict*, p. 10. Also see Lorenzen, "Story's Commentaries on Conflict," pp. 18–19; and William R. Leslie, "The Influence of Joseph Story's Theory of Conflict of Laws on Constitutional Nationalism," 35 *Mississippi Valley Historical Review* (September 1948): 204, 206–8. I have benefited much from Professor Leslie's treatment of Story's conflict theory, particularly his discussion of the Porter-Livermore controversy as a source of Story's ideas. I do not entirely agree with his analysis of Story's preferences for comity as the basis of conflict. Nor do I concur in his argument concerning the impact of comity on slavery.

117. Leslie, "Story's Theory of Conflict," p. 207.

118. Lorenzen, "Story's Commentaries on Conflict," p. 27. Story apologizes for his lack of German and explains it to K. J. Anton Mittermaier in a letter of 14 June 1836, Mittermaier Collection, Universitätsbibliothek Heidelberg, Heidelberg, West Germany. My thanks to Maxwell Bloomfield of Catholic University for calling my attention to the Story letters at the University of Heidelberg.

119. Story, *Commentaries on Conflict*, p. 11 n. 1. Story's sources, including his preference for Huberus (or Huber), are discussed by Lorenzen and Leslie, among others.

120. *LL*, 2:142.

121. Story, *Commentaries on Conflict*, p. 10, sec. 11. Among the several discussions of general conflict theory, two have been especially helpful: Hessel E. Yntema, "The Historic Bases of Private International Law," in AALS, *Selected Readings*, pp. 30–47 (first published in *American Journal of Comparative Law* [1953]; and Elliott E. Cheatham, "American Theories of Conflict of Laws: Their Role and Utility," in AALS, *Selected Readings*, pp. 48–70 (first published in *Harvard Law Review* [1945]).

122. Story, *Commentaries on Conflict*, pp. 8, 32, secs. 7, 34, 35.

123. See advertisement to the 2d ed., reprinted in ibid., v, vi. The second, revised, corrected, and greatly enlarged edition of *Conflict* appeared in 1841.

124. Lorenzen, "Story's Commentaries on Conflict," p. 28. See K. J. A. Mittermaier to Story, 21 November 1835, praising Story's *Conflict*, *LL*, 2:213. Story's letter of thanks (14 June 1836) and seven other letters from Story are found in the Mittermaier Collection. M. Foelix, editor of *Revue Etrangère* (Paris) wrote Story on 17 October 1834 in praise of *Conflict*, *LL*, 2:169–70.

125. Sir John Patteson to Story, 26 April 1841; Lord Langdale to Story, 10 May 1841; John Gurney to Story, 10 June 1841; Sir John B. Bosanquet to Story, 1 May 1841; Lord Erskine to Story, 1 May 1841; Baron Parke to Story, 11 July 1841—all in Story Papers, UT.

126. As quoted in Roscoe Pound, "Story in the Making of American Law," p. 694.

127. Lorenzen, "Story's Commentaries on Conflict," p. 29.

128. See AALS, *Selected Readings*.

129. See Cheatham, "American Theories of Conflict," especially p. 69.

130. Leslie argues this point in "Story's Theory of Conflict."

131. Hopkinson to Story, 30 April 1834, Story Papers, UT.

132. Story, *Commentaries on Conflict*, p. 842, sec. 645.

133. Story to Wilkinson, 26 March 1834, Story Papers, MHS.

134. Lorenzen, "Story's Commentaries on Conflict," p. 29.

135. Cheatham, "American Theories of Conflict," p. 56.

136. William Kent to James Kent, 10 March 1847, Kent Papers.

137. Timothy Walker, *Introduction to American Law*, as quoted in Charles M. Haar, ed., *The Golden Age of American Law* (New York, 1965), p. 77.

138. As quoted in Myers, *Children of Pride*, pp. 45–46.

139. As quoted in Alpheus T. Mason, *Brandeis: A Free Man's Life* (New York, 1946), p. 35.

140. A convenient collection of opinions on Story's contributions is found in *LL*, 2:648–65.

141. Haroldo Valladão, "The Influence of Joseph Story on Latin-American Rules of Conflict of Laws," 3 *American Journal of Comparative Law* (Winter 1954): 27–41, especially 34–38.

142. For sample reviews of his *Commentaries on Conflict* see 11 *American Jurist* (April 1834): 365–408; and 17 *American Quarterly Review* (June 1835): 303–18.

143. Charles Sumner, "Tribute of Friendship: The Late Joseph Story," published in *Boston Daily Advertiser*, 16 September 1845, reprinted in Sumner, *Works*, 1:138 and in *LL*, 2:615.

144. Holmes, "The Use of Law Schools," in *Collected Legal Papers*, p. 41.

145. Charles C. Jones, Jr., to the Reverend and Mrs. C. C. Jones, 13 June 1854, Myers, *Children of Pride*, pp. 45–46.

146. Holmes, "The Use of Law Schools," p. 41.

147. Jabez Fox, "Law and Fact," 12 *Harvard Law Review* (March 1899): 545–52.

148. George T. M. Davis, *Autobiography of the Late Colonel George T. M. Davis . . .* (New York, 1891), p. 53.

149. See Thomas S. Kuhn, *The Structure of Scientific Revolutions*, 2d enlarged ed. (Chicago, 1970), especially pp. 175, 182–88; and Kuhn, "Second Thoughts on Paradigms," in his *Essential Tension: Selected Studies in Scientific Tradition and Change* (Chicago, 1977), pp. 296–319. For a lucid critique of Kuhn's paradigmatic mode of analysis see John C. Greene, "The Kuhnian Paradigm and the Darwin Revolution in Natural History," in *Perspectives in the History of Science and Technology*, ed. Duane H. D. Roller (Norman, Okla., 1971), pp. 3–25.

Chapter Nine

1. Story's letters to Prentiss Mellen are found in the Story Papers, Yale University Library.

2. Story, "Growth of Commercial Law," reprinted in *MW*, p. 279. The first headnote to this chapter comes from p. 287 of this essay.

3. Judicial biographies have not tended to focus much on this problem, but it is explored on a general level in Horwitz, "The Triumph of Contract" and especially in "The Relation between the Bar and Commercial Interests," in his *Transformation of American Law*. Max Lerner's "Supreme Court and American Capitalism," 42 *Yale Law Journal* (March 1933): 668–701, still stands as a good general introduction to the subject, and the previously mentioned studies by the Handlins on Massachusetts (*Commonwealth*) and Hartz on Pennsylvania (*Economic Policy and Democratic Thought*) are rich in information and insights.

4. See his anonymous essay "Courts of the U. States," in Lieber, *Encyclopaedia Americana*, 3:596.

5. Story to Hopkinson, 13 February 1837, Hopkinson Papers.

6. Story to William Williams, 12 January 1838, Story Papers, UT.

7. Story to Peters, 27 November 1842, Peters Papers. Also see Story to McLean, 16 August 1844, McLean Papers.

8. Story to Kent, 10 June 1845, *LL*, 2:538–39. On his plan to resign earlier see Story to Greenleaf, 4 January 1845, Story Letters, HLS.

9. As quoted by his son, *LL*, 2:523.

10. 16 Howard 619; 17 Howard 542; 18 Howard 539.

11. 1 Howard 311.

12. 13 Peters 519.

13. 2 Howard 497.

14. For Story's favorable critique see his letter to Kent, 31 August 1844, Story Papers, MHS.

15. Story explains the formative impact of Marshall on the Court in "Character and Services of Chief Justice Marshall," in *MW*, especially pp. 691–96. Story attempted to institutionalize the principles established by the early Marshall Court in his "Rules of Interpretation," chap. 5, bk. 3, of *Commentaries on the Constitution*, 1:304–49.

16. Something of Story's friendships on the Court is revealed by the fact that during the 1841 term he boarded in "a very comfortable house (Mr Turner's) on the Pennsylvania Avenue opposite the Market House" with "Judges Taney, McLean, Thompson (his wife is not here) & Barbour . . ." (Story to Sarah Story, 23 January 1841, Story Papers, UT). These arrangements altered unexpectedly the following year, and Story ended up rooming with McLean, though close by the three other justices (Story to Sarah Story, 10 January 1842, ibid).

17. McLean to Peters, 17 September 1845, Peters Papers.

18. Story to McLean, 9 October 1843, McLean Papers.

19. Story to Peters, 26 April 1840, Peters Papers.

20. Taney to Peters, 14 November 1845, ibid.

21. Webster to Franklin Haven, 28 December 1847, as quoted in Swisher, *Taney Period*, p. 387.

22. Story, "Sketch of the Character of Philip P. Barbour . . . ," in *MW*, especially p. 828.

23. Swisher, *Taney Period*, p. 55.

24. McLean to Story, 25 January 1843, Story Papers, MHS. The episode is discussed thoroughly in Swisher, *Taney Period*, pp. 300–306. Story's involvement can be traced to the Story-Peters correspondence in the Peters Papers.

25. Story to McLean, 9 February 1845, as quoted in Swisher, *Taney Period*, p. 305.

26. 19 *American Jurist* (April 1838): 9–10.

27. See again Formisano, "Deferential Participant Politics"; and Hofstadter, *Idea of a Party System*.

28. John Catron to James K. Polk, 23 July 1844, as quoted in Swisher, *Taney Period*, pp. 223–24.

29. See Swisher, *Taney Period*, especially pp. 55, 58–66, 68, 112–14, 223–24.

30. For an extended discussion of this point, see my "Story on Circuit," especially p. 113–15.

31. Story to Sumner, 15 March 1838, *LL*, 2:295–97.

32. Daniel's contributions on the Court, as well as his disabilities, are discussed fully in John P. Frank, *Justice Daniel Dissenting: A Biography of Peter V. Daniel, 1784–1860* (Cambridge, Mass., 1964).

33. G. Edward White gives us a superb analysis of Marshall's judging in chap. 1 of *The American Judicial Tradition: Profiles of Leading American Judges* (New York, 1976).

34. Catron to Jackson, 5 February 1838, as paraphrased in Swisher, *Taney Period*, p. 64.

35. Kent to Story, 23 June 1837, *LL*, 2:270–71.

36. Story Papers, MHS.

37. William Story describes his father's domestic habits in *LL*, 2:102–7.

38. Kent to Story, 7 August 1820, Story Papers, MHS.

39. Story to Hopkinson, 16 February 1840, Hopkinson Papers.

40. *Register of Debates*, 19th Cong., 1st sess., 1826, p. 2515.

41. Story to Hopkinson, 16 February 1840, Hopkinson Papers.

42. *Annals of Congress: Debates of the House*, 7th Cong., February 1802, p. 618.

43. *Register of Debates*, 18th Cong., 2d sess., 1825, p. 529.

44. Ibid., 19th Cong., 1st sess., 1826, p. 878.

45. Story to Hopkinson, 9 May 1833, Hopkinson Papers.

46. Catron to McLean, 19 May 1837, McLean Papers.

47. See Ashur Ware to Story, 8 August 1840, Story Papers, MHS, for an example of disagreement and consultation.

48. Story to Hopkinson, 23 March 1839, Hopkinson Papers. "I have no doubt that it is entirely competent for either member of the Circuit Court to hold the circuit court in the absence of the other Judge," wrote Story to Hopkinson, "whether such absence be temporary, or permanent in its character, whether it be from causes accidental, or causes permanent in operation. And such I believe to have been the uniform construction of the Act of 1802 on this subject."

49. See, for example, Story's dedication to Davis in his *Commentaries on Agency*.

50. Story to Peters, 28 September 1844, Peters Papers. Story was referring to the late act of Congress that permitted justices of the Supreme Court to omit every other term of the circuit court.

51. For a sample of the questions asked Story see Charles P. Curtis to Story, 30 May 1820, Story Papers, Essex Institute, Salem, Mass.; A. Robbins to N. Searle, 15 December 1817, Story Papers, LC; Story to the Honorable Daniel Davis, 7 September 1816, Story Letters, Free Library, Philadelphia; and William Sullivan to Story, 27 June 1816, Story Papers, MHS.

52. Requests for patronage recommendations involved such offices as bankruptcy commissioners, master in chancery, surveyor and inspector of the revenue (for the district), revenue collector, clerk of the court, circuit court reporter, district attorney, and district judge. For a sample see George T. Curtis to Story, 30 August 1841, Story Papers, MHS; John Saunders to Story, 22 February 1841, ibid.; Webster to Story, 14 May 1818, ibid.; Benjamin Abbot to Story, 3 September 1827, Story Papers, Essex Institute, Salem, Mass.; and E. Evans to Story, 13 February 1816, ibid.

53. John Pitman to Story, 22 November 1844, Story Papers, Essex Institute, Salem, Mass.

54. Story to John Bailey, 8 December 1823, Story Papers, MHS.

55. [Proceedings on the retirement of Judge John Davis, 9 July 1841], 30 Fed. Cas. 1304.

56. "Proceedings in Maine" at a meeting of the bar of the circuit court, 1 October 1845, in *LL*, 2:633–40.

57. Pitman to Sarah Story, 21 September 1845, Letters to Sarah W. Story, Essex Institute (Salem).

58. Ashur Ware to Story, 2 August 1826, Story Papers, MHS.

59. B. W. Godfrey to Story, 25 April 1841, Story Papers, Essex Institute, Salem, Mass.

60. John Q. Adams, as quoted in Cummings and McFarland, *Federal Justice*, p. 77.

61. Of the seventy-nine lawyers admitted to the Suffolk bar from 1829, when Story assumed duties as Dane Professor, to 1841, twenty-four had studied with him at the Law School. "More than half the younger members [of the Suffolk Bar] had been pupils of the judge," estimated Richard Henry Dana, Jr., as quoted in Warren, *Law School*, 2:41.

62. A clear statement of the crisis in the profession can be found in "Notes on the Early Jurisprudence of Maine," 3 *Law Reporter* (August 1840): 126.

63. Story to Kent, 21 August 1819, LL, 1:330–32.

64. Ibid. Also see Story to Greenleaf, 11 December 1821, Story Letters, HLS.

65. See the statement of district judge Ware in LL, 2:638.

66. The anecdote about Story's confrontation with Dexter is told in Simeon E. Baldwin, *The American Judiciary* (New York, 1905), p. 363.

67. Dane to W. W. Story, 3 May 1851, LL, 2:317–22.

68. See Story to Mellen, 7 October 1824, 23 July, 28 August 1830, 29 January 1831, 30 May 1833, 9 October 1839, 24 March 1840, Story Letters, Yale University Library.

69. Details are supplied in Newmyer, "Daniel Webster as Tocqueville's Lawyer."

70. Wirt to Webster, 8 July 1829, Daniel Webster Papers (typed transcript), LC.

71. "Charge to Grand Jury, 1812," Story Papers, UT.

72. "Charge to Grand Jury, Portland, May Term," ibid.

73. "Charge to Grand Jury, 1818," ibid.

74. Samuel Whitcomb, Jr., to McLean, 13 February 1844, McLean Papers.

75. Undated anecdote, Story Papers, UT.

76. Lerner, "The Supreme Court and American Capitalism," p. 668.

77. 12 *American Jurist* (July 1834): 94.

78. Randall Bridwell and Ralph U. Whitten, in *The Constitution and the Common Law: The Decline of the Doctrines of Separation of Powers and Federalism* (Lexington, Mass., 1977), make this point with persuasive insight in their discussion of Story and *Swift v. Tyson*. I have found their work most useful in understanding Story's work as a commercial judge.

79. 12 *American Jurist* (July 1834): 97.

80. Story, *Commentaries on Promissory Notes*, p. 112. On the same point also see his *Commentaries on Agency*, pp. 2–3, sec. 2; and his *Commentaries on Equity Jurisprudence*, 1:249, sec. 244.

81. John Pickering, "A Lecture on the Alleged Uncertainty of the Law . . . ," 12 *American Jurist* (October 1834): 295.

82. *The George*, 10 Fed. Cas. 205 (No. 5,329) (C.C.D. Mass. 1832); *The Reeside*, 20 Fed. Cas. 458 (No. 11,657) (C.C.D. Mass. 1837). These cases are discussed ably in Bridwell and Whitten, *Constitution and the Common Law*, pp. 54–60.

83. 13 *Merchants' Magazine* (July 1845): 83.

84. 5 Fed. Cas. 719 (No. 2,730) (C.C.D. Mass. 1811).

85. 19 Fed. Cas. 373 (No. 11,035) (C.C.D. Mass.).

86. Denman's letter to Charles Sumner is quoted in LL, 2:576–77. The English decision was *Deveaux v. Salvador*, 4 Adolph. & El. 420.

87. 2 *Merchants' Magazine* (June 1840): 500.

88. 2 *American Jurist* (July 1829): 107.

89. 1 *Merchants' Magazine* (July 1839): 58.

90. (March 1842): 7 ibid. 233–34.

91. (July 1839): 1 ibid. 58.

92. 19 Fed. Cas. 1022 (No. 11,274) (C.C.D. Mass. 1844); Karl N. Llewellyn, *The Common Law Tradition: Deciding Appeals* (Boston, 1960), p. 53.
93. 19 Fed. Cas. 1022–23 (headnote).
94. See Story to Webster, 10 May 1840, *LL*, 2:330–32, in which letter Story recommended that the bill not include corporations. Story spoke in this matter authoritatively, as he put it, for "the corporate capital of New England." Also see Swisher, *Taney Period*, pp. 132–46.
95. S. Doc. 19, 27th Cong., 3d sess., 1842, pp. 27–29. A summary of Story's report appeared in the Report of the Senate Judiciary Committee, S. Doc. 121, 27th Cong., 3d sess., February 1843, pp. 7–9.
96. 9 Fed. Cas. 508 (No. 4,960) (C.C.D. Mass.).
97. Ibid., 514, 512, 518–19.
98. Story to John Berrien, 29 April 1842, *LL*, 2:404–5.
99. Buchanan referred particularly to Story's circuit decisions as evidence of the consolidating nature of the law (*Congressional Globe*, 27th Cong., 2d sess., appendix 385, 1842, as quoted in Swisher, *Taney Period*, p. 137).
100. *Kittredge* v. *Warren*, 14 New Hamp. 509 (1844).
101. 3 Fed. Cas. 138 (No. 1,278) (C.C.D. N.H.). See Swisher, *Taney Period*, p. 143. Story reaffirmed *Ex parte Foster* earlier in *Fiske* v. *Hunt*, 9 Fed. Cas. 169 (No. 4,831) (C.C.D. Mass. 1843).
102. 15 New Hamp. 227; Swisher, *Taney Period*, pp. 143–44.
103. 3 Howard 292.
104. Story to W. W. Story, 1 January 1845, *LL*, 2:508–9.
105. *Peck* v. *Jenness*, 16 New Hamp. 516 (1845).
106. *Peck* v. *Jenness*, 7 Howard 612 (1849), as discussed in Swisher, *Taney Period*, p. 145.
107. Richard H. Dana to Richard H. Dana, Jr., 28 November 1838, Dana Papers.
108. Richard H. Dana, Jr., "Cruelty to Seamen—Case of Nichols and Couch," 12 *American Jurist* (October 1839): 103.
109. Ibid., p. 107.
110. George T. Curtis to Story, 13 December 1844, Story Papers, Essex Institute, Salem, Mass.
111. Especially useful to me in treating this trend have been Albert O. Greef, *The Commercial Paper House in the United States* (Cambridge, Mass., 1938), chap. 1; Ralph W. Hidy, "The Organization and Functions of Anglo-American Merchant Bankers, 1815–1860," 1 *Journal of Economic History*, supp. (December 1941): 53–66; and Glenn Porter and Harold C. Livesay, *Merchants and Manufacturers: Studies in the Changing Structure of Nineteenth Century Marketing* (Baltimore, 1971).
For a lucid discussion of the relationship of these and other economic developments to American law there is no better place to go than Tony A. Freyer, *Forums of Order: The Federal Courts and Business in American History* (Greenwich, Conn., 1979), especially chaps. 1 and 2. Gregory's marvelous study, *Nathan Appleton*, is full of insight on the changing economic world of the nineteenth century.
112. "Theory of Money and Banks," review of George Tucker's *Theory of Money and Banks Investigated*, 1 *Merchants' Magazine* (July 1839): 51.
113. Freyer treats the subject with great clarity in *Forums of Order*.
114. See Chapter 4 above.
115. 1 *U.S. Statutes at Large* 92.
116. 16 Peters 18–19.
117. Tony Freyer, *Harmony and Dissonance: The* Swift *and* Erie *Cases in American Federalism* (New York, 1981), pp. 17–18.
118. 304 U.S. 64.

119. The debate on and off the Court is discussed by Crosskey, *Politics and the Constitution*, 2:902–37. Extremely helpful to me has been Freyer's *Harmony and Dissonance*, chaps. 2 and 3.

120. Crosskey traces this development at length in *Politics and the Constitution*, 2:865–937.

121. 149 U.S. 401 (1893).

122. O. W. Holmes to Sir Frederick Pollock, 17 February 1928, *Holmes-Pollock Letters: The Correspondence of Mr. Justice Holmes and Sir Frederick Pollock, 1874–1932*, ed. Mark DeWolfe Howe, 2 vols. in 1, 2d ed. (Cambridge, Mass., 1961), 2:214–15. See also Holmes to Pollock, 1 January 1910, ibid., 1:157–58. For Holmes's judicial refusal to extend *Swift*, see *Kuhn* v. *Fairmont Coal Co.*, 215 U.S. 349 (1910); and *Black and White Taxicab Co.* v. *Brown and Yellow Taxicab Co.*, 276 U.S. 518 (1928).

123. Charles Warren, "New Light on the History of the Federal Judiciary Act of 1789," 37 *Harvard Law Review* (November 1923): 82–87. Warren's position is seriously undercut by Crosskey, *Politics and the Constitution*, 1:626–27 and 818–937. See Freyer, *Harmony and Dissonance*, pp. 111–13.

124. John Chipman Gray, *The Nature and Sources of the Law* (New York, 1909; reprint, Boston, 1921). For Holmes's approving reference to Gray's book see Holmes to Pollock, 7 January 1910, Howe, *Holmes-Pollock Letters*, 1:157–58.

125. Gray, *Nature and Sources of the Law*, p. 253.

126. See Freyer, *Harmony and Dissonance*, pp. 3–4, 41–42.

127. For William P. Fessenden's arguments concerning negotiability see 16 Peters 6–9. On the more general point of negotiability and the business community see Freyer, *Harmony and Dissonance*, pp. 4–17.

128. This was true also of so-called accommodation notes, in which the person who desired credit drew up a note and persuaded a guarantor to sign it, whereupon the bill could enter the stream of commerce. See J. Milnes Holden, *The History of Negotiable Instruments in English Law* (London, 1955), chap. 10, especially pp. 296–97. Story discussed accommodation notes in his *Commentaries on Bills of Exchange*, and he brought them within the scope of his holding in *Swift* over the objection of Justice Catron, who correctly argued that the issue had not been before the Court (16 Peters 23).

129. Horwitz, *Transformation of American Law*, p. 250, sees a general opposition to the "procommercial legal order" among states, though he does not undertake a full study of this difficult and complex question.

130. This matter is discussed in more detail in Freyer, *Harmony and Dissonance*, pp. 10–11.

131. 16 Peters 18.

132. This would seem to be the direction of recent scholarship. The case for Story was made first and most sweepingly by Crosskey in *Politics and the Constitution*. Neither Bridwell and Whitten, *Constitution and the Common Law*, nor Freyer, *Harmony and Dissonance*, goes the full distance with Crosskey, but both works, from their own perspectives, reject the charge of usurpation.

133. Freyer, *Harmony and Dissonance*, pp. 26–40.

134. 28 Fed. Cas. 1062 (No. 16,871).

135. 15 Fed. Cas. 362 (No. 8,269) (C.C.D. Mass.).

136. 16 Peters 18–19.

137. This point is emphasized by Bridwell and Whitten, *Constitution and Common Law*, especially chap. 4.

138. Horwitz explores the question in *Transformation of American Law*, pp. 245–52, but does not find a satisfactory answer. The difficulty leads him to emphasize the tensions in Story's jurisprudence as a key to understanding his connection with commercial classes.

139. This is Freyer's point in *Harmony and Dissonance*, p. 43.
140. 16 Peters 20.
141. Ibid., 18–19.
142. Holmes to Pollock, 17 February 1928, Howe, *Holmes-Pollock Letters*, 2:214–16.
143. 2 Wheaton 66; 2 Peters 170. See Story at 16 Peters 20.
144. 16 Peters 15–16.
145. Story, *Commentaries on Promissory Notes*, pp. xi–xii.

Chapter Ten

1. Story, *Commentaries on the Constitution*, 2:657–58, sec. 1914.
2. *Liberator*, p. 167. This was the spirit about which Bacon wrote to Story in the letter quoted as the second epigraph to this chapter, Story Papers, UM.
3. 7 Cranch 290 (1813). For a discussion of this case in particular and the Marshall Court on slavery in general, see Donald M. Roper, "In Quest of Judicial Objectivity: The Marshall Court and the Legitimation of Slavery," 21 *Stanford Law Review* (February 1969): 532–47.
4. The status of slavery in American politics and law is discussed in Donald L. Robinson, *Slavery in the Structure of American Politics, 1765–1820* (New York, 1971); and William M. Wiecek, *The Sources of Antislavery Constitutionalism in America, 1760–1848* (Ithaca, N.Y., 1977), especially chap. 3.
5. 8 Fed. Cas. 634 (No. 4,441) (C.C.D. Mass. 1816).
6. *U.S.* v. *La Coste*, 26 Fed. Cas. 826 (No. 15,548) (C.C.D. Mass. 1820); *U.S.* v. *Smith*, 27 Fed. Cas. 1167 (No. 16,338) (C.C.D. Mass. 1820); *The Alexander*, 1 Fed. Cas. 362 (No. 165) (C.C.D. Mass. 1823); *The Plattsburg*, 10 Wheaton 133 (1825); *U.S.* v. *Gooding*, 12 Wheaton 460 (1827).
7. 26 Fed. Cas. 832 (No. 15,551).
8. Ibid., 840.
9. Ibid., 845–46.
10. 10 Wheaton 121–22.
11. 26 Fed. Cas. 840–41 (No. 15,551).
12. Ibid., 842–44.
13. See Warren S. Howard, *American Slavers and the Federal Law, 1837–1862* (Berkeley and Los Angeles, 1963), especially pp. 161–62, where he briefly contrasts Betts and Nelson with Story.
14. Robert M. Cover, *Justice Accused: Antislavery and the Judicial Process* (New Haven, Conn., 1975), p. 102.
15. 26 Fed. Cas. 846 (No. 15,551).
16. Act of May 15, 1820, chap. 113, secs. 4, 5, 3 *U.S. Statutes at Large* 600. For a discussion see Hugh G. Soulsby, *The Right of Search and the Slave Trade in Anglo-American Relations, 1814–1862* (Baltimore, 1933), pp. 847–48.
17. 26 Fed. Cas. 847 (No. 15,551).
18. Webster to Story, 1 December 1821, Story Papers, MHS; Story to Greenleaf, 25 May 1822, Story Letters, HLS.
19. Cover, *Justice Accused*, pp. 104–5.
20. William W. Freehling, "The Founding Fathers and Slavery," 77 *American Historical Review* (February 1972): 81–93.
21. Story to Joseph Tuckerman, 25 July 1837, as cited in Swisher, *Taney Period*, p. 560. Swisher cites the resolutions of the Rhode Island legislature as an example of Story's impact.

22. Story to Bacon, 1 April 1844, *LL*, 2:481.
23. Story to McLean, 16 August 1844, McLean Papers.
24. Story to Sarah Story, 9 February 1845, *LL*, 2:512–13. Also see S. C. Phillips, Charles Allen, and C. F. Adams to Joseph Story, 25 June 1845, Story Papers, UT.
25. Story to Webster, 6 August 1822, *LL*, 1:421–22.
26. Aileen S. Kraditor, *Means and Ends in American Abolitionism: Garrison and His Critics on Strategy and Tactics, 1834–1850* (New York, 1969).
27. Seeing the issue in this light means taking antislavery constitutional thought seriously. Among the works that have been especially useful in making this point are Cover, *Justice Accused*; Paul Finkelman, *An Imperfect Union: Slavery, Federalism, and Comity*, Studies in Legal History (Chapel Hill, N.C., 1981); and Wiecek, *Sources of Antislavery Constitutionalism*. Aviam Soifer's reviews of Wiecek (67 *Georgetown Law Journal* [June 1979]: 1281–89) and Finkelman (10 *Reviews in American History* [June 1982]: 185–93) bring the issues into focus.
28. Story, *Commentaries on the Constitution*, 2:589, 211, secs. 1811, 1335.
29. Ibid., 2:588, 589, secs. 1811, 1812.
30. Ibid., 1:467–68, 470–71, secs. 637, 643.
31. Story dealt with the territorial question only summarily in chap. 31 and did not refer specifically to slavery. But he did accept without question the broad implications for federal governance established in *American Insurance Co.* v. *Canter*, 1 Peters 511 (1828) (*Commentaries on the Constitution*, 2:202–8, secs. 1322–30, especially 1322–26).
32. Finkelman, *Imperfect Union*, p. 32.
33. Story mentioned slavery only briefly in his treatise. His technique was to use slavery to illustrate conflict theory rather than the other way around. Finkelman's *Imperfect Union*, though it deals generally with the comity provisions of the Constitution, is most useful in tracing Story's influence, though Finkelman does so only tangentially to his main objective. His careful, state-by-state approach has served to correct the thesis of William Leslie, who blames Story's conflict theory for the evils of slave rendition. See "Story's Theory of the Conflict."
34. The impact of these cases on American constitutional development is analyzed with admirable clarity in Wiecek, *Sources of Antislavery Constitutionalism*, chap. 1.
35. 35 Mass. 193. Story approved Shaw's decision in *Prigg* v. *Pennsylvania* (1842) and also by implication in his letter to Ellis Gray Loring, 5 November 1836, *LL*, 2:235.
36. 10 Howard 90.
37. Here I have relied on Wiecek's *Sources of Antislavery Constitutionalism*.
38. As quoted in ibid., p. 238.
39. *Liberator*, 11 September 1846, p. 37, as quoted in Oscar Sherwin, *Prophet of Liberty: The Life and Times of Wendell Phillips* (1958; reprint, Westport, Conn., 1975), p. 749.
40. Wiecek, in *Sources of Antislavery Constitutionalism*, chaps. 9 and 11, deals with moderates and radicals respectively.
41. Lysander Spooner, *The Unconstitutionality of Slavery* (1845 [pt. 1]; 1847 [pt. 2]; reprint [pts. 1 and 2], Boston, 1860) pp. 152, 205–36.
42. Story, "Literary Tendencies of the Times," in *MW*, pp. 743, 747.
43. Story to Ticknor, 16 December 1836, Story Papers, UT.
44. Story, "Literary Tendencies of the Times," p. 777.
45. Williams, *Life of Hayes*, 1:37, journal entry of 21 December 1843.
46. Story to McLean, 23 November 1844, McLean Papers. He admitted also to having "sympathized sincerely with the Native Americans in their first movements, because foreign influences have become most mischievous among us . . ." (Story to Greenleaf, 4 January 1845, *LL*, 2:511–12). He withdrew his support, he added to Greenleaf, because he became persuaded "that the party have ulterior views."

47. Story to Peters, 6 July 1844, *LL*, 2:482–83.

48. Story to Williams, 12 January 1836, Story Papers, UT.

49. Writing to Peters on 1 September 1844, on the matter of political corruption, Story noted that the "Abolitionists, as usual, are against the Whigs—simply to defeat Clay, at the same time that they know that by doing so they will aid Polk's Election" (Peters Papers).

50. Lewis Perry argues the point persuasively in *Radical Abolitionism: Anarchy and the Government of God in Antislavery Thought* (Ithaca, N.Y., 1973).

51. Among many letters on this theme see Story to Williams, 12 January 1838, Story Papers, UT.

52. Story to Greenleaf, 16 February 1845, *LL*, 2:513–14.

53. On the ideological character of the Dorr Rebellion I have found George M. Dennison, *The Dorr War: Republicanism on Trial, 1831–1861* (Lexington, Ky., 1976) most useful. The legal aspects are treated in several articles, among which are Michael A. Conron, "Law, Politics, and Chief Justice Taney: A Reconsideration of the *Luther* v. *Borden* Decision," 11 *American Journal of Legal History* (October 1967): 377–88; Mahlon H. Hellerich, "The Luther Cases in the Lower Courts," 11 *Rhode Island History* (April 1952): 33–45; C. Peter Magrath, "Optimistic Democrat: Thomas W. Dorr and the Case of *Luther* v. *Borden*," 29 *Rhode Island History* (October 1970): 94–112; and John S. Schuchman, "The Political Background of the Political-Question Doctrine: The Judges and the Dorr War," 16 *American Journal of Legal History* (April 1972): 111–25. William M. Wiecek deals with *Luther* v. *Borden* as it relates to the guarantee clause in his *Guarantee Clause of the U.S. Constitution* (Ithaca, N.Y., 1975).

54. John Pitman to Story, 30 March 1842, Story Letters, UM. Pitman later congratulated Story "upon the success of the Law and Order party, in the city of New York fought under the Native American Flag" (Pitman to Story, 11 April 1844, Story Papers, MHS).

55. Dennison, *Dorr War*, p. 136.

56. Webster's argument in *Luther* v. *Borden* was printed as a pamphlet: Daniel Webster, *The Rhode Island Question: Mr. Webster's Argument in the Supreme Court of the United States, in the Case of Martin Luther* v. *Luther M. Borden and Others, January 27th 1848* (Washington, D.C., 1848). See pp. 11–12 for Webster's denial of the right of revolution.

57. Story to Webster, 26 April 1842, Webster Papers, New Hampshire Historical Society.

58. Pitman to Story, 26 January 1842, Story Papers, UM.

59. Story to Pitman, 10 February 1842, *LL*, 2:416.

60. Pitman to Story, 30 March 1842, Story Papers, UM.

61. Story to Webster, 26 April 1842, Webster Papers, New Hampshire Historical Society.

62. [J. Story], "Charge to Grand Jury—Treason," 30 Fed. Cas. 1046–47 (C.C.D. R.I. 1842).

63. Meeting of the members of the Bar of the State of Rhode Island, in attendance upon the United States Circuit Court, holden at Newport, 15th June 1842, Story Papers, UM. See Pitman to Story, 27 June 1842, ibid.

64. Joseph Durfee to Story, 5 August 1842, ibid.

65. H. R. 546, 28th Cong., 1st sess., 1843–44. For the entire charge see pp. 991–99, especially 993. Marvin E. Gettleman, *The Dorr Rebellion: A Study in American Radicalism, 1833–1849* (New York, 1973), p. 142, made me aware of this document.

66. H.R. 546, deposition of Martin Luther, p. 322.

67. H.R. 581, 28th Cong., 1st sess., 1844, pp. 158–59.

68. Ibid. Story was also peremptory with John Whipple; indeed, he had a reputation, at least among some of the Rhode Island bar, as a "much-speaking judge" (Payne, *Reminiscences*, p. 37).

69. H.R. 581, pp. 160–61.
70. Dennison, *Dorr War*, p.154.
71. *Luther* v. *Borden*, 7 Howard 40, 51–58 (1849).
72. Wiecek discusses the guarantee clause aspect in *The Guarantee Clause*, chap. 4.
73. 7 Howard 51–53, 69.
74. Ibid., 31.
75. Bureau of the Census, *Negro Population, 1790–1915* (Washington, D.C., 1918), pp. 53–57.
76. "The Latimer Case," 5 *Law Reporter* (March 1843): 481, 486, notes the conflict between different moral standards that underlay this case.
77. 15 Peters 449.
78. 8 Fed. Cas. 493 (No. 4,366) (C.C.D. S.C.).
79. 15 Peters 515.
80. Story to Walker, 22 May 1841, Story Papers, New York Historical Society.
81. 15 Peters 518 (1841).
82. Story to Sarah Story, 28 February 1841, *LL*, 2:348–50.
83. 15 Peters 592, 593, 594–96.
84. Swisher, *Taney Period*, p. 195.
85. Story to Webster, 26 March 1842, Webster, *Writings*, 16:364–65. For Webster's initial letter of inquiry see his letter to Story, 17 March 1842, marked "Private," Story Papers, MHS.
86. Their resolution, printed in the *Congressional Globe*, 27th Cong., 2d sess., 1842, p. 116, is quoted in Swisher, *Taney Period*, p. 197.
87. John T. Noonan, Jr., *Persons and Masks of the Law: Cardozo, Holmes, Jefferson, and Wythe as Makers of the Masks* (New York, 1976), p. 21.
88. 16 Peters 539 (1842).
89. Paul Finkelman is good on the human side of the case: "*Prigg* v. *Pennsylvania* and Northern State Courts: Anti-Slavery Use of a Pro-Slavery Decision," 25 *Civil War History* (March 1979): 5–35.
90. 16 Peters 620.
91. 16 Peters 612.
92. 16 Peters 612, 615. McLean addressed the argument from *Martin* directly and disagreed with it (ibid., 665–66).
93. Ibid., 613. Story did say, however, "that the States, in virtue of their general police power, possess full jurisdiction to arrest and restrain runaway slaves, and remove them from their borders, and otherwise to secure themselves against their depradations and evil example . . ." (ibid., 625).
94. Williams, *Life of Hayes*, 1:37. Hayes quotes Story as saying, "In the case between the states of Pennsylvania and Maryland, I delivered the opinion at the solicitation of my brothers, who adopted unanimously my first draft" (entry of 21 December 1843).
95. This point is not generally recognized, but Story himself called attention to it in his letter to John Berrien, 29 April 1842, quoted in McClellan, *Story*, pp. 262–63.
96. Perhaps the most thorough contemporary defense of Story's position on the whole subject of rendition is found in "The Latimer Case." 481–98. The wide-ranging response is discussed in Dunne, pp. 401–2; Finkelman, "*Prigg* v. *Pennsylvania*"; Thomas D. Morris, *Free Men All: The Personal Liberty Laws of the North, 1780–1861* (Baltimore, 1974), chaps. 6 and 7; Swisher, *Taney Period*, pp. 543–47; and Warren, *Supreme Court*, 2:83–87.
97. His son recounts the matter in *LL*, 2:392. "Triumph of freedom" was Story's phrase, not his son's. Morris, *Free Men All*, has an insightful discussion of the triumph-of-freedom argument, pp. 103–6.

98. *LL*, 2:392.

99. Story quotes Marshall's opinion, 16 Peters 622.

100. Ibid., 617–18. *Houston* v. *Moore* is cited for support, too.

101. The story is told in Morris, *Free Men All*, chap. 7.

102. This is the theme of Cover, *Justice Accused*, which treats Story's decisions on slavery with insight.

103. Morris, *Free Men All*, pp. 113–14. William Story argued, though not convincingly, that *Prigg* did not undercut trial by jury (*LL*, 2:396).

104. 16 Peters 699.

105. "The owner has the same security, and the same remedial justice, and the same exemption from state regulation and control, through however many states he may pass with his fugitive slave in his possession, in transitu, to his own domicile" (16 Peters 624).

106. Joseph C. Burke, "What Did the Prigg Decision Really Decide?" 93 *Pennsylvania Magazine of History and Biography* (January 1969): 80.

107. 16 Peters 636.

108. Ibid.

109. *LL*, 2:392.

110. Burke, "Prigg Decision."

111. 16 Peters 627.

112. Ibid., 617.

113. The standard account of the Latimer case is chap. 6 in Leonard W. Levy, *The Law of the Commonwealth and Chief Justice Shaw* (Cambridge, Mass., 1957). A contemporary account of the case, with a justification of Story's action, can be found in "The Latimer Case."

114. As quoted in "The Latimer Case," p. 486.

115. The act is discussed in detail in Morris, *Free Men All*, chap. 8.

116. Story to Berrien, 29 April 1842. James McClellan discovered this crucial letter in the John Macpherson Berrien Papers, Southern Historical Collection, University of North Carolina, and quoted relevant portions of it in his *Story*, pp. 262–63 n. 94. As McClellan pointed out, Story's son significantly omitted the incriminating part of this letter (*LL*, 2:404–5).

117. *LL*, 2:391–92.

118. Story to Bacon, 19 November 1842, *LL*, 2:430–31. Story made specific reference in this letter to his *Eugenie* opinion, but there can be no doubt that *Prigg* was also on his mind.

119. Young Rutherford B. Hayes recorded Story's lecture verbatim in his journal (Williams, *Life of Hayes*, 1:36–37).

120. William Story said the same thing when he noted that the best argument against the fugitive slave clause was a "naked exposition of it." If the people disliked it they could "move in its amendment" (*LL*, 2:395).

121. The response of Northern conservatives to the Civil War is treated in George M. Fredrickson, *The Inner Civil War: Northern Intellectuals and the Crisis of the Union* (New York, 1965).

Epilogue

1. Story to Bacon, 12 April 1845, *LL*, 2:527–29.

2. *LL*, 2:539.

3. Story to Peters, 1 March 1845, Peters Papers.

4. Story to Kent, 10 June 1845, *LL*, 2:538–39.

5. "Report of the Committee on the Dane Professorship & the Increase of Salary of J. Story in 1845," copy in Story's handwriting, Story Papers, UT.

6. Rufus Choate, "The Position and Function of the American Bar, as an Element of Conservatism in the State . . . ," in *The Works of Rufus Choate, with a Memoir of His Life*, ed. Samuel G. Brown, 2 vols. (Boston, 1862), 1:428. The other epigraphs come, respectively, from Story, "Progress of Jurisprudence," in *MW*, p. 241, and from *Selections from the Correspondence of Theodore Roosevelt and Henry Cabot Lodge* (New York, 1925), as quoted in Felix Frankfurter, *Mr. Justice Holmes and the Supreme Court* (Cambridge, Mass., 1961), pp. 52–53.

7. Conversation as recalled by W. W. Story, *LL*, 2:540.

8. For Sumner's account of the burial see his "Tribute of Friendship," printed in the *Boston Daily Advertiser*, 16 September 1845, and reprinted in Sumner, *Works*, 1:133–48, and in *LL*, 2:613–21.

9. *MW*, pp. 573, 577.

10. Sumner, "Tribute of Friendship," *LL*, 2:615.

11. Ibid.

12. Holmes, "The Use of Law Schools," in *Collected Legal Papers*, p. 41.

13. Summaries of many of these testimonials to Story are contained in the appendix to *LL*, 2:613–47.

14. McClellan, *Story*, p. 3.

15. See, for example, the articles of Hessel E. Yntema, Elliott E. Cheatham, and Walter Wheeler Cook, among others, in AALS, *Selected Readings*.

16. Among the several articles pro and con in leading law journals one might consult Henry J. Friendly, "In Praise of *Erie*—and of the New Federal Common Law," 39 *New York University Law Review* (May 1964): 383–422; Arthur J. Keefe, "In Praise of Joseph Story, *Swift* v. *Tyson* and 'The True National Common Law,'" 18 *American University Law Review* (March 1969): 316–71; and "*Swift* v. *Tyson* Exhumed," 79 *Yale Law Journal* (December 1969): 284–310. Also see the article by John Hart Ely and Abram Chayes, in 87 *Harvard Law Review* (February 1974): 741–62.

17. See, for example, Dunne, "Story and the Modern Corporation."

18. Story to Sumner, 11 August 1845, *LL*, 2:543–44.

19. Charles E. Phelps's account is found in Warren, *Law School*, 2:180–81.

20. Ibid., pp. 168–75.

21. William Kent to James Kent, 10 March 1847, Kent Papers.

22. Holmes, "The Use of Law Schools," p. 41.

23. Grant Gilmore, *The Ages of American Law* (New Haven, Conn., 1977), p. 104.

24. See his "Story in the Making of American Law."

25. Sumner to Story, 5 February 1845, Sumner Papers. Sumner wrote of the "terms" that Webster settled on with "his friends, before he consented to be chosen. They were $50,000 to be subscribed in Boston, & the same sum in N York, to be settled on his life & that of his wife." Also see Otis to G. Harrison, 7 February 1845, Otis Papers. Otis also mentioned a "fund" of $100,000 and noted that this was the third time "that the wind has been raised for him. . . ."

26. Edward Pessen, "The Equalitarian Myth and American Social Reality: Wealth, Mobility and Equality in the 'Era of the Common Man,'" 76 *American Historical Review* (October 1971): 989–1034.

27. Holmes, "The Use of Law Schools," p. 41.

28. See Van Wyck Brooks, *New England: Indian Summer, 1865–1915* (New York, 1940), especially chap. 2, "Cambridge after the Civil War."

Bibliography

Primary Sources

Story Family Documents, Papers, and Correspondence

Elisha Story. Last will and testament, 30 September 1725. No. 5138. Register of Probate, Suffolk County Court House, Boston.

Elisha Story. Last will and testament, 14 October 1805. Trial Court, Probate and Family Court Department, Essex Division, Essex County Court House, Salem, Mass.

Life and Letters of Joseph Story. Edited by William W. Story. 2 vols. London, 1851. (Cited as *LL.*)

Joseph Story Papers. Essex Institute, Salem, Mass.

Joseph Story Letters. Free Library, Philadelphia, Pa.

Joseph Story Letters. Treasure Room, Harvard Law School, Cambridge, Mass.

Joseph Story Letters. College Papers, 2nd ser., Harvard University Archives, Cambridge, Mass.

Joseph Story-Francis Lieber Correspondence. Huntington Library, San Marino, Calif.

Joseph Story Papers. Library of Congress, Washington, D.C.

Story Papers. Marblehead Historical Society, Marblehead, Mass.

Joseph Story Papers. Massachusetts Historical Society, Boston.

Joseph Story Papers. Microfilm. Clements Library, University of Michigan, Ann Arbor.

Joseph Story Papers. Microfilm. New York Historical Society, New York, N.Y.

Joseph Story-Henry Wheaton Correspondence. Pierpont Morgan Library, New York, N.Y.

Story correspondence. *Proceedings of the Massachusetts Historical Society*, 2d ser., 14 (1900–1901), 15 (1901–2), 49 (1915–16), 53 (1919–20).

Joseph Story Papers. Microfilm. University of Texas, Austin.

Joseph Story Papers. Yale University Library, New Haven, Conn.

Writings of Joseph Story (in Chronological Order)

"The Fount: HARVARD PATRIOTIC ODE. Printed in *Columbian Centinel* (Boston). 30 June 1798.

An Eulogy on George Washington, Written at the Request of the Inhabitants of Marblehead and Delivered before Them on the Second Day of January, A.D. 1800. Salem, Mass., 1800.

The Power of Solitude, a Poem in Two Parts. . . . Salem, Mass., 1801.

[Anonymous joint authorship.] *American Precedents of Declarations.* Boston, 1802.

"An Oration," Pronounced at Salem, on the Fouth Day of July, in Commemoration of Our National Independence. Salem, Mass., 1804.

A Selection of Pleadings in Civil Actions, Subsequent to the Declaration. . . . Salem, Mass., 1805.

Address before the Regimental Officers at Salem, July 4, 1808. Salem, Mass., [1808?].

MS digest of various law works [1808–12?]. 3 vols. Treasure Room, Harvard Law School, Cambridge, Mass.

Fee Book. MS. Story Papers. New York Historical Society, New York, N.Y.

Legal Form Book. MS. Story Papers. New York Historical Society, New York, N.Y.

[J. Story.] Act Establishing J. Court of Chancery. 16 January 1808. Report of the Judiciary Committee. Doc. 6413. [Massachusetts] State Archives, Boston.

Practical Treatise on Bills of Exchange: New Edition, from the Second Corrected and Enlarged London Edition with the Addition of Recent English and American Cases by Joseph Story, by Joseph Chitty. Boston, 1809.

A Treatise of the Law Relative to Merchant Ships and Seamen: Second American from the Third English Edition with Annotations by Joseph Story, by Charles Abbott. Newburyport, Mass., 1810.

A Practical Treatise on Pleading, in Assumpsit, with the Addition of American Decisions by Joseph Story, by Edward Lawes. Boston, 1811.

"Charge to Grand Jury, 1812." Story Papers. University of Texas.

"Charge to Grand Jury, 1818." Story Papers. University of Texas.

A Charge to the Grand Juries, in Boston, and Providence, 1819. [1819.]

"Charge to Grand Jury, Portland, May Term, [1820]." Story Papers. University of Texas.

"Memorandums of Arguments in the Supreme Court of the United States Beginning with the January Term, 1831, and Ending with the January Term, 1832." MS. Harvard Law School, Cambridge, Mass.

"Courts of the U. States." In *Encyclopaedia Americana . . .* , edited by Francis Lieber. Philadelphia, 1829–33. New ed. 13 vols., 3:594–96. Philadelphia, 1846.

"Law, Legislation and Codes." in *Encyclopaedia Americana . . .* , 7:576–92. 1846.

"Natural Law." In *Encyclopaedia Americana . . .* , 9:150–58. 1846.

Commentaries on the Law of Bailments, with Illustrations from the Civil and Foreign Law. Cambridge, Mass., 1832. 4th ed. Boston, 1846.

[J.S.] "Art. V—Christianity a Part of the Common Law." 9 *American Jurist and Law Magazine* (April 1833): 346–48.

Commentaries on the Constitution of the United States, with a Preliminary Review of the Constitutional History of the Colonies and States before the Adoption of the Constitution. 3 vols. Boston, 1833. 5th ed. Edited by Melville Bigelow. 2 vols. Boston, 1891. 1st ed. translated as *Commentaire sur la Constitution federale des Etats-Unis . . .* by Paul Odent. 2 vols. Paris, 1843. 1st ed. translated as *Comentario sobre la Constitución federal de los Estados Unidos.* Buenos Aires, 1881.

[J. Story.] "Statesmen—Their Rareness and Importance: Daniel Webster." 7 *New England Magazine* (August 1834): 89–104.

Commentaries on the Conflict of Laws, Foreign and Domestic, in Regard to Contracts, Rights, and Remedies, and Especially in Regard to Marriages, Divorces, Wills, Successions, and Judgments. Boston, 1834. 6th ed. Edited by Isaac Redfield. Boston, 1865.

A Discourse on the Past History, Present State, and Future Prospects of the Law. Edinburgh, 1835.

"American Law." 9 *Kritische Zeitschrift für Rechtswissenschaft und Gesetzgebung des Auslandes* (1836). Reprinted in 3 *American Journal of Comparative Law* (Winter 1954): 9–26.

Commentaries on Equity Jurisprudence, As Administered in England and America. 2 vols. Boston, 1836.

Commentaries on Equity Pleadings, and the Incidents Thereof, According to the Practice of the Courts of Equity of England and America. Boston, 1838.

Commentaries on the Law of Agency as a Branch of Commercial and Maritime Jurisprudence, with Occasional Illustrations from the Civil and Foreign Law. Boston, 1839.

A Familiar Exposition of the Constitution of the United States: Containing a Brief Commentary on Every Clause, Explaining the True Nature, Reasons, and Objects Thereof; Designed for the Use of School Libraries and General Readers; with an Appendix Containing Important Public Documents, Illustrative of the Constitution. Boston, 1840.

Commentaries on the Law of Partnership, as a Branch of Commercial and Maritime Jurisprudence, with Occasional Illustrations from the Civil and Foreign Law. Boston, 1841. 3d ed. Boston, 1850.

[J. Story.] "Charge to Grand Jury—Treason." 30 Fed. Cas. 1046–47 (C.C.D. R.I. 1842).

Commentaries on the Law of Bills of Exchange, Foreign and Inland, as Administered in England and America; with Occasional Illustrations from the Commercial Law of the Nations of Continental Europe. Boston, 1843. 2d ed. Boston, 1847.

Commentaries on the Law of Promissory Notes and Guarantees of Notes, and Checks on Banks and Bankers; with Occasional Illustrations from the Commercial Law of the Nations of Europe. Boston, 1845. 3d ed. Boston, 1851.

The Miscellaneous Writings of Joseph Story. . . . Edited by William W. Story. Boston, 1852. (None of the works listed above is included in this collection of Story's printed essays and speeches, cited as *MW*.)

Contemporary Manuscript Sources

Salmon P. Chase Papers. Historical Society of Pennsylvania, Philadelphia.
Henry Clay Papers. Library of Congress, Washington, D.C.
Crowninshield Papers. Peabody Museum, Salem, Mass.
Richard H. Dana, Jr., Papers. Massachusetts Historical Society, Boston.
Nathan Dane Papers. Massachusetts Historical Society, Boston.
Thomas W. Dorr Collection. John Hay Library, Brown University, Providence, R.I.
Andrew Dunlap Papers. Essex Institute, Salem, Mass.
Stephen DuPonceau Papers. Historical Society of Pennsylvania, Philadelphia.
Edward Everett Papers. Massachusetts Historical Society, Boston.
Galloway, Maxcy, Markoe Papers. Library of Congress, Washington, D.C.
Gideon and Francis Granger Papers. Library of Congress, Washington, D.C.
Robert G. Harper Papers. Library of Congress, Washington, D.C.
Joseph Hopkinson Papers. Historical Society of Pennsylvania, Philadelphia.
Thomas Jefferson Papers. Library of Congress, Washington, D.C.
Thomas Jefferson Papers. Coolidge Collection, Massachusetts Historical Society, Boston.
James Kent Papers. Library of Congress, Washington, D.C.
B. B. Macanulty Letter-books, 1802–7. Essex Institute, Salem, Mass.
McGregor-Madison Papers. McGregor Library, University of Virginia, Charlottesville.
John McLean Papers. Library of Congress, Washington, D.C.
James Madison Papers. University of Virginia, Charlottesville.
John Marshall Papers. Library of Congress, Washington, D.C.
John Marshall Papers. College of William and Mary, Williamsburg, Va.
Karl J. A. Mittermaier-J. Story Letters. Mittermaier Collection, Universitätsbibliothek Heidelberg, Heidelberg, West Germany.
Harrison G. Otis Papers. Massachusetts Historical Society, Boston.
John G. Palfrey Papers. Houghton Library, Harvard University, Cambridge, Mass.
Pedrick Papers. Marblehead Historical Society, Marblehead, Mass.
Richard Peters Papers. Historical Society of Pennsylvania, Philadelphia.
Timothy Pickering Papers. Massachusetts Historical Society, Boston.
Samuel Putnam Papers. Essex Institute, Salem, Mass.
Quinquennial folder of Justice Lemuel Shaw. Harvard University Archives, Cambridge, Mass.
W. C. Rives Papers. Library of Congress, Washington, D.C.
Leverett Saltonstall Papers. Massachusetts Historical Society, Boston.
William Smith Shaw Papers. Boston Athenaeum, Boston, Mass.
Charles Sumner Papers. Houghton Library, Harvard University, Cambridge, Mass.

Upham, Charles W. "Salem Witchcraft Illustrated with Portraits and Autographs." Ch. K. 1.40. Chamberlain Collection, Boston Public Library, Boston, Mass.
Gulian C. Verplanck Papers. New York Historical Society, New York, N.Y.
Autograph file of Webster letters. Houghton Library, Harvard University, Cambridge, Mass.
Daniel Webster Papers (typed transcript). Library of Congress, Washington, D.C.
Daniel Webster Papers. New Hampshire Historical Society, Concord.
Henry Wheaton Papers. Pierpont Morgan Library, New York, N.Y.
William Wirt Papers. Library of Congress, Washington, D.C.
William Wirt Papers. Maryland Historical Society, Baltimore.
Levi Woodbury Papers. Library of Congress, Washington, D.C.

Contemporary (and Earlier) Published Sources

Adams, John. *Diary and Autobiography of John Adams.* Edited by L. H. Butterfield; assistant editors, L. C. Faber and W. D. Garrett. 4 vols. Cambridge, Mass., 1961.
———. *The Works of John Adams.* . . . Edited by C. F. Adams. 10 vols. Boston, 1850–56.
American Jurist and Law Magazine (Boston). 1829–43. (Cited as *American Jurist.*)
American Law Journal (Philadelphia). 1808–17.
American Monthly Review (Cambridge, Mass.). 1832–33.
Angell, Joseph K. *The Law of Watercourses.* . . . Boston, 1824.
Angell, Joseph K., and Ames, Samuel. *A Treatise on the Law of Private Corporations Aggregate.* Boston, 1832.
Bacon, Matthew. *A General Abridgment of Cases in Equity, Argued and Adjudged in the High Court of Chancery.* . . . London, 1732–56.
Baldwin, Henry. *A General View of the Origin and Nature of the Constitution and Government of the United States.* Philadelphia, 1837.
Barton, Charles. *An Historical Treatise of a Suit in Equity.* . . . Dublin, 1796.
Bentham, Jeremy. *The Works of Jeremy Bentham.* . . . Compiled by John Bowring. 1838–43. Reprint. 11 vols. New York, 1962.
Bentley, William. *The Diary of William Bentley, D.D., Pastor of the East Church, Salem, Massachusetts.* 4 vols. Salem, Mass., 1905.
Blackstone, William. *Commentaries on the Laws of England.* 4 vols. Oxford, 1765–69.
Boston Daily Advertiser. 1813–1929.
Boston Gazette. 1800–1815.
Boston Patriot. 1809–31.
"A Catalogue of the Law Library of Harvard. . . ." 26 *American Jurist and Law Magazine* (October 1841): 254–61.
Channing, William Ellery. *Memoir of William Ellery Channing, with Extracts from His Correspondence and Manuscripts.* 3 vols. Boston: 1848.
———. *A Sermon Preached at the Annual Election, May 26, 1830.* . . . Boston, 1830.
———. *The Works of William E. Channing, D.D.* . . . 11th complete ed. 6 vols. Boston, 1849.
Choate, Rufus. "The Position and Functions of the American Bar, as an Element of Conservatism in the State. . . ." In *The Works of Rufus Choate, with a Memoir of His Life,* edited by Samuel G. Brown, 2 vols.,1:414–38. Boston, 1862.
Coke, Edward. *The First Part of the Institutes of the Laws of England; or A Commentary upon Littleton.* 1628. 16th ed., revised and corrected by Francis Hargrave and Charles Butler. London, 1809.
Columbian Centinel (Boston). 1790–1840.
Comyns, John. *A Digest of the Laws of England.* . . . 5 vols. London, 1762–67.
"Corporations." 4 *American Jurist and Law Magazine* (October 1830): 298–308.

Curtis, George Ticknor. *A Treatise on the Rights and Duties of Merchant Seamen.* . . . Boston, 1841.

Dana, Richard H., Jr. "Cruelty to Seamen—Case of Nichols and Couch." 12 *American Jurist and Law Magazine* (October 1839): 92–107.

———. *The Journal of Richard Henry Dana, Jr.* Edited by Robert F. Lucid. 3 vols. Cambridge, Mass., 1968.

———. *The Seamen's Friend, Containing a Treatise on Practical Seamanship.* Boston, 1841.

———. *Two Years before the Mast: A Personal Narrative of Life at Sea.* Boston, 1840.

Dane, Nathan. *A General Abridgment and Digest of American Law.* . . . 9 vols. Boston, 1823–29.

Davis, George T. M. *Autobiography of the Late Colonel George T. M. Davis.* . . . New York, 1891.

Democrat (Boston). 1804–9.

DuPonceau, Stephen. *A Dissertation on the Nature and Extent of the Jurisdiction of the Courts of the United States.* . . . Philadelphia, 1824.

Dwight, Timothy. *Travels in New England and New York.* Edited by Barbara Miller Solomon with the assistance of Patricia M. King. 4 vols. Cambridge, Mass., 1969.

Edgeworth, Maria, and Edgeworth, Richard L. *The Practical Education.* 3 vols. London, 1801.

Enquirer (Richmond). 1804–77.

Essex Register (Salem).

[Everett, Edward.] "Story's Constitutional Law." Review. 37 *North American Review* (January 1834): 63–84.

Farrar, Timothy. *Report of the Case of the Trustees of Dartmouth College against William H. Woodward.* Portsmouth, N.H., 1819.

Fearne, Charles. *An Essay on the Learning of Contingent Remainders and Executory Devises.* . . . London, 1773.

The Federalist, by Alexander Hamilton, James Madison, and John Jay. Edited by Benjamin F. Wright. Cambridge, Mass., 1961.

Fletcher, Calvin. *The Diary of Calvin Fletcher, Including Letters to and from Calvin Fletcher.* Edited by Gayle Thornbrough and Dorothy Riker. 8 vols. to date. Indianapolis, 1972–.

Fonblanque, John. *A Treatise of Equity.* . . . 1793.

Greenleaf, Simon. *A Collection of Cases Overruled, Doubted, or Limited in Their Application, Taken from American and English Reports.* Portland, Maine, 1821.

———. *A Discourse Commemorative of the Life and Character of Joseph Story, 18th of September 1845.* Boston, 1845.

———. *A Treatise on the Law of Evidence.* 3 vols. Boston, 1842–53.

Hale, Mathew. *The History of the Common Law of England.* London, 1713.

Hawkins, William. *A Treatise of the Pleas of the Crown.* . . . [London], 1716.

Hoffman, David. *A Course on Legal Study.* . . . Baltimore, 1817. 2d ed. 2 vols. Baltimore, 1836.

Hopkinson, Joseph. Review of Story's *Commentaries on the Constitution.* 14 *American Quarterly Review* (December 1833): 327–67.

Huber, Ulricus. *Praelectionum Juris Civilis.* . . . 3 vols. Franequerae, 1689–90.

Independent Chronicle (Boston). 1776–1840.

Jefferson, Thomas. *Memoirs, Correspondence, and Private Papers of Thomas Jefferson, Late President of the United States, Now First Published from the Original Manuscripts.* Edited by Thomas Jefferson Randolph. 4 vols. London, 1829.

———. *The Works of Thomas Jefferson.* Federal Ed. 12 vols. New York, 1904–5.

Kent, James. *Commentaries on American Law.* Philadelphia, 1826–30. 12th ed. Edited by O. W. Holmes, Jr. 4 vols. Boston, 1873.

Knox, Viscemius. *Elegant Extracts; or, Useful and Entertaining Passages in Prose, Selected for the Improvement of Scholars at Classical and Other Schools in the Art of Speaking, in Reading, Thinking, Composing; and in the Conduct of Life.* London, ca. 1783.

"The Latimer Case." 5 *Law Reporter* (March 1843): 481–98.

"The Law Institution of Harvard University." 4 *American Jurist and Law Magazine* (July 1830): 217–20.

Lawrence, Amos. *Extracts from the Diary and Correspondence of the Late Amos Lawrence.* . . . Edited by William R. Lawrence. Boston, 1855.

"A Lecture on the Alleged Uncertainty of the Law. . . ." 12 *American Jurist and Law Magazine* (October 1834): 285–311.

Liberator (Boston). 1831–65.

Lieber, Francis. *Manual of Political Ethics, Designed Chiefly for the Use of Colleges and Students at Law.* . . . 2 vols. Boston, 1838–39.

———, ed. *Encyclopaedia Americana* . . . . Philadelphia, 1829–33. New ed. 13 vols. Philadelphia, 1846.

Livermore, Samuel. *Dissertations on Questions Which Arise from the Contrariety of the Positive Laws of Different States and Nations.* New Orleans, 1828.

"Manufacturing Corporations." 2 *American Jurist and Law Magazine* (July 1829): 92–118.

Marshall, John. *The Papers of John Marshall.* Edited by Herbert A. Johnson. Vol. 1. Chapel Hill, N.C., 1974.

Mason, Jeremiah. *Memoir and Correspondence of Jeremiah Mason.* Edited by G. S. Hillard. Cambridge, Mass., 1873.

Merchants' Magazine and Commercial Review [later *Hunt's Merchants' Magazine*] (New York). 1839–70.

Monthly Anthology and Boston Review. 1803–11.

New-England Magazine (Boston). 1831–35.

New England Palladium (Boston). 1793–1840.

Niles' Weekly Register, 1811–49.

North American Review and Miscellaneous Journal (Boston). 1816–.

"Notes on the Early Jurisprudence of Maine." 3 *Law Reporter* (August 1840): 120–27.

Parker, Edward G. *Reminiscences of Rufus Choate, the Great American Advocate.* New York, 1860.

Parker, Theodore. *Additional Speeches, Addresses, and Occasional Sermons.* 2 vols. Boston, 1855.

Parsons, Theophilus, [Jr.]. *Memoir of Theophilus Parsons, Chief Justice of the Supreme Judicial Court of Massachusetts.* . . . Boston, 1859.

Payne, Abraham. *Reminiscences of the Rhode Island Bar.* Providence, R.I., 1855.

Phillips, Mary E. *Reminiscences of William Wetmore Story.* Chicago, 1897.

Phillips, Willard. *The Law of Patents for Inventors.* . . . Boston, 1837.

Pickering, John. "A Lecture on the Alleged Uncertainty of the Law. . . ." 12 *American Jurist and Law Magazine* (October 1834): 285–311.

Pickering, Timothy. *A Review of the Correspondence between the Honorable John Adams, Late President of the United States, and the Late William Cunningham.* . . . Salem, Mass., 1824.

Plumer, William, Jr. *The Life of William Plumer.* . . . Boston, 1857.

[Proceedings on the retirement of Judge John Davis, 9 July 1841.] 30 Fed. Cas. 1302–4.

"Provincial and Colonial Laws." 3 *American Jurist and Law Magazine* (January 1830): 115–21.

Quincy, Josiah. *An Address to the Citizens of Boston . . . [upon] the First Settlement of the City.* Boston, 1830.

————. "Address on the Occasion of the Dedication of Dane Law College." 9 *American Jurist and Law Magazine* (January 1833): 48–66.

————. *The History of Harvard University.* 2 vols. Cambridge, Mass., 1840.

Rantoul, Robert, Jr. *Memoirs, Speeches and Writings of Robert Rantoul, Jr.* Edited by Luther Hamilton. Boston, 1854.

Redesdale, Lord. *A Treatise on the Pleadings in Suits in the Court of Chancery.* . . . London, 1780.

Review of Story's *Commentaries on the Constitution.* 4 *American Monthly Review* (December 1833): 499–513.

Review of Story's *Commentaries on Conflict.* 11 *American Jurist and Law Magazine* (April 1834): 365–408.

Review of Story's *Commentaries on Conflict.* 17 *American Quarterly Review* (June 1835): 303–18.

Review of Story's *Selection of Pleadings.* 2 *Monthly Anthology* (September 1805): 483.

Salem Gazette. 1790–1908.

Salem Register. 1802–7.

A Selection of Eulogies Pronounced in the Several States in Honor of Those Illustrious Patriots and Statesmen, John Adams and Thomas Jefferson. Hartford, Conn., 1826.

Spooner, Lysander. *The Unconstitutionality of Slavery.* 1845 (pt. 1). 1847 (pt. 2). Reprint (pts. 1 and 2). Boston, 1860.

Story, Rev. Isaac. *A Discourse, Delivered February 15, 1795, at the Request of the Proprietors' Committee.* . . . Salem, Mass., 1795.

————. *A Sermon, Preached February 19, 1795* . . . *Being the Federal Thanksgiving.* . . . Salem, Mass., 1795.

"Story's Commentaries—Vol. I." 9 *American Jurist and Law Magazine* (April 1833): 241–88.

"Story's Commentaries—Vols. II and III." 10 *American Jurist and Law Magazine* (July 1833): 119–47.

Sullivan, James. *The History of Land Titles in Massachusetts.* . . . Boston, 1801.

Sumner, Charles. "The Scholar, the Jurist, the Artist, the Philanthropist." In *The Works of Charles Sumner,* 15 vols., 1:245–302. Boston, 1870–73.

————. *Memoir and Letters of Charles Sumner.* Edited by Edward L. Pierce. 4 vols. Boston, 1877–93.

————. "The Position and Duties of the Merchant." In *The Works of Charles Sumner,* 15 vols., 3:479–519. Boston, 1870–73.

————. *The Works of Charles Sumner.* 15 vols. Boston, 1870–73.

Taylor, John. *Construction Construed and Constitutions Vindicated.* Richmond, Va., 1820.

————. *New Views of the Constitution of the United States.* Washington, D.C., 1823.

————. *Tyranny Unmasked.* Washington, D.C., 1822.

"Theory of Money and Banks." Review of George Tucker's *Theory of Money and Banks Investigated.* 1 *Merchant's Magazine and Commercial Review* (July 1839): 50–53.

Tocqueville, Alexis de. *Democracy in America.* Edited by Phillips Bradley. Translated by Henry Reeve. 2 vols. New York: Vintage, 1959.

United States Magazine and Democratic Review (Washington, D.C.). 1837–59.

Walker, Timothy. "Codification. . . ." 1 *Western Law Journal* (July 1844): 433–44.

————. *Introduction to American Law.* . . . Philadelphia, 1837.

Walsh, Michael. *A New System of Mercantile Arithmetic.* . . . Newburyport, Mass., 1801.

Webster, Daniel. *The Rhode Island Question: Mr. Webster's Argument in the Supreme Court of the United States, in the Case of Martin Luther v. Luther M. Borden and Others, January 27th, 1848.* Washington, D.C., 1848.

————. *The Writings and Speeches of Daniel Webster.* National Ed. 18 vols. Boston, 1903.

Western Law Journal (Cincinnati). 1843–53.
Williams, Charles R. *The Life of Rutherford Birchard Hayes, Nineteenth President of the United States.* 2 vols. Boston, 1914.
Wooddeson, Richard. *Elements of Jurisprudence.* . . . London, 1783.
Worthington, Erastus. *An Essay on the Establishment of a Chancery Jurisdiction in Massachusetts.* . . . Boston, 1810.
Young, Edward. *Night Thoughts on Life, Death and Immortality.* . . . London, 1777.

Government Records and Documents

Federal

American State Papers: Miscellaneous. Vol. 1.
Appointment Files for State Department. National Archives.
Circuit Court Docket. 1800–1812. Federal Archives and Records Center, Waltham, Mass.
Circuit Court Records (Massachusetts). Federal Archives and Records Center, Waltham, Mass.
District Court Dockets and Minute Books. 1800–1812. Federal Archives and Records Center, Waltham, Mass.
District Court Records. 1800–1812. Federal Archives and Records Center, Waltham, Mass.
The Federal Cases, Comprising Cases Argued and Determined in the Circuit and District Courts of the United States. . . . 30 vols. (Cited as Fed. Cas.)
Papers of the Attorney General, Massachusetts. Box 1. 1813–41. National Archives.
U.S. Bureau of the Census. *Negro Population, 1790–1915.* Washington, D.C., 1918.
U.S. Congress. *Annals of Congress, 1789–1824. Debates of the House.* 10th Cong., 2d sess., 1808–9; 13th Cong., 1st sess., 1813–14.
———. *Congressional Globe.* 27th Cong., 2d sess., 1841–42.
———. House. H.R. 546. 28th Cong., 1st sess., 1843–44.
———. House. H.R. 581. 28th Cong., 1st sess., 1844.
———. *Register of Debates, 1824–37. Debates of Senate.* 21st Cong., 1st sess., 1830.
———. Senate. 27th Cong., 3d sess., 1842. S. Doc. 19.
———. Senate. 27th Cong., 3d sess., February 1843. S. Doc. 121.
U.S. Reports (Supreme Court).
U.S. Statutes at Large. Vols. 1 and 5.

Commonwealth of Massachusetts

The Charters and General Laws of the Colony and Province of Massachusetts Bay . . . Published by Order of the General Court. Boston, 1841.
Court of Common Pleas (Essex County). Docket Books. Vols. 1–11. 1801–12. Essex County Court House, Salem, Mass.
———. Records. CCP Vol. March–June 1809. Essex County Court House, Salem, Mass.
Justice of the Peace Records of Thomas Bancroft. MSS. Essex Institute, Salem, Mass.
Massachusetts Legislative Documents. 1798–1809. A. State Archives. Boston.
Massachusetts Reports (Supreme Judicial Court). Tyng 2–17 Mass. Rep. 1806–20.
Pickering 18–41 Mass. Rep. 1820–39.

Secondary Sources

Books

Adams, Henry. *History of the United States of America.* 9 vols. New York, 1889–91.

Amory, Cleveland. *The Proper Bostonians.* New York, 1947.

Association of American Law Schools. *Selected Readings on Conflict of Laws.* Saint Paul, Minn., 1956.

Bailyn, Bernard. *Education in the Forming of American Society: Needs and Opportunities for Study.* Chapel Hill, N.C., 1960.

————. *The Ordeal of Thomas Hutchinson.* Cambridge, Mass., 1974.

Baker, Elizabeth F. *Henry Wheaton, 1785–1848.* Philadelphia, 1937.

Baldwin, Simeon E. *The American Judiciary.* New York, 1905.

Banner, James M., Jr. *To the Hartford Convention: The Federalists and the Origins of Party Politics in Massachusetts, 1789–1815.* New York, 1970.

Bauer, Elizabeth Kelly. *Commentaries on the Constitution, 1790–1860.* New York, 1952.

Bemis, Samuel F. *John Quincy Adams and the Union.* New York, 1956.

Berthoff, Rowland T. *An Unsettled People: Social Disorder in American History.* New York, 1971.

Beveridge, Albert J. *The Life of John Marshall.* 4 vols. Boston, 1919.

Billias, George A. *Elbridge Gerry: Founding Father and Republican Statesman.* New York, 1976.

————. *General John Glover and His Marblehead Mariners.* New York, 1960.

Bloomfield, Maxwell H. *American Lawyers in a Changing Society, 1776–1876.* Cambridge, Mass., 1976.

Boorstin, Daniel J. *The Mysterious Science of the Law.* Cambridge, Mass., 1941.

Boyer, Paul S., and Nissenbaum, Stephen. *Salem Possessed: The Social Origins of Witchcraft.* Cambridge, Mass., 1974.

Bridwell, Randall, and Whitten, Ralph U. *The Constitution and the Common Law: The Decline of the Doctrines of Separation of Powers and Federalism.* Lexington, Mass., 1977.

Brooks, Van Wyck. *New England: Indian Summer, 1865–1915.* New York, 1940.

Bruccoli, Matthew J. *The Profession of Authorship in America, 1800–1870: The Papers of William Charvat.* [Columbus, Ohio], 1968.

Bugbee, Bruce W. *Genesis of American Patent and Copyright Law.* Washington, D.C., 1967.

Charvat, William. *Literary Publishing in America, 1790–1850.* Philadelphia, 1959.

Commager, Henry S. "Joseph Story." In Commager, *Gaspar Bacon Lectures on the Constitution of the United States, 1940–1950.* Boston, 1953.

Cook, Charles M. *The American Codification Movement: A Study of Antebellum Legal Reform.* Westport, Conn., 1981.

Cover, Robert M. *Justice Accused: Antislavery and the Judicial Process.* New Haven, Conn., 1975.

Crosskey, William W. *Politics and the Constitution in the History of the United States.* 2 vols. Chicago, 1953.

Cummings, Homer S., and McFarland, Carl. *Federal Justice: Chapters in the History of Justice and the Federal Executive.* New York, 1937.

Curti, Merle E. *The Growth of American Thought.* 2d ed. New York, 1943.

Dangerfield, George. *The Awakening of American Nationalism, 1815–1828.* New York, 1965.

Dauer, Manning J. *The Adams Federalists.* Baltimore, 1953.

Dennison, George M. *The Dorr War: Republicanism on Trial, 1831–1861.* Lexington, Ky., 1976.

Dodd, E. Merrick. *American Business Corporations until 1860, with Special Reference to Massachusetts.* Cambridge, Mass., 1954.

Donald, David H. *Charles Sumner and the Coming of the Civil War.* New York, 1961.

Dorfman, Joseph. *The Economic Mind in American Civilization.* 5 vols. New York, 1946–59.

Dunne, Gerald T. *Justice Joseph Story and the Rise of the Supreme Court.* New York, 1970.

Ellis, Richard E. *The Jeffersonian Crisis: Courts and Politics in the Young Republic.* New York, 1971.

Erikson, Erik H. *Identity: Youth and Crisis.* New York, 1968.

———. *Young Man Luther: A Study in Psychoanalysis and History.* New York, 1958.

Every, Dale Van. *Disinherited: The Lost Birthright of the American Indian.* New York, 1966.

Farber, Bernard. *Guardians of Virtue: Salem Families in 1800.* New York, 1972.

Faulkner, Robert K. *The Jurisprudence of John Marshall.* Princeton, N.J., 1968.

Fifoot, C. H. S. *Lord Mansfield.* Oxford, 1936.

Finkelman, Paul. *An Imperfect Union: Slavery, Federalism, and Comity.* Studies in Legal History. Chapel Hill, N.C., 1981.

Fischer, David H. *The Revolution of American Conservatism: The Federalist Party in the Era of Jeffersonian Democracy.* New York, 1965.

Frank, John P. *Justice Daniel Dissenting: A Biography of Peter V. Daniel, 1784–1860.* Cambridge, Mass., 1964.

Frankfurter, Felix. *Mr. Justice Holmes and the Supreme Court.* Cambridge, Mass., 1961.

Franklin, John Hope. *The Militant South, 1800–1861.* Cambridge, Mass., 1956.

Fredrickson, George M. *The Inner Civil War: Northern Intellectuals and the Crisis of the Union.* New York, 1965.

Freehling, William W. *Prelude to Civil War: The Nullification Controversy in South Carolina, 1816–1836.* New York, 1966.

Freyer, Tony A. *Forums of Order: The Federal Courts and Business in American History.* Greenwich, Conn., 1979.

———. *Harmony and Dissonance: The* Swift *and* Erie *Cases in American Federalism.* New York, 1981.

Friedman, Leon, and Israel, Fred L. eds. *The Justices of the United States Supreme Court, 1789–1969: Their Lives and Major Opinions.* 4 vols. New York, 1969.

Gawalt, Gerard W. *The Promise of Power: The Emergence of the Legal Profession in Massachusetts, 1760–1840.* Westport, Conn., 1979.

Gettleman, Marvin E. *The Dorr Rebellion: A Study in American Radicalism, 1833–1849.* New York, 1973.

Gilmore, Grant. *The Ages of American Law.* New Haven, Conn., 1977.

Goebel, Julius, Jr. *Antecedents and Beginnings to 1801.* Vol. 1 of *Oliver Wendell Holmes Devise History of the Supreme Court of the United States.* New York, 1971.

Goodman, Paul. *The Democratic-Republicans of Massachusetts: Politics in a Young Republic.* Cambridge, Mass., 1964.

Gray, John Chipman. *The Nature and Sources of the Law.* New York, 1909. Reprint. Beacon Press, 1921.

Greef, Albert O. *The Commercial Paper House in the United States.* Cambridge, Mass., 1938.

Gregory, Francis W. *Nathan Appleton: Merchant and Entrepreneur, 1779–1861.* Charlottesville, Va., 1975.

Griffin, Clifford S. *Their Brothers' Keepers: Moral Stewardship in the United States, 1800–1865.* New Brunswick, N.J., 1960.

Gunther, Gerald, ed. *John Marshall's Defense of* McCulloch v. Maryland. Stanford, Calif., 1969.

Gusfield, Joseph R. *Symbolic Crusade: Status Politics and the American Temperance Movement.* Urbana, Ill., 1963.

Haar, Charles M., ed. *The Golden Age of American Law.* New York, 1965.

Haines, Charles G. *The Role of the Supreme Court in American Government and Politics, 1789–1835.* New York, 1960.

Handlin, Oscar, and Handlin, Mary. *Commonwealth: A Study of the Role of Government in the American Economy: Massachusetts, 1774–1861.* New York, 1947.

Hartz, Louis. *Economic Policy and Democratic Thought: Pennsylvania, 1776–1860.* Cambridge, Mass., 1948.

———. *The Liberal Tradition in America: An Interpretation of American Political Thought since the Revolution.* New York, 1955.

Harvard Law School Association. *The Centennial History of the Harvard Law School, 1817–1917.* [Cambridge, Mass.], 1918.

Haskins, George L., and Johnson, Herbert A. *Foundations of Power: John Marshall, 1801–15.* Vol. 2 of *Oliver Wendell Holmes Devise History of the Supreme Court of the United States.* New York, 1981.

Hatch, Nathan O. *The Sacred Cause of Liberty: Republican Thought and the Millennium in Revolutionary New England.* New Haven, Conn., 1977.

Hofstadter, Richard. *Academic Freedom in the Age of the College.* New York, 1955.

———. *The Idea of a Party System: The Rise of Legitimate Opposition in the United States, 1780–1840.* Berkeley and Los Angeles, 1969.

Holden, J. Milnes. *The History of Negotiable Instruments in English Law.* London, 1955.

Holdsworth, William S. *A History of English Law.* 16 vols. London, 1922–66.

Holmes, Oliver Wendell. *Collected Legal Papers.* New York, 1920.

———. *The Common Law.* Edited by Mark DeWolfe Howe. Cambridge, Mass., 1963.

Horwitz, Morton. *The Transformation of American Law, 1780–1860.* Cambridge, Mass., 1977.

Howard, Warren S. *American Slavers and the Federal Law, 1837–1862.* Berkeley and Los Angeles, 1963.

Howe, Daniel Walker. *The Unitarian Conscience: Harvard Moral Philosophy, 1805–1861.* Cambridge, Mass., 1970.

Howe, Mark DeWolfe, ed. *Holmes-Pollock Letters: The Correspondence of Mr. Justice Holmes and Sir Frederick Pollock, 1874–1932.* 2 vols. in 1. 2d ed. Cambridge, Mass., 1961.

———. *Justice Oliver Wendell Holmes.* 2 vols. Cambridge, Mass., 1957–63.

Hurst, J. Willard. *Law and the Conditions of Freedom in the Nineteenth-Century United States.* Madison, Wis., 1956.

Jaher, Frederic C., ed. *The Age of Industrialism in America: Essays in Social Structure and Cultural Values.* New York, 1968.

Jones, W. Melville, ed. *Chief Justice Marshall: A Reappraisal.* Ithaca, N.Y., 1956.

Kammen, Michael G. *People of Paradox: An Inquiry concerning the Origins of American Civilization.* New York, 1973.

Katz, Michael B. *The Irony of Early School Reform: Educational Innovation in Mid-Nineteenth Century Massachusetts.* Cambridge, Mass., 1968.

Kerber, Linda K. *Federalists in Dissent: Imagery and Ideology in Jeffersonian America.* Ithaca, N.Y., 1970.

Kett, Joseph F. *Rites of Passage: Adolescence in America, 1790 to the Present.* New York, 1977.

Konefsky, Alfred S., and King, Andrew J., eds. *The Papers of Daniel Webster: Legal Papers.* 2 vols. Hanover, N.H., 1983.

Kraditor, Aileen S. *Means and Ends in American Abolitionism: Garrison and His Critics on Strategy and Tactics, 1834–1850.* New York, 1969.

Kuhn, Thomas S. *The Essential Tension: Selected Studies in Scientific Tradition and Change.* Chicago, 1977.
————. *The Structure of Scientific Revolutions.* 2d enlarged ed. Chicago, 1970.
Kutler, Stanley I. *Privilege and Creative Destruction: The Charles River Bridge Case.* Philadelphia, 1971.
Lehmann-Haupt, Hellmut. *The Book in America: A History of the Making, the Selling, and the Collecting of Books in the United States.* New York, 1939.
Levy, Leonard W. *Jefferson and Civil Liberties: The Darker Side.* Cambridge, Mass., 1963.
————. *The Law of the Commonwealth and Chief Justice Shaw.* Cambridge, Mass., 1957.
Lewis, R. W. B. *The American Adam: Innocence, Tragedy, and Tradition in the Nineteenth Century.* Chicago, 1955.
Lewis, William Draper, ed. *Great American Lawyers.* . . . 8 vols. Philadelphia, 1907–9.
Livermore, Shaw, Jr. *The Twilight of Federalism: The Disintegration of the Federalist Party, 1815–1830.* Princeton, N.J., 1962.
Llewellyn, Karl N. *The Common Law Tradition: Deciding Appeals.* Boston, 1960.
Lockmiller, David A. *Sir William Blackstone.* Chapel Hill, N.C., 1938.
Lodge, Henry C. *Life and Letters of George Cabot.* Boston, 1877.
McCaughey, Robert A. *Josiah Quincy, 1772–1864: The Last Federalist.* Cambridge, Mass., 1974.
McClellan, James. *Joseph Story and the American Constitution: A Study in Political and Legal Thought with Selected Writings.* Norman, Okla., 1971.
Madison, Charles A. *Book Publishing in America.* New York, 1966.
Mason, Alpheus T. *Brandeis: A Free Man's Life.* New York, 1946.
Meyers, Marvin. *The Jacksonian Persuasion: Politics and Belief.* New York, 1960.
Miller, Perry. *The American Transcendentalists: Their Prose and Poetry.* New York, 1957.
Morgan, Donald G. *Justice William Johnson, The First Dissenter: The Career and Constitutional Philosophy of a Jeffersonian Judge.* Columbia, S.C., 1954.
Morison, Samuel E. *A History of the Constitution of Massachusetts.* Boston, 1917.
————. *The Life and Letters of Harrison Gray Otis, Federalist, 1765–1848.* 2 vols. Boston, 1913.
————. *Three Centuries of Harvard, 1636–1936.* Cambridge, Mass., 1936.
Morris, Thomas D. *Free Men All: The Personal Liberty Laws of the North, 1780–1861.* Baltimore, 1974.
Myers, Gustavus. *History of the Supreme Court of the United States.* Chicago, 1925.
Myers, Robert M., ed. *Children of Pride: A True Story of Georgia and the Civil War.* New Haven, Conn., 1972.
Nelson, William E. *Americanization of the Common Law: The Impact of Legal Change on Massachusetts Society, 1760–1830.* Cambridge, Mass., 1975.
Noonan, John T., Jr. *Persons and Masks of Law: Cardozo, Holmes, Jefferson, and Wythe as Makers of the Masks.* New York, 1976.
Nye, Russel B. *The Cultural Life of the New Nation, 1776–1830.* New York, 1960.
Ortega y Gasset, José. *The Revolt of the Masses.* 25th anniversary ed. New York, 1957.
Parrington, Vernon L. *Main Currents in American Thought: An Interpretation of American Literature from the Beginnings to 1920.* New York, 1927.
Perry, Lewis. *Radical Abolitionism: Anarchy and the Government of God in Antislavery Thought.* Ithaca, N.Y., 1973.
Peterson, Merrill D. *The Jefferson Image in the American Mind.* New York, 1960.
Pierson, George W. *Tocqueville in America.* Abridged by D. C. Lunt. Garden City, N.Y., 1959.
Pocock, J. G. A. *Politics, Language and Time: Essays on Political Thought and History.* New York, 1971.

Porter, Glenn, and Livesay, Harold C. *Merchants and Manufacturers: Studies in the Changing Structure of Nineteenth Century Marketing.* Baltimore, 1971.

Quincy, Josiah, Jr. *Figures of the Past from the Leaves of Old Journals.* Boston, 1883.

Redlich, Josef. *The Common Law and the Case Method in American University Law Schools.* New York, 1914.

Reinhold, Meyer. *The Classick Pages: Classical Reading of Eighteenth-Century Americans.* University Park, Pa., 1975.

Roads, Samuel, Jr. *The History and Traditions of Marblehead.* Boston, 1880.

———. *The Marblehead Manual.* Marblehead, Mass., 1883.

Robinson, Donald L. *Slavery in the Structure of American Politics, 1765–1820.* New York, 1971.

Rudolph, Frederick. *The American College and University: A History.* New York: Vintage, 1965.

Schlesinger, Arthur M. *The Colonial Merchants and the American Revolution, 1763–1776.* New York, 1918.

Schutz, John, and Adair, Douglass, eds. *The Spur of Fame: Dialogues of John Adams and Benjamin Rush, 1805–1813.* San Marino, Calif., 1966.

Sears, Louis M. *Jefferson and the Embargo.* Durham, N.C., 1927.

Shalhope, Robert E. *John Taylor of Caroline: Pastoral Republican.* Columbia, S.C., 1980.

Sherwin, Oscar. *Prophet of Liberty: The Life and Times of Wendell Phillips.* 1958. Reprint. Westport, Conn., 1975.

Soulsby, Hugh G. *The Right of Search and the Slave Trade in Anglo-American Relations, 1814–1862.* Baltimore, 1933.

Spivak, Burton. *Jefferson's English Crisis: Commerce, Embargo, and the Republican Revolution.* Charlottesville, Va., 1979.

Stevens, Robert. *Law School: Legal Education in America from the 1850s to the 1980s.* Sudies in Legal History. Chapel Hill, N.C., 1983.

Stites, Francis N. *Private Interest and Public Gain: The Dartmouth College Case.* Amherst, Mass., 1972.

Story, Ronald. *The Forging of an Aristocracy: Harvard and the Boston Upper Class, 1800–1870.* Middletown, Conn., 1980.

Sutherland, Arthur E. *The Law at Harvard: A History of Ideas and Men, 1817–1967.* Cambridge, Mass., 1967.

Swisher, Carl B. *The Taney Period, 1836–64.* Vol. 5 of *Oliver Wendell Holmes Devise History of the Supreme Court of the United States.* New York, 1974.

Tapley, Harriet S. *Salem Imprints, 1768–1825: A History of the First Fifty Years of Printing in Salem, Massachusetts. . . .* Salem, Mass., 1927.

Tyack, David B. *George Ticknor and the Boston Brahmins.* Cambridge, Mass., 1967.

Vaughan, Floyd L. *The United States Patent System: Legal and Economic Conflicts in American Patent History.* Norman, Okla., 1956.

Wallace, Anthony F. C. *Rockdale: The Growth of an American Village in the Early Industrial Revolution.* New York, 1978.

Warren, Charles. *A History of the American Bar.* Cambridge, Mass., 1912.

———. *History of the Harvard Law School and of Early Legal Conditions in America.* 3 vols. New York, 1908.

———. *Jacobin and Junto.* Cambridge, Mass., 1931.

———. *The Supreme Court in United States History.* New rev. ed. 2 vols. Boston, 1926.

White, G. Edward. *The American Judicial Tradition: Profiles of Leading American Judges.* New York, 1976.

———. *Patterns of American Legal Thought.* Indianapolis, 1978.

Wiecek, William M. *The Guarantee Clause of the U.S. Constitution.* Ithaca, N.Y., 1975.

———. *The Sources of Antislavery Constitutionalism in America, 1769–1848.* Ithaca, N.Y., 1977.

Wood, Gordon S. *Creation of the American Republic, 1776–1787.* Chapel Hill, N.C., 1969.

Young, James Sterling. *The Washington Community, 1800–1828.* New York, 1966.

Articles

Baxter, Maurice G. "Should the Dartmouth College Case Have Been Reargued?" 33 *New England Quarterly* (March 1960): 19–36.

Burke, Joseph C. "The Cherokee Cases: A Study in Law, Politics, and Morality." 21 *Stanford Law Review* (February 1969): 500–531.

———. "What Did the Prigg Decision Really Decide?" 93 *Pennsylvania Magazine of History and Biography* (January 1969): 73–85.

Callender, Guy S. "The Early Transportation and Banking Enterprises of the States in Relation to the Growth of Corporations." 17 *Quarterly Journal of Economics* (November 1902): 111–62.

Chayes, Abram. "The Bead Game." 87 *Harvard Law Review* (February 1974): 741–53.

Cheatham, Elliott E. "American Theories of Conflict of Laws: Their Role and Utility." In Association of American Law Schools, *Selected Readings on Conflict of Laws*, pp. 48–70. Saint Paul, Minn., 1956. (First published in *Harvard Law Review* [1945].)

———. "Federal Control of Conflict of Law." In Association of American Law Schools, *Selected Readings on Conflict of Laws*, pp. 255–74. Saint Paul, Minn., 1956. (First published in 6 *Vanderbilt Law Review* [1953].)

Conron, Michael A. "Law, Politics, and Chief Justice Taney: A Reconsideration of the *Luther* v. *Borden* Decision." 11 *American Journal of Legal History* (October 1967): 377–88.

Derby, Perley. "Elisha Story of Boston and Some of His Descendants, Compiled by Perley Derby, with Additions by Frank A. Gardner, M.D." 50 *Essex Institute Historical Collections* (1914): 297–312; 51 (1915): 41–52.

Dicey, A. V. "The Teaching of English Law at Harvard." 13 *Harvard Law Review* (January 1900): 422–40.

Dowd, Morgan D. "Justice Joseph Story and the Politics of Appointment." 9 *American Journal of Legal History* (October 1965): 265–85.

Dunne, Gerald T. "Joseph Story's First Writing on Equity." 14 *American Journal of Legal History* (January 1970): 76–81.

———. "Justice Story and the Modern Corporation—A Closing Circle?" 17 *American Journal of Legal History* (July 1973): 262–70.

East, Robert A. "Economic Development and New England Federalism, 1803–1814." 10 *New England Quarterly* (September 1937): 430–46.

Ely, John Hart. "The Irrepressible Myth of Erie." 87 *Harvard Law Review* (February 1974): 693–740.

———. "The Necklace." 87 *Harvard Law Review* (February 1974): 753–62.

Finkelman, Paul. "*Prigg* v. *Pennsylvania* and Northern State Courts: Anti-Slavery Use of a Pro-Slavery Decision." 25 *Civil War History* (March 1979): 5–35.

Formisano, Ronald P. "Deferential Participant Politics: The Early Republic's Political Culture, 1789–1840." 68 *American Political Science Review* (June 1974): 473–87.

———. "Political Character, Antipartyism and the Second American Party System." 21 *American Quarterly* (Winter 1969): 683–709.

Fox, Jabez. "Law and Fact." 12 *Harvard Law Review* (March 1899): 545–52.

Freehling, William. "The Founding Fathers and Slavery." 77 *American Historical Review* (February 1972): 81–93.

Friendly, Henry J. "In Praise of *Erie*—and of the New Federal Common Law." 39 *New York University Law Review* (May 1964): 383–422.

"From Judicial Grant to Legislative Power: The Admiralty Clause in the Nineteenth Century." 67 *Harvard Law Review* (May 1954): 1214–37.

Goebel, Julius, Jr., "The Common Law and the Constitution." In *Chief Justice Marshall: A Reappraisal*, ed. W. Melville Jones, pp. 101–23. Ithaca, N.Y., 1956.

Goodman, Paul. "Ethics and Enterprise: The Values of the Boston Elite, 1800–1860." 18 *American Quarterly* (Fall 1966): 437–51.

Greene, John C. "The Kuhnian Paradigm and the Darwin Revolution in Natural History." In *Perspectives in the History of Science and Technology*, edited by Duane H. D. Roller, pp. 3–25. Norman, Okla., 1971.

Hall, Kermit. "Social Backgrounds and Judicial Recruitment." 29 *Western Political Quarterly* (June 1976): 243–57.

Hellerich, Mahlon H. "The Luther Cases in the Lower Courts." 11 *Rhode Island History* (April 1952): 33–45.

Hendrich, Frederick K. "The Development of American Laissez Faire: A General View of the Age of Washington." 3 *Journal of Economic History*, suppl. (December 1943): 51–54.

Hickey, Donald R. "American Trade Restrictions during the War of 1812." 68 *Journal of American History* (December 1981): 517–38.

Hidy, Ralph W. "The Organization and Functions of Anglo-American Merchant Bankers, 1815–1860." 1 *Journal of Economic History*, suppl. (December 1941): 53–66.

Holdsworth, William S. "Blackstone's Treatment of Equity." 43 *Harvard Law Review* (November 1929): 1–32.

Howe, John R. "Republican Thought and the Political Violence of the 1790s." 19 *American Quarterly* (Summer 1967): 147–65.

Jackson, Robert H. "Full Faith and Credit—the Lawyer's Clause of the Constitution." In Association of American Law Schools, *Selected Readings on Conflict of Laws*, pp. 229–54. Saint Paul, Minn., 1956. (First published in 45 *Columbia Law Review* [1945].)

Keefe, Arthur J. "In Praise of Joseph Story, *Swift* v. *Tyson* and 'The True National Common Law.'" 18 *American University Law Review* (March 1969): 316–71.

Kennedy, Duncan. "The Structure of Blackstone's Commentaries." 28 *Buffalo Law Review* (Spring 1979): 205–382.

Lerner, Max. "The Supreme Court and American Capitalism." 42 *Yale Law Journal* (March 1933): 668–701.

Leslie, William R. "The Influence of Joseph Story's Theory of Conflict of Laws on Constitutional Nationalism." 35 *Mississippi Valley Historical Review* (September 1948): 203–20.

Lively, Robert A. "The American System: A Review Article." 29 *Business History Review* (March 1955): 81–96.

Longaker, Richard P. "Andrew Jackson and the Judiciary," 71 *Political Science Quarterly* (September 1956): 341–64.

Lorenzen, Ernest G. "Story's Commentaries on the Conflict of Laws—One Hundred Years After." 48 *Harvard Law Review* (November 1934): 15–38.

McDowell, Gary L. "Joseph Story's 'Science' of Equity." *Supreme Court Review*, 1979, pp. 153–72.

McLaughlin, Andrew. "Social Compact and Constitutional Construction." 5 *American Historical Review* (April 1900): 467–91.

Magrath, C. Peter. "Optimistic Democrat: Thomas W. Dorr and the Case of *Luther* v. *Borden*." 29 *Rhode Island History* (October 1970): 94–112.

Mangus, C. Lee. "Note: Justice Story's Doctrine of Judicial Supremacy and the Uncertain Search for a Neutral Principle in *The Charles River Bridge Case*." 53 *Indiana Law Journal*, no. 2 (1977–78): 327–63.

Marshall, Lynn L. "The Strange Stillbirth of the Whig Party." 72 *American Historical Review* (January 1967): 445–68.

Mathews, William. "Recollections of Judge Story." 4 *Lakeside* (December 1870): 379–87.

Nadelmann, Kurt H. "Joseph Story's Sketch of American Law." 3 *American Journal of Comparative Law* (Winter 1954): 1–26.

Newmyer, R. Kent. "Daniel Webster as Tocqueville's Lawyer: The *Dartmouth College* Case Again." 11 *American Journal of Legal History* (April 1967): 127–47.

———. "Justice Joseph Story on Circuit and a Neglected Phase of American Legal History." 14 *American Journal of Legal History* (April 1970): 112–35.

———. "Justice Joseph Story, the Charles River Bridge Case and the Crisis of Republicanism." 17 *American Journal of Legal History* (July 1973): 232–45.

———. "Justice Joseph Story's Doctrine of 'Public and Private Corporations' and the Rise of the American Business Corporation." 25 *DePaul Law Review* (Summer 1976): 825–41.

———. "A Note on the Whig Politics of Justice Joseph Story." 48 *Mississippi Valley Historical Review* (December 1961): 480–91.

Nolan, Dennis R. "Sir William Blackstone and the New Republic: A Study of Intellectual Impact." 51 *New York University Law Review* (November 1976): 731–68.

"Notes." 37 *American Law Review* (November–December 1903): 899–929.

Pessen, Edward. "The Equalitarian Myth and American Social Reality: Wealth, Mobility and Equality in the 'Era of the Common Man.'" 76 *American Historical Review* (October 1971): 989–1034.

Pound, Roscoe. "The Decadence of Equity." 5 *Columbia Law Review* (January 1905): 20–35.

———. "The Place of Judge Story in the Making of American Law." 48 *American Law Review* (September 1914): 676–97.

Prager, Frank D. "The Changing Views of Justice Story on the Construction of Patents." 4 *American Journal of Legal History* (January 1960): 1–21.

———. "The Influence of Mr. Justice Story on American Patent Law." 5 *American Journal of Legal History* (July 1961): 254–64.

Roper, Donald M. "Judicial Unanimity and the Marshall Court: A Road to Reappraisal." 9 *American Journal of Legal History* (April 1965): 118–34.

———. "In Quest of Judicial Objectivity: The Marshall Court and the Legitimation of Slavery." 21 *Stanford Law Review* (February 1969): 532–47.

Scheiber, Harry N. "Property Law, Expropriation, and Resource Allocation by Government: The United States, 1789–1910." 33 *Journal of Economic History* (March 1973): 232–51.

Schuchman, John S. "The Political Background of the Political Question Doctrine: The Judges and the Dorr War." 16 *American Journal of Legal History* (April 1972): 111–25.

Shalhope, Robert E. "Toward a Republican Synthesis: The Emergence of an Understanding of Republicanism in American Historiography." 29 *William and Mary Quarterly* (January 1972): 49–80.

Stanwood, Edward. "The Massachusetts Election in 1806." 20 *Proceedings of the Massachusetts Historical Society*. 2d ser. (1906, 1907): 12–19.

Story, Ronald. "Class and Culture in Boston: The Athenaeum, 1807–1860." 27 *American Quarterly* (May 1975): 178–99.

Story, Ruth, and Eddy, Devereaux. "The Ancestry of Judge Joseph Story, Justice of the Supreme Court of the United States." 83 *Essex Institute Historical Collections* (January 1947): 59–66.

"*Swift* v. *Tyson* Exhumed." 79 *Yale Law Journal* (December 1969): 284–310.

Tebbe, Jennifer. "Print and American Culture." 32 *American Quarterly* (Bibliography issue, 1980): 259–79.

Thayer, James B. "The Teaching of English Law at Universities." 9 *Harvard Law Review* (October 1895): 169–84.

Tompkins, Silvan. "The Psychology of Commitment: The Constructive Role of Violence and Suffering for the Individual and for His Society." In *The Antislavery Vanguard: New Essays on the Abolitionists*, ed. Martin B. Duberman, pp. 270–98. Princeton, N.J., 1965.

Tucker, Henry St. George. "Judge Story's Position on the So-Called General Welfare Clause." 13 *American Bar Association Journal* (July–August 1927): 363–68; 465–69.

Valladão, Haroldo. "The Influence of Joseph Story on Latin-American Rules of Conflict of Laws." 3 *American Journal of Comparative Law* (Winter 1954): 27–41.

Wallace, Michael. "Changing Concepts of Party in the United States: New York, 1815–1828." 74 *American Historical Review* (December 1968): 453–91.

Warren, Charles. "New Light on the History of the Federal Judiciary Act of 1789." 37 *Harvard Law Review* (November 1923): 49–132.

Wexler, Victor G. "'Made for Man's Delight': Rousseau as Antifeminist." 81 *American Historical Review* (April 1976): 266–91.

Whitney, William T., Jr. "The Crowninshields of Salem, 1800–1808: A Study in the Politics of Commercial Growth." 94 *Essex Institute Historical Collections*, pt. 1 (January 1958): 1–36; pt. 2 (April 1958): 79–118.

Yntema, Hessel E. "The Enforcement of Foreign Judgments in Anglo-American Law." In Association of American Law Schools, *Selected Readings on Conflict of Laws*, pp. 376–403. Saint Paul, Minn., 1956. (First published in 33 *Michigan Law Review* [1935].)

———. "The Historic Bases of Private International Law." In Association of American Law Schools, *Selected Readings on Conflict of Laws*, pp. 30–47. Saint Paul, Minn., 1956. (First published in *American Journal of Comparative Law* [1953].)

Unpublished Works

Campbell, Bruce A. "Law and Experience in the Early Republic: The Evolution of the Dartmouth College Doctrine, 1780–1819." Ph.D. diss., Michigan State University, 1973.

Grimsted, David. "Robbing the Poor to Aid the Rich: The Bank of Maryland Swindle, 1833–1838." Unpublished paper.

Gunther, Gerald. "The Warren Court and the Marshall Court—Strategy in Constitutional Adjudication." Paper prepared for Claremont Seminar, January 1965.

Preyer, Kathryn. "Joseph Story, the Supreme Court and the Question of a Federal Common Law Jurisdiction over Crimes." Paper delivered at the Organization of American Historians meeting, Los Angeles, April 1970.

Sarno (Vontell), Bonnie. "Justice Joseph Story and the Transformation of Seamen's Contract Law, 1790–1872." Honors thesis, University of Connecticut, 1981.

Sheidley, Harlow. "Sectional Nationalism: Massachusetts Conservative Leadership and the Epic of New England, 1820–1836." Research seminar paper, University of Connecticut, 1977.

Thwing, Annie H., comp. "Inhabitants and Estates of the Town of Boston, 1630–1800. . . ." 2 vols. Boston, 1916. Bound typescript in the Massachusetts Historical Society, Boston.

Treon, John F. "*Martin* v. *Hunter's Lessee*: A Case History." Ph.D. diss., University of Virginia, 1970.

Van Burkleo, Sandra F. "Securing the Commonwealth: Law, Politics, and Finance in Kentucky, 1817–1832." Paper presented at the American Historical Association Meeting, Washington, D.C., 30 December 1980.

Warden, G. B. "Preliminary Report: Benjamin Franklin and the Hutchinson Letters." Research paper, 18 January 1971.

Index of Cases

Index